NATIONAL GEOGRAPHIC

ALMANAC OF AMERICAN HISTORY

ALMANAC OF AMERICAN HISTORY

JAMES MILLER AND JOHN THOMPSON
FOREWORD BY HUGH AMBROSE

NATIONAL GEOGRAPHIC
WASHINGTON, D.C.

CONTENTS

The Trylon and Perisphere were the logo of the 1939 World's Fair, a celebration of futuristic technology on the eve of World War II.

Opposite: A portrait of a relatively young-looking George Washington, at age 52, was painted by Charles Wilson Peale in 1780, while the Revolutionary War still raged.
Preceding pages: The popular artist Norman Rockwell created this poster in 1944 urging Americans to "hasten the homecoming" of troops by buying Victory Bonds.

Centuries before contact with Euro-Americans, Native Americans were creating images of humans and animals in rock paintings, or petroglyphs.

Winning women's right to vote in 1920 owed much to suffragists like this New York City woman carrying the flag in a march on Fifth Avenue.

Center of American government, the white marble United States Capitol is one of the most recognized landmarks in the world.

AT A GLANCE

FOREWORD

THE TORRENT OF MEDIA WASHING OVER Americans every day has been described as akin "to a fire hose aimed at a teacup." This observation has become a truism in the 21st century, as the amount of information being communicated and the speed of its transmission grow exponentially. Disconcerting though it can be, the new Age of Information has arrived, and with it, new challenges.

Often, more information has not translated into greater wisdom. Navigating the information ocean can be intimidating: Even with wondrous tools like Google, one can be steered in the wrong direction. Purveyors of information clamor for our attention. Electronic media is easily manipulated, even fabricated. Facts conflict with other facts; statisticians seem to prove anything.

There is so much change and greater complexity in all fields of human endeavor that we are forced to make a rational choice: to claim one area of competency. We become experts in one field, and come to know more—about less. But can we really isolate ourselves this way?

American culture has imbued us with values, traditions, music, art. It holds before us people, events, ideas. All these shape our respective identities. While caught up in our worlds, we may suspect that there is more than meets the eye. And there is. The present—our present—was created by what we call simply "American history," which encompasses all endeavor and experience.

The *Almanac of American History* charts the patterns and cycles of the country's evolution much as a farmer's almanac details weather patterns and crop rotations. Both begin with the land and the sea. We are creatures of geography. True understanding is formed as much by knowing *where* something occurred as knowing *what* occurred, or how. Maps of America's landscape ground us in elemental truth. Every story must "take place."

After orienting us, *The Almanac* offers a section called Milestones—essays of the American experience, which document critical themes and movements in our society. By establishing context—pulling related events, ideas, and individuals together from across the decades—we look beyond facts and figures to deeper truths.

There can be no substitute for browsing the eras of our history. The Eras section not only gives chronology and data, but in gripping narrative gives useful constructs for understanding our past. On display in the White House and the Cotton Club, played out in the boardrooms of blue-chip companies, and across the canvases of great artists, are the passions, ideas, and conflicts that shaped us as a society and as individuals. We watch as something as simple as the novel *Uncle Tom's Cabin* galvanizes public opinion into political force. The resulting change went well beyond any one incident.

Vital information is easy to access in the At a Glance section, including facts about inventors or the Methodist religion. In the Appendix, key documents are featured, because there are times when "Four score and seven years ago . . ." is enough, and there are times when we want to read all that Lincoln said at Gettysburg.

It remains our inalienable right as Americans to interpret the meaning and impact of Lincoln's speech, or of Jackie Robinson's joining the Brooklyn Dodgers, or of the role of telecommunications. Our judgment is the tool with which we decode the present and divine the future. But we need a guide. In a century of existence, the National Geographic Society has gained an unparalleled reputation for disseminating knowledge. This almanac's intent is to describe the grand dynamics of American society and to lay bare the fault lines within its culture.

In the Age of Information, where facts are only a mouse click away, it is wisdom that will sustain us. We are, after all, citizens of a proud republic, with duties as parents, jurors, voters. The good judgment of wise individuals empowers us to progress as a civilization. In our world, we could consider the *Almanac of American History* the desk reference for the American citizen. ■

—HUGH AMBROSE

About This Book

AMERICAN HISTORY IS AN EXCITING AND COMPLICATED affair. To understand the nation today, we must look into its past. The *Almanac of American History* provides a chronological and informative overview of events and people that have shaped America, from its earliest settlers to its diverse cultures of today. The chronological arrangement, overlapping at times, allows the authors to explain America's complex and varied history in a clear and organized fashion.

The *Almanac*'s first section, The Land, gives an overview of America's geologic makeup. The thinking is: To understand how America and its people developed, one must first understand the environment and its effects on the nation's growth, laws, citizens. Next, 12 essays called Milestones reveal topics crucial to shaping America's unique society. Then the body of the book comprises 11 chapters, each focusing on a separate era. Sections within each chapter cover major themes, movements, people, events, and cultures. Each section's title bears dates giving the range of time discussed. Maps provide context and clarify the spread of settlement, the course of major battles, the routes of exploration, and more. Each chapter ends with a World Survey addressing major events elsewhere in the world at that time—and America's link to them; together they give a running commentary on America's rise to global superpower.

At a Glance provides concise entries of America's major events, leaders, native nations, artists, scientists, explorers, and more. Throughout the almanac, photographs, artwork, and maps provide a visual history of each era. Mini-boxes give vital statistics: on child labor, battle casualties, the passage of major laws. Finally, the Appendix presents manuscripts of great documents, including the Constitution and the Gettysburg Address, and a comprehensive index for easy access. All work together to make the *Almanac of American History* an ideal reference for all who value history. ■

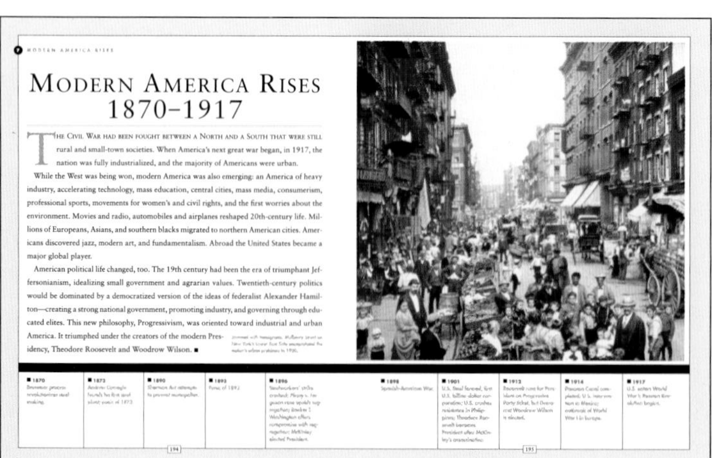

MODERN AMERICA RISES

1870–1917

THE CIVIL WAR HAD BEEN FOUGHT BETWEEN A NORTH AND A SOUTH THAT WERE STILL rural and small-town societies. When America's next great war began, in 1917, the nation was fully industrialized, and the majority of Americans were urban.

While the West was being won, modern America was also emerging: an America of heavy industry, accelerating technology, mass education, central cities, mass media, consumerism, professional sports, movements for women's and civil rights, and the first worries about the environment. Movies and radio, automobiles and airplanes reshaped 20th-century life. Millions of Europeans, Asians, and southern blacks migrated to northern American cities. Americans discovered jazz, modern art, and fundamentalism. Abroad the United States became a major global player.

American political life changed, too. The 19th century had been the era of triumphant Jeffersonianism, idealizing small government and agrarian values. Twentieth-century politics would be dominated by a democratized version of the ideas of federalist Alexander Hamilton—creating a strong national government, promoting industry, and governing through educated elites. This new philosophy, Progressivism, was oriented toward industrial and urban America. It triumphed under the creators of the modern Presidency, Theodore Roosevelt and Woodrow Wilson. ■

■ 1870 ■ 1873 ■ 1890 ■ 1893 ■ 1896 ■ 1898 ■ 1901 ■ 1912 ■ 1914 ■ 1917

194 195

Era Introduction Spread
Each era opens with a short essay that introduces the themes, subjects, and major occurrences that mark the era. A time line highlights the era's ten most important events.

Thematic Spread

Each thematic spread has a narrative that covers the people, events, and achievements of the period. A time line highlights notable dates and events pertinent to the theme. Mini boxes are the "headlines" of an era, giving vital statistics, from immigrations figures to public opinion polls to battle casualties to '20s sports heroes, offering a unique glimpse into each era. Maps illustrate history's ever changing nature.

World Survey Spread

The World Survey spread offers brief synopses of important historical events not otherwise covered within the era chapter. Each event is located geographically on a world map, giving a sense of where concurrent events were taking place, in relation to the events in America.

At a Glance Spread

This spread offers short biographies and summaries of America's religions, human accomplishments, and personalities, from artists and scientists to explorers and sports figures. All are organized alphabetically.

THE LAND

IN THE BEGINNING

No single image better captures the grandeur and the history of the American land than the Grand Canyon.

IN THE BEGINNING

THE GRAND CANYON IS LIKE NO OTHER PLACE ON EARTH. FIVE MILLION YEARS ago, the Colorado River began carving the canyon out of ancient rock. Since then, the relentless erosion of time and weather have battered and reshaped its canyon walls. North America's natural history is written in these rocks.

The universe began in an event called the Big Bang, roughly 15 billion years ago. Our galaxy formed about 8 billion years ago; it took another 3.4 billion years for Earth and the rest of our solar system to form. The oldest identifiable rocks are some 3.5 billion years old. Microscopic life may have begun in chemical processes not long after Earth's formation. Reviewing this immense chronology puts into perspective America's history as well as North America's landforms. It is "only" to 600 million years ago—end of the last ice age—that the North American continent can be dated.

Precambrian Time

Six-hundred million years ago, North America, or Laurentia, included Greenland and lay on the Equator—barren and sculpted by volcanoes, earthquakes, and glaciers. Life, all aquatic, consisted of bacteria, one-cell organisms, and multi-cellular algae. Precambrian time, 80 percent of geologic time, was ending.

The Paleozoic Era

Roughly 514 million years ago occurred history's greatest expansion of life, the Cambrian Explosion. The Paleozoic ("old life") era, and its first subdivision, the Cambrian period (570-500 million years ago) began. Hard-shelled trilobites in Laurentia's shallow seas left much of what we know of Cambrian life. Some 430 million years ago, at the end of the Ordovician period, an ice age caused an extinction that opened the way for new life forms, including early fish. During the Silurian period (435-410 million years ago), fish became the dominant fauna. Plants began colonizing barren coastal lowlands.

About 410 to 360 million years ago, amphibious animal life first reached land and early forests took root. This was the Devonian period, the climax of the age of the fishes. Laurentia—still athwart the Equator—and Baltica, the nearby proto-continent containing northern Europe, crunched together. During the succeeding Carboniferous period (360 to 290 million years ago) early woodlands grew immense, their plants propagating from seeds rather than spores. Decayed Carboniferous vegetation created much of the coal that powered the industrial revolution. Animal life included huge dragonflies and the durable cockroach.

During the Carboniferous and its successor, the Permian period, the continent Gondwanda began creeping northward from over the South Pole. It encompassed

■ **15 billion** YBP (YEARS BEFORE PRESENT)	■ **4.6 billion** YBP	■ **650 million** YBP	■ **570-290 million** YBP	■ **290-240 million** YBP
Big Bang creates universe.	Earth forms; origin of life forms at some time thereafter.	Breakup of super-continent Rodinia; Laurentia (predecessor of North America) not yet formed.	Paleozoic era: Life proliferates; animal life reaches land; creation of North American coal beds; Laurentia and Baltica collide.	Permian period: All continents combine in Pangaea.

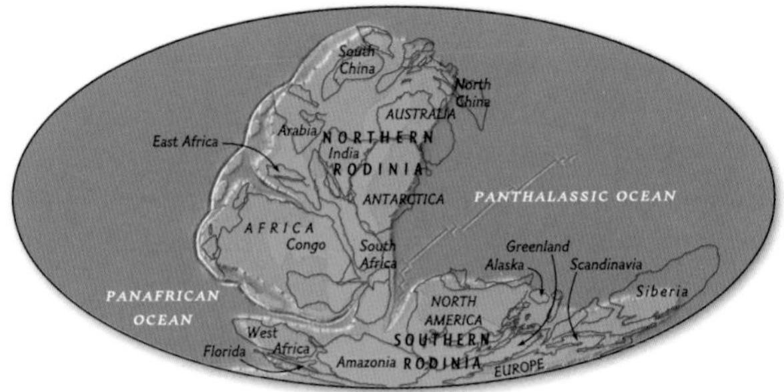

-650 Million Years (Late Proterozoic)

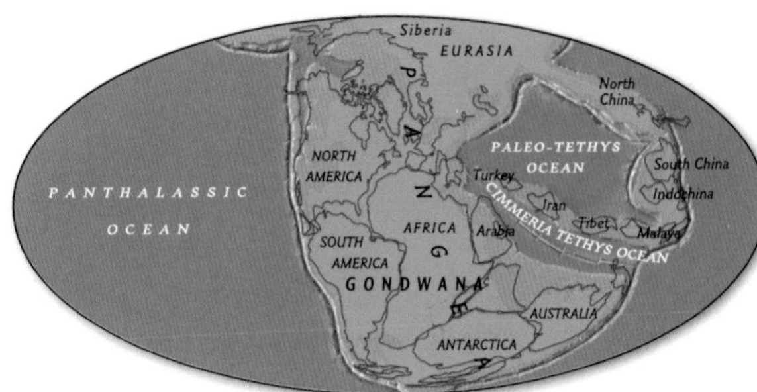

-237 Million Years (Early Triassic)

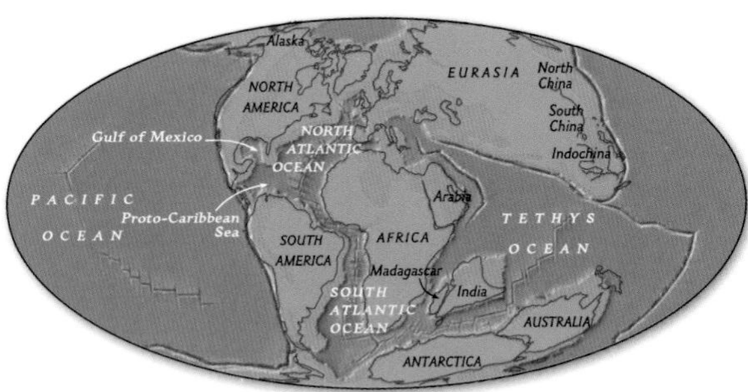

-94 Million Years (Late Cretaceous)

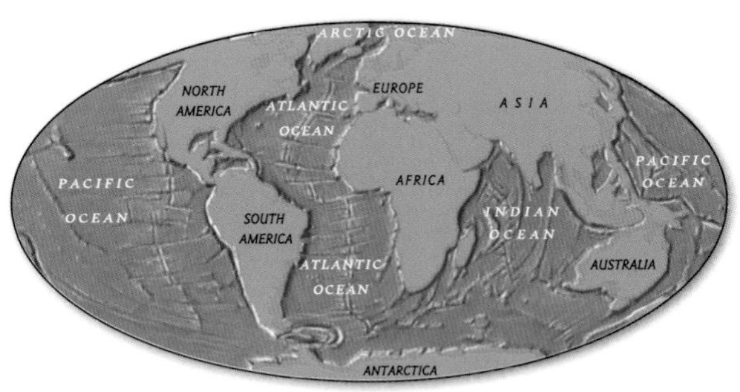

Present

The evolution of the present-day continents and the ways in which their shapes and geologies seem to fit together is explained by the theories of continental drift, first advanced in the 1920s, and plate tectonics, developed in the early 1960s.

present-day South America, Africa, Antarctica, Australia, and India. It rammed into Laurentia, while chunks of Siberia and Scandinavia also approached. From these collisions mountain chains were born, including the Appalachians and Ouachitas in the U.S.

The Permian lasted from 290 to 240 million years ago. Fossil-fuel creation continued, forming huge petroleum beds now in the Gulf of Mexico and nearby. Tectonic forces were pulling landmasses into a single continent, Pangaea. Global warming stimulated coastal life, including ferns and ancestors of seed-plants. But the climate of Pangaea was unstable—much of the land too far inland to receive maritime influences.

Some 240 million years ago, the Great Permian Extinction wiped out 80 percent of all life. Causes probably included climate change and cosmic radiation.

The Mesozoic Era

The Mesozoic ("middle life") era followed, from about 240 to 66 million years ago, with three periods:

■ **240 million YBP**	■ **240-66 million YBP**	■ **66 million YBP**	■ **5 million YBP**	■ **20,000-10,000 YBP**
Great Permian Extinction destroys 80 percent of all species; North America separating from Pangaea.	Mesozoic era: first dinosaurs and mammals; first birds; flowering plants; dinosaurs become extinct; Pangaea has broken apart.	Cenozoic era: evolution of modern mammals; North America assuming more of modern aspect.	Continental uplifting raises western mountain ranges and creates Grand Canyon.	Ancestors of Native Americans enter North America (dating controversial).

Triassic, Jurassic, and Cretaceous. As Pangaea fragmented, North America moved northwestward, reaching its modern latitude by the late Jurassic; collisions with island arcs on the west raised the Rockies and Sierra Nevadas. By the late Cretaceous, North America was separating from Greenland and lay close to Europe. Shallow seas inundated central North America.

Enormous changes occurred in Mesozoic life. Vertebrates survived the Permian extinction better than invertebrates. The evolutionary way was cleared for plants and animals more closely resembling modern life. The first mammals scurried underfoot, and birds evolved from reptiles. Ferns dominated, topped by upper-story conifers. By the Jurassic, conifers and palmlike gymnosperms and cycads proliferated; during the Cretaceous, flowering plants bloomed. Two major extinctions occurred during the Mesozoic. The first, some 208 million years ago, extinguished about 35 percent of all species, but survivors, especially dinosaurs, proved highly adaptable. The second was the environmental crisis that ended the Mesozoic era.

Geological evidence is compelling that the Cretaceous extinction involved a celestial object striking the Gulf of Mexico. But multiple causes seem to have been at work. Whatever ended the dinosaurs' reign, placental mammals survived and beget modern mammals.

The Cenozoic Era

In the last 66 million years tectonics kneaded the globe into its present configurations. Seafloor spreading widened the Atlantic. The Bering land bridge that had connected Alaska and Siberia permitting animal migration was breached about 2.5 million years ago. About the same time, continental uplift created another land bridge to the south, the Isthmus of Panama. Exchanges

Patterns of natural vegetation in what is now the U.S. emerged after the last Ice Age as the ice retreated and the climate warmed over several thousand years. Today, the climate of the lower 48 states ranges from the subtropic in southern Florida to the subarctic at high mountain elevations.

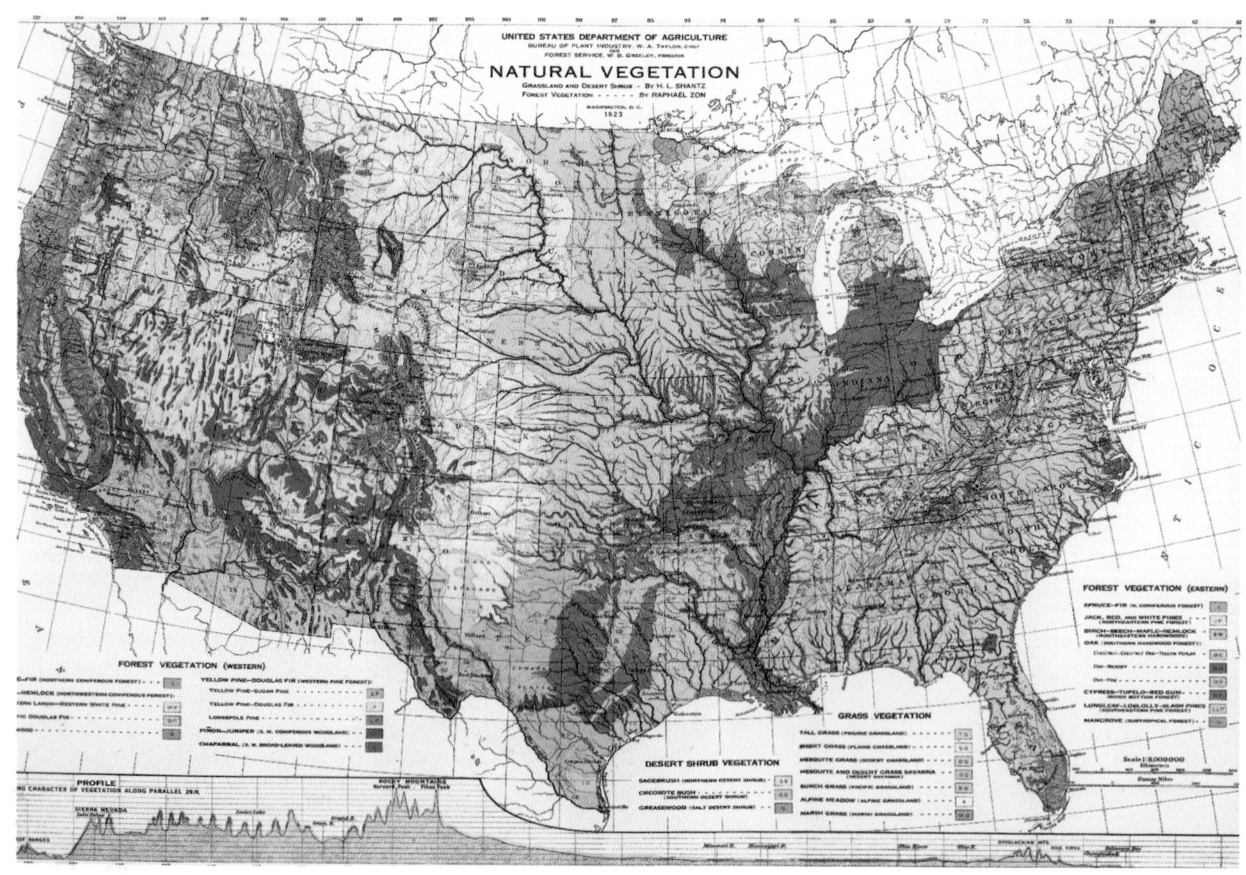

began between the flora and fauna of North and South America. That same uplifting of the North American continent raised the Rockies and other western ranges. Meanwhile the Colorado River cut the awesome gorges of the Grand Canyon, exposing the most extensive record of geological activity on Earth.

Global temperatures began cooling about 50 million years ago. Cooling alternated with warming, but the downward global trend was consistent enough to blanket Antarctica under an icecap for the past 35 million years and to freeze the Arctic Ocean's surface. Beginning about 3 million years ago, successive cooling and warming caused four massive glaciations to build at both Poles of the Earth. As the last Ice Age peaked about 18,000 years ago, glaciers more than a mile thick spread over the Northern Hemisphere, creeping as far south as present-day Kansas, Ohio, and New York City. Glaciers lowered seas and the Bering land bridge reappeared.

Biological evolutionary processes, of course, never stopped. The evolution of mammals continued, filling every ecological niche. Cenozoic North America was exceptional in only one significant case: Primate fossils from the late Cretaceous have been found in Montana. But North America had no part in the evolution of higher primates, including the appearance of hominids, of which modern humans are the sole survivors. Hominids emerged in Africa between 5 and 11 million years ago. Not until 10,000 to 20,000 years ago did hominids set foot in the Western Hemisphere. The human history of America then began.

The Land Today

Across its breadth, the U.S. presents immense contrasts. They grow even more marked when Hawaii and Alaska are added. Although the "lower 48" lie in the temperate zone (save for southernmost Florida), temperature and precipitation swings can be enormous. Central-continental areas and even parts of the Atlantic seaboard receive seasonally alternating patterns of blizzards and intense summer heat, drought and downpours, tornadoes or hurricanes. On the West Coast, cold Pacific currents and seasonal shifts of air masses produce marked contrasts of wet and dry weather. Rain shadows cast by West-Coast mountain systems ensure the perpetual aridity of the interior Great Basin and the intense heat of the southwestern Sonora Desert.

North America's geological history is visible everywhere. In New York, the Adirondacks are a Precambrian remnant. Since the Paleozoic fusion of Laurentia and Baltica, the Appalachians have eroded greatly, though 200 years ago they still impeded westward settlement. East of the Appalachians, the Piedmont and Atlantic seaboard are products of the Mesozoic breakup of Pangaea. Tectonic drift made the mid-Atlantic coast, with its continental shelf, barrier islands, and Tidewater, an emerging shoreline. New England's rock-bound shore results from coastal land sinking under Ice-Age glaciers, followed by oceanic inundation; the present coastline was once interior highlands. Glacial sculpting and runoff from melted glacial water carved New York's magnificent harbor and the deep-water Hudson, with immense significance for North America's development. Ice-Age geomorphology also left behind the Great Lakes, Earth's largest body of fresh water. On the West Coast, colliding plates are subducting the narrow coastline, with spectacular results, while friction along the San Andreas Fault will eventually sever coastal California from the mainland.

The Human Factor

While Native Americans left their imprint on North America, later settlers drastically modified the natural environment. Eastern and southeastern forests fell to farmers and to timber-cutters harvesting lumber to build America's cities. Where great Piedmont and southeastern hardwood forests stood, piney secondary growth now covers areas deforested for tobacco and cotton plantations. Trappers and hunters, then ranchers and farmers, destroyed wildlife populations. Extensive mining, industry, and urbanization have all presented environmental threats.

One of those threats is global warming. All human civilization occurred in the relatively warm 10,000 years since the last glaciers receded. How present-day signs of global warming may fit into these trends is debated—with high stakes. Perhaps, as many experts suggest, global warming will release polar water into the oceans, drowning coastal areas and disrupting such major currents as the Atlantic Gulf Stream. The consequences, paradoxically, could include another deep freeze. It is sobering to ponder how humans and their technology have become key factors in Earth's evolution. ■

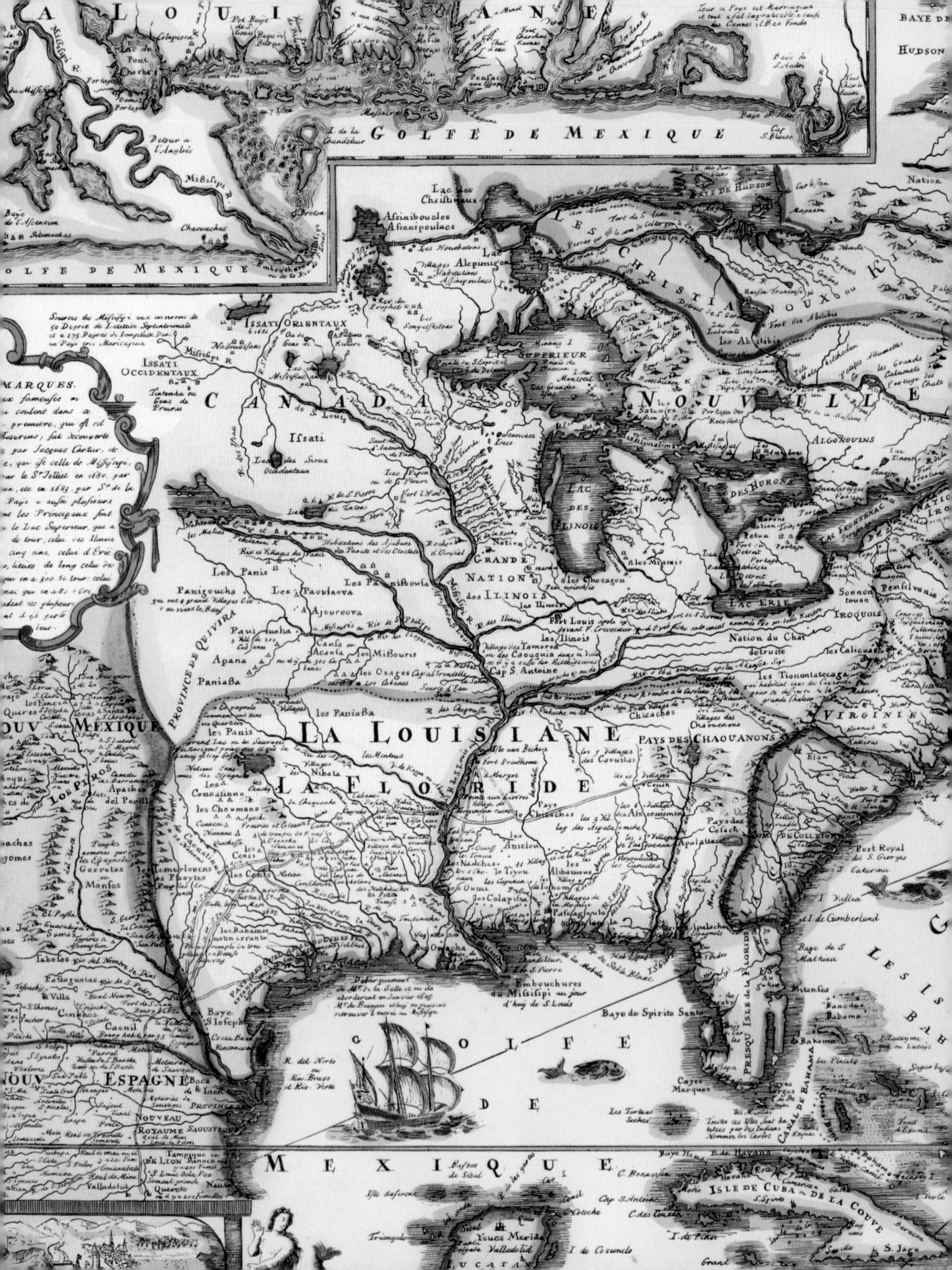

GOLFE DE MEXIQUE
BAYE DE HUDSON
Lac des Christinaux
Assinibouels Assenipoulacs
Lac Alepimigon
LES CHRISTIANOUX ou KIRISTINONS
ISSATI ORIENTAUX
ISSATI OCCIDENTAUX
LAC SUPERIEUR
CANADA
NOUVELLE
Issati
ALGONQUINS
LAC DES ILINOIS
DES HURONS
LAC FRONTENAC
LAC ERIE
GRANDE NATION des ILINOIS
Les Panis
Les Paniassa
Fort Louis
Les Missouris
Les Osages
Cap S. Antoine
PROVINCE DE QUIVIRA
Nation du Chat
IROQUOIS
Pensilvanie
VIRGINIE
PAYS DES CHAOUANONS
LA LOUISIANE
LA FLORIDE
Les Chicachas
NOUV MEXIQUE
LOS PIROS
Apaches
Les Cenis
Embouchures du Missisipi
Baye de Spirito Santo
PRESQU ISLE DE LA FLORIDE
CANAL DE BAHAMA
Baye S. Ioseph
NOUV ESPAGNE
NOUVEAU ROYAUME
GOLFE DE MEXIQUE
ISLE DE CUBA
Port Royal
I. de Cumberland

MILESTONES

- Immmigration
- Religion in America
- Rise of Democracy
- Language
- Legal System
- Slavery
- Industry
- Social Reform
- Conservation & Environment
- Civil Rights
- Space Race
- Global Mission

North America in 1698, two cent
after Columbus made landfall.

IMMIGRATION

AMERICA HAS ALWAYS BEEN A NATION OF NEWCOMERS. STARTING WITH THE earliest English settlers, and continuing up through today, immigrants have arrived on American shores and been greeted with mixed enthusiasm. Indeed, the story of American immigration explains in large part what the country is all about. The story begins in April of 1607 with the arrival of three ships in the Chesapeake Bay. Among the party were Captain John Smith and George Percy.

At first Percy, son of the Earl of Northumberland, raved in his journal about the strawberries, oysters, and plentiful game. But he was not long in changing his tune, what with hunger, disease, and Indians "creeping on all fours from the hills, like bears, with their bows in their mouths." We have no record of what the Indians thought of these founders of Jamestown, but it would likely be a similar recounting of good first impressions that turned sour. This early greet-and-beat was a microcosm of the trials of immigration.

In the early days, it was the newcomers who had the larger impact on the natives, rather than the other way around. The Indians (who themselves had migrated to America thousands of years earlier) were no match for the English tide. East of the Mississippi the native population, around 200,000, was neither organized nor technologically advanced enough to resist invasion. Early wars, such as the Pequot War of 1637 in New England, generally ended in annihilation of the local tribe. European diseases often finished off any possible resistance.

Up through the early 1800s, European immigrants streamed into the colonies and then the United States, primarily from the British Isles. Various groups had intense periods of immigration: In the late 1700s, it was the Scotch-Irish (Scots who had briefly settled in Ireland). From about 1820 to 1880, it was the Irish and Germans. The Irish arrived dirt poor, but the Germans often had a little money and a skill. The Irish took menial jobs, while the Germans went into printing, baking, painting, and the like. Many Germans pushed on to the Midwest, set up farming communities, and maintained old-country traditions.

A second, even larger, wave of immigration hit America around the turn of the century. From 1880 to 1924 some 26 million immigrants arrived—the largest migration in world history. They swelled a population that in 1880 stood at only 50 million. Whereas the earlier wave was primarily from western and northern Europe, the second wave was largely from eastern and southern Europe. Large numbers of Italians came during this period, as well as Jews fleeing persecution in Russia, Poland, and Hungary.

Reaction to the newcomers was mixed. Earlier, there was land ripe for cultivation—and a nation in an expansive mood. Now, with increasing industrialization, growing cities with big factories were in need of cheap labor. But would these people—a kaleidoscope of languages, religions, and customs—fit in?

At around the same time, large numbers of Chinese and Japanese were coming to the West Coast, particularly into the San Francisco area. If the eastern Europeans were different, the Asians were downright foreign. Too much so for some, who worried that all the low-paying jobs were being snatched away from native-born Americans. To limit this latest influx, the government passed the Chinese Exclusion Act in 1882.

English playwright Israel Zangwill wrote in 1908, "America is God's crucible, the great melting pot where all the races of Europe are melting and reforming!" Though the melting pot metaphor may not be the most accurate (a salad with discrete units may be slightly better), it does suggest the nature of America at the time—a changing blend of cultures. Each group affects and is affected by the preexisting culture, yet the result is a more or less homogenous society that speaks the same language and abides by the same laws.

By and large people have immigrated for better opportunities than they could find in their homelands. Large numbers arrived in New York Harbor and were hailed by the poem on the Statue of Liberty's base: "Give me your tired, your poor/ Your huddled masses yearning to breathe free . . . ." America was not a utopian dream, but it was generally better than what they had left behind. Laying railroads, digging canals, and mining coal were not easy, but work was readily available. If the streets weren't lined with gold, they were paved with possibility.

The Immigration and Naturalization Act of 1952 ended the quota system that favored some nationalities over others. Later decades saw the arrival of large numbers of immigrants from places as far-flung as Cuba, El Salvador, Sri Lanka, Vietnam, and India. Debate continues today over numbers and nationalities of immigrants. In 2002 the foreign-born were 11.5 percent of the U.S. population, a rising trend in recent decades, though still below the 14.7 percent of 1910. ■

Faces filled with anxiety, uncertainty, and hope, immigrants arrive in New York aboard the S.S. *Prince Frederick Wilhelm* in 1915. Italians, Russians, Poles, and Hungarians crowded through the portals of America at the turn of the 19th century; by 1920 more than one-third of the nation's population were immigrants and their children.

Religion in America

Americans' religious beliefs are strong. In 2003, 90 percent told pollsters that they believe in God and 84 percent in life after death. In a similar British survey, 60 percent professed belief in God. More significantly, 62 percent of Americans recently said that religion is "very important" in their lives; 60 percent in Mexico, but only 34 percent in Canada, 26 percent in Australia, 18 percent in the United Kingdom, 16 percent in Germany, and 14 percent in France said the same.

By self-identification, more than three-quarters of all Americans—about 225 million—say they are Christians. Jews number about 4 million, Muslims and Buddhists some 1.5 million each; other faiths account for less than a million each. The largest group of dissenters from organized religion—about 39 million Americans—categorize themselves as "nonreligious or secular"; some 3 million are agnostics or atheists. In Britain, 18 percent are "practicing members" of a denomination, and 25 percent nonpracticing; another quarter describe themselves as "spiritually inclined" but don't belong to any religious body; 14 percent and 12 percent, respectively, are self-declared agnostics and atheists. In Canada, 78 percent believe in God, 12 percent are agnostic, and 10 percent unbelievers.

The quest for religious liberty is an enduring theme in Americans' historical identity. The Puritans founded New England so they could worship freely. Maryland's proprietors offered a haven for English Catholics. William Penn, a Quaker, created Pennsylvania as a refuge for victims of religious persecution.

But these religious motives for launching the American 17th-century experiment do not explain modern Americans' strong religiosity. New England's Puritans were not tolerant. They exiled Roger Williams and Anne Hutchinson for challenging orthodoxy, and they exiled, flogged, and even hanged Quakers. In Massachusetts and Connecticut, until the 1830s taxpayers supported the Congregational church. Anglicanism was established in colonial Virginia, the Carolinas, and Georgia, and in Maryland after 1689, but colonial authorities in New York and New Jersey mostly neglected organized religion.

The roots of modern Americans' religiosity lie, rather, in the First and Second Great Awakenings, those vast outpourings that gripped the colonies in the 1740s and swept the U.S. after 1800. By the mid-18th century, New England Puritanism had grown dry and formal, as had southern Anglicanism. In the Awakenings, congregations and individuals sought preachers who would respond to their emotions and promise salvation. From conflicts within churches was born American denominationalism—the conviction that a competition of churches was good. At first, the established churches tried to persecute dissenters. These efforts died with the Revolution and disestablishment. Thomas Jefferson, father of Virginia's Statute on Religious Freedom, had no better friends than the Baptists, once hounded by the Church of England.

Theologically, the Awakenings undermined Puritan Calvinism, which taught that only the predestined would experience salvation. The Awakening's passionate preaching and "revivals" fostered convictions that through faith and reformed living a Christian could make peace with God. Predestination began to disappear from 19th-century American Protestant theology—in part because Baptists, Methodists, and others did not require a seminary-trained clergy. In the communities that took shape as Americans moved west, people proved their character by joining a denomination and living respectably. Salvation became a civic duty. Popular theology adjusted to the democratic religion of 19th-century America—as it still does today.

Because the Awakenings and the Revolution had destroyed established churches, 19th-century Americans never had to resist oppressive state-sponsored religion. Such struggles gave democratic movements in Europe an anti-clerical, anti-religious tone. As Europe industrialized, church attendance dropped sharply. It never recovered. Unlike Americans, Europeans never felt pressures to prove civic virtue by joining churches and doing good works. Only in Ireland and Poland, where Catholicism bolstered resistance to foreign rule, did religion remain a badge of civic solidarity. Present-day comparative measurements of church attendance and religious fervor reflect those contrasting histories and help explain why to many Europeans the U.S. seems a land of religious fanaticism.

Religion remains vibrant in America because for most believers religious affiliation is central to community and family life. The fastest growing religious groups are evangelical denominations and "megachurches" that stress emotional, theologically uncomplicated belief. This has been so since the Great Awakenings. Mainline denominations are losing membership, though this may be a paring down to those who see other strengths—commitment to ideas of social justice and intellectual inquiry—in traditional religion. A mass falling away from religion seems unlikely. ■

Waves of deep religious fervor have repeatedly swept over the United States. Some have called contemporary Americans' commitment to faith the "Third Great Awakening," recalling earlier awakenings of the 18th and 19th centuries.

THE RISE OF DEMOCRACY

COLONIAL AMERICA WAS NOT DEMOCRATIC. DEMOCRATIC SENTIMENTS EXPRESSED during the Revolution did not lead to a democratic federal constitution. The crucial breakthroughs came later. Colonial governance meant maintaining hierarchy. Community leaders competed in politics for acknowledgment of their honor. With differing details, it was the same everywhere. Politics reinforced hierarchy, rather than challenging it.

By driving from the scene the loyalists, the most hierarchy-conscious elements, the Revolution cleared the American ground of the most obdurate opponents of democracy. But the men who headed the Revolution were gentlemen, defending (against British tyranny and popular agitation) their honor as community leaders. Ordinary men were asked to fight for liberty, but under the direction of gentlemen such as George Washington, and insubordination was firmly discouraged. Such democratization that did occur was the overthrow of blatantly unbalanced state legislative representation, whereby Philadelphia and surrounding counties or the Carolina Tidewater had by far outvoted humbler "backcountry" districts. In several states (notably Pennsylvania), legislatures gained authority at governors' expense. But when postwar agitation over debt relief produced Shays's Rebellion in Massachusetts, shuddering gentlemen convened the 1787 Philadelphia Convention. The federal Constitution that it wrote safeguarded the rights of (wellborn) minorities against impulsive majorities. Only in the House of Representatives did the Constitution create a popularly elected organ. The Senate, the federal courts, and the Presidency, which checked and balanced democracy, were implicitly reserved for gentlemen. Anti-Federalists—some with democratic convictions—opposed the Constitution, fearing it would destroy local liberties.

The Federalist period, 1789-1800, saw a bitter struggle between advocates of democratizing American politics, including Thomas Jefferson, and Federalists adamantly opposed. Americans' division into pro- and anti-French Revolution camps helped provoke this struggle; Federalists (including President Washington) feared that the new "democratic republican societies," advocating democracy and a pro-French foreign policy, favored "mob rule." They exaggerated; the societies' members included respectable professional gentlemen and small merchants as well as artisans. Supporting Jefferson for President in 1796 and 1800, they were the core of the Democratic Republican Party.

Jefferson's excruciatingly narrow election in 1800-01 was a triumph for southern gentlemen willing to trust local men to elect their "natural leaders" over hysterical elitists in northeastern cities fearful of "democratical" agitation. Jefferson's Inauguration was epochal in that it represented a peaceful transfer of power; no one was guillotined, French style. But gentlemen remained in command of both federal and state governments, and suffrage often remained restricted to substantial property owners. The Federalists faded, partly because they did not master electioneering and partly because they represented New England—that region had resisted the War of 1812 and was discredited by victory in 1815. By 1820, the Federalists had virtually disappeared; all politicians now belonged to quarreling factions of the Democratic Republican Party. Politics remained a gentleman's game. Voting was done in public, not secretly—and relatively few ordinary men actually voted, even if they qualified.

Democracy emerged between about 1820 and Andrew Jackson's Presidency in 1829-1837, swept in by powerful historical currents. One was the Great

The Declaration of Independence, drafted by Thomas Jefferson with the aid of John Adams and Benjamin Franklin, asserted a fundamental principle of democracy—the people's right to live under a government of their choosing and to alter it if it becomes destructive of their liberties.

Awakening in religion. Traditional Puritan Calvinism had taught that all people were sinners, predestined to hell unless saved by God. Why empower the damned to govern? True, no one claimed that gentlemen were saints (although the 17th-century Puritans had tried to confine voting and officeholding to "converted" church members)—but Calvinism did insist that legitimate "magistrates" (officeholders) ruled by God's will, and they were more apt to be guided by godly clergymen than were ambitious, willful "upstarts" from below. By undermining Calvinism and making individuals responsible for self-improvement, the Great Awakenings legitimated democratic self-rule.

The westward sweep of settlement also abetted democratization. Western pioneers were forming new communities and leaving old hierarchies behind. In the new communities, a person's reputation depended not on known ancestry but on personal qualities—physical prowess, magnetic personality, success in business or farming, and character as revealed by church membership. Everywhere in the new states of the trans-Appalachian West, all grown men had the right to vote, provided they had white skins.

Still another immense change was the advent of the market economy, which also shook old social hierarchies and challenged traditional gentlemanly prerogatives. The wealth created by the capitalist market engendered the myth of the self-made man—a myth because many who thrived had got their start through inherited resources. But the larger point was that being—or claiming to be—"self-made" was now a virtue and a basis for community respect. Always before, being self-made meant being "a mushroom risen upon a dunghill," someone who had got ahead by knavery. In the new capitalist economy, being self-made was the pinnacle of respectability.

Such was the context of the triumph of popular politics—of universal male suffrage, of mass political parties mobilizing ordinary men's votes, of successful politicians boasting of their log-cabin birth even if they had also eaten with silver spoons—in the age of Andrew Jackson. Social and economic hierarchies were not destroyed; indeed, new ones arose, but they were based on success in capitalist enterprise. No one could now assert that it displeased God to empower the people. And since the people could no longer be disfranchised, what more godly calling could there be than to organize movements to put down society's evils—drunkenness, violence, prostitution, slavery, and the oppression of women? All the great reform impulses of Jacksonian America had the common aim of making the people worthy of the unprecedented power that democracy thrust into their hands.

Alexis de Tocqueville, the French visitor of the 1830s who observed American democracy and wrote the greatest book on it, commented repeatedly on the atomization of American society. Replacing old hierarchies, the new American communities were creating churches, volunteer societies, and political clubs. But individuals suffered nagging status insecurity and found it hard to resist majority opinion. ■

LANGUAGE

IN THE FIRST HALF OF THE 17TH-CENTURY WHITE SETTLERS IN NORTH AMERICA hailed predominantly from four regions of England. From the north of England came the Pilgrims and many Quakers peopling Pennsylvania and New Jersey. East Anglian and West-Country Puritans predominated in the 1630s Great Migration to New England. Some Puritans were also from the London area, as were many planters and servants settling the Chesapeake and Pennsylvania.

These English regions had distinctive grammars, accents, and vocabularies, although London was a linguistic melting pot. After the Revolution of 1640-1660, Scotland and the north of Ireland (settled by Scottish and English colonists) supplied most immigrants. These "Scotch-Irish" settlers in central Pennsylvania, the Shenandoah Valley, and the southern Piedmont spoke a distinctive kind of English. Dutch speakers populated the Hudson Valley, the core of the New Netherland colony seized by England in 1664. Germans poured into Pennsylvania and the Shenandoah and Piedmont backcountries during the 18th century. By 1751, so numerous were the Pennsylvania "Dutch" (actually *Deutsch*, or German) that Benjamin Franklin complained that Pennsylvania would soon become German-speaking. French speakers included Protestant (Huguenot) refugees, fur traders from New France (Quebec), and settlers of Louisiana, some of them Acadian ("Cajun") refugees driven from Canada.

By the Revolution, this potpourri produced three American dialects: New England "Yankee" speech; "Midland" speech, from the Hudson Valley to northern Maryland; and Southern speech, from the Chesapeake to Georgia. They remain the major divisions of contemporary "American," although the rise of multicultural New York City added "New Yorkese."

After the Revolution the different accents of American English spread westward. Between the 1790s and the mid-19th century, New Englanders carried their speech into Vermont, upstate New York, and the Great Lakes region. "Midland" speakers settled western Pennsylvania and the Midwest. "Southern" speech, combining Scotch-Irish dialects from the Piedmont and the accents of Tidewater southerners, followed two tracks. One took southern accents and grammar (such as "you all" or "ya'll" for the second person plural) into Tennessee, Alabama, Mississippi, northern Louisiana, and Texas; the second track, taken mostly by Virginians (like Abraham Lincoln's ancestors), crossed the Appalachians into Kentucky and Ohio, Indiana, and Illinois. Post-Civil War migrations took the three American speech patterns to the West Coast.

The American language changed as it moved across the continent. White Northerners and Southerners maintained their distinctiveness because conflicts caused them to live in different regions; speech patterns blended farther west where they settled together. and California became the great melting pot.

Except for the upper class of Boston and other East Coast cities, "American" was not hamstrung by reverence for bookish forms of the language. This freedom from cultural constraint, geographical mobility, and changes in 19th- and early 20th-century life offered limitless opportunities for inventing new words. Americans borrowed freely as they encountered words from other languages—either those of immigrants or of other North American peoples—for things that they needed to talk about. "Prairie," for example, was a French word, adapted by Americans settling the open grasslands of the Midwest where French fur traders had preceded them. "Boss" was a Dutch word, useful in expressing 19th-century market-economy relationships. Mexican Spanish provided a host of expressions related to ranching (from *rancho*) and livestock handling. (*Vaquero* —for cowboy—did not catch on, but bronco, rodeo, lasso, and chaps all did.) Native American words and expressions—like canoe, kayak, moccasin, wigwam, powwow, and bury the hatchet—had been joining white Americans' vocabulary since colonial times. As East European Jews flocked into New York, American speech absorbed many colorful slang words from Yiddish (schlep, heist, shyster, kosher [correct or right], schmoose.) There are even contributions from Chinese (gung-ho).

African-American English dates from the 18th century, as slaves learned to communicate with each other and whites in English. Where they vastly outnumbered whites, notably the Sea Islands of South Carolina and Georgia, blacks developed and retain a pidgin, a language that develops when people of different tongues have to communicate—in this case Gullah, using many West African expressions and grammatical forms. Elsewhere, black English is closer to southern whites' English. As American popular culture interacted with African-American culture, it absorbed much of black origin—jazz, for example (originally an obscenity, reflecting the genre's origin as music performed for white brothel patrons), and cool, from the West African word for "good"—kul.

Today, American English has become every educated foreign person's "second language." It has displaced French as the language of diplomacy, and has become the language of high technology and international business. Universal education and the mass media have smoothed many regional and class differences in American speech. Similarly, the diffusion of American culture and high technology will undoubtedly make American English indispensable in our global future. ■

Altering not just their language but their entire manner of life, the Carlisle Indian Industrial School, founded in 1879, taught thousands of Native American children English and such Euro-American skills as farming and home economics.

Legal System

America, like England, has two streams of law: common law, based on precedent and judges' decisions, and statutory law, which legislatures enact. Like Britons, colonials gloried in "the rights of freeborn Englishmen" and resisted statutory law being imposed on them. They wanted their own legislatures to enact the statutes. Americans and Britons alike contrasted common law with the "despotism" of the Roman (or Civil) Law of continental Europe and Scotland.

Because it was judge-made law, common-law court practice involved an adversarial procedure. The two sides argued before a jury that considered the facts and a judge who ruled, on the basis of precedents, what evidence and procedures were permissible. In civil- law courts, judges, without juries, interrogated both sides before rendering a decision. England also used that procedure under admiralty law, where colonial American smugglers faced trial.

In the 19th century, defining exactly what American law—common or statutory—actually meant was in the hands of "judicial activists," above all Chief Justice John Marshall. Studying and learning to use judge-made precedents was, in addition, the core of American legal education, whether by "reading the law" under an experienced attorney's direction or by taking courses in a school of law.

Since colonial times, however, Americans had to adapt common law to local conditions. This adaptation accelerated with the post-Revolutionary westward push and the rise of democracy. Abolition of primogeniture, redefinitions of divorce and property rights, and the new hazards and liabilities created by industrialization all required statutes changing common-law precedents. So did reforms in the savage common-law punishment of convicted criminals. Slavery, not recognized by the common law, also required statutory regulation in antebellum slave states.

Both state legislatures and Congress used statutory legislation to redefine 19th-century American law. Yet by concentrating in the Supreme Court the power to declare federal and state legislation unconstitutional, a principal first enunciated in *Marbury* v. *Madison* (1803), Marshall made the Court the ultimate arbiter of changes in state and federal law. The Marshall Court (1801-1835) strongly supported updating property rights and commercial transactions to fit the emerging market economy. After the Civil War, the Constitution's scope was enlarged by the 14th Amendment (1868), enacted to extend "the equal protection of the law" to former slaves but used primarily by federal courts to define property rights—usually to the benefit of business and the detriment of labor unions and opponents of monopolies. The Supreme Court narrowly interpreted the 14th Amendment, limiting its civil-rights provisions only to ex-slaves and in 1883 striking down the 1875 Civil Rights Act. This became a bleak era for minorities, epitomized by the Court's 1896 *Plessy* v. *Ferguson* decision upholding "separate but equal" segregation.

Progressivism marked a turning point. The transition was foreshadowed by the influential book *The Common Law* (1881) by Oliver Wendell Holmes, Jr., a Harvard professor and thereafter a justice, first of the Massachusetts supreme court and, after 1902, of the U.S. Supreme Court. Holmes's classic dictum was that "the life of the law is not logic, but experience." He excoriated precedent-bound common-law traditions and insisted that, by intelligent legislation, law should meet changing circumstances. This was the language of pragmatism, an American philosophical school to whose creators Holmes was personally close.

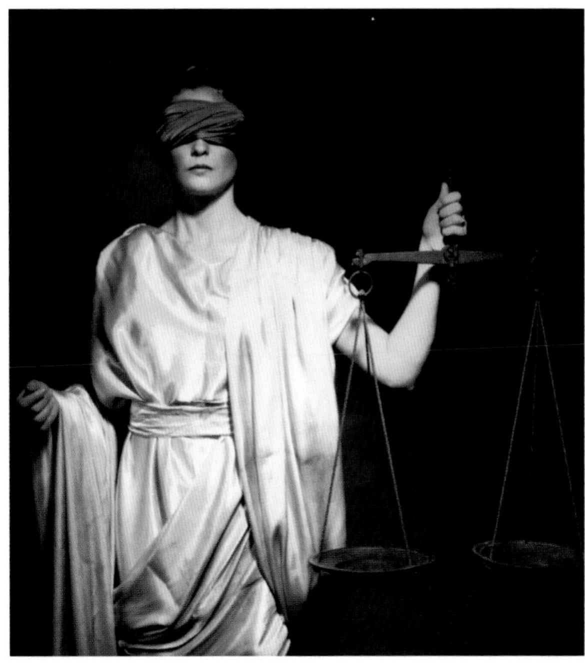

Justice personified as a classically garbed woman, wearing a blindfold and wielding the symbolic scales in which right and wrong can impartially be weighed, has for centuries been the iconic image of the law in Western culture.

Pragmatism dominated American legal thought and education during the progressive era, when federal and state legislation was heavily concerned with labor, public health and safety, and antitrust issues. But by no means did all Court decisions favor progressive causes. Holmes became known as "the great dissenter" from his many disagreements with the Supreme Court's conservative majority.

During the progressive era the legal profession changed enormously, essentially into what it is today. One-on-one apprenticeship gave way to professional study in accredited law schools, and lawyers were licensed to practice only after rigorous examinations by state bar associations. These changes paralleled the emergence of other highly trained, self-regulated professions, notably those of physicians, engineers, architects, and educators.

In the New Deal years, tensions between conservative business interests and progressive reform climaxed. A conservative Supreme Court majority struck down much of the Roosevelt Administration's New Deal legislation, leading FDR in 1937 to try to "pack" the Court with liberal justices. This perceived attack on checks and balances alienated the public, though deaths and retirements soon produced a pro-New Deal Court.

The legal profession's demographics changed after 1945. The expansion of college enrollments during the postwar years swelled the ranks of lawyers in American society; 286,000 lawyers practiced in 1960, and double that number 25 years later, giving the U.S. the world's highest per-capita concentration of attorneys. After the 1960s, women flocked into the profession. The politics of American lawyers, once heavily conservative, now span the spectrum.

The Supreme Court over which Earl Warren presided (1953-1969) was epoch-making, and Warren Burger's Court (1969-1986) continued this process. The Warren Court's basic principle was "incorporation" of Bill of Rights protections into state and federal law. Striking down segregation in the 1954 *Brown* decision, the Court returned to the original emphasis of the 14th Amendment's "equal protection" clause. Subsequent controversial Warren and Burger Court decisions extended constitutional protections in cases involving church-state separation, criminal defendants' rights, pornography, and affirmative action. Searching for a constitutional foundation for its 1973 *Roe* v. *Wade* decision legalizing abortion, the Court found in the "penumbras" of the Bill of Rights an implied "right of privacy," an extrapolation controversial even among some advocates of abortion choice. "Judge-made" law had reached its ultimate extension—save, perhaps, for the Court's intervention in deciding the outcome of the disputed 2000 presidential election in *Gore* v. *Bush*.

Judicial activism became a political shibboleth by 2000. Conservatives denounced it; liberals saw conservative federal courts as a mortal threat. In 2005, the Senate approached collapse over conservatives' demands that Bush have a filibuster-free environment to confirm ultra-conservative federal judges. Arguments over original intent and activist judges ignore the tension between judge-made and statutory law, inherent in Anglo-American legal tradition. "The Americans have given their courts immense political powers," observed Alexis de Tocqueville in 1836. He would say the same today. ■

Slavery

In 1619, a Dutch ship bringing blacks to Jamestown opened the earliest phase in the history of American slavery. We do not know whether these first African Americans were enslaved: All servants, white or black, owed several years' involuntary servitude. Life was short and harsh for virtually everyone who came to the unhealthy tobacco-growing Chesapeake. Many servants did not survive to enjoy their promised freedom. Nevertheless, some black Virginians and Marylanders became free, owned land, and even acquired their own bondspeople. Others were enslaved.

In the late 17th century this phase ended. When Barbados planters helped found Carolina in the 1670s, they brought legal definitions of lifelong servitude from England's Caribbean colonies, where sugar plantations used African slave labor. In Virginia and Maryland it was getting harder to enforce service on whites and Indians, and blacks were singled out for hereditary servitude. By the 1690s, all southern colonies legally defined slavery as a condition for blacks alone.

The years from about 1690 to the American Revolution mark the second phase of American slavery. In the northern and middle colonies, slaves—used for house and shop service—became more numerous as the white population increased and grew more prosperous. In the Chesapeake and the Carolinas, slavery became the foundation of the economy. South Carolina developed a particularly cruel form of bondage after 1690, based on rice cultivation. (Ironically, rice growing was probably brought to the colony by West African slaves.) Southern imports of slaves increased dramatically, mostly from the Caribbean. Natural increase, as well as slave imports, made enslaved blacks the majority in South Carolina and almost so in Virginia. Slavery was brutal and unquestioned, with few slaves learning more than rudimentary English or practicing Christianity, and masters regarded their human property as little different from work animals.

The onset of the Revolution in the 1770s initiated the third phase of American slavery, which continued until 1831. Critics of slavery began speaking out—Quakers, citing religious grounds, claimed that no human was morally fit to own another. Revolutionary rhetoric caused many in the North and some in the Chesapeake to consider slavery incompatible with American liberty. After the Revolution, all states from Pennsylvania north abolished slavery. Only exceptionally, though, did they accord blacks full civil rights.

In the North and South, Christianity reached enslaved populations during these years. The religious movement called the Great Awakening reached across racial lines, and slaves were more readily converted as their command of English increased. After 1808, when the Atlantic slave trade was abolished, the slave population became largely native-born and English speaking. A distinctive African-American culture emerged.

Individual emancipation occurred in the post-Revolutionary South—occasionally. Most slave owners either feared or could not afford to let go; as slave owner Thomas Jefferson put it, "We have the wolf by the ears." Slave conspiracies and revolts after 1800, as well as the bloody and successful slave rebellion in the French colony of St. Domingue (today Haiti), frightened Southerners. No southern states enacted emancipation; antislavery Southerners' main concern was to deport freed slaves. The final nail in the coffin of southern antislavery was driven by Nat Turner's Rebellion in Virginia in 1831, which, though it cost few white lives (and more than a few black lives), convinced almost all Southerners that it was too dangerous to lift the controls that slavery imposed on a presumably vengeful black population.

This romanticized image of entire families of slaves fleeing to northern freedom expresses the aspirations and the idealism of antebellum abolitionists who found slavery more and more intolerable.

The year 1831, which opened the fourth phase of American slavery, was significant not only for Nat Turner's Rebellion but also for the emergence of a militant antislavery movement in the North. Southern whites' response was to assert that slavery was not just a necessary evil, but a "positive good." That became the predominant southern view, and it culminated in secession and the outbreak of the Civil War. Most northern whites did not support abolitionism, regarded as "extremist." But by the 1850s, antislavery in the North became a movement aimed at assuring that the trans-Missouri West would be open only to free white labor. That "Free Soil" definition of antislavery put North and South on a collision course.

The last phase of American slavery was the shortest—that of the Civil War years, from 1861 to 1865. The North fought for the Union, not to destroy slavery, at least until Lincoln's Emancipation Proclamation of 1863 abolished the institution in all states continuing in open rebellion. There were no slave revolts in the Confederacy, but slavery gradually eroded. Slaves fled to invading Union armies, and 180,000 black men volunteered to serve as Union soldiers, an enormous contribution to the war effort. So desperate did the Confederacy become that, in the closing months of the war, it offered freedom to any slave volunteering to fight for southern independence. A few did volunteer, though none served in combat. Defeat on the battlefield—at the cost of more than half a million lives—destroyed southern slavery, and this was ratified by the 13th Amendment in 1865, which formally abolished slavery everywhere in the U.S.

Never was American slavery a benevolent institution, as white apologists claimed. The essence of slavery was the ownership of one human being by another, with all that implied. Individual masters might be kind, but slaves always knew they were powerless.

For 250 years, slavery was a fact of American life. Even today its memory separates African Americans, whose forebears were brought to this land in bondage, from the historical experience shared by the descendants of others who reached America in search of freedom and opportunity. ■

INDUSTRY

IN THE LATTER HALF OF THE 19TH CENTURY, THE UNITED STATES BECAME INCREASINGLY industrialized. The spread of railroads and the rise of new inventions made possible the growth and efficiency of industry, which propelled more advances in technology. The emergence of the petroleum industry, for example, paved the way for transportation, manufacturing, and agriculture on a national scale. Bell's telephone and Edison's affordable electric lighting linked the nation and sped the pace of progress.

This was a time of massive migration from farm to factory. The plow and the sickle were traded in for the assembly line, the forge, and the smokestack. Cities grew at phenomenal rates. Cleveland in the second half of the 1800s grew from a population of 17,000 to 400,000, spurred by the production of locomotives and the founding of Standard Oil Company by John D. Rockefeller in 1870. Also on Lake Erie, Detroit revved into high gear when the Ford Motor Company was established there in 1903 and began mass producing inexpensive automobiles. The country was never the same.

U.S. Steel furnaces belch fumes along the Monongahela River east of Pittsburgh in 1905. Industrialists Andrew Carnegie and Henry Frick combined their steel-making and coal-production concerns into a behemoth enterprise that produced the bulk of the growing nation's steel.

These two women, working as machinists during World War I, build refrigerators for Bohn Refrigerator Company in St. Paul, Minnesota.

Pittsburgh was perhaps the industrial giant of the time. Situated in Pennsylvania hills loaded with iron ore, coal, and limestone, the city was perfect for the iron and steel industries. And with the Monongahela and Allegheny Rivers joining here to form the Ohio, iron and steel could easily be shipped to market. By the late 19th century, half the nation's steel came from "Iron City." Pittsburgh claimed nearly 50 iron and steel foundries, an equal number of glass factories and oil refineries, and hundreds of other production facilities. All that industry resulted in a city described as "Hell with the lid taken off." Skies were black with soot; railroads and machinery banged and huffed day and night; fumes plagued residents; dreary winter days were indistinguishable from night. Little wonder that Pittsburgh had a hard time shaking its image long after it had become clean and modern.

Chicago was in a class by itself. The nation's second largest city (after New York), Chicago grew from a midwestern stockyard into a metropolis with steel mills and shipping. In the 1910s, its factories expanded to churn out material for the war in Europe. It was during this decade that thousands of blacks migrated to Chicago and other northern cities from points south, adding to the heavy immigrant flow. Chicago's black population increased from 44,000 to 109,000, the newcomers lured by the plentiful new factory jobs.

The industrialization and urbanization of America brought new opportunities for many people. A few seized on the limitless possibilities. These captains of industry, or robber barons, cornered the industrial markets. Exploiting a government policy of laissez-faire, or non-interference, the industrialists pooled their capital into corporations that produced goods and services at prices low enough to drive out the competition. Cornelius Vanderbilt took over the shipping and railroad industries; John D. Rockefeller formed an oil trust in 1870; and Andrew Carnegie muscled control of the steel business. By 1900 an elite group had staked out monopolies in the country's leading industries, including sugar, rubber, telephones, and farm machinery.

Carnegie's methods illustrate the principle. Predicting a need for steel as the nation industrialized, Carnegie built modern mills to produce steel fast. Then he began buying coal and iron ore mines around Pittsburgh. Thus armed with a steady supply of cheap raw materials, he bought rail lines to ship his product. He owned everything the industry needed. When a recession hit, he added to his portfolio at low prices; when the economy heated up, he realized huge profits.

While a small cadre of people were growing fabulously wealthy, an increasing number were being left out of the American dream. Mark Twain dubbed this the Gilded Age—it glittered on the surface, but underneath lay base metal. Unchecked by government regulation, greed and corruption flourished.

To counter the powerful forces in control, laborers banded together in unions. A Dutch Jewish immigrant named Samuel Gompers organized a trade union of cigar makers and became a spokesman of the labor movement. In the early 1880s, he formed the American Federation of Labor, one of the first national labor organizations. In 1955 it joined forces with the Congress of Industrial Organizations to become the AFL-CIO, a powerful voice for labor.

Countering the unions and their strikes, big corporations created blacklists of union employees, hired strikebreakers, and used armed guards to intimidate strikers. Between 1881 and 1905, some 37,000 strikes were called around the nation. Most were small and short-lived. Yet by 1900, workers had achieved rights of organizing, striking, and collective bargaining, and had improved their working conditions and wages. ■

SOCIAL REFORM

IN A GOVERNMENT OF THE PEOPLE, BY THE PEOPLE, AND FOR THE PEOPLE, AS THE UNITED States was from the beginning, the excesses of one group will not be tolerated indefinitely if they appear to infringe on the freedom of another. Such was the mood at the turn of the 20th century, when big business seemed to have the government and everyone else in its pocket. Known as the Progressive era, it continued through the first two decades of the 1900s.

It was a time of correcting the abuses and neglect of a hands-off government that had operated since the Civil War. In the late 1890s, half the nation's wealth was owned by one percent of its population. Corrupt city bosses and filthy rich tycoons had more and more power; farmers and working men had less and less. Midwestern Populists advocated a return to the agrarian ideal. With modern farm machinery producing an oversupply of crops, prices were dropping; high freight rates cut further into farm profits. Farmers were being marginalized, left out of the new America. In stepped the great orator William Jennings Bryan, who captured the Populists' imagination and ended up on the Democratic ticket for President in 1896. "The farmer who goes forth in the morning," he roared, "and toils all day is as much of a businessman as the man who goes upon the board and bets upon the price of grain."

Though Bryan lost, his voice was not drowned out. The Progressives pushed for reforms in politics, business, and other facets of American life. Laws were passed to break up trusts, to enact a graduated income tax, to provide referenda on state policies, to recall corrupt officials, to elect senators directly, to give women the vote, to close saloons, and to ensure hygiene in food and housing. Many of these became law by constitutional amendment; the amendment prohibiting the liquor trade was the only one repealed.

The Constitution had been written for an agrarian nation; the reformists tried to adapt it to an urban, industrial society. With Teddy Roosevelt as President, real reform could begin. Stronger than any President since the Civil War, Roosevelt was able to break the Standard Oil Company, Duke's tobacco trust,

An impassioned suffragist exhorts a crowd from the back of an open automobile; in 1920 the 19th Amendment to the Constitution finally gave women the right to vote. During Woodrow Wilson's Presidency (1913-21) many progressive reforms were enacted.

the railroad trust, and many others. Known as a trust-buster, Rosevelt was more showman than die-hard anti-monopolist. In fact, he was all for big business, just against bad business. His weaker successor, President Robert Taft, actually brought more antitrust cases, but Roosevelt set the tone of reform.

Among the significant legislation passed was a series of state laws that restricted child labor. Young children could no longer be employed, and older children were prohibited from working more than ten hours a day and at night and banned from dangerous employment. Safety laws were passed after a devastating fire in New York's Triangle Shirtwaist Company in 1911 left 150 women dead because there were no fire escapes. Public outrage led to the municipal building codes and factory inspection acts that we take for granted today.

Along with legislation, social-minded individuals and institutions rose up to help the less fortunate. Some one hundred settlement houses around the country provided child care for working mothers, offered free hot meals, and helped immigrants and others find jobs.

Hull House, in Chicago, was started by Jane Addams, who had been inspired by a visit to a settlement house in England. The Salvation Army, also originating in England, came to America in 1880 and spread into communities large and small.

Muckraking journalists heeded the call of reform, and wrote damning accounts of sweatshops, the insurance and drug businesses, prostitution, and more. Upton Sinclair's 1906 novel *The Jungle* exposed the unsanitary conditions of Chicago's slaughterhouses. The book led to the Pure Food and Drug Act, outlawing the sale of fraudulently labeled products.

Advanced technology did much to improve workplace safety and efficiency, but big business would not regulate itself. In 1913 alone 25,000 people died from machine accidents. Woodrow Wilson expanded the progressive agenda, proposing legislation in aid of farmers, small businesses, and laborers.

Franklin D. Roosevelt's New Deal put some three million people back to work during the Depression. His Works Progress Administration and Social Security Act were steps toward public welfare, part of his effort to keep the American system from collapsing.

President Lyndon Johnson's Great Society plan of the 1960s was the most ambitious social reform program since the New Deal. One of his main goals was to eliminate poverty in America by providing assistance to the needy and by offering economic opportunities to help people support themselves. He had but modest success. His Job Corps was costly and failed to dent the unemployment rate. Medicare and Medicaid gave access to medical care, but hospitals and doctors billed the government at exorbitant rates, thus raising the cost of medicine.

FDR's social security system was set up to provide a safety net against disability and old age. Reserves in the fund are projected to grow until around 2012, while the baby boom generation continues to contribute to the system. But then that generation will begin retiring and drawing its own social security benefits. Funds could dry up by the year 2037. To ward off this potential disaster, Congress has considered a number of solutions, including tax increases, a higher retirement age, and cuts in benefits. Another possibility, allowing contributors to invest some of their own funds, has stirred recent debate because of the attendant risks. ■

Conservation & Environment

With serious depletions of the nation's wildlife, forests, and other natural resources, a national environmental movement arose at the turn of the 20th century. To "do something for wildness and make the mountains glad," naturalist John Muir founded the Sierra Club in 1892, and in the early 1900s fellow outdoorsman Theodore Roosevelt joined his cause. Though he was supported by big business, Roosevelt became more and more progressive during his Presidency.

He set aside nearly 150 million acres of forest and created the United States Forest Service. He rigidly enforced the lumbering, mining, and grazing laws on the lands in this federal reserve. He also doubled the number of national parks in the system, and put together a National Conservation Conference that led to individual state conservation commisssions.

During the Depression of the 1930s, FDR's Civilian Conservation Corps provided jobs and at the same time helped protect the country's natural heritage. With tree planting, trail clearing, and fire fighting, the CCC focused attention on the nation's forests. The dams erected for the extensive Tennessee Valley Authority and other projects helped control floods that had periodically devastated area farmlands. The Dust Bowl tragedy of the 1930s, in which Great Plains farms and ranches were stripped of topsoil, was caused by poor soil management as much as by drought. The ensuing poverty and migration from the area led to FDR's Soil Conservation Service, promoting long-range soil use.

Along with the growing conservation movement, the new science of ecology combined awe at nature's power and beauty with investigation into its workings. Calling for a "land ethic" that placed humans within the natural world as responsible participants, Aldo Leopold wrote in his 1949 masterpiece, *A Sand County Almanac*: "A thing is right when it tends to preserve the integrity, stability, and beauty of the biotic community. It is wrong when it tends otherwise."

That many things were tending otherwise—dangerously so—had become increasingly clear by the 1960s. Another landmark of environmental writing, Rachel Carson's 1962 *Silent Spring* detailed the pervasiveness of DDT in the food chain. The public was jolted into awareness and the government into action. The National Environmental Policy Act of 1970 pushed major legislation to protect the land, water, and air, and their plant and animal inhabitants. Species near the brink of extinction made comebacks. The 1982 Nuclear Waste Policy Act addressed the future of radioactive refuse. It recommended that high-level detritus from reactors and weapons should be separated from the biosphere—in bedrock, polar ice, and deep ocean basins—for approximately 250,000 years.

Congress created the Office on Environmental Policy in 1993 to coordinate various federal environmental policies. Its objective is to consider the health of overall ecosystems—southeastern wetlands, for example—rather than concentrating on specific species that are in danger. With the protection of whole habitats, the individuals within them would ultimately benefit.

Since the late 1990s the issue of global warming has found America at odds with much of the rest of the world. Emissions of carbon dioxide and other so-called greenhouse gases primarily from the burning of fossil fuels have, according to most climatologists, contributed to an atmospheric greenhouse effect and significantly raised Earth's temperature. Deforestation has added to the effect by reducing trees, which absorb carbon dioxide. Scientific debate today centers on the rate of global warming and its potential future consequences. The gradual melting of the polar

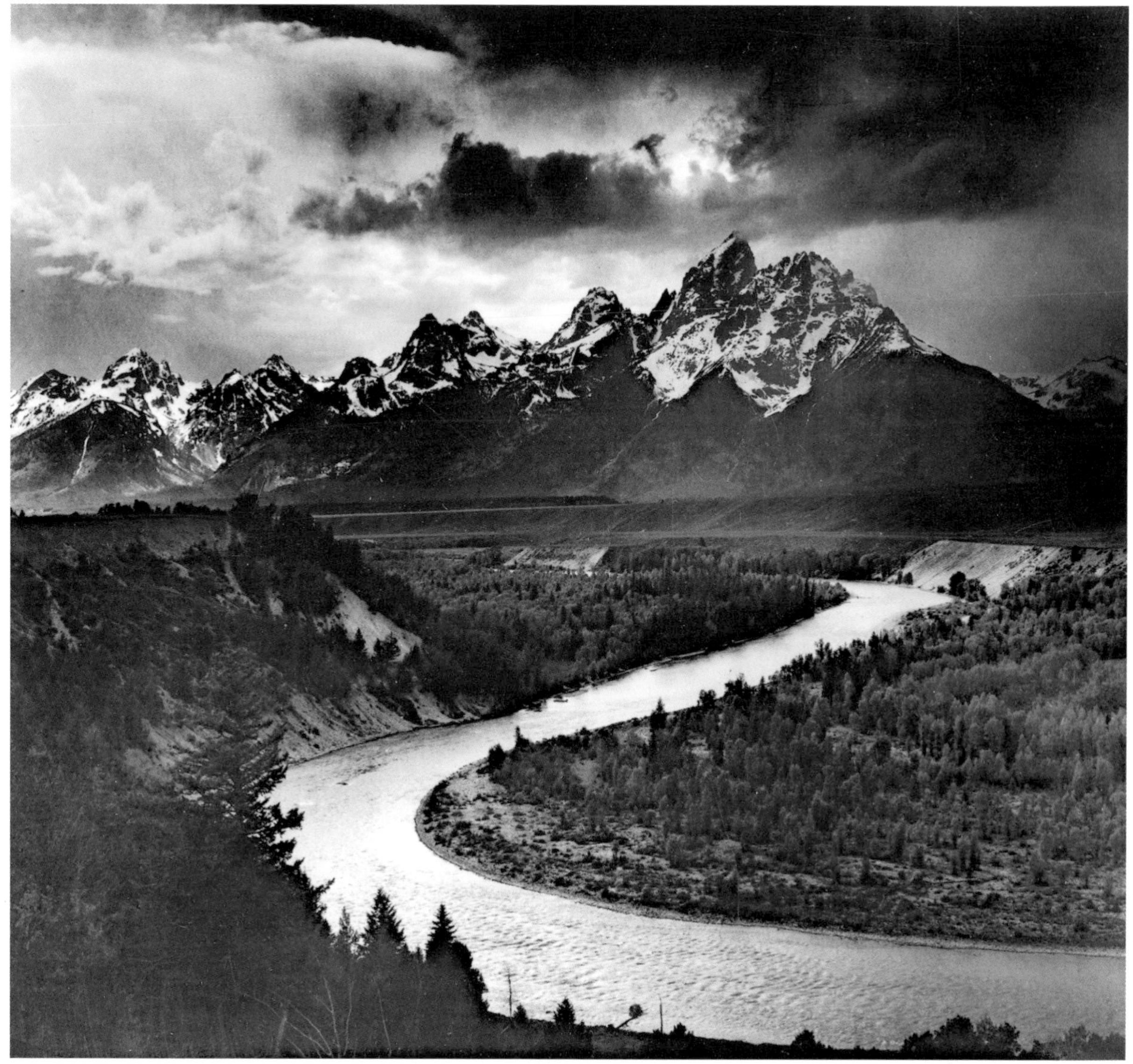

The shining Snake River curves away from the Teton Range in Wyoming in this 1940's Ansel Adams photograph. Adams' straightforward landscapes capture the many moods of the majestic western wilderness; his love of the outdoors led to his support for the conservation movement.

ice caps, for instance, is expected to raise sea levels and thus flood coastal areas; on the other hand, crops could be raised in areas now too cold to farm. In 1997 delegates from 160 countries met in Japan to discuss the issue. The resulting accord, the Kyoto Protocol, calls for the voluntary reduction of greenhouse gas emissions between the years 2008 and 2012.

The main environmental issues in the U.S. in the 21st century are the need for non-oil energy alternatives and for conservation. The latter issue has pitted pro-development forces against slow- or no-development groups. Sustainable development seeks to limit the use of non-renewable natural resources, such as fossil fuels, and to concentrate building within existing cities, leaving large swaths of land untouched.

The newest environmental philosophies take into account the entire planet as an interconnected ecosystem. Many environmental leaders would like to see future public policy conceived around this idea. ■

CIVIL RIGHTS

THE UNITED STATES CONSTITUTION GUARANTEES THE CIVIL RIGHTS OF individuals—specifically, the rights of free speech, religious choice, property ownership, and fair and equal treatment by other individuals and groups. Protecting these rights, especially for minorities, has not always proved easy. Groups unfairly discriminated against have included blacks, women, Jews, Hispanics, American Indians, Asians, homosexuals, and the handicapped.

Since the 1950s a number of legal cases and new laws have been aimed at protecting the civil rights of the nation's largest minority, African Americans. Many blacks had served with distinction during World War II, yet had not been properly recognized; at the same time, the National Association for the Advancement of Colored People was gaining membership and challenging the fairness of the "separate but equal" doctrine handed down by the Supreme Court in 1896. Making white America more receptive to change, the anticommunist witch hunts left many with the fear that basic civil liberties were under attack.

Several Supreme Court rulings in the late 1940s and early 1950s brought progress in the black struggle for equal rights, none more so than the landmark 1954 case *Brown* v. *Board of Education of Topeka*. The suit was filed when the school board in Topeka, Kansas, refused to let a black girl attend a public school near her home. The high Court ruled that segregation in public schools was unconstitutional—separate but equal was no longer acceptable in the eyes of the law.

In Montgomery, Alabama, a bus boycott was staged in 1955 when seamstress Rosa Parks and others refused to give their seats to whites. A local ordinance required blacks to move if whites wanted to sit down. Lasting more than a year, the boycott crippled the bus service. By walking and carpooling, the black community found it could organize peaceful protests and succeed. The bus law was struck down, and the boycott's leader, Reverend Martin Luther King, Jr., emerged as a national civil-rights figure.

During the late 1950s and early 1960s southern schools began slowly to desegregate, sometimes by the use of force. The most newsworthy event was the desegregation of Central High School in Little Rock, Arkansas, in 1957, when Governor Orval M. Faubus brought in the National Guard to prevent a few black students from matriculating. President Eisenhower sent in 1,000 paratroopers to protect the new students from unruly mobs; a handful of soldiers remained throughout the year. Sporadic rioting broke out in other towns, but a majority of the South obeyed the law peacefully, perhaps cowed by the example of Little Rock. Though anti-black discrimination continued, the public schools became the one point of interface in communities large and small.

The next major thrust of the civil-rights movement was for voting rights and equality in public places, including hotels, restaurants, and theaters. King's Southern Christian Leadership Conference joined with other groups of blacks and whites to organize protests, sit-ins, and marches. Students in Greensboro, North Carolina, and other places sat at lunch counters where blacks were traditionally denied service and refused to leave. Groups boarded buses on "freedom rides" to test the efficacy of new laws regarding equality in interstate transportation; they were sometimes targeted by violent mobs. In a march on Washington in 1963, King rallied 200,000 protesters with his famous "I Have a Dream" speech about racial equality.

Splintering off from King's ethic of civil disobedience, militant black groups challenged the entire notion of gaining access within the system. Malcolm X and other Black Muslim leaders believed that blacks should have a separate culture, even a separate state, with its own values. "The Negro," said Malcolm X in 1964, "[must] develop his character and his culture in accord with his own nature." The following year, speaking in suppport of racial harmony, he was assassinated by black followers, who felt betrayed.

Presidents Kennedy and Johnson were finally goaded into action. In 1964 a sweeping Civil Rights Act was passed after a 75-day filibuster in Congress, one of the longest in history. The bill outlawed discrimination by public businesses, employers, and unions. After a protest march from Selma to Montgomery, Alabama, a Voting Rights Act was passed in 1965 barring poll taxes and literacy tests. The Civil Rights Act of 1968 forbade discrimination in housing, and a Supreme Court case ruled that housing sales and rentals were subject to the federal antidiscrimination laws.

In the 1970s, the federal government initiated a policy of "affirmative action" to make up for past injustices against blacks and other minorities. Supreme Court cases since 1978 have ruled that while race could be considered in college admissions and federal programs, quotas and point systems giving preference based on race are unconstitutional. The complexities of the law continue to surface as institutions attempt to level the playing field to be fair to everyone.

Among other groups that have had recent successes with civil-rights issues, the handicapped won a victory in 1990 when Congress passed the Americans with Disabilities Act, requiring that public buildings and mass transit be accessible to the disabled. And in 1996 the high Court overturned an amendment to the Colorado Constitution that banned laws protecting homosexuals from discrimination. In effect, the Supreme Court reversed a position it had taken a decade earlier when it ruled that states could outlaw homosexuality. ■

Three black protesters in Birmingham, Alabama, brace themselves against the searing force of a fire hose wielded by local police in May 1963. Television cameras braodcast the images around the world; outraged viewers spurred action to address long-standing civil-rights abuses.

Space Race

In October of 1957 observers of the nighttime sky saw an unusual object. Moving in a steady trajectory against a background of stars, the first manmade satellite was orbiting Earth. Launched during the Cold War, the Soviet Sputnik satellite touched off the space race, a contest of technology that symbolized the competing ideologies of communism and democracy. The race spurred an unprecedented peacetime advancement of scientific knowledge and achievement.

The National Aeronautics and Space Administration (NASA), established in 1958, has propelled America to the forefront of space exploration; its later cooperation with Russia and other countries has helped breach political gaps while furthering our understanding of the heavens.

Even before Sputnik galvanized the American public, plans were afoot for a U.S. satellite as part of an international effort to obtain more scientific information about our planet. What appeared to be a technological gap between the two countries was more a matter of timing; less than four months after Sputnik the U.S. launched its own Explorer satellite on January 31, 1958. No mere publicity stunt, Explorer helped prove the existence of radiation zones that circle Earth and influence electric charges in the atmosphere.

The competitive nature of the early years of American space exploration helped fuel federal funding, which sped the pace of progress. The U.S. embarked on manned spaceflight missions on May 5, 1961, when Alan B. Shepard, Jr., took a 15-minute suborbital flight as part of the Mercury project. Later that month, President Kennedy announced a hugely ambitious, high-profile objective: "I believe that this nation should commit itself to achieving the goal, before this decade is out, of landing a man on the moon and returning him safely to Earth."

The first American to orbit Earth, astronaut John Glenn became a national hero on February 20, 1962; his three orbits took less than five hours, during which he had to manually correct the attitude of his spacecraft. In 1974, Glenn capitalized on his popularity by winning a Senate seat, and in 1998 he went back into orbit aboard the shuttle *Discovery* to become, at age 77, the oldest person in space.

No space program has generated more excitement than Project Apollo, which was to achieve the dream of taking mankind beyond Earth and onto another planetary body. At a cost of $25.4 billion over 11 years, the Apollo program was the largest non-military technological enterprise the U.S. had ever undertaken, with the possible exception of the Panama Canal. Hundreds of top engineers, rocket scientists, and astrophysicists staked their careers on the job. A fire in 1967 killed three astronauts in an Apollo capsule on the ground, underscoring the dangers of this cutting-edge adventure. By the end of 1968, Apollo 8 was orbiting the moon, its crew stirring the wonder of earthbound people. An unbelievable dream was becoming a reality.

On July 20, 1969, Neil Armstrong piloted the lunar module of Apollo 11 to the moon's surface with less than 30 seconds of fuel left. Then the world watched a grainy, black-and-white transmission of Armstrong descending the module's ladder and setting foot on the moon. "That's one small step for man," he said, "one giant leap for mankind."

Several more successful Apollo missions followed, each a major advance in spaceflight technology. The one exception was Apollo 13, which could have ended in disaster but for the resourcefulness of the crew and ground control. When a fuel tank burst, the mission became a test of grace under pressure: The return of

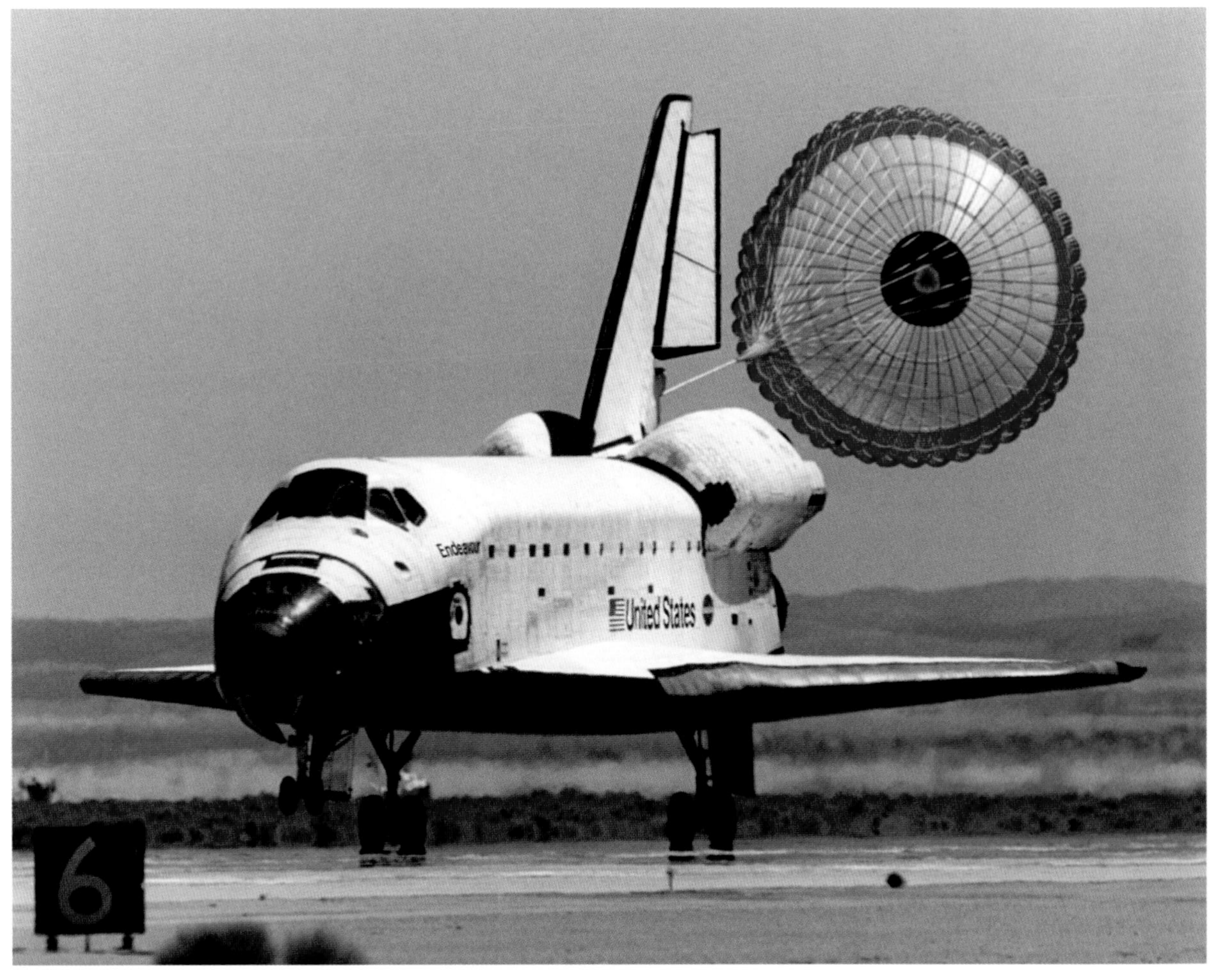

With a drag parachute reducing speed, *Endeavor* lands at Edwards Air Force Base in 2002. After the shuttle completed a smooth journey of 9.3 million kilometers and 217 orbits, bad weather at Cape Canaveral prompted ground control to switch its touchdown to the California site.

the crew safely to Earth was a stirring triumph in itself. During the Apollo program, 12 astronauts walked on the moon in 6 lunar landings.

America's premier space endeavor starting in the early 1980s was a fleet of reusable spacecraft that could be launched on a rocket and landed like an airplane on Earth. The space shuttle program has had huge successes, including a spectacular repair to the Hubble Space Telescope. NASA came under criticism when the explosion of the *Challenger* in 1986 killed all seven crew members. Then in February 2003, after 87 successful shuttle flights, the *Columbia* broke apart on reentry into the atmosphere with loss of the entire crew.

The most research for the money has come from NASA's unmanned interplanetary probes. These "better, faster, cheaper" spacecraft have included several missions to Mars. Two remotely controlled rovers explored Mars's surface in early 2004, finding evidence that the red planet once was drenched with water.

Heralding a thaw in the Cold War, the U.S. and the Soviet Union participated in the first international space mission in 1975, when Apollo and Soyuz spacecraft docked together in space and crews jointly conducted several experiments. Other cooperative missions came in the late 1990s with the space shuttle taking American astronauts to the Russian Mir space station to participate in the creation of an International Space Station. Its focus on overcoming hurdles of long duration in human spaceflight indicate an ongoing commitment toward space as a productive frontier. ■

GLOBAL MISSION

AMERICA IS "A CITY UPON A HILL," AND "WE HAVE THE POWER TO MAKE THE WORLD over." Ronald Reagan, a contemporary exemplar of America's sense of global mission, often quoted those classic words. They were, respectively, spoken by the leader of the Great Migration to America, John Winthrop, to his fellow Puritans in 1630, and written by revolutionary Thomas Paine in his pamphlet "Common Sense," addressed to Americans as they pondered declaring independence in 1776.

John Winthrop was reminding his fellow voyagers of why they had left their native England for the wilds of America. It was not merely to find liberty to practice their Puritan Christianity that Winthrop and his band were "planting" across the Atlantic; they were following God's command to be "a model of Christian charity." God had called them to be a "city upon a hill" so that their success or failure would be an example to the world. And so, Winthrop concluded, let Puritans put aside selfishness, greed, and lack of neighborly concern. They must not fail to give a visible example of humble goodness, or terrible would be God's judgment upon them.

Thomas Paine was an English freethinker, a hater of kings, and a ne'er-do-well who found his voice when he joined Americans' debate on independence. By rejecting monarchy, Americans would give an asylum to Liberty, which "hath been hunted round the world"; by building a democratic republic, they would be a beacon for all who suffered under tyranny's scourge.

Revolutionary-generation Americans had no intention of remaking the world in their image. They, and their 19th-century descendants, wished to withdraw from Old World corruptions and create what Thomas Jefferson called "an Empire of Liberty." Freedom lovers from all over the world—if they had white skins—were welcome. But of reaching out to bring the gifts of liberty to others, Americans had no thought.

Abraham Lincoln, in his Gettysburg Address, reprised Winthrop's city-upon-a-hill theme. America, both declared, was an experiment—in democracy for Lincoln, in Christian charity for Winthrop—and its failure would catastrophically dishearten a watching world. Lincoln spoke in a world where there were no other democracies; Winthrop, in a world that, Puritans believed, knew no true example of godly worship and Christian love. Not to betray the world's trust, not to fail in their dedicated task—such was America's "global mission."

Woodrow Wilson inherited Lincoln's and Paine's faith in democracy as a universal model; as a devout Presbyterian, he was also Winthrop's heir in his conviction that God called Americans to witness to the truth. But when Wilson asked that America make the world "safe for democracy," and when he framed his Fourteen Points as the basis for world peace, he was speaking in a far different context. America was fighting a world war against what Wilson judged a dangerous, aggressive German autocracy, and faced a competition with what he perceived as Russian Bolshevism's revolutionary threat to global liberty and the rule of law. America's safety required joining the other democracies in ensuring that liberty and self-determination did not perish—at first abroad, but ultimately at home. Wilson's call for a League of Nations in which America would participate, which would permanently enforce the peace and defend the weak against the strong, represented a fundamental break from the high and lonely "city upon a hill" that earlier generations of Americans had seen as their nation's mission.

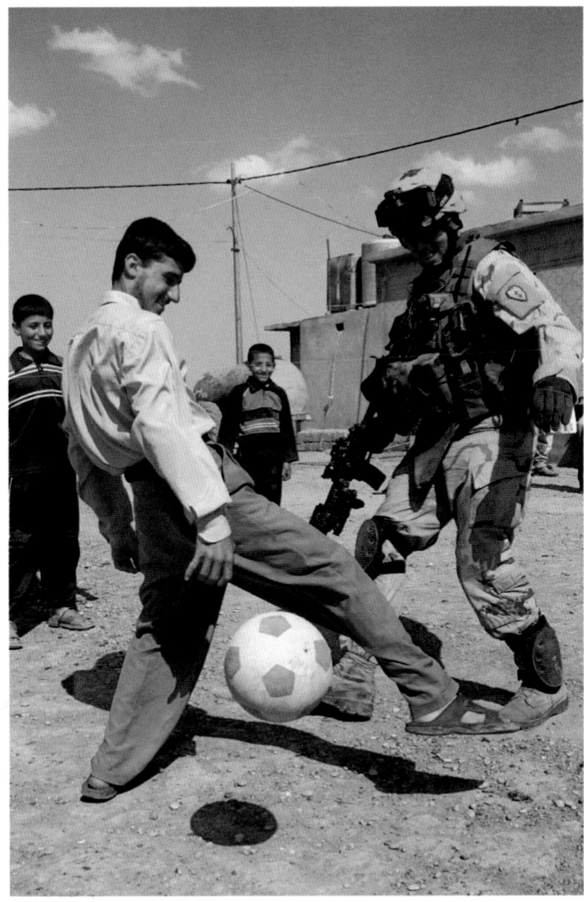

Convincing foreigners of the nation's good intentions has been a key objective of modern American foreign policy. Here an American soldier takes time from his patrol duties in northern Iraq to kick a soccer ball with local boys near Mosul in April 2005.

President Woodrow Wilson prophetically foresaw America's 20th-century role as a democratic bulwark against foreign tyrannies. Unlike the isolated republic of the 19th century, the modern United States was, by virtue of its wealth and power, in a position to defend, if it chose, the cause of global freedom. And again by virtue of that wealth and power, America was bound to attract the envy and enmity of all who saw its democracy as an enemy to be overthrown. Wilson's idealism suffered, in retrospect, from a naïve faith in democracy's transforming power and in the application of such principles as self-determination in resolving ancient enmities. Yet his conviction that it was America's mission to stand with other free nations in a global struggle of Right against Wrong would be the guiding principle of his successors. Presidents Franklin D. Roosevelt in World War II, Harry S. Truman and Dwight D. Eisenhower in the early Cold War, and John F. Kennedy in the 1960s would all echo his call—and in obedience to it, Lyndon B. Johnson would wage war against international communism in the jungles of Vietnam.

An idealistic sense of global mission was not the only tradition guiding America's relationship with the world; there was also a realist tradition that the United States must assert its rights and be guided by its interests in an eternally hostile world. Wilson's political enemies like Theodore Roosevelt and Senator Henry Cabot Lodge advocated such realism. So did George F. Kennan, the chief architect of America's Cold War policy of containing communism; yet Kennan—profoundly skeptical toward democracy—feared that basing foreign policy on popular convictions of right and wrong would lead the nation into disastrous global crusades. So, too, were Richard Nixon and his chief foreign policy advisor, Henry Kissinger, realists who saw the external world in terms of perpetually shifting blocs of states, without permanent principles but always with long-term interests. On the basis of such interests—and not on the basis of idealistic principles—Nixon and Kissinger accomplished two of the 20th century's most remarkable diplomatic revolutions: American recognition of the hitherto-demonized (by the domestic politician Richard Nixon, among others) "Red China" and the policy of détente with the Soviet Union.

Despite the ultimate success of the policy of containment and the end of the Cold War, Americans faced a new challenge at the begining of the 21st century: the prospect of a long and protracted global contest with Islamic movements that see the United States as a godless "Great Satan." With this new and growing challenge, it perhaps would be well for Americans to recall the limits and dangers both of cynically pursuing national self-interest in the name of "realism" and of zealously embarking on "idealistic" crusades to remake the outside world. Maybe recalling the original contexts of John Winthrop's and Thomas Paine's visions would be salutary. ■

Major Eras

1. **Early Americans**
   Prehistory–A.D. 1700
2. **Europe Discovers America**
   1000–1775
3. **The Revolution Era**
   1765–1801
4. **Continental Expansion**
   1803–1853
5. **A Divided Nation**
   1817–1877
6. **From Sea to Shining Sea**
   1867–1896
7. **Modern America Rises**
   1870–1917
8. **Becoming a Great Power**
   1914–1933
9. **Remaking America**
   1929–1945
10. **Cold War America**
    1945–1989
11. **Global Hegemony**
    1985–Present

This statue at the Antietam National Battlefield commemorates the Civil War battle fought there in 1862.

EARLY AMERICANS PREHISTORY–A.D. 1700

THE FIRST PEOPLE LIKELY ARRIVED IN NORTH AMERICA BETWEEN 12,000 AND 20,000 years ago. Although some newcomers walked across the Bering land bridge from Siberia, current theories cast doubt on that route for the earliest arrivals. In the New World, the immigrants fanned out across the Americas, making a living off the abundant wildlife and seafood. They employed a variety of chipped stone and bone weapons and tools, including spears, knives, and scrapers. Early hunters killed animals one by one, but around 10,000 years ago they invented a mass slaughter, in which bison were herded over cliffs or into gullies. Around this same time, the mammoth, mastodon, and other animals went extinct. The mass slaughter of bison continued into the late 19th century. About 1000 B.C. American Indians began shifting from a nomadic to an agricultural existence. Spheres of influence radiated out from the Ohio Valley linking communities in trade networks. Jewelry and ornaments made with shells, stone, pearls, and copper were traded. Corn was the mainstay of communities holding up to several thousand people. Inhabitants built earth mounds 100 feet high for the burial of chiefs and other ceremonies. By the 15th century, the mound culture was in decline. In the Southwest, pueblos had replaced multistory cliff dwellings. Only on the Great Plains did hunter-gatherer tribes live as they had for millennia. ■

Plains hunters stampede long-horned bison over a cliff some 10,000 years ago; the practice yielded meat, clothing, and equipment.

■ **ca 18,000 B.C.** People begin migrating to the New World, by the Bering land bridge or perhaps by sea.

■ **ca 8000 B.C.** Hunters begin using the "bison jump" technique to kill herds.

■ **ca 5000 B.C.** Villagers in Mesopotamia begin practicing irrigation.

■ **ca 1000 B.C.** Eastern Indians begin constructing burial mounds.

■ **ca 300 B.C.** Irrigation canals are dug in the desert Southwest.

■ ca A.D. 900	■ ca 1100	■ ca 1200	■ ca 1500	■ 1539-1542
Environmental stresses and increased conflict contribute to the collapse of Maya civilization, resulting in the destruction or abandonment of most urban areas.	Anasazi community in Chaco Canyon, New Mexico, is in its prime.	Mound village at Cahokia, Illinois, reaches its peak.	Peru's 2,500-mile Inca Empire reaches its height, extending from present-day Ecuador to Chile.	Hernando de Soto explores Florida, Alabama, Tennessee, Mississippi, Arkansas, Oklahoma, and Louisiana, spreading ill will.

Paleolithic and Archaic Indians

18,000–1000 B.C.

PREVAILING THEORIES OF THE original immigrants to North America hold that sometime between about 12,000 and 20,000 years ago, people walked from Siberia to what is now Alaska. This was made possible by the 50-mile-long Bering land bridge—land exposed when ice sheets during the last Ice Age locked up enough of the world's water that sea levels were lowered by as much as 300 feet. By 10,000 years ago, glacial masses were melting, and rising seas closed off the route. Today the sea at the Bering Strait is about 200 feet deep.

Called Beringia, the land bridge measured more than a thousand miles wide in places. Tundra carpeted the bridge, and mammoths, mastodons, elk, and giant bison came to graze. Following them were predators such as saber-toothed cats and humans. Working down through North America, over the Isthmus of Panama and to the tip of South America took about 7,000 years, or some 350 generations, if we accept the figure of 8,000 years ago for the first occurrence of man in southern South America. Because of scant evidence, no clear consensus exists for the timing and patterns of these earliest migrations; the excitement of American prehistory is that it can change dramatically with each discovery.

Evidence of early human occupation has come to light in numerous places in the Americas, including Idaho, Oregon, Missouri, and Pennsylvania. But investigators subject every claim of extreme antiquity to rigorous scrutiny. To be accepted, a find must lie sealed under unbroken layers of later sediment, yield diagnostic artifacts, be in close association with now extinct mammals like the mammoth, and yield radiocarbon dates older than 10,000 years ago. Time after time, new finds where ages of 12,000 to 20,000 B.C. or more seem to be indicated fail to meet one or more of these criteria. Of possible exceptions, one is Meadowcroft Shelter near Pittsburgh. The excavator originally claimed an age of 17,000 B.C. The claim sparked instant controversy. Although the radiocarbon assay came from cultural material, the sample may have been contaminated with microscopic coal bits because the shelter is in a coalfield. Moreover, animal bones recovered were from modern species. The excavator now supports a younger age, but the matter is still debated.

The New Land

The oldest reliable skeletal remains are less than 12,000 years old, yet they offer a basis for reconstructing the appearance of hunters who first trod the New World. From a ranch near Midland, Texas, came the fragmentary skull of a delicately boned female. On the Marmes ranch in southeastern Washington, scientists found fragments of three skulls. All are of fully *Homo sapiens* type, yet they show neither Asiatic nor specifically American Indian attributes.

From such evidence, and from modern Indians, experts envision the first Americans. Today's Indians, like eastern Asians, have straight black hair, high cheekbones, and little body hair. The aboriginal Indians were, unlike any major population groups of today, long-headed and slender. With the land bridge and the corridor south occasionally closed by glaciation, only sporadic inputs of new racial stock were possible. This left the early Indian to evolve into a population unlike any other.

When these pioneers stepped into North America they were walking into a game park teeming with food: wooly mammoths, great short-faced bears, stag-moose, camels, lionlike cats, and musk oxen. Indeed, the extinction of the mammoth and other Pleistocene animals may have been hastened by these early invaders. Climate changes likely altered the feeding grounds of herd animals; nomadic hunters could then have pushed stressed populations over the brink.

The diversity of terrain was tremendous. The Sierra Nevada and Rocky Mountains offered low

Successful Makah whale hunters return to their village on Washington's Olympic Peninsula some 500 years ago.

passes where travelers could cross; the Appalachian Mountains posed even less of a problem. The continent fell rather neatly into five major environments—and because the Indian lived by exploiting local resources, his culture types fell into the same five physiographic areas. The plains were rich in big game; east of the Mississippi River game and a variety of vegetable foods characterized the woodlands. In the arid Southwest and Great Basin animals and edible plants were in shorter supply. Cultures of the West Coast looked to the rivers or the sea for food. And the Arctic cultures depended on mammals of both land and sea.

Clovis and Folsom Hunters

In 1952 an Arizona rancher noticed huge teeth and bones embedded in an arroyo. When University of Arizona scholars examined the find, they found the best record of mammoth hunts yet unearthed in the Americas. On the banks of an ancient stream lay dismembered skeletons of nine mammoths. With the remains were lance points, a type called Clovis Fluted, found thus far only at mammoth kills and as isolated surface finds. Animals had been butchered about 9500 B.C. and remains covered with sediment as the stream valley filled in.

One of the most famous ancient sites was discovered near Folsom, New Mexico, in 1926. Again a cowman, again a chance exposure of bones in a gully—but these were remains of long-horned bison, 23 of them, killed in a box canyon. With the bones were several slender points, each with a long flake scar from base to tip. Distinct from the Clovis style, these have come to be known as Folsom Fluted.

The people who fashioned the Clovis points seem to have felled their prey one by one, perhaps surrounding a beast trapped in the

NOTABLE DATES

■ **ca 18,000-10,000 B.C.**
Paleo-Indians enter the New World via the Bering land bridge from Siberia, and possibly by other routes from Polynesia, Australia, and Europe.

■ **ca 9500 B.C.**
Clovis people leave records of a mammoth hunt near Clovis, New Mexico, as well as in Arizona; their artifacts are found in Pennsylvania, Virginia, and other places. They make distinctive blades and spear points by chipping flint; possibly they used atlatls—throwing devices.

■ **ca 9000-7000 B.C.**
Folsom people hunt long-horned bison over cliffs, into deep arroyos, and into dead-end canyons as at Folsom, New Mexico.

■ **ca 8000-1000 B.C.**
Archaic peoples spread throughout the Americas, living by hunting, fishing, and plant collection. Semi-permanent campsites are established; food grinding tools are used. Trade and ceremony become important late in the period.

■ **ca 6500 B.C.**
Hunters stampede 200 bison into a narrow arroyo near Big Sandy Creek, Colorado.

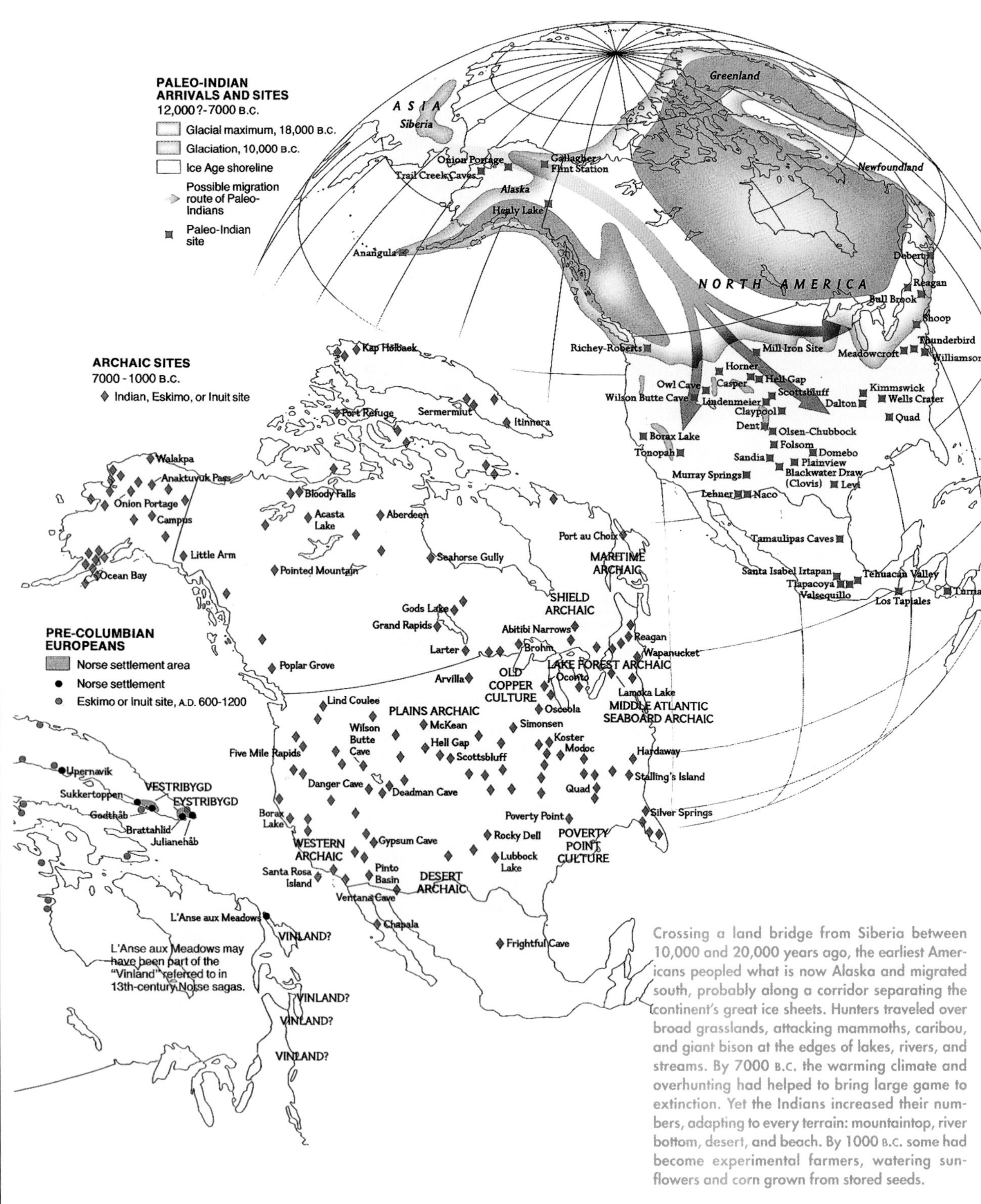

Crossing a land bridge from Siberia between 10,000 and 20,000 years ago, the earliest Americans peopled what is now Alaska and migrated south, probably along a corridor separating the continent's great ice sheets. Hunters traveled over broad grasslands, attacking mammoths, caribou, and giant bison at the edges of lakes, rivers, and streams. By 7000 B.C. the warming climate and overhunting had helped to bring large game to extinction. Yet the Indians increased their numbers, adapting to every terrain: mountaintop, river bottom, desert, and beach. By 1000 B.C. some had become experimental farmers, watering sunflowers and corn grown from stored seeds.

mud, then jabbing and stoning until its bellowing ceased. But by the time of the Folsom people a major invention developed: the jump, a simple hunting method that lasted for 10,000 years until the late 19th century. The technique was important socially, too, because it required hunters to act cooperatively, probably under one leader, in tasks no small family band could handle. Hunters would rise up yelling on three sides of a bison herd. Animals stampeded out the open side, thundering over a cliff.

By about 8000 B.C., the world of the Folsom hunters had begun to change. As the glacial ice retreated, the climate became drier, particularly west of the Rockies. The great beasts of the Pleistocene died out. Old lifestyles no longer worked; the Paleo-Indian had to adapt.

The Archaic Era

A variety of adaptations makes up the next era in Indian prehistory, the Archaic. Lifestyles were based on collecting vegetable foods and hunting game. Family bands moved with the seasons, using portable tools for harvesting tasks.

Eventually the foraging way of life covered the continent. In western deserts, game was sparse; seeds, bulbs, fruits, and nuts were the staples. In eastern woodlands, game and plants were abundant, and Archaic peoples developed at least the *concept* of horticulture. Unusual seeds have turned up—leading to the theory that some species were cultivated, possibly even planted in locations where yields would be bigger or better. ■

Beringia Challenged

One problem with the Beringia migration theory is that glaciers in what is now British Columbia sometimes joined with glaciers to the east to pinch off the corridor into the rest of North America. Some paleontologists now believe that this corridor was not open until 11,000 years ago—or about 1,000 years prior to the end of the Ice Age—and that any migration into America before that was by another route. One possibility is that South America was inhabited before North America, the colonizers arriving by the Pacific from Polynesia or Australia. Some early South American skeletons show marked similarities to Polynesians.

Other scientists are investigating links between the Clovis people of North America and the Solutreans of Paleolithic Europe to suggest that Atlantic crossings some 18,000 years ago brought the first people to America. So far, no boats from the period have been found, but the two cultures share similar flintknapping techniques. Glaciation in Europe and depleted resources may have forced a migration by sea, or along the southern edges of the Atlantic sea ice.

Still, with the biological and linguistic evidence piling up in favor of northeastern Asian ancestry, the northwest coast seems the most likely entry point for the first Americans, whether or not they actually crossed via Beringia. With no animal bones yet found on the ice-free corridor south of Beringia dating from 11,500 to 21,000 years ago, there is a great chance that if Indians arrived in the Americas more than 11,500 years ago they came by another way. ■

Paleo-Indian projectile points included chipped Clovis points (9200 B.C.), fluted Folsom points (after 9000 B.C.), Inuit slate points (2500 B.C.), and hammered spear points (3000-1200 B.C.).

Woodland Era

1000 B.C.–A.D. 1400

By around 1000 B.C. the nomadic, hunting-gathering traditions were giving over to a more settled way of life. Except for inhabitants of the Great Plains, agriculture and villages became more prevalent. Woodland Indians lived in villages of 50 to 70 people and sustained themselves by hunting and foraging and cultivating edible seeds and squash. Communities clustered principally in river valleys abundant with fish and game. Far-ranging traders made use of the rivers for transportation.

The Indians of the desert Southwest became farmers. Corn, squash, and the protein-packed bean, imports from Mesoamerica, emerged as staples. Each could be eaten from the field or dried and stored for years. Populations surged. With a more sedentary way of life, some villagers turned out pottery or jewelry or music; others tracked the sun and moon.

Two waves of culture rolled across the East: the Adena way of life (named for a landowner on whose property many mounds were discovered), which flourished from about 500 to 1 B.C., and the more complex Hopewell cluture (named for a large Ohio mound excavated in the 1800s), which peaked between A.D. 1 and 300. Both cultures were centered in the Ohio Valley and obsessed with the afterlife. Both cultures crossed linguistic and geographic barriers, and spread their influence throughout the northeastern and southeastern areas. Communities learned about each other's crops, pottery, and mound building in trading expeditions. Traders may have been selected by their tribes or were perhaps individual adventurers.

Early Mounds

North America's oldest Indian mounds are the large rings of piled shells that dot coastal and river sites from South Carolina to Florida. One of the largest of these, on Sapelo Island, Georgia, measures more than 300 feet across—a mysterious, seven-foot-high palisade of saltwater shells constructed some 4,000 years ago. And within these mounds archaeologists have found examples of the first pottery to appear on the continent. It was made of clay tempered with plant fibers; some pieces bore geometric designs around the rims. Before the Woodland period, American Indians may have made long coastal voyages from South America to Georgia and South Carolina, bringing elements to enrich the Archaic cultures of the North American eastern area.

The first burial mounds began to appear after 1000 B.C. Thousands of them—some small, others manmade hills—still dot the east. In the period around 1000 B.C. to A.D. 700 the mounds contained tombs. Later they were built as flat-topped bases for temples. Some even depict birds, beasts, and men in sprawling effigies too large to be read from the ground; only from an aerial vantage point do the great images take shape. The world's largest serpent effigy, a coiled quarter-mile of heaped earth in Adams County, Ohio was likely built for ritual use in the middle Woodland period. Even with area farming, the Great Serpent Mound still measures five feet high. Perched on a cliff 100 feet above a stream, the snake's open mouth appears to be holding an egg. The purpose of this giant earthen sculpture is still unknown.

Well-made pottery, ornate art objects, copper beads, stone gorgets, and tubular smoking pipes have been unearthed from the early mounds of the Adena culture in Ohio and Kentucky. Pipes carved from Ohio pipestone were traded throughout the northern part of what is now the United States and have turned up in Illinois, Iowa, and New York. Such artwork, as well as the mysterious mounds, suggest an upper class able to command large labor forces for public works. All these products are seemingly based on an obsessive preoccupation with honoring the dead.

Marietta, Ohio, portrayed in 1847, grew on layers of history: a grave mound of the Adena era (500 to 1 B.C.), earthen walls of Hopewell design (A.D. 1 to 300) and platform mounds, perhaps Mississippian (A.D. 800 to 1500).

Gradually cultivation began to appear. Within a few centuries of the Adena culture, the Hopewell arose in Illinois with an intensified expression of the death-ritual cult and hints of agriculture. Large burial mounds containing elaborate log tombs full of rich offerings were built in Illinois, Ohio, and New York. Specialists in art appeared: potters, stone carvers, coppersmiths, workers in shell and mica. Their raw material flowed in as trade or tribute from sources far distant. Obsidian came from what is now Yellowstone Park, more than a thousand miles away. Huge conch shells for ceremonial vessels and ornaments were imported from the Gulf of Mexico. Embossed breastplates, ear ornaments, and ritual weapons were hammered from copper picked up as nuggets or mined around the Great Lakes. Pearls by the thousand were plucked from river mussels, drilled, and sewn on garments or strung about throat, wrist, and ankle.

Like ever widening ripples on a pond, the influence of the Hopewell culture spread southward, and then languished through quiet centuries peopled by what one scholar called "the good gray cultures." But by about A.D. 700 a vibrant, well-organized way of life called the Mississippian culture arose, geared to farming and with a strongly Mexican flavor to its arts. This dominant culture would transform the entire eastern area. ■

NOTABLE DATES

■ **ca 1000 B.C.-100 B.C.**
In the early Woodland era, people depend upon hunting, fishing, and plant collection; planting of squash and sunflowers begins; pottery is used for food storage.

■ **ca 500 B.C.-100 B.C.**
The Adena culture spreads over the Ohio Valley, responsible for large earthen burial mounds.

■ **ca 100 B.C.-A.D. 500**
Middle Woodland period sees more settled communities throughout America.

■ **ca 100 B.C.-A.D. 400**
Hopewell sphere of influence spreads from Ohio across Northeast, with ceremonial mounds, trade networks, and prevalent use of shells, copper, mica, obsidian.

■ **ca A.D. 500**
Teotihuacan, great urban center in the Valley of Mexico, nears the height of its influence in Mesoamerica.

■ **ca 500 B.C.-A.D. 1400**
In late Woodland period, population grows, with larger villages and fewer scattered communities; agriculture increases, crops include goosefoot and corn.

Complex Societies

A.D. 1000–1540

SOMETIME BETWEEN A.D. 800 and 1000, a new way of life took root in the southern area, when corn became a staple crop. Shaped by corn and, later, bean agriculture, farming settlements began to appear along the Mississippi River. The culture of the Mississippi peoples spread northward and westward.

The Mississippians raised huge pyramidal hills, usually built around a central plaza with temples on the flat summits—strong evidence of a powerful class of ruler-priests. Supporting each center and its priests, nobles, and craftsmen were the surrounding villages where farmers, hunters, and traders toiled to provide the necessities of life for themselves and their betters at the temple complex.

From its apparent beginnings in the fertile lands of the lower Mississippi Valley, the new culture spawned famous centers hundreds of miles away. Dozens of these temple mounds still rear their great

Cofitachequi town, reconstructed for a diorama in the South Carolina State Museum, shows the main building on platform mounds, the great plaza, and surrounding thatched-roof dwellings as they may have looked in spring 1540.

hulks, many preserved in state or national parklands. Most are situated in the rich, broad bottomlands along southern rivers, but the largest of all rises at Cahokia in western Illinois. The crown jewel of the Mississippian culture sprawled along Cahokia Creek for miles and boasted perhaps 20,000 residents in its heyday. Its central mound looms 100 feet high, while satellite mound-clusters dot the fertile plain for miles around. In the 12th century, Cahokia was a fully developed urban center with clustered housing, rigid social strata, and specialists in the arts.

Some Cahokia residents built clay-and-pole homes inside a 15-foot-high stockade, rebuilding on the ashes of the old home if sparks from cooking fires ignited its thatched roof. On fertile lands outside, farmers with flint hoes tended corn, beans, and squash. Hunters bagged deer, ducks, geese, and swans; fishermen worked lakes and streams. Canoes brought raw materials and bore the artisans' wares afar.

Life focused on the great mound, its 16-acre base surpassing that of Egypt's Great Pyramid. From its top, chiefs gazed across a plaza to a truncated pyramid where nobles were prepared for burial in a conical knoll nearby. The great mound, some 700 by 1,000 feet, is not even partly a natural hill; thousands of laborers without wheels or draft animals built it by the basketful in at least 14 stages between A.D. 900 and 1100.

Mounds by the score held temples, burials, and homes of the elite. One yielded a noble and six slain retainers; nearby lay 53 women in a mass grave, apparently sent with their master to the afterlife. Diggers also found remains of "Woodhenges"—circles hundreds of feet across, once ringed with massive posts whose alignment with the sun may have told farmers when to sow. Cahokia reached its peak about A.D. 1200, then faded as nearby centers grew. Eventually it was abandoned.

Influence From the South

From A.D. 1250 through the 15th century, the largest settlement north of Mexico was Moundville, in present-day Alabama, home to as many as 3,000 people. Its rulers also governed villages along 75 miles of the Black Warrior River. The town's core, enclosed by a wooden stockade, contained mounds topped by temples and elite residences, ceremonial plazas, and ponds stocked with fish. Workshops produced pottery, often distinguished by a filmy black finish, as well as woven goods and beads.

Throughout the Mississippian culture are echoes of the Hopewell people's concern with death. But by about A.D. 1300, rulers were going to their graves amid the temple mounds with an array of offerings ascribed to a new southern cult. Motifs reminiscent of Mexico appeared. The plumed rattlesnake, for example, appears on pottery at Moundville, Alabama. On a stone pipe from Spiro, Oklahoma, an executioner cleaves his victim's skull. Ritual must have pervaded life. Even children in tombs wore sacred feather capes with ritual weapons in miniature.

NOTABLE DATES

■ ca 900-1400
Mississippian culture flourishes in the south and beyond, centered on ceremonial earthen mounds and the cultivation of corn.

■ ca 1050-1300
The Anasazi flourish in the southwest, especially at Chaco Canyon and Mesa Verde, before suddenly disappearing.

■ 1492
Christopher Columbus departs Italy; his expeditions will open the New World to Europe.

■ 1539
Francisco de Coronado enters New Mexico looking for gold and defeats Zuni Pueblo.

■ 1539-1542
Army of Hernando de Soto explores the southeast, captures numerous Indians, and spreads fear and disease among the native population.

The Mississippian splendor was already fading when the first Europeans arrived. In short order the invaders destroyed the rich and fascinating culture they found, both by conquest and by diseases for which the Indians had no immunity. But some early explorers left tantalizing glimpses of the Mississippian culture. Garcilaso de la Vega, chronicler of de Soto's expedition of 1539-1542, wrote of a temple, probably somewhere in present-day South Carolina, whose "ceiling . . . from the walls upward, was adorned like the roof outside with designs of shells interspersed with strands of pearls. Among those decorations were great headdresses of different colors of feathers . . . it was an agreeable sight to behold." Although it died out elsewhere, the Mississippian lifeway remained potent among the Natchez of Louisiana well into the 18th century.

The Anasazi

In the west, complex societies had been in the making since the early Woodland period in the east. Some two millennia ago, the Hohokam coaxed corn, beans, and squash from the arid ground of present-day Arizona, leading water from rivers to fragile crops in elaborate networks of canals. Diversion dams on the Salt and Gila Rivers supplied more than 500 miles of irrigation canals. The oldest canal measures three miles long and dates from 2,300 years ago. One early artery was two feet deep and twenty feet wide; later branches were built narrow to slow evaporation. The canals were so efficient that Mormon farmers used portions of the network in the 19th century. Also among Hohokam artifacts, researchers have found the Western world's first etchings, made by daubing shells with pitch and bathing them in acid—probably fermented cactus juice.

The Hohokam people of Snaketown and many other southwestern desert communities derived their culture from Mexico. There were platform mounds, arenas similar to Mexican ball courts, and tiny copper bells like those made in western Mexico. In turn, the influence of the Hohokam farmers radiated across the southwestern area throughout the existence of Snaketown, a span of around 1,500 years.

The pinnacle of southwestern tradition was reached by the Anasazi, concentrated around today's Four Corners area. Elaborate apartment complexes nestled in the cliffs of Mesa Verde in southwestern Colorado, and imposing stone buildings arose in Chaco Canyon in northwestern New Mexico. Bones from Anasazi burials show close kinship to present-day Indians who live in pueblos of Arizona and New Mexico. Some of the tools and beautifully designed pottery in use there today can hardly be distinguished from those found in the cliff dwellings.

As the Anasazi tradition developed, the pit house—a log-and-mud

Pages of Prehistory

Largest Mississippian community: Cahokia, Illinois; population 20,000 (peak A.D. 1200)

World's largest serpent effigy: Great Serpent Mound, near Cincinnati; 1,254 feet long, 20 feet wide, 5 feet high; over 2,000 years old

Largest settlement north of Mexico when Columbus arrived in New World: Moundville, Alabama; population 3,000

Largest cache of Eastern Archaic artifacts from a single dig: 55,000 items from Indian Knoll, Kentucky

Numbers of items from a Hopewell era (100 B.C.-A.D. 400) site in Hamilton County, Ohio: 12,000 unperforated pearls, 20,000 shell beads, 35,000 pearl beads, and nuggets of copper, meteoric iron, and silver

A Mississippian chief holds a long bow in this post-contact portrait. A hallmark of the Mississippian culture was reliance on farming as the main food source. Keenly territorial, these Indians wrested land from each other and dispatched warriors to carry on tribal feuds.

superstructure over a shallow pit—evolved in two directions. By A.D. 700 or 800, dwellings became surface affairs of stone, often joined in sprawling pueblos with populations in the hundreds. The concept of a house partly underground also led to the development of the round subterranean chamber called the kiva, an exclusive preserve where the men carried on their sedentary chores, spinning yarn of cotton fibers and weaving warm blankets of feathers plucked from domesticated turkeys. Here they performed a variety of religious ceremonies, dancing on a hard clay floor that in some kivas was buffed with rubbing stones to a surface resembling cement. Many kivas had a small round hole in the floor, occasionally lined with the neck of a broken pot; this was the *sipapu*, gateway to and from the spirit world.

From historic accounts and from existing archaeological evidence, researchers have guessed at kiva ceremonies for rain and fertility, for example. Gourd rattles would imitate the pattering sound of rain; fringed sashes around the dancers' waist would suggest the look of falling torrents. A roof hole had the dual purpose of letting fire smoke out and letting guests in. No women were allowed to join in these secret rites, although at certain times they may have entered to bring food, or perhaps even to witness special rituals. Between the ceremonies, the men would sit on the hard clay floor to spin, weave, and gossip, or stretch out for a night's sleep, in this combination workshop, men's club, ritual center, and bachelor dormitory.

Alaska's Indigenous People

With Alaska serving as a conduit for the rest of the Americas, there were inevitably people who chose to stay and make a living in this harsh, unforgiving country. No one knows eactly when or how the ancestors of today's Inuit (Eskimos) arrived in North America, only that they were likely the last aboriginal people to populate the continent. Some archaeologists believe the original home of these ancestral Inuit was the surface of the Bering land bridge, and that as the seas rose to inundate it about 10,000 years ago, they moved to Alaska and to the eastern extremity of Asia.

In the western Arctic, along the coast of the Beaufort Sea, a culture known as Thule emerged. Although skilled at hunting seals, polar bears, and other creatures, the Thule people were especially noted as whale hunters. They ranged the open waters in skin-covered boats—kayaks and the larger umiaks—in search of sea mammals. They had sleds drawn by dogs and probably wore caribou-skin clothing. Their domed, semisubterranean dwellings had walls and roofs of sod laid over slabs of limestone and rafters of whale rib. About A.D. 800, the Thule people began a rapid sweep eastward. In less than 300 years they overran the entire Arctic. Little is known about them, but their tools resemble those used by Inuit in historic times. While predators have scattered most human remains, those that have been found suggest that today's Inuit descended directly from forebears of Thule and earlier times. ■

An Inuit hunter watches walrus herds on the clam shoals at Bristol Bay, Alaska; by the late 1700s Russian fur traders were forcing native Alaskans to hunt for them.

Bering Strait
ARCTIC OCEAN
NORTH ALASKAN INUPIAQ
SEWARD PENINSULA INUPIAQ
Greenland
(Denmark)
HOLIKACHUK
UPPER KUSKOKWIM
KOYUKON
CENTRAL ALASKAN YUPIK
Alaska
(U.S.)
KUTCHIN
(GWICH'IN)
TANAINA
(DENA'INA)
LOWER TANANA
ALEUT
HAN
TANACROSS
AHTNA
ALUTIIQ
UPPER TANANA
EYAK
NORTHERN TUTCHONE
SOUTHERN TUTCHONE
KASKA
TAGISH
TLINGIT
TAHLTAN
TSETSAUT
SEKANI
HAIDA
NASS-GITKSAN
(NISGA'A, GITXSAN)
HAISLA
BABINE-WITSUWIT'EN
COAST TSIMSHIAN
HEILTSUK-OOWEKYALA
BELLA COOLA
(NUXALK)
CARRIER
(DAKELH)
KWAKIUTL
(KWAKW'ALA)
CHILCOTIN
(TSILHQOXT'IN)
SHUSWAP
(SECWEPMECTSIN)
LILLOOET
(ST'AT'IMCETS)
NOOTKA
(NUUCHANULTH)
NITINAHT
MAKAH
QUILEUTE
QUINAULT
CHEHALIS
LUSHOOTSEED
NICOLA
COLUMBIAN
KOOTENAI
CHINOOK
CLATSKANIE
TILLAMOOK
ALSEAN
SIUSLAW
COOSAN
KALAPUYA
SPOKANE
COEUR D'ALENE
SAHAPTIN
FLATHEAD
(SALISH)
CAYUSE
NEZ PERCE
(NIMÍIPUU)
MOLALA
OREGON ATHABASKAN
TOLOWA
KLAMATH
YUROK
WIYOT
SHASTAN
HUPA
CALIFORNIA ATHABASKAN
YUKIAN
POMOAN
WAPPO
YANA
MAIDUAN
WASHOE
MIWOK
COSTANOAN
ESSELEN
SALINAN
YOKUTSAN
MONO
PANAMINT
CHUMASH
KITANEMUK
SERRANO
GABRIELINO
LUISEÑO
CAHUILLA
CUPEÑO
IPAI
KUMEYAAY
TIPAI
PAIPAI
KILIWA
QUECHAN
MARICOPA
MOHAVE
YAVAPAI
WALAPAI
HAVASUPAI
HOPI
NAVAJO
JEMEZ
ZUNI
TAOS
JICARILLA
PECOS
S. TIWA
PIRO
WESTERN APACHE
CHIRICAHUA
MESCALERO
UPPER PIMAN
ÓPATA
SERI
LOWER PIMAN
EUDEVE
JOVA
YAQUI
GUARIJÍO
TARAHUMARA
TUBAR
MAYO
NORTHERN TEPEHUAN
BORJEÑO
IGNACIEÑO
CADEGOMEÑO
MONQUI-DIDIU
GUAICURA
HUCHITÍ
PERICÚ
ACAXEE
TARACAHITIAN
SOUTHERN TEPEHUAN
HUICHOL
CORA
TEPECANO
CHICHIMECO
NAOLAN
PAME
MARATINO
HUASTEC
OTOMI
MAZAHUA
MATLAZINCA
OCUILTEC
NAHUATL
TOTONAC
CUITLATEC
CUICATEC
IXCATEC
MIXTEC
ZAPOTECAN
MIXE-ZOQUEAN
HUAVE
TLAPANEC
AMUZGO
CHATINO
TEQUISTLATECAN
CHOCHO
CHONTAL
CHOL
YUCATEC MAYA
CHOLTI
CHUJ
ITZA
MOPAN
Q'EQCHI'
GUATEMALA
BELIZE
CHICOMUCELTEC
MOTOCINTLEC
TAPACHULTEC
MAM
TECO
KAQCHIKEL
PIPIL
TZ'UTUJIL
XINCAN
LENCAN
HONDURAS
JICAQUEAN
PAYA
MISKITO
SUMU
MATAGALPA
ULWA
EL SALVADOR
CACAOPERA
SUBTIABA
MANGUE
NICARAO
NICARAGUA
RAMA
BRIBRI
COSTA RICA
BORUCA
TIRIBI
GUAYMI
PANAMA
CUNA
SOUTH AMERICA
PACIFIC OCEAN
HARE
BEARLAKE
MOUNTAIN
DOGRIB
YELLOWKNIFE
SLAVE
(DENEDHA)
CHIPEWYAN
(DENE)
BEAVER
(DUNNEZA)
ROCKY
MOUNTAINS
GREAT PLAINS
PLAINS CREE
STONEY
SARCEE
BLACKFOOT
(SIKSIKA)
GROS VENTRE
ASSINIBOINE
WOODS CREE
WESTERN SWAMPY CREE
SEVERN OJIBWA
EASTERN SWAMPY CREE
SAULTEAUX
CENTRAL SOUTHERN OJIBWA
CROW
HIDATSA
MANDAN
ARIKARA
NORTHERN SHOSHONE
(AQUI-DIKA)
EASTERN SHOSHONE
(SO-SO-GOI)
NORTHERN PAIUTE
WESTERN SHOSHONE
(SO-SO-GOI)
SOUTHERN PAIUTE
UTE
CHEYENNE
YANKTON-YANKTONAI
TETON
(LAKOTA)
SANTEE-SISSETON
BESAWUNENA
ARAPAHO
PAWNEE
OTOE
IOWA
OMAHA
KANSA
MISSOURI
NAWATHINEHENA
KIOWA
KIOWA APACHE
OSAGE
COMANCHE
WICHITA
CADDO
QUAPAW
TUNICA
YATASI
ADAI
NATCHEZ
KITSAI
LIPAN
TONKAWA
BIDAI
ATAKAPA
ARANAMA
KARANKAWA
COAHUILTECO
SOLANO
COTONAME
GARZA
COMECRUDO
QUINIGUA
CHITIMACHA
WASHA
BILOXI
PENSACOLA
MOBILE
CHOCTAW
CHICKASAW
CHAKCHIUMA
ALABAMA
TAWASA
CREEK
(MUSKOGEE)
KOASATI
HITCHITI
APALACHEE
TIMUCUA
YAMASEE
GUALE
CUSABO
AIS
CALUSA
TEKESTA
YUCHI
OFO
MICHIGAMEA
CHEROKEE
CATAWBA
WATEREE
WOCCON
TUSCARORA
CAROLINA ALGONQUIAN
NOTTOWAY
MEHERRIN
VIRGINIA ALGONQUIAN
TUTELO-SAPONI
NANTICOKE-CONOY
SHAWNEE
MIAMI
ILLINOIS
KICKAPOO
(MESKWAKI) FOX
SAUK
WINNEBAGO
(HO-CHUNK)
MENOMINEE
POTAWATOMI
OTTAWA
(ODAWA)
HURON
(WENDAT)
ERIE
SUSQUEHANNOCK
SENECA
ONEIDA
MOHAWK
MAHICAN
MUNSEE
DELAWARE
UNAMI DELAWARE
QUIRIPI-UNQUACHOG
MOHEGAN-PEQUOT
LOUP
MASSACHUSETT-NARRAGANSETT
WESTERN ABENAKI
EASTERN ABENAKI
ETCHEMIN
PASSAMAQUODDY
MALISEET
MICMAC
LAURENTIAN
ATTIKAMEK
NORTHERN ALGONQUIN
OLD ALGONQUIN
EASTERN OJIBWA
EAST CREE
MONTAGNAIS
(INNU-AIMUN)
NASKAPI
(INNU-AIMUN)
BEOTHUK
WESTERN CANADIAN INUIT
(INUKTITUT)
EASTERN CANADIAN
INUIT
(INUKTITUT)
Hudson Bay
Baffin Bay
UNINHABITED
WEST GREENLANDIC
EAST GREENLANDIC
EUROPE
ICELAND
CANADA
UNITED STATES
MEXICO
Gulf of Mexico
ATLANTIC OCEAN
BAHAMAS
TAINO
CIBONEY
CUBA
HAITI
DOMINICAN REPUBLIC
JAMAICA
Puerto
Caribbean Sea
0 300 mi
0 500 km
Native American Cultures at Contact
1 Eskimo-Aleut
2 Eyak-Athabaskan
3 Wakashan
4 Salishan
5 Plateau-Penutian
6 Kiowa-Tanoan
7 Uto-Aztecan
8 Cochimí-Yuman
9 Otomanguean
10 Mayan
11 Algic
12 Siouan-Catawba
13 Iroquoian
14 Caddoan
15 Muskogean
16 Timucuan
17 Arawakan
18 Chibchan
19 Unclassified
20 Other language families
WINNEBAGO Native American language
(HO-CHUNK) Indigenous name for language
Keyed to the colors and numbers at left, this map approximates language-family extent at the time of first European contact. Explorers encountered many of these groups during the 16th century, but some were not contacted until the 20th century.

North American cultures at European contact can be grouped into at least ten major areas. Hunting was practiced by all native peoples, and it was the principal means of livelihood on at least half of the continent.

Mesa Verde and Chaco Canyon

Two awestruck cowboys in 1888 were the first white men to discover the abandoned cliff dwellings of Mesa Verde, home to the Anasazi for 700 years. First in pit houses, then in stone peublos with up to 75 rooms, these hunter-farmers inhabited the flat mesa top, digging pools and ditches to gather rainwater for their corn, beans, and squash. They kept dogs and turkeys, probably using the birds less for food than for the feathers their men worked into warm leggings and blankets. About A.D. 1150 they began to abandon mesa-top homes and to crowd into cliff-hung citadels whence they clambered by toeholds cut in rock to tend fields, fetch water, and hunt bighorn sheep and deer. About 100 years later they left even these.

To the south, Chaco Canyon dazzled visitors in the 11th and 12th centuries with its splendor. Hub of the Anasazi culture, Chaco had villages, irrigation ditches, and fields surrounding great walled pueblos, where diplomats and astronomer-priests may have brought news to the locals, who numbered perhaps 5,000. Traders hawked turquoise, scarlet macaws, and shell jewelry from the south. Some 400 miles of perfectly straight roads ran to and beyond outlying pueblos. Largest of Chaco's 12 great towns, Pueblo Bonito was both the political and the religious center of the Chaco Anasazi. The pueblo towered five stories on the strength of the Anasazi builders' innovative masonry. Some 650 living and storage rooms surrounded the plaza.

The early architects of Chaco Canyon seem to have developed their own local style. But in later features there are indications of Mexican influence—features like colonnades and round towers, or the distinctive technique of building a wall like a vertical sandwich, with a core of rubble between two layers of cut sandstone. There is even a suggestion of a cult of Quetzalcoatl, the feathered serpent worshiped in middle America.

There was never a long decline in the Anasazi tradition. The Anasazi culture simply disappeared, and with a suddenness that left no firm clues as to why. A prolonged, unrelenting drought? Attack by invaders? An overloading of the environment by peaceful immigrants? Any one of these is possible, but the best guess is that drought and soil loss forced the Anasazi southward to better land, where their descendants still live in the pueblos there today. With no written language, this advanced civilization left no record of its rulers, battles, and daily struggles—nor of its ultimate disappearance.

Arrival of the Spanish

In 1539 Spanish explorers led by Francisco de Coronado came looking for the fabled Seven Cities of Cibola. The Spanish harbored an old legend that told of seven cities, rich in gold and jewels, settled by oppressed Christians from Moorish Spain. Seeing the Zuni Pueblo in New Mexico ahead, they believed they had struck gold. Instead of fabulous treasure, however, Coronado and his men found a "little, crowded village . . . crumpled all up together."

The Zuni warriors stood ready to defend their town. They sprinkled sacred cornmeal in a line and warned the Spaniards not to cross. Coronado was reluctant to start a fight, but when a shower of Zuni arrows struck his ranks, he attacked. Stones and arrows were no match for Spanish armor and harquebus, or heavy guns. After plundering the town's food stores, the conquerors set out for other pueblos, then turned eastward to explore along the Rio Grande. It was not long before Roman Catholic missions appeared in Pueblo country; Indians who did not comply with the new religion were punished or killed.

At about the same time, Spanish explorer Hernando de Soto and his 600 soldiers were plundering much of the present-day South in search of riches. Indians were generally regarded as either a nuisance or a potential source of information. If they could contribute information that the explorers deemed necessary, they were impressed into service; the uncooperative were often tortured. After an odyssey of some three years, de Soto became ill with a fever and died by the Mississippi River in 1542. Hernando de Soto's and Francisco Coronado's exploits and expeditionary forces spread turmoil and disease throughout much of North America, heralding the end of the Indian cultures. ■

At Contact

1492–1700

THE NATIVE PEOPLES OF NORTH America may have numbered two million or more at the time Christopher Columbus arrived in 1492. All were hunters and gatherers; in addition, the settled peoples of the East, Southwest, and Great Plains cultivated crops of corn, squash, and beans. Copper-skinned, black-haired Indians were scattered across the continent in hundreds of culturally distinct groups: They spoke some 200 languages, respresenting perhaps 17 language families. Cultural boundaries were rarely sharply defined, and European immigration, especially immigrants to the East Coast, forced major shifts in the native population.

Some tribal groups were bound together politically—most notably the five neighboring tribes of the Iroquois confederacy, formed to end fraternal warfare. Tribes speaking Iroquoian languages ranged from the Cherokee to the south, through the Erie and Susquehanna in Ohio and Pennsylvania, to the Huron around Georgian Bay to the north. But the five tribes grouped as the Iroquois—the Mohawk, Oneida, Onondaga, Cayuga, and Seneca—held a land across central New York State "full of chesnutts and oakes" and passenger pigeons so abundant "that in a nett 15 or 1600 att once might be taken," according to the account of an early scribe.

The Iroquois lived in bark-covered longhouses flanking the central street of villages ringed by log stockades as tall as 20 feet. A dozen or more families had allotted spaces in each longhouse, a structure likened by one writer to a noisy "prison [with] four other great discomforts—cold, heat, smoke, and dogs." Outside the palisades lay fields "of all sides of Indian corne" tended by the women, whose child-rearing abilities, the Iroquois believed, were magically associated with the productivity of Mother Earth.

As woodland farmers, the Iroquois had agricultural rites tied to such events as the maturing of the corn or the ripening of wild strawberries. As northern hunters, the Iroquois also had shamans with supernatural powers to deal with the spirits. Religion wove itself into every aspect of daily life. Dreams had significance and offered guidance, and often were recounted in a ceremony at the beginning of the year. Through everything ran a force Mohawks called *orenda*, the mystic essence that bound all things. Individuals could accumulate orenda for inner strength. A shaman had powerful orenda, and members of one tribal society gained orenda to intercede with the False Faces—grotesque bodiless beings that roamed the dark forests and bewitched people into illness.

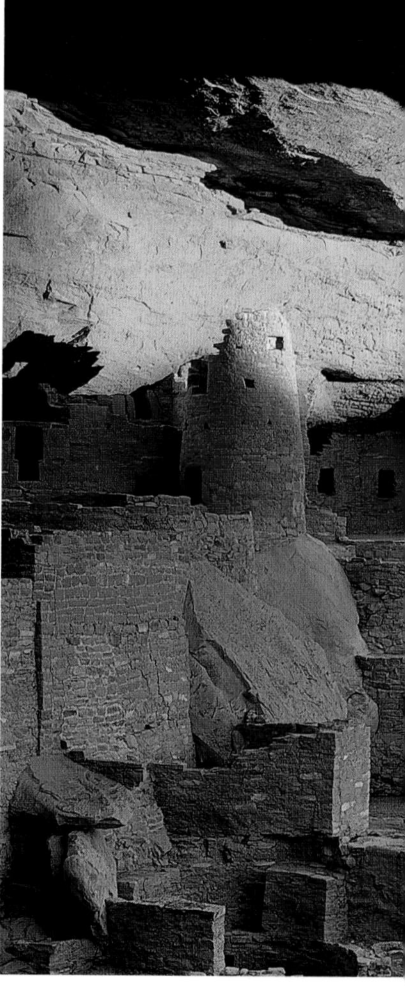

A Colorado sunset illuminates the masonry walls of Cliff Palace in Mesa Verde National Park. Built between A.D. 1190 and 1280, it housed some hundred Anasazi or "ancient ones," a term later applied to these Indians.

NOTABLE DATES

■ **1492**
Christopher Columbus lands on Caribbean islands in the New World.

■ **1565**
Pedro Menendez founds St. Augustine, Florida.

■ **1607**
The first enduring English settlement in the New World begins at Jamestown, Virginia.

■ **1676**
Fierce Indian war in New England ends with the death of numerous Narragansett Indians.

■ **1683**
William Penn signs a treaty with the Delaware Indians and pays them for lands in Pennsylvania.

A Matriarchal Society

The Iroquois woman had a freer, more influential place in the world she lived in than her European counterpart. Like many tribes, the Iroquois traced descent on the mother's side. A matriarch ruled each longhouse, and within it all the women were related; when a girl married, the husband moved, not the wife. Women named the children and raised them. Women owned the houses and belongings and fields—to the extent, at least, that anyone could be considered to own land. Indians all over the continent generally held that tribal terrain was a trust to be used, and no more saleable than the air.

The Iroquois tribes differed from other matrilineal societies in the amount of power women held. Matriarchs chose the chiefs and could depose them. Men held tribal offices and did the speaking, but women exerted genuine influence behind the scenes. And when a captive was brought home from a raid, it was the women who had final say in whether the captive would be adopted or executed—put to death by torture.

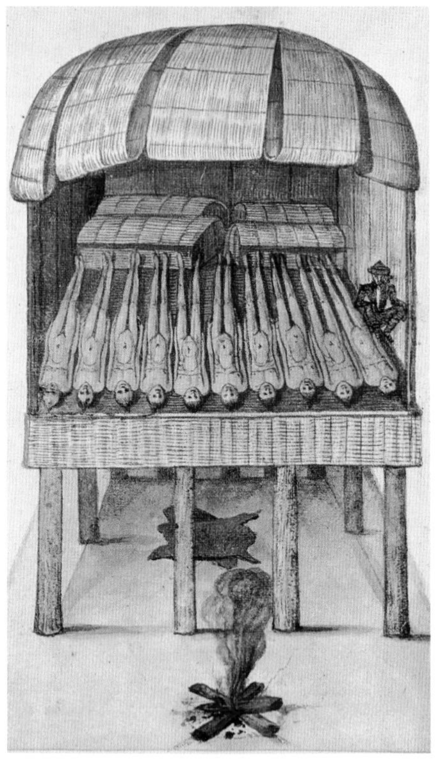

For tidewater Algonquins, ceremonial dances were a "sport . . . almost . . . as necessary as their meat and drynck." John White, governor of the Raleigh colony in 1580s, painted Indians circling stakes topped by carved faces, right. He also depicted burial customs in a watercolor of the tomb of their "cheefe lordes," above.

Indian warfare, before white contact, was as much a ceremony as a deadly business. Through war a young man could prove valor and win status. A swift commando raid by a small war party was the usual pattern. A prisoner taken in a raid faced punishment along the trail to the Iroquois village. Once there, he had to run a gauntlet of women and children wielding sticks, thongs, and branches. If he survived all this bravely, he might be adopted into the tribe by a family that had lost a warrior in battle. If marked for death, he faced hours of agony at the hands of enemies who "delight to tormente men in the most bloodie manner . . .; fleaing some alive . . . cutting of[f] . . . joynts of others by peese-meale and broiling on the coles, eate the collops of their flesh . . . while they live."

Though brutal, the torture had overtones of religious sacrifice. Victims might be feasted before their ordeal, treated with deference through it. Eating a bit of the body was a way to get some of the fortitude of an especially courageous sufferer. The victim had a role and played it—defiantly singing his death song, taunting his captors.

Fierce fighters though they were, the Iroquois also had an edge in tactical training and organization. That organization was reflected in the novel political system—perhaps the most complicated north of Mexico—that linked the five tribes.

The League of the Iroquois began in the 1500s. Before then, the five tribes were feuding kin. They constantly raided each other and—because of their division—suffered at the hands of their Algonquin neighbors. But a visionary Huron named Deganawidah dreamed of a mighty tree of "Great Peace" anchored by roots among the Five Nations. He and a disciple named Hiawatha—an Onondaga, not the imaginary Ojibwa hero of Longfellow's famous poem—traveled among the tribes to forge that unity. The resulting league formed a primitive sort of democracy with an oral constitution and governing council. (The five became six when the Tuscarora, pushed out of Carolina by white setlement, were admitted about 1722.)

The Pueblo

The first major European contact for the Pueblo people in the Southwest occurred with Coronado's 1539 expedition. At that time, about 90 pueblos were inhabited. (Today there are 30.) Coronado's soldiers saw young men living in underground council chambers—kivas—and women plastering their adobe houses and grinding corn.

The men of the pueblos put in long hours cultivating corn, beans, squash, and cotton. Hunting parties stalked deer and antelope, and communal rabbit hunts were organized in most villages. Varieties of tobacco grew wild in Pueblo country. Smoking the dried leaves in a "cloud blower"—clay pipe—was ceremonial rather than pleasurable or relaxing. Youths could smoke only when they proved they were good hunters. At Isleta Pueblo, near present-day Albuquerque, New Mexico, this meant killing a Navajo, the Pueblos' traditional enemy to the north.

Black-haird Pueblo matrons, wrapped in dark blankets fastened to leave the left shoulder bare, fashioned pots of coiled clay or bent over stone slabs baking *piki*, a paper-thin bread. Women enjoyed a privileged place in society, especially among the Hopi, where they owned the houses and fields. Children became members of the mother's clan and inherited

Indian Dwellings

NATIVE HOUSING COULD BE AS BASIC AS the Paiute's summer windbreaks or as highly developed as the Zuni's multistory pueblos. Design and construction depended upon available materials, climate, traditions, and the mobility of the tribe. Many groups used more than one type of dwelling, according to the season. Indians tied to a central location by farming built permanent homes, as, for example, did the fishermen of the Northwest Coast. Hunters and gatherers raised shelters they could easily carry or rebuild.

Within a culture area Indians built similar housing, though each tribe had distinctive variations. Wattle-and-daub houses, common in the Southeast, were raised with split saplings, withes, or canes that were woven around poles. The gaps were packed with a mud-and-moss mixture and then plastered with clay. Roofs were usually thatched with local grasses. In the Great Lakes area, wigwams were homes for one to two families; these small, domelike structures were framed with saplings and covered with bark and reed mats. A fire pit, which vented through a central roof hole, was used for heating and cooking.

Rectagular earth lodges, sod-covered structures shored by heavy cottonwood frames, were predominant on the Great Plains during the pre-Columbian era, before the advent of the horse. By European contact in the mid-1700s, earth lodges were circular in shape. The Mandan built them in permanent villages near their Missouri floodplain gardens but lived in buffalo-hide tepees during the hunting season. ■

A John White watercolor of the village of Secotan, probably located along the Pamlico River near present-day Bonnerton, North Carolina, limns an entire agricultural season.

property through her. Pueblo marriage was monogamous, although divorce and remating were fairly frequent. A Hopi husband who found his possessions stacked outside the door knew that he was not expected to return. At Taos and Acoma, adultery was punished by public whipping. If a boy wanted a girl to be his bride, he would make a "bundle" for her—clothing and fine white buckskin moccasins, which he left on her doorstep. If they were accepted, so was he. When a wedding followed, there were elaborate festivities, with an exchange of gifts by the two families.

The peaceful Pueblos, content in their close-knit village life, went to war only when necessary—to defend themselves or to avenge a raid by enemy Indians. Their weapons were arrows, clubs, and stone knives; from their belts hung a bag of *pinole*—meal made from roasted corn, rations for the journey. The war priest held ceremonies for as long as three nights to guarantee the expedition's success and the warriors' safe return. The Pueblo warriors would attack at dawn, rushing on surprised enemies as they came stumbling out of their shelters. They took a few scalps, gouging out a small, circular piece from the top of the head. When attacking from a distance, they shot arrows, sometimes tipped with rattlesnake venom. Before a counterattack could be organized, the warriors fled, hurrying through enemy country, back to the pueblo. If they were carrying scalps, they did not enter but camped outside, for a scalp was dangerous and full of supernatural power. The scalp had to be cleansed and then it became a friend, bringing good instead of evil.

Hunters of the Plains

The Great Plains, a sea of grass that sustained the buffalo, also nurtured the tribesmen who would become the stereotype of all American Indians: Blackfoot and Dakota (Sioux), Crow and Cheyenne, Comanche and Pawnee. Most roamed as hunters, moving their tepee camps in pursuit of the buffalo. Some clustered in villages, built houses of bark or covered with grass or earth, tilled riverside tracts, and traded with nomadic tribes. Though the Plains Indians had no common tongue, they could communicate in sign language.

Coronado's conquistadores, exploring the southern plains in the spring of 1541, marveled at these Indians. Instead of growing maize, they killed strange, shaggy wild cattle with bows and arrows. They pursued the great herds across the grasslands. "Troops of dogs" moved with them, dragging tent poles and bearing burdens. The skins of the "cattle," as the Spaniards called the bison, gave not only shelter but also clothes and shoes, rope and wool. They made thread of the sinews, awls of its bones, jugs of its bladder. Even the dung was used—for fires, "since there is no fuel in that land."

The Plains Indians made a living as they had for thousands of years. For a brief period of time—after they had acquired the horse and before they lost their tribal independence—they were among the finest horsemen and ablest mounted warriors in the world. The awe the Indians must have felt at first seeing horses is echoed in an 18th-century account of a Cree's first sight of a horse on the

As the morning sun rises behind the sandstone pillar of Fajada Butte, an Anasazi sun priest greets it with a ritual offering of ground maize, crushed shell, and turquoise.

northern plains. The old Indian told a white trader how, about 1730, he and other young warriors had trekked to a fallen horse, killed by an arrow in a battle with a tribe that was mounted.

"Numbers of us went to see him" he remembered, "and we all admired him. He put us in mind of a stag that had lost his horns; and we did not know what name to give him. But as he was a slave to Man, like the dog, which carried our things, he was named the Big Dog." The knowledge of horses spread across the plains, tribe by tribe. There is no historic foundation to the story that strays from Coronado's expedition provided the first horses to the Plains Indians. Instead, there was a slow and prolonged process of cultural diffusion. Mounted Indians appeared in northern Mexico in the latter half of the 16th century, and later around Spanish settlements in the Southwest. But two centuries would elapse between Coronado's exploration and acquisition of horses by distant tribes on the northern plains. As the Big Dog came into their lives—undoubtedly by intertribal trading—the Plains Indians were transformed from plodding followers of the buffalo into a pastoral people concerned with the breeding, daily care, and protection of large herds of domesticated animals.

Pacific Northwest

On the rocky and rainy coasts of the Pacific Northwest, there are few extensive beaches. But wherever a river delta or a protected inlet broke the forest, the native people settled, taking a rich, abundant livelihood from the streams and the ocean. One of the most aristocratic, richest Indian cultures north of Mexico flourished here—a land of salmon, cedar, potlatch, and totem pole.

From northern California to southeastern Alaska, an estimated 150,000 Indians lived at the beginning of the historical period. There were dozens of tribal groups, quite separate, yet the conditions of nature under which they lived and their responses were sufficiently alike to define a distinct cultural unit. The larger tribes, sorted by language groupings, included the Tlingit in southeastern Alaska; the Haida of the Queen Charlotte Islands; the Tsimshian, Kwakiutl, and Salish on the mainland; the Nootka on Vancouver Island; and the Chinook along the lower Columbia River. A number of smaller tribes held the coastal area from Washington State south into California.

Indians at Contact

Number of Indians in North America in 1492: 2,000,000

North American languages in 1492: 200

Pueblo villages in existence during Coronado's 1539 visit: about 90

Missionary chapels in Pueblo country by 1630: 90

Pueblo Indians converted to Christianity by 1630: 60,000

Tribal population density of coastal New York and Connecticut compared to that of Viginia and North Carolina: 3 times

Maritime specialization deeply affected all aspects of the culture—material, social, spiritual. Villages of sturdy houses were sited with an eye to a beach where canoes could be drawn up. Tools and implements included a vast array of devices for fishing and for hunting sea mammals. And religion, both rituals and deities, centered on aquatic creatures that were the staff of life. Fish was the main article of diet, salmon the mainstay. If the Salmon Beings were treated with respect, people believed, their spirits would return to the Salmon House under the sea, acquire new bodies, and make the sacrificial run again. All along the coast from Monterey Bay north, Indians held some sort of salmon ritual. Its basic purpose was a kind of game management since, as part of the rite, provision was made for enough salmon to ascend and spawn to ensure their return.

In addition to the summer village on the beach, tribes had a winter seat at the head of a protected inlet or in a fjord sheltered from the lash of storms. Rough terrain and dense evergreen forests, with an obstacle course of fallen timber, shrubs, and vines beneath the canopy, discouraged overland travel. There were few trails. Most people traveled by canoe rather than on foot. The heavy framework of both winter and summer houses was stationary, but planks for roofs and walls moved with the occupants. Soft, straight-grained cedar wood was readily split into house planks or carved into totem poles, tools, or utensils. The bark, too, had a multitude of uses—from baskets and clothing to whaling ropes. ■

WORLD SURVEY

PREHISTORY–A.D. 1700

While America was being populated by nomadic Indians, settled civilizations in other parts of the world were developing technologies and ways of life that would spread across the globe. The civilizations of the dominant nations would become defined as "advanced," and that of the aboriginals "primitive."

The Fertile Crescent

Some 8,000 years ago neolithic settlements in the Fertile Crescent—stretching from the southeastern coast of the Mediterranean Sea to the Syrian Desert—were domesticating animals and using agricultural techniques. About 5,000 years ago, settlements in the Mesopotamian Tigris-Euphrates Valley and the Nile River Valley were using irrigation to increase their agricultural production.

Within this junction of Asia and Africa, the next millennium saw the rise of cities and powerful city-states, kingdoms, and empires, as cooperative settlements pooled their resources under strong leadership. The parallel emergence of written language in this same region was a tremendous leap forward, for it marked the beginning of recorded history. By contrast, American Indians north of Mexico relied solely on oral language before the arrival of Europeans.

China

Isolated from civilizations elsewhere, the Chinese began to form villages along the middle Yellow River and its tributaries by about 5000 B.C. In the wetlands along the Yangtze to the south, villagers began cultivating rice, and they soon began to harvest silk from the cocoons of caterpillars that fed on mulberry leaves.

It is unclear exactly when a kingdom first emerged in China, but by 1750 B.C. rulers of the Shang dynasty had gained control over much of the Yellow River Valley. Chieftains loyal to the Shang ruled the kingdom's provinces with an iron hand and paid their ruler tribute in the form of troops and taxes. In China, as in Mesopotomia, rulers claimed kinship with the gods and were offered human sacrifices when they died.

Around 1100 B.C. rebels from western China overthrew the Shang and formed the Zhou dynasty. Just as Rome was coming to power, China was entering its own golden age under the Qin and Han dynasties (403 B.C.-A.D. 220), an era of stability and prosperity.

With the end of the Han dynasty in 220, China entered a period of disunity akin to Europe's Dark Ages, in which central control was lost. By the mid-1300s the Mongols, who had seized control of China in the late 1200s, were in decline, and the Ming dynasty began a 300-year reign.

Central and South America

By around 6000 B.C. Indians had spread throughout the Americas, down to the tip of South America. As in North America, they lived for millennia in small bands of hunter-gatherers. The Indians eventually began to settle in villages and farm corn, cacao, lima beans, potatoes, peanuts, squash, and tobacco.

The Olmec civilization arose in eastern Mexico around 1200 B.C. and flourished for the next eight centuries. The Maya gained control of southern Mexico and northern Central America from about A.D. 250 to 900, making splendid contributions in the fields of sculpture, painting, pottery, and architecture. They also had a written language, were well versed in astronomy, and used irrigation canals. The Toltec and Aztec civilizations followed, the latter thriving until the early 1500s. During the Aztec reign, the Inca built a dominant empire along South America's west coast, excelling at architecture and farming.

Starting with the landing of Hernan Cortés in Mexico in 1519, the Spanish conquistadores subjugated the great Indian civilizations within a few decades. Indians were enslaved; the mineral and agricultural resources of the new colonies brought great wealth to Europe.

■ Europe

The cradle of Western civilization, southern Europe began its rise around 3000 B.C. on the Aegean islands. With the Roman Empire (509 B.C.-A.D. 476) and the ascension of Greece in the fourth and fifth centuries B.C., Mediterranean civilization reached its full flowering. Greeks took the arts, philosophy, and democratic government to new heights, while fending off invasions from Persia. Athens emerged as one of the largest, most powerful, and most innovative of the Greek city-states. In the fourth century B.C. Alexander the Great defeated Persia and extended the reach of Greece all the way to northern India.

In the second century A.D., the Roman world stretched from England to the Persian Gulf and the Caspian Sea. Roman theaters were built in Africa, aqueducts carried water in France, villages with indoor latrines sprang up in Britain. Fifty thousand miles of hard-surface roads knit the empire together, and stone walls kept the barbarians out.

Following the decline of the Roman Empire, the Middle Ages began in Europe. While the Roman Catholic Church remained a strong influence througout Europe, there were no dominant nations. With the beginning of the Renaissance in the early 1300s, a new period of European prosperity and enlightenment began. Advancements in the arts and education led to a period of sweeping achievements in economics, politics, and science. The emergence of European nations as world powers followed, setting the stage for colonization in Asia, in Africa, and in the Americas. ■

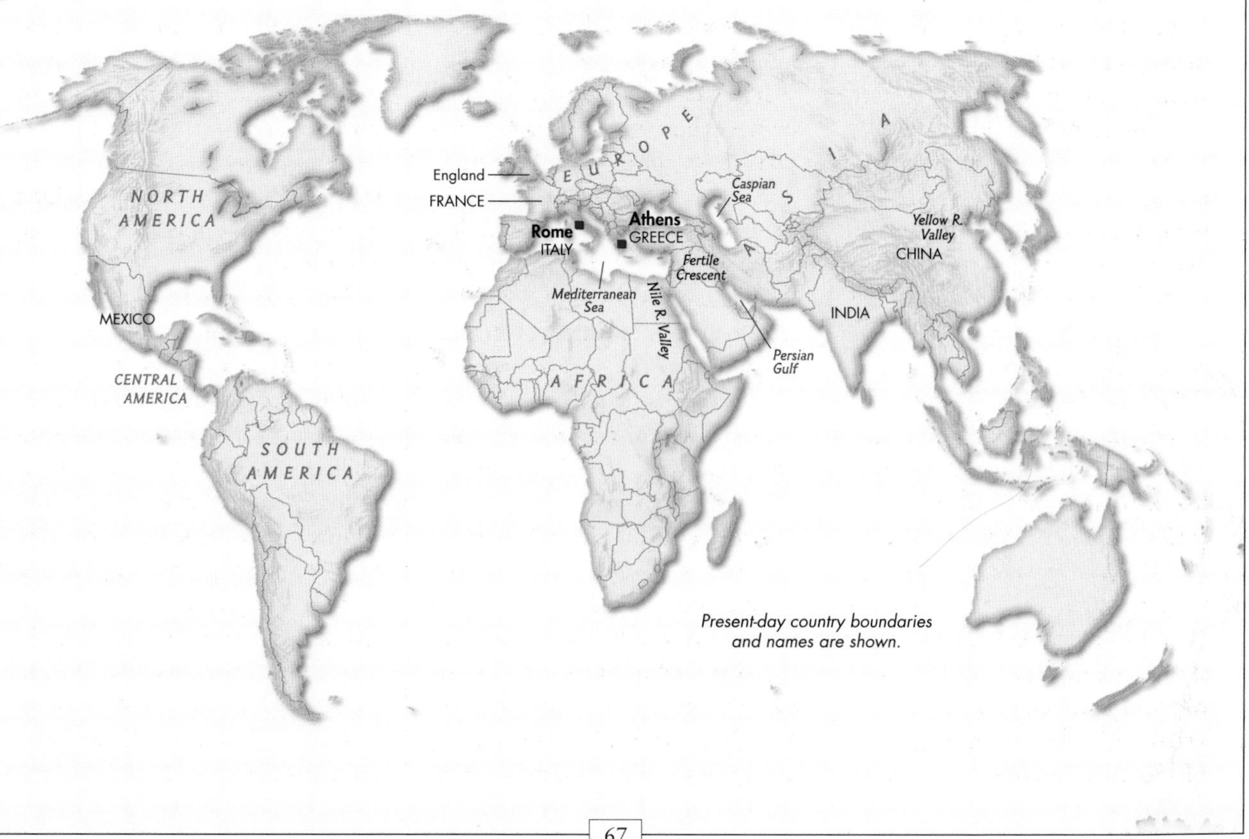

EUROPE DISCOVERS AMERICA 1000–1775

THOUGH THE VIKINGS WERE THE FIRST EUROPEANS TO SET FOOT IN THE NEW WORLD around the year 1000, their impressive feat was lost to history until relatively recently. The age of discovery waited until Christopher Columbus, sailing for Spain, made landfall in the Caribbean in 1492. What followed was an avalanche of exploration and conquest—devastating for American Indians, highly lucrative for European powerbrokers. Aided by cannon and muskets, Europe placed colonies in South America, then in North America. The Spanish gained footholds in Florida in the mid-1500s and the Southwest in the early 1600s, while Holland established New Netherland in present-day New York in the 1620s. But the real contest for control of North America was between France and England. French holdings extended from Quebec to the Great Lakes, with posts in the Ohio and Mississippi Valleys, while British colonies ran along the Atlantic; boundaries were indistinct. A series of long wars, known as the French and Indian Wars, played out across the North American frontier in the 1700s, as the two leading European nations struggled for territory and control of fishing and fur trading. England's ultimate triumph in North America and in other theaters around the world meant that the colonies would be British. But the victory whoop was cut short as England began overtaxing her American possessions to pay down the enormous debt incurred during the struggle with France. Revolution was in the wind. ■

Hudson River-school artist Alexander Wyant chose the unkempt wilds of the Cumberland Plateau for his 1866 landscape "Tennessee."

■ ca 1000	■ 1492	■ 1565	■ 1607	■ 1608
Leif Eriksson lands on the North American mainland, likely in Newfoundland; after several years, settlement attempts are abandoned.	Columbus opens the New World to European exploration.	Pedro Menendez founds St. Augustine in Florida.	Three boatloads of settlers establish Jamestown, England's first permanent New World settlement.	Samuel de Champlain establishes Quebec, the first permanent French settlement in North America.

■ 1619	■ 1689-1763	■ 1692	■ 1774	■ 1775
A Dutch ship unloads Virginia's first cargo of slaves at Jamestown.	The French and Indian Wars end with France all but banished from North America; Britain's costly triumph sets the Revolution in motion.	The Salem witch trials end with 19 executions; after a period of denial, Massachusetts reels with shame and admits the evils of narrowminded cultism.	The First Continental Congress, a meeting of colonial leaders, maps out a course of action against Britain's oppressive control.	William Bartram, America's first naturalist, explores the Cherokee country in the mountains of North Carolina.

Vikings

793–1042

While the Vikings had no direct influence on the settlement of America, they were likely the first Europeans to set foot there, and their influence on France and England established a hostile relationship between those two countries that lasted through the colonial era.

Hailing from Scandinavia, which now includes Norway, Sweden, and Denmark, the Vikings were a group of dreaded seafaring warriors who raided and plundered coastal towns all over Europe. The term "Viking" has come to mean all Norsemen from the Viking period, even though most were peaceful farmers.

Their homeland surrounded by frigid seas and dotted with deep fjords, the Vikings became master mariners, their skill and bravery in the open waters unmatched in their times. Expert shipbuilders chose timber from dense Scandinavian forests; a shallow draft and light weight meant the boats could travel up streams. Large woolen sails powered the boats at sea. The addition of a keel to vessels added stability, aided steering, and increased speed and the distance an expedition could travel. Merchant ships, or *knorrs*, measured about 50 feet in length; warships were built up to 95 feet long and 17 feet wide. In addition to the sail, some 15 to 30 pairs of rock-muscled oarsmen provided power.

Commanded by Leif Eriksson, a Viking landing boat rows toward Vinland, probably near present-day Newfoundland. The landing, about A.D. 1000, is the earliest known European presence in North America; five centuries elapsed before Europe really arrived in the New World.

Viking Conquests

Living for conquest, the Vikings terrorized dwellers of the European coastline. Churches were often targeted for silver and gold objects; churchgoers even said a special prayer, "God, deliver us from the fury of the Northmen." A typical warring party of two to ten Viking ships would land at a small, unprotected port, and several hundred warriors would storm in. Showing no mercy to men, women, or children, the Vikings often left towns in smoking ruins. Surprise attacks were lightning fast—over before the defenders could organize a resistance. Sometimes the Vikings massed a fleet of several hundred warships; warriors would swoop into a region and overwhelm it with sheer numbers. The warriors were wild in battle, shooting arrows, throwing spears, and swinging broadaxes to chop off limbs.

As explorers, the Vikings constantly pushed into new territory. At first using only the sun for navigation, they developed by the late 900s a system for estimating latitude by the use of a table showing the sun's midday height for each week. Sometimes they released a raven—known for its ability to find land—and then steered their ship in the bird's flight path.

The discoverers of America, the Norwegian Vikings initiated a reign of terror in 793. They attacked English monasteries, fertile English farms, and later European towns. But by the late 800s the Norwegians were reaching out across the North Atlantic, using as landmarks the Shetland and Faroe Islands. By the mid-900s some 25,000 Vikings had colonized Iceland. It was but a few hundred miles from there to Greenland, and in 982 explorer Erik the Red landed there with his family and soon was joined by several hundred stalwart Icelanders.

The New World

Not long afterward, Captain Bjarni Herjulfsson sailed off course from Iceland to Greenland and caught sight of a new land—presumably the first European sighting of North America. Sometime around the year 1000, Erik's son Leif Eriksson went in search of this new land. He and his crew wintered on a North American site that he termed Vinland (Wineland) for the grapes he found there; some scholars believe the fruit may have been cranberries or gooseberries. A colony was soon established but overrun by local Indians. The discovery in 1961 of a Viking settlement at L'Anse aux Meadows in Newfoundland indicates this as Eriksson's colony, though some historians believe it could have been located as far south as Cape Cod, Massachusetts. Though no maps or records of Vinland survive, Icelandic sagas describe it as a scene of several settlements over the next 20 years.

While Norwegian Vikings were exploring new worlds, Danish Vikings were making inroads in the old. Invading England in the 800s and 900s, they unified the country, ruling it until 1042. A Viking descendant called William the Conqueror led French Normandy (itself a Viking establishment) to victory against the English in 1066. The stage was thus set for enmity between France and England. ■

NOTABLE DATES

■ 793
Norwegian Vikings sack the monastery of Lindisfarne on an island off the east coast of England.

■ 839-845
Norwegian pirate Turgeis preys on Ireland and founds Dublin as his base.

■ ca 870
Norwegian settlers emigrate to Iceland.

■ 982
Erik the Red sails with his family to Greenland.

■ 985
Settlers journey from Iceland to Greenland and establish a colony.

■ ca 1000
Leif Eriksson and a crew of 35 land on North America, likely in Newfoundland, and establish a short-lived settlement.

■ 1042
Danish rule of England ends.

Spain in North America

1492–1800

IN 1492, NEARLY 500 YEARS after Leif Eriksson's failed Newfoundland settlement, Spain commissioned the Italian mariner Christopher Columbus to find a new sea route to the East. His landing in the Caribbean opened a new world to European profit and settlement. He made landfall on October 12, 1492, possibly on the Bahamian island of San Salvador; his three ships then continued to Cuba and Hispaniola.

For the next 50 years, the Spanish embarked on numerous expeditions, primarily into Central and South America and mainly for the purpose of conquest and plunder. By recruiting Indian allies discontent with the Aztec demands for tribute and sacrificial victims, Hernan Cortés laid waste the Aztec empire in a two-year campaign ending in 1521. Francisco Pizarro used a similar strategy in his 1531-36 defeat of the Inca.

By late summer of 1492, Columbus's three ships were ready to sail, loaded with supplies, cannons, money, and trinkets to trade for gold. The decked ship *Santa Maria* measured about 117 feet long, the caravels *Pinta* and *Niña* 50 feet. The fleet set sail on August 3 and within nine days had raised the Canary Islands; here they stopped for fresh supplies. They then sailed into the unknown. Columbus's talents as a mariner and leader soon came to the fore when fainthearted members of his crew began having doubts about the whole enterprise. There were incessant worries, one of which was that there would be no wind for a return trip. Columbus, who had begun to feel a divine providence guiding him, was not surprised when a facing wind blew in, calming the fears of his mates.

After several false sightings of land, on October 12 a sailor on the *Pinta* beheld the New World. The Bahamian island of San Salvador was a paradise of soft color

European powers contest territory overseas in this rendering of Spanish ships firing on John Smith's ship off the coast of New England in 1614. By this time Spain's hold on the New World was beginning to shrink.

in the dawn light. Columbus went ashore and planted the flag of Spain, laying claim to the land. For two weeks they sailed among the islands, looking for gold, considering the other natural resources that might be profitable, including the natives. They explored Hispaniola and Cuba, which Columbus thought was Japan. When the *Santa Maria* ran aground and wrecked, he left 38 men at a place he called Villa de la Navidad (in Haiti), and the other two ships left for Spain in early January. On the return, storms threatened to annihilate the mission. Fearing the anonymity of death, Columbus wrote out his tale, sealed it in a cask, and tossed it overboard. He later admitted that he had withheld key distances to make it hard for others to re-create his feat.

He hailed land on March 4, 1493, was received by the king of Portugal, and from there headed to Spain. The captain of the *Pinta*, Martin Pinzon, wiped out by the expedition, died on March 20. The monarchs of Spain, Ferdinand and Isabella, were so impressed with Columbus's success, they immediately funded a second, much larger, expedition, partly to keep ahead of Portugal.

During this second trip, he sent home the news that the Spaniards at Villa de la Navidad had all been killed by Indians, and his benefactors began having doubts about his judgment. On this and his two subsequent voyages of up to three years, Columbus explored the Caribbean and the coast of Central and South America, while constantly dealing with native unrest, mutinies, shortages of food, bad weather, and illness. He found his authority eroding as he pushed for discoveries while abusing his role as governor of the island bases. Simply put, he was a much better admiral than administator, and his supporters knew it.

Even before Columbus's final voyage in 1502, the seas were no longer his alone—France and England had launched their own dreams of empire. "They all made fun of my plan then," he wrote, "now even tailors wish to discover." Though he had made a fortune, it was honor that he mostly sought. Ferdinand was generous with Columbus but refused his

NOTABLE DATES

■ 1492
Columbus explores the Caribbean and builds a fort on island of Hispaniola.

■ 1511
Diego Velazquez conquers Cuba and becomes the governor of Spanish colonists.

■ 1513
Vasco Nuñez de Balboa crosses the Panamanian Isthmus and reaches the Pacific Ocean.

■ 1519
Hernan Cortés leaves Cuba for Mexico, where he completes his conquest of the Aztec Empire in 1521.

■ 1531
Francisco Pizarro reaches Peru and embarks on his conquest of the Inca Empire, completed in 1536.

■ 1542
Hernando de Soto dies near the Mississippi River while searching for wealth in the Southeast; Francisco Vasquez de Coronado returns to Mexico after a similar expedition across the Southwest.

■ 1565
Spanish colonists land in Florida and found St. Augustine.

■ ca 1609
Spanish colonists found Santa Fe, which becomes the colonial capital of New Mexico.

■ 1762
France cedes Louisiana west of the Mississippi to Spain.

■ 1769
Spanish missionaries and troops reach San Diego harbor from Baja California and found the colony of Alta California.

audacious request of "the government and possession of the Indies." The man who had opened up the New World died in 1506, a year and half after returning from his final voyage.

But the conquistadores who explored North America found no great wealth or native empires to exploit. Instead, they encountered tribes fiercely resistant to outside control. Explorerer Juan Ponce de Leon was the first European of record to make landfall on the coast of Florida, when he arrived somewhere between present-day St. Augustine and the St. Johns River in 1513. On a return trip eight years later he was attacked by Indians and mortally wounded. He died in Cuba a few weeks later.

La Florida

The Florida territory (*La Florida*), covering an expanse west to the Mississippi River and north to the Carolinas, did not yield easily to colonization. For his work in conquering Cuba, Panfilo de Narvaez received a Spanish patent to settle Florida in 1527. Landing in Tampa Bay, he and some 200 men marched north, sending ships on ahead to meet them. The ships failing to appear, Narvaez and his crew built several boats and attempted to reach Mexico; most of them perished in a storm somewhere in the Gulf.

Hernando de Soto was a more capable explorer, but his epic journey also ended in ultimate failure. In 1539 he sailed into Tampa Bay with nine ships and more than 600 soldiers. Armed with harquebuses, crossbows, and other weapons, the group embarked on a 4,000-mile journey north through present-day Georgia and the Carolinas, then back down to Alabama and the Mississippi River. After four years of searching, they found no gold. Instead, they were in near constant conflict with Indians, using them when they could and punishing them if they did not cooperate. Their greed spread resentment through the native populations and cost the lives of half the crew, including de Soto himself.

A Deadly Toll

Number of Tainos (Hispaniola natives) Columbus shipped to Spain in 1596: 500

Number that survived the voyage: 300

Number of soldiers Cortés took to Mexico in 1519: 600

Number of natives Cortés recruited to help defeat the Aztecs: 200,000

Number of men Pizarro took to Peru in 1531: 200

Number of Incas Pizarro killed by luring them unarmed into the Spanish camp: 6,000

Number of years Pizarro lived after capturing Cuzco (before being killed by natives): 8

A Spanish attempt to establish a settlement at Pensacola Bay in 1559 ended when storms and hunger caused strife among the sailors. For a while, Florida looked to Spain like a lost cause; plenty of gold and silver was already flowing in from Peru and Mexico. But holding the peninsula was important to Spain's defense against pirates operating between the Caribbean and the Straits of Florida. Thus when France built Fort Caroline at the mouth of the St. Johns River in 1565, Spain responded by sending Pedro Menendez de Aviles to found St. Augustine, which became the first permanent European settlement in the United States. After establishing his base at St. Augustine, Menendez went up the coast and attacked Fort Caroline, then chased down the fort's 50 unarmed survivors and slaughtered them on the beach. But the French took their revenge three years later, returning to burn the Spanish-held fort and massacre its occupants; the Spanish rebuilt it,only to abandon it soon after.

With a garrison at St. Augustine and, by the end of the century, another at Pensacola, the Spanish built some hundred missions in the Florida country. The first mission chain stretched along the Atlantic coast up to present-day Georgia; the second, built primarily in the 1600s, went across the Florida Panhandle. The missions served as strategic defense posts as well as reeducation centers where potentially hostile Indians could be tamed, converted, and then subjugated for labor. By the early 1700s most of the missions had been burned by the British and their Indian allies. Built of wood and palm thatch, the missions soon deteriorated, leaving no traces of those turbulent years.

Spain relinquished Florida to Britain from 1763 to 1783 under the Treaty of Paris, but then regained the western part by treaty, holding it from 1784 to 1821.

Christopher Columbus

Born around 1451 in the Italian port of Genoa, Christopher Columbus became one of the greatest mariners of all time. His egomania and overbearing temperament, amounting almost to mental illness, brought about a reversal of fortune in his later life. But his accidental discovery of the New World—the result of his persistence, daring, and lively imagination—sets him apart as a man of towering achievement.

Eyes on the prize: Traveling from court to court to obtain financial backing, Columbus and his son pause at water's edge in this symbolic colored woodcut.

The son of a weaver, Columbus went to sea at age 14 and by his early 20s was a pirate, his life filled with adventure. During a battle off Cape St. Vincent, his ship caught fire and he had to swim to the Portuguese shore. He stayed briefly in Portugal, then the center of cosmographic and astronomic ferment and the staging point for world exploration. Columbus was soon off on a voyage to Iceland, honing his skills as a navigator. During this mid-1470s journey, he was already dreaming up a westward expedition to "Cathay," or China. In 1478 he married into the Portuguese aristocracy and lived for a while on Porto Santo in the Madeira Islands; his journeys from here into the South Atlantic included trips to the Gold Coast of Africa, then the southernmost point of the known world.

Columbus's radical idea that the Orient could be reached by sailing west was derived from a number of sources, as varied as Marco Polo, Ptolemy, and the Apocrypha. He based his belief on the assumption that, if the world was round, it was a shorter distance by sea to the Orient than by land. By Columbus's calculations, "India" lay only 3,900 miles west of the Canary Islands—little did he know that it was almost exactly that distance to America.

Inflamed by his imagination, Columbus envisioned both new lands and new routes to old lands, and great glory and wealth for himself. He presented his proposal to the king of Portugal in 1484, but was rejected. Turning to Spain, he was passed over by various nobles before finally getting a hearing in 1486 witih King Ferdinand and Queen Isabella. Spain was then a rising world power; Columbus's scheme could enrich Spanish coffers. The monarchs created a commission to study the proposal. Partly owing to Columbus's incoherence, the commission took four years to deem the project not worthwhile. Friends got him another audience with the monarchs, who asked his price: He wanted a knighthood, ten percent of the profits, and to be appointed grand admiral and viceroy. The king and queen were stunned, but Columbus refused to compromise. As he was leaving Spain in early 1492, he was recalled to court and granted everything he had requested. ■

Mission San Francisco de Asis (St. Francis of Assisi) near Taos, New Mexico, was dedicated by Franciscans to the founder of the order. Spanish missions played a vital role in colonizing the New World, particularly in the Southwest.

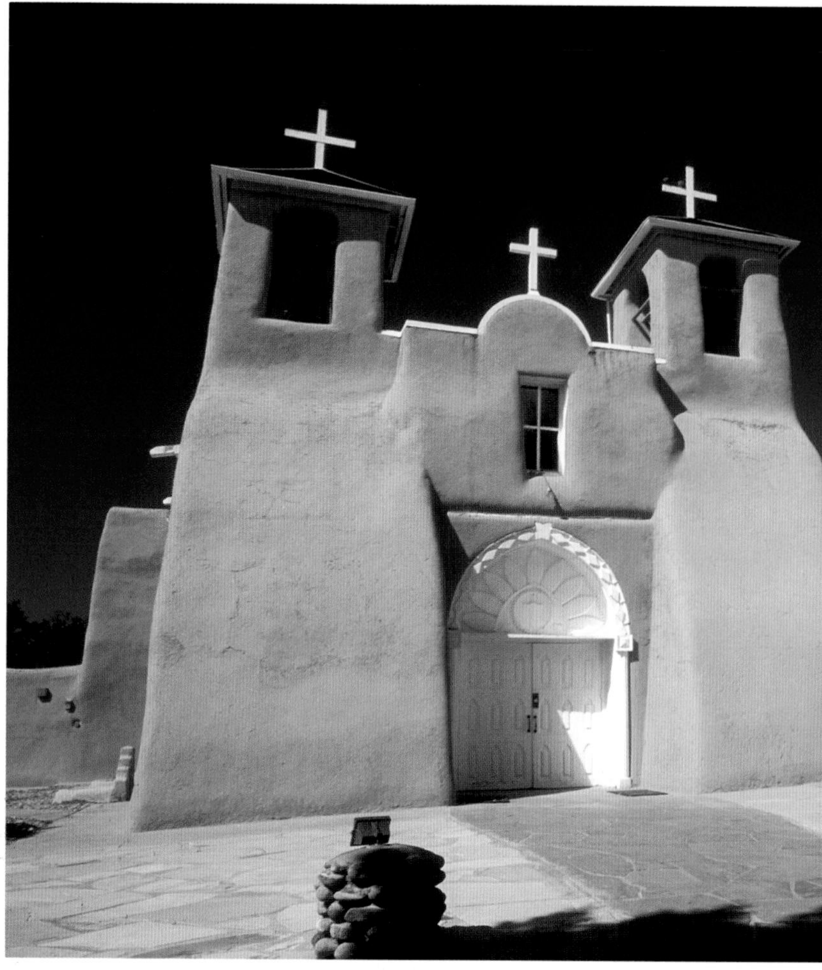

Missions in the West

The Spanish mission system gained firmer footing in the West than in the Southeast. In the Spanish colonies of California, Texas, and New Mexico, Franciscan friars established scores of missions in desert outposts where few settlers dared attempt to make a living. Indians in the Southwest were somewhat more tractable than in the Southeast, or at least more willing to accept the newcomers and their strange rituals. Francisco Vasquez de Coronado's 1540 search for the fabled Seven Cities of Cibola certainly wreaked havoc among Pueblo Indians, but it was a shorter and generally less brutal outing than de Soto's simultaneous venture in the Southeast.

Through the end of the 1500s, soldiers and friars made a few random incursions into New Mexico. Then, in 1610, Juan de Onate founded Santa Fe, the first permanent white settlement in the territory. Conflict with the Indians and the excesses of missionary zeal brought a backlash in 1680 when the Indians revolted and massacred hundreds of white settlers. In the process many Spanish horses found their way into the hands of nearby Plains Indians, greatly enchancing their skills as hunters and warriors. After a few years, Spanish colonists crept back in and eventually came to terms with the Pueblos, who served with them in expeditions against hostile tribes. Albuquerque was founded in 1706, giving New Mexico both a southern and a northern outpost.

Meanwhile, Juan Rodriguez Cabrillo was exploring the coast of California for Spain in 1542, making landings at Catalina Island and the sites of San Diego, Santa Monica, and other places. But it was not for another 40 years, once England had taken an interest in the area, that Spain returned on reconnaissance missions. The real settlements, though, worked their way north from Baja California in a chain of missions. The first mission in Alta California (present-day California) was at San Diego in 1769, more than 150 years after the founding of Santa Fe. During the next 54 years, 20 more missions were added to the chain, each about a day's journey apart. This mission chain, linked by El Camino Real (the Royal Highway), owed its existence largely to the efforts of Father Junipero Serra (1713-84), a Franciscan monk born on the Spanish island of Majorca. He was 36 years old when he became a missionary in Mexico, continuing his well-intentioned, faithful work with unstinting energy even though he was lame.

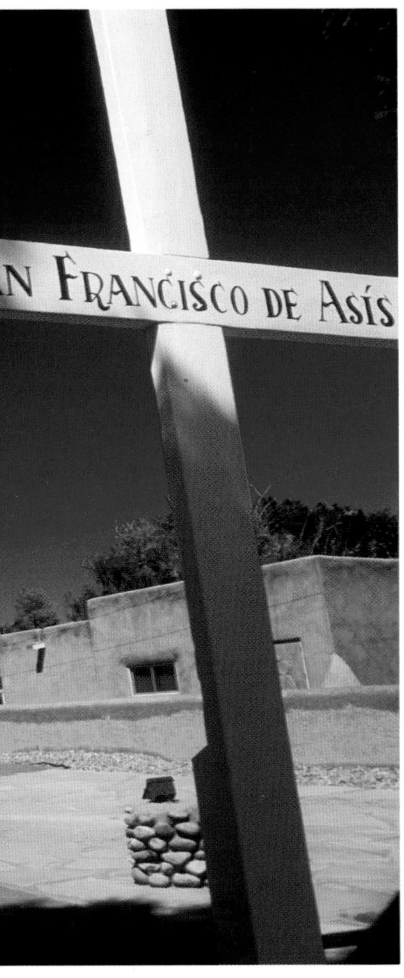

Overall, the missions of the Southwest converted tens of thousands of Indians to Christianity, and introduced them to Spanish customs and to the Spanish language. By the late 18th century the missions and the farms and ranches attached to them offered Indians some security at a time when their livelihood was threatened by the incursions of colonists and the variety of diseases they communicated. On the other hand, the concentration of native people at the missions sometimes made the epidemics of diseases brought by the Europeans even worse.

Spanish troops went in pursuit of runaways and sometimes forced unbaptized Indians into missions. Even willing converts disliked the strict mission regimen that banned "pagan" practices such as the worship of kachinas—spirits sacred to the Pueblos—and handed out bodily punishments for a variety of offenses. Many missionaries allowed Indians to engage in their traditional customs, such as tribal dances, but some were the kind of harsh and punitive disciplinarians who arouse violent and long-standing resentments.

Missions in New Mexico were heavily subsidized by Spain, while those in California were largely self-supporting. Aided by California's mild climate, friars and their Indian converts reaped large harvests from irrigated fields, tended cattle and sheep, and built handsome mission buildings where Indians practiced traditional crafts like pottery and basketmaking and mastered such new skillls as masonry and tanning hides. Yet even these seemingly successful missions were shadowed by disease and discord.

Spanish America Falters

California missions were supposed to disband after ten years; at that time their occupants would become part of colonial society, which needed to assimilate Indians to compensate for the small numbers of Spanish settlers. Franciscans postponed that transition indefinitely, arguing that mission Indians were not ready for independence. Here, as elsewhere, the mission system helped the colony get started but failed to promote its continued growth and resuscitate the declining Spanish-American empire.

On the eastern side of New Mexico, the Spanish colony of Texas also consisted largely of missions for Indians guarded by small numbers of troops. Texas had more than 30 missions by 1800. Yet here and elsewhere the missions as centers of settlement never really took off in the way the Spanish had hoped. Even the prosperous California missions, with their well-tended fields and gardens, were plagued by disease and unrest, and no large towns arose outside their walls. Some Spanish settlements founded in the 1700s would later grow into major cities, including San Antonio in Texas and Los Angeles in California. But for the most part, the rugged Southwest remained lightly inhabited throughout the colonial period.

Spanish America reached its greatest extent in the late 1700s after France ceded to Spain the city of New Orleans and the rest of Louisiana west of the Mississippi. Yet this huge empire extending from the Canadian border to Cape Horn was impressive only on paper. It was lightly defended and Spain's fortunes had been in decline since the 1588 defeat of its armada by the British. Its North American empire would soon crumble as Anglo-Americans encroached on the borderlands, and Spanish colonists in Central and South America—weary of a colonial system that extracted their resources while restricting their economic and political development—began agitating for independence. ■

France

1534–1763

FRENCH EXPLORATION OF North America got underway in earnest in 1534, when Jacques Cartier entered the Gulf of St. Lawrence. His expedition was the first to penetrate Canada—a name of Indian origin for the land the French called New France.

Like Columbus, Cartier hoped to find a passage to the Indies and returned to Canada in 1535 to explore that possibility. At first the broad St. Lawrence looked promising, but it narrowed as he and his crew went westward; soon they encountered rapids that proved impassable. This was no passage to India, but the countryside along the St. Lawrence looked fertile and inviting. Climbing a hill he dubbed Mont Royal, Cartier admired the broad river valley. It was "the most beautiful land," he wrote, "covered with the most magnificent trees."

Cartier returned to Canada in 1541 and founded a settlement at Quebec. It lasted only two years before the colonists headed home, discouraged by the harsh climate, the inhospitable Indians, and the absence of precious metals. Europeans remained obsessed with finding mineral wealth in the New World and paid little attention to other resources. By 1600, however, there was a demand in Europe for beaver pelts, used to make hats, and that profitable trade helped spur the development of New France.

Colonizing Canada

In 1608 Samuel de Champlain founded the first permanent French settlement in Canada at Quebec. Champlain understood that the French needed Indians as allies and trading partners in order to succeed in the fur trade, and he forged ties with several tribes, notably the Huron living between Lake Ontario and Georgian Bay. Soon Jesuit missionaries from France were living among the Huron, introducing them to Christianity.

The colony of New France grew and prospered. Enterprising fur traders called *coureurs du bois*, or voyageurs, set out from Quebec and the nearby town of Montreal, founded in 1642, and ranged far to the west, traveling along rivers or lakes. By 1670 the French had a trading post at Sault Ste. Marie and were exploring Lakes Superior and Michigan. The founding of the Hudson's Bay Company by the English that same year provided competition for the Canadian fur trade and encouraged the French to broaden their scope.

Meanwhile Montreal, Quebec, and other settlements along the St. Lawrence were gradually increasing in population as new colonists arrived from France and raised families. The French authorities expanded the colonies by granting territory to landlords, who then recruited settlers and provided them with hundred-acre homesteads in exchange for rent and services. The system was based on feudalism, but unlike serfs in Europe, settlers in New France had a legal claim to their land.

Founding Louisiana

After reconnoitering the Great Lakes, French explorers pushed southward along the Mississippi River and its tributaries. In 1673 Father Jacques Marquette and French-Canadian Louis Jolliet, traveling with five voyageurs, paddled their canoes far down the Mississippi past the mouths of the Missouri and Ohio Rivers. The venturesome French seigneur Rene-Robert Cavelier, Sieur de la Salle, reached the mouth of the Mississippi in 1682. La Salle claimed for France all the country watered by the Mississippi and its tributaries, including the Ohio and Missouri, which extended a thousand miles or more in either direction.

Known as Louisiana in honor of King Louis XIV, this vast country extending from the Appalachians to the Rockies went largely unsettled by the French, and both Spain and England contested La Salle's claim. Nonetheless, France was planting settlements along the

Indians trade furs for guns in a Hudson's Bay Company trading post. Founded in London in 1670, the company helped settle Canada all the way to the west coast; today it ranks as the country's leading department store retailer.

lower Mississippi River, including New Orleans, founded in 1718. French numbers there were bolstered in the mid-1700s by the arrival of several thousand Acadians, exiled from their homeland in Nova Scotia (long disputed by England and France), which came under British control in 1713.

A Losing Struggle

The treaty by which France lost Nova Scotia, Newfoundland, and other territory to Great Britain ended Queen Anne's War, one of several conflicts between the two powers that culminated in the British conquest of Canada.

After King George's War ended inconclusively in 1748, the French tried to halt the westward expansion of the British by occupying the Ohio Valley. British colonial authorities responded in 1754 by sending out militia under George Washington to challenge the French at Fort Duquesne in present-day Pittsburgh. Washington lost in a battle that inaugurated the epic conflict known as the French and Indian War. In 1758, the British gained the upper hand by shipping more troops to North America. In 1759 British troops captured Quebec and took control of Canada.

Elsewhere, savage fighting continued between British colonists and Indian allies of the French until peace was negotiated in 1763. France renounced its claims to Canada and all of Louisiana east of the Mississippi except New Orleans, having ceded it and western Louisiana to Spain a year earlier. Spain ceded Lousiana back to France in 1800, and three years later the United States made the Louisiana Purchase. The French adventure in North America had come to an end. ■

NOTABLE DATES

■ 1534
Jacques Cartier explores the Gulf of St. Lawrence on the first of three pioneering expeditions to Canada.

■ 1608
Samuel de Champlain founds Quebec, the first permanent French settlement in Canada.

■ 1682
La Salle reaches the mouth of the Mississippi and claims all the land watered by that river and its tributaries for France under the name of Louisiana.

■ 1685
La Salle lands at Matagorda Bay after failing to locate the mouth of the Mississippi by sea and explores Texas.

■ 1713
France surrenders Newfoundland and other territory in North America to England at the conclusion of Queen Anne's War.

■ 1718
New Orleans is founded by French settlers.

■ 1759
British forces capture Quebec and take control of Canada in the decisive battle of the French and Indian War.

■ 1762
France cedes New Orleans and all of Louisiana west of the Mississippi to Spain.

■ 1763
France surrenders its remaining territory in North America by conceding British control of Canada and transferring the eastern portion of Louisiana to Britain.

Northern Europe

1621–1867

WHILE THE FRENCH WERE gaining ground in Canada, countries in northern Europe were also staking claims in the New World. In 1621 traders in the Netherlands organized the Dutch West India Company and began to colonize New Netherland in a region now containing parts of Connecticut, New York, New Jersey, and Delaware.

The Dutch had already established several trading posts along the lower Hudson River in the early 1600s and built a successful business with local Indians. Then in 1624, 30 families sponsored by the Dutch West India Company settled in the area. A group of these settlers founded Fort Orange (now Albany). In 1625 other Dutch settlers founded New Amsterdam—present-day New York City—at the mouth of the Hudson. The next year New Netherland governor Peter Minuit made one of the country's most famous real estate deals when he bought Manhattan Island from the Indians for goods worth some 60 guilders, about 24 dollars.

Fur trading posts and settlements soon sprang up in other locations, including present-day Hartford, Trenton, Schenectady, Brooklyn (originally Brueckelen), Kingston (Wiltwyck), and Rensselaer (Rensselaerswyck). Under the Charter of Privileges of Patroons (landowners), members of the Dutch West India Company received tremendous parcels of land if they could colonize them with 50 settlers. The longest-lived patroon holding, lasting until the 1700s, was in the family of diamond merchant Kilaen Van Rensselaer, his tract encompassing much of Albany, Columbia, and Rensselaer counties.

In the meantime, Peter Minuit, relieved of his position in New Netherland in 1631, took a group of Swedish settlers south to the Delaware River and founded the colony of New Sweden. Their first settlement, Fort Christina was built at future Wilmington. Swedish and Finnish immigrants, in constant friction with the Dutch, continued to augment the colony's population. The Swedes took over Dutch Fort Casimir (at current New Castle) in 1654, but the next year the Dutch annexed all of New Sweden.

English explorer Henry Hudson meets with Native Americans along the Hudson River. He attempted on four voyages, from 1607 to 1611, to find an inland passage from the Atlantic to the Pacific; he sailed farther north than anyone ever had.

After a few short decades of relative peace (with sporadic fighting against the French and their Indian allies), the Dutch began to come into conflict with the English over boundaries and trade disagreements. In 1664 the competition was pushed to the brink of violence when English King Charles II granted his brother, the Duke of York, the whole territory between Maryland and Connecticut. To seal the agreement three English warships appeared before New Amsterdam, then a town of some 1,500 people. Though the director general of New Netherland and the adjacent regions, Peter Stuyvesant, said he'd sooner be "carried out dead" than surrender, the colonists refused to back him. He had no choice but to give in, and so without bloodshed New Amsterdam became New York. Stuyvesant left for Holland, but returned in a few years and settled on his farm in New York's present-day Bowery. The Dutch in New York were content to become British citizens in the new country, and it was not long before the remaining Dutch settlements gave in to British authority. Merchants back in Amsterdam shrugged off the loss—their main colonial interests lay in the Far East.

Russians

Though not interested in colonizing the New World, Russia had a large stake in its natural resources, particularly in the fur industry. Under the Russian flag in 1725, the Danish navigator Vitus Bering set off on a 6,000-mile journey across Russia and Asia; on the coast, he built a ship and sailed through the strait, now bearing his name, that separates northeastern Asia from North America. Fog kept him from seeing the North American mainland. Again given a commission by Russia, Bering made another North Pacific trip in 1741 and landed on Kayak and Southeast Islands in southern Alaska. Journeying home in the winter, Bering's ship ran aground off the coast of Siberia. While trying to wait out the bad weather, he and 19 crew members died of scurvy; the others rebuilt their ship, and survived on fish they caught until they could finally sail for home.

Back home, the Russian fur traders were less interested in the expeditioners' tale of hardship than in the otter pelts the survivors brought with them. It was not long before more Russian vessels appeared in the waters off Alaska and as far south as California. Forts sprang up along the coast, with headquarters at Novo Arkangelsk (New Archangel), now Sitka, on Baranof Island. Alexander Baranov in 1799 created the Russian-American Company, a fur trading concern. To satiate Chinese demand for furs, the Russians in the late 1700s and the early 1800s enslaved the local Aleuts and nearly destroyed the Pacific Northwest's marine mammal kingdom: The sea otter population plummeted from four million to 100,000. With stiff competition from both British and American traders and the decline of the fur industry, the Russians began scaling back, finally selling Alaska to America in 1867, for $7.2 million. ■

NOTABLE DATES

■ 1621
Holland founds the Dutch West India Company and colonizes New Netherland.

■ 1625
New Amsterdam is founded on the site of New York City.

■ 1626
Governor Peter Minuit buys Manhattan Island from the Algonquins for the equivalent of $24.

■ mid-1600s
Dutch painters Rembrandt and Vermeer at their creative height.

■ 1655
The Dutch take over New Sweden in Delaware.

■ 1664
Peter Stuyvesant surrenders New Amsterdam to the British.

■ 1741
Commissioned by the Tsar of Russia, Vitus Bering explores the coast of southern Alaska; Russian fur posts follow.

England
1584–1732

IT WAS THE ENGLISH WHO WOULD colonize America most aggressively, and the English influence would dominate American culture until an American identity gradually emerged. The first attempts at English colonization fared poorly. In 1584 explorers sent out by Sir Walter Raleigh, who held a grant from Queen Elizabeth I to colonize the New World, found a likely site for settlement on Roanoke Island. In 1585 settlers arrived at Roanoke Island, off the coast of what is now North Carolina, inaugurating the first English colony in America. Short of provisions, they grew dependent on Indians for food and ended clashing with them and abandoning the island. A second expedition in 1587 brought a party that included women and children to Roanoke, where they, too, suffered from lack of supplies.Their leader, John White, returned to England for help, leaving behind his married daughter and her infant, Virginia Dare, the first English colonist born in the New World. When White returned in1590, and he found the settlement deserted. The fate of White's "Lost Colony" remains a mystery.

Jamestown

Similar trials beset the next English colony in America, founded in

Pilgrims and Indians share food and count their blessings in painter Jean Louis Gerome Ferris's rendering of the first Thanksgiving; the harvest celebration of 1621 between English Protestants and Cape Cod natives started a tradition.

Virginia in 1607 at a site called Jamestown in honor of King James I. Located in a marshy area along the James River, the colony was plagued by malaria. Hostilities, disease, and starvation nearly wiped it out, but new settlers arrived and began working the land. They found a cash crop in 1612 when colonist John Rolfe succeeded in growing tobacco. This set the stage for colonial expansion, but settlers first had to reckon with fierce resistance from Powhatan, leader of a confederacy of Algonquin tribes. Powhatan relented after the English captured his daughter Pocahontas, who wed John Rolfe.

The men of early Jamestown were a hardy lot. At times nearly wiped out by starvation and Indian raids, they were given a boost in 1619 when a ship arrived from England carrying 90 "young maidens" who were wed to eager colonists. That same year Jamestown, with a population of 2,000, started a precedent-setting representative government—the first legislative meeting consisted of a governor, six councilors, and burgesses from ten plantations.

Though the Anglican Church took root in the South, it did not find good soil. In England, villages were close and well connected with roads; in America there was wilderness. Church attendance was sparse, and ministers barely eked out a living.

Puritans in New England

Among dissidents seeking refuge in America were the Puritans: Protestants at odds with the Church of England. Some were ready to separate from that faith and England. One such group of Separatists migrated first to Holland in 1608 and then sailed for the New World aboard the *Mayflower* in 1620, landing on Cape Cod. They called themselves Pilgrims and settled at Plymouth, where they met with Indians who had been devastated by diseases communicated by earlier European visitors and wanted to avoid hostilities. The settlers learned from them how to plant corn and other native crops and joined with them to celebrate the harvest in 1621—the first Thanksgiving celebration.

This small Plymouth colony endured, but it was soon eclipsed by a massive colonization effort by Puritans who reached Massachusetts Bay in 1630 and founded the town of Boston and nearby settlements. The Puritans did not start out as Separatists, but they took advantage of their newfound freedom by dispensing with Anglican rules that gave bishops authority over local parishes and instead granted each congregation the "liberty to stand alone," as one minister put it. Ironically, that did not mean colonists could worship as they pleased. Massachusetts was Puritan, and nonconformists had no place there. Puritans were conservatives, bent on creating a church-state. Dissenters pushed into new territory.

Breakaway Colonies

Two notable dissenters, Roger Williams and Anne Hutchinson, advocated the separation of church and state; they found refuge in the wilds of adjacent Rhode Island. In 1636 Roger Williams founded

NOTABLE DATES

■ 1585
The first English colony in the New World is established at Roanoke Island, off the coast of North Carolina, where efforts to establish a permanent settlement falter.

■ 1607
Colonists arrive at Jamestown, the first enduring English settlement in North America.

■ 1620
Puritan Separatists known as Pilgrims land on Cape Cod and settle at Plymouth.

■ 1636
Religious dissident Roger Williams founds Providence.

■ 1670
Charleston, first town in Carolina, is founded.

■ 1682
William Penn, proprietor of Pennsylvania, establishes the town of Philadelphia.

■ 1732
James Oglethorpe founds the colony of Georgia.

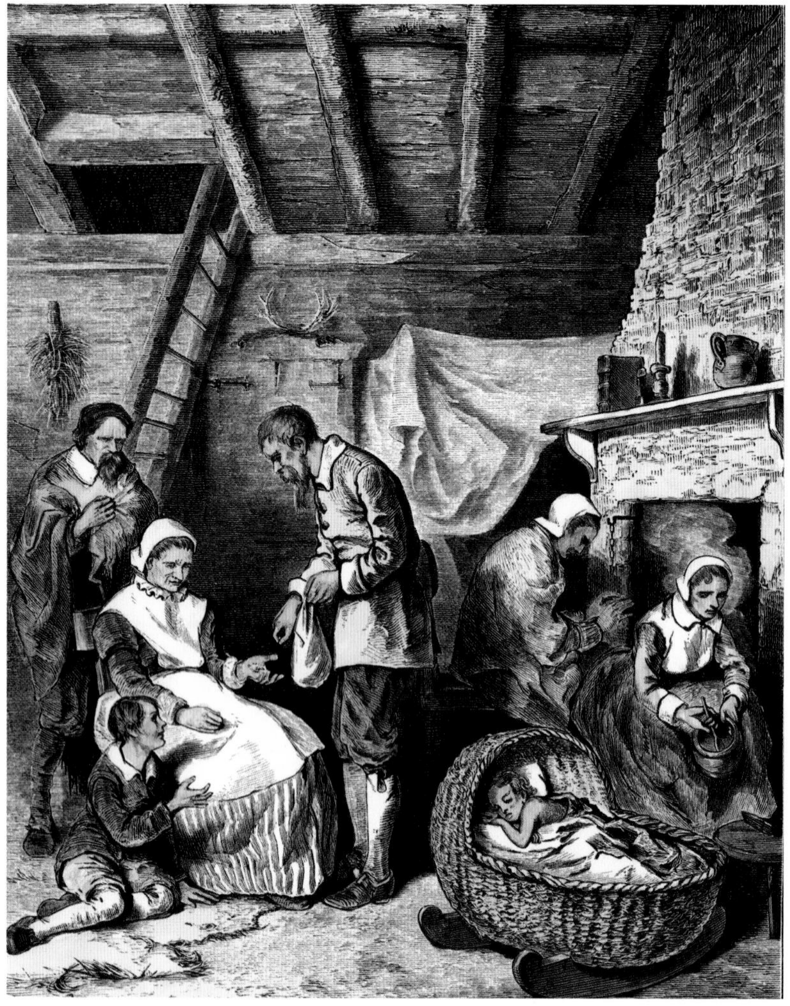

A Jamestown colonist doles out the last few kernels of corn during a particularly bad winter. After relief ships reached the colony in May 1610, the haggard survivors convinced their countrymen to take them home.

Providence, a place of true religious tolerance. A graduate of England's Cambridge University, Williams rejected the Puritans' belief in theocracy. Massachusetts Bay colony officials demanded his return to England, but once he had escaped to Rhode Island, he was beyond their reach. Hutchinson was a similarly radical thinker. The first woman to play a key role in America's religious and political life, she preached ideas similar to 19th-century transcendentalism. In her view the spirit, not the laws of church or state, held primacy over individuals. Convicted of "traducing the ministers and their ministry" in 1637, she was banished from Massachusetts. After four years in Rhode Island she and her family moved to New York, where they were massacred by Indians.

Other religious nonconformists, led by Reverend Thomas Hooker, left Massachusetts to settle in Connecticut. Another colony came into being in 1634 when the forward-thinking Cecilius Calvert, second Baron Baltimore, settled in Maryland. Calvert and his cronies were English Catholics, but the common settlers were Protestants; from the beginning Maryland operated on the principle of religious tolerance.

One of the last colonies formed, Pennsylvania was the largest in size. The brainchild of English Quaker William Penn, this middle-Atlantic colony began as a "holy experiment" of religious and political freedom. King Charles II granted the 50,000-square-mile tract to pay a debt he owed Penn's deceased

Hard Facts

Distance from England to the New World: 3,000 miles

Length of transatlantic voyage: 6-8 weeks

Amount Sir Walter Raleigh lost in overseas ventures: 40,000 pounds

Number of settlers in the first Jamestown voyage: 100

Names of the ships: *Susan Constant, Discovery, Godspeed*

Amount the London Company lost on the Jamestown venture from 1606 to 1622: more than 160,000 pounds

Number of settlers sent during that period: 6,000

Number alive in 1625: 1,300

Only profits realized: by a joint-stock company transporting eligible women to the colony

Worst Indian attack in Jamestown: 1622; 347 colonists died

Amount spent by Massachusetts for title to Maine in 1677: 1,250 pounds

Debt forgiven by William Penn in exchange for Pennsylvania: 16,000 pounds

father. Dubbed "Penn's woods" in 1681, the colony began attracting settlers the following year with the founding of Philadelphia. To ease relations with the locals, Penn paid the Indians for their land and penned a friendship treaty. French philospher Voltaire called it "the only treaty never sworn to" (Quakers being forbidden to swear) "and never broken."

Colonial Governments

Throughout the English colonies, citizens were technically given the same rights and freedoms, according to Virginia's first charter, "as if they had been abiding and born within this our Realm of England." Yet from the outset, the colonists had to agitate for these freedoms within their evolving brand of representative government. As in Virginia, so in Massachusetts Bay a representative system developed. More of a theocracy, with legislators chosen from within the church, it still was an elected assembly with upper and lower houses and the power to pass laws in the hands of the people.

By the early 1700s colonists had achieved a measure of independence. Two features distinguished colonial governments. First, the Americans put a high value on written laws and agreements. America was a land of charters granting specific rights. Second, the royal governors and popularly elected legislatures were in constant conflict, with legislatures insisting on their rights to control appropriations and elections and a governor floating above with a royal mandate. These two elements would direct the future of the colonies. ■

John Smith

English adventurer John Smith was the perfect person for journeying to a wild new world with the intention of establishing a settlement. A daring, difficult enterprise called for a man who lived for adventure. Born in 1580, Smith left home at age 16 and became a soldier of fortune, first fighting for the Dutch against the Spanish, then with the Austrians against the Turks. According to his writings, which were often exaggerated, he was captured and sold into Turkish slavery. He escaped into Russia, then traveled extensively in Europe and North Africa.

Captain John Smith, stalwart leader of the Jamestown colony, chronicled England's early ventures in the New World.

Back in England, Smith grew restless and cast about for his next adventure. He soon found it. In December 1606 Captain Smith was on board one of three ships bound for Virginia. During the voyage a sealed box listing the names of the seven men who would govern the new colony was opened; Smith's name was there. After more than four months at sea the ships landed at a place the newcomers called Jamestown.

Disease, hunger, and hostile Indians made the settlers' lives a misery. Smith emerged as a leader, fought the Indians, and was captured. Impressed by his confidence and moved by the intercession of chief Powhatan's daughter Pocahontas, the Indians spared his life. While the colony suffered from internal bickering, laziness, and attempts at desertion, Smith explored the Chesapeake Bay for supplies. He was elected president of the colony in 1608, though many objected to his rigid rule—some aristocratic-born colonists rankled under the authority of a farmer's son. Injured by a powder burn, Smith returned to England in 1609. He made one more journey to the New World, but spent most of his remaining life writing, promoting colonization. He died in 1631. ■

Colonial Life

1612–1752

DURING THE 150-PLUS YEARS of colonial life, America began to assume an identity unique in the world. Two main factors contributed to the shaping of the American character: the people and the land.

By the time of the Revolution, approximately 75 percent of the white colonists were of English origin. The customs, language, and religion were English, a fact that helped forge a national unity. At the same time, there were heavy infusions of Germans and Scotch-Irish, and minor waves of Dutch and French settlers. This diversity created from the outset a sense of newness, an awareness that America was something altogether different from England and Europe.

After the Dutch had been assimilated into English colonial life, the next major influx of non-Brits was from the German principalities, spurred by the persecution of Lutherans, Moravians, Mennonites, and other religious sects. The Germans settled primarily in the middle colonies, especially in Pennsylvania, where they laid out tidy wheat farms that made the region the breadbasket of the colonies.

Next came the indomitable Scotch-Irish, every bit as thrifty and hardworking as the Germans. They pioneered into the Shenandoah Valley and upland Carolina country and pushed into Georgia and Kentucky. Many were Presbyterians of Scotch origin whose families had settled briefly in Ireland, fleeing English tyranny. More comfortable with the wilderness than the Germans, the Scotch-Irish made a living with their guns as well as their hoes, and built log cabins in clearings in the woods. They loved the independent life, disliked the Indians, and were so acquisitive that it was said of them, "They kept the Sabbath and everything else they could lay their hands on." From this tough, resilient stock came such noteworthy Americans as Andrew Jackson, John C. Calhoun, James Polk, and Sam Houston.

Landscape

The other factor that molded the American character was the land. Some of the early settlers had been naïve about the demands of the new environment. Instead of preparing for a long-shot experiment in survival, they dabbled with glass-blowing and silk-raising. Later colonists came ready for the almost unimaginable physical and mental

Pilgrims build houses in Plymouth, Massachusetts, in the 1620s. The Mayflower Compact established a design for self-government; protection from hunger and cold was another matter. Half their number perished by spring.

demands of an inhospitable wilderness. From the marshy coast, out through the swamps and the piedmont forests, and on to the mountains, America was untamed wild country filled with dangerous animals, natives, and weather. Those who could adapt, who could learn from the natives how to plant and fertilize corn or tan deerskins, could survive until a community could be established, and perhaps eventually a town. Each new region required a similar process of pioneering, land clearing, and settlement—the work of generations.

The egalitarian nature of pioneering produced a democracy of the spirit. Class distinctions, especially along the edges of the wilderness, were blurred. Pluck and self-reliance were of great value, noble lineage was worthless. As John Smith said, "He who does not work, will not eat."

The size of the new continent was unknown. There was a sense of almost limitless space, which made it easier for people of different backgrounds to get along together. They knew that in America there was a chance for a fresh start, that with hard work the land's abundant natural resources would pay off. Frenchman St. John Crevecoeur wrote of the emerging American type in 1759: "A European when he first arrives, seems limited in his intentions as well as in his views; but he very suddenly alters his scale. He no sooner breathes our air than he forms new schemes, and embarks on designs he never would have thought of in his own country. . . . He begins to feel the effects of a sort of resurrection; hitherto he had not lived, but simply vegetated; he now feels himself a man."

Herded by her Narragansett captors, Mary Rowlandson bundles her child against the cold. Captured during the 1675-76 King Philip's War, she wrote a popular account of her captivity.

Regional Lifestyles

The 1.5 million British-American subjects inhabiting the 13 colonies by 1750 lived according to several regional variations. New England, middle, and Southern colonies, and the backcountry formed four distinct regions, each with its own characteristics and lifestyles.

The New England colonies consisted of Massachusetts (including Maine), Connecticut, Rhode Island, and New Hampshire (including the Vermont country). Here farmers tilled small rocky parcels of land, or lived by lumbering. Along the coast, cod fishermen and whalers profited from the bounty of the Atlantic, and maritime traders and shipowners

NOTABLE DATES

■ 1612
John Rolfe, husband of Pocahontas, introduces West Indian tobacco to Jamestown soil; milder than the local tobacco, the product brings financial benefit to the colony.

■ 1639
First American printing press set up, in Cambridge, Mass.

■ 1692
Witch trials in Salem, Massachusetts, result in 19 executions.

■ 1732
Franklin's *Poor Richard's Almanack* begins annual publication, lasting until 1757.

■ 1735
John Peter Zenger, editor of *New York Weekly Journal* is acquitted of libel; his criticism of Governor Cosby is sanctioned as a landmark for freedom of the press.

■ 1752
Flying a kite in a thunderstorm, Franklin proves lightning is electricity; he invents the lightning rod.

in Boston began building lucrative businesses. In town and country, Yankees were known for their industry, stubbornness, prudence, and piety. Puritans were adamant believers in public education; literacy in New England was promulgated like nowhere else in the world. Religious austerity relaxed somewhat during the 18th century. True, the Sabbath was strictly observed, during which no one could travel, work, enter a tavern, or play a game. But Christmas became a merry celebration; new fashions like periwigs were accepted; and romance and ambition became a major part of life.

In the middle colonies of New York, New Jersey, Pennsylvania, and Delaware, life was not as rigidly circumscribed. The total population, like that of New England, was about 700,000 at the time of the Revolution. A more varied economy had people working not just on small farms, but on large estates in the Hudson Valley, in iron furnaces and other manufacturing operations, as mechanics and tradesmen. Merchants exported grain, fur, lumber, and imported fine china, textiles, and furniture from London. Another exchange route had grain going to the West Indies, and slaves and molasses coming back. New York and Philadelphia became cosmopolitan centers, where people could attend plays, concerts, and balls. Multitalented Philadelphian Benjamin Franklin (1706-90) published *The Pennsylvania Gazette* and the popular *Poor Richard's Almanack*, which, with its blend of moral advice and witty aphorisms, began to generate a mass American culture.

Success Stories

Annual fisheries exports from Massachusetts to Europe and West Indies by 1770: $1.25 million

Number of vessels involved in Boston's foreign commerce in 1770: 600

Length and width of colonies from Maine to Georgia: 2,000 miles by 50 miles

Tobacco produced from 2-3 acres: 2,500 pounds

Profit realized: over 200 percent

Tobacco production in America in 1616: 2,500 pounds

Tobacco production in America in 1700: 30,000,000 pounds

South Carolina rice production in 1700: 100,000 pounds

South Carolina rice production in1775: 65,000,000 pounds

Life in the South was far different from that in the North. With Charleston, Savannah, and Baltimore the only towns of note, the South had a more rural character. Large plantation owners supplied the leadership and hence created a political monopoly. And the South had a clearly defined class structure: At the top were the major planters; the middle class was composed of small farmers and a few tradesmen; in the lower class were tenant farmers and poor whites, many of them convicts and indentured servants from England. Beneath, and supporting, this structure were blacks, mostly slaves, who made up nearly half of the entire population of 1,000,000 in the South.

Southern culture was confined mostly to the self-sufficient plantations, strung along the low country from tidewater Virginia to the St. Johns River. Brick and stone mansions held mahogany furniture and extensive libraries. Lavish entertainments lasting for days included hunting, racing, cards, and big dinners.

The fourth major section of America was the frontier, running from the Green Mountains of Vermont, down through the Mohawk Valley and the Alleghenies, to the foothills of Georgia. As the country pushed west, the backcountry came to define the American spirit of can-do optimism. Rough of manners, simple in tastes, these backwoods pioneers wore homespun hunting shirts, deerskin leggings, and fabrics made on the cabin loom. They ate local game and fish, built forts for protection, and participated in quilting bees and shooting matches. The archetype of resourceful frontiersmen, Daniel Boone opened up the Kentucky country to settlement just before the Revolution.

American Culture

American education established itself solidly during the colonial period. In New England there were Harvard, Yale, Dartmouth, and the College of Rhode Island (now Brown); the middle colonies had King's College (Columbia), the College of Philadelphia (University of Pennsylvania), and the forerunner of Princeton. The College of William and Mary in Virginia educated many prominent citizens, including Thomas Jefferson. Many

Southerners, however, completed their higher education in England.

The first American printing press went into operation in Cambridge in 1639. By the time of the Revolution, Boston had five newspapers, Philadelphia three. Among colonial scribes, Franklin attained enduring fame for his writings on science and politics, as did Jonathan Edwards in theology. Quaker farmer John Bartram was the father of American botany; son William became the country's first great nature writer, his work influencing the Romantic poets of Europe.

Among ideas generated during America's colonial years, two guided the emerging nation. First was the concept of democracy. The freedoms enjoyed by the colonists, from elbow room to representative government to an egalitarian society, gave Americans a belief in equality for all citizens. The second was that America was a land of opportunity, that providence had offered this New World for people to create something truly special. As St. John Crevecoeur observed, "Americans are the western pilgrims, who are carrying along with them that great mass of arts, sciences, vigor and industry which began long since in the East; they will finish the great circle." Buoyed by a keen sense of destiny, America was ready to expand and achieve. ■

Witches in Salem

AMONG THE DARKER CHAPTERS OF COLONIAL life, the Salem witch trials of 1692 hold a special place. About 20 miles north of Boston, the village of Salem had a citizenry, like many small towns, that did not always live in harmony. Some families supported the new minister, Harvard dropout Samuel Parris; others did not. Previously a merchant in the Caribbean, Parris had taken up preaching only three years before coming to Salem. With him were his wife, daughter, niece, and a West Indian slave, who dabbled in magic.

It was but two years before opponents of Parris were calling for his ouster. At about this time, the two girls and a friend began behaving oddly, making strange gestures and statements. A doctor declared them "bewitched." The slave and two women with poor reputations were questioned by court deputies. The girls' contortions during interrogation convinced them to send the women to jail on suspicion of witchcraft.

A Modeſt Enquiry
Into the Nature of
Witchcraft,
AND
How Perſons Guilty of that Crime may be *Convicted*: And the means uſed for their Diſcovery Diſcuſſed, both *Negatively* and *Affirmatively*, according to *SCRIPTURE* and *EXPERIENCE*.

By John Hale,
Paſtor of the Church of Chriſt in *Beverley*, *Anno Domini* 1697.

When they ſay unto you, ſeek unto them that have Familiar Spirits and unto Wizzards, that peep, &c. To the Law and to the Teſtimony; if they ſpeak not according to this word, it is becauſe there is no light in them, Iſaiah VIII. 19, 20.
That which I ſee not teach thou me, Job 34. 32.

BOSTON in N. E.
Printed by *B. Green*, and *J. Allen*, for *Benjamin Eliot* under the Town Houſe. 1702

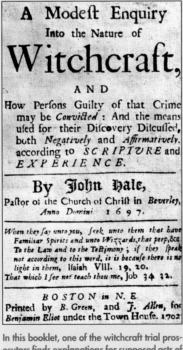

In this booklet, one of the witchcraft trial prosecutors finds explanations for supposed acts of witchcraft after his wife is charged with sorcery.

The hysteria soon spread to other villages and counties, with feuding neighbors making ugly accusations across the God-fearing countryside. Within three months 150 people had been charged of practicing witchcraft; 28 were convicted. In all, 19 people were hanged; one man, convicted of being a wizard, was buried alive under a pile of stones. Finally, ministers urged the governor to intercede to halt further executions.

Parris was fired, and many other ministers came away from the episode with their reputations in tatters. Cotton Mather, who became a famous religious writer, had goaded hangmen into doing "their duty" to eradicate the demons from the commonwealth. He later changed his position. By then the idea of a Puritan community was on the ropes. ■

Slave Trade

1619–1775

THE SAME YEAR THAT A SHIP arrived in Jamestown carrying bartered brides-to-be, another came bearing a cargo of a different sort. On this Dutch ship in 1619 were the first black slaves in what would become the United States; settlers bought 20. Slaves were not new to the New World. With Indians succumbing to introduced diseases, European colonists needed another source of cheap labor. In the 1500s, they began importing Africans to sugar and coffee plantations in the Caribbean and Brazil. By the early 1600s, about 400,000 slaves had been imported. The Jamestown slaves were the next step in an expanding New World economy.

The spread of slavery in the North American colonies was slow at first. By 1650 only 300 blacks lived in Virginia. In 1664 New York had 700 slaves in a total population of 8,000. Slaves were an expensive proposition to the early colonists—costing five times the amount of an indentured servant.

A Permanent Solution

Until the late 1600s, labor was supplied mainly by indentured servants, apprentices who worked for room and board for a stated period—usually five years—before gaining their freedom. But as

The first Africans to enter the English colonies of North America arrived in 1619. Dutch sailors captured them from a Spanish ship and exchanged them for food with Jamestown settlers. Though the first blacks were likely freed, in two decades they were considered slaves for life.

settlements expanded, available good land was harder to find. Freed servants ended up on the margins of large plantations; when owners tried to remove them, they claimed squatters' rights—the right to buy the land from the owner. Legal conflicts sometimes led to violence. The indentured servitude system soon became more trouble than it was worth. Colonists and their financial backers in England saw black slavery as a permanent solution.

With slavery, the colonies would have an entire class of servants, identified by race, who would never be free, never have legal rights, and thus never offer any competition for land or political power. The English were new to the slave trade, but they had the Spanish and Portuguese as models, and likely there was already prejudice against Africans that cancelled any moral scruples about enslaving them. At any rate, like the Indians the Africans could be caught and made to work. Black slavery ensued.

Importers in Boston, Newport, New York, and Charleston made fortunes in the slave business. Slaves were brought from West Africa directly, or by way of the West Indies, to markets at these ports, where planters paid cash for them. Sometimes a middleman would buy them in lots, in return for tobacco, rice, or indigo, then sell them to plantation owners.

The Rice Culture

While slaves in Virginia toiled in the tobacco fields, in South Carolina they produced indigo and rice. The cultivation of indigo, an asparagus-like plant used for dye, lasted from the 1740s to the 1790s. Madagascar rice, introduced in the 1690s, was produced until the late 1800s. This staple crop grew well in the tidelands along creeks and rivers. By the mid-1700s, slaves outnumbered whites in South Carolina two to one; in some areas the ratio was higher. Adapting African techniques, slaves turned the low country into a rice empire, raising exports from 100,000 pounds in 1770 to 65 million pounds in 1775.

First slaves cleared cypress and other trees from the soupy ground; then they built dirt banks, dug ditches, drained the fields, and plowed them. They planted rice seeds in the spring on flooded fields, draining them through gates every few days to let the shoots grow in the sun. Boys ran through the fields beating pots and pans to scare away birds. In late summer men and women harvested the crop, threshed it with flailing sticks, and tied it in sheaves. In the winnowing house, grain was sifted through grates to separate out the chaff.

With slave labor, the South relied almost exclusively on agriculture, retarding the development of a diversified economy. Manufacturing was almost non-existent on the eve of the Revolution; finished goods were imported from England. In the middle colonies, slaves, though fewer, also became an accepted form of reliable labor. The system was too profitable to abandon, and the inherent evils of one class having complete domination over another were thus unleashed into American life. A few Quakers voiced objections, but even some Quakers owned slaves themselves. ■

NOTABLE DATES

■ 1619
A Dutch slave ship arrives in Jamestown; colonists buy 20 slaves.

■ 1650
Chattel slavery is legally recognized in Virginia.

■ 1676
Nathaniel Bacon of Virginia leads frontiersmen in a revolt against the colonial governor who opposes westward expansion; Bacon dies and 23 followers are executed.

■ 1690
Competition in the slave trade makes slave prices fall.

■ 1712
Slaves revolt in New York; 6 commit suicide and 21 are executed.

■ 1741
Another slave revolt in New York ends with 13 hanged, 13 burned, and 71 deported.

■ 1750
Slaves appear in Georgia, a colony founded in 1732 as a refuge for free labor.

Colonial Wars

1675–1775

UNTIL THE MID-1700S, TENsions between colonists and the motherland were overshadowed by conflicts with the French and their Indian allies. A series of four protracted struggles, called the French and Indian Wars, pitted England and France against each other from 1689 to 1763. These colonial wars were extensions of wars in Europe. In North America, France gained control of the St. Lawrence and the Great Lakes, with outposts along the Mississippi. British colonies extended up and down the Atlantic seaboard. The two nations, with their Indian recruits, battled over the fur trade, boundaries, and unclaimed territory. But ultimate British triumph contained the seeds of a stunning defeat by American colonists 20 years later.

Before the French and Indian Wars, colonists in search of good land came into conflict with the Indians. Encroaching settlers' treatment of Indians in New England infuriated Chief Metacomet of the Wampanoag. Known to the English as King Philip, he enlisted other tribes in a fiery uprising in 1675. Some 600 colonists in Massachusetts were killed and many captured before the English struck back and won King Philip's War with the help of the Iroquois.

French and Indian Wars

The first French and Indian War, King William's War, lasted from 1689 to 1697. The action in North America was concentrated in New York, New Hampshire, and Canada; it ended in a stalemate. Queen Anne's War began in 1702 with a French and Indian invasion of New England settlements. At war's end, in 1713, France ceded Newfoundland and other Canadian holdings to Britain, but the boundaries were unclear. By the time of King George's War from 1744 to 1748, Britain was beginning to gain the upper hand.

During the final conflict, the French and Indian War from 1754 to 1763, Britain finally put an end to French hopes of empire in North America. British regulars aided the colonials in taking back Louisburg, gaining the Ohio Valley, and seizing the greatest prize of all—Quebec. In 1754 British colonial authorities sent militia under George Washington to challenge the French and their tribal allies in the Ohio Valley. He was beaten at Fort Necessity, but the following year helped stave off disaster at Fort Duquesne in present-day Pittsburgh. After a series of defeats, Britain pressed colonists into service and won a decisive battle at Quebec in 1759, securing control of Canada.

France Capitulates

The victory of General James Wolfe over the Marquis de Montcalm at Quebec marked the high point of the British Empire in the New World and the beginning of its decline. Wolfe was a doomed figure even before the battle, gravely ill with tuberculosis. Yet he agreed to undertake this grueling campaign, knowing that the capture of Quebec might well decide the century-old struggle between Britain and France for control of North America. Ships carried his forces up the St. Lawrence to Quebec, perched high atop a cliff and seemingly impregnable. Wolfe and his troops scaled the cliff and surprised Montcalm's forces at the city's edge. In a furious battle on September 13 that lasted barely an hour, both comanders were mortally wounded. Wolfe lived long enough to learn of his victory.

Just days later, Quebec was in British hands; the remaining French forces in Canada surrendered the next year. In the Treaty of Paris, France gave up all its North American holdings except two small islands south of Newfoundland.

Beginnings of Rebellion

Once the French threat was removed, Americans were less inclined to defer to the motherland.

In this hand-colored woodcut, British are ambushed near Lake George, New York, in the French and Indian War (1754-63). With British expansion westward, the French and Indians felt threatened; local antagonisms led to war.

British-American relations were further strained when Parliament taxed the colonists to cover the huge expense of winning the war. The Stamp Act of 1765 taxed newspapers and other printed material. Many American colonists, now literate, resented a measure that penalized the press and imposed taxation without representation.

Parliament added fuel to the fire by repealing the contentious taxes, except one—on tea. Bostonians protested by dressing as Indians, boarding ships loaded with East India Company tea, and dumping it into the harbor. The Boston Tea Party led Parliament to pass the Coercive Acts, which closed the port of Boston and curbed the Massachusetts Assembly. In response, delegates from the 13 colonies met in Philadelphia in September 1774 for the First Continental Congress to spell out grievances and approve military preparations for the defense of Massachusetts. The stage was set for the Revolutionary War. ■

NOTABLE DATES

■ 1675
An Indian uprising in Massachusetts results in 600 dead colonists; British strike back and defeat the Indians.

■ 1689-97
King William's War, first French and Indian War, starts with English raids on French settlements near Montreal.

■ 1702-13
Queen Anne's War again pits French against British forces, with their Indian allies; France concedes Newfoundland and part of Nova Scotia.

■ 1744-48
King George's War ends with no net gain in territory for either side.

■ 1754-63
The French and Indian War results in France's loss of most North American holdings.

■ 1764
The Sugar Act places duties on molasses, rum, lumber, and foodstuffs to help pay the war debt.

■ 1765
The Stamp Act is passed by Parliament, triggering colonial protests against taxation without representation.

■ 1767
Townshend Acts tax glass, painter's lead, and tea.

■ 1773
The Boston Tea Party on December 16 protests the tea tax.

■ 1774
The First Continental Congress convenes in Philadelphia as a showdown looms between British troops and rebellious colonists in Massachusetts.

WORLD SURVEY

1000–1775

DURING THE MEDIEVAL ERA, power shifted from one kingdom to another. As explorers, conquerors, and settlers spread around the globe, Europe emerged as the dominant continent, its nations vying for hegemony in long wars that played out in minor theaters throughout the world.

■ Europe

During the medieval and Renaissance periods, Europe rapidly underwent a number of major upheavals. The Roman Catholic Church played dominant roles in both politics and religion, and it influenced the art and culture of the times. From the 11th to 13th centuries, thousands of knights went on crusades to the Middle East to try to regain the Holy Land by battling the Muslims. From 1337 to 1453, England and France engaged in the destructive Hundred Years' War, which resulted in the English being pushed out of nearly all of France.

With the discovery of the New World in 1492, the European powers began to extend their grasp out across the globe. Imperial ambitions were fueled by natural resources in the colonies. In addition to the Americas, most of Africa and one-third of Asia were colonized by Europe. Meanwhile, great changes swept Europe after 1517, the year Martin Luther sparked the Protestant Reformation with his critique of the excesses of the Catholic Church. The 1700s marked the beginning of the Age of Reason, or Enlightenment, as well as the Industrial Revolution, during which new scientific knowledge brought life-changing technological advances.

■ Asia

The medieval era was a time of increasing cultural interaction in Asia, particularly in the sea-lanes of the Indian Ocean and South China Sea. Major trading cities grew up throughout Southeast Asia, India, Ceylon, East Africa, Arabia, China, Japan, and Korea. Arab and Venetian traders transported Asian goods to the middle East and Europe—spices, silk, jewels, and other luxury items, as well as building materials. Ports throughout Asia became wealthy, bustling cities hosting merchants of all races and religions.

During the last great period of nomads, Ghenghis Khan in the early 1200s led the newly united Mongols into northern China, where they set up a Mongol state. In 1279, they brought down China's Song dynasty. Under medieval shoguns, Japan fended off Mongol attacks and suffered through civil wars among competing barons. The austere and meditative lifestyle of the samurai warrior class encouraged the spread of Zen Buddhism.

In the mid-East, Ottoman Turks overwhelmed the long-established Byzantine Empire in 1453, and Constantinople was renamed Istanbul. While Europe was becoming an industrial center, Asia remained largely agrarian and unmechanized.

■ Africa

Around the year 1000 trade routes across the Sahara brought wealth to west African kingdoms, where gold and kola nuts were exchanged for Saharan copper and salt. Gao and Timbuktu were among the cities that prospered as centers of commerce. At about the same time in eastern Africa, Muslim traders established coastal settlements and created commercial links across the Indian Ocean with India and China—gold and ivory were exported in exchange for silk, cotton, and porcelain.

By the 15th century, Portuguese adventurers began setting up outposts on the Gold Coast (current Ghana). They also started exporting African slaves to Europe. Two centuries later the Dutch took control of the west African ports and founded Cape Town in southern Africa. African and Muslim slave traders had been involved in slave exportation before European colonization, but the market increased dramatically with the discovery of the New World. Within about 300 years, some 10 million slaves had been sent to the Americas.

■ Australia

Though forebears of Australia's Aborigines arrived from Asia via New Guinea some 65,000 years ago, it was not until 1609 that whites discovered the existence of the southern continent. A Dutch sailor that year sailed along the northeastern edge, thinking it was New Guinea. In succeeding decades other Dutch explorers made passes along other sides of Australia and were unimpressed with the dry, desert conditions. It was only in 1770 that British navigator James Cook became the first European to explore the east coast; he claimed it for Great Britain and called it New South Wales. White settlement did not take place for another 18 years.

■ Latin America

While the conquistadors were routing the Indian civilizations in the 1500s, Portuguese and Spanish settlers began streaming into the continent. Plantations of coffee, sugarcane, and tobacco sprang up, worked by Indian slaves and later African slaves. Power in the colonies rested with landowners, the Roman Catholic clergy, and with government officials appointed by rulers in Europe. The goals of colonization were to exploit the mineral and agricultural resources and also to convert the natives to Christianity, in that order. With European-imposed restrictions on manufacturing and trade, and on self-rule, many Latin Americans yearned for greater freedom; independence movements, however, did not begin until after the American Revolution. ■

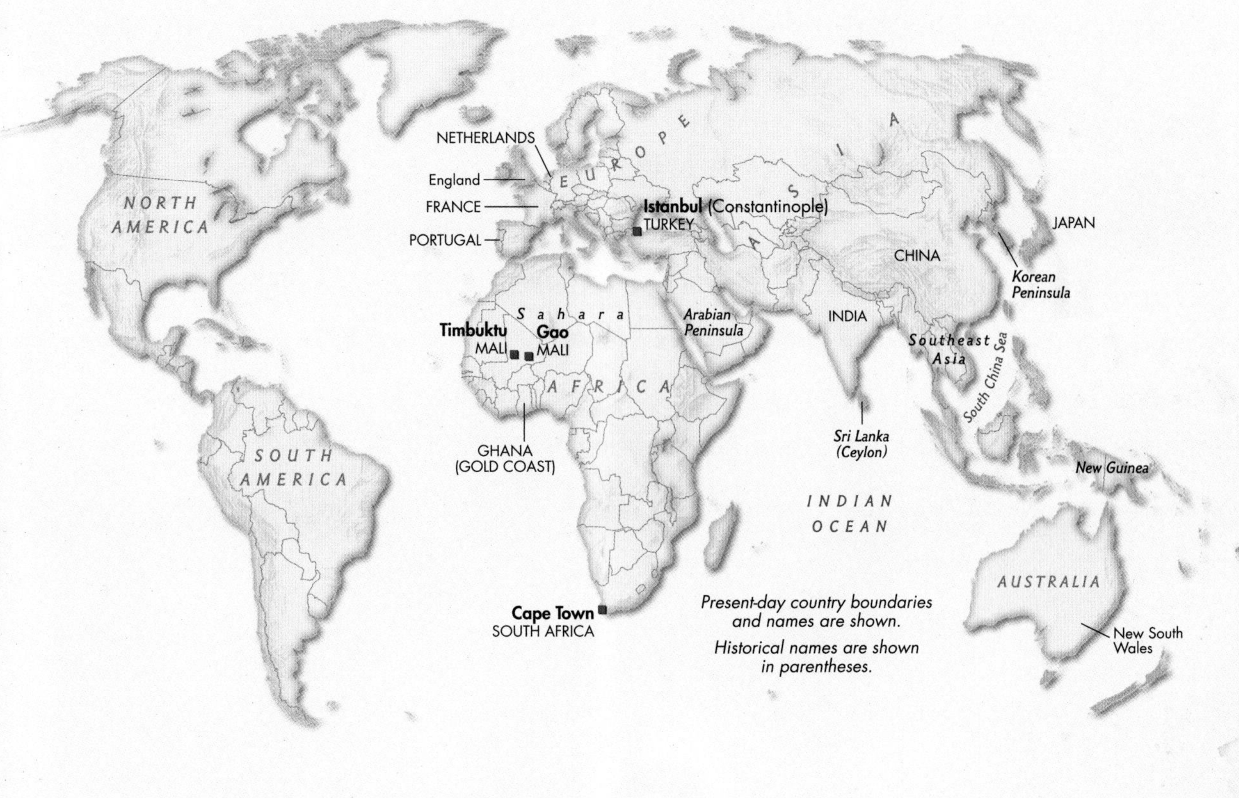

The Revolution Era 1765–1801

IN THE YEARS LEADING UP TO THE REVOLUTION, RELATIONS BETWEEN BRITAIN AND AMERICA grew increasingly strained. Facing tremendous debts and the cost of maintaining troops in North America, Parliament turned to Americans to shoulder some of the burden. Long accustomed to governing and taxing themselves, Americans saw no reason to pay the mother country's bills. Thus began a cycle of repressive British measures, followed by American protests, followed by punishment. There were periods of appeasement and calm, but the trend was toward conflict. Finally, in 1775 the powder keg blew and the war was on. At first Americans were fighting for their rights as British citizens; after 1776, for independence. Unwavering, undaunted General George Washington united the colonies in a common cause and became the symbol of the Revolution. A patriot victory at Saratoga in 1777 brought France into the war as an American ally. After the loss of a massive army at Yorktown in 1781, Britain began peace negotiations with the U. S. A period of economic depression and unrest followed. Creation of the U.S. Constitution, a major world event, spelled out the form of the federal government and gave it power to tax and move the country forward. Advocates of a strong central government—Federalists—were checked in the press and legislatures by those favoring a more democratic government. Leader of the latter group, Thomas Jefferson became the country's third President in 1801.■

Noted Revolutionary War artist John Trumbull painted "Death of General Warren at the Battle of Bunker Hill."

■ **1775**
War begins in Lexington and Concord, Massachusetts.

■ **1776**
Delegates to the Second Continental Congress in Philadelphia approve the Declaration of Independence.

■ **1777**
An American victory over British forces at Saratoga, New York, attracts French support for the Revolution.

■ **1781**
George Washington, aided by French forces on land and sea, wins a decisive victory at Yorktown, Virginia.

■ **1783**
Great Britain recognizes American independence and, with an eye to future trade, offers generous terms under the Treaty of Paris.

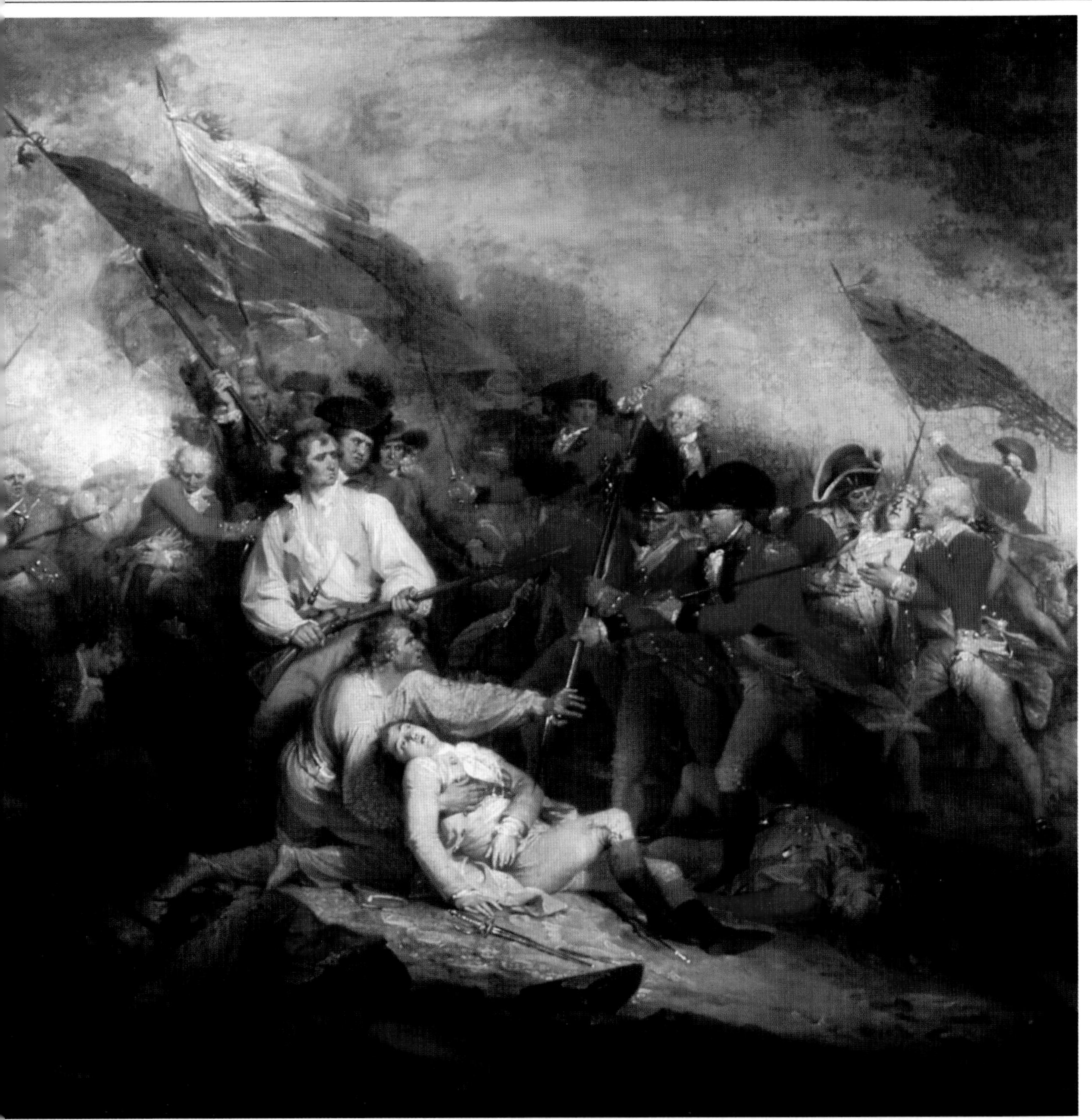

■ 1787	■ 1788	■ 1789	■ 1794	■ 1798
The Constitutional Convention meets in Philadelphia to formulate a new federal government.	The states ratify the U.S. Constitution.	Americans hold the first election under the Constitution and choose George Washington as the nation's first President.	Washington puts down the Whiskey Rebellion in Pennsylvania, the first exercise of federal force under the Constitution.	Congress passes the protective Alien and Sedition Acts; the suppression of government criticism costs Adams a second term as President.

The Revolution Begins

1765–1775

ATTEMPTING TO PAY OFF THE debt incurred by the French and Indian War, the English began taxing the colonists. When the colonists resisted, Parliament applied more pressure, sometimes in a punitive way. The reaction in the colonies grew from irritation to outrage. With a central government 3,000 miles across an ocean, America began feeling itself unrepresented and ill-used. It was almost inevitable that, bit by bit, violence would break out.

The Stamp Act of 1765 caused a heated reaction. According to the law, legal and business documents, as well as many everyday items, had to be made of paper bearing an embossed impression. Americans felt the act was unfair—the cost of the stamped paper was modest, but penalties could be assessed for noncompliance. Citizens in Boston hanged the stamp officer in effigy and hounded him out of office. In ports up and down the coast, stamps were destroyed, and stamp officers resigned in fear. Some members of Parliament insisted that force should be used to put the Americans in their place. For the moment, however, wiser heads prevailed, and the law was repealed.

Now the question was, if the colonists got their way this time, what was to keep them from doing it again, and again? Parliament responded with new duties on British glass, paper, paint, and tea arriving in colonial ports, the income to be used to pay colonial governors and judges. Colonists started boycotting English goods.

First Blood

Tension between townspeople and soldiers was especially bad in Boston. Name-calling had turned to brawls on more than one occasion. Then, on March 5, 1770, a restive mob of about 50 people gathered around a sentinel in front of the customs house. The sentinel called for backup. The mob began swearing at the soldiers, then throwing snowballs and rocks. When it was clear they could no longer keep order, the troops fired. When the smoke from the muskets had cleared, five civilians lay dead.

Though it would be five more years before war broke out, the so-called Boston Massacre was treated in the American press, inflamed by master propagandist Samuel Adams, as an intolerable act of aggression. The trial was put off until tempers could cool and the accused receive fair play. Two of the seven soliders were convicted of manslaughter; future U.S. President John Adams defended the soliders, in part to prove that Americans were law-abiding people.

Parliament's repeal of all duties except on tea did not look like conciliation to the Americans; it still smacked of coercion. The tea tax reminded Americans that Britain maintained the right to tax.

The colonies settled back down for two more years of relative peace and quiet, dropping their general boycott of British goods but still refusing to buy British tea. Britain imprudently decided to meddle. Lord North, prime minister for nearly the entire American Revolution, devised a scheme whereby the East India Tea Company could sell tea stripped of all duties except the American tea tax. Americans would get cheaper tea, and the company could unload its warehouses of boycotted tea.

The Party's Over

North underestimated American reaction. To them it looked like bribery. On December 16, 1773, Bostonians boarded three East India ships and tossed 342 chests of tea into the harbor. Other ports staged similar "tea parties." Britain answered with a series of repressive laws, known in America as the Intolerable Acts and in Britain as the Coercive Acts. The most offensive of all was the Boston Port Act, which ordered the port blockaded and closed to commerce.

Into this untenable situation came Thomas Gage, newly

Protesting the British tea tax, colonists dressed as Mohawks dump imported tea into Boston Harbor in December 1773; 16 months later Britain and America were at war.

appointed governor of Massachusetts Bay. When he found that the colony's legislature would not pay for the spilt tea, he declared it dissolved and ordered more troops sent to the city. On September 1, 1774, afraid that a Yankee militia would take 125 barrels of gunpowder from a storehouse in Cambridge, Gage sent 250 British Redcoats to seize it. The move was seen by locals as hostile and invasive.

Representatives from 12 of the 13 colonies met to form the First Continental Congress in Philadelphia to consider ways to safeguard American liberties. At this illegal convention, there was no talk yet of independence, merely of redress for their grievances as free British

NOTABLE DATES

■ 1770
In the Boston Massacre, British soldiers shoot into a crowd and kill five.

■ 1774
Britain passes the Intolerable Acts, which include the closing of the port of Boston.

■ 1775
General Gage sends Redcoats to seize ammunition stored in Cambridge; Parliament votes not to make concessions to the Americans.

Battles of the American Revolution 1775–1783
BRITISH NORTH AMERICA
APPALACHIAN MOUNTAINS
SPANISH LOUISIANA
ATLANTIC OCEAN
Gulf of Mexico
EAST FLORIDA (Under British control from 1763-1783)
Lake Michigan
Lake Huron
Lake Ontario
Lake Erie
St. Lawrence
Mississippi
Ohio
Tennessee
Alabama
Savannah
Potomac
James
Chesapeake Bay
Hudson
Quebec
Montreal
MASS. (DISTRICT OF MAINE)
FT. TICONDEROGA
N.H.
Oriskany
Saratoga
Bennington
Lexington
Albany
MASS.
Concord
Bunker Hill
Boston
FT. DETROIT
NEW YORK
CONN.
R.I.
WEST POINT
White Plains
November 1776
Wyoming Massacre
PA.
New York
FT. LEE AND FT. WASHINGTON
FORT AUGUSTA
Morristown
Long Island
FT. PITT
Princeton
Germantown
Monmouth Courthouse
VALLEY FORGE
Trenton
FT. HENRY
Brandywine
Philadelphia
MARYLAND
N.J.
DEL.
Cahokia
Vincennes
Kaskaskia
VIRGINIA
Richmond
Williamsburg
Yorktown
Guilford Courthouse
NORTH CAROLINA
Cowpens
Charlotte
King's Mountain
FT. NINETY SIX
Camden
Wilmington
SOUTH CAROLINA
Augusta
GEORGIA
Charleston
Savannah
British North America, 1775 (excluding 13 colonies)
The 13 Colonies
Spanish possessions
American victory
British victory
Indecisive battle
Fort
0 miles 200
0 kilometers 300

From Savannah to Quebec, from the Atlantic to the Mississippi, battles of the Revolution raged; at issue was who would govern the colonies—how they would be governed was decided later.

subjects. For the first time the colonies began to unite with a single voice. Citizens began seeing themselves as more American than British. And they resented the superior attitude of their European cousins.

Britain Votes for War

Parliament's response to the Continental Congress was further repression. For the next several months, the patriots (as they had begun calling themselves) and the British began preparations for war. In London, the monarch seemed content. "I am not sorry," wrote George III, "that the line of conduct seems now chalked out. . . . The New England Governments are in a state of rebellion." Determining that force was the only way to put the unruly Americans in their place, the British dispatched more troops to Boston.

As 1774 drew to a close, armed conflict appeared more and more likely. The choice was to accept moderate oppression or reach for uncertain freedom, even possible chaos. Political lines were being drawn between loyalists (Tories) and patriots. Organizations like the Sons of Liberty practiced their own kind of tyranny by boycotting British goods, and sometimes resorting to outright violence. Those who disagreed with them were censured and sometimes tarred and feathered. Families often were divided in their sympathies; small tragedies began unfolding across the land at the dawn of America's first civil war.

Paul Revere

THANKS TO HENRY WADSWORTH Longfellow's poem of 1863, Paul Revere's nighttime ride on the eve of the Revolution is an American classic. Yet the Boston silversmith's accomplishments far outweigh that deed. He took on management of a thriving silver shop at the age of 19, when his father died. A 1787 advertisement indicates its variety of wares: tea and coffee urns, tankards, sugar tongs, porringers, and butter boats.

Courier Paul Revere rides through the Massachusetts countryside warning villagers of the movement of British troops.

A leader of the city's artisan class when rustlings of revolution traveled through the streets of Boston, Revere helped organize American resistance efforts. Dressed as a Mohawk, he participated in the Boston Tea Party. As the main courier for Boston's Committee of Safety, he rode to New York and Philadelphia to carry information of patriot activity. On April 16, 1775, Revere rode to Concord to warn locals to move their military stores. Two nights later he made his famous ride to alert Lexington of the movement of British troops.

Narrowly avoiding capture as he set out, he was arrested between Lexington and Concord. An officer "clapped his pistol to my head," he wrote later, "and told me . . . if I did not give him true answers, he would blow my brains out." After the interrogation, he rode on to warn John Hancock and Samuel Adams. If the British had followed him, they might have bagged Boston's two foremost agitators. During the war, he was a lieutenant colonel. He also engraved the first Continental money and drew political cartoons. After the war, he designed the official seal of the United States. In old age he cut a quaint figure about town in his Revolutionary garb. He died in 1818 at age 83. ■

By a majority of two to one, Parliament determined in early 1775 that the colonies should bow to Britain. In a series of famous speeches seeking conciliation with America, Edmund Burke tried once again to appeal to his fellow parliamentarians, cautioning wisely on March 22, "The use of force alone is but *temporary*. It may subdue for a moment; but it does not remove the necessity of subduing again; and a nation is not governed, which is perpetually to be conquered." The speeches of the Whigs were in vain; by the next month the war had begun.

In the early months of 1775, General Gage built up his forces until about 4,000 soldiers had crossed the Atlantic to join him in the American colonies. He sent repeated requests back to his homeland, asking for an army 20,000 strong, but they were repeatedly denied by the British cabinet. Frustrated, he sent what trooops he had on training marches into the countryside, readying them for action.

Revere's Ride

Meanwhile, an illegal body called the Provincial Congress of Massachusetts held meetings in Cambridge and Concord. As their president the congress appointed 38-year-old John Hancock, a wealthy merchant and member of the Massachusetts General Court. He urged citizens to defend themselves against the encroachments of the British Army. Local militia units were appointed as the vanguard of defense. Intending to be ready at a minutes' notice, they took the name "minutemen" and gathered a cache of military supplies at Concord.

Gage's spies reported back on these developments. So that the rebels would not seize the advantage, Gage sent a detachment of 700 troops on the night of April 18, 1775, to destroy the supplies at Concord. Patriot spies had been just as busy, and before the Redcoats had set foot on the mainland, patriot couriers were riding hard out of Boston, spreading word of the enemy's approach. Paul Revere, 40-year-old silversmith, was the main rider. He set off toward Lexington, assigned to alert Samuel Adams and John Hancock that the British were after them. On the way to Concord, Revere and two other riders were arrested by the British; the two others escaped, and Revere was quickly released.

By then the countryside was aroused by a relay system of lights, drums, and church bells. Early in the morning, a motley group of 70 militiamen assembled on the village green of Lexington. It was not long before the British advance guard came through town, with 400 heavily armed men. "Stand your ground," ordered John Parker, captain of the American militia. "Don't fire unless fired upon but if they mean to have a war, let it begin here!" It was unclear who fired the first shot, but it triggered volleys from both sides. Within two minutes the melee was over. Eight Americans were killed, including Parker, with ten wounded. One British soldier was grazed in the leg.

Joined by genadiers, who had formed the detachment's rear guard, the entire British force marched a few miles on to Concord, were they found that most of the military stores had already been moved by the rebels. At the North Bridge over the Concord River, several hundred militiamen from surrounding towns came out against the Redcoats. After a heated exchange, the Redcoats converged back on the town. Then, marching back along the road to Boston, they became easy targets for the enraged patriots. From stone walls and orchards, barns and houses, the guns of the milita blazed away, picking off the highly visible Redcoats. Soldiers by the dozen fell dead in the road. All the British could do was hustle back to the city and the protection of the navy. Britain's total casualties for the engagement were 273 (including wounded and missing); America's were 95.

In Perspective

Tea destroyed in Boston Tea Party in modern dollars: $150,000

Population of Great Britain in 1775: 11 million

Population of American colonies 1775: 2.5 million

Growth since 1770: ten times

Population of Philadelphia 1775: 40,000

Population of New York 1775: 25,000

Population of Boston 1775: 16,000

Population of Charleston 1775: 12,000

Population of Newport 1775: 10,000

Population of Norfolk 1775: 7,000

Boston Besieged

April 19, 1775, was in many ways a microcosm of the great struggle to come. The Americans would take a beating; then the British would pursue them deeper into the interior and hence farther from their supply bases. The deeper in the British went, the more militia swarmed around them, forcing them back.

The battle news spread so quickly through New England that by the morning of April 20, a ragtag army of 15,000 patriots had assembled around Boston, hemming the British in. Attempts at negotiating a quick resolution evaporated in the next few weeks.

Britain faced a daunting task in subduing her colonies. Time and again, the British would count on loyalist support in America—and end up disappointed. The terrain in America was more rugged than the European battlefields. And more than 1,000 miles, connected by poor roads, separated the villages of New England from the rice plantations of Georgia. Even more troublesome, there was no capital—no one strategic and symbolic city—to be conquered. Even when Philadelphia was the meeting place for the Continental Congress, it was not that meaningful a prize to capture: Congress could (and did) simply move elsewhere.

Another difficulty the British faced was that supplies, messages, and troops had to sail across the Atlantic: a six-week journey—in favorable weather. On the other hand, Great Britain was the world's dominant colonial empire, her military the envy of the world. ■

George III

WHO WAS THIS MAN WHOM AMERICANS BEGAN MORE AND more to personify as their enemy? Thomas Paine dubbed King George III the "royal brute." In fact, he was not a ruthless tyrant, nor a brilliant strategist, nor a fool. He assumed the throne in 1760 at the age of 22. He ruled in the wake of a bitter civil war, which had ended by vesting sovereign power in Parliament. Moderately talented, he wanted to be known as a benevolent monarch. He respected the governing body's authority but manipulated it to gain his own ends, frequently changing ministers to assure that Parliamentary decrees followed the traditional Tory paths.

King George III (1738-1820) supported repressive policies that eventually led to war with America.

During the American Revolution, the relationship between George III and his ministers was poorly understood, especially in America. Not until Thomas Paine published his incendiary "Common Sense" did the target of American opposition to Britain's repressive policies encompass not only Parliament but also King George himself. It finally dawned on the colonists—with a strong nudge from Thomas Paine—that their king was not simply being misguided, but that in fact he was the one who was wielding the punishing rod.

As a child George was a slow learner, and thereafter never much of a reader. Lacking the will and intelligence to be a strong leader, he was obliged to fulfill a role in history he was never quite up to. He suffered a bout of mental illness at age 27, but not again until 1788, long after the war was over. His increasingly muddled mind made it imperative that his son serve as regent from 1811 until his death in 1820. ■

Revolutionary War

1775–1781

At the Second Continental Congress in Philadelphia on May 10, 1775, one of the main orders of business was the designation of a commander for the new Continental Army. Among the attendees were Patrick Henry, Samuel and John Adams (distant cousins), John Jay, Benjamin Franklin, and Thomas Jefferson. They chose Virginia plantation owner George Washington, who had proved himself a brave and capable leader in the French and Indian War, though he had not won a battle.

In June British and American forces jockeyed for position on the heights of Charlestown peninsula, just north of Boston, laying the groundwork for the war's first major battle. On June 17 General William Howe attacked the American left flank on Breed's Hill, adjacent to Bunker Hill. American General Israel Putnam cautioned his men, "Don't fire until you see the whites of their eyes." The resolute Americans shocked the British by holding their ground through three assault waves, breaking only when their ammunition ran out. Known afterwards as the Battle of Bunker Hill, the day served as a lesson for the British. They had won a peninsula, but at a very high cost: 50 percent casualties out of 2,200 troops, against 30 percent patriot casualties of 1,500 fighters.

Independence

Until 1776 Americans were not fighting for independence, but for their rights as British citizens. American leaders began to realize that by fighting for independence, they could possibly enlist the aid of France, Britain's long-standing enemy. In the meantime, Britain started recruiting Hessian

Her husband wounded, Mary Hays takes his place in an artillery crew at the Battle of Monmouth in 1778. Earlier on that sweltering June day, she carried water to the men in battle, earning her the nickname Molly Pitcher.

mercenaries, American Indians, and black slaves; each of these moves further alarmed and infuriated the patriots.

The publication in January 1776 of Thomas Paine's pamphlet "Common Sense" put words to the thoughts and feelings of many Americans. In highly emotional language, the English-born writer dismantled the whole idea of hereditary monarchy and advocated a complete separation from the motherland. He reminded his readers that "virtue is not hereditary." Above all, he declared, "We are not Englishmen; we are Americans!"

At the meeting of Congress on June 7, 1776, Virginian Richard Henry Lee introduced a resolution calling for a public proclamation "that these United States are, and of right ought to be, free and independent states." That announcement ended up, practically word for word, in the Declaration of Independence, drafted by 32-year-old planter-statesman Thomas Jefferson. Incorporating political philosophy dating back to 17th-century English philosopher John Locke, the 1,817-word document asserted that "all men are created equal," and that among the rights all were born with were "life, liberty, and the pursuit of happiness." On July 4, the Declaration was adopted by vote of Congress. Broadside copies were sent to various corners of the country, as well as to London. Now the new United States had to settle down to the serious business of actually gaining its independence.

Washington in Trouble

In the summer of 1776, British forces were converging on New York to mete out punishment. By August New York Harbor was white with sails: Some 24,000 troops massed on Staten Island, supported by 30 man-of-war battleships and nearly 400 transport ships—the largest overseas expedition ever undertaken by the British. Over in the village of Brooklyn, Washington ordered a third of his army of 28,000 to dig in and wait. He did not expect to defeat the greatly superior British force, only to inflict as much harm as he could.

NOTABLE DATES

■ **1775**
Battle of Bunker Hill results in 1,150 British casualties, versus 450 American casualties.

■ **1776**
The Declaration of Independence is ratified on July 4 by the Continental Congress.

■ **1777**
Maj. Gen. John Burgoyne surrenders at Saratoga, New York, October 17.

■ **1778**
The French formally agree on February 6 to aid the U.S.

■ **1779**
On September 23 John Paul Jones's *Bonhomme Richard* captures H.M.S. *Serapis* off the British coast.

■ **1780**
The treason of Maj. Gen. Benedict Arnold is discovered on September 23 at West Point, New York; he becomes a British brigadier general.

■ **1781**
After a nine-day siege, Cornwallis surrenders his army at Yorktown, Virginia, October 19.

Just as Bunker Hill had been the strategic key to Boston, so Brooklyn Heights was paramount to controlling New York. Instead of a frontal advance, Howe sent a shock force around to the east to attack the Americans' undefended left flank. A Hessian bayonet attack surprised and devastated the patriot forces. But thanks to Washington's clear thinking and ingenuity, a rout was turned into a brilliant getaway, as the Continental Army slipped across the East River in a predawn blanket of fog.

On September 7, 1776, General Washington held a council of war with his generals to decide whether to try to hold New York, as Congress wanted, or to take the more prudent course and evacuate. He decided to try to do both, by splitting his army. It was a mistake that nearly cost him his army, if not the war. Howe's forces easily took New York City, then chased the Continentals north and captured Forts Washington and Lee, two strategic posts on the Hudson River, along with thousands of prisoners and a cache of weapons and equipment. All Washington could do was beat a hasty retreat, leading his depleted, dispirited army over New Jersey's muddy roads.

The Crossing

On the west side of the Delaware River, in mid-December 1776, General Washington began hatching a daring plan that could spell disaster for his army. His troops were battered, and at the end of the month most of his men's one-year enlistments would expire. Across the river, 3,500 Hessians were positioned at Trenton and Bordentown. On December 19, another Thomas Paine pamphlet appeared, filled with exactly the kind of inspiration the Continentals needed. Washington ordered copies of "The Crisis" sent and read to all his brigades. Up and down the river, troops listened to Paine's words of encouragement: "These are the times that try men's souls. . . . But he that stands it now, deserves the love and thanks of man and woman."

Silver gorgets, attached to the collar, were vestiges of the throat protection worn by knights in armor. A gorget distinguished its wearer as a British officer—and a valuable target.

While the Hessians feasted and drank on Christmas day, the Continentals began preparing to launch a surprise attack. That night, in driving sleet, the army crossed the river, shoving ice floes out of the way, then hiked to the Hessian encampment. In an early morning rain, the Continentals handily took Trenton in an hour. They followed up by taking Princeton, and much of New Jersey that they had lost only recently. In just over a week, the Continental Army had turned its fortunes completely around, proving to themselves that they could fight, and win.

Saratoga

After two years of war, the British were growing frustrated. It did not seem to matter how many battles they had won; the Americans still would not concede. The British government decided to focus attention on Canada and try an invasion from the north. In June 1777 Gen. John Burgoyne's army of more than 7,000 British and German troops began heading south from Fort St. John, near Montreal. With them were several hundred Tories, Indians, and French Canadians. In early July, they took Fort Ticonderoga, located on the south end of New York's Lake Champlain. The British considered this fort, controlling the St. Lawrence-Hudson waterway, a grander prize than it really was. George III crowed at the news of Ticonderoga's fall: "I have beat all the Americans!"

Shortly thereafter, Burgoyne got bogged down in the dense forests north of Albany. His supply line was stretched to the breaking point and was constantly harassed by patriot skirmishers. He sent a raiding party out into the Vermont country for food, horses, and wagons, but the party was thrashed by militia under the command of John Stark, a veteran of Trenton and other battles.

To oppose Burgoyne, patriots under Horatio Gates moved in early September to Bemis Heights, 25 miles north of Albany. Later in September, the first of the two battles of Saratoga ended with the British falling back. A second battle on October 7 convinced Burgoyne that he could not break through to the south, where he hoped to join with Howe's army. Ten days later, Burgoyne was forced to surrender his entire army. The loss was the worst defeat yet in the war, and it marked the turning point of the Revolution. In Europe, the news shook Parliament as well as Lord North's war machine. It also convinced France to join with the Americans. In February, France and the United States signed an alliance, and the Revolution became a world war.

After Valley Forge

During the Saratoga campaign, Washington kept an eye on Howe in New York. Battles at Brandywine Creek and Germantown left the Continental Army reeling but not defeated. They went into winter quarters at Valley Forge, Pennsylvania. The winter of 1777-78 was marked by deprivation. Congress, with no power to tax, could not raise money to feed and clothe its own army properly. Yet Valley Forge proved a pivot point for the Continental Army, marked by the arrival of Baron von Steuben, a Prussian army captain with an inflated résumé. Von Steuben began training the ragged soldiers, drilling them in the fundamentals.

A much more confident army took to the field in June. Late that month the two armies met at Monmouth Courthouse, New Jersey. In one of his finest

Benjamin Franklin

One of the leading lights of the Revolution, Benjamin Franklin (1706-90) was remarkable for his contributions to American life throughout a long and varied career. When the war broke out he was 69, not an age when many men would embrace a radical antiestablishment cause. He had already left an impressive body of scientific and literary work. The lightning rod, bifocals, and Franklin stove are some of his enduring creations, and his writings on thrift and industry in *Poor Richard's Almanack* established him as both a civic leader and a prototype of the American humorist.

Statesman, philosopher, and scientist, Benjamin Franklin did more than any man, except George Washington, to found the nation.

Yet when the Revolution came he threw himself into wider public service, ushering in the new nation with paternal care. As envoy to France he was known as a sharp negotiator. A bon vivant, ladies man, and raconteur, he became the darling of Paris salons, symbolizing in his beaver cap the enlightened rustic wit, and putting the lie to perceptions of Americans as ignorant lowlifes. Playing his part to the hilt, he helped bring France and its war chest into the Revolution, a crucial factor in the patriot victory. Afterwards, he worked on the peace treaty, which provided generous boundaries for the new nation. In his eighties he had a hand in drafting the Constitution, just as he had earlier with the Declaration of Independence.

Philadelphia honored Franklin with the largest funeral the city had ever known. Among tributes was one from French economist Turgot: "He snatched the thunderbolt from heaven, then the sceptre from tyrants." When Jefferson was asked in Paris if he had come to replace Franklin, he said, "I succeed him; no one could replace him." ■

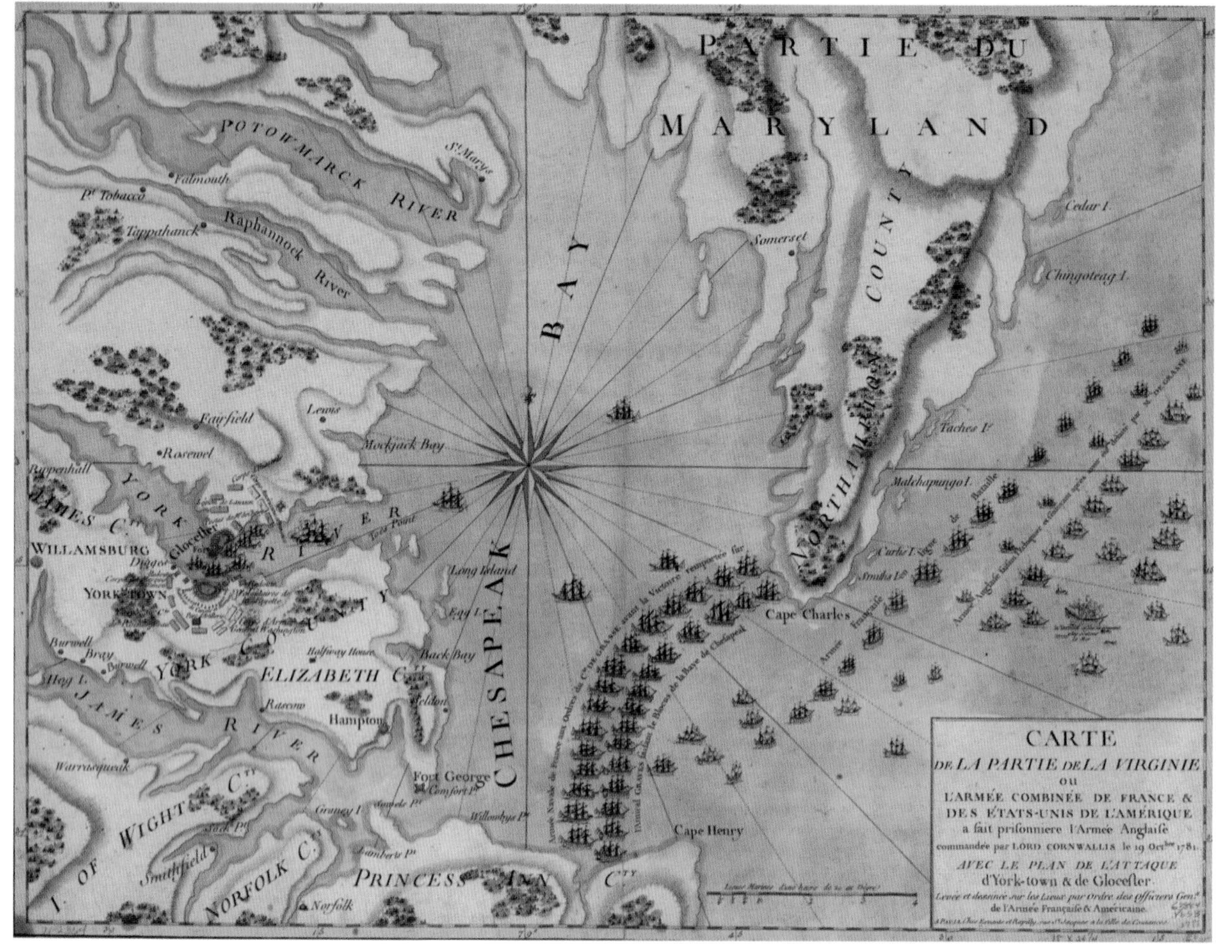

This French map of the lower Chesapeake Bay was drawn on-site at the Battle of Yorktown. The geography of the region's waterways and the disposition of French ships made escape for General Lord Cornwallis a near impossibility and helped ensure allied victory.

moments, Washington rallied his troops and turned a retreat into a fierce attack. A tactical draw, the engagement went down as an American victory since it ended with a British withdrawal.

By autumn of 1778, the war had stalled out in the North. Parliament was convinced now that New England was gone. But they had hope of regaining Georgia and the Carolinas, and perhaps Virginia. Part of this hope was based on the belief that there were more loyalists in the South than in the North. In January 1779, British forces captured Savannah, then were repulsed at Charleston. The following year, 10,000 British forces under the command of Henry Clinton laid siege to Charleston and finally brought it under submission. The capture of Charleston's 5,500 patriot troops was the worst American defeat of the war. Yet guerilla raiders such as Francis Marion (the "Swamp Fox") continued to heckle British detachments throughout South Carolina.

On to Yorktown

Clinton departed for New York, leaving Charles Cornwallis with instructions to take a defensive posture and then, if prudent, to advance northward. Cornwallis soon was on the move, and in August of 1780 he met an American force near Camden, South Carolina; here Horatio Gates, victor of Saratoga, suffered a humiliating defeat. The venture ended his career in the Continental Army. Cornwallis was the new hero, his stock soaring among southern loyalists. Yet defeats at Kings Mountain in October and the Cowpens in January—both near the border of North and South Carolina—checked his advance. A major battle in March 1781 against American forces under Nathanael Greene gave a tactical victory to Cornwallis at Guilford Courthouse, North Carolina, but the high number of British casualties left Cornwallis reeling.

Still hoping to strike a blow that would end the war, Cornwallis marched his men northward into Virginia. By early August 1781 he was fortifying his position at Yorktown, on the Chesapeake Bay. Meanwhile, Washington had learned in May that the French intended again to offer assistance. A potent fleet under the command of the Comte de Grasse was en route from the Caribbean to North America. Washington decided to attempt to capture Cornwallis in a pincer of both sea and land forces, including those under the command of the self-financed 23-year- old Marquis de Lafayette. The timing would have to be absolutely perfect—never something one could rely on with uncertain sailing weather and communications that could take weeks.

Thinking the Americans would focus on capturing New York, the British command realized too late that Cornwallis was in a trap. A brief naval engagement in early September forced British ships out of the Chesapeake. There were now 36 French warships in place, while a juggernaut of 16,000 allied troops was gathering around Yorktown. Cornwallis was in check. The allies dug siege lines and on October 9 began an around-the-clock bombardment.

Finally, on the night of October 14-15, 1781, bayonets in hand, the allies stormed two important redoubts. To ensure silence, Washington ordered his men to go in with unloaded guns. The French, planning to capture an adjacent redoubt, were allowed to load their guns but expected not to shoot them. Both fortresses fell in less than 30 minutes, in one of the few instances of hand-to-hand action during the entire Yorktown campaign. The fall of Cornwalllis's two fortresses meant that siege lines could move even closer. The allies could now bomb any spot in Yorktown with devastating accuracy. In the process, half of the town ended up destroyed.

The siege had lasted another three days before a British drummer appeared on the ramparts, solemnly tapping out a request for a ceasefire. Not until October 17 did Clinton, in New York, set sail to the south, with a force of 7,000. But with de Grasse's fleet blocking the bay, he could not have reached Cornwallis—and before he and his fleet had even made it that far, Cornwallis had surrendered.

Cornwallis sent word to Washington that he was prepared to lay down arms, on condition that his troops could sail back to England. Washington demanded complete surrender. Backed into a corner, Lord Cornwalllis had to submit.

On the afternoon of October 19, the British troops paraded through the allied ranks and laid—or, in some cases, flung—down their weapons in a pile. The British and French soldiers were resplendent in their clean, neat uniforms. The American soldiers were a different lot. Washington and his staff came formally decked out, but the rank and file were a ragged bunch of hungry-eyed, battle-hardened soldiers, scruffy in appearance yet every inch proud victors.

Dejected, even tearful, the British behaved honorably, as did their captors. Cornwallis could not bring himself to attend the ceremony. He sent General Charles O'Hara to offer the sword of surrender. Washington delegated a second to receive it. It is said that a British military band played a popular contemporary ballad, "The World Turned Upside Down."

The capture of 8,000 British soldiers and seamen at Yorktown spelled the climax of the Revolution. Though Washington did not declare the war officially over until March 1783, Yorktown marked the end of major hostilities. ■

Yankee Doodle Stats

Number of Hessian troops recruited by Britain: 30,000

Copies of "Common Sense" sold in 3 months: 100,000

Major battles of the war: 20

Number of battles Washington commanded: 9

Battles Washington won: 3

Miles George Rogers Clark traveled in the winter of 1778-79 to claim the frontier to the Mississippi: 1,200

Number of men with him: 200

Number of cannon balls shot by allies during nine-day siege of Yorktown: 15,000

The New Nation

1782–1801

WITH YORKTOWN IN 1781, the formal battles were over, though guerilla struggles would bloody the southern landscape for another year, as they would the midwestern territory then known as the Northwest. George Washington returned to New York to keep watch over the British forces there.

The politicians had already begun negotiating a peace deal. Congress in 1781 designated a peace commission consisting of John Adams, Benjamin Franklin, John Jay, Thomas Jefferson, and Henry Laurens. The diplomats were hard at work while soldiers were still on the battlefield. In early 1782 Parliament passed a motion to stop aggression against her colonies. At first, George III tried to marshal support to continue

After the French and Indian Wars in 1763, Britain had the upper hand on the continent. Twenty years later, British territory amounted to Canada alone.

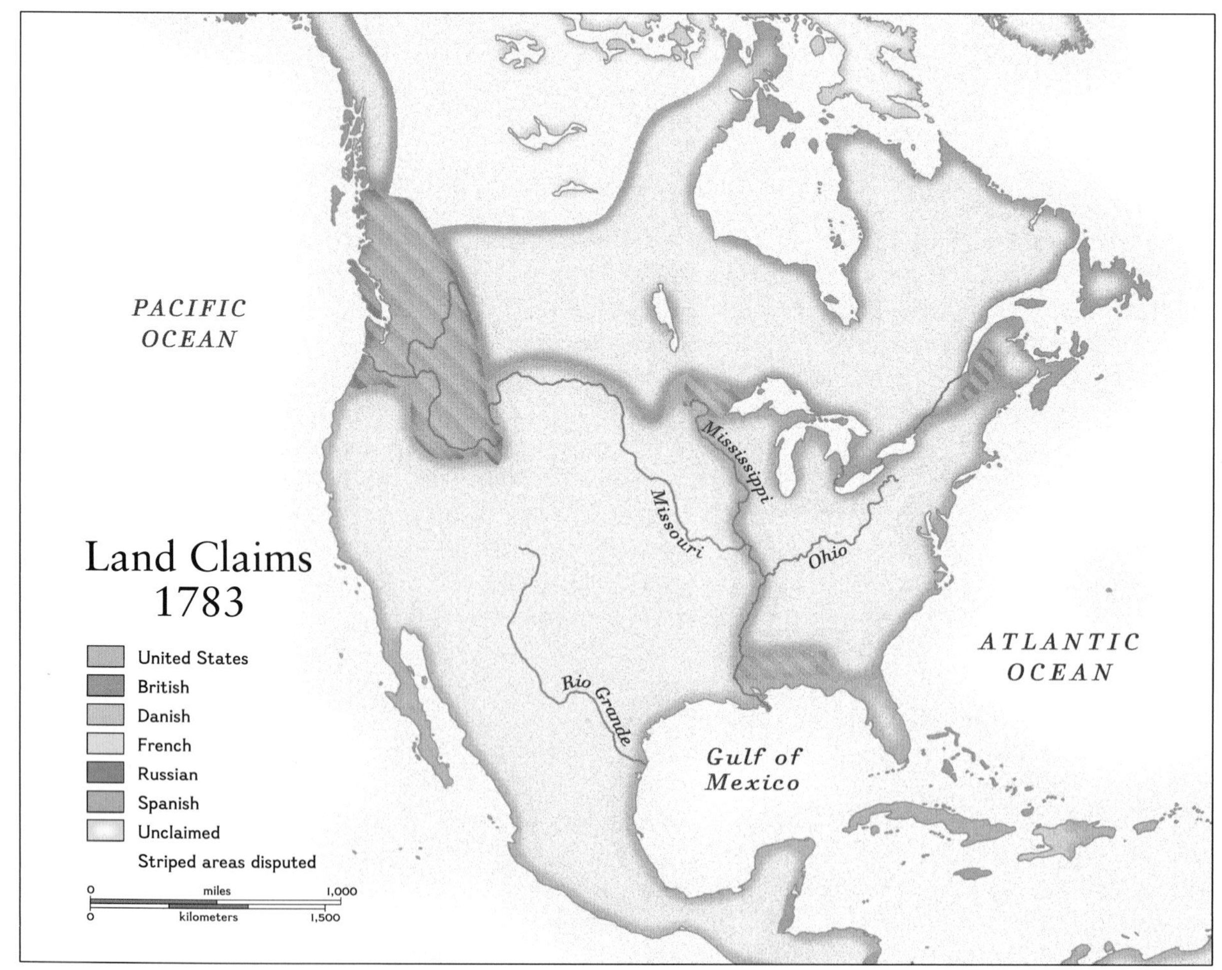

fighting, but not long after Parliament's decision he capitulated to the new state of affairs.

The Peace

The peace talks in Paris went on through the spring and summer of 1782 before much progress was made. Negotiators representing France, Great Britain, the United States, and Spain spent months hammering out a complex series of deals. France came out the biggest loser, retaining only her few sugar islands in the West Indies and her trading posts in the East. Spain came away with Britain's holdings in Florida.

Franklin, age 75, became the major spokesman for his country. The American commissioners first of all wanted independence. In the end they got much more than they had hoped for. Among the articles of peace were the recognition of an independent United States of America, American fishing rights on the Grand Banks off Newfoundland, the end of all hostilities, the evacuation of British troops from American soil, and free navigation by both countries of the Mississippi River. Boundaries were agreed upon: west to the Mississippi and north to more or less the current borderline. Benjamin Franklin and John Jay tried to get Canada as the 14th state, but finally conceded it to Britain. The United States worked out a deal to gain possession of Florida, although it was not finally resolved until an 1819 agreement with Spain. The vague boundary lines between Maine and Canada were not clearly defined until 1842.

Congress ratified the peace treaty in April 1783, and all parties signed it in Paris on September 3. Late in November the final British troops marched into ships waiting at harbor and sailed away. Within a few minutes the Stars and Stripes was hoisted on New York City's Battery flagpole. Washington bade an emotional farewell to his troops in Fraunces Tavern on December 4, then hurried south to his Virginia plantation home, Mount Vernon.

Constitutional Convention

During the first few years after the war, several more battles were fought—in the legislature. The "united" part of United States was as yet more an ideal than a legal fact. Congress in 1781 had approved a document called the Articles of Confederation, which kept central authority so weak that it was a government in little more than name only. To most Americans, strong governments ran the risk of becoming despotic. From 1781 to 1787, the job of the United States was to make war and peace, coin money, create a postal service, and manage Indian affairs. It was hampered by being unable to collect taxes. As a result, soldiers and officers were not paid, the Navy was scuttled, borders and maritime trade were unprotected, and the sovereignty of the new United States was questioned by other nations. Britain, for instance did not bother sending a minister to the United States.

With neither chief executive nor federal courts, the government had little authority. Instability and economic depression finally led to

NOTABLE DATES

■ 1783
Britain declares an end to war with the U.S.

■ 1784
Congress narrowly defeats Jefferson's proposal to ban slavery in new territories after 1800.

■ 1787
Shays's Rebellion of debt-laden farmers fails in Massachusetts; the Northwest Ordinance provides for the division of the Territory Northwest of the Ohio River into three to five states; Delaware is the first state to ratify the new Constitution, followed by Pennsylvania.

■ 1792
The national mint is established in Philadelphia; Washington is reelected; New York Stock Exchange begins as a written agreement among 24 brokers and merchants.

■ 1794
The Whiskey Rebellion—western Pennsylvania farmers protesting the whiskey tax—is put down by militia, setting a precedent for the federal government enforcing its laws.

■ 1795
General "Mad" Anthony Wayne signs a treaty with 12 defeated Indian tribes at Fort Greenville, ending Indian control of present-day Ohio.

■ 1795
Farmers gain free access to the Mississippi River through a treaty with Spain.

■ 1797
French seizure of 300 U.S. ships and demands for bribes lead to a three-year undeclared naval war.

■ 1798
Congress passes Alien and Sedition Acts to suppress opposition.

The Stars and Stripes

NO ONE KNOWS FOR SURE WHO DESIGNED THE UNITED STATES flag or whether it flew during any Revolutionary War battle. General Washington was issued no official flags until the spring of 1783, when peace was being negotiated.

Various heraldic standards began to appear in the early years of the Revolution. One popular motif was the rattlesnake—a native American reptile much feared by European soldiers—on a yellow or red-and-white striped field, often accompanied by the phrase, "Don't Tread on Me." From 1775 to 1777 the unofficial American flag was the Continental Colors, or Grand Union flag. Consisting of 13 alternating red and white stripes with a British Union Jack in the upper left-hand corner, the Grand Union suited colonies still attached to the mother country.

The Stars and Stripes rose over New York Harbor when the British departed in November 1783.

After the Declaration of Independence, the main business of the day was to fight a war. But Congress found time on June 14, 1777, to issue a resolution "that the flag of the United States be thirteen stripes, alternate red and white; that the union be thirteen stars, white in a blue field, representing a new constellation." Flags began appearing with different arrangements—13 stars in a circle, or 12 circling a central star, or (most popular) stars in horizontal rows. Betsy Ross did make flags for Pennsylvania, but the first we know of her association with the Stars and Stripes is when her grandson claimed in 1870 that she designed it at the request of George Washington. It is likely that Francis Hopkinson, artist and delegate to the Continental Congress, had some say in the design.

The new American flag was first saluted in a foreign port on February 14, 1778, when John Paul Jones sailed the *Ranger* into Quiberon Bay, France. A flag at the battle of Yorktown in 1781 inspired Private Joseph Martin to write, "I felt a secret pride swell in my heart when I saw the 'star-spangled banner' waving majestically." ■

mutiny in Massachusetts, when a group of farmers, threatened with losing their debt-ridden property, tried to take over a national arsenal in January 1787. Led by Daniel Shays, who had served as an officer in the Revolution, a band of 1,200 converged on the Springfield arsenal on January 26. The governor called out the Massachusetts state militia, who forced the rebels back. In the process, they killed four of Shays's followers.

Shays's Rebellion spurred Congress to act. From May 25 to September 17, a group of some 55 influential American leaders—lawyers, planters, and merchants—met in Philadelphia. Chosen by state conventions, they argued and compromised and finally turned out a document considered one of the most imporant in the history of the world, the United States Constitution. Virginian James Madison became the visionary leader of this august gathering.

One thorny problem the convention tackled was representation in Congress. Small states wanted an equal voice, while those from large states thought population size—and hence tax payments—should grant them more seats. The solution was a bicameral legislature with a lower house representing states in proportion to population, the House of Representatives, and an upper house with two members from each state, the Senate. There was still the question of how slaves should be counted. Northerners thought slaves should be counted the same as whites for purposes of taxation, but not for representation. Southerners natu-

George Washington leads federal troops in September 1794 to put down the Whiskey Rebellion in western Pennsylvania—the first such deployment under the U.S. Constitution.

rally argued for the opposite, there being so many more slaves in the South. Madison proposed having five slaves count as three whites for both purposes, and the motion carried. Constitutional phrasing also distinguished the legislative, the executive, and the judiciary branches of government, and described the checks and balances necessary to keep any one of those three branches from gaining too much power.

The First President

Within a year, the Constitution was adopted, though several states were concerned that it lacked a Bill of Rights. The Constitution only spelled out the form and function of government but did not mention the rights of the governed. By 1791, under Madison's sponsorship, the Constitution was augmented with ten amendments, the Bill of Rights.

The electoral college unanimously designated George Washington as President. In the spring of 1789, he mounted his horse and headed north again, crowds cheering along the way. The buoyancy of the 1789 Inauguration was soon deflated. To bring economic order, Washington's Administration in 1790 instituted brilliant but severe measures devised by Treasury Secretary Alexander Hamilton, the 35-year-old West Indian prodigy who had fought alongside Washington in the war. The federal government paid off its own debts and the debts of the states. Speculators—including congressmen—who had bought up old certificates from farmers and veterans for as little as 15 cents on the dollar laughed all the way to the national bank, which had just opened in Philadelphia.

Farmers, particularly in the South and on the frontier, banked only bitterness. Their resentment deepened with news of a whiskey tax, a 25 percent excise per gallon. Distilling corn or wheat was the best way for poor farmers to transport those crops to market. With coins and bank notes scarce, whiskey also served as local currency. Suspected delinquents were summoned to Philadelphia. At Pittsburgh a protest convention sought legal redress with little success. In 1794 the farmers rebelled. They attacked federal militia, burned houses, and later marched —5,000 strong—through

Pittsburgh. Washington quickly ordered 15,000 federal troops there—the government's first use of armed force under the Constitution—personally leading them part of the way. The Whiskey Rebellion collapsed. Distillers, now suddenly flush with coin from thirsty soldiers, began paying the tax, although fairly sporadically.

Federalists vs. Democrats

Many Americans were alarmed by the strongarm use of the federal government. Fearing a return to the kind of tyranny they had broken with in the Revolution, they favored a freer, less centralized government. At their head: Virginia planter and Secretary of State Thomas Jefferson. They were passionate about France's own revolution, the rights of states, and the role of independent farmers. Jefferson retired as Secretary of State in 1793; three years later he returned as Vice President. He presided over the Federalist Senate during the nation's undeclared war with France, a difficult position for one who had embraced that country's bloody revolution.

On the other side of the political fence were those nationalists who believed the country needed more unity. Their spokesman was Alexander Hamilton. In private coffeehouses Hamilton's followers—the Federalists—spoke in favor of Britain, industry, and a strong central government. Jefferson and Hamilton faced each other at cabinet meetings "like two [pitted] cocks." Civil in public, they fought through the anonymous pages of subsidized newspapers.

Early Reckonings

U.S. population at first census, 1790: 3,929,214

National debt in 1790: $56 million

Acreage of the Northwest Territory (northwest of Ohio River): 1.5 million acres

Number of essays in "The Federalist," 1787-88 series by Hamilton, Madison, and Jay, defending greater national powers: 85

Number of yellow fever victims in 1793 Philadelphia epidemic: 4,000

Philip Freneau, whom Jefferson had added to the State Department's payroll, edited the Democratic-Republican paper.

These two opposing points of view—Jeffersonian democracy and Hamiltonian nationalism—influenced American history from 1790 to 1830 more than anything, with the exception of the country's westward expansion. At times in outright conflict, they balanced the early ship of state, keeping it from listing too far to one side. The two-party system—called Democrat-Republican and Federalist—grew from those two outlooks.

Washington and his successor Adams were basically Federalists at a time when the country needed to establish its sovereignty. In 1796 President Washington retired after two terms, refusing a third term for fear that if he were to die in office it would establish the precedent of a lifelong Presidency. At his farewell address, he cautioned Americans against large public debts, permanent alliances with foreign powers, an overlarge military establishment, and the efforts of a "small, artful, enterprising minority" to manipulate the government. At the age of 65, he went home and spent the final two and a half years of his life managing his beloved Mount Vernon.

Alien and Sedition Acts

Adams, never the popular leader that Washington had been, soon found himself in political hot water. Principled, headstrong, and cantankerous, Adams distanced himself from Hamilton and thus from his political base. Adams's wisdom served the country well in avoiding war with France after its seizure of numerous United States ships. And during the XYZ Affair, in which three French agents demanded bribes from the U.S., he refused to yield and thus became somethng of a national hero.

But on the domestic front, Adams ran into trouble when he passed a series of repressive measures called the Alien and Sedition Acts. These controversial laws increased from 5 to 14 years the period an alien had to live in the U.S. before gaining citizenship, gave the President power (for 2 years) to order dangerous aliens out of the country, allowed aliens to be held without trial and deported during a time of war, and made it a crime to conspire against a legal measure or to criticize a public officer. In short, the new laws sent foreign agents packing and opposition editors to jail. The acts did more than make martyrs of the editors: Defense measures increased the federal budget between 1796 and 1800, necessitating heavy taxes.

As shown in this diorama, the New York Stock Exchange began on May 17, 1792, at 68 Wall Street, when 24 stockbrokers and merchants signed an agreement under a buttonwood tree.

In 1801, John Adams was out, Thomas Jefferson in. Jefferson tied with his running mate, Aaron Burr of New York. Each held 73 electoral votes. The House of Representatives voted 35 times before choosing Jefferson, whom they believed more willing than Burr to maintain the public credit, the Navy, and many Federalist civil servants. In one of his shining moments, Jefferson's arch-rival Hamiliton saw that the people's choice was clearly Jefferson and made sure that the House voted him in.

Jefferson was the first President to take office in Washington, the new capital city on the Potomac. As the voice of the working man and of the farmer, Jefferson immediately unstuffed the shirts of the federal government—wearing plain clothes he walked from his boardinghouse to the Capitol, trailed by his friends. After taking the oath of office, he made a pitch for national unity. "We are all republicans," he reminded his audience, "we are all federalists." He advocated justice to all, freedom of religion, and freedom of the press. "If there be any among us who would wish to dissolve this Union or to change its republican form, let them stand undisturbed as monuments of the safety with which error of opinion may be tolerated where reason is left free to combat it."

Jefferson set about encouraging western settlement and immigration, reducing the national debt, ending property ownership as a requirement for voting and holding office, and pressing for humane treatment of debtors and criminals. But by the end of his term, the nation was once again on the brink of war, again with Great Britain. ■

WORLD SURVEY

1765–1801

Events in America in the late 1700s upstaged events everywhere else in the world. That colonies could break away from the dominant world power, then establish a free, democratic form of government, was new to the world. The Revolution touched off similar regime changes in France and Latin America.

■ Europe

A gradual shift from an agricultural to an industrial way of life swept Europe in the late 1700s, culminating in the establishment of large factories and the mass production of textiles, all of which was made possible by machines such as James Watt's steam engine, patented in 1769, and James Hargreaves's spinning jenny, patented in 1770.

Since the early 1700s, Europe had been under the influence of the philosophies of Locke, Voltaire, and Montesquieu, who believed that reason could solve virtually every human problem and that the course of history was a tale of continuous progress. Originating in Great Britain and France, this optimistic outlook was the underpinning of the Age of Reason, or Enlightenment, which reflected scientific advances taking place such as the development of the microscope and the subsequent discovery of bacteria. Philosopher Jean-Jacques Rousseau countered the primacy of reason by arguing for the importance of sentiment and innate moral sense. Governments in general corrupted people, he believed, so people should change them if necessary.

These philosophies had a great sway on American intellectual life, leading to the Declaration of Independence—stressing the inalienable rights of man—and the U.S. Constitution. Six years after peace was declared, bringing an end to the American Revolution, the French Revolution was underway; lasting from 1789 to 1799, it abolished the monarchy and temporarily established a republic in France.

■ Asia

Much of Asia in the 18th century closed its doors on modernization and trade with the West. In Japan, the Tokugawa rulers banned all Spanish and Portuguese traders, allowing only one Dutch ship per year at Nagasaki. China's Qing dynasty of the Manchus permitted foreign vessels only at Guangzhou (Canton). British merchants looked to Southeast Asia, eventually colonizing most of India; the Dutch meanwhile took control of Indonesia, and the Spanish gained the Philippines. The Russians expanded eastward from Europe into Siberia.

By the mid-1700s Vietnam had reached approximately its present size. The country emerged from earlier Chinese domination with nationalist pride, but it was also beset by debt and was divided into two parts, north and south, led by separate families. These parts were rejoined during the 1770s through a rebellion led by the three Tay Son brothers, who called for the redistribution of property from rich to poor and abolition of taxes.

■ Africa

The island of Madagascar was divided into a number of small states in the 1600s. Located along key trade routes in the Indian Ocean, it had a diverse population of both African and Asian ancestry that was enriched by European and Arab visitors. Some unity came to the island under the rule of King Andrianampoinimerina, who in 1797, after 15 years of war with 3 other kngs, joined the kingdom of

Imerina on the central plateau of Madagascar.

Andrianampoinimerina established a network of provincial governors, created a uniform system of laws, and sold slaves to the French in exchange for guns. He died admonishing his son to extend the kingdom as far as the sea.

Some parts of west Africa in the 1700s profited from the export of gold and slaves. Into African ports, Europeans brought corn and cassava, which became major crops. The Africans were also introduced to European guns, which were used in internecine wars as well as against the Europeans. In the latter part of the century, Europeans began penetrating deeper into the interior of Africa, planting the seeds of Christianity and establishing trade relations based on palm oil, minerals, and other natural resources. The development of a market in raw materials helped bring about the end of the slave trade by the early 1800s.

■ Australia

After the American Revolution, Britain could no longer use America as a dumping ground for convicts from overcrowded prisons. In 1786, it opened a penal colony in New South Wales. Retired naval captain Arthur Phillip was charged with setting up the new colony and acting as its governor. In May of 1787, his party of 11 ships left England with some 570 male and 170 female convicts, 200 soldiers, 30 soldiers' wives, and several children. On Jan. 18, 1788, they reached Botany Bay on the east coast of Australia. About seven miles north of Botany Bay, at present-day Sydney, the colonists established the continent's first white settlement.

By the 1790s, Britain was offering land grants to officers and freed convicts, and new settlers began arriving. In the late 1790s and early 1800s navigators explored the uncharted perimeters of Australia and determined that it was indeed the land mass—*Terra Australis*, southern continent—that had since the 1500s been rumored to exist. ■

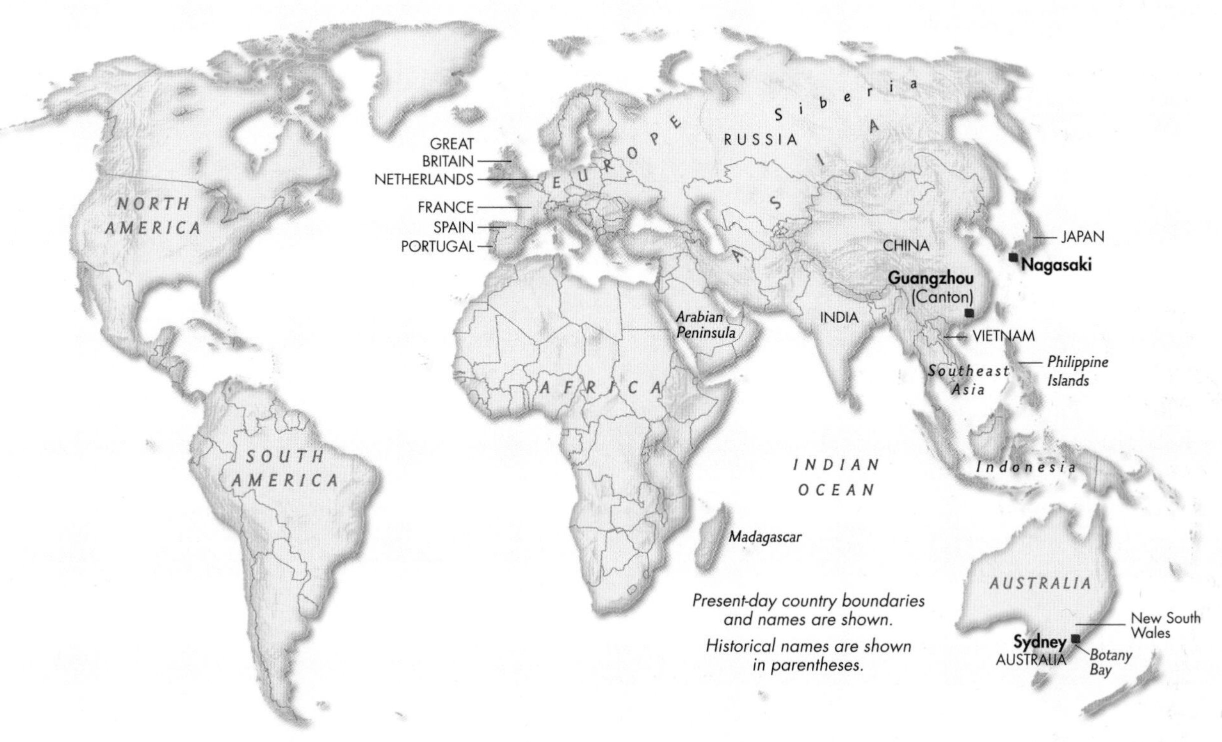

Continental Expansion 1803–1853

When Thomas Jefferson became President in 1801, the Mississippi formed the western boundary of the U.S. By 1860, when Abraham Lincoln was elected President, the nation stretched to the Pacific. This expansion brought new sources of wealth and opportunity. The first step in American expansion occurred in 1803, when Jefferson concluded the Louisiana Purchase. For 15 million dollars, the U.S. obtained from France its claim to the 909,380-square-mile Louisiana Territory. In 1804 Meriwether Lewis and William Clark left St. Louis and headed up the Missouri on an expedition that would take them to the source of that river in Montana and on to the Pacific. They returned to St. Louis in 1806 after charting a path soon to be followed by trappers and fur traders. After the War of 1812, settlers surged westward by river and trail, and work began on the Erie Canal, linking the Hudson River with Lake Erie. Tensions between the U.S. and Mexico escalated in 1845 when President James Polk, a fervent expansionist, won approval from Congress to annex Texas. U.S. and Mexican troops clashed along the border in early 1846, and the U.S. went to war in May. The treaty of 1848 kept Mexico intact below the Rio Grande while ceding to the U.S. New Mexico (including what is now Arizona), California, and other territory in the Southwest. The discovery of gold in California that same year hastened a migration already underway to the West. ■

On the open range, longhorns overtake a mounted cowboy in this illustration by the noted Western artist Frederic Remington.

■ 1803
U.S. embarks on an era of rapid territorial expansion by purchasing the Louisiana Territory from France.

■ 1807
The steamboat era begins with Robert Fulton's *Clermont* making a 5-day round trip from New York City to Albany.

■ 1812
U.S. Senate votes for war with Britain to protect "free trade and sailors' rights." Peace is made December 1814.

■ 1815
Defeat of Napoleon Bonaparte at Waterloo brings French imperial expansion in Europe to an end. Congress of Vienna restores France to its 1792 borders.

■ 1817
Erie Canal construction begins in New York.

■ 1819	■ 1836	■ 1846	■ 1848	■ 1848
A treaty cedes Spanish Florida to the U.S.	Texas settlers declare their independence from Mexico.	The Mexican War begins.	Mexico cedes Texas, New Mexico, California, and other parts of the Southwest to the U.S. in a treaty ending the Mexican War.	The discovery of gold in California spurs a massive migration westward.

Moving West

1803–1819

SHORTLY AFTER JEFFERSON assumed the Presidency, Napoleon Bonaparte forced Spain to cede back the Louisiana Territory to France. The idea that the world's most powerful nation now controlled access to the lower Mississippi River and might set up a French empire in the West set alarms ringing in Washington. New Orleans was an essential port for flour, salt pork, whiskey, and other products from the Ohio and the Mississippi Valleys. "There is on the globe one single spot," Jefferson wrote, "the possessor of which is our natural and habitual enemy. It is New Orleans." President Jefferson admitted that if France moved in next door, "from that moment we must marry ourselves to the British fleet and nation."

But Napoleon, too, had his qualms. He knew that an Anglo-American attack would come in Louisiana. Special envoy James Monroe was en route to Paris, authorized to pay up to $10 million for New Orleans and Florida, when the situation turned in favor of America. Napoleon had just lost almost an entire army of 20,000 in Haiti, where it had failed to crush a slave rebellion and instead contracted yellow fever. Strapped for cash, Napoleon decided to make the most of the situation by selling off Louisiana, and make friends with America in the bargain. Diplomat Robert Livingston had only been angling for New Orleans and Florida; he was shocked when France's foreign affairs minister Talleyrand wanted to know how much America would pay for the entire Louisiana Territory, which included New Orleans and everything west of the Mississippi River up to the headwaters of its tributaries in the Rocky Mountains.

Louisiana Purchase

When Jefferson became President he had said that America had enough land already for the next thousand years; on the other hand, here was an obvious opportunity. Robert Livingston quickly composed himself and offered $5 million. French minister Talleyrand thought the offer too low. For the next couple of days Livingston had to figure what to do. Since he could not wait two to three months to send for and receive instructions, he and Monroe haggled with Talleyrand and finally agreed to buy the Louisiana Territory for 60 million francs, about $15 million. Talleyrand had no idea of the real

Swiss artist Karl Bodmer traveled up the Missouri River in 1833-34, painting scenes like this riverside camp, as well as the daily life of the Plains Indians.

size of the territory. "I can give you no direction," he told Livingston. "You have made a noble bargain for yourselves, and I suppose you will make the most of it." Never did the United States, wrote historian Henry Adams, "get so much for so little."

But in approving the transaction, Jefferson exceeded the powers granted by the U.S. Constitution, which nowhere authorized the President to purchase foreign territory. He had criticized the Federalists for assuming "implied powers" of the Constitution. He tried putting forth an amendment, but that idea was squelched. He finally justified it for "the good sense of our country," and decided "that the less we say about constitutional difficulties the better." Congress went ahead and ratified the deal. History has judged this the greatest act of Jefferson's Presidency. The Louisiana Purchase of 1803 doubled the size of the country, adding an area larger than present-day Great Britain, France, Germany, Italy, and Spain—space enough for all or part of 13 states.

As Jefferson's stock rose in the South and West, the power of New England Federalists declined. Sensing their party's demise, a few Federalists contemplated seceding from the Union, and even formed a group called the Essex Junto in 1804. Dour conservative Timothy Pickering, former secretary of state, led this unlikely attempt to form a "Northern Confederacy." The Junto backed Vice President Aaron Burr, a long-shot candidate for governor of New York.

Though Burr lost and the Junto folded, a national tragedy ensued. Alexander Hamilton had campaigned against Burr, whom he considered a tyrant in the making. Afterwards, Aaron Burr challenged Hamilton to a duel. The latter objected to dueling, having lost a son this way. Yet he agreed to the challenge and the two met at Weehawken, New Jersey, on July 11, 1804. After Hamilton purposely missed, Burr aimed carefully and shot Hamilton. The country lost an early hero.

Lewis and Clark

Even before the Louisiana Purchase, Jefferson had his eye on the West. With an appropriation of a mere $2,500, in 1804 the expedition of Meriwether Lewis and William Clark was underway, probing the nation's newest territory, penciling in the first lines on the blank map of the American West. The 31 men (plus the invaluable Sacagawea) were searching for a good water route to the Pacific. Though they found none, they brought back a trove of knowledge about the plants, animals, minerals, landforms, and native peoples of the interior—all new information that the expanding country needed. They traveled up the Missouri, over the Rockies, and into the disputed Northwest Territory—there and back in two and a half years. The epic trip, a military expedition with flags waving, had the added benefit of announcing the nation's presence to English and French fur traders in the north, the Spanish in the south, and Indians all along the way.

NOTABLE DATES

■ 1803
The Louisiana Purchase gives the U.S. claim to a vast area west of the Mississippi River formerly claimed by France.

■ 1803
The Supreme Court under Chief Justice John Marshall rules an act of Congress null and void in *Marbury v. Madison*, establishing itself the ultimate interpreter of the Constitution.

■ 1804
Vice President Aaron Burr kills Alexander Hamilton in a duel incited by a published attack on Burr, who flees south and conspires to create an independent republic.

■ 1804-06
Lewis and Clark journey overland from the Mississippi to the Pacific.

■ 1819
Spain cedes Florida to the U.S. in exchange for American recognition of a boundary line in the West that confirms Spanish possession of Texas, New Mexico, and California—territory later assumed by Mexico when it won independence from Spain in 1821.

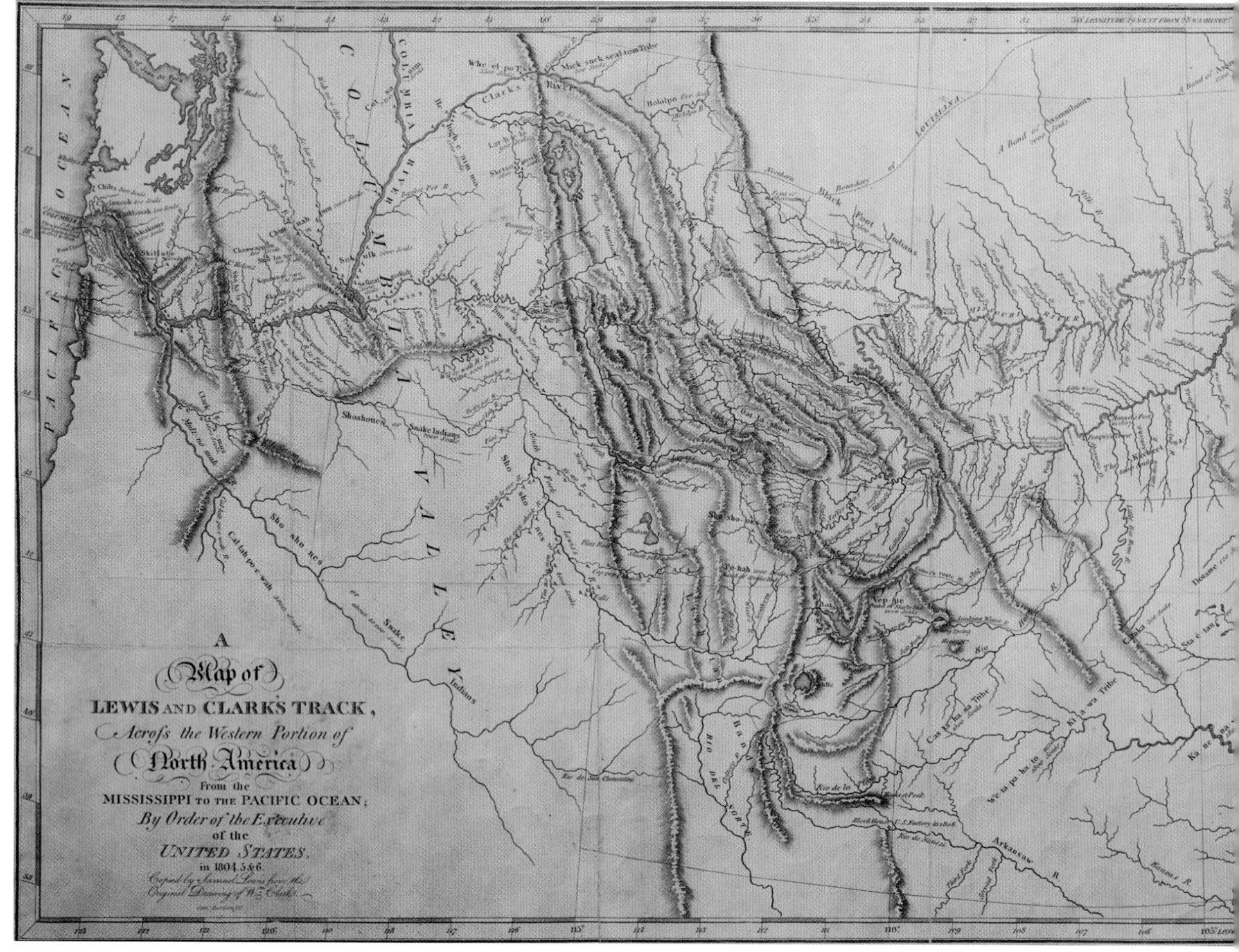

Filling in *terra incognita*, this 1814 map was the first composite map of the Lewis and Clark expedition route; their journey proved there was no waterway to the Pacific.

Enduring biting winds, grizzly attacks, near drownings, starvation rations, tense Indian situations, grueling portages, and clouds of "musquitrs and knats" so thick they had to build large, smoky fires, the explorers traversed 8,000 miles between St. Louis and the Pacific. In the whole journey there was only one death—near the outset—caused by a ruptured appendix. "Never did a similar event excite more joy thro' the United States," wrote Jefferson on the return of Lewis and Clark. Their diaries noted 122 new species and subspecies of birds, fish, amphibians, mammals, and reptiles; and nearly 200 new plants, many of them edible or medicinal. Among the finds sent to Jefferson was a caged and yelping prairie dog—caught after hours of pouring river water down its burrow, and two grizzly bear cubs, which lived for a while in a stone pit on the White House lawn.

In 1806, the year Lewis and Clark returned, Zebulon Pike explored the Arkansas River to its source in the Rockies. In 1807 he was captured by Spanish troops and held prisoner for several months—a reminder that much of the West remained disputed territory. In the Colorado region he discovered the peak now bearing his name. He explored to Santa Fe and the upper Rio Grande.

Not long after the Lewis and Clark expedition, Clark's Missouri Fur Company set up posts along the Missouri, and John Jacob Astor's American Fur Company established an American presence in the Northwest. By 1812, some 75,000 settlers had moved into the territory west of St. Louis.

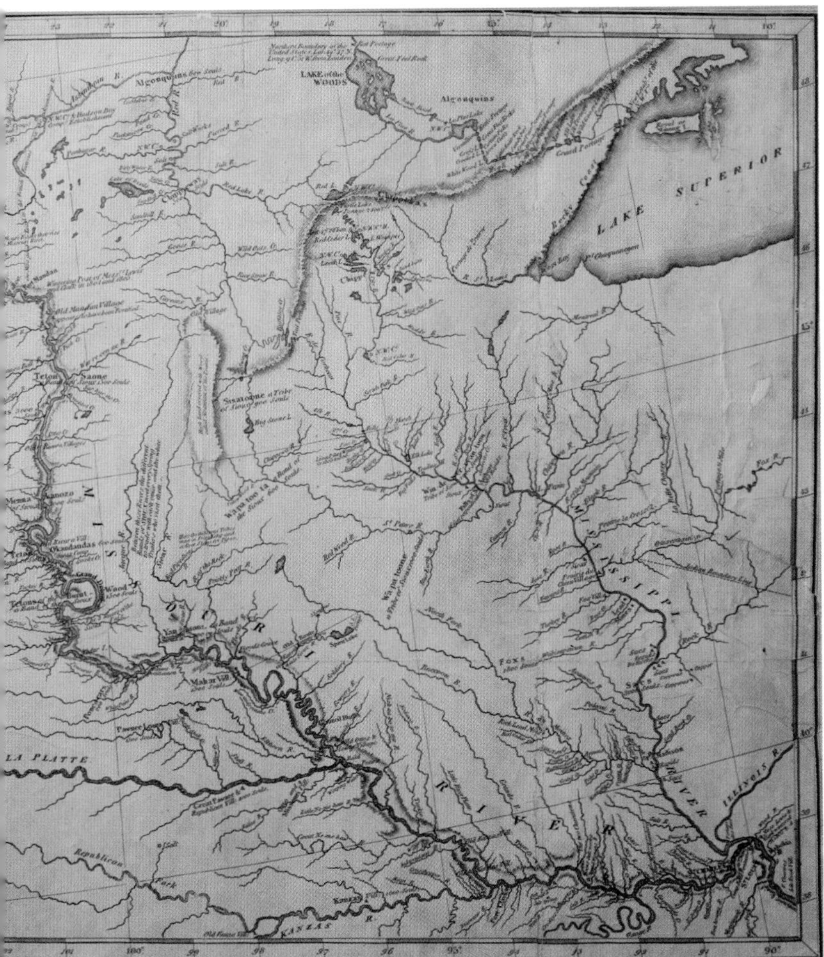

More Land

East of the Mississippi, about 100,000 settlers had pushed into Kentucky and Tennessee by 1790; six years later these territories were admitted as states. Ohio followed in 1803. By 1820 the Old Southwest territory had been carved into three states—Alabama, Mississippi, and Louisiana—and in the Old Northwest, Indiana and Illinois became full-fledged states.

The Louisiana Purchase did not extend all the way to the Pacific, only to about the western edge of present-day Montana, and the southern boundaries were vaguely defined. Spain held this southwestern territory. After the War of 1812, the U.S. was in a position to push out its boundaries. Britain and the United States agreed to the 49th parallel for the northern boundary. In 1818 President James Monroe sent General Andrew Jackson to clear the Seminoles away from American territory and push them into Spanish Florida. The following year, Spain gave up west Florida; the treaty was ratified in 1821.

It became clear to Spain that American settlers would soon be moving in. They went to the bargaining table to salvage what they could of the Southwest by giving up Florida. In Washington, Spanish minister Luis de Onis met with Secretary of State John Quincy Adams. Onis wanted the boundary set in the middle of current Louisiana. A shrewd negotiator, Adams pressed for a line much farther west—through what is now Texas. After some high-minded talk about "reason and justice," Onis could only capitulate.

The U.S. now owned the territory north of the Arkansas River and the 42nd parallel (the Oregon-California line). Adams also insisted that where the line coincided with a river, the U.S. owned the river. The entire deal cost $5 million, not payable to Spain but to Americans who held notes against the Spanish government. Called the Transcontinental Treaty, the deal was signed in 1819, though not ratified until 1821. Florida looked like the best part of the deal to most Americans. Yet Adams confided to his diary, "The acquisition of a definite line of boundary to the [Pacific] forms a great epoch in our history." ■

Pushing West

Number of miles Lewis and Clark traveled in 2.5 years: 8,000

Cost of Louisiana Purchase: $11.25 million in bonds, and $3.75 million indemnities to Americans with claims against France.

Residents in Louisiana Territory in1803: 50,000

Residents in Louisiana Territory in1812: 75,000

War of 1812

1812–1815

PRESIDENT JEFFERSON, IN OFFICE from 1801 to 1809,extended the federal reach not just in buying new territory but in trying to keep America out of the war raging between France and Great Britain. The infant nation needed time to grow and prosper. Its foreign trade suffered as France and Britain used America like a pawn. A British blockade of Napoleon's shipping meant seizing American vessels trading in French ports. The French responded with their own blockade and the capture of American and other ships that had called at British ports. In effect, America could not carry on reliable trade with either country— and the economy began to suffer.

Another especially intolerable measure was the impressment of American sailors by the British. The Royal Navy had in 1805 crushed the French fleet at the Battle of Trafalgar. To keep its country safe from attack and its trade routes open, Great Britain continued to maintain a beefed-up navy of 700 warships and almost 150,000 sailors and marines. But with low pay and a steady stream of desertions, she had to find alternative sources of manpower. Hence seized American ships were routinely searched for deserters—many Brits having opted for the freer life of an American sailor—and Britain refused to recognize former Brits as American citizens. By 1811 upwards of 6,000 American seamen had been impressed and held in bondage.

Andrew Jackson became the "hero of New Orleans" after his forces killed or wounded 2,000 British soldiers at the end of the War of 1812; U.S. casualities numbered only 71. His fame helped earn the Presidency 14 years later.

Edging Toward War

In 1807 the British warship *Leopard* ordered the U.S.S. *Chesapeake*, at the mouth of the James River, to give up its deserters. The latter balked, and the British began firing, killing 3 and wounding 18. They seized four men—only one a real deserter, who was hanged. Jefferson responded by declaring a total trade embargo. In 1808, American trade plummeted to one-fifth its total.

Pushing the country further toward war, frontier settlers were outraged by British support for Indians in the Northwest Territory, who were uniting under the powerful Shawnee warrior Tecumseh.

Three days before he left office, Jefferson repealed the embargo. But the damage had been done. In 1812, Madison called for war on Britain. On June 17, 1812, the Senate barely voted for war to protect "free trade and sailors' rights." What the war hawks actually wanted was to annex Canada, expand western and southern frontiers, and remove the threat of alliance between Britain and the Indians in the Great Lakes region.

A small, untrained U.S. Army invaded Canada. At the outset, Detroit was surrendered without one shot fired. Sunken morale was raised, if briefly, by victories in scattered naval engagements. Captain Oliver Perry's defeat of a British squadron on Lake Erie eased the threat of British attacks from the west. "We have met the enemy and they are ours," he reported. But by 1814 the Royal Navy had blocked the U.S. Navy in ports and reduced trade to six percent of the 1807 peak.

Final Peace with Britain

Things got worse. Having defeated Napoleon, Britain sent toughened veterans to crush the upstart Yankees. Had not Captain Thomas Macdonough held Lake Champlain and the garrison at Fort McHenry defended Baltimore, the British might have prevailed. British forces torched the White House and the Capitol.

General Andrew Jackson defeated a British force at New Orleans—not knowing that peace had been made 15 days earlier, on Christmas Eve, 1814. The war ended essentially a draw. Americans turned from making war to buying land and making money. ■

Summing Up The New Republic

American exports 1807: $108 million

American imports 1807: $139

American exports 1808 (during the trade embargo): $22 million

American imports 1808: $57 million

American frigates 1812: 7

British frigates 1812: 34, plus 7 ships of the line

British vessels captured in the War of 1812 by American merchant ships: over 1,300

Casualties on Perry's flagship during 1813 Lake Erie battle: 85 out of 103 men

Blacks fighting with Perry: 25 percent

Shells that fell on Fort McHenry in 25-hour bombardment, Sept. 13-14, 1814: 1,800

NOTABLE DATES

■ **1807** U.S. embargoes trade with all foreign countries, hoping to force Britain and France to stop interfering with U.S. shipping.

■ **1811**
William Henry Harrison defeats Shawnees in the Battle of Tippecanoe.

■ **1812**
U.S. declares war on Great Britain.

■ **1813**
Oliver H. Perry defeats a British fleet in the Battle of Lake Erie.

■ **1814**
Francis Scott Key writes "The Star-Spangled Banner" after the shelling of Fort McHenry. The Treaty of Ghent ends the war.

■ **1815**
Barbary pirates end raids on American commercial shipping after a U.S. flotilla under Capt. Stephen Decatur captures warships and forces treaties.

Transportation Revolution

1794–1855

After the War of 1812, settlers still had to get to the territories on foot or, if they were lucky, by horse or Conestoga wagon. They would travel hundreds of miles on potholed and muddy trails that were in many cases unimproved since colonial times. The technological advances that spurred settlement and allowed the settlers to contribute to the national economy were primarily advances in transportation. Only with better transportation could people in the new country get their products to market, and thus improve the value of their land.

Early road builders took on the forbidding task of linking the East with the West. To cut through the rugged Appalachians, forests had to be cleared, steep grades reduced, streams bridged, and drainage ditches dug; then the roads were covered with gravel so that they could endure the heavy tread of boot, hoof, and wagon wheel. All this was done with no more machinery than mules. Roads cost an average of $6,500 per mile to build, though they could cost twice that. By 1821, New York had about 4,000 miles of roads; most places had far fewer, especially in the West.

The federal government as early as the Jefferson Administration proposed a national road plan. But owing to political fights none was developed in the 1800s. Instead, a haphazard system of public and private roads began to vein out from east to west. Venture capitalists, sometimes with government assistance, built turnpikes—roads on which tolls were collected and a gate literally "turned" open so the traveler could proceed. A Philadelphia to Lancaster, Pennsylvania, turnpike opened in 1794. With road maintenance costs high and traffic low, pike owners usually made a poor return on their investment. Following the lay of the land, public roads called "shunpikes" often ran parallel to the turnpikes, further cutting into profits.

The earliest major thoroughfare, the Cumberland Road (Old National Road) ran from Cumberland, Maryland, west over the mountains to Wheeling at the Ohio River. Started in 1811, this main artery eventually stretched all the way to Illinois. At completion it was 600 miles long and 60 feet wide, with a paved center strip 20 feet wide. But this and other roads were uneconomical for transporting anything much heavier than mail. People in the hinterlands wanted furniture, books, clothes, and hardware. But the cost of shipping freight the 300 miles from Philadelphia to Pittsburgh, for example, was more expensive than shipping it west on the Ohio, south on the Mississippi, and around by the Atlantic—a journey of more than 3,000 miles.

The experimental locomotive Tom Thumb makes a trial run in 1830. The nation's first locomotive operated on the new Baltimore and Ohio Railroad, the nation's first railroad, whose first section ran from Baltimore to Ellicott's Mills.

NOTABLE DATES

■ **1819**
The *Savannah* makes the first partly steam-powered crossing of the Atlantic in 29 days.

■ **1820**
S.S. *Robert Fulton* steams from New York City to Havana, Cuba—the first steamship to make that voyage.

■ **1823**
James Fenimore Cooper publishes *The Pioneers,* a detailed account of frontier life and the first of the Leatherstocking tales.

■ **1825**
The Erie Canal opens, connecting the Great Lakes with the Atlantic at New York.

■ **1830**
The Baltimore and Ohio, America's first commercial railroad, opens.

■ **1838**
Steamer *Moselle* explodes on the Ohio River; more than 130 people die.

■ **1844**
Inventor Samuel F.B. Morse sends the first message over a telegraph line from Washington to Baltimore: "What hath God wrought?"

From Roads to Waterways

The answer was to improve boats and waterways. Flatboats, rafts, and barges were good for the downstream trip to New Orleans, where roustabouts would offload cargoes of grain, pelts, pork, venison, and flour. But there was no waterway back north—the boatmen would break up the raft, sell the lumber, and begin the trudge. Steamboats came to the rescue.

Steamboats had been in commercial operation since 1790, but their use did not become widespread for another 20 years. While in Paris working on the Louisiana Purchase, Robert Livington met artist and engineer Robert Fulton and offered to finance his work on an improved steamboat. Back in New York, Fulton in 1807 built the 142-foot-long *Clermont*, a sidewheeler capable of 5 miles per hour. Instead of a strikingly new design, the *Clermont*'s integrated engine, boiler, hull, and paddle wheels gave the boat new balance and efficiency.

Soon paddle-wheelers were churning up and down the Mississippi. On luxury steamers like the 1819 *General Pike* with its plush carpets, marble columns, gilt mirrors, and heavy curtains, passengers could gamble and dance the night away. Between 1820 and

An 1876 Currier & Ives print illustrates the progress of the 19th century: the lightning steam press, the electric telegraph, the locomotive, and the steamboat. The new technologies made the continent's distances seem less vast.

1830 the number of steamers running between Louisville and New Orleans jumped from 60 to over 200. Commerce in the Mississippi Valley made the same leap. The tonnage of freight coming into New Orleans from upriver ports jumped almost sevenfold between 1817 and 1841.

Interestingly, the rise of steamboats did not spell doom for flatboats. In fact, more boats of all kinds made their way to New Orleans, where farmers and lumbermen could sell their wares and imbibe the carnival atmosphere of the most outlandish city in the United States, a polyglot melting pot of Spanish, French, Creoles, blacks, pirates, prostitutes, bums, fortunetellers, and speculators.

As it did on the inland waterways, so steam fueled the engines of progress on the ocean. With their higher average speed, steamships were by the late 1840s outcompeting clipper ships in passenger, mail, and first-class freight traffic. It was not long before steamships were crossing the Atlantic in under ten days.

Canals

At the same time that steamboats were proliferating, canals were spreading out from east to west, linking the established cities with the frontier. Though they were more expensive to build than roads, canals had the advantage of less friction; thus a horse or mule walking a towpath could pull much more in a canal boat than in a wagon. The most impressive canal was the 363-mile Erie Canal linking Albany with Buffalo. There were only 570 feet of elevation to overcome with locks along the route. To raise money for construction, New York's Mayor DeWitt Clinton promoted it: "As an organ of communication between the Hudson, the Mississippi, the St. Lawrence, the great lakes of the north and west, and their tributary rivers, [the canal] will create the greatest inland trade ever witnessed."

When construction began in 1817, the longest canal in the nation measured only 28 miles long. The digging of the "Big Ditch" was perhaps the greatest feat of civil engineering the young nation had known. Engineers invented a waterproof cement of native limestone, and cut through dense woodlands, completing the project in eight years. It was not long before the Erie Canal had recovered its $7 million cost and was bringing in some $3 million a year. By connecting Lake Erie with the Hudson River and thus with New York City, the canal brought great prosperity to the state; a later road and canal connected Buffalo to the Ohio River and hence to the entire heartland. A canal boom followed the Erie, but, since New York's geography made it particularly suitable for a canal, few other such projects were as successful.

Getting There

Freight brought to New Orleans from upriver 1816-17: 80,000 tons

Freight brought to New Orleans from upriver 1840-41: 542,000 tons

Canals in 1830: 1,277 miles

Canals in 1840: 3,326 miles

Railroads in 1830: 13 miles

Railroads in 1840: 3,328 miles

Railroads in 1860: 30,636 miles

The Railroad Age Begins

If steam transport and canals kicked off the American economy, the railroads pushed it into high gear. The first American rail line, a 13-mile section of the Baltimore and Ohio, opened in 1830. By the end of the decade, the U.S. had 3,328 miles of track—the same as the canal mileage and double that of Europe's rail lines. The early railroads did not put the canals out of business as they were nearly all east of the Appalachians and had not yet evolved into an interconnected system. Some lines, in fact, were built with different widths so that competing companies could not horn in on local business.

The railroads had a tremendous impact on farm production. In the Midwest, corn and wheat output soared so high that labor was hard to find. With the high cost of labor, new machinery such as John Deere's steel plowshare and Cyrus McCormick's horse-drawn reaper made farm production more economical. Railroads also stimulated the growth of cities. When Chicago in the early 1850s suddenly became a hub for 2,200 miles of railroads, it became the most important city in the Midwest. The early railroad industry was an unregulated free-for-all in which a few shrewd financiers grabbed control, some by outright dishonesty. They issued free shares of stock to themselves, manipulated corporate books, and profited on inside information. The shenanigans of railroad investors grew out of control in the laissez-faire decades following the Civil War. ■

Robert Fulton

THOUGH HE DID NOT INVENT THE STEAMBOAT, ROBERT FULTON (1765-1815) deserves more credit than anyone else for ushering in the golden era of steamboating. Born on a Pennsylvania farm, Fulton showed early promise as a painter. Tall, good-looking, and well-spoken, he had no trouble getting financial support to study art in London. However, with poor reception of his art abroad, he began experimenting in boat propulsion.

By age 29 he had given up art in favor of canal engineering. He then turned to the mechanics of submarines. He moved to Paris in 1797 where he designed a submarine for the French. It was never used in an attack, and he later tried to sell the design to the British. In Paris in 1801, he met Robert R. Livingston, minister to France, who held a 20-year charter on steamboat navigation in New York. Livingston agreed to help finance a Fulton-designed steamboat.

Back in the U.S. in 1806 Fulton went to work on the new steamboat. In 1807 it was ready for test runs. The single-cylinder steam engine propelled two 15-foot-wide side-wheels. On a 150-mile trial from New York to Albany, the boat averaged 4.7 miles per hour, beating the 4 miles per hour required by the steamboat charter. His steamboat had accomplished in 32 hours what took sailboats 4 days. Fulton soon began commercial and freight runs. The newly outfitted boat, the *Clermont*, was registered in 1808. In 1812 Fulton sat on the commission recommending the building of the Erie Canal. He spent his last years building boats— and giving away money to family and young artists. ■

Steamboats ply the upper Mississippi River. By 1840 some 500 steamboats operated on the river; their numbers declined in the early 1900s.

The Jacksonian Period

1829–1837

NOT LONG AFTER THE WAR of 1812, James Monroe began his eight-year tenure as President (1817-25) during a time of national expansion. Not highly popular, Monroe nevertheless, said his successor John Quincy Adams, had "a mind sound in its ultimate judgments, and firm in its final conclusions." He is best known for promulgating the Monroe Doctrine, a policy of barring Europe from intervention in the Americas. In the 1824 election Andrew Jackson won the most popular votes, but with no majority of electoral votes the decision went to the House of Representatives. When Kentucky Congressman Henry Clay decided to back Adams over front-runner Jackson, the House vote put John Quincy Adams into office. Jackson's supporters claimed Adams had stolen the election in a backstage deal, and Clay's subsequent appointment as Adams's secretary of state did nothing to soothe their outrage. Jackson pronounced the appointment a "corrupt bargain," resigned from the Senate, and began planning for the next election. The brilliant, austere, high-minded Adams—who, as Monroe's secretary of state, had written much of the Monroe Doctrine—had a one-term Presidency, hampered by unpopularity.

The hero of the Battle of New Orleans, Jackson swept to victory in 1828 on a tide of support like no President had enjoyed since Washington. The champion of the commoners had thrown out the aristocrats. Bitterness between Adams and Jackson was so intense that President-elect Jackson decided not to pay the traditional visit to the sitting President, and

A piece of mock currency skewers the failing monetary programs of Presidents Jackson and Van Buren. Jackson and Senator Thomas Hart Benton pursue the "Gold Humbug" butterfly, while Van Buren deviates toward Bank of U.S.

Adams refused to ride to the Capitol with Jackson. The Inauguration was an extravanganza of gloating southern and western Democrats who had felt disenfranchised by the Eastern elite. They surged into the White House to get a glimpse of Old Hickory, as Jackson was called, helping themselves to the free punch and getting muddy boots on the furniture. "I never saw such a mixture," observed a Supreme Court justice, "The reign of King Mob seemed triumphant."

Massachusetts Senator Daniel Webster said during the 1829 Inaugural, "Persons have come five hndred miles to see General Jackson, and they really seem to think that the country is rescued from some dreadful danger!" Here was the man, they thought, who could return the government to the high ideals recalled by Revolutionary hero Marquis de Lafayette in his triumphal 1824 tour of the United States. In battle Jackson had earned the devotion of his soldiers by being both unyielding (he had once had a soldier shot for disobeying orders) and comforting (he nursed his men with bandages and fatherly advice). He was a man who dueled over principles.

Hot-tempered, high-handed, and keen of intellect, Jackson was born in poverty in western North Carolina in 1767. Though not an able administrator, he had a persuasive, winning personality. He became known for his bravery and audacity in the War of 1812 and in fighting the Seminoles. As a lawyer and senator he spoke for the underprivileged. And as President he went gunning for special interests and monopolies that concentrated political and economic power in the hands of the few. He made a show of his reforms, purging civil servants and vetoing the requests of America's rising entrepreneurs, who sought aid in building and insuring their canals, roads, and factories. He vetoed more bills than all the Presidents before him combined, and it was Jackson who initiated the pocket veto, whereby a President sits on an unsigned bill until the legislature adjourns. He simplified the uniforms worn by U.S. ministers abroad and sought to simplify the economy, with mixed results.

His championing of the underclass by no means extended to everyone. It was Jackson's policies that led to the removal of the southeastern Indians from their homeland in the bitter Trail of Tears. Nor was Jackson an abolitionist. The owner of as many as 200 slaves, Jackson fully supported states' rights—that is, until South Carolina threatened to nullify a federal law regarding tariffs.

The Nullification Crisis

When the sanctity of the Union was endangered, Jackson drew a line, and rallied public opinion against state nullification. During a banquet in 1830, he fixed Vice President and South Carolina leader John C. Calhoun in the eye and made a toast: "Our Union—it must be preserved." Two years later he sent a naval unit to Charleston along with General Winfield Scott, and he warned a South Carolina representative that "if one drop of blood be shed there in defiance of

NOTABLE DATES

■ 1832
South Carolina passes an Ordinance of Nullification to nullify a federal law, and threatens to withdraw from the Union over a permanent tariff.

■ 1833
A tariff compromise induces South Carolina to repeal the 1832 ordinance.

■ 1835
The national debt is paid off through tariffs and land sales.

■ 1837
Some 600 banks fail at the start of a seven-year depression sparked by land speculation.

■ 1840
Whig William Henry Harrison unseats incumbent President Martin Van Buren.

the laws of the United States, I will hang the first man of them I can get my hands on to the first tree I can find." Later in life Jackson confided that he was sorry he had not hanged Calhoun himself.

Fiery high priest of states' rights, Calhoun began his career promoting nationalism, including a tariff to protect manufacturers. By 1832 he had done an about-face. He was the voice of the South, a man "who would rather rule in hell, than be subordinate in heaven," wrote an irate Andrew Jackson. In 1818 prosperity had reigned in the South: A pound of cotton earned planters 31 cents. By 1831—battered by depression and a sated world market—a pound of cotton brought only 8 cents. Congress ignored southern distress, almost doubling the hated tariff in 1828. In reaction, Charleston flags flew at half-mast. Equally feared was the rising din of abolitionists and slave uprisings. Vice President Calhoun's pen flew at top speed, explaining for South Carolina legislators his doctrine that no state could be bound by a federal law it believed to be unconstitutional.

Thus when Congress renewed high tariffs in 1832, South Carolina igorned Jackson's warnings and went ahead and passed an Ordinance of Nullification that outlawed the collection of tariff duties. Jackson responded with a Proclamation to the People of South Carolina. "The laws of the United States must be executed," he asserted. "I have no discretionary power on the subject. . . . Those who told you that you might peaceably prevent their execution deceived you. . . . Disunion by armed force is *treason*. Are you really ready to incur its guilt?"

Old Hickory's New Politics

Miles traveled by de Tocqueville in his 1831-32 tour of America: 7,000

Ballots cast in the 1824 election: 300,000

Ballots cast in the 1828 election: 1.2 million

Popular votes in 1828: Jackson 647,231, Adams 509,097

Electoral votes in 1828: Jackson 178, Adams 83

Popular votes in 1832: Jackson 687,502, Clay 530,189

Electoral votes in 1832: Jackson 219, Clay 49

Federal government workers in 1828: 10,000

Bills Jackson vetoed: 12

New Hampshire Senator Daniel Webster, in one of his many memorable speeches, declaimed against South Carolina's resistance in 1833: "Liberty and Union, now and forever, one and inseparable!" The crisis was finally swept under the rug when Kentucky Senator Henry Clay, known as the "Great Pacificator," worked out a compromise that lowered the tariff. For now, civil war was avoided and the Union remained intact.

Taking Down the Bank

In 1832, in opposition to Henry Clay, the Whig Party, and Philadelphia financier Nicholas Biddle, Jackson used his veto to prevent Congress from extending the charter of the second Bank of the United States. In his veto message President Jackson appealed directly to the public for support against this "hydra of corruption," which catered to the wealthy. Taking his landslide reelection that same year as a mandate, Jackson drained the bank of government deposits and sent them out to "pet" state banks. Uncontrolled land speculation followed, creating a bubble of prosperity. By 1835 the national debt was erased, thanks to tariffs and land sales. But the bubble burst during the administration of Martin Van Buren, Jackson's Vice President and handpicked successor. And debt returned.

A statesman with a sound business sense, Van Buren in general considered himself a Jeffersonian, favoring state over national legislation. But he approached individual issues in a practical fashion. Coming to office in 1837, he inherited the financial panic that burst over the country. During the short-lived panic, banks ceased trading currency for gold and silver; as a result, interest rates dropped and loans became easier to get. But with a bumper crop of cotton in 1839, prices collapsed and road and other building projects began defaulting on their debts. Foreign investors walked away. The resulting depression lasted until 1843. By then, Martin Van Buren had been voted out of office.

Van Buren's reaction to the financial crisis was not in keeping with the idea of the Jacksonians as caretakers of the common people. His policy was to worry first and foremost about the federal government: "The less government interferes with private pursuits the better for the general prosperity." And, in fact, the individual states could and did take measures to promote greater prosperity and economic growth.

The election of 1840 hinged not on Van Buren's fiscal policies, but rather on the Whig Party's shrewdly organized campaign strategy. Instead of choosing the popular but controversial orators, Daniel Webster or Henry Clay, they went—as the Democrats had with Jackson—with a military hero. General Harrison had defeated the Indians at Tippecanoe; his running mate, John Tyler, was a states' rights advocate and former Democrat and could thus appeal to both sides. In other words, the Whigs beat Van Buren not on the issues but on the strength of their ticket. By casting William Henry Harrison as a rustic man of the people and Martin Van Buren as a sophisticated insider, the Whigs cleverly turned the stereotypes inside out. Never mind the fact that Harrison was a well-educated son of a Virginia governor, and that he had no more familiarity with a log cabin than did Van Buren. Harrison won by a landslide. During his Inauguration he caught pneumonia; he died a month later, leaving John Tyler to complete his full, four-year term. ■

Alexis de Tocqueville

During Jackson's presidency, the French writer Alexis de Tocqueville made an extended visit to the United States. His perceptive account of the new nation, *Democracy in America*, analyzed American government and society as only an outsider could. During nine months from 1831 to 1832 he and fellow critic Gustave de Beaumont interviewed 250 people ranging from Chippewa Indians to President Jackson. One of Tocqueville's most important observations was that "in America, men are nearer equality than in any other country in the world." Education, intelligence, social standing, and wealth did not count for near as much in America as they did in Europe. "Such wealth," he wrote, "is not at all permanent; it is within reach of all."

De Tocqueville's 1835 classic *Democracy in America* depicts an idealized rural life, reflecting the book's spin on American society.

Of course, Tocqueville's generalizations were not entirely true, but he caught the essential optimism of the new democracy. Moreover, he understood that the American social structure was evolving, producing a large class of people who were "not exactly rich nor yet quite poor." As he put it, "The whole society seems to have turned into one middle class." As for the government's system of checks and balances, he noted that "the power vested in the American courts of justice of pronouncing a statute to be unconstitutional forms one of the most powerful barriers that have ever been devised against the tyranny of political assemblies."

Tocqueville's visit coincided with a period in which everything from manners to religion was becoming more democratized and less formal. Baptism, Methodism, and Presbyterianism were spreading with the western frontier, the first two in particular emphasizing an emotional rather than intellectual spiritualism, complete with shouting, singing, and personal conversion. And Democratic ideas were being promulgated as well by such writers as James Fenimore Cooper and Washington Irving. ■

Texas Joins the Union

1836–1848

THE TRANSCONTINENTAL Treaty of 1819 gave most of present-day Texas to Spain; in a few years the territory was part of Mexico. But by 1830 only a few thousand Mexicans lived there, sharing it with 20,000-odd white Americans and 2,000 slaves. And more on the way.

President John Quincy Adams had offered $1 million for Texas; Jackson upped the ante to $5 million. Mexico declined both offers. But it grew increasingly uneasy about the flood of American settlers. Most did not bother learning much Spanish; most were Protestant, even though Mexico required its immigrants to be Catholic. Mexico also had abolished slavery. The settlers neatly worked their way around the law by freeing their slaves, then having them sign on for lifetime indentures. Finally, Mexico outlawed further American settlement in Texas. But the Americans kept coming anyway, planting the fertile soil with cotton and raising homesteads.

Republic of Texas

With their rights restricted, the Texans bristled for independence. After a few skirmishes, rebellion

The southwestern U.S. expanded by leaps and bounds in the mid-19th century. Annexation of Texas added 390,000 square miles; territory acquired after Mexican War, 529,000 square miles; Gadsden Purchase, 30,000 square miles.

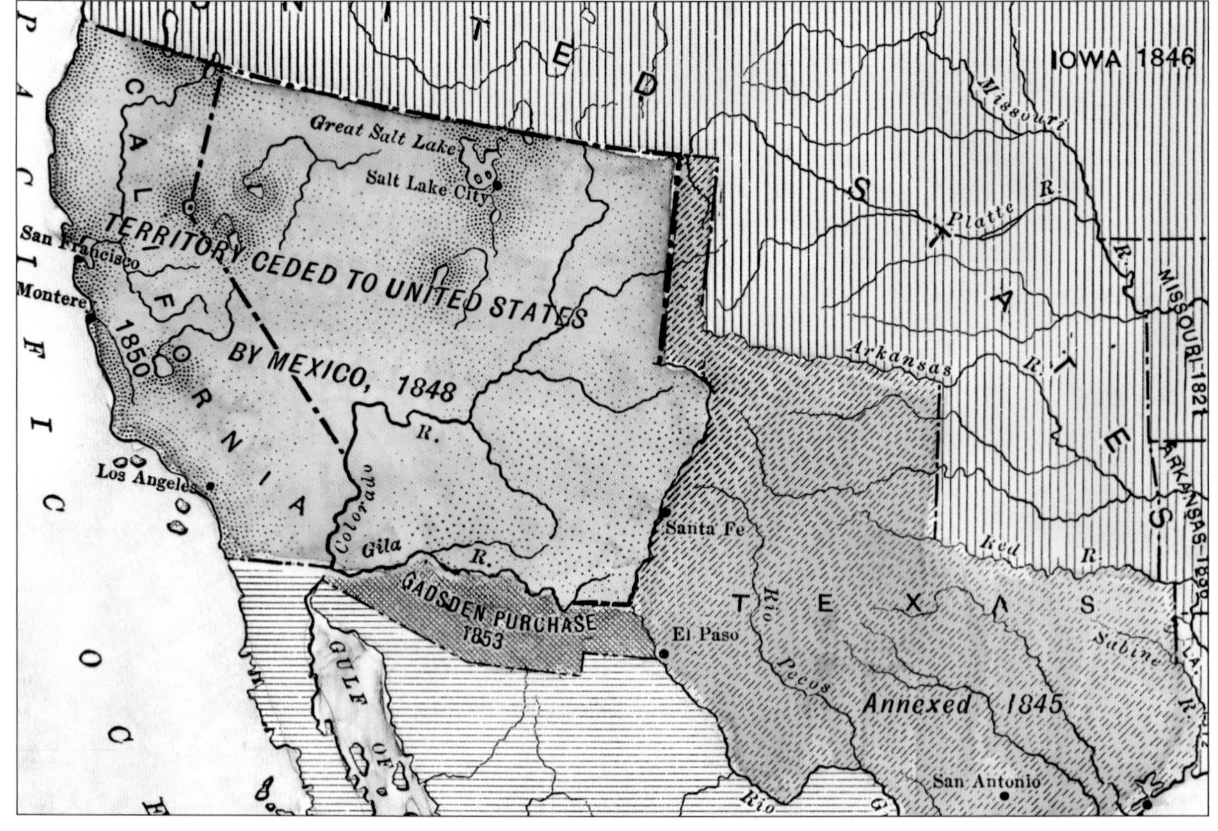

had broken out by 1835. Mexican President Antonio Lopez de Santa Anna and 4,000 troops marched north, arriving at San Antonio in February 1836. There, Colonel William B. Travis and about 150 men holed up in the Alamo, a former mission. After a 13-day siege, the Mexicans overwhelmed the Alamo, killing all its defenders. The slaughter further outraged the Texans and strengthened the movement for independence. Sam Houston, Indian fighter and former congressman and Tennessee governor, led the rebel army. At first, all Houston could do was retreat in front of Santa Anna's larger army, but on April 21, 1836, he attacked the Mexicans at the San Jacinto River, forcing them to retreat all the way back across the Rio Grande. In the fall Houston was elected president of the Republic of Texas.

The vast majority of Texans voted to join the Union. President Jackson, near the end of his term, was hesitant to stir up trouble with Mexico. On his final day in office he officially recognized the republic, but made no move to annex it. Nor did Van Buren. For several years, then, Texas was an independent nation. Britain was happy to import its cotton without having to pay American tariffs. The American South, on the other hand, was anxious about having a British-friendly neighbor that might outlaw slavery. John Tyler, President from 1841-45, was in favor of annexing Texas, and his secretary of state had a treaty in the works in early 1844 when he was killed by an exploding ship cannon.

Tyler made a political miscalculation when he appointed John C. Calhoun the new secretary of state. The South was already in favor of annexing Texas; appointing the South Carolina firebrand of states' rights caused anger in the North. The Senate voted against the treaty, and Texans stewed in resentment.

Young Hickory

The election of 1844 turned on the question of Texas statehood. Instead of the bungling incumbent Tyler, the Whigs nominated Henry Clay, who opposed expansion in general. Tyler considered running independently but was persuaded against it. The Democratic convention put forth Van Buren and Calhoun, but with neither able to marshal a two-thirds majority, the nomination went to dark horse James K. Polk, former speaker of the House and governor of Tennessee. Polk, "Young Hickory," was very much a Jacksonian; he opposed high tarrifs and the establishment of a new national bank. The Democratic platform called for Texas to be "reannexed" (even though it had never belonged to the United States) and for Oregon to be "reoccupied" (though it was held jointly by the United States and Britain). Polk vowed to serve only one term, thus not waste his energy campaigning for another; his slogan, "54-40 or Fight!" meant that he intended to claim the whole Oregon Territory up to that latitude.

Polk squeaked out a victory, handing Clay his second defeat (after the 1832 loss to Jackson). Congress immediately voted to

NOTABLE DATES

■ 1836
Republic of Texas is proclaimed by settlers outraged over taxes and restrictions on slavery imposed by Mexican President Santa Anna.

■ 1840
U.S. population reaches 17 million.

■ 1845
Texas, after repeatedly petitioning for annexation, is admitted to the Union as a slave state.

■ 1846
President Polk orders Gen. Zachary Taylor to take the disputed Texas territory; treaty with Britain sets Oregon Territory's northern boundary at 49th parallel (current northern boundary of Washington State).

■ 1847
Mexico City falls to Gen. Winfield Scott.

■ 1848
The Treaty of Guadalupe Hidalgo gives the U.S. claim to Texas, California, Arizona, New Mexico, Nevada, Utah, and part of Colorado.

accept Texas into the Union, and in December of 1845 Texas became a state.

The hard-working, goal-oriented, stiff-backed Polk then rolled up his sleeves and went after Oregon. As in Texas, Oregon's population of American settlers far outnumbered that of the other occupying nation—in this case Great Britain. A Massachusetts congressman, echoing the popular cry of the year, stated that it was "our manifest destiny to spread over this whole continent." In May 1846, Polk informed Britain that the joint occupation was no longer in effect. Britain decided to compromise, to pull back its Hudson's Bay Company base to Vancouver Island. Polk agreed to the 49th parallel as a border, with both nations having access to the Strait of Juan de Fuca. In June the Senate okayed the deal, and the United States had clear title all the way to the Pacfic.

The Mexican War

Meanwhile, back in Texas, not everybody was happy. Specifically, Mexico was not keen on the United States simply grabbing a large parcel of land and calling it a new state. Before Texas was declared a state, Polk had tried to buy it by cancelling $2 million worth of Mexican debts. Furthermore, he offered $30 million for part or all of California and New Mexico. Mexico needed the money, and should have seen the inevitable expansion of the United States into those territories. Instead, she chose to fight.

By March 1846, Gen. Zachary Taylor and some 4,000 soldiers were positioned on the north bank of the Rio Grande, opposite the town of Matamoros in extreme southern Texas. In late April, a Mexican force crossed the river and attacked. Polk could report to Congress that a state of war existed, and thus for the first time a President launched a war without the formal declaration of war required by the Constitution.

From the outset, the war went badly for the Mexicans. Poorly equipped and led, they suffered a humiliating defeat at Palo Alto against a smaller American force. Then, south of the Rio Grande, 1,700 Americans crushed a Mexican force of 7,500. Polk capably managed the war all the way from overall strategy down to the purchasing of mules. His plan was a three-part operation. The first order of business was to take over Texas and the northern provinces of Mexico; then he would seize California and New Mexico; and finally he would take Mexico City.

With Taylor carrying out the first part of the plan, settlers in the Sacramento Valley took the initiative in June 1846 and hoisted the "Bear Flag" of the republic of California. They were backed up by explorer John C. Fremont, who had taken time off from an expedition to attack the Mexicans at Monterey. A U.S. naval squadron then helped capture Monterey, and took San Francisco in July. By February 1847 the United States had gained control of nearly all of Mexico north of its capital. For the third phase of the war, Polk, suspicious of the political capital accruing to Zachary Taylor, deployed Gen. Winfield Scott, a veteran of the War of 1812. Tall, smart, and somewhat arrogant, Scott was a Whig with political ambitions of his own, but Congress twisted Polk's arm to choose him.

Treaty of Guadalupe Hidalgo

Scott landed his army of 10,000 just south of Veracruz, and in March 1847 began laying siege. Within three weeks the city had fallen and the Americans began marching west toward Mexico City. Decisive victories against larger forces at Cerro Gorda and Puebla opened the way to the capital. On the outskirts of the city, Scott's army suffered about 1,000 casualties, while inflicting 4,000 and taking 3,000 prisoners. Finally, in mid-September, Scott pounded his way into the city.

Throughout the campaign the Americans had been far outnumbered yet had scored thorough victories and taken far fewer casualties. But even though they were completely whipped, the Mexicans did not accept defeat easily. President Polk dispatched an able peace commissioner by the name of Nicholas P. Trist, chief clerk at the State Department. Somewhat pompous, Trist was married to a granddaughter of Thomas Jefferson and had served as a secretary to Andrew Jackson; having acted as consul in Havana, he was fluent in Spanish.

Trist had been with Scott since May and the two had not hit it off. To Scott it was a "personal dishonor" to take orders from what he thought of as a State Department lackey, whose idea of communication was to send Scott a 30-page letter expounding upon the purpose of the campaign. But Scott was big enough to realize that cooperation would prove to be of mutual benefit; when Trist got sick, Scott made amends by sending him a jar of guava marmalade—and the gesture did much to advance the cause of national expansion. Because of the collapsing Mexican government, though, Trist was unable to begin negotiations until January 1848.

Negotiations dragged on for months. At one point Polk considered demanding more territory for less money, but Trist foresaw an imminent collapse of the Mexican government and decided to proceed on his own before no one was left to treaty with. The Treaty of Guadalupe Hidalgo agreed on the Rio Grande as a boundary, with Mexico ceding California and New Mexico, a territory including current Arizona, Nevada, Utah, and part of Colorado. The United States agreed to pay $15 million and to assume $3.25 million of American citizens' claims against Mexico. When Polk discovered that Trist had disobeyed him, he fired him and ordered him arrested. Yet with the growing anti-war sentiment in the North, Polk had to submit the treaty to Congress, which ratified it 38 to 14. For very little expense, the United States had acquired a vast amount of new land. In January 1848, while peace negotiations were in progress, gold was discovered in the Sacramento Valley. Soon fortune seekers and settlers by the thousands were pouring into the newly acquired territory. ■

The Alamo

The total defeat of Americans defending the Alamo holds a special place in American history as much for its story as for its impetus in uniting Texans against Mexican authority. Established in 1718, the Roman Catholic mission was named for the surrounding cottonwood trees. When General Santa Anna marched north to San Antonio in early 1836 to put down a nascent rebellion, about 150 men under Colonel William Barret Travis took cover in the Alamo. Their hope was to defend the city against an army of 4,000. Travis sent for help, with the declaration, "I shall never surrender or retreat."

Mexican troops overwhelm the Alamo in March 1836; the small holding force was annihilated.

A small force of Texans broke through the Mexican lines, upping the Alamo's numbers to 189. A larger relief unit of about 400 never made it to San Antonio. The Mexicans, meanwhile, had begun laying siege to the Alamo on February 23. By March 5, the Texans' position was dire. They were nearly out of ammunition. Among the fighters were noted frontiersmen Davy Crockett and James Bowie. The 50-year-old Davy Crockett had fought Indians with Jackson and served in the U.S. House of Representatives from Tennessee.

The firepower coming from the Alamo was deadly, but when it died out the Mexicans stormed the walls. On March 6, the carnage began. The Texans used their guns as clubs, but to no avail. No prisoners were taken. The only survivors were an officer's wife, her baby and nurse, and a slave. The victors poured oil on the dead and burned them.

Rallying his troops with the cry, "Remember the Alamo," Sam Houston turned the tables on the Mexicans at the Battle of San Jacinto in April. His small force made a surprise attack during siesta time and in 18 minutes destroyed a detachment of 1,200. The next day he caught Santa Anna and made him sign a treaty giving Texas its independence. ■

Indian Removals

1830–1850

BETWEEN ABOUT 1830 AND 1850 an estimated 100,000 Choctaws, Creeks, Chickasaws, Cherokees, and Seminoles were forced from their homelands to the new "Indian Territory" beyond the Mississippi. Their massive eviction is one of the sadder chapters in American history, the price exacted by a seemingly endless stream of land-hungry white settlers. President Andrew Jackson's Indian Removal Act of 1830 ultimately added 100 million acres of land to the public domain.

While most Indians went peacefully, albeit reluctantly, the Seminoles fought back. In 1835 U.S. troops arrived in Florida after a three-year grace period had run out. No Seminoles had left during that period. Led by cunning chief Osceola, the Seminoles ambushed an Army unit north of present-day Tampa. In late 1837 the Army used a truce flag to lure Osceola into a camp near St. Augustine. He was captured and sent to prison at Fort Moultrie in Charleston, where he died the following year. Four years later the Seminole quit fighting; about 3,000 Indians and blacks were sent to Oklahoma, while a few hundred disappeared into the Everglades.

The Creeks, Chickasaws, and Choctaws migrated voluntarily. Between 1831 and 1833, about 15,000 Choctaws made the long trek from Mississippi and western Alabama to the Indian territory west of Arkansas. But the Cherokees were a different story. They held out until the deadline for leaving had come and gone, trying to prove that they could adapt to white culture. Their 800-mile journey in the fall and winter of 1838-39 has become known as the Trail of Tears.

Forced to leave their homes, Cherokee men, women, and children trekked along the aptly named Trail of Tears. "Long time we travel on way to new land, many days pass and people die very much," one survivor recalled.

Trail of Tears

At the time of the American Revolution, Cherokee territory included most of Tennessee, Georgia, and Kentucky—and parts of South Carolina, Virginia, West Virginia, Mississippi, and Alabama. By 1820, after dozens of treaties, their land was down to ten percent of its original size. The state of Georgia declared that it would secede from the Union if all Indians in the South were not relocated west of the Mississippi. The state then began holding lotteries to distribute Cherokee land to white newcomers.

The Cherokee at first tried to resist. By 1830, they had their own newspaper, printed in both English and a written form of Cherokee developed in 1820s by Sequoyah; many of them were partially white and lived in small houses with white picket fences; some operated plantations and even owned slaves. They took the case to the U.S. courts. Delivering a speech in New York in 1832, Cherokee spokesman John Ridge said, "You asked us to throw off the hunter and warrior state—we did so. You asked us to form a republican government—we did so. You asked us to cultivate the earth and learn the mechanical arts—we did so. You asked us to cast away our idols and worship your God—we did so."

That same year, the Supreme Court ruled that Georgia's laws against the Cherokee were unconstitutional. Yet Jackson refused to enforce the ruling of the highest court in the land, maintaining that it was "absurd" to think that a sovereign nation could operate independently within the United States.

In 1835, 20 Cherokees signed a treaty at New Echota, Georgia, agreeing their nation would move in exchange for five million dollars. The U.S. Congress ratified it by one vote. But the vast majority of Cherokees stayed put. Finally in May 1838, soldiers began going door to door. Individuals were given no time to collect possessions or locate family members; those who resisted were beaten or put in chains; the old and infirm were pushed out at bayonet point; women were molested. Wrote one soldier: "I fought through the Civil War and have seen men . . . slaughtered by the thousands, but the Cherokee removal was the cruelest work I ever knew."

More than 16,000 Cherokees were herded into stockades—disease-ridden camps that claimed many lives. Some were moved west in the summer, but drought and sickness took a toll. Most were allowed to wait until fall. Heavy rains slowed their progress, and then came a bitter winter. Ice floes on the Mississippi bogged down some groups for weeks. Women tried to gather edible plants from the forest to supplement rations of white flour and old salt pork, yet many plants were unfamiliar. Deaths from malnutrition and exposure were common. Most families lost at least one member. In all, some 4,000 Cherokees died—nearly a fifth of their entire population. ■

Indians' Tragic Trail

Number of southeastern Indians removed in the 1830s: 100,000

Number of treaties signed by tribes during the Indian removal period: 70

Number of acres added to public domain: 100,000,000

Number of Cherokee forced out: 16,000

Number who died on the Trail of Tears: 4,000

NOTABLE DATES

■ **1830**
Indian Removal Act is signed by President Jackson.

■ **1832**
The Black Hawk War forces the Sauk and Fox Indians of Illinois and Wisconsin west of the Mississippi.

■ **1835**
Under chief Osceola, the Seminoles begin attacking U.S. forces in resistance to removal.

■ **1838**
Cherokee embark on the Trail of Tears to Oklahoma.

■ **1842**
Seminole War ends; Seminoles are sent to Oklahoma.

Westward Expansion

1821–1853

DURING THE SECOND QUARTER of the 19th century, the United States bulged westward across North America to the Pacific Ocean. With a flood of settlers and new immigrants in search of open land, Texas was added to the Union in 1845, the Oregon Territory in 1846, the Mexican Southwest in 1848, and the Gadsden Purchase in 1853—a total of 869 million acres in eight years. This amazing acquisition—a stunning 46 percent of the entire area of the country at that time—completed the outlines of the continental United States, excluding Alaska.

The final piece of the puzzle, the Gadsden Purchase gave the United States a strip of land south of the Gila River that provided a workable railroad route to the Pacific Ocean. James Gadsden, United States minister to Mexico and railroad entrepreneur, negotiated the purchase with Mexican President Antonio Lopez de Santa Anna,

Forty-niners man a long tom, or sluice box, in the gold fields of California around mid-century. The rush began when flakes of precious metal were found in the tailrace of John Sutter's mill in 1848.

with the United States paying, in the end, $10 million for the 29,640-square-mile parcel. Only five years earlier, at the conclusion of the Mexican War, the United States had paid Mexico the equivalent of $18 million for an area 18 times larger. Such were the fortunes of war. Especially unpopular among the Mexican population, the selling of the Gadsden area led to President Santa Anna's banishment two years later. It was unpopular, too, with abolitionists in the United States Senate, who suspected the consequent addition to slaveholding territory as a ploy by pro-slavers to expand the slave system. Though its outcome was undoubtedly a boon to the nation's economy—the new territory not only facilitated a southern railroad route to the Pacific, it also opened up new opportunities for exploiting the region's mineral wealth—the Gadsden Purchase also added fuel to the fire of sectional conflict that was to result in the full-scale conflagration of the Civil War.

Santa Fe and Oregon Trails

Several well-trod trails etched the American West, bringing commerce and settlement. One of the first, the Santa Fe Trail, was a trade route started in 1821, as Mexico acquired independence from Spain and lifted the trade sanctions that had prohibited United States traders from selling goods in New Mexico. Soon big Conestoga wagons pulled by parades of oxen were making their way across 800 miles of prairie and plains from Independence, Missouri, to Santa Fe, New Mexico, on a regular basis. By 1835 the total value of the Santa Fe Trail trade was $140,000; in 1860 it was $3.5 million, or about $53 million in today's dollars. From Mexico came the raw goods the United States needed—silver, wool, furs, mules; going the other way were goods manufactured in the United States—everything from printed cotton and playing cards to tools and mirrors.

Anything could occur on that eight-week wagon journey—wild storms, flooded rivers, buffalo stampedes, dry heat that shrank wooden wheels from their iron rims, and Indian attacks. These adventures were interspersed among long days of dust, mud, and mosquitoes. When the railroad pushed into Santa Fe in 1880, the trail became obsolete.

The famous Oregon Trail carried one of the most extensive migrations in peacetime history: some 500,000 people moving more than 2,000 miles from 1841 to 1869. In 1841 a group of 500 people started out together from Independence, Missouri. Unorganized, they had no guide and no clue about the route; most eventually turned back, although a few struggled on to California and about 30 made it to Oregon.

Over the ensuing years many would begin with a common destination, then, after crossing the Continental Divide in western Wyoming, some would head to Oregon, others to California. Trail rumors could change minds overnight—farming was better in Oregon, or opportunities were wider in California. In any event, what had started as an exercise in

NOTABLE DATES

■ 1821
Trader William Becknell arrives in Santa Fe, initiating the Santa Fe Trail.

■ 1836
Narcissa Whitman becomes the first white woman to cross the Plains; she and other missionaries are killed in 1847 by Indians near Fort Walla Walla in present-day Washington.

■ 1841
The first party of settlers reaches California and Oregon.

■ 1843
Nearly 1,000 pioneers make the trip from Missouri to Oregon.

■ 1848
Gold is discovered at Sutter's Mill inCalifornia, precipitating a rush of immigrants.

■ 1850
California becomes a state.

■ 1851
Irish immigration peaks at 221,253.

■ 1853
The Gadsden Purchase rounds out the U.S. boundaries in the lower 48 states; the treaty with Mexico is ratified in 1854.

navigation along old Indian and trapper routes grew to a veritable highway of prairie schooners, complete with traffic jams at river crossings. In 1850 some 65,000 people used the trail, primarily heading out during a 45-day period in late spring that allowed them to be over the mountains before the first snow.

Manifest Destiny

The reasons so many travelers were willing to leave their homes and risk the trail were many. A financial depression convinced many to sell their farms and try their luck out West. To missionaries, western Indians were fertile soil for sowing God's word. Some went for the adventure, with no intention of staying. And over this whole movement hovered the notion that it was America's destiny to extend from the Atlantic to the Pacific. In 1845 New York journalist John O'Sullivan expressed the spirit of divine providence that Americans felt about their expanding nation. It was, he wrote, "our *manifest destiny* to overspread the continent allotted by Providence for the free development of our yearly multiplying millions."

The Oregon Trail followed the Kansas River west of Missouri, then the muddy Platte, the North Platte, and the Sweetwater River out beyond Fort Laramie to the Rocky Mountains. The emigrants crossed the Continental Divide about halfway along the trek through South Pass—a mere 7,550 feet in elevation, slipping between 13,000-foot peaks. They turned left to Fort Bridger, in Wyoming, and northwest to the Snake River Valley. The final pitch of the five-month-long ordeal was a treacherous ride down the Columbia River or an arduous climb around Mount Hood, with wagons lowered over steep places by ropesand drags.

Six to ten percent of the pioneers—roughly ten per mile—died on the way, often from disease or accidents. Though not as dangerous as advertised, Indians did kill several hundred of the overlanders. While Indians saw the first few wagon trains as curiosities, they considered succeeding hordes a threat—emigrants took game and forage, and spread disease andsuspicion. Still, more Indians were killed by pioneers than vice versa. In sum, the trip overland was, according to one historian, a "remorseless, unending, weather-scoured, nerve-rasping plod on and on and on and on, foot by aching foot." As soon as they arrived in their promised land, the pioneers had plenty more hard work ahead of them.

Trail Ways

Length of Santa Fe Trail: 800 miles

Duration of trip: 8 weeks

Average length of trek from Missouri to Oregon: 2,000 miles

Duration of trip: 5 months

Number of Oregon Trail travelers in 1841-69: 500,000

Number of overlanders to California in 1848-50: 200,000

Territory added to the U.S. in 1845-53: 869 million acres, or 1.36 million square miles

Total U.S. territory by 1853: 3 million square miles

In southwestern Wyoming, those who were headed for Oregon branched to the right, those headed for California to the left. Along the trail into California, there were nearly 20 cutoffs and alternate routes, chosen according to trail conditions and depending on one's ultimate destination. Prior to 1848 most people went to California for the good climate and soil, as they did to Oregon. Afterwards came the gold rush—and then what really pounded the trail into dust were the wagons and the boots of the gold seekers.

California Bound

One day in January 1848 in the Sacramento Valley east of San Francisco, sawmill foreman James W. Marshall noticed some yellow flakes in a millrace along the American River. He tested them and found that they were pure gold. Gold had been discovered before in California, but this discovery started a stampede. And for good reason—$200 million was extracted in four years. By the end of 1849, as many as 80,000 "Forty-niners" had left friends, families, and half-plowed fields to pan, sift, or mine for California gold or, better yet, to establish a gold claim. For many, the gold rush was proof positive of the righteousness of manifest destiny. Those with the fare booked passage on steam or clipper ships, pounded around storm-tossed Cape Horn, and put ashore in San Francisco after three or four months. But the majority went by land. From 1848 through the 1850s, more than 200,000 journeyed overland to California.

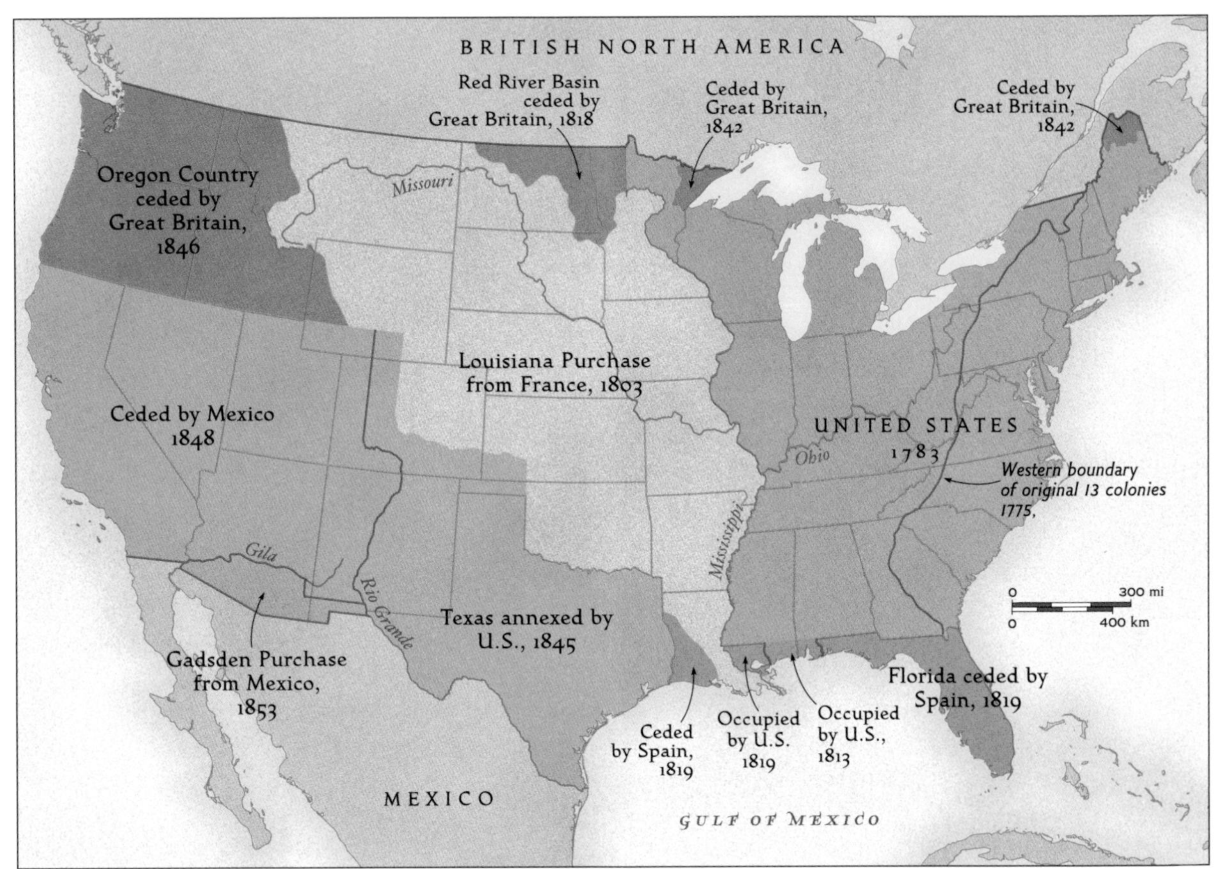

With the 1840s acquisition of the Oregon Country and California, the U.S. owned a swath of land from the Atlantic to the Pacific. Miners and settlers pushing into these new territories gave rise to the idea of America's manifest destiny.

The first part of the forty-niners' journey took them across the length of Nebraska, from the tall-grass prairies to the plains. Then on they went to the broken-up lands of the high plains, counting off one landmark after another—Chimney Rock, Soctts Bluff, Fort Laramie, and Register Cliff. At Independence Rock in what is now central Wyoming, the travelers stopped to carve their names or paint them in wagon tar. They were on schedule if they arrived on or around July 4, the day that some members of an 1830 wagon train named the granite slab while celebrating the nation's birthday.

After a quick jog into Idaho, California-bound pioneers veered off the Oregon Trail and began to cross the hellish deserts of the Great Basin, a high-elevation land of salt faults and dead-end streams between the Rockies and the Sierra Nevada. It was here that many realized there was no easy way to easy street, that their El Dorado was not waiting for them at the end of a rainbow. Getting over the Sierra Nevadas before snowfall meant being in North America's largest desert at the worst possible time—in the scorching heat of August.

Entering present-day Nevada, the trail dropped down to the curving Humboldt River, the pioneers' lifeline in the desert. But it was hardly a rushing source of clear water and lush banks. The river grew smaller as it went downstream, finally disappearing altogether in the Humboldt Sink. Its water often was a thin gruel of warm brackish mud. Local springs were either scalding hot or so alkaline they were poisonous. What little grass grew along the trail that wasn't dried by the summer sun was sheathed in salt crystals. At night it was so cold water would freeze; during the day the sun would bake the ground. A powder-fine dust, kicked up by the animals

The Donner Party

"Westward ho! Who wants to go to California without costing them anything?" began an ad placed by George Donner for ox-team drivers. The cost, he found, could be everything. The Donner party of 1846 was the last wagon train of the season. To speed things up they unwisely took advice from a letter written by a man no one had even heard of, thus wasting precious weeks hacking a road through the mountains of Utah in a vain attempt to save time, livestock, and their possessions. Exhausted, the group, which contained people mostly under the age of 20, disintegrated into a bickering, leaderless bunch of families.

Bad luck played a part too. Winter came early to the Sierras, penning the Donners on the east side of the mountains in late October. Drifts up to 20 feet high plagued the party—the sort of drifts that would not be seen in the area again for 100 years. Timing was everything.

"Never take no cutoffs, and hurry along as fast as you can," wrote 13-year-old Donner party member Virginia Reed in a letter. What she endured beggars description. Of the 91 people that started together, 42 succumbed to starvation and exposure, their bodies becoming food for the survivors. Along Alder Creek, Tamsen Donner stayed with her dying husband, refusing to leave with rescue parties. When they returned in the spring, she was dead.

Yet if the Donner saga of 1846 was a cautionary story, it was not enough to stop the legions from coming. They kept pouring into the Sierra foothills, the land of golden dreams. ■

A stagecoach embarks for California. So attractive was the lure of the West that no stories of hardship and death could stop the tide of human traffic.

and wagon wheels, coated every crevice of clothing and skin. The mules and oxen, desperate for water, would sometimes stampede into the wasteland where they would die. Other times they simply dropped dead in their harnesses. One traveler counted 163 dead oxen, mules, and horses in just a 16-mile stretch.

The number of journals written by one-time authors indicates that these migrants knew they were part of something bigger than themselves and their quest for riches, that they were swept up in a major historical movement. One traveler wrote, "It will be received as a legend on the borderland of myth." Most of the newcomers did not expect to stay. But once they were there, they discovered that the true riches of the Sacramento Valley were to be found in planting instead of panning, and so they put down roots. The farmers, ranchers, and merchants were the ones who struck pay dirt, and on their sturdy shoulders the golden state was built. Even though the gold rush did not peak until 1852, the momentum of foot traffic and settlement helped to hasten the statehood of California; only two years after being acquired from Mexico in 1848, it was admitted to the Union as the 31st state.

The Saints

Another major western migratory movement was that of the Mormons. Of the many religious groups to spring up in 19th-century America, the most successful was the Church of Jesus Christ of Latter-Day Saints (LDS),

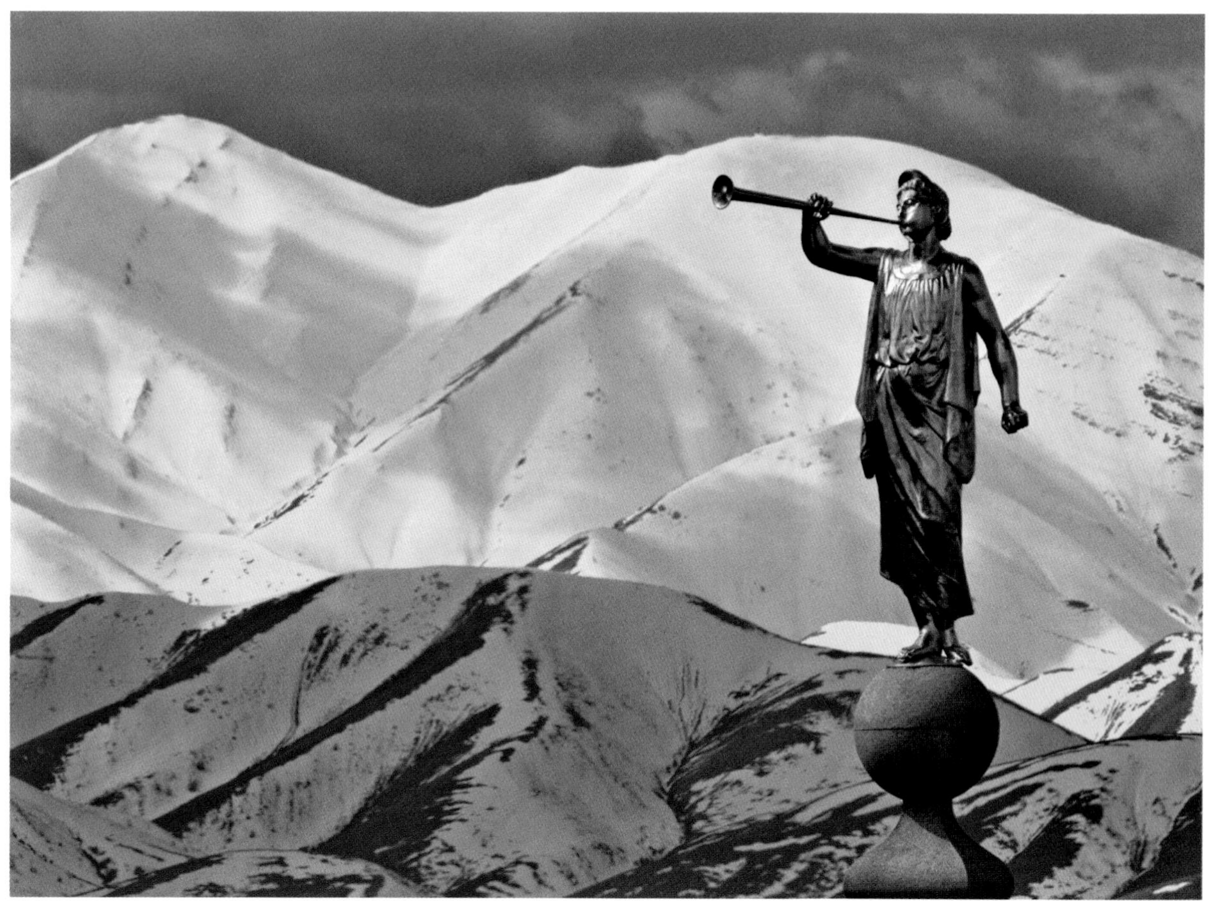

The angel Moroni trumpets atop the Mormon Temple in Salt Lake City, Utah; Moroni revealed the sacred Book of Mormon to Joseph Smith in 1827.

or the Mormons. Founded in 1830 by 25-year-old leader Joseph Smith, the LDS moved by stages from New York State to Nauvoo, Illinois, where in 1844 Smith was assassinated by an angry mob. An expanding church-state of industrious zealots, led by polygamous men who organized their own milita, was more than the provincial town could bear. The Mormons knew it was time to move west. Their new leader, Brigham Young, had the blue-chip management style to organize and motivate 70,000 willing, but untested, followers and get them across the Great Plains and the Rockies to the fertile valleys of the Great Salt Lake.

They set up a staging area north of present-day Omaha, Nebraska, and in 1847 they began heading west in companies of up to about a hundred people. Much of their route, until Fort Bridger in southwestern Wyoming, followed the Oregon Trail, but on the opposite side of the river. This self-imposed segregation was primarily to avoid hate mongers. The most organized of the migratory movements, the Mormons set up way stations to help later companies, invented an odometer to click off the precise distances, and even published a guidebook with the impressive title, *The Latter-Day Saints' Emigrants' Guide: Being a Table of Distances, showing all the springs, creeks, rivers, hills, mountains, camping places, and all other notable places from Council Bluffs to the Valley of the Great Salt Lake*. For Mormons and non-Mormons alike, it proved to be one of the most useful and comforting books on the arduous trail. Until railroad tracks spanned the continent with the completion of the transcontinental railroad in 1869, the trail to their Utah utopia was for Mormons a rite of passage. ■

WORLD SURVEY

1803–1853

WHILE THE UNITED States was spreading out across the continent, the forces of imperialism, industrialization, and independence continued to sweep the globe, with some countries gaining ground and others losing it. Imperialism brought the world closer, but proved deeply disruptive for many native peoples.

Europe

The chaos following the French Revolution ended when Napoleon rose to power. In 1804 he became emperor with the consent of the French people, who approved him as their monarch by a vote of 3,572,329 to 2,569. His Napoleonic Code promised all male citizens equality before the law; he instituted public education and reformed the tax system. But he dispensed with other democratic ideals fostered during the revolution, including freedom of expression and representative government. By 1812, Napoleon's armies had taken over most of western Europe, including all of Italy and much of Germany. His invasion of Russia in 1812 was a disaster—he lost some 500,000 troops to battle, starvation, and exposure. Three years later he was finished off by allied powers at the Battle of Waterloo in Belgium.

At the Congress of Vienna in 1814 and 1815, European leaders attempted to restore monarchies toppled by Napoleon. But popular uprisings, ignited by the spirit of the French Revolution, made these restorations short-lived. Democratic revolutions in Italy and Spain in 1820, Greece in 1821, and Poland, Belgium, and France in the early 1830s began replacing kings with constitutions.

Asia

European colonialism continued to spread through Asia in the early 1800s. European powers sought colonies as cheap sources of raw materials and markets for manufactured goods; India served Britain in both respects and was thus the jewel in Britain's crown. Among goods imported by India was British cloth, which overran India's textile trade. Among the items Britain exported from India was opium. The British introduced it to China, where millions grew addicted to it. Britain twice went to war with China in the mid-1800s when authorities there tried to halt the flow of opium. British forces took control of parts of Burma in 1824 to safeguard India and later colonized Malaya for the same reason. In 1842 China opened its ports to limited trade with Great Britain, and in 1844 began trading with France and the United States.

Imperialists helped modernize India and other countries by introducing technologies such as steam power and railroads, but they kept those nations economically dependent on Europe and thwarted progress toward economic and political self-determination. After decades of capitalist involvement, primarily through the East India Company, Great Britain quashed a violent uprising and finally took formal control of India in 1858. The East India Company disbanded, and subsequently the British government ruled India directly.

Japan offered less opportunity for trade than India or China, and for many years Western countries left it alone. But by the mid-1800s more American ships were plying the Pacific; Japan's potential value as a supply and repair base became obvious. In 1853 Commodore Matthew Perry arrived in Tokyo Bay with four steam-powered warships and presented a request that Japan open its ports to U.S. trade. Threat of force was clear. When

Perry returned the next year, Japan signed a treaty of cooperation.

■ Africa

In the 1800s the transatlantic slave trade ended. Western public opinion had turned against slavery, and it was not suited to modern industrial economies. In 1807 the British government outlawed buying and selling slaves, and in 1833 abolished slavery itself in the British Empire. Other powers followed suit. Western explorers, missionaries, and traders spread into Africa seeking geographic and scientific knowledge, Christian converts, and potential profits. To the south, white settlements were spreading inland as well.

■ Latin America

Struggles for independence swept Latin America after 1800, triggered by the decline of Spanish power. Spain reached the height of its wealth and influence in the 16th century. Subsequently, the Spanish -American empire became less rewarding. Colonizing North American provinces such as Florida and New Mexico became a drain on the royal treasury.

By 1800 Spain's position in Europe had deteriorated; King Charles IV was virtually a pawn of Napoleon. In 1808, when Charles was forced to abdicate in favor of his son Ferdinand VII, Napoleon stepped in and put his brother, Joseph, on the throne. Spaniards rebelled, joining neighboring Portugal in a guerrilla war against Napoleon that lasted until he abdicated as emperor of France in 1814.

The collapse of the Spanish monarchy in 1808 opened the floodgates of rebellion in Latin America. One country after another broke away until only Cuba and Puerto Rico remained under Spanish control. The independence movement was dominated by two remarkable freedom fighters—Simon Bolivar (*El Libertador*) and José de San Martín. Bolivar's campaign began in his native Venezuela and spread south, while San Martín launched his revolution in Argentina and moved north. Their paths converged in Peru, where Bolivar took control. ■

Present-day country boundaries and names are shown.

A DIVIDED NATION 1817–1877

WITH THE NATION NOT YET 50 YEARS OLD, THE INSTITUTION OF SLAVERY BEGAN driving a wedge between North and South. As the country expanded west, each prospective state became the centerpiece of debate on the issue of slavery. Should the territories and new states allow slavery? The Missouri Compromise of 1820 kept the balance of free and slave states. The Compromise of 1850 attempted to appease both sides by allowing "popular sovereignty" in the territories, in effect putting the decision off to a later time. The Supreme Court became involved, ruling in the Dred Scott case in 1857 that Congress could not ban slavery from the territories. Meanwhile, abolitionists grew increasingly outraged. In reaction, southern firebrands shot back with equal invective. In 1860 the Democratic Party ruptured across sectional lines, and the final ties holding the nation were severed. War broke out in South Carolina and spread into Virginia and other states. With the South in a defensive posture, the first two years swung in its favor. But after the Battle of Gettysburg and the fall of Vicksburg in July 1863, the North and its industrial might began overcoming the impoverished South. The assassination of President Lincoln at war's end in 1865 deepened the nation's tragedy, leaving the wounded country without direction. The Reconstruction period began the slow process of reuniting South with North and enfranchising millions of freed slaves. ■

The Union entered the war with the support of the free states and control of the border states; most major battles were fought in the South.

■ **1820**
The Missouri Compromise temporarily resolves the issue of slavery in the western territories.

■ **1831**
British scientist Michael Faraday harnesses electromagnetism by inventing the dynamo, or electrical generator.

■ **1850**
The Compromise of 1850 admits California as a free state while allowing other western territories to decide the issue of slavery for themselves.

■ **1860**
Abraham Lincoln is elected President, prompting southern states to secede.

■ **1861**
The Civil War begins when southern forces fire on federal troops at Fort Sumter, in Charleston Harbor.

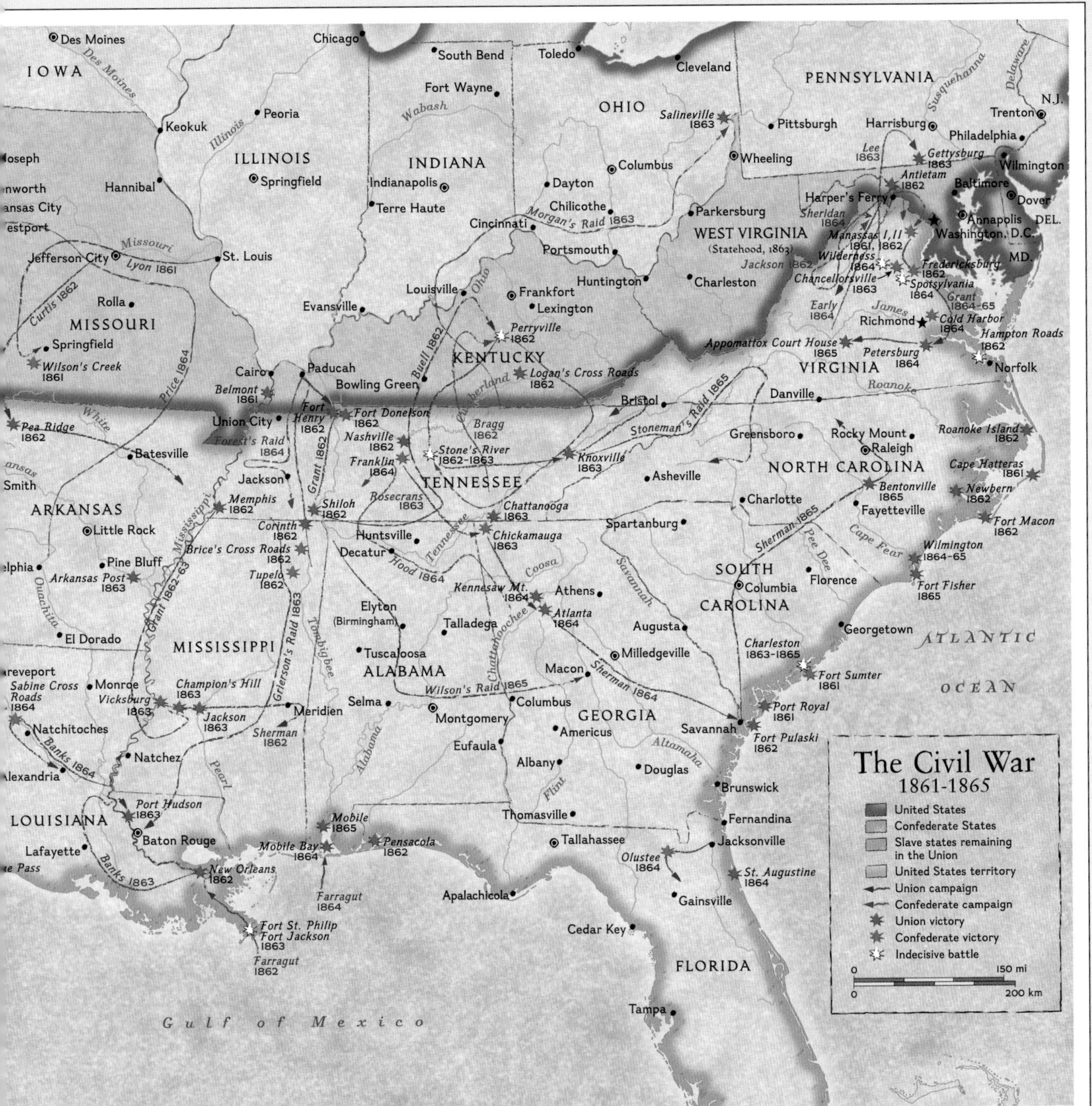

■ **1863**
The decisive Battle of Gettysburg ends July 3 in a Union victory, forcing Robert E. Lee's Confederates out of the North. The following day Vicksburg falls to Ulysses S. Grant and the Mississippi is again in Union hands.

■ **1865**
Lee surrenders to Grant at Appomattox, Virginia, on April 9. Lincoln is assassinated five days later.

■ **1867**
Congressional representatives favoring radical reconstruction of the South impeach Johnson but fail to convict him.

■ **1868**
Ulysses S. Grant is elected to succeed Andrew Johnson as President.

Missouri Compromise

1817–1821

Before 1819 the issue of slavery caused little national friction. The federal government had outlawed importation of slaves in 1808, though some illegal trade continued. But with the country's expansion, a sectional division took shape—the North opposing slavery, the South in favor. With a boom in cotton in the early 1800s, the South became even more dependent on slavery. Eli Whitney's cotton gin of 1793 made removing the seeds so easy that a slave could clean 50 times that done by hand. Annual cotton rose from 3,000 bales in 1790 to more than 400,000 in the early 1820s.

By 1819 there were 22 states, equally divided between slave and free. As a slave state was added, it was balanced by the addition of a free state, thus preserving a balance in the Senate. Of the original 13 states, six permitted slavery—Delaware, Virginia, Maryland, North Carolina, South Carolina, and Georgia. Of new states, Kentucky, Tennessee, Louisiana, Mississippi, and Alabama permitted slavery. Seven original states did not permit slavery—New Hampshire, Massachusetts, Rhode Island, Connecticut, New York, Pennsylvania, and New Jersey. Vermont, Ohio, Indiana, and Illinois were free states. Western territories tended to side with the South—many settlers were from the South, and much of the West's produce was marketed to plantations.

A map of the U S. shows free and slave states and territories after the 1820 Missouri Compromise. Slavery's spread westward became political dynamite in succeeding decades.

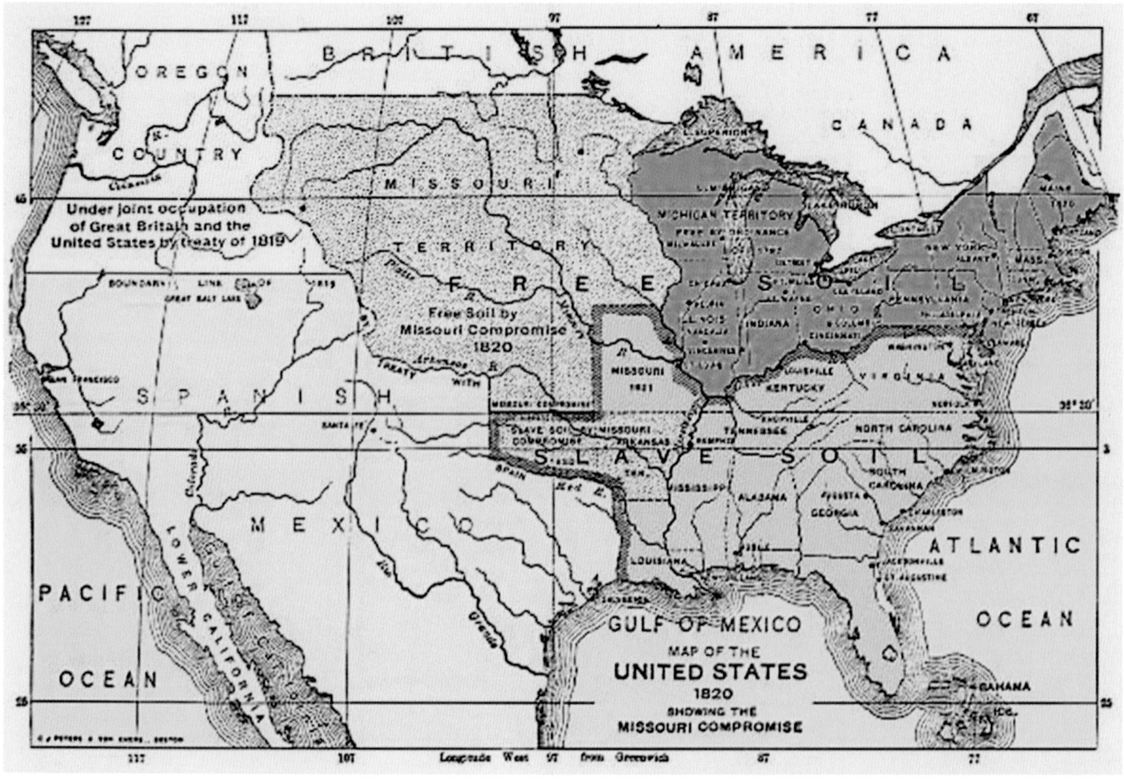

Jefferson Predicts

In a letter dated April 22,1820, the 77-year-old Jefferson wrote of the Missouri Compromise:

> "But this momentous question, like a firebell in the night awakened and filled me with terror. I considered it the knell of the Union. . . . It is hushed, indeed, for the moment. But this is a reprieve only, not a final sentence. A geographical line, coinciding with a marked principle, moral and political, once conceived and held up to the angry passions of men, will never be obliterated; and every new irritation will mark it deeper and deeper."

In 1817, Missouri requested admission to the Union. Many of her 60,000 citizens were southern slaveholders who had settled in the Arkansas and Missouri River Valleys. The Ohio River and Mason and Dixon's line defining the southern border of Pennsylvania had separated free from slave states. Bordering on both free and slave states, Missouri became a thorny question. In 1819 New York congressman James Tallmadge proposed an amendent to the bill allowing Missouri statehood, and a spirited debate followed. The amendment would prohibit more slaves from entering the state, and would grant freedom to slaves born in Missouri once they reached age 25. Dominated by northern representatives, the House passed the amendment; the Senate rejected it.

When Congress reconvened in December 1819, the Missouri issue surfaced immediately. Heated debate ensued. Instead of questioning the morality of slavery, the debate focused on the balance of representation in Congress. Northerners complained that the influx of slaves into Missouri would increase its population enough to give the South an unfair advantage.

The Wolf by the Ears

When Maine applied for statehood in 1820, the Missouri Compromise was proposed by Illinois senator Jesse B. Thomas. Maine would be admitted as a free state, Missouri as a slave state. Slavery would be forever banned in the Louisiana Purchase north of latitude 36° 30', the westward extension of Missouri's southern boundary. Despite the lack of territory south of this line, Southerners accepted this solution, while Northerners thought lands north and west of Missouri—now carpeted in grain fields—worthless prairie.

Before being admitted to the Union, Missouri submitted a constitution to Congress for approval. In violation of the U.S. Constitution, it barred free blacks from entering the state, though once in they were supposed to be treated as full citizens. Thus Congress neatly danced around the issue of slavery, admitting Missouri to the Union in 1821. And the Union went teetering on. "We have the wolf by the ears," wrote Thomas Jefferson a month later "and we can neither safely hold him, nor safely let him go." Secretary of State John Quincy Adams foresaw the compromise as "the title page to a great tragic volume." ■

NOTABLE DATES

■ 1817
Missouri petitions for statehood.

■ 1819
The Tallmadge amendment to the Missouri Enabling Act stirs controversy by outlining a process for eventual emancipation in the new state.

■ 1820
The Missouri Compromise bans slavery in the Louisiana Purchase lands above latitude 36° 30', excepting Missouri; Maine is admitted to the Union as a free state.

■ 1821
Henry Clay works out another compromise to allow Missouri to ban free blacks in violation of the Constitution, and Missouri becomes a state.

Road to War

1822–1860

The importation of new slaves swelled in anticipation of the 1808 ban, and as northern opposition to slavery grew more vocal southern slavery became more firmly entrenched and justified as an economic institution. Slavery was defended on the grounds that it provided for workers in old age and infirmity, exempted the South from labor strikes, made Christians of heathens, and was the onlyway of controlling a tremendous population of blacks. Opponents, including some outspoken Southerners, pointed out that slavery broke up black families, allowed cruelty, prevented the advancement of the black race, retarded economic development of the South, and was morally harmful to both master and slave.

Slave insurrections, greatly feared though few in number, hardened southern attitudes against freeing slaves. In 1822 Denmark Vesey, who had purchased his

In the cover of deep woods, Nat Turner preaches bloody insurrection, knowing that he has great influence "over the minds of my fellow-servants." His rebellion in 1831 in Virginia spurred a backlash against runaways and rebels.

freedom with lottery winnings, was accused of plotting a revolt in Charleston—at least 35 slaves were hanged, and some 30 more were deported. After a rebellion in Louisiana, 16 were decapitated, their heads left on poles as a warning. In Tidewater Virginia, Nat Turner led an uprising in which 57 whites were killed; in reprisal, 100 blacks were killed. After a two-month search, Turner was found and hanged. As a result of these outbreaks, laws controlling slaves and runaways became harsher. In 1859 only 3,000 out of 4 million southern slaves were granted freedom, many of them too old to be of further use.

States' Rights vs. Abolition

The nullification crisis of the early 1830s (see chapter 4) deepened a division of the country along sectional lines. South Carolina's attempts to nullify a protective federal tariff from 1828 to 1832 tested the U.S. Constitution and the resolve of President Jackson, himself a Southerner. Henry L. Pinckney, editor of the Charleston *Mercury,* warned his readers that if they did not fight this issue, which was not even related to slavery, then "abolition will become the order of the day." Vice President John C. Calhoun argued cleverly for states' rights, but Jackson saw that underlying the rhetoric was a clear challenge to the integrity of the Union. If a state could nullify a federal law, there was no federal authority, hence no Union. He told a South Carolina representative in 1832 that "the Nullifiers . . . can talk and write resolutions and print threats to their hearts' content." But in no uncertain terms would he allow them to defy the laws of the United States.

Once again, it was Henry Clay, now a senator, who came up with a compromise solution. Clay and Calhoun put a lowered tariff through Congress in 1833, and the issue died off. But South Carolina planters had become convinced that secession was the only way of preserving slavery, and that enlisting other states to their cause was the only way to succeed. Calhoun made reference to ancient Greece when extolling the virtues of slavery as the underpinning of a great civilization. College of William and Mary professor Thomas Dew published a book defending the institution, and Governor Hammond of South Carolina in 1835 declared it "the cornerstone of our republican edifice."

On the Brink

1850 U.S. population: 23,200,000

1850 slave population: 3,200,000

Number of citizens owning 200 or more slaves in 1850: 254

Number of whites out of 8 million owning up to 20 slaves in 1860: 46,000

Cost to feed, clothe, and house a slave in 1859: $32 a year

Average cotton yield per slave: $78.78 a year

Eligible voters in Kansas in 1855: 2,905

Votes cast (with the addition of border ruffians): 6,307

Number killed in Bleeding Kansas by 1856: 200

NOTABLE DATES

1822
Freed slave Denmark Vesey plans rebellion in Charleston; 35 or more are hanged.

1831
Nat Turner's revolt, a two-day rampage by Virginia field slaves, claims the lives of 57 whites before militiamen crush it.

1849
Henry David Thoreau publishes "Civil Disobedience."

1850
Senator Henry Clay's Compromise of 1850 admits California as a free state, and enacts the Fugitive Slave Law, cracking down on free slaves.

1851
Herman Melville publishes *Moby Dick.*

1852
Harriet Beecher Stowe publishes *Uncle Tom's Cabin,* firing northern hatred of slavery.

1855
Poet Walt Whitman publishes *Leaves of Grass.*

1857
The Supreme Court decides 7 to 2 that Dred Scott was still a slave even though he had been taken into free territory; the court also rules the Missouri Compromise unconstitutional.

1859
Abolitionist John Brown and 21 cohorts seize a U.S. armory at Harpers Ferry; he is hanged for treason.

1860
Republican Abraham Lincoln is elected President in a four-way race.

With the help of his friend Reverend Samuel A. Smith, Henry Brown prepares himself for shipment on the Underground Railroad; "Box Brown" spent 26 hours in a wooden crate.

While the South was coming together to protect slavery, forces in the North were becoming more outspoken against it. One influential outlet, William Lloyd Garrison's *Liberator* was founded in 1831 in Boston. Just as vociferous in promoting free-soil and outright abolition was a group in New York led by Arthur Tappan, and one in Ohio led by agitator Theodore Weld and preacher C.G. Finney. When a mob attacked an abolitionist press in Illinois in 1837, killing owner Elijah P. Lovejoy, the campaign gained followers who decried threats to first amendment rights. A mob attack on Garrison enlisted the support of the outspoken Wendell Phillips; similarly, the well-heeled Gerrit Smith of New York and future Ohio senator Salmon P. Chase were inspired to join the crusade by attacks in their states. One of the most convincing antislavery spokesmen was former slave Frederick Douglass, whose 1845 *Narrative of the Life of Frederick Douglass* recounted in gripping detail the life of a slave.

Compromise of 1850

The Missouri Compromise kept the issue at bay until the acquistion of California and the Southwest in 1848, following the Mexican War. Once again, slavery became a Constitutional concern. Once again, a compromise kept the Union intact, with Henry Clay as the designer. Calhoun and others insisted that slavery should be permitted to enter new territories; free-soilers asserted that slavery would cripple free enterprise in the West and was a moral blight. An independent Free-Soil party nominated Van Buren for President in 1848, under the platform "Free Soil, Free Speech, Free labor, and Free Men." They took an amazing 11 percent of the vote, but the nation went with war hero Zachary Taylor, who became the last Whig President.

Moderates in Congress began offering solutions to the Western situation. Some proposed extending the Missouri Compromise line all the way to the Pacific; others favored letting the territories decide the slavery issue themselves once they were organized into states. In late 1849, Georgia Representative Robert Toombs shouted about a northern bill, "If it should pass, I am for disunion!" But Clay's Compromise of 1850 kept things from falling apart. Clay and Illinois Senator Stephen A. Douglas crafted a plan whereby California would become a free state, New Mexico and Utah would be organized as territories with the slavery issue deferred, the slave trade would be abolished in Washington, D.C., and fugitive slaves would be returned more speedily to their masters. Thus both sides had to yield something.

The Senate debates on the compromise were among the most brilliant in American history. On one side were the aging Calhoun, whose speech was read by a colleague, and Jefferson Davis of Mississippi; on the other were Salmon Chase and Senator William H. Seward of New York. In the middle were Stephen Douglas and elder statesmen Henry Clay and Daniel Webster. In his last great speech, Webster spoke "not as a Massachusetts man, nor as a northern man, but as an American." He took criticism for supporting the fugitive slave provision, but his eloquence for unity helped win the day for the moderates.

Kansas-Nebraska Act

But the abolition movement continued unabated. The new Fugitive Slave Law only stirred anger, and attempts to capture the 20,000 escaped slaves often caused rioting. Many Northerners were involved in helping more slaves escape through an "Underground Railroad," with hideouts along various routes, including rivers, the coast, and the Appalachians. Northern

Uncle Tom's Cabin

THE FUGITIVE SLAVE ACT, PART OF THE COMPROMISE OF 1850, outraged many Northerners, who felt that once a slave had escaped to freedom he was permanently free. Neither a professional writer nor an abolitionist, Harriet Beecher Stowe was so moved that she wrote a novel. She tossed it off quickly; it was the work of God, she explained. The result was the popular and influential *Uncle Tom's Cabin*. Published in 1852, it sold 300,000 copies in the first year, giving many their first vivid depiction of the evils of slavery.

The sister of clergyman Henry Ward Beecher, Stowe grew up in Cincinnati, Ohio, on the border of free and slave states. She had visited plantations in Kentucky, though much of her material was gathered from abolitionist acquaintances. Calling the Fugitive Slave Act a "nightmare abomination," she went to work. *Uncle Tom's Cabin* details the plight of an old black slave, Uncle Tom, who is beaten by a cruel driver, Simon Legree. The dignified Uncle Tom is devoted to Eva, daughter of the plantation owner. The death of Eva and the escape of a slave girl across the frozen Ohio River wrung tears from audiences of the stage version.

The setting is Kentucky and Louisiana, but Stowe keeps balance by having Legree hail from the North and by depicting kind Southerners. Though too melodramatic to be a great literary work, the book's drama made it very successful. Southerners accused Stowe of trying to "awaken rancorous hatred"; Northerners dismissed such criticism as biased. ■

"The Flight of Eliza" depicts a dramatic slave escape in an early edition of *Uncle Tom's Cabin*.

Lincoln-Douglas Debates

THE ILLINOIS RACE FOR U.S. SENATE IN 1858 PRODUCED ONE OF the most eloquent series of debates in American history. Republican Abraham Lincoln and Democrat Stephen Douglas did not, in fact, differ greatly in their positions, but as politicians they tried to exaggerate each other's stances to make them seem out of touch with reality.

Lincoln gains a wide audience in his highly publicized debates with Senator Stephen Douglas.

Lincoln challenged Douglas to seven debates in different venues throughout the state; Douglas accepted. The debates were well attended and widely reported. The main issue of the day was the extension of slavery into the territories, but the first thing audiences noticed was the debaters' style. Douglas, the "Little Giant," was short, stout, deep-voiced, and so full of energy he could not keep still. Lincoln was a complete contrast—tall, thin, high-voiced, and very deliberate in his speech. Douglas was a flashy dresser; Lincoln wore rumpled, poorly fitting suits.

Douglas was known as a great debater; the newcomer Lincoln scored points that would accrue later. Lincoln depicted Douglas as a proslavery defender of the Dred Scott decision, which ruled that slavery could not be banned in the territories. "Slavery is an unqualified evil to the Negro, to the white man, to the soil, and to the State," Lincoln said. Yet he watered down his stance by stating, "I am not . . . in favor of bringing about . . . the social and political equality of the white and black races." In a debate on the Dred Scott decision, Lincoln pressed Douglas to admit that "the people have the lawful means to introduce or exclude [slavery] as they please." This may have won Douglas the Senate seat, but it cost him the presidential nomination in 1860, when southern fire-eaters walked out on him. The man who warned that "a house divided against itself cannot stand" was in 1860 the last contender standing. ■

states even passed "personal liberty laws," which nullified the onerous provisions of the Fugitive Slave Law.

Then in 1854 the issue of slavery in the territories again reared its head. Radical Southerners wanted to abolish the Missouri Compromise, because it ensured that the territory west of Missouri, now Kansas and Nebraska, would be free-soil. Instead of a barren desert, that area was proving quite fertile, and Missouri slaveholders feared that new states there would become a haven for runaways. Northerners were eager to see states organized in this territory, for they could become the linchpin of a railroad running from Chicago to the Pacific Ocean. Stephen Douglas, who speculated in real estate, proposed a "popular sovereignty" bill that would let the new states, such as Utah and New Mexico, decide the slavery issue for themselves. Not an opponent of slavery, Douglas also had presidential ambitions and knew his proposal would look good in the South.

The Kansas-Nebraska Bill opened up a new round of angry debates. Free-soil presses and northern churches attacked it. Douglas professed that he could journey from Washington to Chicago by the light of fires burning him in effigy. When the bill passed in the Senate, the South celebrated with cannon fire; in Chicago flags were lowered to half mast. As a result of Senator Douglas's bill, the Whig Party evaporated and the Republican Party arose, full of fresh young talent and embracing the free-soil movement. Right off the bat they nearly won the 1856 presidential election by nominating a dashing explorer named John C. Fremont. Among the rising stars of this new party was a tall lean lawyer from Illinois, Abraham Lincoln, who thought slavery should be contained with the controversial and much-debated Missouri Compromise.

Bleeding Kansas

Meanwhile settlers moved into "Bleeding Kansas," the scene of ugly guerrilla warfare in the 1850s. Northern settlers came armed with "Beecher's Bibles," so called after influential minister Henry Ward Beecher suggested that a rifle was of better persuasion in the territory than a Bible. Thousands of "border ruffians" crossed from the state of Missouri to vote illegally and harass the free-soilers. President James Buchanan erred when he urged Congress to admit Kansas as a slave state; the North was outraged anew.

In the late 1850s, the tone of the debate rose to a fevered pitch. After a virulent speech by Massachusetts Congressman Charles Sumner, South Carolina Representative Preston Brooks cane-whipped him so severely that he was an invalid for years. In the Dred Scott case of 1857, the United States Supreme Court ruled that government could not exclude slavery from the territories. It was a tangled, much denounced legal argument relying on the unconstitutionality of the Missouri Compromise. The courts and the legislatures were tying themselves in knots to defend an institution that more and more people were considering not only immoral but also indefensible.

The Illinois race for the United States Senate in 1858 featured a remarkable series of debates between the candidates, Douglas and Lincoln. Each forcefully articulated the consitutional issues surrounding slavery, with Lincoln shrewdly getting Douglas to admit that the Dred Scott decision did not necessarily prohibit popular sovereignty in the territories. Douglas won the race, and Lincoln became a national figure. The following year abolitionist John Brown raided a United States arsenal at Harpers Ferry in western Virginia. His attempt to arm slaves failed, but when he and six of his disciples were hanged, he became for many a powerful symbol and a martyr to freedom.

The 1860 Democratic Convention

Because of a split in the Democratic Party, the Republicans were able to win the White House in the election of 1860. When Stephen Douglas, the Democratic frontrunner, made clear his belief that the Dred Scott decision did not contravene local territorial laws prohibiting slavery, leaders in the South challenged him, saying that settlers should be allowed to bring their property to wherever they decided to go. But there were no laws specifically protecting property in a territory. "I tell you, gentlemen of the South," said Douglas, "in all candor, I do not believe a Democratic candidate can ever carry any one Democratic state of the North on the platform that it is the duty of the Federal government to force the people of a territory to have slavery when they do not want it."

The Democratic convention met in Charleston, South Carolina. The weak incumbent James Buchanan was not interested in reelection. Instead, the drama centered on the continuing fight between Stephen Douglas and the radical South. Jefferson Davis and others tried to force Douglas to tow the southern line, but he refused. The Alabama delegation walked out in protest, followed by the delegates from South Carolina and from other states. The party split along northern and southern sectional lines meant that the Democratic Party could not win; it also meant the end of one of the last great ties holding the country together.

The nomination was sacrificed to principle. The radical South chose Vice President John C. Breckenridge; the mainstream Democrats went with Douglas. The Republicans enthusiastically backed Lincoln. The Southerner Breckinridge carried every southern state except for Virginia, Tennessee, and his own Kentucky, which voted for the Constitutional Union candidate John Bell of Tennessee. Douglas took only Missouri and part of New Jersey. Lincoln won the election, 180 to 123 electoral votes, though he polled only 40 percent of the popular vote.

The divided country had voted for the restriction of slavery and for peace. But in the South, the extremists had taken charge; the country's delicate balance had tipped. ■

Civil War

1861–1865

On December 20, 1860, shortly after Lincoln's election, the South Carolina legislature voted unanimously to secede from the Union. By February 1861, Georgia, Alabama, Mississippi, Louisiana, Texas, and Florida had followed suit. In early February a provisional government of the Confederate States of America was set up in Montgomery, Alabama. Virginia, North Carolina, Tennessee, and Arkansas declared that they would secede if armed force were used against the South.

Many Southerners were devoted to the United States and accepted the decision to secede reluctantly. In fact, there was no compelling reason for secession at the time. There had been no force or threat of force. Democrats were still in control of Congress and the Supreme Court. But the fear of the North's powerful industrial economy and its increasing antislavery stance, together with the goading of the radical southern press, was enough to make the South take this bold step. "We must either submit to degradation, and to the loss of property worth four billions," stated the Mississippi convention,

Bodies lie decomposing on the Antietam battlefield; the furious battle in 1862 cost both sides an unprecedented one-day toll of 22,000 men, a casualty rate of 20 percent. Lee's advance northward was temporarily checked.

"or we must secede." A few hundred wealthy landowners stood to lose the most, and they were the most influential voices in the South. Some Northerners refused to accept that the South really intended a permanent break. Lincoln considered the move a bluff to gain further compromises. The lame-duck President Buchanan sat on his hands and did nothing to conciliate or bring the South to heel, merely waiting for his term to expire in March. In Virginia, Col. Robert E. Lee expressed the feeling of many when he wrote, "I see only that a fearful calamity is upon us. There is no sacrifice I am not ready to make for the preservation of the Union save that of honour. If a disruption takes place, I shall go back in sorrow to my people & share the misery of my native state."

The War Begins

Political analysts found it odd that Lincoln seemed unalarmed, that he presented no early plan, but spent the time up to his Inauguration picking his Cabinet. That he picked a balanced group of moderates and radicals, instead of members who agreed with each other, struck many as a sign of weakness. In his Inaugural speech he reminded listeners that, "We are not enemies, but friends. . . . The mystic chords of memory, stretching from every battlefield and patriot grave to every living heart . . . will yet swell the chorus of the Union when again touched, as surely they will be, by the better angels of our nature." Although some found courage in these words, others saw in them a sign that the President was soft in the head.

One thing Lincoln was clear on—secession was illegal. Although federal property had been seized by Confederates in the Deep South, Fort Sumter at Charleston and Fort Pickens in Pensacola were still manned by United States forces. Lincoln did not want to give these up without at least some effort. Neither did he want a big show of force—conciliation, he believed, could still avert a disaster. After weeks of hesitation, Lincoln sent a relief naval expedition to Fort Sumter, to supply the men with food. Before the ships could land, Confederates fired on the fort on April 12. After a 34-hour bombardment the fort surrendered. The Civil War was on.

Lincoln immediately called for 75,000 soldiers to enlist. This move was interpreted as an act of aggression, prompting Virginia, North Carolina, Tennessee, and Arkansas to secede. The southern position was that it had been attacked and was being forced into submission. Lincoln's stance was that the South by seceeding was rejecting the Constitution and therefore democracy. "The central idea of secession is the essence of anarchy," he maintained. Only at the ballot box could the people change their government. Thus from the outset the war itself was fought against the principle of secession, though slavery had been the reason for secession in the first place. Lincoln wanted above all to save the Union: "If I could save the Union without freeing *any* slave, I would do it; and if I could save it by freeing *all* the slaves, I would do it."

NOTABLE DATES

■ 1861
Civil War begins in April when secessionists in Charleston, South Carolina, attack federal troops at Fort Sumter.

■ 1862
Federal troops repulse Confederates in Maryland at the Battle of Antietam in September; Lincoln pledges to free slaves in the Confederacy under the Emancipation Proclamation.

■ 1863
Federal troops under George Meade repel Robert E. Lee's Confederates at the Battle of Gettysburg, forcing them to retreat from Pennsylvania. Ulysses S. Grant captures Vicksburg, Mississippi.

■ 1864
Federals commanded by William Tecumseh Sherman capture Atlanta in September and drive across Georgia to the sea.

■ 1865
Lee surrenders to Grant at Appomattox on April 9; Lincoln assassinated on April 14 and succeeded by Andrew Johnson.

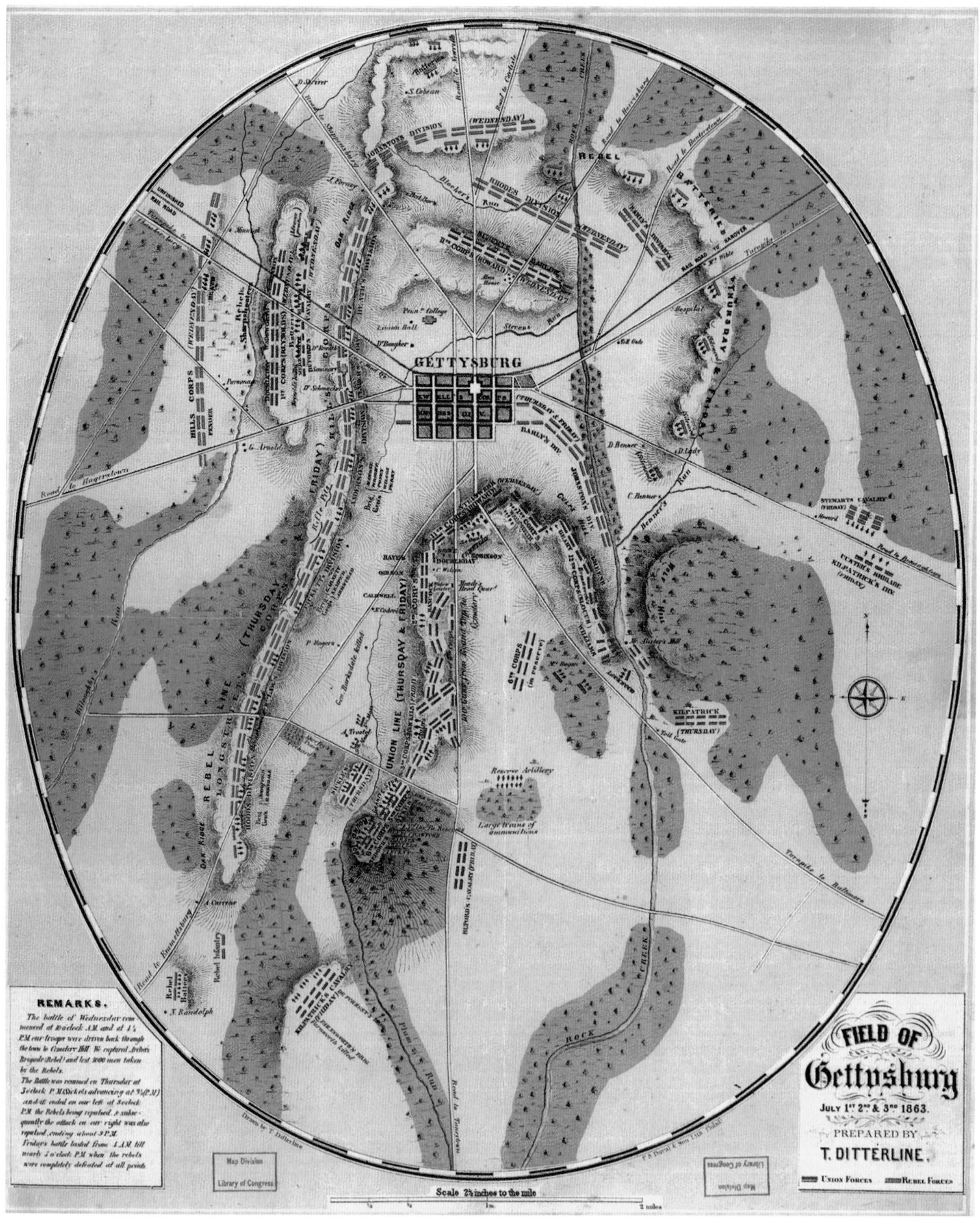

A map of Gettysburg shows the placement of troops at the beginning of the three-day battle in early July 1863. Despite fierce Confederate assaults, the Union held its advantage on slightly higher ground, thus winning the key battle of the war.

Northern Advantages

As the conflict opened, the North possessed a tremendous advantage in men and materiel. The population of the North stood at 20 million, that of the South at 9 million, including 3.5 million slaves who were not going to be trusted with guns. The North had seven times as much manufacturing as the South, a better railroad system, and the U.S. Navy could easily blockade Confederate ports. On the plus side for the South was that the North counted on southern markets for its products. The South also need only fight a defensive war, and perhaps an invasion by a hostile army would gain sympathy for the South by other nations. The North claimed some 300 West Point-trained officers, the South 180. In Robert E. Lee the South was lucky to have the most able military commander in the country. For years the North struggled to find commanders who were not indecisive and incompetent.

For head of state, the North had a much better edge. Lincoln proved that he was up to the gravest responsibility a sitting President had ever faced. He confronted problems head on, thought them through carefully, and acted decisively. He began to rise in the esteem of his Cabinet, and then of the people, who found him both strong and gentle, humble and wise. Though only 52 when he took office, he was soon known affectionately as Old Abe.

The Confederacy had to start from scratch. Its form of government was borrowed from the United States government—in fact, federal laws were to remain in effect unless individually repealed. But a major problem was that the Confederacy was founded on a principle of states' rights, thus many states ignored orders from Richmond, the seat of government, and did as they pleased. Created and operating during a war, the Confederate government had to function, sometimes literally, on the fly. Confederate President Jefferson Davis had been a hardworking, intellectually powerful senator from Mississippi, but he was too thin-skinned and reserved to be popular. His wife called him "abnormally sensitive to disapprobation." Nor was he a great military strategist. People supported him for his dedication to the Confederacy, but they did not love him the way Lincoln, or Lee, was loved.

Strength in Numbers

White population 1860: North 20,275,000, South 5,449,000

Manufacturing establishments 1860: North 110,000, South 18,000

Value of firearms manufactured 1860: North $2,270,000, South $73,000

Locomotives manufactured: North 451, South 19

Railroad mileage: North 21,973, South 9,283

Damage inflicted on the South by Sherman: $100 million

Amount stolen: 15,000 horses and mules, 20,000 cattle, 50,000 hogs, 100,000 bushels of sweet potatoes, 500,000 bushels of corn

Peak year of both Union and Confederate forces on duty: 1863, with nearly 700,000 Union and 275,000 Confederate troops

Number of dissenters and others arrested and held without trial during the North's suspension of habeas corpus: 13,000

Number of Alabama planters exempt from military service because they owned at least 20 slaves: almost 1,500

Casualties during Battle of Gettysburg, July 1-3, 1863: more than 20,000 on each side

Total Union casualties during the war: 1,566,678; of these 275, 175 were wounded, 110,070 died of wounds, 249,458 died of disease

Total Confederate casualties: 1,082,119; 100,000 wounded, 94,000 died of wounds, 164,000 died of disease

Death rates: 23% of Union soldiers, 24% of Confederate soldiers; about twice as many soldiers died of disease than of wounds

Electoral votes in 1864 election: Lincoln 212, McClellan 21

Bull Run and the Peninsula Campaign

On July 21, the first major battle was fought 20 miles west of Washington at Manassas Junction, Virginia. About 30,000 men attacked an equal-size Confederate Army there at Bull Run, a branch of the Potomac River. Though at first the North seized the advantage, pushing aside the Confederate left flank, the Confederates rallied around a Virginia brigade led by Thomas J. Jackson who was standing "like a stone wall against the enemy." Stonewall Jackson would prove time and again a formidable enemy. The northern advance stalled out, and the Confederates counterattacked from a strategic hill. The retreating soldiers fled in panic back to Washington, dropping their guns and scattering picnickers who had come to watch the action. Not experienced or organized enough to take advantage of the rout, the Confederates gave up the chase.

The total victory was praised in the South. The North settled down to the prospect of a long struggle. Lincoln began planning a much broader strategy. Among top priorities were control of the Mississippi, a tight blockade of southern ports, and an invasion of Virginia by a new army. Congress authorized the enlistment of 500,000 volunteers for a period of three years. To lead this army, Lincoln appointed 34-year-old Gen. George B. McClellan, a veteran of the Mexican War. Gen. McClellan had already successfully cleared Confederates from the Unionist western Virginia, a small-scale operation that opened that area for upcoming statehood. Though he was somewhat vainglorious, McClellan, a West Pointer, was a capable organizer and careful planner—sometimes too careful.

After innumerable delays, McClellan was finally ready in the spring of 1862 to move. He sent his Army by water down to Yorktown where they could work their way up the York and James peninsula and then march toward Richmond. In March the U.S.S. *Monitor* had defeated the Confederate *Merrimack*, in the first battle of ironclad ships, thus clearing the way for McClellan's army. McClellan stalled, waiting for more men, envisioning glory, but in fact not lionhearted enough to want an all-out fight. A lightning attack with his 80,000 men might have ended the

Sherman's March to the Sea

On December 24, 1864, President Lincoln received a telegram: "I beg to present to you as a Christmas gift the city of Savannah." The sender was 44-year-old William Tecumseh Sherman. Earlier in the war, Sherman's erratic behavior had led to newspaper reports that he was insane. But Grant trusted him, giving him rein to launch an assault on Atlanta. His overall plan was to demoralize the enemy, to destroy the enemy's ability to fight by destroying its will. Though the South "cannot be made to love us," he said, it "can be made to fear us." After sacking Atlanta, Sherman and his 62,000 men set out on their epic march to the sea.

They found little resistance. Instead, they engaged in demolition. Sherman never called for the destruction of private property, but he rarely punished anyone for it. "The devil himself couldn't restrain my men," he explained. Across the countryside they swept in a barely contained anarchy—plundering railroads, poultry, potatoes, sheep, furniture, everything they could lay hands on. To a distraught farm woman, one soldier politely vowed, "Madam, we're going to suppress this rebellion if it takes every last chicken in the Confederacy."

Outside Savannah, Sherman took a key fort after a fierce hand-to-hand battle. The losses were worth it. As Sherman wrote to Atlanta's mayor: "You cannot qualify war in harsher terms than I will. War is cruelty and you cannot refine it. . . . But, my dear sirs, when peace does come, you may call on me for any thing." Such was the hatred of Sherman in the South, it is unlikely many accepted his offer. ■

General William Tecumseh Sherman watches troop movement through binoculars during his epic 1864 march from Atlanta to Savannah; the campaign opened up a wound 60 miles wide in the heart of the South.

Alexander Gardner, protégé of Mathew Brady, photographed this devastated landscape following the 1862 battle at Antietam.

war, but he dallied and deliberated, edging forward with great care.

On to Antietam

Lee meanwhile had assumed command of the Army of Northern Virginia after Gen. Joseph Johnston was wounded. Lee was McClellan's opposite—quiet, self-assured, intuitively brilliant with tactics, and almost recklessly daring. He had proved in the Mexican War that he was a natural fighter. A master of battle psychology, he geared each fight differently depending upon whom he faced. He now sent Stonewall Jackson out to mop up the Shenandoah Valley, and thus divert the Union's focus. After Jackson's successful campaign, he returned to Richmond. In late June, Lee struck hard at McClellan, who was good at defense. After seven days, McClellan staggered back, having suffered 15,800 casualties; Lee's army suffered 20,000.

In a secure position, McClellan could have pressed his advantage. Instead, he hesitated. Lincoln did not. He replaced him and ordered him to join Gen. John Pope, who was then gearing up forces between Washington and Richmond. With the opposition gone, Lee moved north, striking at Pope in late August back at Bull Run and pushing him off the field. Exasperated, Lincoln put McClellan back in command. "We must use what tools we have," he said. Lee knew that it was only a matter of time before the North's endless resources would overcome the Confederacy. His only hope was for quick, bold action, and so he took the lead, marching north into Maryland with a force of 60,000. McClellan pursued at his usual hesitant, lackluster pace.

Lee then split his Army—always a risky tactic—and sent Jackson to take Harpers Ferry. Then on September 17, he and McClellan clashed at Antietam Creek, near Sharpsburg. At the end of this, the single bloodiest day of the war, over 22,000 men lay dead or wounded. In a perilous position, its back to the Potomac, Lee's exhausted Army could not safely retreat. But McClellan did not seize the initiative, and thus let Lee melt away. This time, Lincoln dismissed McClellan for good.

In the western theater, forces under Ulysses S. Grant invaded Tennessee from the north, taking Forts Henry and Donelson in early 1862. Then 40,000 Confederates led by Albert Sidney Johnston moved to stop Grant's southward advance. A surprise attack at Shiloh in April caught Grant off guard; he managed after two days to push the Confederates back, but the losses on both sides during the Battle of Shiloh were so high that neither was able to re-engage. For not following up his momentum, Grant was relieved of command at this point.

Emancipation Proclamation

After the costly victory at Antietam, Lincoln decided to bolster the war effort with a political move. The North had become increasingly hostile to the South; abolitionism had grown in popularity as a result, partly because it flew in the face of a southern institution. In April of 1862, Congress abolished slavery in the District of Columbia. This was followed by abolition in the territories. Lincoln was in favor of individual states freeing slaves and providing compensation to slaveowners; federal aid would help

Bodies strew the battlefield at Gettysburg in a grim harvest of death, the price of all-out war. The photographer's original caption said the Confederates "paid with life the price of their treason."

slaves who wanted to leave the country. But no loyal state was willing to make this move. Convinced that foreign nations would sympathize with an antislavery position, Lincoln finally took the step of issuing the Emancipation Proclamation on September 22, 1862. It proclaimed that starting in 1863 slaves in Confederate states "shall be then, thenceforward, and forever free."

Since it only applied to the rebel states, not the loyal or border states, no slaves were actually freed by the proclamation, not even those in Union-controlled areas of the South such as New Orleans and Norfolk, Virginia. The London *Spectator* scoffed at this half-measure: "The principle is not that a human being cannot justly own another, but that he cannot own him unless he is loyal to the United States." Yet Frederick Douglass expressed the hope the proclamation kindled when he wrote, "I took the proclamation for a little more than it purported, and saw in its spirit a life and power far beyond its letter." Many in the North considered it either illegal or, contrarily, not near enough. The South bristled at the prospect of slave insurrections resulting from the proclamation. Slaves pretended to their masters that they didn't know about it, but when federal troops came through they dropped their cotton sacks and ran off.

Racial prejudice in both the North and the South flared—though millions were against slavery they were also against racial equality. Some recoiled at the idea of a northward migration of blacks, who would compete for jobs, reduce wages, and raise the crime rate. One immediate effect of the ill will caused by the Emancipation Proclamation was a drop in enlistments. Congress then passed a conscription law for all men from 20 to 45 (the Confederacy already had conscription). The rich had the advantage of being able to pay for a substitute, and thus avoid the draft. Draft riots broke out in several cities. The $300 exemption was for many people a year's earnings. Poor Irish workers and others were furious at the notion of being forced to hazard their lives to free slaves, who would then compete with them for jobs. In mid-July 1863, a four-day riot erupted in New York City; buildings and houses were burned, and more than 100 blacks were killed.

In backlash to the riots, even conservatives began considering the idea of giving blacks the vote. Many whites began changing their opinion of blacks. Though blacks had fought in the Revolution and the War of 1812, a 1792 law prevented them from serving in the military. With the pressing need for more troops, Secretary of War Edwin M. Stanton authorized the enlistment of slaves on the captured sea islands of South Carolina. Among black regiments was the Massachusetts 54th commanded by Col. Robert Gould Shaw, a white as were all commanders of black troops. The blacks' fighting spirit and bravery impressed Northerners and Southerners alike.

Lee Wins Again . . . and Again

Lincoln replaced McClellan with Gen. Ambrose E. Burnside, known for his long side whiskers—now named sideburns in his honor. Not as reluctant a warrior as McClellan, Burnside was sometimes lacking in judgment. As he took the Army of the Potomac south toward Richmond, he and his 120,000-man Army got bogged down with foul weather and supply problems. In mid-December 1862, he encountered Lee, who had been fortifying a position in Fredericksburg with 75,000 soldiers. Aggressive to a fault, Burnside led wave after wave of uphill assaults, wasting thousands

The Cost of War

When the Civil War erupted, the federal government could not foresee its duration and cost. Secretary of the Treasury Salmon P. Chase requested much too small an appropriation from Congress. In the summer of 1861 Congress passed an income tax requirement of 3 percent for annual incomes over $800; later a top tier of 10 percent for incomes over $10,000 was assessed. Each state also was taxed, and loans of $140 million were authorized. As the war continued, excise taxes on innumerable goods and services were added. More borrowing was required. By war's end the government had borrowed $2.2 billion and collected $667 million in taxes. The banking system had been reorganized and the first "greenbacks" issued—$431 million of unredeemable bills.

Financial problems were much worse in the South. With ports blockaded, tariffs were insufficient. In addition to an income tax and excise taxes, the Confederacy levied a tax of one-tenth of every farmer's production. The Confederacy also borrowed a total of $712 million. But the South's chief means of raising money was to print it—over $1.5 billion dollars' worth. Near the end of the war, a Confederate dollar was worth less than 2 cents in gold. On the plus side, blockade runners slipped through with goods and weapons. It is safe to say that no major battle was lost because the South lacked weapons or equipment. ■

Confederate sailors run a Union blockade into Wilmington Harbour, North Carolina.

of men in a futile effort. Watching the action, Lee remarked, "It is well that war is so terrible—we should grow too fond of it!" Burnside evacuated in tears; he was soon replaced with Gen. Joseph Hooker.

Lincoln was reluctant to put vile-tempered "Fighting Joe" Hooker in charge, but he felt he had no better choice. In spring 1863, Hooker crossed the Rappahannock ten miles west of Fredericksburg at Chancellorsville with 125,000 men. Once again, superior numbers meant nothing. Instead of immediately attacking an Army half his in size, he waited. Lee used the opportunity to send Jackson around through the woods with 28,000 men. Near sunset on May 2, Jackson's troops emerged and blew out Hooker's right wing while the men were at dinner. It was perhaps the most brilliant battle plan of the entire war, and, were darkness not gathering, could have destroyed Hooker. In the event, Hooker retreated, and, unfortunately for the South, Jackson was killed by friendly fire.

The Turning Point

Knowing that Vicksburg, and thus the Mississippi, was in jeopardy, Lee decided to follow up his victory with another invasion of the North. It would be his last. On July 1, he faced off with Gen. George G. Meade in Gettysburg, Pennsylvania for the decisive battle of the war. The Union controlled the best position, on Cemetery Ridge. On the third day of the battle, Gen. George F. Pickett led a heroic and doomed assault of 15,000 men against the rock-solid federal lines. A few made it all the way to the federal position, but the assault melted back under heavy fire. On July 4, the whipped Confederates began retreating; the seemingly invincible Lee had finally been beaten. Meade decided not to follow up and deliver a fatal blow.

The North had more good news that same July 4. General Grant had captured the strategic town of Vicksburg, Mississippi, which guarded a 150-mile piece of the river. The shabbily dressed, cigar-smoking, hard-drinking general had surreptitiously moved his troops down and around Vicksburg so that he could attack it from the east, dispatching Confederate forces along the way. Then laying siege to Vicksburg in mid-May, Grant finally prevailed in July. Now Texas and Arkansas were cut off from the rest of the Confederacy. Lincoln had not endorsed Grant's audacious plan, but a victory was a victory. In March 1864, Lincoln made Grant supreme commander of the United States Army.

After 1863 the Confederacy went into steady decline. Economically, the South was ravaged, its inability to centralize government only exacerbating its hardships. Its ports blocked in and its presses cranking out currency, the South endured runaway inflation. A pound of butter cost $25, an officer's coat $2,000. Meanwhile, the North was beginning to prosper, the economy stimulated by wartime production. The Homestead Act of 1862 opened up lands in the West; money was allocated for a transcontinental railroad; and a national banking act created a uniform currency.

Artists such as Alfred R. Waud, sketching here at Devil's Den in the 1863 Battle of Gettysburg, captured action that slow cameras could not.

The Final Blow

Still, the war had yet to be concluded. Grant had a simple, dogged plan—ram like a juggernaut against Lee and Richmond, while sending Gen. William T. Sherman around to devastate the lower South; the two armies would then meet. They headed out in May 1864 with more than 100,000 men each. In drawn-out, grim battles at the Wilderness, near Chancellorsville and Spotsylvania Courthouse, Grant lost some 30,000 men, but instead of retreating he kept moving South, trying to outflank Lee and go for Richmond, barely giving Lee's played-out army a chance to keep up. By June, after a costly battle at Cold Harbor, Grant pushed around to Petersburg and laid siege. He had lost 60,000 men. Lee had far fewer.

Grant's massive losses disheartened many in the North, but he pressed implacably on. As did Sherman, who after a hard slog took Atlanta on September 2. He now headed for the port of Savannah, scything a 60-mile-wide swath through Georgia. Under Sherman's total war, southern resistance finally began to weaken. By February of 1865 he had captured Columbia, South Carolina, and two months later he forced the army of Joseph Johnston to surrender in North Carolina. Meanwhile, with the tide turning in favor of the North, Lincoln was reelected, and Grant had finally cornered Lee. With 30,000 able-bodied men against 115,000, Lee surrendered at Appomattox Court House on April 9, 1865. The war was effectively over. ■

Lee and Grant at Appomattox

One of the most famous and moving tableaux of American history was the surrender of Robert E. Lee to Ulysses S. Grant. Under the constant and overwhelming pressure of Grant's forces during a nine-month siege, Lee dropped back from Petersburg in early April 1865. Realizing that further fighting would be a pointless waste of life, Lee agreed to meet with Grant on April 9 at Appomattox Court House.

Dignified to the end, Lee appeared in a new dress uniform with an embroidered red sash; his polished boots held gold spurs. Grant showed up with muddy boots and a slouch hat, but he was gracious, even admiring, of his old adversary. "I met you once before, General Lee," he said, "while we were serving in Mexico. I have always remembered your appearance, and I think I should have recognized you anywhere."

The terms of surrender were simply that the Confederates lay down their arms. Lee hinted that his men might need their horses for the spring planting, and Grant agreed. He also offered to send rations to Lee's emaciated army. Then astride his horse Traveller, Lee rode through his ranks. "Men," he said, "we have fought the war together, and I have done the best I could for you. My heart is too full to say more."Grant recalled that he "felt like anything rather than rejoicing at the downfall of a foe who had fought so long and valiantly." The two sides saluted each other, and the Confederates stacked their arms. And so with great chivalry and honor, two men set the tone for the peace ahead. ■

In a crisp, clean uniform, Gen. Robert E. Lee accepts the generous surrender terms offered by Gen. Ulysses S. Grant at Appomattox, bringing about the end of major hostilities.

Reconstruction

1865–1877

The President whose patience and wisdom had guided the Union through its most turbulent years had been fervent in his belief in reconciliation instead of punishment for the South. Among his masterful speeches, his Second Inaugural Address specified, "With malice toward none, with charity for all . . . let us strive on to finish the work we are in, to bind up the nation's wounds." In early April 1865 Lincoln gave a speech on post-war Reconstruction, recommending fairness and leniency. Thus when a conspiracy of southern agitators plotted his assassination, they worked against the best interest of the South's easy re-entry into the Union.

On April 14 Lincoln attended a play at Ford's Theatre. One of the conspirators, a half-crazy actor named John Wilkes Booth, snuck into the President's box and shot him in the head. He died early the next morning. The poet James Russell Lowell wrote, "Never before that startled April morning did such multitudes of men shed tears for the death of one they had

Refugees await a boat on the swollen Mississippi River. After federal intervention ended in the post-war South in 1877 and state laws limited rights of ex-slaves, many headed West.

never seen . . . . " The national mood shifted, not toward revenge exactly, but toward a more entrenched bitterness and grim determination to bring the South to its knees.

President Johnson

The new President, Tenneseean Andrew Johnson, inherited the nearly impossible task of reuniting and readjusting the nation. A former Democrat, now at the helm of the nation and the Republicans, Johnson found no support in Congress. He found it difficult to adjust to the demands of the job and was constantly on the defensive. In attempting to protect the authority of states, he tried to stymie a Civil Rights Act and bills that would aid blacks through a Freedmen's Bureau. He lost control of Congress to Radicals bent on retribution. Radical leader Thaddeus Stevens of Pennsylvania exhorted, "Dead men cannot raise themselves. Dead states cannot restore their existence 'as it was.'"

Stevens, Charles Sumner (recovered from his caning by Preston Brooks), and others did not trust white Southerners to grant blacks equality. As proof they cited race riots in Memphis and New Orleans and newly enacted repressive "black codes." When Johnson departed from a prepared text of an 1866 speech to call three Radical Republicans "traitors," even his supporters were appalled. A Republican Congress passed the Civil Rights Act and other laws over his veto. Then, over his veto, they passed a possibly unconstitutional bill forbidding the President to dismiss certain officials without congressional consent. When he tested it by trying to fire Secretary of War Edwin Stanton, the House impeached him in 1868 for "high crimes and misdemeanors." He was spared removal by one vote in the Senate.

The aims of federal Reconstruction were three: to bring the South back into the Union, to guarantee political and civil rights to the newly freed slaves, and to bolster the economy by continuing earlier policies on tariffs, banking, and western territory. One way to achieve these ends was by amending the Constitution, and thus the 13th Amendment abolished

Back to Business

- Grant's margin of victory over Democrat Horatio Seymour in 1868: 214 to 80 electoral votes; 3 million to 2.7 million popular votes.
- Grant's margin of victory over Liberal Republican Horace Greeley in 1872: 286 to 66 electoral votes; 3.6 million to 2.8 million popular votes
- Schools established by Freedmen's Bureau: 4,329, attended by 250,000 ex-slaves
- Cotton produced by the South in 1860: 5 million bales
- Cotton produced by the South in 1870: 3 million bales
- Tobacco produced by the South in 1860: 200 million pounds
- Tobacco produced by the South in 1870: 75 million pounds
- Sugar produced by the South in 1860: 230 million pounds
- Sugar produced by the South in 1870: 100 million pounds

NOTABLE DATES

■ 1865
Lincoln is assassinated. The 13th Amendment abolishes slavery.

■ 1866
Tennessee voters ratify a new state constitution and the state is readmitted to the Union.

■ 1868
The 14th Amendment grants citizenship to blacks; President Johnson issues amnesty to all parties in the rebellion; Arkansas, North Carolina, South Carolina, Alabama, Louisiana, and Florida readmitted to the Union.

■ 1870
Viginia, Georgia, and Texas readmitted to the Union.

■ 1871
The Great Fire of Chicago destroys the city October 8-11; damage estimated at $196 million.

■ 1872
The Amnesty Act restores citizenship to Southerners, except for 500 Confederate leaders.

■ 1873
A panic on Wall Street prompted by unbridled speculation and overexpansion in industry, agriculture, and commerce closes the stock exchange for 11 days.

■ 1876
Mark Twain publishes *Tom Sawyer*.

■ 1877
The last federal troops patrolling the South are withdrawn from Louisiana and South Carolina; the policy of Reconstruction is effectively terminated.

Reconstruction Legislatures

During Reconstruction a strange amalgam of politicians filled the vacuum left by deposed southern Democrats. The so-called black Republican state governments were primarily white, composed of scalawags and carpetbaggers. The former were Southerners who were sympathetic to the new regime, many of them old planters and merchants who had been Whigs, and others out for personal gain. The carpetbaggers (named for their valises) were a mixed group of Northerners, also willing to work with freed slaves—some were idealistic, others purely profit- or revenge-driven.

Blacks also came to political power. Less than five years after becoming free, they could vote and hold office. Fewer than 20 actually made it to Congress, yet many held minor state offices and one became a state supreme court justice.

Though some black lawmakers were capable, few had the experience necessary to pass laws benefitting their race—the South Carolina legislature, for instance, often split into quarelling factions. Described as a spectacle, the legislators, dressed in old frock coats, would pontificate on subjects they knew little about. A northern commentator called it "a wonder and a shame to modern civilization." Yet few black officeholders were vindictive, and there was no more corruption than among city bosses in the North. Further, Reconstruction governments made progress putting the South back in order—rebuilding railroads and levees, enlarging social services, and financing public education. ■

An allegory of the reconciliation of North and South shows the U.S., as a pavilion, undergoing reconstruction; under military supervision, civilians put the new columns into place.

slavery in 1865, the 14th granted citizenship to blacks in 1868, and the 15th granted suffrage in 1870.

Return of White Supremacy

Faced with the 14th Amendment, granting equal protection of the law to all races, the southern legislatures rejected it. Now the question was, who was in charge of Reconstruction? Radicals were for waiting until the states were contrite and rehabilitated. Moderates wanted to speedily heal the nation's wounds. The election of 1866 tipped the balance in Congress in favor of the Radical side, and a new military authority took control of the South. Readmission to the Union would be determined by legislatures ratifying the 14th and 15th Amendments.

Another way Reconstruction was approached was by a strengthening of the Republican Party in the South. The military melted away as reconstructed governments took over. Composed of blacks, Republicans, and carpetbaggers—northern politicians and businessmen with often dubious intentions—these new governments were in charge for up to seven years. Some were incompetent, others corrupt, but they all made an attempt at reform. Then one by one, the Radicals yielded to the return of "home rule," the white Democrats who knew the lay of the political land.

The administration of Ulysses Grant, President from 1869 to 1877, proved inept in dealing with economic turmoil and ineffective in coping with a united white front in the South. There were too many

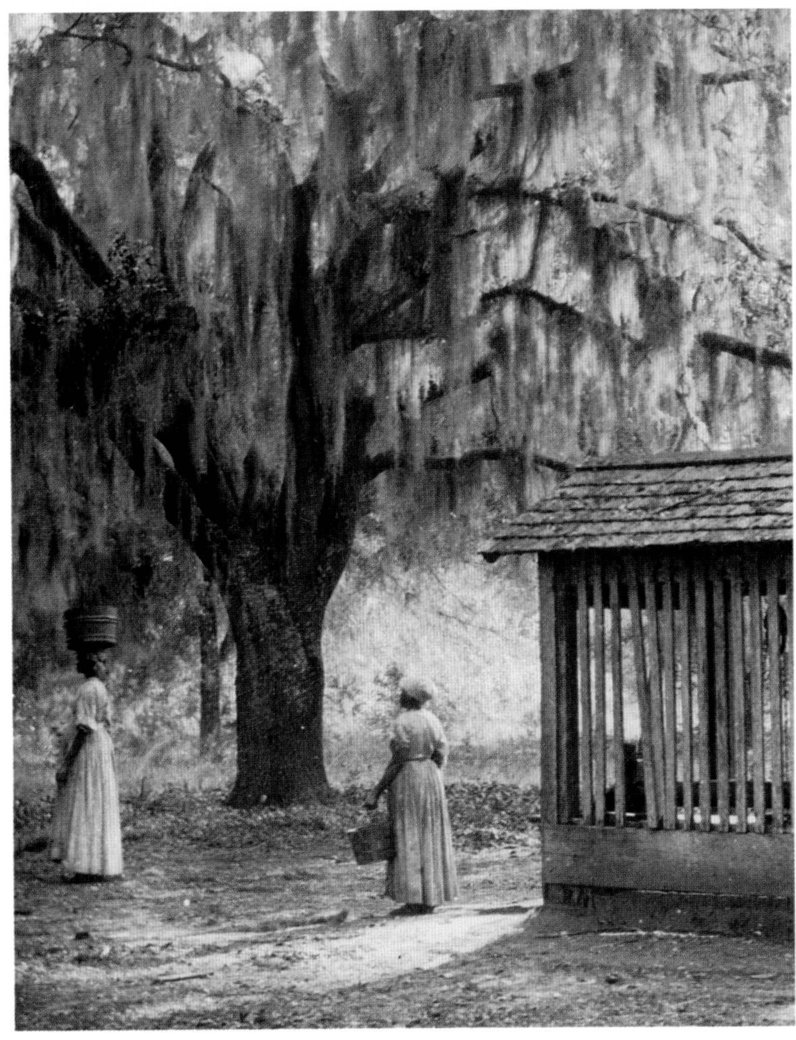

Under streamers of Spanish moss, freed slaves carry water on a Georgia plantation. Many ex-slaves continued to work for former masters.

other pressing problems. Locally, governments were unable to meet the needs of emerging cities. Industrialization and an influx of immigrants increased demands for services. City bosses answered those needs with political machines organized to trade patronage and favors for loyalty and votes. In the West deceit, theft, and neglect marked the government's policy toward the Indians. After the Civil War the government began driving them onto reservations.

Military Occupation Ends

The 1876 presidential election delivered the final blow to Reconstruction. Republican Rutherford B. Hayes, governor of Ohio, lost the popular vote to Democrat Samuel J. Tilden, governor of New York. Tilden seemed to have a clear majority of electoral votes as well, but results were contested in Florida, Oregon, South Carolina, and Louisiana. An electoral commission awarded all the votes to Hayes, giving him a one-vote edge. To avoid another civil war, the parties agreed to give Hayes victory if he would remove troops from the South. Reconstruction was over, and black civil rights would languish until the mid-20th century.

The Civil War and Reconstruction were an unparalleled national tragedy. The loss of over 600,000 soldiers was greater than in all other U.S. wars combined. The South was left in ruins, and the North and South with a distrust and hatred that took decades to repair. So too, the establishment of blacks as equal members of society would require the passage of generations. In his Gettysburg Address, dedicating the battlefield in 1863, Lincoln had called for "a new birth of freedom." Yet the ideal democracy was still a distant dream. Partisanship reigned in Congress—it was 20 years before a Democrat would become President, and 50 before a Southerner (Woodrow Wilson) won the White House. In politics and business the war spawned an age of greed.

Yet without the war, it is unlikely that slavery would have died out soon. The South's economy was to some degree liberated with the freeing of the slaves. Though cruel, the war showed that democracy could be tested and prevail, that government of the people, by the people, and for the people, as Lincoln said, would not perish from the earth. Emerging from an epic four-year struggle, the people realized they had a set of shared experiences that tied North and South together like nothing else could. ■

WORLD SURVEY

1817–1877

While the United States was pausing in its rise to world power to fight a civil war, Europe maintained dominance. Social and political upheavals prompted by spreading industrialism and nationalism were commonplace, and radical new ideas about the workers' place in society were propagated.

Europe

The French Revolution and the Napoleonic Wars shook Europe to its foundations. Rulers could no longer safely ignore the will of the people. Napoleon acknowledged as much by confirming the legal rights of French citizens and seeking their approval in plebiscites. After he was ousted, European monarchs tried to maintain absolute power by repressing nationalist movements. In the long run, however, rulers risked rebellion and defeat if they failed to reckon with nationalism and turn it to their advantage.

The rise of nationalism was accompanied by a surge in radicalism among Europe's industrial workers. In Britain they drew up a People's Charter in 1838, demanding an end to property requirements that prevented the poor from voting. Agitation led Parliament to pass economic reforms in the 1840s, but social philosophers like Karl Marx, a German emigrant, argued that a revolution by the working class against the ruling class was inevitable. Marx and his colleague Friedrich Engels called on workers of the world to unite in the Communist Manifesto, published in 1848.

Nineteenth-century Russia had fallen behind its European counterparts socially, politically, and technologically. In 1855 Tsar Alexander II came to power intent on change. In his 26-year reign Alexander greatly reformed and modernized Russian society. He reformed laws, spread state-sponsored education, and increased literacy. But the tsar's greatest reform was the emancipation of Russia's tens of millions of serfs in 1861, two years before Lincoln's Emancipation Proclamation.

Canada

By the mid-19th century, Canada existed as a number of separate provinces. As immigrants moved in, as the power of the United States grew, and as Canadian politicians saw the need to secure the northwest for expansion, a coalition of Canadian leaders agreed to form a union. In 1867 Nova Scotia, New Brunswick, and Canada East and West (now Quebec and Ontario) became the Dominion of Canada under the British North America Act. In 1869 the country purchased the Northwest Territories from the Hudson's Bay Company, and in 1871 British Columbia joined the union.

With the addition of extensive western lands, a transcontinental railway became a primary goal. The Canadian Pacific Railway reached Vancouver in 1887, giving the county access to the Pacific. Between 1891 and 1914, more than three million immigrants followed the railway, settling east to west.

Mexico

After losing territory to the United States in 1848, Mexico was in disarray. Liberals turned against President Antonio Lopez de Santa Anna and drove him from power in 1855. A few years later, Benito Juarez, a liberal leader of Zapotec Indian descent, became president and pressed ahead with a controversial program of reforms that included separating church and state and confiscating church property not used for worship. In 1860 Juarez defeated Mexican conservatives who revolted against his policies, but rebels in exile then encouraged the French Emperor Louis Napoleon to intervene on their behalf. In 1861, after Juarez suspended payment of foreign debts, France, Britain, and Spain sent troops to Mexico. Britain and Spain soon withdrew, but French forces persisted. On May 5, 1862, Mexican troops repulsed the French in the Battle of Puebla—a victory that inspired the Mexican festival known as Cinco de Mayo (Fifth of May).

Louis Napoleon sent more troops. They captured Mexico City and installed Napoleon's puppet, Prince Maximilian of Austria, as emperor. Juarez continued to wage guerrilla warfare against the regime with support from the United States, which had protested the French occupation as a violation of the Monroe Doctrine, prohibiting European intervention in the Americas. In 1866 Napoleon bowed to U.S. pressure and withdrew his forces; Juarez regained power and captured Maximilian, who was tried by court-martial and executed.

■ Egypt

The history of Egypt in the 19th century can be divided into two parts—before and after the Suez Canal. In the first part of the 1800s, Ottoman Turks joined the British in ousting Napoleon's troops from Egypt. In the following years, a forward-looking soldier named Muhammad Ali became pasha and undertook military, social, and economic reforms. He modernized the army, expanded industry, and increased production of crops such as cotton and indigo. After Ali's death in 1849, his successors, known as the khedives, were unable to continue his reforms and began to fall into debt to European financiers. This debt was increased by the cost of the Suez Canal, completed in 1869. Eventually, Egypt was forced to sell many of its shares in the canal to the British. Increasingly, Egypt came under European domination. Nationalists staged a revolt against the outsiders in 1882, but were crushed by British forces. By 1900 Britain was in control of the country. ■

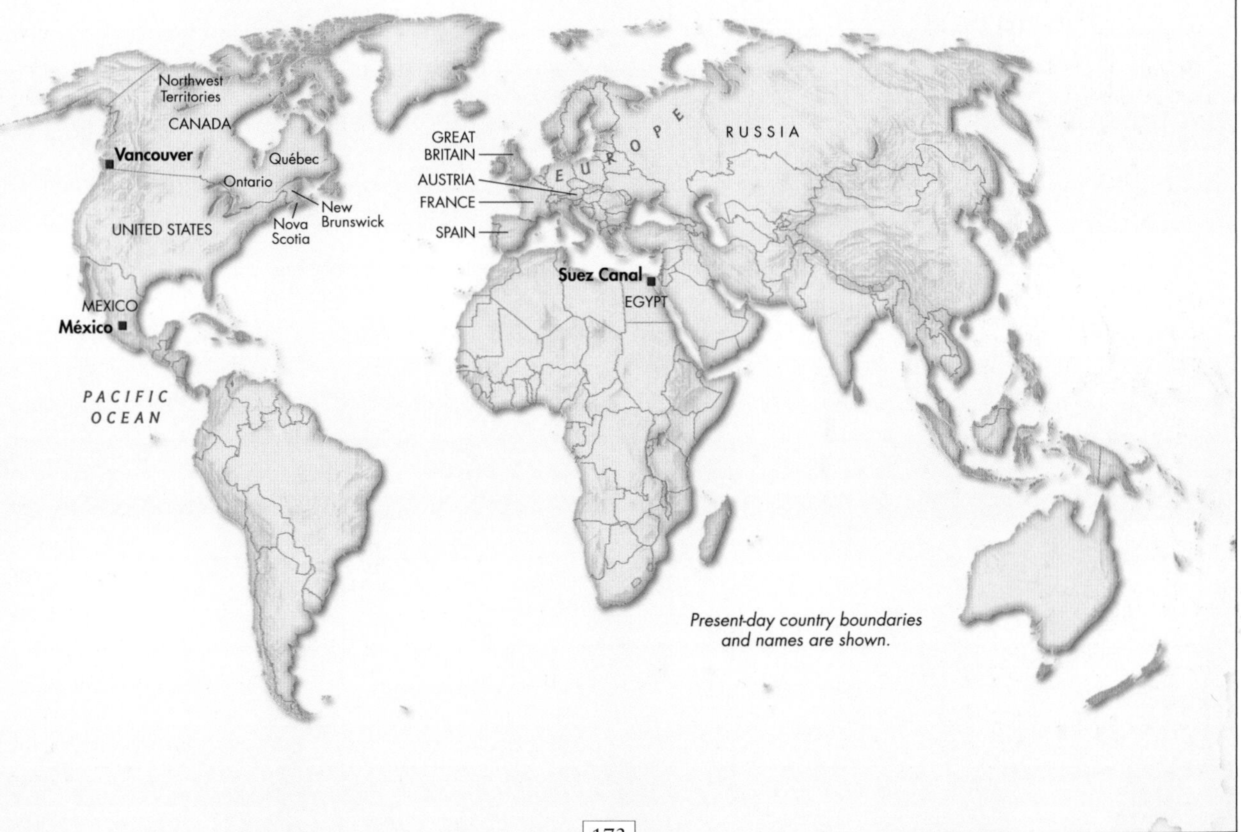

Present-day country boundaries and names are shown.

FROM SEA TO SHINING SEA 1867–1896

WITH THE CIVIL WAR OVER, THE VICTORIOUS NORTHERNERS TURNED THEIR ENERGIES back to the westward surge of antebellum days. Tens of thousands of Union veterans yearned for family farms. Immigrants who had flocked into the Union Army or wartime factories were now available for railroad construction or dreamed of a western farm of their own. Industries that had churned out uniforms and weapons redirected production toward farm implements and work clothing. American capital invested in wartime industry and foreign capital withheld when the Union's future remained in doubt now could fund westward expansion. Opportunity beckoned, and Yankee optimism knew no bounds.

No longer did southern congressmen block legislation that would open up the West on northern terms. In 1862, the Republican-dominated Congress passed the Homestead Act, which granted a 160-acre farm on western federal lands to anyone who settled on and developed the plot for five years. That same year Congress chartered two companies to build a transcontinental railroad between the Missouri River and California.

The "way west" lay open. Neither nature nor the West's native and Hispanic peoples now seemed a barrier to the realization of what, for a generation, Americans had assumed was their "Manifest Destiny" to sweep across the entire continent. ■

This 1885 train trestle may look rickety, but it was sturdier than wooden ones thrown up to carry the first transcontinental railroad in 1869.

■ **1867**
Nebraska admitted as a state; Alaska purchased.

■ **1869**
Completion of first transcontinental railroad.

■ **1876**
Colorado admitted as a state; "Custer's Last Stand" at Little Bighorn.

■ **1881**
Helen Hunt Jackson publishes *A Century of Dishonor.*

■ **1886**
Great Plains drought and severe winter wipe out many ranchers and farmers.

■ 1887	■ 1889	■ 1890	■ 1893	■ 1896
Dawes Severalty Act breaks up large reservations, provides for individual farms.	Oklahoma opened to non-Indian settlement; North Dakota, South Dakota, Montana, and Washington admitted as states.	Ghost Dance spreads to Plains Indians; Wounded Knee massacre; U.S. Census Office declares the western frontier closed; Wyoming and Idaho admitted as states.	Frederick Jackson Turner reads his paper, "The Significance of the Frontier in American History.	Utah admitted as a state.

Tracks Across the Continent

1865–1890

As debate erupted in Washington over policy on Reconstruction, across the nation many were avidly following telegraphed news of the construction of the first transcontinental railroad. In San Francisco, the group of wealthy merchants (their fortunes dated from the gold rush days) who organized the Central Pacific Company planned the daunting task of laying tracks from Sacramento eastward across the towering Sierra Nevada Range and the Nevada desert. In the East, the Union Pacific Company contracted with a European-based construction firm called Crédit Mobilier to build westward from Omaha.

Beginning in 1865, the two companies raced against each other. At stake was the vast acreage that the federal government promised for every mile of track laid. The Union Pacific had the easier task, following a route—already surveyed by Army engineers—across Nebraska and present-day Wyoming that often paralleled the Oregon and

These Indians of the Atsina tribe—a branch of the Arapaho nation—are performing part of a ritual dance known as "Flight of the Arrows."

Western Women Voting

American women gained the vote in 1920 with the 19th Amendment. But the territory of Wyoming gave women the vote in 1869, and women kept that right when Wyoming became a state in 1890. Since 1870, women—70,000 of them—voted in the Utah Territory and (after 1896) the state of Utah. Colorado enacted women's suffrage in 1893; Idaho, in 1896. Women could vote in Montana school-board elections after 1896. Because Western states were eager to increase their populations and attract educated women as teachers, women's suffrage enjoyed early progress in the West.

Mormon Trails. Logistical problems, however, made laying the track in record time a challenge. The workers, mostly Irish and Mexican immigrants, as well as blacks, had to be provisioned as they crossed virtually unsettled country. Massive buffalo hunts organized by Col. William F. Cody (later to gain fame as the showman Buffalo Bill) provided most of the food. Supplies had to be continuously brought in by rail as the tracks went down; discipline had to be maintained in the rowdy construction settlements that sprang up along the way. There was worry about Indian attacks, and the U.S. Cavalry stood guard, but in fact the Plains tribes largely kept their distance. Under these conditions, the Union Pacific stretched westward at a feverish pace.

Building eastward from California posed greater challenges. Narrow shelves for the right-of-way had to be cut alongside raging whitewater. Trestles had to be thrown across high gorges, and tunnels blasted through mountains. The hard-driving Central Pacific bosses bullied their crews, eager that the company lay enough track and claim enough land to make the venture profitable. American-born workers rebelled at the seemingly impossible job. Most of the Central Pacific's workforce came to consist of Chinese laborers—10,000 in all, some veterans of the gold rush days, others brought from South China to California specifically for the job. Their work was hazardous in the extreme: for example, being lowered by ropes in flimsy baskets to hammer holes into sheer rock faces, in which highly volatile explosives were then detonated.

On May 10, 1869, the job was done. At a spot in the Utah Territory called Promontory, on the northern edge of the Great Salt Lake, the two lines met. A golden spike was driven to join the tracks, the hammer blows telegraphed across the nation and the leaders of the two rival lines shaking hands for the photographers. Church bells rang out the news that track bound together the United States from sea to sea. It was now possible to travel overland from New York to San Francisco in a week—and soon, thanks to the Pullman Company's slumber coaches and dining cars, in great comfort. Already, the West was being opened to tourists; Yellowstone National Park (the first of its kind) was created in 1872 for visitors

NOTABLE DATES

■ 1865
Building of Central Pacific and Union Pacific railroads begins.

■ 1867
United States purchases Alaska from Russia.

■ 1869
Central Pacific and Union Pacific lines meet in Utah, completing the first transcontinental railroad.

■ 1872
Yellowstone National Park opens; Crédit Mobilier scandal in connection with Union Pacific railroad construction uncovered.

■ 1890
Yosemite National Park opens; the western frontier declared closed following U.S. Census.

"Seward's Ice Box"

ALASKA BECAME RUSSIAN TERRITORY IN THE MID-18TH CENTURY. In 1799 the Russian-American Company was chartered to tap the lucrative commerce in seal and sea otter pelts, and the Orthodox Church set up a few missions. North of Spanish-controlled San Francisco Bay, Russians established Fort Ross in 1812. The United States took no notice except when, in 1823, Russia edged closer to formally claiming the whole Pacific Coast down to San Francisco. But Fort Ross proved unprofitable and was abandoned in 1841, and Russia retracted its claims back to 54°40′, the northern limit of the Oregon Country.

William H. Seward served as secretary of state all through the Civil War and under Andrew Johnson. He is considered one of the greatest occupants of that office.

In the 1860s, Russia faced critical foreign policy choices. Alaska was vulnerable to being picked off by the British in the event of war. Selling off the distant territory—of diminishing value as overhunting depleted fur-bearing animals—seemed prudent. Russia's relations with the United States had been good during the Civil War, when both governments resented British meddling in their internal affairs. (Russia faced a revolt of its Polish provinces at the same time that the Union was fighting southern secessionists, who like the Poles counted on European intervention.) So, when in 1867 Russia approached Secretary of State William Seward with an offer to sell Alaska for $7.2 million, the deal was promptly accepted. Seward, mindful of protecting American interests along the sea route to East Asia, persuaded President Johnson and a skepticalCongress to appropriate the money, despite scoffing about buyingfrozen "Walrussia."

Still, Alaska remained little known. It was not farming country, and few Americans homesteaded. Gold strikes in Alaska and the Klondike region of the nearby Canadian Yukon caused "rushes." But it was the 20th-century discovery of Alaska's mineral and petroleum wealth, as well as its significance during World War II and the Cold War, that in retrospect made Seward's strategic vision obvious. ■

who came by train followed by long stagecoach rides, and from the beginning it was well furnished with tourist facilities. (A second transcontinental line, the Northern Pacific, soon made Yellowstone Park much more accessible.) Yosemite National Park in California followed in 1890.

Much of the railroad construction was shoddy. Within a few years, tracks had to be re-laid, and (after several tragic accidents) rickety trestles had to be replaced. The transcontinental railroad companies (like so many others in this era of quick and shady money) proved to be grossly mismanaged. Crédit Mobilier was especially corrupt, and its bribery ensnared prominent politicians including Vice President Schuyler Colfax.

An Epic Achievement

Still, building the first transcontinental railroad—as well as the construction of other lines during the next decades crossing the Northwest and the Southwest—was an enormous step. It speeded up enormously the trans-Missouri West's economic, social, and political development and the vast region's integration into the nation as a whole. Over the years, railroads brought settlers west by the hundreds of thousands. Because the government had granted them large tracts along the right-of-way, the railroads had plenty of choice land to sell to settlers. Those who settled down—to farm, to mine, or to populate the region's mushrooming towns—found themselves instantly dependent on the railroads to bring their output to east-

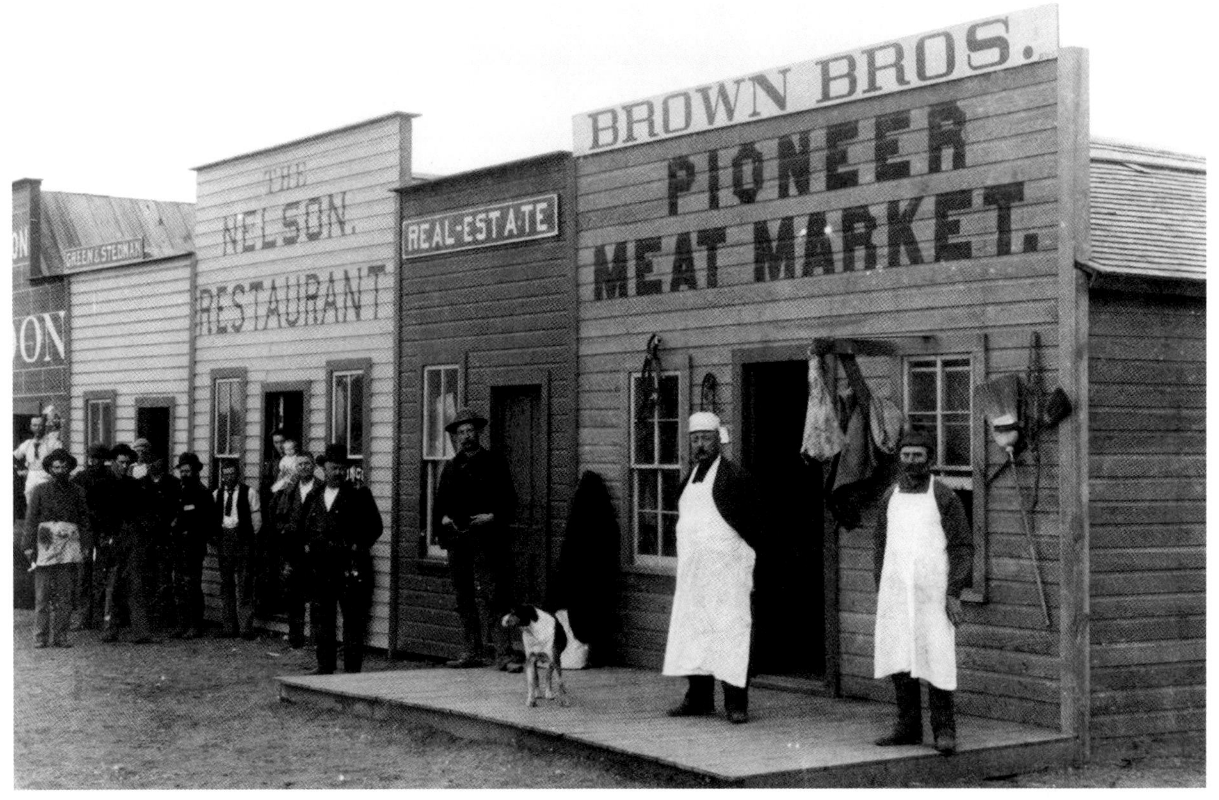

Townsmen pose in Round Pond in Oklahoma Territory in January 1894. Growth of towns and the birth of civic pride were important parts of the settlement of the western frontier.

ern processing plants and markets and to keep them supplied with manufactured goods. That dependency would cost the new western communities dearly in the late nineteenth century, spurring demands for radical political reform. For example, the People's (or Populist) Party, a third-party protest movement that gained much support in the Midwest and West in the early 1890s, took the lead in denouncing the railroads as a menace to the interests of farmers and small-town businessmen. "In their delirium of greed," orated the Populists' 1892 presidential candidate, James B. Weaver, "the managers of our transportation systems disregard both private right and public welfare. Today they will combine and bankrupt their weak rivals, and by the expenditure of a trivial sum possess themselves of properties which cost the outlay of millions. Tomorrow they will capitalize their booty for five times the cost, issue their bonds, and proceed to levy tariffs upon the people to pay dividends upon the fraud."

Momentously, in 1890 the federal census authorities declared that the western frontier—the imaginary line separating settled from unsettled lands—no longer existed. Only 21 years had passed since the driving of the golden spike. By that frontier-closing year, almost all the Great Plains and Rocky Mountain region had achieved statehood. (Utah waited until 1896, when the Mormon church withdrew its sanction for polygamy to meet congressional requirements; Arizona, New Mexico, Oklahoma became states early in the 20th century.)

The heaviest cost of building the transcontinental railroads fell upon the native populations of the West. Their traditional hunting grounds and grazing ranges disrupted by rail lines and barbed wire, their lands seized by unequal treaties for settlers' farms, the buffalo herds on which they depended for survival almost wiped out by predatory hunters, the Indians of the Plains were soon driven into desperate revolts in a futile effort to stop the progress of the white man. By the 1890s, they too would be all but totally crushed. ■

The Last Indian Wars

1862–1900

THE NATIVE PEOPLES OF THE Great Plains and northwestern plateau region best embody the familiar image of "American Indians," complete with feathered war bonnets and war paint. Since acquiring horses from the Spanish in the late 16th century and later firearms from European traders, they had developed into fierce, skillful hunters and warriors, proud of their independent, often nomadic way of life. The Sioux, Arapaho, Pawnee, Northern Cheyenne, Blackfoot, Crow, and Nez Perce nations captured the imaginations, and eventually also the consciences, of "back east" Americans and Europeans. Yet they were by no means the only Native Americans to stand in the way of advancing white settlers. In the Southwest, settled agricultural peoples such as Hopi and Zuni had maintained wary relationships with the region's Spanish-speaking settlers since about 1600, and they often had to defend themselves against such warlike invaders as the Navajo and Apache—who also stubbornly resisted white conquest. The native peoples of California and the Great Basin, whose non-agricultural way of life outsiders patronized as "primitive," were often overwhelmed by the mid-century gold rush immigrants; by the century's end, most had been reduced to meager remnants. In the Northwest, the Chinook and other coastal peoples struggled hard to maintain their salmon streams against the logging companies of Oregon and Washington State.

About 360,000 native peoples inhabited all the regions of the trans-Mississippi West in 1865. On the High Plains and in the northwestern plateau country, most Indian nations migrated seasonally over traditional hunting grounds. But at least as many Indians, particularly in the Southwest and the Northwest, lived in permanent village communities, and the once-warlike Navajo were taking up more peaceful ways as sheepherders. Everywhere during the next 35 years, western Indian communities were devastated by diseases such as smallpox, against which Indian people had little natural resistance, and by alcoholism encouraged by white traders, to which Indians were particularly susceptible. And in many places, a brutal, sometimes violent, struggle also ensued between the white man's vision of progress and the native people's defense of their traditional land and way of life. In the end it was always the natives who would lose.

Guns blazing, in this romanticized 1889 lithograph, George A. Custer and his men make their last stand on the Little Bighorn. In 1876, Custer's death came as a great shock to a nation preparing to celebrate its centennial.

Indian-white relations had been relatively peaceful during the great westward migrations to Oregon, California, and Utah during the 1840s. But the uneasy peace began to break down during the Civil

War. In Minnesota in 1862, the Sioux rebelled against advancing white settlement; after the militia crushed the insurrection, 38 Sioux (about a tenth of those originally condemned) were hanged for murder or rape on President Lincoln's order. In the southern Plains, some tribes sided with the Confederates and occasionally clashed with Union soldiers. In Colorado, raiding mining communities was always a temptation for the Plains people after a gold rush started there in 1859. In retaliation, in 1864 the territorial militia massacred, without provocation, a large band of Arapahos encamped at Sand Creek. Then, in 1866, the Teton Sioux ferociously battled the cavalry in Wyoming, trying to stop construction of a road to a gold-mining field across their sacred grounds.

A New Policy

These outbreaks of violence shocked many in the East, and in response Congress enacted a new Indian policy in 1868. Natives were supposed to confine themselves to two large "reservations,"

NOTABLE DATES

■ **1862**
Sioux uprising in Minnesota; 38 leaders hanged.

■ **1864**
Colorado militia massacres Arapahos at Sand Creek.

■ **1866**
Teton Sioux clash with U.S. Cavalry in Wyoming Territory.

■ **1868**
New federal reservation policy announced, moving Indians away from transcontinental railroad.

■ **1869**
Transcontinental railroad completed, passing through Plains Indian country.

■ **1870**
Full-scale Indian War engulfs Plains.

■ **1876**
Custer and his men wiped out in Battle of Little Bighorn in Montana Territory.

■ **1877**
Chief Joseph and the Nez Perce surrender and accept transfer to reservation.

■ **1879**
Carlisle Indian School established to educate young Indians in Euro-American ways.

■ **1881**
Helen Hunt Jackson publishes *A Century of Dishonor.*

■ **1887**
Dawes Severality Act breaks up reservations by giving Indians small farmsteads.

■ **1890**
Ghost Dance spreads; death of Sitting Bull; Wounded knee massacre.

Carlisle School

Having defeated the tribes of the Plains militarily, the United States government undertook a massive campaign to transform the Indians culturally and economically. The goals were to eradicate "Indianness" and to assimilate Indians into white society. The best way to accomplish this, officials believed, was to educate Indian children.

The flagship of the government boarding schools was the Carlisle Indian Industrial School, established in Army barracks in southern Pennsylvania by Capt. Richard H. Pratt. After managing the Indian prison at Fort Marion, Pratt became committed to improving the lives and futures of Indian children. Ten thousand children enrolled in his school during its 40-year existence. The school flourished from 1879 to 1918, by which time it and similar schools were falling out of favor.

Richard Pratt, a veteran of the Indian Wars, was one of the well-meaning whites who hoped to "save" the Indians by training them in the whites' way of life.

At these schools, the young Indians learned skilled trades, farming, and home economics, but they received little more than an eighth-grade education. When they graduated, they faced tremendous difficulties. Successfully educated out of their traditional cultural patterns, they still did not easily fit into the white culture that had transformed them, and hence they did not comfortably belong to either culture.

At the time, though, it was impossible to predict such a difficult future for the children of the Carlisle School. Even Indians praised the work that Pratt was doing. Geronimo visited the school in 1905 and told the children he met there, "You are here to study, to learn the ways of white men, do it well." ■

on which they would—it was hoped, with help from Protestant missionaries—eventually settle down as Christian farmers. One reservation lay north of Nebraska, the other south of Kansas. Through the intervening corridor (through which the new transcontinental railroad ran), white settlement was encouraged and protected against Indian raiders. But the policy quickly broke down: Indians simply refused to stay out of lands where traditionally they had hunted. "We do not want to live like the white man," said a Sioux chief. "Our fathers have taught us to hunt and live on the Plains, and we are contented." Many Plains people simply had to extend their hunting grounds as far as possible as a result of the huge killing of buffalo that attended the building of the transcontinental railroad. That extermination continued as train-riding sportsmen came west, and the Army encouraged the slaughter simply to weaken potential Indian enemies.

When Indian raids on the settled corridor continued, the cavalry struck back hard. By 1870, full-scale war raged on the Great Plains. By now, most of the remaining United States Army units (except for those still occupying the South) were committed to the struggle against the Plains warriors. Not only did Indian raids on white settlers continue to provoke military counterattacks, but whites also insisted on pressing into lands that Indians thought had been guaranteed as theirs forever—and not only did the Army do little to prevent them, but it sometimes encouraged them outright. Thus in 1874 Gen. William Tecumseh Sherman, of Civil War fame, sent the flamboyant cavalry commander George Armstrong Custer into the Black Hills region of present-day South Dakota. Ostensibly, his orders were to find the site for a new fort, but Custer was also on the lookout for good farmland and to confirm rumors of gold. When he found evidence of both, he sent glowing reports to the eastern newspapers, sparking a new rush of settlers into lands that the Sioux held sacred. The Sioux responded by organizing an alliance led by Sitting Bull. On June 25, 1876, having tracked down Sitting Bull's warriors, Custer and 211 cavalrymen rashly attacked a much larger encampment of Sioux warriors on the Little Bighorn River in southeastern Montana. Custer and all his men perished. News of "Custer's Last

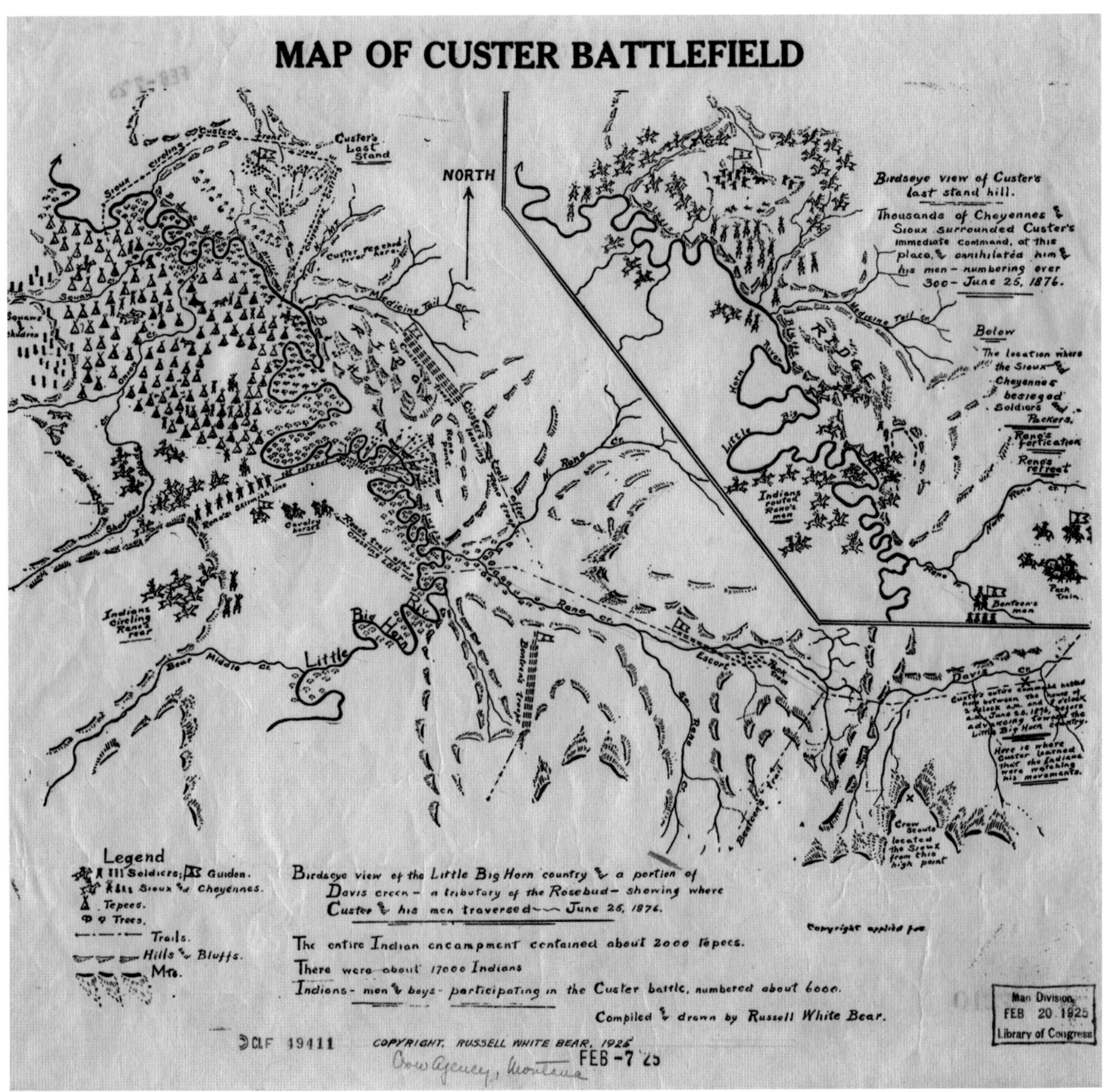

Custer foolishly blundered into his unplanned, fateful battle with the Sioux in June 1876. This map was drawn much later, as the U.S. Army was struggling to reassess its tactics in fighting the Plains Indians.

The Ghost Dance and Wounded Knee

As the demoralization of the western Indians hit rockbottom in the late 1880s, the ecstatic movement known as the Ghost Dance spread across the region.

Originating among the Paiute people of Nevada, the Ghost Dance was propagated by a native healer named Wovoka. By performing a hypnotic communal dance, Wovoka promised, the spirits of the native people's ancestors would come back to life; if Indians gave up white ways and lived honest lives, the invaders would be driven from the land and America restored to it true owners. And, he added, performing rituals would keep warriors safe from white bullets. This faith combined native traditions with bits of Christianity, culled from missionaries. Federal authorities saw the Ghost Dance as an incitement, and tried to ban it.

These leaders of the Ghost Dance movement led more than a thousand Indians into the Dakota Territory before the Wounded Knee Massacre.

In 1890, the Ghost Dance reached Sioux reservations in the Dakota Territory. Sitting Bull encouraged his people to perform it and took part in the ritual himself. That December, a federal marshal arrived at the reservation to enforce the ban and arrest Sitting Bull. In the confusion, a gun went off, and one of the panicked federal agents killed the chief with a point-blank shot.

Only weeks later, on the same Sioux reservation, at Wounded Knee, in present-day South Dakota, United States troops were rounding up freezing, hungry Indians to move them to a new location. One desperate Sioux fired a concealed rifle. No soldiers were injured, but they responded with a machine gun, raking the huddled, frightened natives. More than 300 Indians fell dead, some of them small children. All the bodies were dumped into a mass grave. ■

Stand," telegraphed to a nation that had come to admire the showy cavalry hero, cast a pall over the hundredth-anniversary celebrations of independence. Some Americans were shocked at the aggressive campaign the Army was waging. A *New York Herald* writer spoke for most, however, when he declared that "to allow the Indian to roam over a country as fine as that around the Black Hills . . . can never be. This region must be taken from the Indian."

Military leaders in the West agreed, but the memory of Custer's grim fate instilled caution. Rather than attempting knockout blows, the Army sought to wear down Indian bands and slowly to drive the Native Americans into ever-smaller reservations. Bands who refused to stay on reservations were hunted down and imprisoned—and some who tried to escape were killed. A favorite tactic was to wipe out buffalo herds and destroy winter food supplies. This war of attrition slowly had its effect. In 1877, Chief Joseph of the Nez Perce gave up after having led his people on an epic retreat from the northwestern plateau into Canada. "I will fight no more forever," he pledged in his famous surrender agreement, by which the Nez Perce were exiled to the distant plains of present-day Oklahoma. The same fate befell Sitting Bull and his Sioux in 1881—and the great chief was forced to endure the ignominy of being paid to sit like a sideshow freak, staring balefully at gawking eastern visitors to Buffalo Bill's "Wild West" show.

Twilight of a Nation

The brutal Indian wars and the despoiling of the western tribes shocked many Easterners. But these "friends of the Indian" almost invariably thought in terms of white values. Richard Pratt, a retired Army officer, in 1879 founded the Carlisle School in Pennsylvania with the watchword "Kill the Indian, save the man." Young Indians, voluntarily sent by their families to the school (or others like it), were reeducated. They received new names, wore "proper" clothing, learned trades, were converted to Christianity, and were subjected to every possible pressure to make them forget their native heritage. Few Carlisle graduates matured into confident and well-adjusted adults. Another well-meaning white attempt to encourage justice for Native Americans was Helen Hunt Jackson's widely read 1881 book, *A Century of Dishonor,* documenting the long trail of broken treaties between the United States government and the Indian nations.

Called upon by such reformers to "do right," Congress in 1887 enacted one of the most important pieces of legislation affecting Native Americans, the Dawes Severalty Act. The idea, basically humanitarian and rooted in middle-class white values, was to give individual Indians secure property rights, to encourage them to take up farming, and to wean them away from "outmoded" tribalism. Actually, it did great damage to Indians' cultural identity, morale, and individual well-being, The act broke up the large reservations on which most western Indians had already been forced, and on which they felt badly limited in their ability to pursue their traditional nomadic existence. Instead, individual Indians were now asked to accept 160-acre plots carved out of the reservations for individual farms, or 320-acre plots for grazing land. Whatever remained of tribal reservation land after these allotments were made was then sold to white settlers. Naturally, the best land tended to wind up being sold off, leaving the Indians with farms or grazing land that was practically useless—too small, too isolated, too arid, and too infertile to actually support a family.

The reservations quickly became squalid, hopeless dumping grounds for dispossessed, unwanted human beings. Alcoholism, despair, and silent rage grew endemic. Few Native Americans had any idea of how to farm or ranch in the white man's way. White traders continued to cheat the Indians with impunity, and education was limited to the bare minimum, in a language and with cultural assumptions that few Indians could understand.

Resistance slowly died. The last great Indian uprisings took place from 1882-1886, when the Apache chief Geronimo led a stubborn guerrilla war (as we would call it today) in the borderlands of New Mexico, Arizona, and Mexico. For the next decade, violent conflict in the West was sporadic, usually in response to actions by U.S. Army troops.

By 1900, the population of the Plains Indians had dropped below 100,000—down by at least half in 45 years. Only the Navajo, by giving up marauding and becoming pastoralists, were increasing their numbers. Not until 1924 would all Indians even enjoy American citizenship. The story of the Native American and the destruction of the Indian nations was one of the saddest sagas in U.S. history, weighing with increasing heaviness on the modern American conscience. ■

Wiping Out the Buffalo

In the mid-19th century buffalo may have numbered 32 million head. In the 1870s American carriage riders developed a fashion for buffalo robes, and factories needed hides for machinery belts. The Sioux made good money supplying these needs. William F. (Buffalo Bill) Cody organized mass hunts to supply meat to crews building the Union Pacific railroad, and afterwards excursion trains of hunters from the East slaughtered the animals for "sport"—nine million animals in the years1872-75 alone. The United States Army encouraged these slaughters as a way of depriving hostile Indians of their food supply. By the 1880s, the great herds were gone—buffalo were down to a few thousand head.

Closing the Frontier

1865–1896

Most new settlers of the West moved from nearby midwestern states. Homesteaders made up only a fraction of them, and an even smaller proportion of those who settled successfully. The railroads used their generous federal land grants to sell, very profitably, the best tracts to farmers who could pay well for gaining ready access to transportation. Speculators also bought from the government, and then parceled out, blocks of what they claimed (not always accurately) to be good farmland. Homesteaders usually had to stake claims to acreage far from rail lines, on land no one else wanted. Many were foreign-born. Almost none, however, were city workers without prior experience in farming.

Favorable climatic conditions in the 1870s lured many westward, and railroads and land promoters spread encouraging stories that plowing virgin soil stimulated the clouds above to yield plentiful rainfall. But this weather was unusual. By the 1880s, the weather on the Great Plains was cycling back to its normal, semi-arid conditions, and would-be settlers who were slow to learn "dry farming" methods (combining deep plowing and constant harrowing) suffered catastrophic losses. Swarms of

Helena, Montana, was a boomtown after the discovery of gold there in 1864—at Last Chance Gulch, which later became this main street in the town, photographed in 1870. Unlike other gold-rush towns, Helena became a thriving city.

Bread Basket Distress

After the 1870s American farmers faced declining prices. Improvements in agricultural machinery, the expansion of settlement and railroads, and foreign competition produced these annual per-bushel averages of wholesale wheat—and distress and political protest throughout agrarian America.

1870	$1.37	**1884**	$.93
1871	$1.58	**1885**	$.86
1872	$1.78	**1886**	$.80
1873	$1.78	**1887**	$.77
1874	$1.52	**1888**	$.87
1875	$1.43	**1889**	$.89
1876	$1.30	**1890**	$.89
1877	$1.68	**1891**	$.96
1878	$1.25	**1892**	$.79
1879	$1.22	**1893**	$.68
1880	$1.06	**1894**	$.60
1881	$1.15	**1895**	$.60
1882	$1.12	**1896**	$.64
1883	$1.04	**1897**	$.79

crop-devouring locusts wrought disasters of biblical proportions. Yields from homestead plots of 160 acres proved pitifully inadequate to support farm families on the dry lands beyond the 100th meridian. Life on the treeless, windswept Plains, often in a sod house and with neighbors few and far between, could be desperately lonely, especially for women who had left behind networks of kin and friends. Western farmers soon found that their cash crops—wheat or corn—were perilously dependent on global market conditions, and years of glut and tumbling prices would wipe them out. Railroads and grain-elevator operators ruthlessly used their control of access to markets to extract what farmers considered extortionate profits, and the federal government's tight-money policies kept the price of credit high. In short, western farming was no bonanza. Speaking for thousands of others, one woebegone family trekked back eastward to seek refuge among relatives, its wagon painted "In God we trusted, in Kansas we busted." In places like North Dakota's Red River Valley, corporate wheat farms with steam-powered machinery began taking over where homesteaders had failed, foreshadowing the development of 20th-century agribusiness.

The Open Range

The cattle boom followed a similar trajectory. In the 1870s, railroads facilitated grazing vast herds on the open range, especially in Texas and the Wyoming Territory. Ranchers marketed their animals by driving them to railhead cow towns like Dodge City or Cheyenne. From there, trains hauled them to the Chicago and Kansas City slaughterhouses. Big money could be made in cattle, but it required capital, a significant share of which came from Europe.

The hard work of range riding and herding fell to poorly paid cowboys, whose skills and jargon mostly came from Mexico. (So did many cowboys.) Out of all this emerged, somehow, a new American folk hero. In the 1870s and 1880s, paperback "dime novels" about Deadeye Dick thrilled eastern readers of all ages. Dick was a real cowboy, though wildly romanticized and with inconvenient details left out. For example, most of the cowboys' meager earn-

NOTABLE DATES

■ 1870s-early 1880s
Abnormally wet weather conditions lure many white settlers into the Great Plains regions.

■ Late1880s
Great Plains weather reverts to normally arid conditions.

■ 1885-1886
Blizzards devastate Great Plains cattle ranching.

■ 1889
Great Oklahoma land rush.

■ 1890
Following U.S. Census, western frontier declared "closed."

■ 1892
People's, or Populist, Party nominates James B. Weaver for President.

■ 1892
Frederick Jackson Turner reads his influential paper, "The Significance of the Frontier in American History."

■ 1896
Democrat and Populist candidate William J. Bryan loses presidential race to William McKinley.

In 1867, this ambulance wagon, which also featured a portable darkroom, rumbled across the Carson Desert in Nevada during a geological survey conducted by the government. Such surveys were crucial in developing the West's mineral resources.

ings wound up in (to middle-class readers) highly disreputable cow town establishments like saloons, dance halls, gambling houses, and brothels. It was also not revealed that the real Dick was black, like many other cowboys—former slaves who accepted this hard work as an escape from southern sharecropping.

The cattle boom came at a high cost. As both the cattlemen and the farmers moved onto the Plains, "range wars" erupted between crop growers stringing barbed-wire fences and ranchers trying to maximize the free range. As more and more land was fenced off, overgrazing on what was left of the range destroyed the grass cover and—like many farmers' inappropriate cultivation—caused severe erosion and topsoil losses; the full consequences would only appear in the 1930s Dust Bowl. More immediately, the abnormally cold and snowy winter of 1886-1887 devastated herds, by now too large to find enough natural forage, and ruined many a rancher—just as drought, insects, overproduction, and tumbling prices brought terrible distress to farmers.

The extractive industries—mining and lumbering—all entailed big business; a few individual miners might strike it rich at panning or prospecting, but sustained enterprise was impossible without heavy investment. Over time, the ghost towns multiplied—settlements like Virginia City, Nevada, and Cripple Creek, Colorado, that in the heyday of the gold and silver rushes had flourished with as many as 10,000 residents, only to be abandoned when the rush was over and opportunity beckoned elsewhere. But some of the mining "strikes" turned into cities with real industrial bases, such as Helena, Montana, with its rich copper mining pits and smelting works. Lumbering, which housed workers in camps, was more mobile, but also attracted capital and just as diverse a labor force.

Chinese, blacks, Mexicans, and eastern and southern Europeans all were drawn—often more readily than old-stock Americans of north European ancestry—to the hard industrial labor needed for the West's diversifying economy and its booming cities in the late 19th century. Collisions between these poorly paid workers, their angry white co-workers, and their corporate employers also produced some of the bitterest, bloodiest labor strife in American history. Class conflict and income inequalities were, in fact, greater during the 1880s and 1890s than at almost any other time in American history. The tensions inherent in these situations deeply influenced western life at the close of the 19th century—and through the West, the nation's destiny as well.

Protest Parties

Agrarian distress in the Plains states (and in the South too) produced a raft of protest and political third parties. Common threads running through these movements were demands that credit be eased, more dollars be put into circulation, and the monopolistic rates of railroads and grain-storage operators be regulated. Not only farmers and ranchers but also many western merchants, bankers, and other small-business owners supported these protests, usually with little lasting success. Labor agitation, responding to the anti-unionizing efforts of mining and lumbering companies and fighting the alleged willingness of Chinese laborers to accept low wages, also became explosive. Rural and small-town grievances coalesced in the movement called populism, which mounted a serious though unsuccessful effort to capture the Presidency in 1892. In 1896 the populist movement captured the Democratic Party itself with the nomination of William Jennings Bryan, an orator whose sole issue was a demand for the free coinage of silver in hopes of curing the national depression by inflating the currency.

Bryan lost the election of 1896; Republican William McKinley triumphed, with his "sound money" platform that appealed to eastern bankers, industrialists, and urban workers. McKinley, not Bryan, set the stage for 20th-century politics.

The mystique of the frontier, however, would live on in American culture, at least through the mid-1960s, in the popular appeal of "western" fiction and movies in which "manly" men and spirited women defied the odds, and right triumphed over wrong. Not only dime novels trumpeted this vision; in 1893, historian Frederick Jackson Turner read an influential paper to a historical convention arguing that the frontier—recently declared "closed" by the Census Office—had always been the seedbed of American democracy, liberty, and individuality. (Turner said little about the Indians' fate.) The western myth was just that—a myth, and one that ignored much that was ugly and evil—yet it contained enough reality to help define bedrock American virtues. ■

The Great Land Rush

IN THE 19TH CENTURY, WHAT IS NOW OKLAHOMA WAS CALLED THE Indian Territory. Here refuge had been granted to remnants of the "Five Civilized Tribes," evicted from the Southern Appalachians, Alabama, and Mississippi in the1830s and driven west on the Trail of Tears. The prairie land they found differed in many ways from their forested homelands, but some Indians prospered; a number of slaveholding tribes fought for the Confederacy. As punishment, during the subsequent Indian Wars much of the territory was broken up into reservations, onto which Plains tribes were forced southward to make room for the white settlers pouring into Kansas and Nebraska. Among the Indians forced in, at the expense of the pro-Confederate nations, were the Cheyenne, Arapaho, Osage, Comanche, and Apache, each assigned its own reservation. Federal law still kept the Territory off-limits to whites.

These homesteaders rushed into Oklahoma Territory staking claims to 160-acre farms—on lands once guaranteed to Indians moved from the Southeast.

By the late 1880s, as agrarian distress gripped the Plains, pressure became irresistible for Congress to make more good land available to white settlers. On April 22, 1889, canceling government promises of the land belonging to the Indians forever, "the great Oklahoma land rush" began. Thousands of white farmers stampeded into parts of the future state to stake out claims on two million acres of formerly Indian-held federal land. (Settlers discovered that some of the best tracts had been grabbed by white "sooners" who had sneaked in illegally.) The new soil transferred to whites, originally promised to Indians, was often better watered by rainfall and more fertile than other western reservation land. Over the next decade, other tribal lands were broken up under the Dawes Act, which gave homestead plots to individual Indian families but sold the "surplus" to the general public. By 1907, when Oklahoma received statehood, all the large reservations had been dissolved and most Indian land had passed to whites. ■

Gilded Age Politics

1873–1896

In 1873, Mark Twain and journalist Charles Dudley Warner co-authored a satirical novel about Washington life that gave the late 19th century in America its indelible name: *The Gilded Age*. This was not the first time in American history that corruption ran amok, nor was it the last. An argument can be made, though, that seldom was dishonesty in American public life more blatant, nor did the gap ever yawn more widely between untaxed wealth and the modest incomes of working- and middle-class people. There was no income tax; federal revenues came mainly from tariffs, excise taxes, and the sale of public lands. Virtually every city had its political boss at the head of a crooked "machine"; New York City's notorious Tammany Hall was only the best known of the kind. Most state legislatures were cesspools of corruption in which large corporations freely bought favors. Oil company bosses did everything they wanted to the Pennsylvania legislature, someone quipped, except refine it. Many congressmen were openly "on the take." Until the Pendleton Act (1883), patronage controlled

This drawing of the mysterious explosion aboard the U.S.S. *Maine* in Havana Harbor on February 15, 1898, helped inflame public opinion in the U.S., leading to the brief Spanish-American War.

almost all federal jobs, down to the local postmasterships.

Nevertheless, this was also an era of vibrant democratic participation, at least among white males. Between 1876 and 1896, participation in presidential elections *averaged* 78.5 percent of eligible voters—a far higher rate than at any time in the 20th century. Political passions boiled hot, and although many states were "solid" for one party, in national elections Democrats and Republicans were almost equally balanced. From 1868 through 1892, presidential elections were always very close, although only one Democrat was elected—Grover Cleveland, for two non-consecutive terms. Control of Congress seesawed. All elections were bitterly fought, amid a great hoopla of flowery speeches, torchlight processions, marching bands, and street brawls. For many males, politics was virtually a participant—even a contact—sport. One reason why many men objected to the idea of women's suffrage was their attitude that political loyalties were a form of male bonding, forged in saloons.

In this era, the federal government's powers were more limited than they would be in the century to come, and after the Civil War, Congress not the President was the chief initiator of policy. Similarly in the states, legislatures, not governors, generally ruled. Gilded Age Presidents were mostly good, earnest, bewhiskered men who could do little about the corruption of the day. James Garfield was assassinated in 1881 by a crazed and disappointed office seeker, a tragedy that helped push his successor, Chester A. Arthur, into signing the Pendleton Act, establishing the Civil Service system. Democrat Cleveland made his reputation chiefly by vetoing more pension bills and special-interest legislation than all other Gilded Age Presidents combined. These Presidents saw their job as administrators, not as policy makers. Vetoing a bill to give Texas farmers relief from a crop failure, Cleveland declared that in the United States, "though the people support the Government, the Government should not support the people."

Gilded Age politics may seem boring and petty, but not so to contemporaries. Should certain industries and workers be protected, or should tariffs be cut to lower the price of goods? Should credit to farmers and small businessmen be tight or loose? Should railroads and corporations be regulated? How generous should the federal government be in compensating aging Union Army veterans and their families?

Women did not vote, despite momentum building for women's suffrage after the Civil War. Resistance to giving women the vote was fierce in the older states, spearheaded by men who thought politics was the last refuge of "manly" men. "Politics ain't bean-bag," observed fictional Chicago Irish bartender "Mr. Dooley," a creation of 1890s newspaper humorist Finley Peter Dunne. "'Tis a man's game, an' women, childer, cripples an' prohybitionists 'd do well to keep out iv it." ■

NOTABLE DATES

■ 1873
Mark Twain and Charles Dudley Warner publish satirical novel, *The Gilded Age.*

■ 1876–1877
Rutherford B. Hayes becomes President after a hotly disputed election.

■ 1880
James A. Garfield elected President.

■ 1881
Garfield assassinated; Chester A. Arthur becomes President.

■ 1883
Pendleton Act establishes U.S. Civil Service System.

■ 1884
Grover Cleveland elected President.

■ 1888
Benjamin Harrison elected President.

■ 1892
Cleveland elected to second, non-consecutive term as President.

■ 1896
William McKinley elected President.

WORLD SURVEY

1867–1896

ALL OVER THE GLOBE, 19TH-century populations were rising, people were on the move, and empires were growing. People flocking in from rural hinterlands in search of industrial jobs sustained the massive growth of industrial cities in Europe, North America, and Japan. European peasants who were not absorbed by Old World cities crossed the seas in search of new homes, rural and urban, not only in the United States but also in Canada, Australia, New Zealand, and South America's "Southern Cone" countries.

Great Britain, France, Italy, Germany, Belgium, and Portugal were all building or expanding colonial empires; so was Japan. Imperialism sprouted from the same soil of nationalist, economic, social, and racial superiority as did the motivations for American westward expansion, and imperialism harbored a similar mixture of arrogant as well as humanitarian impulses.

Russia and China

In Russia, a rural population surge was relieved partly by early industrialization and partly by migration to Siberia. Between 1891 and 1903, this expansion of Russia's eastern frontier was facilitated by the building of the Trans-Siberian Railroad, an epic comparable to the construction of North America's transcontinental lines. Although many Russian peasants voluntarily migrated eastward seeking greater personal freedom and more land, others of Siberia's settlers were convicts and political prisoners, released from prison camps on condition that they never go home.

In China, where there was as yet virtually no industrialization, the 19th-century population boom simply forced peasants to migrate to inhospitable places such as frigid, heavily forested Manchuria, high-altitude Tibet, and China's arid far west, as well as out of China itself—to Southeast Asia and to North and South America.

Argentina, Australia, and New Zealand

Farmers in the post-Civil War American West were eager to feed the world's burgeoning cities. But Russia, Argentina, and Australia were also helping create a global grain market. American farmers who produced for that market found themselves subject to sharp, uncontrollable swings of supply and demand—that is, to booms and gluts, driven partly by local climate and partly by worldwide market conditions. Those wild gyrations help explain much of the agrarian distress that periodically gripped the late 19th-century American West.

The expansion of settlement in Australia closely resembled America's, and "down under" British colonial authorities' attempts to control and direct settlement aroused deep resentment. In the United States and Australia alike, the coming of big-business mining concerns and heavily capitalized sheep ranches gave a major spur to development.

Foreign capital and heavy European immigration in the 1860s and 1870s likewise spurred Argentina into rapid development, which included the rise of vast wheat farms and a heavily capitalized ranching industry; the proud and hard-working gauchos who herded cattle on the Argentine pampas became as important a part of their country's self-image as did the cowboys for Americans.

It is little comfort for Americans to know that other countries' experiences with displacing "primitive" indigenous populations in favor of newcomers were at least as disturbing. Thus in Australia indigenous peoples (or "Aborigines") resisted fiercely and died in droves, both from violence and disease. In New Zealand, British colonial authorities' efforts to oversee immigrants' purchase of land from the indigenous Maori people broke down amid incessant pressure from would-be settlers and escalating violence; decimated by European diseases, the Maori were cheated of their lands and driven deep into the islands' interior.

■ Canada

In the Canadian prairie and mountain provinces, the authorities generally managed to apportion land to designated groups of settlers and used the Royal Canadian Mounted Police to keep order among them—a policy very different from Americans' individualistic westward surge.

During the 1870s the Canadian government also confined the western Indians to reservations, usually by peaceful negotiation. In part this was because Canada offered modest financial and educational inducements, and in part because Canadian native peoples did not wish to share the fate of their resisting kinfolk south of the 49th parallel. Reservation land in Canada, as in the United States, tended to be places whites shunned, and in the long run Canadian native peoples who moved to reservations did not fare much better than did those in the U.S.

In the 19th century, "progress" was practically an article of religious faith. "Backward" peoples were expected to make way. As racism acquired pseudo-scientific underpinnings, such reasoning acquired respectability: "primitive" societies stood in the way of progress, condemned by their "backwardness" to succumb. Even if native peoples did not deserve extermination, many well-intentioned people thought they should be lifted out of their benighted ways and given the benefit of a superior civilization. If "the only good Indian is a dead Indian" was a chilling American proverb, the Carlisle School founder's motto "Kill the Indian, save the man" smugly justified cultural genocide. ■

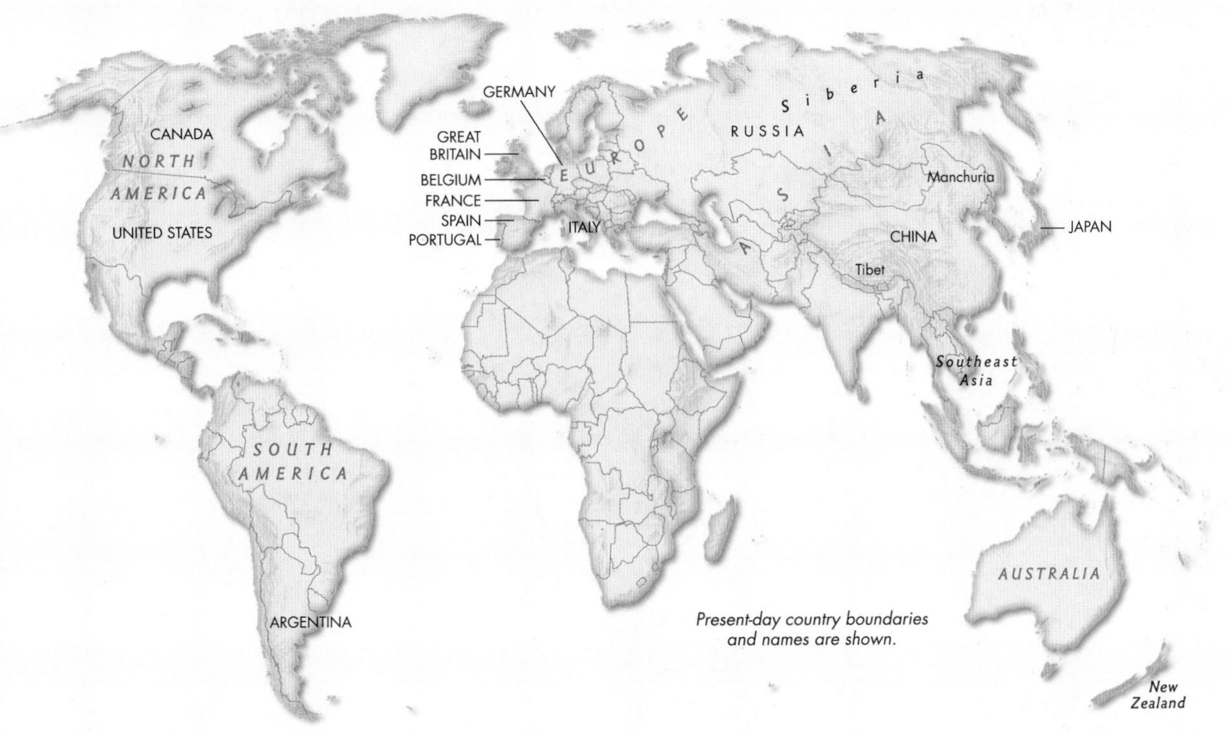

Present-day country boundaries and names are shown.

Modern America Rises 1870–1917

The Civil War had been fought between a North and a South that were still rural and small-town societies. When America's next great war began, in 1917, the nation was fully industrialized, and the majority of Americans were urban.

While the West was being won, modern America was also emerging: an America of heavy industry, accelerating technology, mass education, central cities, mass media, consumerism, professional sports, movements for women's and civil rights, and the first worries about the environment. Movies and radio, automobiles and airplanes reshaped 20th-century life. Millions of Europeans, Asians, and southern blacks migrated to northern American cities. Americans discovered jazz, modern art, and fundamentalism. Abroad the United States became a major global player.

American political life changed, too. The 19th century had been the era of triumphant Jeffersonianism, idealizing small government and agrarian values. Twentieth-century politics would be dominated by a democratized version of the ideas of federalist Alexander Hamilton—creating a strong national government, promoting industry, and governing through educated elites. This new philosophy, Progressivism, was oriented toward industrial and urban America. It triumphed under the creators of the modern Presidency, Theodore Roosevelt and Woodrow Wilson. ■

Jammed with immigrants, Mulberry Street on New York's Lower East Side encapsulated the nation's urban problems in 1900.

■ 1870
Bessemer process revolutionizes steel-making.

■ 1873
Andrew Carnegie founds his first steel plant; panic of 1873.

■ 1890
Sherman Act attempts to prevent monopolies.

■ 1893
Panic of 1893.

■ 1896
Steelworkers' strike crushed; *Plessy* v. *Ferguson* case upolds segregation; Booker T. Washington offers compromise with segregation; McKinley elected President.

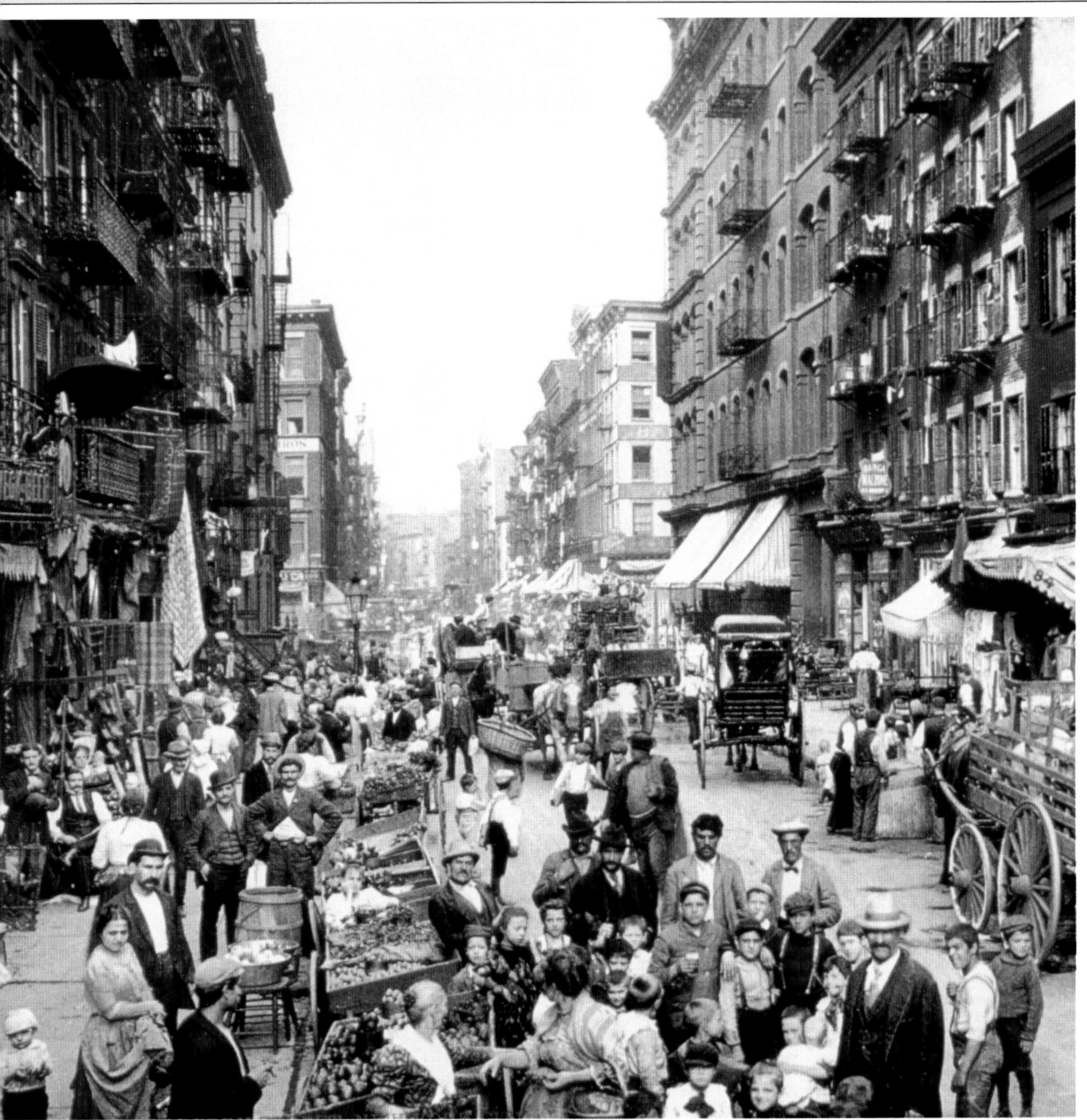

■ 1898
Spanish-American War.

■ 1901
U.S. Steel formed, first U.S. billion-dollar corporation; U.S. crushes resistance in Philippines; Theodore Roosevelt becomes President after McKinley's assassination.

■ 1912
Roosevelt runs for President on Progressive Party ticket, but Democrat Woodrow Wilson is elected.

■ 1914
Panama Canal completed; U.S. intervention in Mexico; outbreak of World War I in Europe.

■ 1917
U.S. enters World War I; Russian Revolution begins.

The Birth of Industrial America

1859–1911

EIGHTEENTH-CENTURY GREAT Britain had led the world in developing new sources of energy for making textiles and concentrating the process in factories. This was the Industrial Revolution. In New England, small factories first appeared in the 1790s. Thereafter, the proportion of manufacturing carried out in northern factories, as opposed to artisan workshops or rural households, steadily rose. By 1850, Americans were pioneering ways to mass-produce clocks and firearms using interchangeable, machine-made parts. Goods poured out of New England and midwestern factories. Steelmaking also spread, using the traditional open-hearth process. Industrialization lagged in the South, though it was not unknown.

The Civil War boosted northern manufacturing, and the Union's ability to churn out what it needed doomed the Confederacy. The loss of southern railroads and wealth (invested in land and slaves) set the region further behind the North.

Suggesting an exotic, luxurious, and slightly erotic ambiance, this 1900 advertisement tried to lure middle-class buyers into purchasing General Electric's latest lightbulb.

Railroads led the way into the post-Civil War industrial boom. Not only building the transcontinental lines but also extending them and rebuilding lines in the South created huge demands for steel—and American steelmakers responded. Soon after 1870, the newly invented Bessemer steelmaking technology reached the U.S. from Great Britain. Melting iron ore at high temperatures in a blast furnace, it produced harder, purer steel than traditional metallurgy. It slashed production costs and yielded steel better suited to the needs of the railroads and modern industry. It also made possible the building of steel-framed "skyscrapers" that by 1900 were reshaping Chicago and New York.

American railroads developed new organizational models. By 1860, elaborate bureaucratic systems were needed. The era's infamous "robber barons" mostly headed—and looted—railroad companies, while "watering" the stock to swindle investors. Still, railroads pioneered modern corporate management.

Captains of Industry

Andrew Carnegie's career illustrates this process. Born in Scotland, Carnegie came to America at age 12 in 1848 and worked in a Pittsburgh textile mill. Later, as a messenger boy with Western Union telegraph company, he learned Morse code and business practices. At 17, Carnegie became the personal secretary and telegrapher to one of the Pennsylvania Railroad's regional superintendents. By 1859, when his boss moved up, Carnegie took his place. Then, during a six-year span, Carnegie applied cost-benefit and efficiency analysis to increase the capacity of his section of the railroad to generate profits. He was a wealthy man by 1870.

In 1873, Carnegie switched to steel, building a steel plant near Pittsburgh. Exploiting the latest technology, Carnegie adopted the Bessemer process and paid attention to efficiency. By cutting costs he beat out all competitors. A ruthless businessman, Carnegie joined price-fixing pools, undersold his rivals, and acquired them after they went bankrupt. He also reaped enormous advantages through "vertical integration"—gaining control of the sources of raw materials. In 1881, he formed a partnership with Henry Clay Frick, whose company produced coke (the vital fuel for blast furnaces); ten years later he was buying up iron ore mines in Minnesota. Continuing his cost cutting, Carnegie built the firm into one of America's great corporations. In 1901 he sold Carnegie Steel to banker J.P. Morgan for half a billion dollars. Morgan combined Carnegie Steel with Federal Steel to form U.S. Steel (now USX Corporation), capitalized at $1.4 billion—the nation's first billion-dollar corporation, worth three times the government's annual expenditures. Carnegie devoted his last years to the philanthropy that he had argued was the duty of every wealthy man.

Other industries followed the same path. The discovery of petroleum in Pennsylvania in 1859 led to the oil-refining industry by 1870. Kerosene—used for cooking,

NOTABLE DATES

■ **1859**
Discovery of oil in Pennsylvania.

■ **1870**
Bessemer process introduced in British steel industry; John D. Rockefeller forms Standard Oil of Ohio.

■ **1873**
Andrew Carnegie enters steelmaking business.

■ **1876**
Alexander Graham Bell exhibits first telephone.

■ **1878**
Four-stroke gasoline engine invented in Germany.

■ **1881**
Rockefeller forms Standard Oil as the United States' first trust.

■ **1892**
General Electric Corporation formed by merger of Edison's electric company and several smaller firms.

■ **1896**
Homestead Strike by Pittsburgh steelworkers against Carnegie's company.

■ **1901**
Carnegie Steel bought by J.P. Morgan and merged with other firms to form U.S. Steel.

■ **1903**
Wright brothers test first successful airplane at Kitty Hawk, North Carolina.

■ **1908**
General Motors Corporation formed; Henry Ford introduces assembly-line production of automobiles.

■ **1911**
Supreme Court breaks up Standard Oil as a monopoly.

Ford's Model T was designed to be assembled quickly by workers trained to do only one part of the operation. Here, two workers add components to a Model T as it rolls down the line.

heating, lighting—was the first great commodity produced by the American oil industry. John D. Rockefeller became as notorious as Carnegie in creating a gigantic, vertically integrated industrial juggernaut. Meapacking grew into a major industry after 1870 as a stream of cattle cars from the West rolled into Chicago and Kansas City. Gustavus Swift and Philip Armour, whose firms still exist, proved as adept as Carnegie and Rockefeller in maximizing efficiency, minimizing costs, and exploiting inventions—in their case, refrigerated railroad cars rushing meat to the nation's cities.

Giants of Invention

Inventiveness itself created entire industries, enormous consumer demands, and modern corporate giants. Alexander Graham Bell by 1876 created the first telephone, one of many marvels on display at the American Centennial Exhibition in Philadelphia. The first telephone was installed in the White House during Rutherford Hayes's administration (1877-1881), and when it occasionally rang the President usually answered. By 1900 the Bell Telephone Company (later called American Telephone and Telegraph) installed some 800,000 telephones in the U.S. Bell's rival, Thomas A. Edison, turned out a torrent of ingenious inventions, beginning in 1868 with a telegraphic machine that sent multiple messages simultaneously. In 1877, having established a research and development facility in New Jersey, Edison followed with the phonograph. In 1879 came Edison's electric light bulb, and in 1882 he won Morgan's financial backing to establish the Edison Illuminating Company, which lit up New York City's financial district. In the 1890s one of Edison's companies produced the first crude motion pictures. Competition with Edison spurred George Westinghouse to develop alternating current (AC) as a cheaper substitute for the direct current (DC) that Edison used. Edison then merged with several competitors in 1892 to create the General Electric Company.

Scientists joined hands with tinkerers like Edison. Much innovation in the late 19th century emanated from Germany, where researchers laid the foundations of modern electrical engineering and organic chemistry. German chemical and pharmaceutical companies

America's Industrial Spurt

Between the late 1860s and the early 1900s, the creation of national wealth by American industry and the extraction of raw materials (minerals, timber, and fossil fuels) increased dramatically; farms and ranches contributed modestly to economic growth. The following figures, calculated as five-year aveages, and expressed in 1929 dollars, show that vividly.

1869-1878 — Out ot a total GDP of $10. 9 billion, $6.8 billion came from the non-farm, or industrial, sector; $4.1 billion from the farm sector.

1892-1896 — Out of a total GDP of $28.5 billion, $21.7 billion came from the non-farm sector; $6.8 billion from the farm sector.

1907-1911 — Out of a total GDP of $55.1 billion, $43.7 billion came from the non-farmsector; $9.2 billion from the farm sector.

dominated these industries in the U.S. until World War I. Bayer, the chemical giant that first synthesized aspirin (and heroin, like aspirin sold over the counter as a painkiller), was one of the notable German companies turned over to American owners as enemy assets during the war.

Other wonders appeared at the turn of the century. In 1901, Italian inventor Guglielmo Marconi flashed the first radio signal across the Atlantic. It was the first step toward long-distance commercial broadcasting and an American radio industry. Meanwhile, on December 17, 1903, humanity's age-old quest to fly culminated at Kitty Hawk, North Carolina, when Wilbur and Orville Wright flew the world's first powered aircraft. Subsequently the brothers helped create the aircraft industry.

Back in 1878, a German inventor had created the first four-stroke gasoline-powered engine, and experiments in Europe and the U.S. using such an engine produced dozens of tiny American car companies by 1900. But their expensive, hand-built "horseless carriages" lacked a mass market. In 1908, General Motors Corporation was formed by the consolidation of several smaller companies. That same year, Henry Ford revolutionized the industry by using assembly lines to build a cheap, easily maintained car—the Model T. It was a classic instance of an industry jump-started by mass production, cost cutting, and innovative design. In their Fords, Americans would roar into the Automobile Age in the 1920s. ■

Coal-Oil Johnny

The public image of John D. Rockefeller (1839-1937) was that of a pinch-faced old man, solemnly bestowing a dime on some worthy child. This cold and colorless tycoon's saga was crucial to American industrialization.

Born in New York State, Rockefeller came to Cleveland in 1853 and entered business. He saw his chance when oil was struck in Pennsylvania. The refinery he built in 1863 was within two years the biggest in Cleveland. In 1870 he formed Standard Oil of Ohio.

Like Carnegie, Rockefeller got rich by mastering details, adopting new technologies, and cutting costs. Once, he eliminated a single drop of solder from the operation sealing the red cans in which Standard Oil kerosene ("coal-oil") was sold. Such penny-pinching put Rockefeller in control of all refining in Cleveland by 1872 and in the whole country ten years later—a process hastened by his use of monopoly power to demand cheap transportation rates and acquire pipelines.

In 1881, Rockefeller turned Standard Oil into America's first trust, combining the stock of oil-related firms under a board of trustees that he chaired. From exploration to sales, it vertically dominated the American petroleum industry. Rockefeller ruined any rival. To curb him, the Sherman Act of 1890 and various state anti-monopoly laws were passed. His lawyers outfoxed them all. Only in 1911 did the Supreme Court split Standard Oil into competing firms whose modern names are Exxon and Mobile (now recombined), Chevron (today Chevron-Texaco), and Amoco (part of BP). Rockefeller, now a billionaire, had already retired, devoting the rest of his 98 years to philanthropy. ■

John D. Rockefeller was one of the most hated and feared businessmen of his time, accused of controlling both the national government and the nation's oil industry.

Booms, Busts, and Labor Struggles

1869–1912

INDUSTRIALIZATION CAME AT A high price. Factories polluted the air and water; indiscriminate mining and lumbering and farming raped the land. The consequences would not become apparent soon. At the time, these seemed proud symbols of progress.

But prosperity and plentiful jobs were not always to be had. In 1873, 1884, 1893, and 1907, Wall Street "panics" turned into depressions that lasted for years and cost untold workers their livelihoods. The nation's currency and banking systems were mismanaged, intensifying booms and busts. Agrarian distress was brought on by overly tight credit. Technological innovation, mass production, and cost cutting put downward pressure on prices and wages for most of the post-Civil War period.

Immigrant Factory Workers

The nation's booming factories—at least when they were booming—drew millions of Europeans to the East and Midwest, as well as several hundred thousand Chinese and Japanese to the West Coast. Uncounted immigrants also flocked into the West from Mexico. Industrial work, mining, and railroad construction attracted foreign peasants, lacking money and craft skills. Some—Chinese and southern Italians especially—intended to

Resisting company efforts to slash wages, Baltimore and Ohio Railroad workers went on strike. It turned violent when President Hayes used troops to crush it on July 20, 1877.

New Immigration

1890	1900	1910
All Countries Recorded		
455,302	448,572	1,041,570
Northern Europe		
Great Britain		
69,730	12,509	68,941
Ireland		
53,024	35,730	29,855
Scandinavia		
50,368	31,151	48,267
Germany		
92,427	18,507	31,283
Other		
20,575	5,822	23,852
Central Europe		
30,575	5,822	23,852
Austria-Hungary and Polish lands		
67,272	114,847	258,737
Russia and Eastern Europe		
36,327	188,426	212,079
Southern Europe		
Italy		
52,003	100,135	215,537
Other		
3,960	8,369	37,740

stay briefly in America, save money, and return when rich enough to buy land.

Native-born Americans stereotyped factory work as "immigrant labor." And so it was. Industrial recruiters scoured Eastern Europe for factory hands. Certain ethnic groups gravitated toward particular industries, in which workers and foremen spoke the same dialect and lived in enclaves near the plant. Jewish and Slavic immigrants from Eastern Europe, where peasants traditionally earned a little money by doing piecework making clothing, found jobs in New York City's sweatshop garment industry.

"Deskilling" helps explain why immigrants took factory jobs. Though hard and dangerous, factory work required little training. Ford's assembly line may have been efficient, but it was also mind deadening. Traditional shoemaking in 19th-century artisan workshops (often where the shoemaker and his apprentices lived together) was a craft of finely honed skills; doing just one phase of the cutting and stitching of leather in a shoe factory was considered degrading by trained shoemakers—but economic pressure was forcing many shoemakers into low-wage factories. American-born workers tried to avoid such jobs and clung to skilled trades or remained farmers, shopkeepers, or office workers.

Unions and Strikes

Industrialization and workers' attempts to organize had gone hand in hand since the 1830s. The largest postwar labor union was the Knights of Labor, a fraternal organization founded in 1869 to improve earnings, working conditions, and fellowship among "producers." The Knights were open to small business owners and artisans, factory workers, and women. Only gamblers, bankers, liquor dealers, and lawyers were not welcome. Their espousal of "producers'" values displayed the Knights' old-fashioned orientation, rooted in Jeffersonian republicanism; for them, the struggle was between the many who worked or employed workers, and the few who lived off other people's labor. Because they

NOTABLE DATES

■ **1869**
Knights of Labor founded.

■ **1873**
Panic of 1873.

■ **1877**
Great Railroad Strike crushed by federal troops.

■ **1884**
Panic of 1884.

■ **1885**
Statue of Liberty dedicated in New York Harbor.

■ **1886**
American Federation of Labor founded; Haymarket riot in Chicago.

■ **1892**
Ellis Island becomes gateway for immigrants entering New York; Homestead strike in Pittsburgh.

■ **1893**
Panic of 1893, worst depression in American history before 1929.

■ **1894**
Pullman strike in Chicago.

■ **1907**
Panic of 1907.

■ **1912**
IWW leads strike in Lawrence, Massachusetts; Eugene Debs wins 900,000 votes as Socialist Party candidate for President.

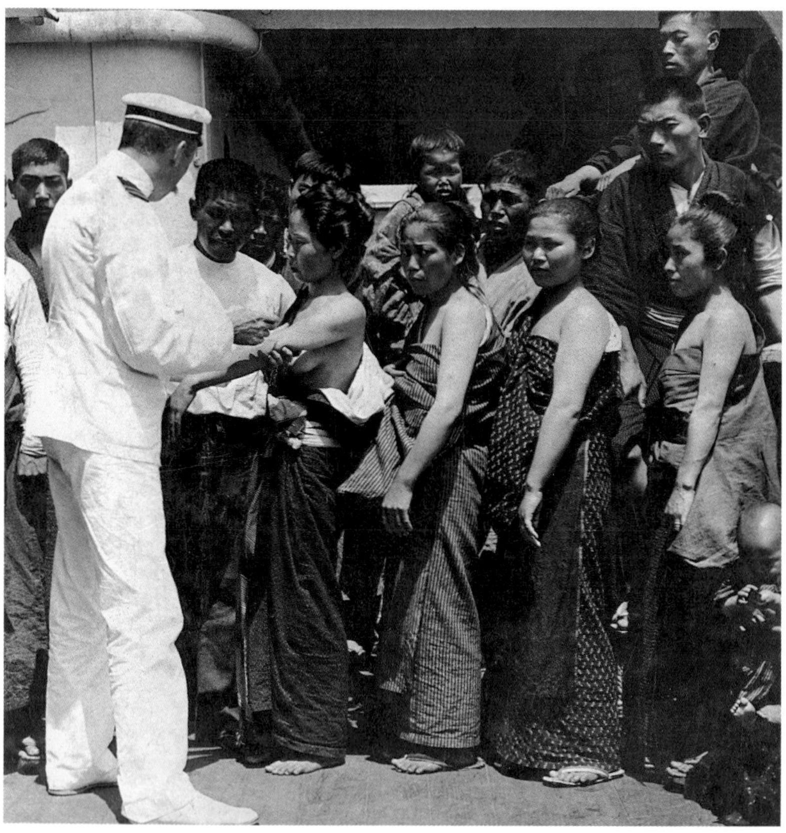

These Japanese immigrants are being vaccinated as their steamship approaches Hawaii in 1904. The immigration of Japanese workers to Hawaii's sugarcane plantations was heavy.

minimized class-conflict rhetoric and sought employers as well as wage earners as members, the Knights were squeamish about calling strikes. They also ignored immigrants. Especially during the depression that began in 1893, the Knights proved totally ineffectual—and so disappeared. In their place, the American Federation of Labor (A.F. of L.) organized workers in the skilled trades. The A.F. of L. was not afraid to strike. But its leader, cigar maker Samuel Gompers, had only one aim: "More"—higher wages for shorter hours. Gompers steered the A.F. of L. away from utopian visions and ignored industrial workers. (Many immigrants, not speaking English and intent on earning what they could before going home, had no interest in unions and were willing to "scab.") Organizing factory workers was left to the radical International Workers of the World (IWW), an early 20th-century movement that agitated in northern factories, western mines, and lumber camps, giving the middle class nightmares of "anarchy."

An American socialist movement did arise in the late 19th century, climaxing in 1912 when Socialist Party presidential candidate Eugene V. Debs won 900,000 votes—6 percent of the total. Debs and his party (unlike the IWW) were more reformers than revolutionaries; they aimed to win power through the ballot box. Some native-born Americans—Debs, for example—converted to socialism out of Jeffersonian hopes for a just "producers'" society and considered themselves heirs of Thomas Jefferson. But most members of American socialist parties were immigrants who brought to America the left-wing traditions of the working class in their homelands. Most Americans rejected socialism as a foreign idea.

Employers hated unions. Where they could, they got federal court injunctions to block unionization on grounds it violated the Fourteenth Amendment's "equal protection" clause or the Sherman Act's ban on "unreasonable restraint of trade." Some bosses hired Pinkerton Company agents to use espionage and brutal tactics to stop organizing. Economic downturns, paradoxically, hampered unionization because many workers, desperate for work, took the jobs of those who struck to protest wage cuts. Nevertheless, there were also severe outbreaks of labor unrest, paraticularly in hard times. In 1877, a nationwide railroad strike ended violently when President Hayes called in the Army to ensure that the mail went through. In 1886, Chicago police broke up a peaceful rally at the Haymarket, a gathering place where German-speaking anarchists were haranguing workers demanding an eight-hour day. Someone (no one knows who) threw a bomb. Seven policemen were killed, sixty bystanders were injured, and four anarchists were later hanged. (One committed suicide.)

The Panic of 1893—the worst depression yet—brought immense suffering to the unemployed, generating many local labor disturbances and several major strikes. The largest of these were the strikes of steel workers at Carnegie's Homestead plant in Pittsburgh in 1892 and of the Pullman Company workers in Chicago in 1894. Both were quelled with bloodshed. Mining towns like Cripple Creek and Ludlow, Colorado, and Coeur d'Alene, Idaho, saw deadly confrontations between strikers and state militias. In 1912, an IWW-sponsored strike of textile workers in Lawrence, Massachusetts, dragged on for months before the workers' resistance collapsed. Such labor violence caused many Americans to fear—and a few on the far left to hope—that the nation was on the verge of class war.

Some labor disputes had racist overtones. On the West Coast, white workers accused Chinese, Japanese, and Mexicans of depressing wages to "starvation" levels. The anti-Chinese "Workingman's Party" flourished in California in the 1870s, and ugly agitation there led to the federal Chinese Exclusion Act of 1882, severely limiting immigration. Japanese immigration was similarly limited by treaties—considered insulting in Japan—that were negotiated by President Theodore Roosevelt. And throughout the West, Mexican workers, facing overwhelming workplace discrimination, were limited to jobs that Anglos thought too menial. ■

"Give Me Your Tired, Your Poor . . . "

In 1885 the French Republic presented to the United States the majestic Statue of Liberty. Raising her lamp, Lady Liberty greeted ships carrying immigrants into New York harbor, inspiring poet Emma Lazarus to imagine her welcoming the world's "refuse . . . , tempest-tost" to the "golden door." Sadly, old-stock Americans' greetings to "the huddled masses" were often churlish. First came intrusive medical examinations at Ellis Island, the immigrants' gateway to New York after 1892. Once through the golden door, a life of low wages and the disdain of "native" Americans awaited.

In this idealized scene, Jewish immigrants sail past the Statue of Liberty in 1892.

No matter—on they came. Some 10 million arrived, mostly from the British Isles and northern Europe, between 1870 and 1890. Then, as the numbers of northern Europeans fell, came ever more southern and eastern Europeans and, after 1905, eastern Asians. Between 1890 and 1920, the number of foreign-born swelled by 18 million.

Most immigrants went where they could find friends and relatives, marriage partners, familiar places of worship, and ethnic food. Poles, Slovaks, and Hungarians recruited for factory jobs created enclaves in Pittsburgh, Cleveland, and Chicago, and Chinese packed into squalid "Chinatowns." Jews gathered in neighborhoods where they could find sweatshop work. Southern Italians chose homes and jobs largely on the basis of ancestry, whether Sicilian, Neapolitan, or Calabrian.

Immigrant life was hard but not hopeless. Newcomers avoided conscription, and eastern European Jews gave thanks to escape murderous pogroms. Immigrants who raised families wanted their children to learn English and rise economically. Dreams of freedom and opportunity brought them, as so many before, to the land of Second Chance. ■

The New South

1865–1909

THE POSTWAR SOUTHERN economy remained largely agricultural. Sharecropping replaced slavery, but cotton remained "king"—for cotton usually sold readily, and that was what creditors demanded in repayment of loans to farmers, black or white. Discriminatory tariffs and railroad rates kept manufactured goods in the South relatively expensive, and regional impoverishment made capital hard to find locally.

In the 1870s some southern politicians and newspaper editors began calling for a "New South" of bustling industry and more diverse agriculture. By the 1880s, the initiatives they championed were beginning to occur—although the region's agriculture would remain cotton-dominated until far into the 20th century. Some capital came from rich Southerners, but more was northern. Railroads were rebuilt and extended, in part because southern legislatures offered land grants to northern railroad companies, which developed the timber and mining resources they gained. With transportation assured, Birmingham, Alabama,

In 1908, the employment of children was common in North Carolina's textile mills. Work was exhausting and ill paid, and opportunities for education almost nonexistent.

The Quality of Life for African Americans, 1900

There are many possible ways to measure the quality of life; perhaps the most all-encompassing is life expectancy. When used to compare different groups, life-expectancy statistics reveal much about the levels of public health and sanitation, medical care, education, working conditions, and violence in which these groups live—and, of course, they differ by gender, since females enjoy slightly longer expectations of life than do males. In 1900, census data showed the following patterns for white and black Americans (the latter living for the most part in the South): White male 46.6; white female 48.7; Negro male 32.5, Negro female 33.5.

grew into a major steel-producing center between 1871 and 1900. The regional transportation and distribution hub of Atlanta, rebuilt after wartime devastation, got its start toward becoming the South's premier city.

Textiles became the New South's most important industry. After the Civil War, rising costs forced New England textile-mill owners to look southward. Landowners and merchants also realized how profitable a clothmaking industry that took advantage of the cheap labor and raw cotton could be. From the Carolinas to northern Alabama, in the 1880s the Piedmont became dotted with mill towns. Whole families of poor white farmers and mountain folk took mill jobs, children alongside parents. Southern mill owners, many of them former shopkeepers, established "company stores" where mill families bought everything they needed—on credit, with repayment deducted from earnings. Most found themselves entrapped in debts, their children growing up with stunted stature, bad health, and little education. About the only consolations mill workers enjoyed were evangelical religion and the assurance of not having to work alongside blacks. African Americans were seldom hired by the mills. This process of job segregation, however, led to blacks predominating in the Birmingham steel works—ironically, at wages above those of mill workers.

The New South and Jim Crow grew up together. The South in the 1870s swept away Reconstruction governments dependent on African-American votes to safeguard black civil rights. By the 1890s, southern state legislatures were writing Jim Crow laws to keep blacks at the bottom. When the Supreme Court ruled in *Plessy* v. *Ferguson* (1896) that the South could provide "separate but equal" facilities for the two races, the last barrier to segregation fell.

Southern states circumvented the Fifteenth Amendment by imposing rules that effectively barred all blacks from voting. Congress stood aside. Intimidation, backed by threats of violence and loss of livelihood, completed the disfranchisement of southern blacks, even as lynching terrorized them into submission. New South promoters never lifted a finger or a voice to halt the oppression, and they profited from the social and economic subordination of black people. ■

NOTABLE DATES

■ 1865
Civil War ends; slavery abolished by the 13th Amendment.

■ 1866
Radical Reconstruction begins under congressional leadership; Ku Klux Klan founded.

■ 1868
The 14th Amendment guarantees former slaves equal protection of the law.

■ 1870
The 15th Amendment guarantees black men the right to vote.

■ 1871
Birmingham, Alabama, begins to develop as an industrial center.

■ 1875
Civil RIghts Act enacted.

■ 1877
Northern occupation of South ends and last Republican-controlled state governments overthrown in South; "redemption" of South by white-supremacist Democrats begins.

■ 1890
Climax of Jim Crow legislation, imposing rigid segregation in the South.

■ 1895
Booker T. Washington's "Atlanta Compromise" speech.

■ 1896
Supreme Court in *Plessy* v. *Ferguson* accepts principle of "separate but equal."

■ 1909
National Association for the Advancement of Colored People (NAACP) founded.

Urban Growth in the North

1870–1917

FED BY MILLIONS OF IMMIgrants, American cities grew rapidly after 1870. Much of this growth was chaotic; industrial districts and slums made painful eyesores. But the development of mass transit systems—first streetcars, later subways—also killed the pre-Civil War "walking city." In such cities, everyone had clustered in a central area, with residences and work accessible on foot. Post-Civil War cities became too big for that, and better-off residents wanted to escape smokestacks and tenements. The first suburbs appeared in the late 19th century, home to people who could afford nicer neighborhoods and rode streetcars to work.

Class conflicts were sharper in late 19th- and early 20th-century America than ever before or since, matching the concentration of wealth at the top. Wealthy families lived in fantastic ostentation. Not until 1916 was the modern federal income tax levied, but only on the largest incomes. At that time, the richest one percent of Americans held about 38 percent of national wealth. (In 2000, the top one percent controlled a still-generous 21 percent of national wealth.)

Immigrants constituted the overwhelming majority of the northern urban poor between 1870 and 1917; rural southern blacks' migration into northern cities contributed only a small proportion to the urban population before World War I. For the foreign-born, often confined to

Coney Island amusement park, on Brooklyn's Atlantic shore, offered cheap entertainment to the city's working poor. This photo from about 1900 shows the popular roller coaster chute.

Growth of American Cities, 1870-1920

For almost a century after the Revolution the vast majority of Americans lived on farms or in small towns. But New York City's rise as a great metropolis dated from the 1820s, and by the Civil War the Northeast and parts of the Midwest were becoming significantly urbanized. Industrialization continued this trend, as the following census snapshots—of locales with populations under 2,500 and over 250,000—demonstrate:

Rural Residents (under 2,500)	**Urban Residents** (250,000-1 million)
1870	
28,656,000	3,140,000
1890	
40,841,000	3,254,000
1920	
51,533,000	10, 765,000

By 1920, there were 4,541,000 residents living in cities with populations of more than 1 million.

industrial and sweatshop labor, life was harsh. Yet it was devoid neither of hope for upward mobility nor of pleasures unknown in the newcomers' homelands. Listen, for example, to the words of a Polish-born Jewish girl, 17 years old in 1902, as she describes her life on New York City's Lower East Side: "At seven o'clock we all sit down to our machines and the boss brings to each one a pile of work that he or she is to finish during the day. . . . Sometimes the work is not all finished by six o'clock and then the one who is behind must work overtime. . . . All the time we are working the boss walks about examining finished garments and making us do them over again if they are not just right. So we have to be careful as well as swift. But I am getting so good at the work that within a year I will be making $7 a week, and then I can save at least $3.50 a week. I have over $200 saved now . . . . But you must get out and get air, and have some pleasure. . . . I go out, generally with Henry [her 19-year-old boyfriend]. Sometimes we go to Coney Island, where there are good dancing places."

Late 19th-century industrialization enabled the middle class to expand both its numbers and the quality of its life. These years saw the birth of urban department stores, while the Sears and the Montgomery Ward catalogues brought that lifestyle (if only in dreams) to rural and small-town Americans. Advertising conjured up needs and brand loyalties. Mass circulation newspapers, vaudeville shows and amusement parks, bicycles and spectator sports, and movies and phonograph records helped standardize tastes and created the popular culture that still binds most Americans together.

American cities were exciting and turbulent. Plutocrats' mansions, pleasant middle-class homes, grimy working-class areas, and appalling slums matched the shopping districts, libraries, museums, universities, and concert halls—often donated by philanthropists like Carnegie and Rockefeller—in which the middle class found time for self-improvement.

But philanthropy could not solve all the nation's ills. During the troubled 1890s, urban America's gathering problems—from public health to boss rule to what Theodore Roosevelt would call "the malefactors of great wealth"—brought into focus a potent reform movement. ■

NOTABLE DATES

■ **1876**
Alexander Graham Bell exhibits first telephone at Philadelphia's Centennial Exposition.

■ **1877**
Thomas A. Edison introduces his phonograph.

■ **1879**
Edison invents electric light bulb.

■ **1882**
Edison establishes his Illuminating Company for New York's financial district.

■ **1889**
Andrew Carnegie publishes his *Gospel of Wealth*.

■ **1890**
Beginning of waves of immigration of southern and eastern Euorpeans.

■ **1901**
First radio signal broadcast across the Atlantic Ocean.

■ **1908**
Henry Ford introduces the Model T.

■ **1916**
Federal income tax begins to tax the wealthy.

Progressivism

1887–1916

In the 1890s, America's cities and their issues rose on the scale of national priorities, just as returning farm prosperity after 1896 took the edge off rural populist protest. The movement called progressivism was taking shape.

Progressives were middle-class, urban-oriented, and educated. Their leaders included journalists, educators, and ministers, as well as politicians for whom reform was a winning issue. Some of the most enthusiastic progressives belonged to the professions that America's new system of university education was licensing: lawyers, physicians, engineers, college professors, teachers, and social workers.

Progressives were reformers, not revolutionaries. They believed in efficiency, honesty, and applying practical knowledge to solve public issues. They were overwhelmingly native-born and Protestant. All were moralistic, some deeply religious. They were intensely patriotic, concerned with assimilating immigrants. Some were sympathetic to African Americans. But all were intent on rousing the public against abuses. "Muckrakers," President Theodore Roosevelt in 1906 called the progressive journalists whose sensationalist magazine articles uncovered corruption and corporate malfeasance. Roosevelt thought that often the muckrakers went too far. But his jibe became a badge of honor.

A Religious Divide

One enduring legacy of the progressive era was a schism between modernists and "fundamentalists" in religion. Charles Darwin's theory of evolution and advances in theological scholarship cast doubt on literal interpretations of biblical texts, and some Americans began reinterpreting Christianity in the light of the era's dizzying changes. The "Social Gospel," which some Protestant clergy began preaching, applied Christian ethics to modern society. The settlement house movement and the popularity of such "helping" professions as education and social work reflected these tugs of conscience. Theologically conservative believers strenuously objected. Whether to read the Bible literally or metaphorically became a burning issue. In 1902, conservative theologians at Princeton Theological Seminary threw down the gauntlet by insisting on the fundamentals of literal belief in Scripture. From then on, struggles between "fundamentalists" and "modernists" gripped most Protestant denominations. It spilled over into the Roman Catholic Church, arousing papal alarm about the errors of "Americanism." Around 1900, there was also a rapid proliferation of charismatic Pentecostal groups, practicing faith healing in humble storefront tabernacles or at backwoods revivals. Midway between all these groups stood the Salvation Army, a religious movement of British origin

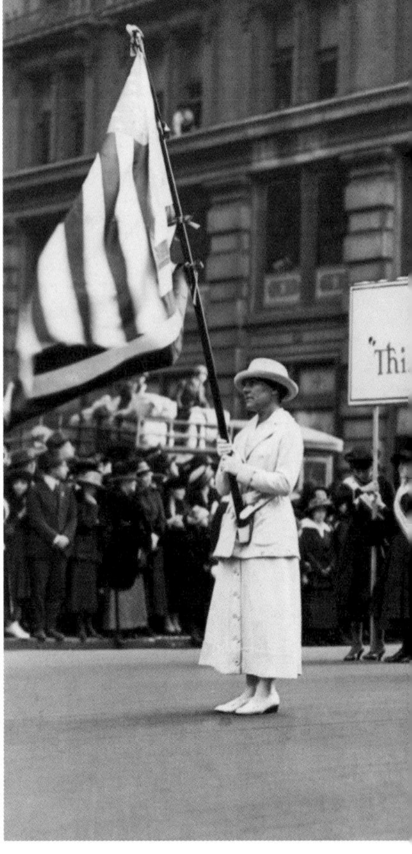

Woodrow Wilson initially opposed votes for women, not popular with the Democratic machine of the Northeast. By 1916 he changed his mind and supported the suffragists' cause.

and pseudo-military trappings that offered food and shelter to down-and-outs with an insistent but upbeat stress on repentance.

Jews felt these strains, too, fissuring into Reform, Conservative, and Orthodox. "Assimilated" Jews abandoned or modified dietary rules and formed synagogues that modernized religious observances and supported social reforms. Old World Jews, mostly recent immigrants, clung to traditional piety.

These rifts had political ramifications. Protestant progressives embraced the Social Gospel; Jewish progressives sometimes supported the secular ideology of Zionism or anti-religious socialism; Catholic progressives appealed to recent papal pronouncements on social justice. But fundamentalists usually grew apolitical or conservative, downplaying "worldly" concerns. Fundamentalism became dominant across the rural Midwest and South, opening rifts between those regions and the urban Northeast, as well as between highly educated and ordinary Americans. Those rifts still remain.

Progressive Policies

Progressives would today be called liberals. They believed in mobilizing government—city, state, and federal—to deal with local and national problems. And, indeed, liberals' shift away from distrusting state power (thinking typical of

NOTABLE DATES

■ 1887
Interstate Commerce Commission (ICC) established.

■ 1890
Sherman Anti-Trust Act enacted.

■ 1896
William McKinley (Republican) elected President over William Jennings Bryan (Democrat).

■ 1900
McKinley reelected President, with Theodore Roosevelt as Vice President.

■ 1901
McKinley assassinated; Roosevelt becomes President.

■ 1902
Fundamentalist movement challenges liberal Christianity.

■ 1904
Roosevelt elected President in his own right.

■ 1906
The Jungle by Upton Sinclair exposes the meatpacking industry.

■ 1908
William Howard Taft (Republican) elected President.

■ 1909
National Association for the Advancement of Colored People founded.

■ 1911
Triangle Shirtwaist Company fire in New York City.

■ 1912
Woodrow Wilson (Democrat) elected President over Roosevelt (Progressive) and Taft (Republican).

■ 1913
Federal Reserve System established.

the 19th century) to embracing it was one of the major changes in political ideas of the past century. Meanwhile, conservatives, once advocates of a powerful, paternalistic state, fought progressive initiatives by adopting the once liberal "leave-it-alone" (laissez-faire) stance toward business.

Progressivism inherited from populism worries about concentration of economic power. As early as 1887, populist pressure resulted in the creation of the Interstate Commerce Commission, a federal agency charged with preventing discriminatory railroad rate setting. The ICC had not been successful. Nor did much come of the Sherman Act, an 1890 law forbidding "combinations in unreasonable restraint of trade." By the 1890s, trusts—legally constituted combinations of firms, led by the likes of Rockefeller and J.P. Morgan—were gaining control over railroads, oil, steel, meatpacking, sugar refining, and other industries. Public fears grew that monopolistic trusts would dictate prices. The Supreme Court disagreed. In 1895, it found the American Sugar Refining Company, in conrol of 98 percent of the sugar industry, not "in restraint of trade." Progressives found such logic outrageous.

Beginning on the state and local level, in the 1890s progressives tackled issues that plagued middle-

A Hot Time in the Old Town Tonight

THAT CATCHY TUNE BLARED EVERYWHERE AS Theodore Roosevelt, the hero of San Juan Hill , landed in New York in 1898, launching a whirlwind campaign for governor that would soon lead him (accidentally) to the White House.

America was becoming a mass-entertainment, mass-media society. Manufacturers of consumer goods captured loyalties with brands and logos; some still sell, like Shredded Wheat and Ivory soap. The "yellow journalism" of cheap mass newspapers, especially the rival Hearst and Pulitzer chains, produced war with Spain in 1898. The 1890s bicycle craze foreshadowed the auto mania of the Model T era. New York's Coney Island drew thrillseekers and taught young people to date with corrosive effects on parental-controlled courtship. Spread by the phonograph, ragtime music evolved into jazz, while opera star Enrico Caruso won fans by pouring his voice into Victrola records. Edison's filmstrips of the 1890s led to *The Great Train Robbery* of 1903, the first "action" film with a plot, and D.W. Griffith's silent epic *Birth of a Nation* in 1915, its cinematography glorifying the Ku Klux Klan.

In 1910 Americans avidly followed baseball and its heroes, either at the ballpark or in the sports pages of the newspaper.

America also went sports-mad. Professional baseball soon became "the national pastime," followed by millions of fans and played on every sandlot. Football, mainly a collegiate sport and played without protective gear, survived a national scandal about high fatalities. Basketball was invented in 1891 to give restless young men something to do in winter. And boxing was already a national craze when black heavyweight Jack Johnson won the world championship in 1908, setting off white America's quest for "the Great White Hope." ■

class city people. Boss rule was high on the list: It involved corrupt links between politicians and business interests and winked at moral offenses like gambling and prostitution. Bosses' power, moreover, usually rested on the votes of "ignorant" immigrants. In mid-size industrial cities like Toledo and Cleveland, reform politicians swept into the mayors' offices with solid middle-class backing. In San Francisco, crusading district attorney Hiram Johnson sent the city's boss to prison and won a Senate seat. In Wisconsin, Robert "Fighting Bob" La Follette thwarted corrupt interests to become governor and unleash a flood of reforms, eventually joining Johnson as a progressive Republican senator. Local reformers championed bringing utilities under public control or regulation, correcting bad working conditions, improving sanitation, and providing building codes, urban zoning, parks, and playgrounds. State-level reformers regulated business abuses, improved education, and taxed corporations.

The Progressive Presidents

Progressivism reached the White House with Theodore Roosevelt. "TR" or "Teddy," as he became known, had been elected Vice President with McKinley in 1900. McKinley was no progressive, but his defeats of William Jennings Bryan in 1896 and 1900 made the Republicans the country's dominant party—and one oriented toward urban interests. When an anarchist assassinated McKinley in 1901, Roosevelt became President. By turning his office into "a bully pulpit," Roosevelt created the modern Presidency. No longer the mere administrator of congressional policies, as his Gilded Age predecessors had been, TR was the formulator and drumbeater of a dynamic policy agenda.

During the Spanish American War, crowds gathered outside *New York Tribune* headquarters to catch the latest news. Newspapers had played a major role in bringing about the war.

Roosevelt, the youngest man ever to be President, was a human dynamo. Born to a wealthy family for whom public service was a duty, a Harvard-educated intellectual who had ranched in North Dakota, and a tireless self-promoter, he enthusiastically became the nation's number-one reformer. In his seven-and-a-half years as President (he was elected in his own right in 1904), TR tried to break up or bring under federal regulation trusts that he believed violated the public interest. (Not all did, he thought.) Sickened by reading novelist Upton Sinclair's *The Jungle*, which exposed unsanitary practices of the meatpacking industry, Roosevelt pressured Congress into establishing the Food and Drug Administration. He sponsored legislation to regulate railroads, and he mediated a settlement between miners and mine owners that threatened to provoke a national strike. An avid outdoorsman, he advocated conservation and federal management of natural resources. But he did not go as far as his friend John Muir, the founder of the Sierra Club, in advocating wilderness preservation.

In 1908, honoring the two-term tradition, Roosevelt turned over the Presidency to his obese friend William Howard Taft and left for an African safari. (With him went a prayer that "a lion would do its duty" from trust-builder J.P. Morgan.) Taft, Roosevelt assumed, was a sound progressive, and could handle Morgan.

But Taft was nowhere near as successful as Roosevelt in making himself a progressive hero—even though more trusts were "busted" during his administration than during TR's. In 1912, Roosevelt challenged Taft; and when the GOP refused to nominate him, TR ran on his own Progressive Party ticket. He drew more votes than Taft—opening the White House door for a progressive Democrat, Woodrow Wilson, the governor of New Jersey and former president of Princeton University.

Like TR, Wilson was a well-read intellectual. He was also the first (and so far only) Ph.D. to sit in the White House. But his progressivism differed from Roosevelt's. Wilson wanted to break up trusts, not regulate them. Born in Virginia, Wilson had more respect than did Roosevelt for the small-government Jeffersonian tradition. Wilson was also a deeply religious Presbyterian with a strong sense of doing God's work.

The most important legislation of the Wilson Administration, in 1913, created the Federal Reserve System to reform the nation's banking institutions and (it was hoped) end boom-and-bust cycles. The reform avoided giving total power to federal authorities and Wall Street, which Republicans would have done. Instead, "the Fed" combined the functions of a national bank with a strong role for local banks.

The Progressive Balance Sheet

Many of progressivism's causes still seem bright and forward-looking. The Triangle Shirtwaist Company fire in New York City in 1911 prompted progressives to demand inspections of industrial workplaces. Child labor became a major target. Many male progressives (including Roosevelt and belatedly Wilson) supported women's suffrage and paid lip service to the women's rights movement gaining momentum after 1900. Sometimes prosecuted for "immorality," progressive feminist Margaret Sanger championed birth control. Progressive education, personified by Columbia professor John Dewey, called for child-centered schooling emphasizing "life-adjustment" and "practical" subjects. With more urban students completing that brand-new institution, high school, progressive education exerted a wide reach, with mixed results.

Booker T. Washington was the most widely known and respected African-American leader long before his death in 1915. Here he addresses an audience in Louisiana.

African-American Progressives

Turn-of-the-century African Americans not only resisted racist denigration but also laid foundations for the 20th-century civil-rights movement. Black journalist Ida Wells-Barnett, fleeing from a Memphis mob to Chicago, courageously fought to rouse consciences against the epidemic of lynching terrorizing southern blacks. In segregated black communities everywhere, clergy kept alive dignity and self-respect. And two great spokesmen arose with differing strategies for winning black freedom.

Booker T. Washington, born a slave in Virginia, preached black self-help. In a famous address to a white audience in Atlanta in 1895, Washington seemingly accepted Jim Crow but offered white America a deal. Blacks, he said, would not threaten the racial status quo; in return, Washington asked whites to help blacks improve their lot. He founded and dominated the Tuskegee Institute in Alabama, a school that offered young blacks training in the humble trades to which white America consigned them. "A credit to his race," condescending whites called him. But Washington secretly gave financial support to blacks fighting Jim Crow, and he saw self-help as a prelude to a struggle for equality.

No one ever called W.E.B. Du Bois an Uncle Tom. Northern-born and educated at Harvard and the University of Berlin, Du Bois was the first African American to earn a Ph.D. A brilliant intellectual who taught at all-black Atlanta University, Du Bois advocated training the "Talented Tenth" of black America. He hoped that his black elite would join whites in spearheading progressivism, while serving as role models for African Americans. With black and white progressives, Du Bois co-founded the National Association for the Advancement of Colored People (NAACP) in 1909 and for years used his editorship of its magazine, *The Crisis*, to advocate resisting racism.

Du Bois and Washington became bitter rivals. Given the realities of the times, both men were necessary as African-American champions, and ultimately their strategies were complementary. They rank among the most important of progressive-era American leaders. ■

The Triangle Shirtwaist Fire

On March 25, 1911, at Washington Place in New York City, the Triangle Shirtwaist Company was keeping its workers busy. Packed into the eighth and ninth floors, hundreds of young women huddled over sewing machines to assemble garments under the supervision of a handful of men. They were paid by the "pieces" they turned out. It was a Saturday afternoon, a normal workday.

At the New York City morgue, grief-stricken parents come to identify loved ones killed in the Triangle Shirtwaist Company fire.

A fire broke out, and with it panic when it was discovered that most doors were locked. A few women slid down an elevator cable. But then the cable snapped. In desperation, some jumped from the windows, to certain death. Many more perished amid the bolts of material on which they had been working.

One hundred forty six died. Bodies, reported the *New York Times*, were "strewn on the street outside"; there were "piles of dead" inside. Parents, searching for their daughters, all that night kept calling out "a dozen pet names in Italian and Yiddish . . . in shrill agony above the deeper moan of the throng."

The disaster horrified the middle-class public and progressive reformers. Consciences were awakened about conditions under which immigrants worked, for long hours and a pittance. Worse, it was outrageous that a sweatshop such as Triangle had so few safety precautions and that the owners had even locked the doors. City and state legislators convened inquiries and passed laws to toughen workplace inspection. The progressive era's women's movement saw the plight of young immigrant laborers as a gender issue. And America's small but vocal socialist parties redoubled efforts to organize workers. One of the few American labor organizations that historically had a strong socialist presence, energized by the Triangle Fire, was the International Ladies' Garment Workers Union. ■

America Builds an Empire

1889–1917

Post-Civil War America had its collective hands full with subduing and developing the West, but even so, some American businessmen were looking for opportunities in East Asia, the Pacific islands, and Latin America. Christian missionaries saw in China a vast opportunity for winning souls. Far-sighted naval strategist Alfred T. Mahan urged the United States to build a fleet capable of defending its interests on the high seas, and the generally somnolent administration of President Benjamin Harrison (1889-1893) bestirred itself to start modernizing the Navy.

American Imperialism

Suddenly, in the century's last decade, the United States emerged as a world power, with imperial ambitions. The U.S. Navy narrowly avoided a clash with Germany over who should control Samoa. American sugar- and pineapple-growers engineered a "revolution" in Hawaii that toppled the native queen and sought annexation to the U.S.; only President Cleveland's aversion to imperial expansion blocked this sordid deal.

The sugar-rich Spanish colony of Cuba had long topped the wish list of American expansionists. A bloody Cuban revolt in the 1890s attracted incessant attention in the yellow press, whose illustrated stories of Spanish horrors sometimes were actually true. In February 1898, the American warship U.S.S. *Maine* blew up in Havana harbor, with heavy loss of life—almost certainly a shipboard accident (as both contemporary naval inquiries and subsequent investigations con-

Building the Panama Canal was an engineering triumph. Here, a year before the canal was finished, work is proceeding on the huge locks that raise ships passing from ocean to ocean.

firmed), but presented as a sneaky Spanish attack by American newspapers screaming "Remember the Maine!" President McKinley succumbed to the uproar, and in April 1898 he asked Congress to declare war. Congress did, though anti-expansionist senators insisted on making promises that the United States would not annex the island.

The Spanish-American War was short, glorious, and mercifully light on casualties. (Five thousand American servicemen died of yellow fever but only 379 from hostile action, and Spanish losses were also low.) A bungled invasion of Cuba culminated in the well-publicized charge up San Juan Hill by a volunteer regiment of western Rough Riders led by Theodore Roosevelt, hitherto Assistant Secretary of the Navy and soon to be elected governor of New York and then Vice President. American forces seized Spanish-ruled Puerto Rico against virtually no opposition. On July 17, 1898, Spain gave up the fight, its aging navy shattered by the American fleet.

The worst bloodshed came after the peace treaty was signed. The U.S. annexed not only Puerto Rico but also Spain's Philippine Islands (which Japan or another imperialist power would have seized if the U.S. had not). Already a brutal guerrilla conflict with Filipino nationalists was under way, eerily foreshadowing the Vietnam War. Before it was over in 1901, at least 20,000 Filipino fighters died as well as 4,000 Americans. War-related deaths among the Philippines' civilian population ran much higher.

The new American empire now took shape. Cuba, nominally independent, was in fact an American puppet state, run by corrupt Cuban politicians and American investors. Puerto Rico was at first simply a colony; only in 1924 did its people become American citizens, and in 1952 the island became a self-governing commonwealth. The Philippines, too, were ruled as a colony, but in 1933 independence was promised within 10 years. (Delayed by World War II, Philippine independence actually came in 1946.) In 1899 the United States overcame earlier squeamishness

The American Colonial Empire, 1898-1917

American Samoa — acquired 1899, independent U.S. territory since 1960

Canal Zone — acquired1903, part of Colombia under U.S. administration by 1903 treaty with Panama, returned to Panamanian sovereignty 1977

Cuba — acquired 1898 from Spain, U.S. protectorate until 1899, independent but dominated by American business interests until 1958 revolution

Guam — acquired 1898 from Spain, U.S. territory since 1950

Hawaii — acquired 1898, independent U.S. state (since 1959)

Philippines — acquired 1898 from Spain, U.S. territory until granted independence 1946

Puerto Rico — acquired 1898 from Spain, self-governing commonwealth since 1952

Virgin Islands — acquired 1917 from Denmark, U.S. territory since 1954

NOTABLE DATES

■ **1898**
Spanish-American War; U.S. annexes Puerto Rico, Guam, and Philippines; Philippine resistance to U.S. occupation begins; Cuba nominally independent; Hawaii annexed.

■ **1899**
Anti-Imperialist League organized to oppose U.S. imperialism.

■ **1901**
U.S. forces defeat Filipino insurgency.

■ **1903**
U.S. sponsors Panamanian independence and takes Canal Zone; construction of Panama Canal begins.

■ **1910**
Mexican Revolution begins.

■ **1912**
U.S. forces intervene in Nicaragua.

■ **1914**
Panama Canal completed; World War I (Great War) begins in Europe; U.S. occupies Veracruz in Mexico.

■ **1915**
Lusitania sunk by German submarine.

■ **1916**
U.S. Army invades Mexico to pursue Pancho Villa in Mexico; Wilson re-elected President.

■ **1917**
U.S. purchases Virgin Islands from Denmark; U.S. enters World War I.

Anti-Imperialists and Imperialists

SOME AMERICANS OBJECTED TO IMPERIALISM, convinced that republicanism and democracy were incompatible with colonialism. A mixed group of citizens, ranging from Andrew Carnegie to William Jennings Bryan, Mark Twain, and Jane Addams, founded the Anti-Imperialist League. (Carnegie put his money where his principles were, endowing the Carnegie Foundation for International Peace, which still exercises great influence in formulating American global policy.) "We hold that the policy known as imperialism is hostile to liberty and tends toward militarism, an evil from which it has been our glory to be free," declared the League. "We regret that it has become necessary in the land of Washington and Lincoln to reaffirm that all men, of whatever race or color, are entitled to life, liberty, and the pursuit of happiness. We maintain that governments derive their just powers from the consent of the governed. We insist that the subjugation of any people is 'criminal aggression' and open disloyalty to the distinctive principles of our Government."

Andrew Carnegie was a supporter of the peace movement and considered himself a humanitarian dedicated to philanthropy.

In response, the British poet Rudyard Kipling published his famous appeal: "Take up the White Man's burden/ The savage wars of peace/ Fill full the mouth of famine/ And bid the sickness cease." Kipling saw imperialism as a burden that the civilized West—and in particular the democratic Anglo-Saxon lands of Great Britain and the United States—must shoulder for the sake of progress in the world.

Whether or not Rudyard Kipling's words persuaded them, most Americans were in favor of expansionism, proud to see the flag flying gloriously beyond the seas. The presidential election of 1900 served as a referendum on imperialism, with the Democratic nominee, Bryan, urging an end to the war in the Philippines and supporting giving the islands their freedom. But McKinley, who before the war had confessed to not knowing where "those darned islands" even were, won overwhelmingly. ■

and annexed Hawaii, providing—along with the formerly Spanish island of Guam—a series of naval-base stepping stones to the Philippines and East Asia. China itself escaped partition by the world's imperialist powers, in part because of American insistence that the vast but struggling empire remain independent with an "Open Door" to investors and missionaries from all "civilized [read: Western] countries." The United States in 1899 divided the Samoan islands with Germany, and later, in 1917, purchased the Virgin Islands from Denmark.

As President, Theodore Roosevelt and many progressives noisily applauded imperial expansion. Memorably, Roosevelt said that his foreign policy was to "speak softly but carry a big stick." His "big stick" was a much-expanded and heavily armored Navy—nor was his voice very soft. In 1903 he engineered Panama's independence from the Republic of Colombia and as a reward seized a strip of territory through which American army engineers by 1914 dug the Panama Canal. "I took the Canal Zone," TR candidly boasted.

Roosevelt was not interested in further territorial expansion, but he did make the U.S. the dominant imperial power throughout most of Latin America. Under the Roosevelt Corollary to the Monroe Doctrine, he asserted U.S. prerogative to intervene in any Latin American nation whose "chronic wrongdoing" demanded that a "civilized country" take over its financial affairs and safeguard property. He also saw that Kaiser Wilhelm II's Germany was a dangerous future rival and presided over a rapprochement—but no open alliance—with Great Britain portending the 20th-century "special relationship" between the two largest English-speaking nations.

Taft and Wilson continued Roosevelt's foreign policy. Under Taft, the watchword was "dollar diplomacy," stressing the protection of such large American corporate investments as those of the United Fruit Company, which virtually controlled several Central American governments. And guns backed up the dollars. In 1912, Taft sent in the Marines to quell a revolt against a pro-U.S. president in Nicaragua; they would occupy the country until 1933. Wilson was just as proactive, dispatching the Marines to Haiti and the Dominican Republic. He also became embroiled in the Mexican Revolution, which began in 1910, when reformers overthrew Mexico's long-time dictator. Wilson, offended by the "butchers" who were clawing their way into power south of the border, decided to "teach the South American republics to elect good men." Instilling that lesson, Wilson outraged Mexicans by occupying Veracruz in 1914. He compounded his heavy-handed pedagogy in 1916 by sending troops into Mexico to hunt down the bandit Pancho Villa, who had sacked the border town of Columbus, New Mexico. (The Army never caught Villa.)

The Philippine Insurrection, one of the bloodiest and least-known U.S. conflicts, in some ways eerily foreshadowed the Vietnam War.

The Looming Great War

But Wilson had larger matters to worry about. In August 1914, World War I (called the Great War at the time) broke out in Europe, with Germany and its allies pitted against Great Britain, France, and Russia. An ardent Anglophile, Wilson wished for an Anglo-French victory, but he also desperately hoped to keep out of the fighting. So did most Americans.

In May 1915, off the coast of Ireland, a German submarine torpedoed without warning the British liner *Lusitania*, sending to their deaths 1,198 crew and passengers, of whom 128 were American citizens. Germany's attack was illegal under international law, but so was the British practice of using such civilian ships to carry munitions. While Roosevelt howled for war, Wilson held the line; he did extract a promise from the Germans to abstain from further attacks. Wilson had prescient fears of what bringing the U.S. into this struggle would do to the nation's civil liberties, tolerance, and prospects for political reform. In the election, he ran as the "peace candidate" who had kept America neutral. Wilson narrowly won, beating out fence-straddling Republican Supreme Court justice Charles Evans Hughes. The year 1917 opened with the world still at war and an air of apprehension engulfing the United States. ■

WORLD SURVEY

1870–1917

As the U.S. modernized, comparable transformations were under way elsewhere, generating the strains, tensions, and creativity as within American society.

■ Europe at Its Zenith

In 1870 Great Britain was at the height of its power, supplying much of the capital that developed the U.S. But Britain's industrial plant was aging. Germany became a united country, but not a democracy, in 1871, when Prussia gathered other small German states into an empire. Imperial Germany industrialized swiftly and dazzled the world with its superb higher education and science. France was torn by divisive, bitter politics; Italy was hampered by a deep gulf between an industrializing north and a poverty-stricken south, from which millions emigrated. Austria-Hungary, Germany's multinational ally, was sapped by endemic conflicts. Unfortunately, Germany from 1890 onward was bidding for "world power"—causing Britain, France, Russia, and Italy to pull together.

All Western countries—except Russia, but including Canada, Australia, and New Zealand—were developing social safety net institutions similar to those of progressive-era America. In fact, most of them outpaced the U.S. in providing old-age, health, and unemployment insurance. All had women's rights movements, but nowhere before World War I did women vote in national elections. And all Western countries, including Russia, had socialist movements more formidable than the U.S. Historians debate why, but it seems that Americans' deep attachment to republicanism and to the belief that anyone could rise by personal effort kept this country from embracing class-conflict models of politics.

Russia most clearly illustrates the perils of an autocracy facing modernization. In 1870 the tsar reigned as an absolute monarch, heading a bureaucratized but economically backward state, most of whose people had recently been serfs. In 1917 the tsar was still an autocrat, though Russia had begun developing industries, built railroads, and was settling Siberia. But a revolution in 1905 almost toppled the autocracy. The parliament that emerged was weak, persecution drove millions of Jews abroad, and several revolutionary movements aspired to lead the peasantry and the urban proletariat in overthrowing tsarism. Russia barely managed to cope with World War I, and in 1917 would enter another revolution.

■ The Non-West Stirs

Almost everywhere outside North America, Europe, and Australia, these were decades of rule by the empire-building industrial societies. China, sinking into chaos and with an uncontrollably mushrooming population, barely escaped imperialist partition; its Qing Dynasty collapsed in 1911-1912. Most of the Middle East was still ruled by the multinational Ottoman Empire, in which attempts at internal reform collided with the stirrings of Arab and Turkish nationalism and an Islamic revival. Another ancient Islamic society, Persia (now Iran), contended with the same modernizing pressures and barely stayed independent of Russia and Britain. India seemed firmly under British control, though Mohandas Gandhi was already planning the nonviolent protest strategy that would by 1947 win Indian independence. Africa in the 1880s had almost entirely been partitioned among European powers. Much of Latin America was, economically, virtually a colony of the U.S.;

only South America's southern cone showed signs of dynamism, made possible by distance from the U.S. and European immigration.

The world's most successful non-Western society was Japan. Seeing the danger of Western encroachment, in 1868 the Japanese samurai class restored to power the emperor and initiated sweeping modernization. Within a few decades, Japan acquired modern industry and business organization, Western-style education, bureaucratic and parliamentary government—and also militarism and a taste for Western-style imperialism.

■ Modernism in Science and Culture

Cultural change accelerated breathtakingly in the years after 1870. Darwinian evolution dominated biology. Atomic structures and X-rays became objects of research. The old certainties of Newtonian physics dissolved after Max Planck in 1900 initiated quantum theory and Albert Einstein in 1905 published his first paper on relativity. Friedrich Nietzsche and Sigmund Freud questioned confidence that rationality governed the human mind and opened deep recesses of irrationality. Modern art and music were born when the Impressionists strove to capture light and movement, when Cubists such as Pablo Picasso offered abstract representations of fractured planes, and when composer Richard Wagner stretched musical tonality to its limits and Arnold Schoenberg then dissolved it. Novelists and poets abandoned straightforward narrative in favor of attempts to reproduce inner consciousness.

Europeans took the lead in cultural and scientific modernization. The U.S. made its contribution when black musicians in New Orleans combined African and European traditions in the rhythms of jazz. Middle-class Americans felt bewildered on encountering modernism. The Armory Show, opening in New York City in 1913, elicited howls of derision at the abstract works of Picasso, Marcel Duchamps, and other European masters. But the shock jolted American artists like Georgia O'Keeffe into a life of creativity. ■

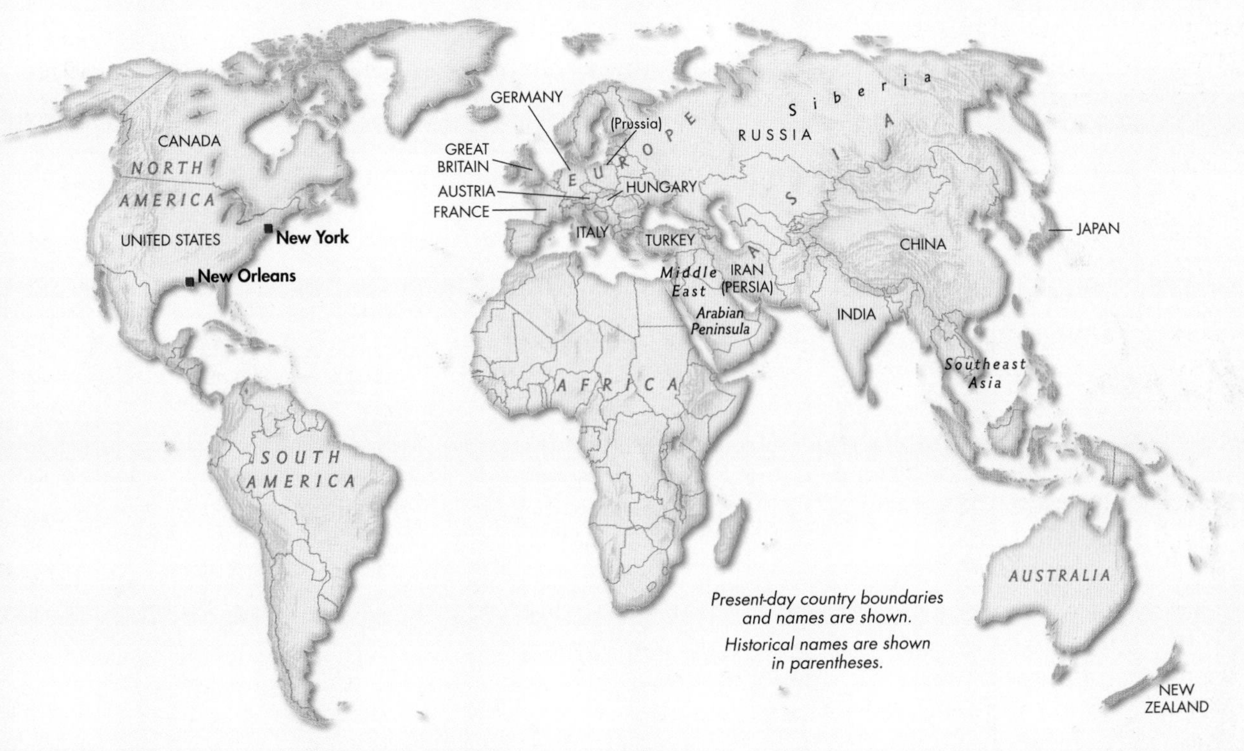

BECOMING A GREAT POWER 1914–1933

ON JUNE 28, 1914, A SERB ASSASSINATED THE HEIR TO THE AUSTRO-HUNGARIAN THRONE. When Serbia refused Austria-Hungary's demand to crush the nationalist movement behind the assassination, Austria-Hungary declared war. As Serbia's Russian ally mobilized, Germany declared war—and when France (Russia's ally) refused to promise neutrality, Germany struck France through Belgium. Great Britain declared war. By August 4, 1914, Europe was aflame. Bulgaria and the Ottoman Empire joined Germany and Austria-Hungary to form the Central Powers, and Japan and Italy joined the Allies.

Every belligerent country expected a quick triumph. But by Christmas 1914, millions of troops were dug into muddy trenches from the English Channel to Switzerland. In Eastern Europe, fighting also deadlocked. Britain blockaded Germany, which responded by sending U-boats to sink any ship approaching the British Isles.

By the beginning of 1917 signs of crisis multiplied ominously. Russia reached the limits of its endurance. Mutiny rumbled through the French Army. Germany's generals persuaded the Kaiser that unleashing the U-boats would bring Great Britain and France to their knees before a single American soldier could land in Europe. On February 1, 1917, Germany broke its pledge to Wilson that its U-boats would not indiscriminately sink vessels in the Atlantic. ■

Camp Dix in New Jersey was one of the chief training camps of America's World War I Army. These men are lucky: The war ended before they went overseas and they are being mustered out.

■ 1917	■ 1918	■ 1919	■ 1920	■ 1923
U.S. enters WordWar I (also known as the Great War); Russian Revolution.	Wilson announces Fourteen Points; World War I ends; influenza pandemic kills millions worldwide.	Treaty of Versailles; 19th Amendment adopted, permitting prohibition.	Prohibition begins; 18th Amendment adopted, giving women the vote; Warren G. Harding elected President.	Calvin Coolidge becomes President on Harding's death.

■ 1924	■ 1928	■ 1929	■ 1932	■ 1933
Scopes "Monkey Trial" in Tennessee spotlights fundamentalist-modernist clash; Coolidge elected President.	Herbert Hoover elected President.	Wall Street crash ushers in the Great Depression.	Franklin D. Roosevelt elected President.	Roosevelt's Inauguration marks beginning of the New Deal; Prohibiton ends; Hitler comes to power in Germany, inaugurating the Nazi regime.

Into the Great War

1914–1918

Woodrow Wilson was pro-Allied—and feared for the world's future if Imperial Germany dominated Europe. American companies and banks sold and lent to the Allies far more than to the Central Powers. Thus the U.S. gained an economic stake in an Allied victory. Britain controlled the flow of war news, to which Allied propagandists added horrific tales of German barbarism.

Opposition to entering the war, however, remained strong. Many Irish- and German-Americans were passionately anti-British. A peace movement had arisen during the progressive era. Wilson's secretary of state, William Jennings Bryan, resigned after the *Lusitania* incident because he thought the President's response insufficiently even-handed. The Socialist Party denounced the war. Above all, there was the pull of American isolationism, which branded Europe's wars as just an Old World vice.

Going to war would be the death knell of progressive reform, Wilson feared. "Once lead this people into war, and they'll forget there ever was such a thing as tolerance," he mused. But Germany's challenge to neutral rights and American lives was too blatant to ignore. On February 24 the British released an intercepted cable in which Germany offered Mexico an alliance and the return of Texas, New Mexico, and Arizona. On April 2, after Germany ignored warnings to call off the U-boats, Wilson asked Congress to declare war. The motion passed on April 6.

Declaring war was the easy part. The small U.S. Army was busy occupying Central American and Caribbean countries, policing the Philippines, and chasing Pancho Villa. Although 1.3 million Americans volunteered, a huge army had to be drafted and trained. Ultimately, 3 million Americans were drafted. But the idea of

Off to fight "over there," these American soldiers leave on a troop train from Philadelphia in 1917. Enthusiasm was often high until troops reached the trenches of the westerm front.

dispatching these troops into battle was neither welcomed nor even expected. One senator was shocked that the administration planned to send troops to the western front—he assumed that the Navy would pursue U-boats but leave ground fighting to the Europeans.

Selling the war to the public required an enormous public-relations effort that escalated into hysteria. A progressive advertising executive, George Creel, headed a national information service that flooded the country with patriotic hoopla and warnings of subversion. Wild claims about the menacing "Hun" were the least of the excesses. People of foreign birth or ancestry were exhorted to become "100-percent Americans." German-Americans were prime targets. At least one young German-American was lynched; uncounted thousands were harassed. Schools banned teaching German, orchestras refused to play Beethoven, and sauerkraut became "liberty cabbage."

At Wilson's urging, Congress enacted a sedition law that made it a federal crime to question the war, the draft, or the nation's leaders. Eugene Debs got a ten-year sentence for saying, in a speech, that it was a rich man's war but a poor man's fight. "Seditious" publications were banned from the mails.

Many citizens threw themselves into the war effort, eager to mobilize. Wartime prohibition was enacted, ostensibly to increase efficiency—but reformers pointed out that German-Americans had the sinister, morale-sapping habit of drinking beer.

These earnest crusades may now seem silly, but the mobilization of industry to boost the production of armaments, ammunition, and supplies was impressive. Women took drafted men's places in the labor force—working in factories, running streetcars, even barbering. The federal mobilization of American industry provided a template for efforts during the New Deal and World War II to bring industry under government control. Most impressive of all was the work of the Food Commission, which rationed what consumers could buy while stockpiling food for troops and starving refugees. The name of the progressive businessman who headed it would become well known to Americans: Herbert Hoover. ■

Hysteria and Repression

1917

April – U.S. declares war on Germany; government creates Committee on Public Information to promote war.

June – Espionage Act threatens imprisonment for "disloyal, profane, scurrilous or abusive language" about the war, government, flag, or military.

September– Justice Department agents arrest 113 IWW leaders.

1918

April – Robert Prager, a German-American, lynched in St. Louis.

May – Sedition Act threatens imprisonment for protesting the draft or criticizing the government.

November – Armistice ends fighting.

1919

January – Socialist Congressman Victor Berger denied seat, sentenced 20 years for antiwar articles.

March – Supreme Court upholds Espionage Act convictions.

NOTABLE DATES

■ 1914
Outbreak of the Great War.

■ 1916
Wilson reelected President.

■ 1917
Germany resumes unconditional submarine warfare; United States declares war on Germany; tsar overthrown in Russia; Bolsheviks seize power in Russia and promise an immediate peace.

■ 1918-19
Flu pandemic sickens one billion people, kills some 20 million; in the U.S. alone some 550,000 die—more than would be killed in both world wars.

A World "Safe for Democracy"

1918–1920

IN JANUARY 1918, WOODROW Wilson announced before Congress his Fourteen Points—the foundation for a just and lasting peace. They received worldwide publicity.

American troops had not yet reached Europe, where morale in the French Army was cracking. In Russia, weak democratic forces taking over from the failed tsarist regime had given way in November 1917 to the Bolsheviks, radical Marxists who promised immediate peace. The Bolshevik leader V. I. Lenin exhorted workers to overthrow the capitalists who had caused the war. Wilson's Fourteen Points were an answer to Lenin's call for world revolution.

In the Fourteen Points, Wilson redefined Allied war aims as a struggle for democracy. Belgium and Poland must regain independence and Alsace-Lorraine return to France. Other territorial changes should depend on plebiscites and "free national development."

"Making the world safe for democracy" had been Wilson's aim in asking Congress to declare war on Germany. He saw a democratic world as essential for American security. His justification for using American power to ensure that peaceful world order still echoes. But Germany still had the initiative. In March 1918 the Bolsheviks signed the harsh Treaty of Brest-Litovsk, by which the Central Powers stripped Russia of all its western lands. The Germans then shipped troops, once tied down fighting Russia, to deliver a knockout punch on the western front.

On the Western Front

"The Yanks are coming," promised Broadway songwriter George M. Cohan in "Over There," the war's most memorable tune. And by the spring of 1918 the Yanks did start coming. (When French Premier Georges Clemenceau offered to provide brothels, the secretary of war warned: "For God's sake, don't show this to the President, or he'll stop the war.") In June the American Second Division helped repulse a German advance at Château-Thierry. In summer, more Yanks reached France. But they were green. Since 1914, French, British, Belgian, and Canadian soldiers had endured trench life, often among rotting corpses, poison-gas attacks, savage artillery bombardments, and charges against machine-gun nests. Into this hell went American draftees.

In July 1918, weary German soldiers ripped through the Allied

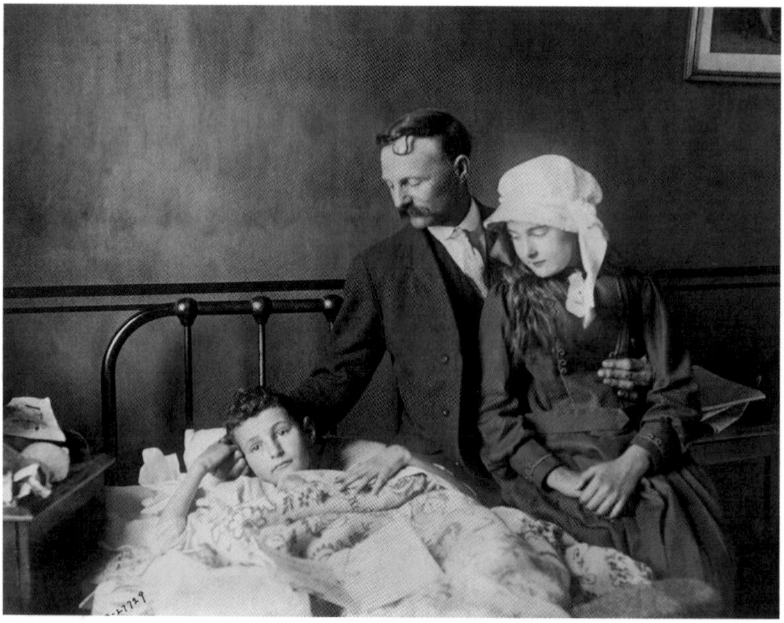

This father and his children were among few survivors of the sinking of the *Lusitania*. The boy jumped; the father and daughter swam until rescued and were reunited in a hospital in Ireland.

trenches, advancing toward Paris. American doughboys bore the brunt of the onslaught at several key spots along the western front. In September, counterattacking Allied and American troops penetrated the Germans' defensive barrier. On September 29, his generals told the Kaiser their army could hold out no longer, and in Berlin liberal and socialist leaders took power. They asked for peace on the basis of Wilson's Fourteen Points. Kaiser Wilhelm fled, and a democratic republic was proclaimed. As the Austro-Hungarian army collapsed, Czechs, Slovaks, Yugoslavs, Hungarians, and Poles declared independence. On November 11, 1918, the armistice was signed.

Wilson the Peacemaker

American prestige has never stood higher than when, in December 1918, Wilson went to Europe to lead the American delegation at the Paris Peace Conference. Throngs of French, British, and Italians cheered. Wilson vowed to carry out the Fourteen Points, but he could not live up to the extravagant faith that the words evoked.

Boundaries could not be redrawn without mortally offending someone. The war's monetary and human costs were too high for leaders of the victorious powers to defy popular demands that Germany pay (as British Prime Minister David Lloyd George promised) "till the pips squeak." French leaders insisted that only a harsh peace settlement would keep their country safe. Hunger stalked the continent—Herbert Hoover made his reputation as a great humanitarian by distributing food to famished populations—and an influenza pandemic decimated the globe. For a while it seemed that Bolshevism might engulf Central Europe, leading the Allies and the United States to intervene in Russia's civil war. Wilson's attempts to insist on basing the peace on the Fourteen Points were bound to suffer. The passionately anti-German Clemenceau sneered at Wilson's "naiveté"—why, even the Good Lord had confined Himself to Ten Commandments!

At Paris, Wilson had to give way on issue after issue. In the resulting Treaty of Versailles, signed in June 1919, Germany sustained serious territorial losses, and huge reparations were imposed to force Germany alone to repay the whole cost of the war. Germany lost its colonies and its navy, was limited to an army of 100,000 men, and had its Rhineland region demilitarized, while millions of ethnic Germans remained outside Germany's shrunken borders. All this was justified by a clause branding Germany uniquely responsible for the war. Other peace treaties ratified the creation of the new republic of Czechoslovakia out of part of Austria-Hungary, and awarded huge chunks of that defunct empire to Italy, Romania, Poland, and Yugoslavia (a greater Serbia). Austria and Hungary were left as barely viable. The Ottoman Empire was reduced to part of Anatolia as Britain and France occupied the Arab regions and turned over other areas to the Greeks and Armenians. (The Ottoman carve-up was modified when the

NOTABLE DATES

■ 1918
Wilson announces Fourteen Points; Russia signs Treaty of Brest-Litovsk with Germany and its Central Powers allies, surrendering all western borderlands; American troops join fighting on western front; Germany defeated; Austria-Hungary disintegrates; Great War ends.

■ 1919
Wilson negotiates at Paris Peace Conference Treaty of Versailles and other peace treaties with defeated Central Powers; debate on League of Nations in United States; Wilson suffers stroke; Red Scare begins in United States.

■ 1920
Climax and dampening of U.S. Red Scare; Senate rejects Treaty of Versailles and League of Nations; Warren G. Harding elected President.

On the western front, these American troops of the 23rd Infantry are firing a 37-mm gun at German lines on April 3, 1918—one of the earliest engagements in which American soldiers participated.

new Turkish Republic fought back ferociously.)

Wilson justified his compromises by insisting that the League of Nations be created under an agreement with the biblical name the Covenant. Wilson dreamed of a League embracing all peace-loving countries. Its council could impose sanctions and authorize military action to stop aggression.

The "war to end all wars" had ended in fear and cynicism. Being forced to sign the treaty labeled the democratic leaders of Germany traitors to right-wingers and ultranationalists. Italy came away deeply disappointed. Soviet Russia remained a pariah, and the democratic German Republic schemed to revise Versailles and develop forbidden weaponry on Soviet soil.

The long-range effectiveness of the peace settlement depended on the willingness of the U.S. to continue playing the global role it had assumed in 1917-1919. Wilson understood this. He had to win a two-thirds Senate vote to ratify the Treaty and the Covenant. But his exclusion from the peace-talk delegation of sympathetic Republicans came back to haunt him. A majority of Republican senators would accept the League of Nations with reservations (reflecting concerns that foreign governments might force the U.S. into war or undermine the Monroe Doctrine). Other Republicans rejected the League. The rejectionists were mostly progressives, appalled by domestic wartime excesses; they blamed American participation on international bankers and demanded a return to American isolation.

Wilson fought both the rejectionists and the advocates of "reservations," going on a national speaking tour to rally support for the League. But in September 1919 he suffered a stroke. From his sickbed, Wilson forced Senate Democrats to vote only for the unchanged Covenant. It, along with the Treaty, was therefore rejected. In 1920, the pro-League Democratic presidential and vice-presidential candidates, James M. Cox and young Franklin Delano Roosevelt, were swamped by Republicans Warren G. Harding and Calvin Coolidge.

The Red Scare

War-bred hysteria roared on. Race riots greeted returning African-American troops. And the Great Red Scare panicked the nation. Bolshevism and anarchism took the Kaiser's place as national nightmares. A postwar economic bust caused distress; strikes in several cities were crushed. Remnants of the prewar IWW (resistant to the war) were wiped out with methods that included lynch mobs. Radical aliens were deported to Soviet Russia. A few caused fatal bombings, and an American Communist Party was formed. Wilson's Attorney General A. Mitchell Palmer predicted a Bolshevik uprising on May Day, 1920. A new Federal Office of Investigation, the precursor of today's FBI, was founded to pursue radicals, headed by Palmer's young aide, J. Edgar Hoover. But when nothing happened, Palmer—"the Fighting Quaker"—became "the Quaking Fighter." By the end of 1920, fear of the Reds was ebbing. When Harding gave his Inaugural Address in 1921, he averred that he saw America returning to "normalcy." ■

Harlem Hellfighters

OF 380,000 AFRICAN-AMERICAN MEN DRAFTED, 200,000 served in Europe, but only 42,000 of them saw combat. All of them served in segregated units. The Army reluctantly agreed to train a few black officers, but only to command black soldiers. Most white officers disliked being assigned to command a black unit, did not respect the men they were supposed to lead, and deprecated their fighting ability. But given a fair chance, blacks fought in the Great War with bravery and skill.

One of the first American units to reach the western front was the 369th Infantry—the Harlem Hellfighters. These tough regulars, all black, served under fire longer than any American unit in the war—191 days—and compiled one of the most envied records of gallantry of the war.

"My men never retire, they go forward or they die," reported their white commander. In May 1918, Corporal Henry Johnson and Private Needham Roberts were attacked by Germans at a front-line outpost; wounded and against overwhelming odds, they fought until the Germans fell back. For this they won France's highest decoration, the Croix de Guerre. In decisive and bloody battles at Château Thierry and Belleau Wood, the 369th helped weary French fighters stop the German offensive. The 369th was the first American unit to reach the Rhine.

The entire 369th received the Croix de Guerre. They marched up Fifth Avenue in a victory parade in February 1919, to the beat of a band led by one of their own, jazz musician James Reese Europe. But their valor made little difference at the time. Not until the Korean War did black and white American soldiers fight shoulder to shoulder. ■

Harlem Hellfighters emerge from a woodland to engage the Germans in battle. Their heroism belied racist talk about the unfitness of African-American troops during the Great War.

Normalcy and Cultural Conflict

1921–1929

THE REPUBLICAN PARTY dominated American politics from 1921 to 1930. All three Presidents during those years were Republicans.

The Republican Presidents

First came genial, silver-maned, and empty-headed Harding, an Ohio newspaper publisher whom a political kingmaker once had spotted having his shoes shined and decided that he "looked like a President." Harding died in 1923, just before revelations emerged of the sordid corruption he had tolerated among his friends. The worst of the scandals involved the illegal leasing of rights to extract oil on a federal tract in Wyoming known as Teapot Dome. It resulted in a prison term for Harding's secretary of the interior, the first ex-cabinet officer imprisoned in American history. Within a few years of Harding's death, it was learned that he had fathered an illegitimate child while in the White House.

Harding's death elevated to the White House the flinty New Englander Calvin Coolidge, equally conservative but honest and straight-laced to the point of insufferable dullness; Theodore Roosevelt's daughter said that he had a face that looked like he had been "weaned on a pickle," and the public called him Silent Cal because he talked so little and slept so much. Coolidge handily won reelection in 1924, beating colorless Democratic Wall Street lawyer John W. Davis and doughty old Robert La Follette, who carried only his native Wisconsin.

"I do not chose to run for President in 1928," Coolidge told the press with typical tartness, clearing the way for dour but brainy Herbert Hoover—an old progressive who had drifted to the right. Hoover's opponent was New York's capable governor Al Smith, a product of the Lower East Side known for his machine politician's derby hat and cigar, his New York City accent (he said "radio" with a nasal a), and his Roman Catholic faith. Smith's nomination signaled the growing clout of the urban Northeast within the Democratic Party, but his Catholicism and his opposition to Prohibition were the big issues. Hoover won in a landslide, taking several southern states where Smith's religion had stirred fears that he would turn over America to the pope.

The New Era's Political Economy

After sharp wartime inflation and a short but serious postwar recession that lasted until 1921, the American industrial economy shifted into a rapid-growth mode. Republican administrations of the twenties were unabashedly pro-business; they slashed wartime income taxes and raised tariff barriers to protect favored industries. Consumer industries like electrical appliances and equipment (where General Electric led the pack) and autos (dominated by Ford and General Motors) created full employment for their workers and large profits for stockholders.

The auto industry effected some of the most sweeping changes in American life—still with us, in the form of the overwhelming majority of Americans' love affair with

Booms and Busts, 1920-1930

In the 1920s the rate of GNP growth or contraction reflected the boom-and-bust pattern of the business cycle: A sharp postwar depression in 1920-21, a strong recovery in 1922-23, another contraction in 1924, and then three years (1925-1928) in which another boom slowly flattened. In 1929 it looked like another boom was beginning; then came the Wall Street crash. In annual percentages of growth:

1920	– 4.3%	**1926**	5.9%
1921	– 8.6%	**1927**	0%
1922	15.8%	**1928**	.6%
1923	12.1%	**1929**	6.7%
1924	–.2%	**1930**	–9.8%
1925	8.4%		

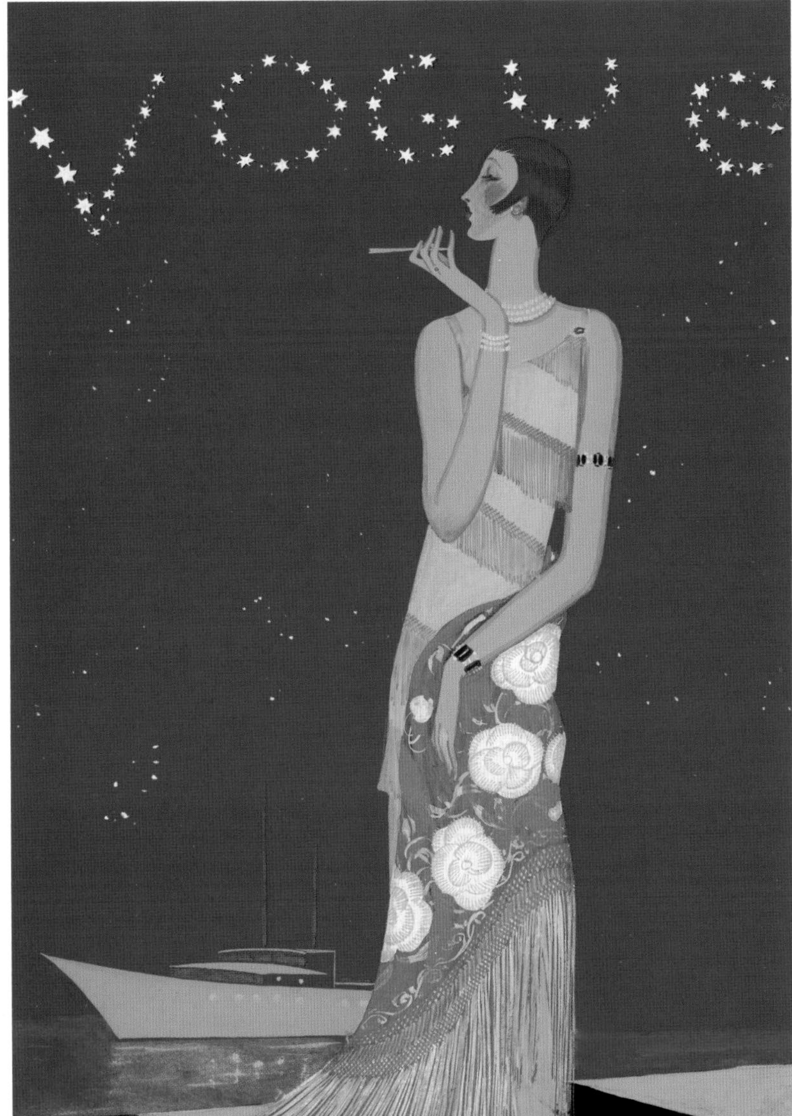

In this 1926 magazine cover, a flapper flaunts her sophistication while puffing a cigarette as an ocean liner awaits in the background.

the car, regardless of ominous environmental consequences. Gasoline-powered vehicles first challenged the hitherto unchallenged railroads for a growing share of intercity goods haulage, and the auto would have vanquished the trains even sooner had not pre-World War II American highways been so wretched. In rural America, where many farm families replaced "the old gray mare" with a Ford "flivver," vehicles provided a cheaper, faster way of getting produce to market. They also allowed consolidated high schools to bring to classes farm children who formerly would have had no education beyond the one-room rural schoolhouse. As teenagers acquired access to cars, parents lost much of

NOTABLE DATES

■ **1920**
Commercial radio broadcasting begins; Ku Klux Klan revival begins.

■ **1921**
Postwar recession ends and twenties prosperity begins; Harding, in Inaugural Address, announces the return of "normalcy."

■ **1923**
Harding dies, shortly before revelations emerge of Teapot Dome and other scandals; Calvin Coolidge becomes President.

■ **1924**
Ku Klux Klan reaches maximum national influence; Coolidge elected President.

■ **1925**
Scopes Trial in Tennessee occasions national debate about teaching evolution in public schools.

■ **1926**
NBC, first national radio network, created.

■ **1927**
First motion picture with sound.

■ **1928**
Herbert Hoover elected President.

■ **1929**
Wall Street crash ushers in Great Depression.

George "Machine Gun" Kelly was one of the most notorious gangsters of the early 1930s. In this October 1933 photograph he is escorted from the Memphis jail.

the control that they had once exerted, with profound implications for sexual behavior. The words "necking" and "petting" were coined in the twenties—doubtless in fathers' Model Ts. The first precursors of motels, primitive "tourist cabins," were also products of the twenties, much to the consternation of moralists. Old-fashioned, parentally supervised courtship vanished everywhere except in remote rural America, again thanks to cars. In general, the emergence of a youth culture, distinct from (and sometimes hostile to) the adult world, with its defining tastes in music and dancing, dress and slang, and above all sex, owed more to the auto than to any other facet of twenties life, with the possible exceptions of the radio and the movies.

Despite the coming of the car, rural America suffered during the twenties. During World War I, American farmers had expanded their production to feed the troops and Europe's starving refugees—and often had gone deeply into debt investing in new equipment powered by gasoline engines. Such risk-taking boomeranged as postwar European nations restored their own farms to productivity and erected tariff barriers to keep out American produce. Much of the farm economy sank into serious recession even as urban America got richer. The McNary-Haugen bill, which would have guaranteed farmers a minimum price for their produce, several times passed in Congress but was vetoed by Coolidge and Hoover as anathema under orthodox economic theory. Southern and midwestern farmers were right: Their interests were ignored by the rest of America. Yet the full economic implications of rural distress did not sink in until the Great Depression.

The Republican administrations used the catchphrase the "New Era" to promote their policies. Hoover, the secretary of commerce under both Harding and Coolidge before he himself entered the White House in 1929, was the driving force of New Era policies. Twenties Presidents avoided the often acrimonious clashes between government and business interests that had marked the Roosevelt and Wilson Administrations. "The business of America," averred the avuncular Coolidge, "is business." An engineer by training, a pre-war progressive, and a prominent World War I administrator, Hoover was obsessed with "efficiency." The key idea of his New Era was a partnership between Washington and big business and a flow of economic information from the government to corporate decision makers.

This was, indeed, an era of more business consolidations, continuing trends that had begun in the late 19th century. Trust-busting was a curiosity of the bygone days of TR (who had died, prematurely old and sick, in 1919). And consolidation reached directly into the heart of American life.

Characteristic of these years, and with a considerable impact on American society, was the emergence of the first big grocery chains, A&P and Acme. Although huge supermarkets would not come until the 1950s, the twenties chains combined hundreds of medium-size grocery stores throughout urban

America. The chain stores touted their cleanliness, and a few experimented with open shelves from which shoppers made their own selections rather than having someone behind a counter hand across a requested item (plucked with a cherry picker from high on the wall). Unlike old-time neighborhood groceries, which sold bulk commodities out of open barrels, the chains offered standard brands and paid close attention to packaging and advertising. And because the chains achieved economies of scale, they undersold the mom-and-pops. Such inducements convinced large numbers of younger women to do their food shopping at chain stores and to abandon their mothers' familiar groceries. But women gave up something by shopping at the modern, efficient chains. Prices were set; there was no haggling. The chains never gave credit, as old-fashioned groceries usually did. And the chain stores all looked the same; gone were the community bulletin boards and the gossip (for immigrants, in their native language), and the cozy ambiance of neighborhood shopping. The chains were "modern America," and in big cities like Chicago they were one more way of "Americanizing" Italian, Polish, or Czech families, who of course could not find at the A&P the familiar kinds of mushrooms or sausage that their ethnic shops had featured. But as the chains became popular, the grubby old mom-and-pops were steadily disappearing.

Radio was still another force for assimilating "hyphenated Americans" in the twenties. Its impact

The Scopes Trial

THE SHARPEST BATTLE LINE BETWEEN RELIGIOUS FUNDAMENTALISM and modern science and religion was Darwin's theory of evolution. To fundamentalists, evolution starkly denied the Genesis account of God's special creation of all living creatures, including humans. To modernists, evolution was incontrovertible science. In 1925 the Tennessee legislature forbade the teaching of anything in the public schools that denied divine creation. When Dayton, Tennessee, high school teacher John Scopes taught his biology class about evolution, he was arrested and indicted. The ensuing "monkey trial"—so-called because anti-evolutionists caricatured Darwin's theory as claiming that humans descended from monkeys—mesmerized the nation.

John Scopes, the biology teacher charged with teaching evolution, is flanked by the local procsecutor (replaced by Bryan) and another citizen.

Famous defense lawyer Clarence Darrow, an agnostic, served as Scopes' attorney. William Jennings Bryan volunteered to prosecute Scopes. Bryan, a fundamentalist, also objected to evolution on the grouds that Darwinism justified the division of human beings into "fit" and "unfit"—exactly the point that *Baltimore Sun* journalist H.L. Mencken kept making in his columns, which kept urban America howling at the "simian antics" of southern anti-evolutionists.

The climax of the trial came when Darrow put Bryan on the stand as an "expert" on the Bible and got him to state his unshakeable belief that the prophet Jonah had been swallowed and disgorged by a whale. Scopes was convicted and paid a $100 fine, later struck down by the state's supreme court as excessive. A few days after the trial, Bryan died of a heart attack, brought on by heat, stress, and humiliation. In a nasty obituary Mencken likened him to a cock crowing on a dunghill. But the struggle between modern science and "creationists," as anti-evolutionists would later label themselves, was far from over. ■

was probably even greater than that of its successor—television—simply because of radio's unprecedented newness as a mass medium. TV later would only build on what radio had initiated.

Like so much else in American life, broadcasting's evolution was part of the New Era economy. Not until after World War I did Marconi's pioneering work with transmitting long-distance radio signals begin translating into a consumer good. Americans' first radio sets were for hobbyists, who assembled kits with crystals, tightly wound wires, and headphones to pick up dim local signals. The first commercial radio station, KDKA in Pittsburgh, dated from 1920. It flashed, to a handful of local listeners, news of Harding's election. Over the next few years, radio stations proliferated, and building kits became easier and more widespread. But all this was local. Religious and ethnic groups controlled a surprising amount of broadcasting, much of it foreign-language outreach to ingrown communities. In its first few years, radio was serving mainly to perpetuate "otherness." Only in the mid-1920s did the federal government—largely at the behest of Secretary of Commerce Hoover—begin to encourage the amalgamation of local broadcasting into larger networks and to sell broadcast frequencies accordingly. NBC, the first network, was created in 1926, followed by CBS. Rapidly they enlarged broadcasting "space" at the expense of small-market radio stations; and because the emerging national networks had plenty of money (from the sale of advertising) to invest in programming, they could offer "modern"—but by def-

Brandishing an American flag and a blazing cross, the supreme leader of the Ku Klux Klan swears allegiance to God and country in this December 1922 photograph. The Klan reached the height of its influence in the mid-1920s.

Edward Daheny, at center, stands with his lawyers prior to the Senate hearing on the Teapot Dome scandal.

inition homogeneous—fare that appealed to vast audiences. Masses of listeners tuned in to comedy, adventure, and suspense programs, music, sports, news, and the first "soap operas." (These 15-minute tear-jerking serials were sponsored by the corporate makers of dish-washing and laundry soaps and were aimed at housewives doing chores just before the children got home from school.) Making receivers for all budgets, by the late 1920s the Radio Corporation of America (RCA) mushroomed; its fancy models became as prized a living-room icon as the post-World War II TV set.

Rural America

Farm families had few or no modern conveniences—in most rural areas, there were no telephones and no electricity because private utilities saw no profit in stringing lines from one isolated farm to the next. Almost the only new popular commodity that cities and the country shared was Coca Cola, a drink invented in 1891 by Atlantan Asa G. Chandler and heavily marketed in both North and South. In most aspects of modern life, the gap between rural and urban America was widening.

For much of the 1920s, rural and small-town America's backlash against urban values was expressed by a new Ku Klux Klan. D.W.Griffith's silent-film classic *Birth of a Nation* had thrilled millions, thanks to a technical wizardry never before seen on the screen. "History written in lightning" had been Woodrow Wilson's approving verdict. But in glorifying the post-Civil War Klan the film presented blacks as cowardly "race mixers"—a horrendous message. Recognizing the power of Griffith's romanticization of the white-robed terrorists, some enterprising Southerners set about reviving the Klan itself. By 1920, "klaverns" were sprouting up in the South, the rural Midwest, and the West. Many joined in the same spirit that Americans flocked to innumerable other harmless fraternal organizations like the Elks and the Odd Fellows—for fellowship and the exciting mumbo-jumbo of ritual, which diminished the tedium of small-town life. Many Klansmen were upstanding community leaders, their faces always hidden behind white hoods. In some places, membership in the Klan was necessary to achieve community status, business contacts, or votes. But the new Klan, like the original one, was sinister. It preached virulent hatred of blacks, Roman Catholics, Jews, and immigrants, and it did not hold back from terrorist acts like midnight riding, cross burning, and lynching. As it spread, it gained power in some states through the men elected to office. The Indiana, Oklahoma, and Oregon legislatures and governorships were at various times virtually controlled by the Klan. KKK values kept alive the worst excesses of the postwar Red Scare, including the suppression of all dissent from "100-percent Americanism," fundamentalist religion, and of course virulent racism.

The Klan's downfall came chiefly because the Indiana Klan's "grand dragon" was exposed for murder, sex offenses, and embezzlement. But while it lasted, the Klan was an ugly stain on the United States, and in many ways it gave a frightening voice to traditionalist and nativist resentment against modernity. There was no sadder example of the decade-long culture war. ■

The Stresses of Modernization

1920–1930

IN 1920 THE NINETEENTH Amendment was added to the Constitution, at long last giving the vote to women everywhere. The participation of so many women in the wartime workforce had helped tip the balance.

Women's Rights

Considering the passionate debates, pro and con, that the prewar suffragist movement had generated, actual voting by women proved anticlimactic. Progressives, who generally supported women's suffrage, had hoped that politics would be "cleaned up" and that concerns such as child labor, education, and health would be better addressed. But the actual impact of women voting was minimal. There was no gender gap in twenties elections: Women voted along party lines in almost the same ways that men did.

Women's "liberation" (no one used that word at the time) consisted mostly of young flappers smoking cigarettes, bobbing their hair, wearing short skirts, flattening their breasts, talking about sex, dancing the Charleston, and—despite Prohibition—drinking in "speakeasies." In all these ways, young women were defying parental values and traditional ideas, but such rebellions were most common among well-off young women. Working-class women lived as they always had—underpaid, overworked, under the authority of parents and husbands, but still enjoying (while young) such pleasures as dating, movies, jazz on the radio, and the Tunnel of Love ride at the amusement park. Middle-class women could buy vacuum cleaners and washing machines, and often learned to drive Fords and Chevies like their husbands. And great numbers of middle-class white women employed live-in black women, at abysmally low wages, to ease the drudgeries of housework. For black women, there was virtually no change at all—and, if they lived in the South, neither they nor black men could vote.

Immigration "Reform"

Given the prewar concern that the nation was being inundated with low-class foreigners speaking outlandish languages, immigration might have been one of the great postwar political issues. The hysteria of the World War I years certainly showed how worried "old stock" patriots were about the loyalty of "hyphenated Americans." In 1916, a New York socialite named Madison Grant had published a widely read book, *The Passing of the Great Race*, dismally predicting America's incipient "mongrelization." The fact that so many "mongrels" rallied to the flag during World War I may have allayed nativist fears, but the Red Scare rekindled them. Then, in 1921, the return of peace and prosperity touched off another wave of transatlantic immigration. America was still the Promised Land. It was time for the conservative majority in Congress to get to work.

In 1921 Congress cut immigration to 350,000. In 1924 it shrank the influx to164,000 and imposed severe limitations on immigrants by their place of origin. Henceforth, foreigners' access to the Golden Door would depend on where they were coming from. Each country was assigned an annual quota of immigrants—a number corresponding to the proportion of each ethnic group within the general population as of 1890. By making 1890 the crucial year, Congress was setting the clock back to just before the U.S. was flooded with immigrants from eastern and southern Europe. Thus countries like Italy, Greece, Poland, and Yugoslavia got tiny quotas, whereas Great Britain, Ireland, Germany, and Scandinavia received such large quotas that in many years they went unfilled. Despite blatant discrimination against those most anxious to enter, the quota system was accepted by old-stock Americans as a wise measure. It remained in force until 1965.

Before the 1920s, respectable American women did not smoke, at least in public. Here, a photographer and a friend humorously poke fun at the era's New Woman image by brazenly smoking in petticoats and masks.

NOTABLE DATES

■ **1920**
The 19th Amendment gives women the right to vote; Volstead Act enacts national prohibition; Census Bureau finds that for the first time urban dwellers are a majority of the U.S. population.

■ **1921**
Large-scale immigration resumes; Congress imposes first immigration restriction.

■ **1924**
Immigration restriction enacted, drastically limiting immigration from southern and eastern Europe.

■ **1929**
Al Capone's gang in Chicago carries out St. Valentine's Day Massacre of its enemies.

■ **1930**
Capone convicted of tax evasion.

Prohibition and Crime

"Resolution" of the immigration "crisis" left Prohibition as the political issue of the decade. Wartime prohibition had paved the way for broader acceptance of what Hoover in 1928 would call "a great . . . experiment, noble in motive and far-reaching in purpose." In 1919 the Eighteenth Amendment was ratified, empowering Congress to ban the manufacture, sale, and importation of intoxicating beverages. Congress duly passed the Volstead Act in 1920, imposing Prohibition.

Prohibition was the triumph of two forces: evangelical religion, and the moral purity obsessions of urban progressives. Alcoholism was undoubtedly a serious social problem, and a connection between saloons and machine politics had long been assumed. But in the old-stock American mind, public consumption of alcohol was associated with foreigners—beer-swilling Germans, superstitious Roman Catholics, and swarthy Jews. Prohibition was a way of accelerating aliens' Americanization.

All through the 1920s, whether to repeal or vigorously enforce Prohibition was the hot issue. Republicans and old-fashioned Protestants were "dry." But a split in the

Democratic Party pitted "dry" southern whites against "wet" working-class northern urbanites.

Prohibition may have been a noble experiment, but it had sordid consequences. In simple dollars-and-cents terms, it was a disaster because the federal government gave up excise revenues that legal alcohol would have generated, while spending on futile law enforcement. Overall, Americans may have drunk less while it was in force (modern statistical attempts to calculate this are controversial), but those who did want a drink invariably got it. Defying the law became a mark of sophistication. (Before the war, respectable women did not drink in public.) Sometimes the "home brew" and "bathtub gin" that was consumed turned out to be poison. More likely, the booze was good—and supplied by organized crime. Gangs had been part of the American urban scene since the 18th century, but immigration of the late 19th century had created fresh underworlds, often in shady partnerships with corrupt politicians and police. These criminal and semi-criminal outfits usually preyed upon their own ethnic communities: extortion, loan-sharking, numbers rackets, gambling, prostitution, and untaxed liquor were their usual sources of profit. Neapolitan and Sicilian mafias ("brotherhoods" and "families" rooted for hundreds of years in the Old Country) established themselves in big-city "Little Italies," using codes of silence, extended-family networks, close-knit loyalties, and terror to keep their illegal

The House That Ruth Built

The 1920s were the Golden Age of American sports, from golf, tennis, boxing, and racecars to college football and professional baseball. Hyped by radio and newsreels, twenties sports heroes became legends. The most beloved was an orphan from Baltimore, George Herman "Babe" Ruth.

Baseball, like so much in America, hit a crisis in 1919. American League champions, the Chicago White Sox, unaccountably lost the World Series, and soon it was clear why: Team members and gamblers had thrown it. In 1921 a retired federal judge, Kennesaw Mountain Landis, appointed Commissioner of Baseball to clean up the mess, banned the offenders from the sport for life. The White Sox became the "Black Sox."

Ruth slugs a pitch at a hitting exhibition staged in another New York City stadium, the National League Giants' Polo Grounds.

Landis's stern crackdown, the "live ball" (a new baseball that could be hit spectacularly long distances), and Ruth saved the game. Equally skilled as a pitcher and batter (though too slow to be a great centerfielder), he was sold by the Boston Red Sox to the undistinguished New York Yankees in 1920. The Sultan of Swat transformed his team and captured the public's imagination as a live ball slugger. His 60 home runs in 1927 and his career total of 714 homers stood for decades. He enriched the Yankees' owners, who assembled a team of other great players. So mighty did the Yankees grow, with their "Murderers' Row" lineup and matching stable of starting pitchers, that fans outside New York City loved to hate them—another American tradition. The new Yankee Stadium became "the House that Ruth Built." His venereal diseases and boozing were hushed up. But a reinvigorated sport was Ruth's true legacy. Epitomizing the 1920s spirit, "the Babe" lives on as one of America's great folk heroes. ■

activities secret from the authorities. But among other ethnic groups, including Irish, Jews, and Chinese, equally ruthless gangs operated by similar rules.

With Prohibition, the underworld vastly increased its scope and profit, and for the first time reached into middle-class American life, where the demand for illegal alcohol seemed insatiable. "Running" liquor in from across the border and from ships just outside the twelve-mile limit defining American territorial waters became a big business; so did supplying the bootleggers and the speakeasies that retailed booze. Because all this was illegal and therefore the object of federal interdiction, gangs fought savage turf wars to control it. In all this, ruthless gangsters like Chicago's Al Capone and the godfathers of Mafia families flourished. Capone himself was only brought down in 1930 on federal tax-evasion charges.

Cultural Clash

Prohibition was only one of the issues comprising what would today be called a culture war. In fact, it is quite possible to see the decade's cultural clash as a precursor of divisions that still divide Americans. For that reason, the twenties are as dominated by the theme of modernization as are the years of the Great War, when the U.S. first faced—and flinched at—the challenge of global leadership.

At the root of many tensions over modernization was the fact that after the 1920 Census it was officially announced that for the first time a majority of the American people lived in "urban areas." The era of rural and small-town America setting the tone for the nation's life was gone forever. There were racial implications as well. In 1917-1918 millions of African Americans left the rural South to work in war industries. They made for cities like Los Angeles, Chicago, and New York, creating large black communities like once-white Harlem. A little later, the explosive growth of the automobile industry made Detroit a city with a large African-American minority—as well as a serious race problem. However hard life might be in "Motown" or Harlem or Chicago's South Side, black residents now could vote, were safe from southern lynch mobs, and developed more freely their distinctive cultural style.

In a host of ways, urban America was coming to hold values critical of rural America. Not just tension over Prohibition but also a craze for "movies," universal access to the radio and to popular jazz music, and the availability of professional sports allowed even poor urbanites to see themselves as different from the "hicks."

Hollywood's emergence as an American icon was a product of the twenties. The movie industry was created by a hard-driving group of Russian-Jewish entrepreneurs with roots in prewar vaudeville and Old Country Yiddish theater. Men like Samuel Goldwyn and Jack Warner were fascinated with the dynamism, flash, and opportunity that America represented to enterprising immigrants, and their vision of American life literally got projected into the movies. They also invented the famed—and exploitative—studio system, in which movie stars and writers, directors, and cameramen truly "belonged" to their producers. Hollywood, part of the growing southern California metropolis centered on Los Angeles, became the embodiment of America long before the twenties were over. And Hollywood's films sold to audiences around the globe a vision of America that was upwardly mobile, fun, glamorous, and ever-so-slightly sexy.

Throwing off Puritanism

Among sophisticated urban Americans, the twenties were an exciting decade of revolt against old-time values, maliciously caricatured as Puritanism. "Someone with the nagging fear that someone, somewhere, is happy"—so Baltimore journalist and literary critic H.L. Mencken blasted the Puritan tradition. A master of the no-holds-barred style, Mencken denounced everything that Americans held dear. Democracy, progress, religion, businessmen, jazz, movies, idealism, and—naturally—Prohibition were pilloried in his monthly magazine *The American Mercury* and in his *Baltimore Sun* columns. After the war he poked fun at Jews, Christians, blacks, "the Archangel Woodrow," "Lord Hoover," and thousands of other squirming targets. The South received some of his sharpest barbs, to the delight of thousands of aspiring southern intellectuals, including the young African-American writer Richard Wright. "Why do you still live in the United States?" someone asked. "Why do men visit zoos?" Mencken retorted. ■

The Jazz Age

1920–1929

SOME AMERICAN ENTHUSIASMS of the twenties crossed all social and cultural boundaries. One was baseball. Some of the greatest players were in the segregated Negro League. Fans followed games on the radio.

A second unifying craze was enthusiasm for the shy young Midwesterner who in 1927 won the competition to be the first to pilot, single-handedly, an airplane from the U.S. to Paris. Charles Lindbergh and his *Spirit of St. Louis* embodied, for all his compatriots, America's can-do character, its mechanical knack, its rebuke to Old World arrogance, and its individualism.

Jazz was a third popular craze, but by no means a universal one. Musical traditionalists thought jazz "brittle"; in general, the older generation did not become jazz buffs. But young people of the twenties embraced jazz—like the car and illegal booze—as an exciting expression of their own impatience with tradition. Radio and record players spread jazz like wildfire. And jazz steadily became a more sophisticated and varied art form, shaped by such artists as Jelly Roll Morton, Louis Armstrong, Duke Ellington, and Billie Holiday.

The writer F. Scott Fitzgerald memorably defined the twenties as "the Jazz Age," though he did not have much to say about jazz. Fitzgerald's greatest novel of the twenties, *The Great Gatsby*, largely written in Europe, illuminated the ambiguities of the American dream as it oscillated between respect for tradition and the temptations of money and success.

American popular culture mesmerized Europeans. The Jazz Age was a transatlantic phenomenon, and the gifted African-American modern dancer Josephine Baker was the rage of Paris. Not all American writers stayed in the U.S.; some, like Ernest Hemingway, were expatriates, living cheaply in Paris and free of the stultifying values of Main Street—the title of the first novel of another great twenties writer, Sinclair Lewis.

All the notable American writers of the decade were shaped by the modernist styles of prewar, European-rooted literature. Under this influence, yet searching for distinctively American themes and

A huge crowd waits outside Warners' Theatre to see Al Jolson in *The Jazz Singer* in 1927.

expressiveness, all rebelling in various ways against older America, some of the greatest writers in the nation's history came to the fore. Besides Fitzgerald, Hemingway, and Lewis, the pantheon included playwright Eugene O'Neill and poets T.S. Eliot, Ezra Pound, Carl Sandberg, and Edna St. Vincent Millay. Especially notable was the Harlem Renaissance, in which white patrons gave encouragement and financial support to a group of gifted black writers, above all poet Langston Hughes.

Modernist values sank deeper roots into the urban-influenced American mind during the twenties. Einstein's theory of relativity became widely known, if hardly understood. (When the great physicist was introduced at the White House, a newspaper headlined: "Einstein Theory Puzzles Harding.") German, Austrian, and British, but not U.S., universities trained American researchers in the "new physics." And all but the most scientifically literate Americans missed the significance of European physicists' theorizing about quantum mechanics. Among the greatest achievements of the twenties, its significance would not be broadly known for many years.

The king of scientific sophistication in postwar America was Vienna's Sigmund Freud. Getting psychoanalyzed became fairly common among urban Americans with money to spend years on the couch. Freud introduced to American middle-class discourse talk of repression, the unconscious, and sex, and exerted a powerful impact on American culture. Other experts scolded parents to attend to cleanliness and rigid feeding schedules and tried to discourage "unsanitary" breastfeeding. In all these dimensions, "up-to-date" scientific efficiency was the watchword.

During the twenties, however, taboos in favor of the double standard and against flaunted sexuality remained strong. Movies were self-censored. Sexuality in fiction had to be expressed in euphemisms. (The novel *Ulysses*, masterpiece of the great Irish writer James Joyce, could not legally be sold in the United States until 1934 because of its sexual language.) Birth control was widespread among the middle class, but abortion was illegal. The twenties were in fact an ambiguous age, tentative in exploring new sensations, but still tied strongly to older traditions. Full cultural revolution had to await the sixties and seventies. ■

Heroes of the 1920s

Baseball Babe Ruth's 60 home runs in one season and career total of 714 homers was unsurpassed for decades; Ty Cobb amasses .357 batting average; Rogers Hornsby bats .424 in 1924.

Football "Four Horsemen" of Notre Dame backfield and Red Grange popularize college and professional teams.

Golf Bobby Jones's amateur career climaxes in winning the four big titles (1930): British Amateur, British Open, U.S. Amateur, U.S. Open.

Boxing Popular pros include Jack Dempsey, Gene Tunney; black champion Jack Johnson banned from fighting in U.S.

NOTABLE DATES

■ 1919
"Black Sox" scandal in baseball.

■ 1920
Babe Ruth sold by Boston Red Sox to the New York Yankees, beginning the Yankee's dominance in major league baseball.

■ 1925
F. Scott Fitzgerald publishes *The Great Gatsby*.

■ 1927
Charles Lindbergh's solo transatlantic flight; Babe Ruth hits 60 home runs in one season, a long-standing record; *The Jazz Singer*, first movie with sound, released.

WORLD SURVEY

1914–1933

THE UNITED STATES NEVER joined the League, and isolationism remained strong. But much had changed. Before 1914, the U.S. was a creditor nation, but Europe's war debts to the U.S. ran into the billions, and Wilson's idealism fell short when it came to the U.S. taking advantage of the war to pressure competitors to liquidate their Latin American investments in favor of the U.S. Throughout the twenties, American economic influence remained paramount in Latin America; American troops occupied Nicaragua, Haiti, and the Dominican Republic. Relations with Mexico stabilized, in 1927, but Mexicans did not forget Wilson's intervention.

■ Asia

The U.S. stayed closely engaged with global affairs. In 1922 it hosted a major international conference in Washington, at which the U.S., Britain, and Japan reduced their naval fleets to a 10:10:7 ratio. (That favored Japan, which concentrated its fleet in the western Pacific and secretly fortified the islands that it acquired from Germany.) China suffered domestic turmoil during the 1920s, including civil war between the Nationalist regime (headed by Chiang Kai-shek) and the Communists. But Americans dismissed this as East Asia's endemic disorder; the Open Door remained ajar, and thousands of American Christian missionaries labored to win Chinese souls.

■ Europe

Restoring Europe's economic stability was delayed by a devastating inflation in Germany in 1923. Washington worked out a stabilization program that cycled dollars to Germany as loans with which to pay reparations—out of which the Allies could pay on their war debts to America. The plan allowed the democratic German Republic to consolidate. International reconciliation seemingly reached its pinnacle in 1928, when the United States sponsored the Kellogg Pact. Each signatory pledged never to go to war with the others. But one U.S. senator gave a more accurate assessment: "An international kiss."

Europe's recovery rested on the flow of dollars, and it was flimsy because high tariff walls on both sides hampered international trade. American protectionism blocked Europeans from selling industrial goods to Americans while paying war debts; European barriers to agricultural imports worsened American farmers' depression. Coolidge refused to consider reducing debts: "They hired the money, didn't they?" The French called America "Uncle Shylock."

The Great War had sapped white prestige in many European colonies. In India, the gentle Hindu lawyer Mohandas Gandhi began preaching nonviolent civil disobedience; in French Indochina, the young Communist Ho Chi Minh was preparing to fight for independence. Arab nationalism and an Islamic revival made it difficult for the British government to fulfill promises to the Zionists in 1917 to create a Jewish Homeland in Palestine. Long before Israel existed, the Arab-Israeli struggle had begun.

European nationalist hatreds never dimmed. Germans dreamed of throwing off "the shackles of Versailles," although Adolf Hitler's first bid for power in November 1923 failed miserably. Italy, though, succumbed to dictatorship in 1922 when Benito Mussolini led his Fascist Party followers in a March on Rome and seized emergency powers. Never mind that the strutting Duce's Fascist dictatorship was rarely as "totalitarian" in practice as it bragged (he did not even get the trains to run on time); Il Duce's many foreign admirers praised him for achieving efficiency and for crushing communism.

■ U.S.S.R.

In 1924, the year Lenin died, Soviet Russia became the Union of Soviet Socialist Republics. Throughout most of the twenties, "the great Soviet experiment" evoked both interest and disdain among Westerners. But the radicalism of the experiment dimmed somewhat when Lenin decreed the restoration of private property to revive food and industrial production. Within limits, creative experimentation was permitted in literature, art, and film. Lenin's death, however, unleashed a power struggle within the Communist Party, and by 1928 the contest ended in the victory of cunning Joseph Stalin. Soon after taking power, Stalin launched a drive to industrialize and abolished private farming by herding peasants into collective farms. Simultaneously, the first of many bloody purges of potential political opponents was unleashed in Moscow.

In 1928, the United States still refused to recognize the Soviet Union. But by now few Americans feared Bolsheviks lurking under their beds. The Cold War between Wilson and Lenin in 1918 had been temporarily shelved. Stalin spoke of "building socialism in one country," and nothing seemed to challenge American capitalism.

But with the collapse of Wall Street, one by one the capitalist countries sank into economic depression. Hard times gave the Japanese military the excuse in 1931 to seize mineral-rich Manchuria from China, touching off war in East Asia. By 1931-32, banks were crashing in Central Europe and unemployment was soaring. Germany's democratic parties failed to stop the disaster; the race to take power between the Communists and Hitler's Nazis was on. Hitler won, by a combination of democratic votes and backroom political intrigue. On January 30, 1933, Hitler became the chancellor of Germany, and within weeks he was establishing a dictatorship. ■

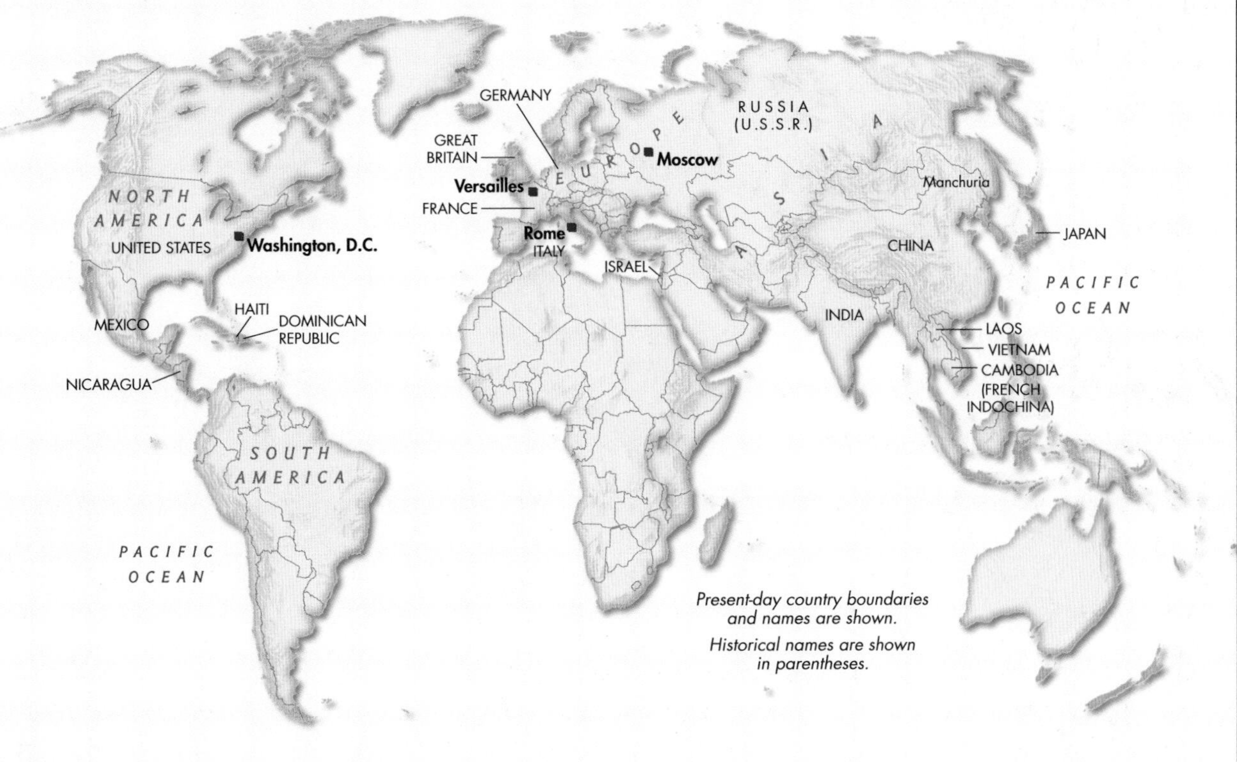

REMAKING AMERICA 1929–1945

THE WALL STREET CRASH OF 1929 WAS A DISASTER FOR AMERICA. IT SHATTERED ILLUSIONS of automatic economic growth and shook faith in democratic capitalism. It blighted a generation, making the thirties a decade of shriveled hopes. One of America's greatest Presidents did restore morale, but even he could not end the Great Depression.

Depression hit Central Europe even harder than the United States, destabilizing the fragile democratic German republic. The Nazi Party, which took power in January 1933, reopened the struggle for mastery in Europe that had merely been suspended by what appears in retrospect as the truce of November 1918. In East Asia, economic disaster spurred Japanese leaders into seizing the resources that their island nation lacked by conquering Manchuria in 1931 and invading China in 1937. Germany's aggressive drive to overthrow Versailles and Japan's equally aggressive determination to rule "Greater East Asia" culminated in 1939 with World War II. By December 1941, the United States and the remnants of the democratic world were fighting for survival against murderous tyrannies. America and Britain had to find common cause with Stalin, who had no more respect for liberal democracy than did Hitler. In winning the war, the United States in August 1945 unleashed the most destructive weapon ever built by human hands, the nuclear bomb. ■

With Germany about to collapse in the spring of 1945, the U.S. Army liberated this German POW camp, freeing 6,000 American prisoners of war. Jubilantly, they pour out of confinement.

■ **1929**
Wall Street crash begins worldwide Great Depression.

■ **1933**
New Deal begins with many emergency and reform measures; Hitler establishes dictatorship in Germany.

■ **1935**
Social Security Act; Hitler begins German rearmament.

■ **1938**
Hitler annexes Austria and begins carving up Czechoslovakia.

■ **1939**
Hitler-Stalin non-aggression pact; German attack on Poland starts World War II; Einstein's warning to Roosevelt initiates U.S. research on nuclear weapon.

■ **1940**
Germany conquers most of Western Europe but fails to defeat Great Britain by air attacks; U.S. begins defense preparations; Roosevelt elected to third term.

■ **1941**
U.S. extends Lend-Lease aid to nations resisting Hitler; Germany invades U.S.S.R.; Japan attacks Pearl Harbor, bringing U.S. into World War II.

■ **1942**
U.S. defeats Japan at Coral Sea and Midway; first self-sustaning nuclear reaction advances work toward atom bomb; Nazis begin to exterminate Jews.

■ **1943**
German defeat at Stalingrad marks turning point in World War II in Europe; U.S. invades southern Italy.

■ **1944**
Normandy invasion and liberation of France; Soviet army advances into Eastern Europe; U.S. forces close in on Japan.

The Great Depression

1929–1933

In September 1929, a leading American economist, Irving Fischer, announced that stock prices had reached "a permanent high plateau." Everyone was buying on credit. But the truly savvy were pulling out of the overheated stock market. On October 24, 1929, Black Thursday, Wall Street crashed. The twenties were over.

Severe and prolonged economic downturns had punctuated 19th-century American history at ten- to twenty-year intervals. They were called panics—those of 1819, 1837, 1857, 1873, 1882, 1893, and 1907. But none had been as profound and prolonged as the Depression (a word coined by the Hoover Administration as a supposedly reassuring euphemism) that began in 1929.

The causes of the Great Depression are still debated. But most agree that a high-flying securities market could not sustain the "bubble" prices to which buyers had bid stocks. The bubble burst, ruining those who could not ride out the sudden drop—often because they had bought "on the margin" and now had to pay up or lose everything. But although the skid in the Dow Jones index in October 1929 was sharper than had ever occurred before, this was not the whole story of the oncoming disaster: The Dow would fall very hard, too, in October 1987 without making a second Great Depression. The reasons for the worst crisis of American capitalism go much deeper.

First, there were the inherent weaknesses in the twenties economy. Corporate profits and upper-bracket incomes were rising much faster than incomes of ordinary Americans on whose spending a modern consumer-oriented economy always rests. With low wages and industrial laborers lacking unions to represent their interests, worker-consumers were not making enough to buy the flood of goods they were producing. Farmers, a much larger segment of the general population in the 1920s than today, were in chronic economic trouble. Protectionism distorted international trade, preventing the exporting of enough industrial goods and the importing of cheaper goods, and keeping the farm economy depressed.

Second, once the economy began to tank, in 1929-1930, there was no safety net to check the collapse, no automatic stabilizers to right the capsizing boat. There was no unemployment insurance to help laid-off workers survive temporary job loss, no old-age pensions to support the elderly or disabled, and no health insurance to pay medical bills not met out of pocket. Bank accounts were not insured; if banks failed, depositors lost everything. No government agencies inspected the books of corporations that sold stock or banks that borrowed and lent money, so that fraudulent practices could lead the country, unknowingly, to financial disaster.

Third, the New Era government failed miserably. Not only had the late-twenties speculative mania roared on with few warnings of risk, but economic policy makers made almost every possible mistake after the market "corrected" in October 1929. What could have been merely a big blip on the charts became a downward spiral. The Federal Reserve tightened credit

Unemployment, 1929-1933

The Wall Street crash did not immediately throw millions out of work. It came late in the year, and employers hoped it was only temporary. Only as recession deepened and pessimism engulfed the nation did unemployment begin to rise steeply. By 1933, when joblessness hit its peak, the situation was truly frightening.

Average Annual Unemployment for Workers 14 Years and Older

Year	Number	Percent
1929	1,550,000	3.2
1930	4,340,000	8.7
1931	8,020,000	15.9
1932	12,060,000	23.6
1933	12,830,000	24.9

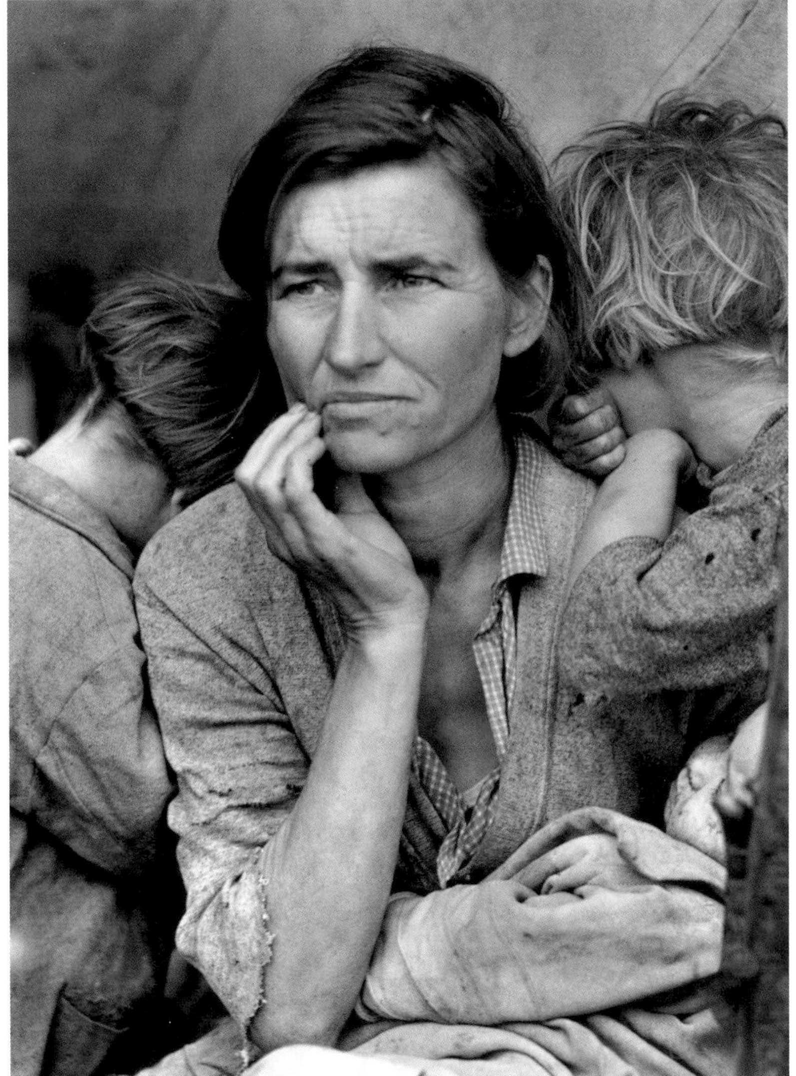

This famous Dorothea Lange image of Dust Bowl migrants is emblematic of Depression victims.

and the money supply where it should have immediately slashed interest rates and put more dollars into circulation. The Republican Congress and President Hoover raised tariff barriers still higher when they should have reduced them to free international trade. Hoover ordered drastic government economies and belt-tightening when he should have called for extra public spending to offset the recession; the Democrats criticized him for not cutting waste even more. Constant talk from the White House about recovery being just around the corner, intended as a confidence-builder, turned into a sick joke. Hoover was not a heartless fool; he grieved deeply for victims of the Depression, and he knew as much as anyone about orthodox economics. But he was hamstrung by that very orthodoxy,

NOTABLE DATES

■ **1929**
Herbert Hoover becomes President; Black Thursday (October 24) Wall Street crash begins the Great Depression.

■ **1930**
Smoot-Hawley Tariff raises protectionist barriers to highest level yet; amid deepening economic distress, Democrats sweep midterm elections.

■ **1931**
Farm foreclosures stimulate rural radicalism; Hoover announces moratorium on repayment of foreign war debts; Japan seizes Manchuria from China.

■ **1932**
Reconstruction Finance Corporation (RFC) established, to lend federal funds to struggling businesses; bank failures increase in U.S., Europe; Bonus Marchers evicted from Washington, D.C.; Democrats nominate Franklin D. Roosevelt, who promises a "new deal"; Roosevelt elected President.

■ **1933**
Adolf Hitler takes power in Germany; with unemployment peaking and bank failures multiplying, Roosevelt inaugurated as President.

and by a personal faith in rugged individualism that told him that federal relief to citizens would destroy their self-reliance and subject them to intolerable governmental control.

The last accomplishment—in the GOP's eyes—of the Republican Congresses of the interwar years was to enact the Smoot-Hawley Tariff of 1930, a measure touted as protecting American workers from foreign competition by setting trade barriers higher than ever before. That fall, the Democrats won large majorities to both houses of Congress and many state legislatures, and in New York they reelected as governor Franklin D. Roosevelt, a distant Democratic cousin of TR. As governor of what was then the nation's largest state, Roosevelt automatically became a contender for the Presidency.

Hoover fought the Depression. In 1932, he and Congress established the Reconstruction Finance Corporation (RFC), which throughout the thirties lent billions to beleaguered corporations struggling to maintain payrolls. Hoover was dead-set against offering relief to individuals, but the RFC continued his faith in government-business partnership.

Such measures did nothing to drag the economy out of its morass. What economists call a deflationary liquidity trap was taking hold. With prices trending relentlessly downward, employers and individuals had every incentive to save today because they expected prices and costs would fall tomorrow. So payrolls got slashed, cash went under mattresses, and the stock market remained mired at rock bottom. (A few bold souls did take the risk, acquiring the stock and real estate portfolios that would make them rich decades later.) People lucky enough to keep their jobs faced wage cuts, but at least prices were falling too. Unemployed workers' savings were exhausted, and the resources ordinary people counted on "against a rainy day"—insurance, fraternal and ethnic organizations' mutual savings societies, credit at the local store, and loans from relatives—collapsed one by one. In rural America, farmers struggling with dropping prices and inexorable demands to repay debts faced bank foreclosure. By 1931 and 1932, such foreclosures were stirring stolid rural communities into a radicalism more passionate than anything seen since the heyday of populism; neighbors tried banding together to stop farm foreclosures by threat of armed force, and in Republican Iowa farmers muttered that if they could no longer march under the American flag they would fly the red flag of Communism.

By 1932, runs on banks were becoming common, as panicky savers swarmed in to close their accounts. Banks in turn called in their loans—and often discovered that they had no more money to pay desperate depositors. Community after community sank into the doldrums, their economies at a standstill and their citizens reduced to despair. The American Dream was fading into a will-o'-the-wisp.

Local governments, churches, and community organizations tried to help. Soup kitchens offered what they could. These were the years of jobless apple-sellers lingering on street corners, cadging a few dimes from passersby. And they were the years of Hoovervilles in which the homeless and hopeless congregated. Hoboes rode the rails, looking for work and thieving. In 1932, demands raced through the ranks of unemployed World War I veterans that a promised lump-sum bonus be paid early to relieve the distress. In June 1932, 10,000 desperate veterans and their families assembled peacefully in Washington, D.C., to press for payment of the bonus, only to meet Hoover's cold refusal. For weeks there was a standoff as the Bonus Army camped in swampy Anacostia Flats; then Hoover ordered Army regulars commanded by a swaggering colonel named Douglas MacArthur to disperse the demon-

America's Hit Parade, 1936

Life magazine began, Dale Carnegie's *How to Win Friends and Influence People* topped the nonfiction list, and Margaret Mitchell's *Gone with the Wind* sold a million copies in its first six months. On Broadway, Robert Sherman's antiwar *Idiot's Delight* and Richard Rodgers' musical *On Your Toes* were hits. Popular movies included Charlie Chaplin's *Modern Times* and *Mr. Deeds Goes to Town*, starring Gary Cooper. "Major Bowes' Amateur Hour" was the new sensation on radio. Hit songs included Cole Porter's "I've Got You Under My Skin," Irving Berlin's "Let's Face the Music and Dance," and the Yale Glee Club's "Whiffenpoof Song."

stration. Both men were convinced (on almost no evidence) that communists were manipulating the Bonus Army. MacArthur did as he was ordered with zeal. The whole incident underscored how great the gulf had grown between Hoover and those who elected him in 1928.

In the summer of 1932, Democrats nominated Franklin D. Roosevelt for President. He flew to the convention (a first) to accept the nomination—promising "a new deal" for America. Besides a sunny smile and the fact that he was not Herbert Hoover, what FDR had to offer was unclear. His advocacy of repealing Prohibition was hardly an overwhelming issue; he also denounced Hoover for spending too much money.

Hoover campaigned grimly, warning that "grass would grow in the streets" if Roosevelt won. No matter. Voters swept "the Great Engineer" out of the White House by even bigger margins than those by which they had sent him there four years earlier.

The winter of 1932-1933 was the worst yet. Unemployment peaked at 25 percent of the entire workforce, and bank failures multiplied. Hoover reached his wits' end. In 1931, trying to stanch the downward slide of the world economy, he had agreed to an international debt moratorium, and in early 1933 an international conference was scheduled to meet in London to stabilize currencies and revive international trade. Roosevelt, fearing to be bound by Hoover's policies, refused to signal what he might do after his Inauguration on March 4, 1933. ■

Henry Ford–Revolutionary and Reactionary

All the tensions haunting 20th-century America permeated the life of industrialist Henry Ford (1863-1947). Born to Irish immigrant parents on a farm near Detroit, Ford cherished a warm affection for rural America, an emotion which is celebrated in his museum village in Dearborn, Michigan.

Apprenticed in a machine shop, Ford tinkered with gas engines and learned enough to become chief engineer in an Edison utility. In the 1890s he started building cars, and in 1903 formed Ford Motor Company. It made its first Model T in 1908.

A dapper Henry Ford poses proudly in one of his earliest automobiles, pre-Model T.

Having to meet demand for the Model T spurred Ford to invent the assembly line. During the twenties and thirties his manufacturing technique drew observers from all over the world. Ford pioneered giving consumers what they really wanted (a cheap, easily maintained car, in any color—he said—as long as it was black). He understood that everyone benefited if workers could buy what they manufactured. He put the auto into the hands of the American middle class. Ford's high wages shocked other employers, accustomed to squeezing payrolls.

Ford had a dark side. In 1918 he bought an obscure newspaper and filled his *Dearborn Defender* with diatribes against "the international Jew." He blamed that mythical monster for World War I, but his arguments were as vile as those of the Nazi propagandists. Ford sold and repudiated the paper in 1928.

Ford fought unions his whole life. During the Depression there was constant unrest among his assembly-line workers, and in 1937 workers fought bloody battles with Ford's private security forces.

Ford's anti-Semitism, his resistance to labor organizers, and his dictum that "history is bunk" were the screams of a traditional man for whom modernity—which he played a huge part in creating—meant the destruction of a misremembered, vanished rural youth. ■

The New Deal

1933–1940

FDR was born to privilege. He graduated from Harvard, married TR's niece Eleanor, and entered politics out of patrician obligation. During World War I, he was Assistant Secretary of the Navy, TR's old job. The Democrats nominated him for Vice President in 1920. Then, in 1921, his life changed when polio paralyzed his legs. Rather than retire, he drove himself to regain mobility. In 1928, he was elected governor of New York. He came to the White House with no plan except to shore up American capitalism and preserve liberties—and with optimism conveyed in his Inaugural Address's ringing words: "Let me state my firm belief that we have nothing to fear but fear itself."

The Hundred Days

On March 4, 1933, Inauguration Day, the nation's banking system was collapsing. Frantic depositors lined up to withdraw life savings from every bank in the land. Roosevelt declared a bank holiday, while government inspectors went through banks' books. Sound banks reopened quickly; unsound banks were merged with solvent ones. Roosevelt went on the radio for his first fireside chat, explaining what had been done. The panic stopped. Soon the President pushed legislation through Congress to establish federal insurance for deposits and inspections of banks.

Most of Roosevelt's cabinet members, like FDR, were moderate progressives. But Roosevelt sought advice from many quarters, including his informal Brain Trust. He committed to as little as possible and sometimes pursued contradictory policies, juggling results into something that he could reassure the public was working.

Roosevelt refused to join the London Economic Conference, determined to meet America's crisis in isolation. Outraging conservatives, he took the dollar off the gold standard so he could fight the Depression by inducing inflation while negotiating with trading partners to cut tariffs.

Laws creating "alphabet soup" agencies poured out of Congress in the Hundred Days of 1933. The National Recovery Administration (NRA) suspended antitrust rules, allowed companies to set prices and quotas, and granted workers greater collective bargaining rights. The Agricultural Adjustment Act (AAA) gave farmers price supports and limited production. The Public Works Administration (PWA) put the jobless to work on government projects.

FDR's voice made him master of the radio as a means of connecting with the American public. Here, on November 4, 1938, he makes a pre-election broadcast from Hyde Park, New York.

The Great Depression Economy

Overall, 1929 had been a boom year, cut short by the Wall Street crash; for the rest of Hoover's Administration everything went downhill. The NRA and early New Deal government spending helped reverse the plunge, but the economy slowed again in 1936; it was only preparation for war that ended the Depression in 1939-1940.

Rate of GNP Change 1929-1940

1929	6.7%
1930	–9.8%
1931	–7.6%
1932	–14.7%
1933	–1.8%
1934	9.1%
1935	9.9%
1936	5.3%
1937	–5.0%
1938	8.6%
1939	8.5%
1940	16.1%

The Civilian Conservation Corps (CCC) sent the sons of unemployed families to rural camps to reforest eroded hillsides, plant windbreaks, and build trails in national parks. (The Appalachian Trail was a CCC project.) The Federal Housing Administration (FHA) guaranteed home loans. The Rural Electrification Administration (REA) brought electricity to rural areas ignored by private utilities. To reassure investors and stop wild speculation, the Securities and Exchange Commission (SEC) forced companies to disclose their financial condition and limited margin trading. Cunningly, Roosevelt appointed one of the most notorious stock manipulators of the 1920s, who knew all the dirty tricks to head the SEC: Joseph P. Kennedy, patriarch of the Kennedy clan. Finally, the Democratic Congress passed an amendment repealing Prohibition, and by year's end the states ratified it.

This did not stop the Great Depression; it just relieved its worst symptoms. Roosevelt's optimism, his jauntily tilted cigarette holder, his glowing radio voice, and his warmhearted wife, Eleanor, were reassuring after four years of Hoover's gloom. But they were not enough. A lingering drought gripped the Plains, causing prairie soil, mistreated for half a century, to turn into a dust bowl. Refugees fled to California's farm-labor camps, their saga recounted in John Steinbeck's great 1939 novel *The Grapes of Wrath*. Urban unemployment failed to drop. Elderly people unable to work, without savings, and with unemployed grown children faced starvation. The NRA and its red tape became the "National Run Around."

The Second New Deal

By 1935, the New Deal was in crisis. On the right, the Supreme Court struck down the NRA. Republicans and the wealthy cursed "that man in the White House" for inciting the poor against the rich. On the left, Louisiana Senator Huey Long touted a "share our wealth" program and California dentist Dr. Francis Townsend advocated generous old-age monthly pensions, which recipients would have to spend within 30 days. Radio priest Father Charles Coughlin, whose weekly broadcast reached millions, railed against Roosevelt and his

NOTABLE DATES

■ 1932
Franklin D. Roosevelt elected President.

■ 1933
New Deal begins: bank crisis; NRA allows emergency business collusion; AAA gives farm price supports; PWA and CCC hire the unemployed; FHA guarantees home mortgages; REA promotes rural electrification; SEC regulates stock market.

■ 1935
Supreme Court declares NRA unconstitutional; Huey Long, Francis Townsend, and Father Coughlin attack New Deal; Social Security established; Wagner Act extends labor union rights.

■ 1936
Roosevelt reelected.

■ 1937
Roosevelt tries unsuccessfully to pack the Supreme Court; economic improvement ends in severe recession; labor violence spreads as CIO organizes major industries.

■ 1938
House Un-American Activities Committee investigates alleged communist influence; Republicans gain in midterm elections.

Crusading against "Reds" in 1935, a delegation of Elks petitions lawmakers at the Capitol to root out subversive activities. Here, the delegation meets Speaker of the House Joseph T. Byrnes and Vice President John Nance Garner.

"Jew banker" allies. Roosevelt had to shift gears. The result was what historians call the Second New Deal of 1935-36, with two seminal pieces of legislation.

The Wagner Act of 1935 ensured unions the right to organize and strike. It outlawed unfair labor practices and set up federally supervised procedures for workers to vote on being organized. The Social Security Act of 1935 created old age, disability, and survivor pensions, financed by a payroll tax on employers and employees. A welfare program—Aid to Families with Dependent Children (AFDC), part of Social Security—offered help to single mothers. Finally, the act provided for unemployment insurance, which gave laid-off workers a small temporary income.

Social Security programs were intended neither to build retirement wealth nor to create a welfare state. They were insurance, to guarantee a minimal safety net in the event of job loss, disability, or old age. (In 1940, when the first Social Security checks went out, the life expectancy of white males was 62 years, and 67 years for white females; for blacks, it was about 10 years less.) Large groups were excluded, including largely nonwhite farm and domestic workers. Nor was there health insurance. But FDR gave working people an entitlement that, he boasted, "no damn politician" could ever scrap.

The election of 1936 ratified the New Deal political realignment. Republicans furiously attacked everything Roosevelt stood for. But FDR did not have to face a threat from the left, for in September 1935 an assassin killed Huey Long, while Social Security stole Dr. Townsend's thunder and Father Coughlin revealed himself to be a Jew-baiting windbag. The GOP nominated moderate Kansas governor Alfred E. Landon, but the Democrats "defined" the Republicans as reactionaries. FDR swamped Landon.

Roosevelt's New Deal coalition dominated American politics until 1968. It included southern whites, northern workers, Roman Catholics, Jews, "ethnics," and intellectuals—and also northern African Americans, who could vote. Depression-era miseries drove African Americans in large numbers away from the party of Lincoln, which now looked like the party of Hoover. Blacks were the last to benefit from the New Deal, and in the South were still oppressed by the lily-white Democratic Party. Still, FDR had won black allegiance, and his Democratic heirs would keep it.

The New Deal Balance Sheet.
Roosevelt was at the height of his power after his 1936 reelection, with a huge Democratic majority in Congress. But his second term was not very successful. With the Supreme Court poised to strike down New Deal legislation, FDR tried to pack it with New Deal partisans. The public turned against this move, and Roosevelt had to back off. But two justices started voting in a more consistently New Deal-friendly way, and the conservatives died or retired. Roosevelt had a liberal Court by 1939.

Signs of recovery appeared in 1937, luring FDR into a massive mistake. He cut federal spending—and the stock market plunged, recession returned, and unemployment rose sharply.

Roosevelt's understanding of the modern American economy was no better than Hoover's. In Britain, economist John Maynard Keynes developed macroeconomic theory to explain the Depression. In an economic downturn, he advised, governments should spend heavily, cut taxes, and run deficits. With recovery, spending should be cut and taxes increased to prevent inflation. Keynes tried to persuade FDR to spend—and most modern economists agree that he was right. But, bewildered by John Keynes' "rigmarole of figures," Roosevelt stuck to his old-fashioned views.

Although the New Deal never embraced Keynesianism, in other ways it marked the emergence of modern liberalism, looking to the state as the proper focus of reform. Old-fashioned, small-government liberals gravitated toward the Republicans. Some Republicans remained progressives. Increasingly, though, liberals were Democrats and conservatives (unless they were southern) were going to vote the Republican ticket.

Roosevelt saved American capitalism. Cleaning up Wall Street, insuring bank accounts, encouraging workers to organize, and creating Social Security reshaped the American political economy. Building stabilizers into the economy, such as pensions and unemployment insurance that kicked in as unemployment rose, probably prevented later Great Depressions. ■

HUAC Investigates Un-American Activities, 1938

By 1938, groups such as the German-American *Bund*, who dressed in Nazi-style uniforms and aped Nazi marches and anti-Semitic harangues ("Halloween Nazis," mocked H.L. Mencken), were attracting a great deal of attention.

Texas Congressman Martin Dies got the House of Representatives to let him head a committee to investigate such "un-American" activities, and it actually did grill some American admirers of Hitler and Mussolini. But Dies was targeting bigger game.

Congressman Martin Dies, right, conducts hearings on subversive activities in the film industry. Here, he grills Humphrey Bogart, at far left.

A Democrat, Dies had supported the New Deal until 1937, but—like a number of southern politicians—had turned against the President and formed a bloc with Republicans that stymied most of FDR's second-term initiatives. (That conservative coalition would dominate the House until the mid-1960s.) Dies' bugbear was not homegrown Nazis; it was Communists. He was convinced Reds had infiltrated New Deal agencies and posed a danger to the American way of life. He and his committee (its name was quickly compressed to HUAC, pronounced "hew-ack") became notorious for badgering witnesses, assuming guilt by association, and threatening non-cooperators with contempt of Congress—which could mean jail and ruined reputations.

Dies' main targets were labor unions and New Deal agencies such as the Federal Writer's Project. One "Communist" named at Dies' hearings was Christopher Marlowe—Shakespeare's contemporary. By 1940 Dies claimed to have unmasked more Communists than the FBI. He turned HUAC—which he continued to chair until 1945—into an engine of innuendo against the New Deal and a model for the postwar anti-communist witch hunts of Joseph McCarthy. ■

Culture and Life in the Depression

1933–1939

THE NEW DEAL ALSO LEFT A physical legacy. The Tennessee Valley Authority (TVA), a network of government-built and -owned dams and power plants in Tennessee and adjoining states, transformed the poverty-stricken Southeast into a region that blossomed in the late 20th century. Conservation and reclamation in other parts of the country spurred economic development, brought water to southern California and Arizona, and helped prevent future Dust Bowls. The PWA and its successor, the Works Progress Administration (WPA), erected landmark buildings around the country—and saved millions by giving them useful work in years of immense unemployment. Writers, musicians, and theater people had creative WPA projects and produced much of lasting value.

Depression Culture

During the Depression and New Deal years, the culture wars of the 1920s abated. Times were tough for everyone, urban or rural. But everyone could afford cheap movies, and Hollywood thrived. The hit novel and film of the decade was the romantic Civil War epic *Gone with the Wind.* (It reeked of racist condescension toward blacks, but that was hardly noticed at the time.) Where twenties intellectuals had sneered at Main Street and hicks in the benighted hinterland, thirties intellectuals and liberals celebrated the era of the common man. In American classical music, the modernism that the young composer Aaron Copland had produced for tiny avant-garde audiences in the 1920s gave way to his popular 1930s dance pieces based on American folk tunes, like *Rodeo* and *Appalachian Spring.* Rural suffering evoked deep sympathy from novelists like John Steinbeck, and he passed on his reactions to middle-class readers of *The Grapes of Wrath.* Upbeat big band music like that of Glenn Miller (a white trombonist) and Earl "Fatha" Hines (a black jazz pianist) appealed across the generations. It was radio's golden age, offering entertainment that ranged from the Burns and Allen comedy team to the drama of Orson Welles's "War of the Worlds." And for kids there was the Lone Ranger.

Class Conflict and Consensus

Class defined most lines of conflict. Struggling farmers, embattled or

Actress Vivien Leigh won an Academy Award in 1939 as Scarlett O'Hara in *Gone With the Wind*, one of the most popular movies ever made in America. Its portrayal of the antebellum South was highly misleading.

unemployed workers, and backs-to-the-wall middle-class types confronted those whose material circumstances made it possible for them to hate FDR and all he stood for. Lines of ethnic provincialism, which had begun to blur under the impact of the 1920s mass media, got fuzzier still in the Depression years. Workers gained a sense of themselves as embattled workers rather than ethnics facing WASP sneers. Movies and radio drew Americans closer in a shared popular culture. The exhortation to pull together and hope for better times was a common theme in Depression-era films and music.

The youth culture, a product of the affluent twenties, did not disappear in the thirties. But during the Depression years it was hard for any but the most privileged teens and young adults to assume the economic autonomy and psychological independence that their predecessors in the Roaring Twenties had taken as a birthright—or that their children and grandchildren would claim in the sixties. Young people of the thirties often had to stick close to the parental home—unless that home disintegrated in economic disaster, in which case they might find themselves drifting with a youth gang. Depression-era teenagers felt themselves under pressure to complete high school and to contribute whatever they could earn to a family budget. With virtually no new housing being constructed, newlyweds often doubled up with in-laws, and many couples had to postpone marriage. Both factors explain why the thirties birthrates were the lowest in the 20th century. In retrospect, the twenties' youth culture seemed shallow and silly to youngsters struggling for survival.

Hard times in the thirties sometimes splintered marriages, destroyed self-respect, and caused children and elders to be abused. But privation could also tighten family bonds. Few who lived through this traumatic decade ever forgot it.

Crime and Justice

Even crime seemed to follow class lines during the Great Depression. Urban desperadoes like John Dillinger and Bonnie and Clyde put themselves forward—or were half-admired—as Robin Hoods. It did not seem to matter so much that they were coldblooded killers more interested in money than in abstractions of social justice. The public avidly followed the sagas of their crimes and the law's pursuit of them.

J. Edgar Hoover's FBI gained extraordinary power during the gang-war era of the early thirties. This was partly due to his ability to blackmail politicians by collecting embarrassing details about their private lives; partly it resulted from his encouragement of the press to glamorize G-men as they tracked down the kidnapper and killer of Charles Lindbergh's toddler son, the tragic crime of the decade. The consolidation of power by the FBI and its director was one of the most significant, and ominous, trends in Washington during the New Deal era, and would better have fit conservative admonitions about power corrupting than "creeping socialism" bromides. ■

NOTABLE DATES

■ 1933
Tennessee Valley Authority (TVA) established to bring electricity and conservation to Tennessee and adjacent states.

■ 1934
Gangster John Dillinger killed in Chicago shootout with FBI agents; Clyde Barrow and Bonnie Parker killed in Louisiana ambush after robbing banks across rural America.

■ 1935
Dust Bowl droughts in Midwest and Oklahoma at their worst; Works Progress Administration WPA) established.

■ 1936
Bruno Richard Hauptmann, kidnapper of Charles Lindbergh's son, executed for the boy's murder.

■ 1938
Orson Welles broadcasts radio drama of a fictional Martian invasion.

■ 1939
Gone With the Wind reinforces stereotypes about the Civil War, blacks, and slavery; John Steinbeck publishes *The Grapes of Wrath.*

The Road to World War II

1931–1941

In 1935-36, Hitler remilitarized Germany, allied with Japan and Italy, and supported pro-Fascist General Francisco Franco's revolt against Spain's republican government. No one stopped him. Again without resistance in 1938 he annexed Austria and demanded Czechoslovakia's German-speaking border regions. France and Great Britain forced Czechoslovakia, at the Munich Conference in September 1938, to give in to Hitler. Within six months, Hitler seized the rest of Czechoslovakia. Meanwhile, since 1937 Japan had been mounting a full-scale invasion of China.

Isolationism

Americans wanted no repetition of having been sucked into World War I. In Senate hearings, North Dakota's Gerald Nye grilled bankers and the "merchants of death" and demanded tough neutrality laws. Pacifism spread on campuses. Hitler, with his silly mustache and his oratorical rants,

In this dramatic photograph taken on December 7, 1941, sailors from the U.S.S. *California*, one of the battleships bombed at Pearl Harbor, try to escape the flames. Many did not make it to safety.

seemed to Americans more comical than sinister, and Americans belittled "Japs" on racist grounds.

In 1937 Roosevelt called on democracies to "quarantine the dictators." Reactions were vehemently negative. Isolationism reached a nadir in June 1939 when the liner *St. Louis*, carrying 900 Jewish refugees, attempted unsuccessfully to dock at Fort Lauderdale, Florida. People feared the refugees would compete for American jobs. They went back to Europe and died in the Holocaust.

War

On August 23, 1939, Hitler and Stalin signed a nonaggression pact, providing for the partition of Poland. On September 1, Hitler attacked Poland; it fell within a month. Britain and France declared war but could not help the Poles. In spring 1940, Hitler struck again. He seized Denmark and Norway; then, in May, he unleashed a blitzkrieg (lightning war) on the Low Countries and France. By June 22, France surrendered. Britain, standing alone, under the leadership of Prime Minister Winston Churchill, endured bombardment by the German Luftwaffe.

Amid these storms, Americans prepared for elections. The New Deal had lost steam, and unemployment remained high. The Democrats renominated FDR. The Republicans nominated Wendell Willkie, who shared some of the New Deal's liberal objectives. The public liked the maverick Willkie. Both candidates pledged that the U.S. would maintain neutrality. In September, Congress enacted America's first peacetime draft. Both candidates endorsed giving Great Britain all help short of war. An isolationist America First movement backed Willkie. In the end, Roosevelt's promise not to send American boys into war reelected him.

Isolationists in Congress insisted that the U.S. sell to belligerents only on a "cash-and-carry" basis. By late 1940, Britain had no cash. In January 1941 Roosevelt persuaded Congress to allow the government to "lend or lease" war materiel to countries resisting Nazi Germany. The American defense industry geared up. By 1945, 17 million jobs would be created.

In July 1940 Roosevelt cut off shipments to Japan of oil and scrap iron. Without oil, Japan had to choose between dropping its imperial ambitions or fighting the U.S. On December 7, 1941, the blow finally came. In a magnificently organized sneak attack, Japanese carrier-based bombers devastated the naval base at Pearl Harbor. Roosevelt responded, on December 8, to the "day which will live in infamy" by asking Congress to declare war on Japan. It did so unanimously—with one exception. Representative Jeanette Rankin, who had voted against World War I, once again cast her pacifist vote against war.

A crafty Hitler might have stayed out of the U.S.-Japanese War; it is doubtful whether FDR could have persuaded Congress to take on Germany too. Hitler took the decision out of American hands by declaring war on the "half Jewish, . . . half Negrified" U.S. And so he sealed his doom. ■

NOTABLE DATES

■ **1931**
Japan seizes Manchuria from China.

■ **1935**
Hitler begins German rearmament.

■ **1936**
Spanish Civil War begins, with Germany and Italy supporting pro-Fascist Nationalist Party.

■ **1937**
Japan invades China; U.S. Neutrality Act prohibits war loans and arms sales to belligerents except on a "cash-and-carry" basis.

■ **1938**
Hitler annexes Austria; Great Britain and France, following policy of appeasement, force Czechoslovakia to surrender borderlands to Germany.

■ **1939**
Liner *St. Louis* barred from landing Jewish refugees in U.S.; Hitler and Stalin conclude nonaggression pact; Germany attacks Poland, and Britain and France declare war.

■ **1940**
Germany occupies Norway and Denmark, attacks Low Countries and France; France falls and is occupied by German troops; in Battle of Britain, British withstand German bombing and prevent invasion; U.S. begins industrial mobilization for war and enacts military draft; Roosevelt elected to third term.

■ **1941**
U.S. begins "lend-lease" aid to countries resisting Germany; Hitler conquers Balkans and invades U.S.S.R.; Japanese attack Pearl Harbor; U.S. declares war on Japan; Hitler declares war on U.S.

At War

1941–1945

WAR ENDED THE GREAT Depression, and unemployment disappeared. About 16 million men served in the military; in addition, 400,000 women volunteered for the medical corps and women's units. Almost 250,000 men served in the Merchant Marine, whose casualty rate exceeded that of any branch of the military.

The Home Front

As millions of housewives went to work, women's participation in the workforce rose from 25 to 37 percent. For Rosie the Riveter's defense-contractor employers, cost-plus contracts guaranteed handsome profits in return for meeting tight production schedules.

Virtually everyone felt the war through rationing, price controls, shortages, and taxes. For the first time, workers paid income tax, deducted from paychecks. These measures prevented inflation but caused constant grumbling. In the 1942 elections, conservatives made a strong comeback by denouncing Washington red tape.

Overwhelmingly, Americans saw the war as a necessary evil. There was hysteria only against the Japanese. Conscientious objectors were tolerated if, like Quakers, they belonged to a "peace church" and did alternative service. But 5,000 pacifists went to prison for refusing induction. The authorities controlled public opinion by censoring information, and war movies were always upbeat.

World War II brought immense change to America. The size and scope of government, enlarged by the New Deal, grew exponentially. Washington, D.C., became the epicenter of what was later named the military-industrial complex. In Arlington, Virginia, the world's largest office building—the Pentagon—was built. Into Washington flocked representatives of thousands of contract-seeking firms, the

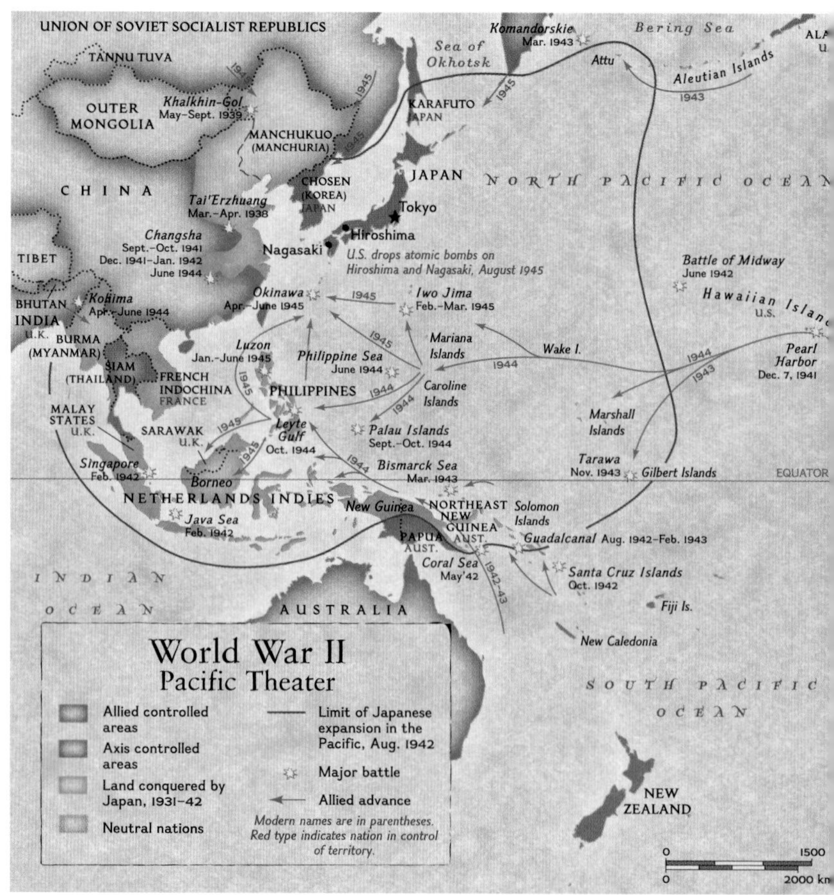

In World War II American and British strategists concentrated on defeating Nazi Germany first. Not until 1944 could the Allies invade France. The U.S.S.R. meanwhile bore most of the burden of fighting the German Army.

nucleus of today's vast influence-peddling industry. Outside Detroit, Ford built the world's biggest factory to build tanks and trucks. From the South poured in poor farmers in search of defense-plant jobs, and Mexican *braceros* flocked into American agribusiness. The war created Sun Belt industrial centers from Los Angeles's aircraft plants to Norfolk's shipyards.

Racial Tensions

Little housing had been built in the Depression, and overcrowded cities seethed with racial antagonisms. A race riot devastated Detroit in July 1943. In Los Angeles, sailors beat up Mexican workers—supposedly draft dodgers, but mostly draft-exempt foreigners—who disported themselves after work in "zoot suits." By FDR's landmark 1940 executive order, racial discrimination was banned in hiring or paying defense workers. The order was wrung from Roosevelt by the threat of a march on Washington by A. Philip Randolph, president of the railroad porters' union and a champion of racial justice.

A determination to win a "double V"—victory over enemies abroad and victory over discrimination at home—spread through the wartime African-American community. Not only the military was segregated; German POWs in

NOTABLE DATES

■ 1939
World War II begins in Europe; Einstein warns Roosevelt of danger that Germany may build a nuclear weapon.

■ 1940
Fall of France and Battle of Britain; Roosevelt bans racial discrimination in war-industry employment; Roosevelt elected to third term.

■ 1941
Germany invades U.S.S.R.; Japan attacks Pearl Harbor, bringing U.S. into World War II.

■ 1942
Nazis launch Holocaust to exterminate Jews; Japanese interned in U.S.; Japan conquers Philippines and Southeast Asia but is defeated at Coral Sea and Midway; Battle of Stalingrad begins; Fermi achieves first self-sustaining nucler reaction; U.S. invades North Africa.

■ 1943
Germans capitulate at Stalingrad and Soviets clear South Russia; Anglo-American invasion of Italy begins, Mussolini falls; race riots in Detroit; Roosevelt, Churchill meet Stalin at Tehran.

■ 1944
Western Allies invade and liberate France; Soviet Army advances across Poland, occupies Balkans; Allied advance stalls in Battle of the Bulge; U.S. island hopping in Pacific liberates Philippines; Roosevelt elected to fourth term.

■ 1945
Roosevelt, Churchill, and Stalin meet at Yalta; Nazi Germany conquered by Allies, U.S.S.R., Hitler commits suicide; U.S. takes Iwo Jima and Okinawa; Roosevelt dies, succeeded by Truman; Potsdam Conference; Hiroshima and Nagasaki destroyed by atomic bombs; Japan surrenders, ending WWII.

The air war in the Pacific theater cost many pilots their lives. Here, in November 1943, Lt. Walter Chewning, the catapult officer on the aircraft carrier, attempts to rescue Ens. Byron Johnson, the pilot of a downed F6F Hellcat fighter.

southern camps got privileges that blacks were denied, such as the right, on leave, to eat at "white-only" lunch-counters. White consciences were moved by a powerful study published in 1944 by Swedish social scientist Gunnar Myrdal, *An American Dilemma*, pointing to the contradiction between Americans' profession of faith in equality and the realities of segregation.

A Global Struggle

The U. S. joined the war as the Axis Powers—Germany, Italy, and Japan—reached their widest sway. Japan battled a communist army in northern China while Chiang Kai-shek's Nationalists hoarded air-lifted Anglo-American weapons for a showdown with Mao. Japan overran Southeast Asia and the Dutch East Indies, thrust toward Australia, and planned to follow up Pearl Harbor by wiping out America's aircraft carriers. By December 1941 the Nazi Army besieged Leningrad but fell back from Moscow with the onset of winter and a Red Army counter-attack. In the North Atlantic, Nazi U-boats threatened vital sea lanes to Britain and the U.S.S.R.

Such was the global chessboard when British and American strategists, including Army Chief of Staff George C. Marshall, met in Washington to map the road to victory. They saw Germany as the gravest threat, but an assault on Europe was not yet possible. Churchill clashed with American strategists. Memories of World War I trenches filled the British with dread. Churchill urged attacking Europe's "soft underbelly," the Mediterranean. But to Marshall and FDR, this was folly.

In the Pacific, early 1942 brought heartbreaking defeats. MacArthur fled the Philippines, vowing "I shall return," while surrendering U.S. and Filipino troops endured the Bataan Death March and subsequent years of starvation.

The American Navy stopped the Japanese fleet in the Coral Sea on May 7, 1942, saving Australia from invasion. A month later the Japanese were defeated again at Midway. These were two of history's most momentous naval battles—the first time that aircraft carriers projected the decisive margin of firepower. At Midway Island, American fighter pilots' sudden descent from behind clouds to sink several Japanese carriers won the day. In August 1942 Marines and Army landed on Guadalcanal and the Solomon Islands, beginning "the road back." In the Central Pacific an island-hopping campaign secured some Japanese islands while isolating others. Admiral Yamamoto, the planner of Pearl Harbor, was right: Japan had awakened a sleeping giant. Yamamoto perished in 1943 when Americans shot down his aircraft.

Science at War

Winning at Midway and killing Yamamoto were possible because of American knowledge of enemy codes. Before the war, Polish cryptographers had broken the German code, Enigma. After the fall of Poland, this secret was conveyed to Britain. And American code breakers also learned to read Japan's communications.

Wartime needs begot world-changing technologies. Discovering how to inject penicillin in 1940 saved countless lives on the battlefield and opened up a vast postwar future for antibiotics. The British perfected radar more quickly than did the Germans. British cryptographer Alan Turing spun off fundamental theoretical insights on which postwar computer science would rest.

The most epoch-making wartime scientific work of all led to unleashing the elemental physical forces in the nucleus of the atom. The uranium atom was first split in Berlin in late 1938. In October 1939 Roosevelt recieved a letter from Einstein warning him that Hitler might build a nuclear weapon. Roosevelt gave the go-ahead to American nuclear research. Code-named the Manhattan Project, the British were let in on the secret. Some of the world's greatest physicists, refugees from Nazi-ruled Europe, were enlisted under young American theoretician J. Robert Oppenheimer. On December 2, 1942, Italian

Japanese-American Internment

UNLIKE IN THE GREAT WAR, THERE WAS little wartime ethnic hysteria—with one glaring exception. After Pearl Harbor, fears ran rampant of a Japanese attack on the West Coast and of enemy espionage and sabotage. These legitimate fears were compounded by racist feelings toward "Orientals," in particular toward the Japanese, hated and envied as aliens and for their success as farmers and small-business owners. President Roosevelt was beset with demands from politicians on the West Coast—including California governor Earl Warren. In February 1942 the President ordered the removal of all Japanese residents in the western states. Before being interned in camps, they had to sell their property, invariably at a great loss. Anglos profited enormously. Both foreign-born (*Issei*) and U.S.-born (*Nisei*) Japanese were interned; the only possible escape was to volunteer for service in the U.S. military. In all, about 120,000 Japanese Americans were interned. A handful of German and Italian "enemy aliens" were also sent to the camps.

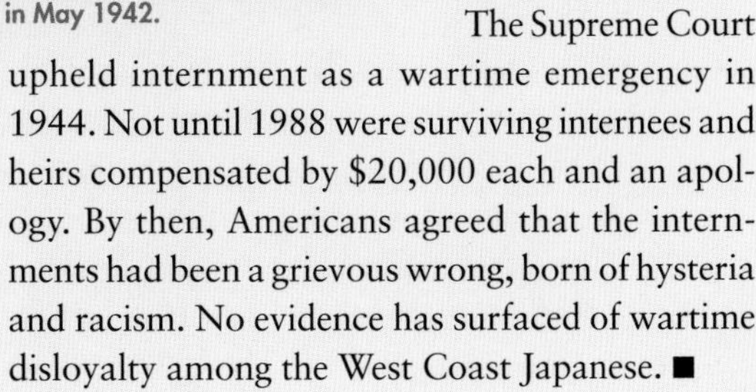

Japanese Americans have their belongings inspected in Turlock, California, prior to being sent to an internment camp in May 1942.

The ten camps were bleak. They were located in isolated, barren areas from California to Wyoming and Arkansas. Privacy was minimal, living conditions difficult, food inadequate, and petty humiliations frequent.

Japanese residents of Hawaii were exempted from internment because that territory (which became a state in 1959) was under martial law until late in the war. Deporting these residents would have been a logistical nightmare, and, in any case, ethnic Japanese in the islands were vital to the local economy.

The Supreme Court upheld internment as a wartime emergency in 1944. Not until 1988 were surviving internees and heirs compensated by $20,000 each and an apology. By then, Americans agreed that the internments had been a grievous wrong, born of hysteria and racism. No evidence has surfaced of wartime disloyalty among the West Coast Japanese. ■

physicist Enrico Fermi achieved the first self-sustaining nuclear reaction, and the race was on to incorporate this power into a bomb. At three secret facilities—Los Alamos, New Mexico; Hanford, Washington; and Oak Ridge, Tennessee—theoretical and engineering problems were explored. More than $2 billion was spent secretly, and congressional probers into wartime waste, including Senator Harry Truman, were encouraged to look the other way. The Manhattan Project remained secret—except to Stalin, who learned enough, from communist physicists at Los Alamos, to start a Soviet nuclear program.

German researchers also tried to build a bomb but blundered into blind alleys. The Nazi authorities gave priority to jet propulsion and rocketry. In 1944 German V-1 and V-2 rockets terrorized London, and in early 1945 the first German jet fighters took to the skies, though a lack of fuel kept them from doing much harm. After the war, U.S. and Soviet authorities took advantage of German innovations.

The Tide Turns

On November 8, 1942, after FDR gave in to Churchill's Mediterranean strategy, American troops landed in French North Africa. The inexperienced Americans were battered in their first battle with the Germans. Almost simultaneously, at El Alamein in Egypt, the British stopped the Nazis short of Suez. By May 1943, British and Americans drove the Axis from North Africa.

One of the most decisive battles was fought at Stalingrad (now Volgograd) in Russia, the gateway to Russia's oil region, where the Germans attacked in September 1942. In November 1942 the Soviets counterattacked, and Hitler rejected the pleas of his generals to pull back. On February 2, 1943, 100,000 starving Germans surrendered. Nazi losses amounted to a half-million men.

On July 10, Anglo-American and Canadian armies landed in Sicily, conquering the island within six weeks. Mussolini had followed Hitler into the war in 1940, but his armies performed poorly. A coup ousted Il Duce on July 26, producing a new Italian government seeking an armistice. But German commandoes rescued Mussolini, while the German Army occupied central Italy. Every mile of Anglo-American advance up the Italian "boot" came at a heavy cost.

Americans' Wartime Service

Some 16 million Americans served in uniform, 12 million of them draftees from an under-26 pool of 30 million men. Many won exemptions by having "essential" jobs. About 37,000 men received conscientious objector status on religious grounds and did alternative service. From a prewar strength of 55,000, the Merchant Marine swelled to 215,000 men; deaths were higher here than in any other branch of service: about 9,300, or 1 in 26. More than 250,000 women served in women's branches, and 70,000 as military nurses. In all, 18.1 percent of American families had at least one member in the armed forces

The Western Allies faced great obstacles in invading Fortress Europe. American, British, and Canadian Armies trained in England, augmented by refugee Polish units and exiled French forces led by General Charles De Gaulle. Staggering logistical problems were overcome. Command of Operation Overlord was entrusted to General Dwight D. Eisenhower. With his reassuring smile and steady manner, he was much respected by ordinary soldiers, who called him Ike.

The date for D-Day was June 6, 1944. At the last minute bad weather almost forced postponement. But after receiving sophisticated meteorological analysis, Ike gave the word: Go.

The invasion hit Normandy—rather than farther north as the Germans expected. Hitler thought that Normandy was a diversion. Holding too long in reserve heavy armor reinforcements, the Germans failed to drive the invaders from the beachhead, allowing the Allies to land supplies and manpower. Not everything went as planned. But Allied bombing of French roads, bridges, and railroads, plus fuel shortages, made it difficult to repel the invaders.

By early 1944, Allied bombing raids were crippling Germany's war industries. World War II bombing was called strategic—designed to target precise facilities—but the bombs rarely landed on target. They were effective chiefly because they rained down indiscriminately. British air commanders turned with increasing ferocity to terror bombing, intended to break the enemy's will. Instead, civilian will continued to stiffen against the Allies.

In July 1944 soldiers take refuge in a ditch near St. Lô in Normandy after encountering German mortar and machine-gun fire. In the first six weeks after D-Day, the Allied advance into German-occupied France was slow and costly.

In July 1944, Allied Armies broke out in Normandy. American General George C. Patton led a tank charge across northern France. As Americans neared Paris, the populace revolted and the Nazi occupiers fled—ignoring Hitler's order to burn the city. That might have happened in Warsaw, too, as the Soviet Army approached in late July. But when the anticommunist Polish underground triggered an insurrection, Stalin allowed the Germans to destroy Warsaw, and 100,000 civilians. Stalin expelled the Germans from Romania and Bulgaria, while communist-led guerrillas prevailed in Yugoslavia. Hitler escaped assassination on July20 by German officers.

The Holocaust

As the Allies closed in, Nazi leaders redoubled efforts to achieve their aim: exterminating Europe's Jews. Since January 1942 "the Final Solution" had been under way. On the eastern front, Jews were massacred on the spot. In Central and Western Europe, the more "efficient" means was to ship Jews in cattle cars from urban ghettos to death camps. There Jews, Gypsies, and homosexuals were either worked and starved to death or immediately exterminated. About six million Jews—most of European Jewry—were slaughtered. Sometimes Jews were able to resist, though never successfully, as in the 1943 Warsaw Ghetto uprising, and brave non-Jews risked their lives to save victims.

Allied leaders learned about the Holocaust in 1942. They did nothing, arguing that concentrating on Germany's defeat would save more lives. The true horrors were not revealed until Soviet and Western Armies liberated the death camps.

Hitler's Downfall

Hitler held off the Allies in December 1944 along Germany's western border, ordering the last major German offensive. American troops suffered a setback in the Battle of the Bulge. But by January 1945 they regained the offensive. Simultaneously, the Soviet Army resumed its push toward Berlin. In February 1945 Dresden—crowded with refugees and home to great art but without military significance—was firebombed, killing between 25,000 and 135,000 civilians.

In March 1945 American troops crossed the Rhine River. From his Berlin bunker, Hitler ordered nonexistent German Armies to march hither and thither and decreed a "scorched earth" policy to destroy his own country. His chief accomplices tried to save their skins with peace offers. The Americans and British insisted on unconditional surrender—and worried that Stalin and Hitler just might strike a last-minute deal.

When FDR won a fourth term in November 1944, his health was in shocking decline. On April 12, 1945, he died of a cerebral hemorrhage. His Vice President, the little-known Harry Truman—whom Roosevelt had kept in the dark about everything—stepped uncertainly to the helm. Hitler for an instant thought FDR's death a portent of his own coming victory.

The Navajo Code Talkers

Despite the formidable mathematics involved in World War II codes such as Enigma, the most effective cryptography was the languages of American Indians. Soon after Pearl Harbor, a World War I veteran named Philip Johnston proposed to the Marine Corps that Navajo speakers be recruited as "code talkers." The son of missionary parents, Johnston had grown up on a Navajo reservation and spoke the language. He also knew that Navajo was one of the world's most difficult languages. Navajo had no alphabet, and its grammar had received little study. Moreover, the Navajos were one of the largest native peoples in the U .S., offering a large recruiting pool. Ultimately more than 400 Navajo men, fluent in both their own language and in English, were recruited or drafted.

Navajos who served in the Pacific islands as code talkers performed indispensable missions at the front lines.

The first code talkers began on Guadalcanal in August 1942, and served throughout the Pacific war. "Were it not for the Navajos, the Marines would never have taken Iwo Jima," said the signal officer of the Fifth Marine Division on that hard-fought island. Their frontline work was dangerous—and some were even captured by suspicious Marines, thinking them Japanese disguised in American uniforms. Eventually each code talker had his own bodyguard.

They simply used their own impenetrable language to communicate over the open radio between battlefield and headquarters. Much of the vocabulary of modern warfare—tank, airplane, grenade, submarine, and sailor, for example—did not exist in Navajo, requiring the code talkers to memorize 508 substitutes using native words. The Japanese never broke the "code." The role of Navajo and other Native American code talkers (a smaller number of Chocktaws and Comanches did similar work in the European theater) was not revealed until 1969; the Cold War military wished to keep it secret. ■

But with Soviet troops within blocks of his hideout, the end had finally come. Mussolini was shot, while trying to flee, and hung upside-down by Italian guerrillas on April 28. On April 30, the Führer shot himself; his mistress took poison. A week later, on May 7, 1945, Germany, at last, unconditionally surrendered.

Postwar Plans

Churchill and Roosevelt had been planning for this moment for years, and twice, at Tehran, Iran (December 1943), and at Yalta in the Crimea (February 1945), they had met Stalin. Remembering Wilson's mistakes in being too specific with the Fourteen Points, Roosevelt preferred vague postwar plans. But he did insist on creating a stronger successor to the League, the United Nations. Roosevelt projected a global American presence, including lowering tariffs and creating international financial organs—the World Bank and the International Monetary Fund—to ensure recovery. These plans upset the British, but the anti-imperialist Roosevelt had no patience. Mighty, unscathed America would dominate the postwar world.

At Yalta, Roosevelt finally had to commit himself. The Soviet Army controlled Eastern Europe and Stalin had to be enlisted for the final assault on Japan. Not willing to start a new war with Stalin, Roosevelt and Churchill had to agree that the pro-Soviet Polish government could take power, and while Poland was supposed to be "friendly" toward Moscow, free elections were also promised. But when they were held, in 1946, communists intimidated the democratic opposition. Stalin pledged to enter the war against Japan three months after Germany's defeat. He was promised territories lost by Russia to Japan earlier in the century, economic concessions in Manchuria, and a share in the occupation of Korea. In return, Stalin agreed to join the United Nations. Roosevelt, like Wilson, hoped that an international peacekeeping body could right the wrongs of flawed peace agreements, and he expected that the "carrot" of American economic aid would restrain Stalin.

Defeating Japan

Throughout 1943 and 1944, a two-pronged American offensive took one island stronghold after another. Then in October 1944, MacArthur returned to the liberated Philippines; in the struggle, Japan lost most of its remaining fleet. Americans began bombing Japan, and the bloody conquest of Iwo Jima and Okinawa, in February and April 1945, brought war closer to the home islands. At least 80,000 died when Tokyo was firebombed on March 9-10, 1945. But the Japanese could still launch kamikazes against American warships, exacting a deadly toll. American military planners projected a million battle deaths should U.S. troops invade Japan.

As 1945 opened, the Manhattan Project was closing in on the final secrets of nuclear weaponry. No one who knew of the project doubted that the bomb, if ready, would be used against Nazi Germany. Those not in the know included Harry Truman; only after he became President was he told about the Manhattan Project. In New Mexico on July 16, 1945, the bomb was first tested. "Now I am become death, the destroyer of worlds," murmured Oppenheimer on seeing the fireball, quoting from ancient Indian scripture.

Truman learned of the test at Potsdam, outside Berlin, while meeting with Stalin and Clement Atlee, the new British prime minister, to hammer out plans for postwar Germany and Japan. Observers sensed that after learning of the successful test, Truman grew more assertive with Stalin. A handful of the bomb's scientific fathers urged that the enemy be warned with a test blast. Others urged following up hints from Tokyo of willingness to surrender if the sacred emperor could keep his throne. Such proposals were rejected. What if a demonstration failed? What if the Japanese military leaders still demanded a fight to the death? And—asked Truman—what if the American public discovered that $2 billion had been spent to build a war-winning bomb that was never used? Truman—on whose desk, he said, "the buck stopped"—had no doubts.

On August 6, 1945, an American B-29 took off from the Marianas carrying a single atom bomb. It was detonated with a blinding flash over Hiroshima. About 80,000 people died in the blast, most of them in an instant but some after suffering horrendous burns or radiation sickness. Countless other lives were cut short by radiation-induced cancers.

Truman called on Japan to surrender or face more atomic bombs dropped on Japanese cities. Emperor Hirohito and civilian leaders realized the time had come, but the military refused. The Japanese dithered, and Truman ordered a nuclear attack on Nagasaki on August 9. Some 60,000 perished. Finally, Hirohito went on the radio to admit that the war situation "had developed not necessarily in Japan's favor."

On August 14, 1945—V-J Day—Japan indicated that it would surrender. On September 2, on the U.S.S. *Missouri* in Tokyo Bay, formally attired Japanese officials signed under the proud eye of Douglas MacArthur. America had surmounted its 20th-century crisis. The atomic age had begun. ■

Depression, War, and the Declining Farm Population

In 1930, farmers numbered 30.5 million, or 24.9 percent of Americans. Foreclosures and the Dust Bowl devastated farmers, and New Deal policies mostly helped larger operators; by 1940, farmers still numbered 30.5 million, but represented only 23.2 percent of the population. World War II brought sweeping changes: mechanized cotton harvesting, agribusiness, and migrations of black and white sharecroppers into defense industries. (Farm workers were exempt from the draft.) By 1945, there were 24,420,000 farmers—17.5 percent of the population. These trends continued after the war. Today, fewer than 2 million Americans—out of 293 million—are "principal farm operators."

WORLD SURVEY

1929–1945

UNLESS THEY LOST A loved one, Americans had it easy compared to the sufferings of civilians in war-torn countries, let alone the victims of the Holocaust. The United States lost almost 400,000 lives in World War II, which made it the nation's most costly war besides the Civil War. (About a million were also seriously wounded.) But to understand the true immensity of this war, set America's losses against the *at least* 19 million military and civilian dead in the Soviet Union, or China's at least 10 million, or Poland's perhaps 6 million (many of them Holocaust victims), or Germany's perhaps 5.5 million, or Japan's 2-3 million—the very vagueness of those statistics suggests the immensity and impersonality of the slaughter, for the true numbers will never be known. And aside from Japan's attack on Pearl Harbor (which struck only military targets) and its invasion of a remote Aleutian island, American soil was entirely spared during the war, unlike the devastation visited upon every belligerent country in Europe and East Asia. The U.S. emerged from the war with its cities unscathed and its factories humming in high gear.

■ Europe

The Great Depression had seared every industrial nation in the capitalist world. It had destroyed Germany's fragile democracy and strengthened Japanese militarism; in both cases, disastrous wars and national ruin were the consequences. In France, the economic crisis unleashed bitter struggles between left and right; by 1940 the Third Republic was vulnerable to the defeatism and treason that destroyed it with the German invasion and occupation. Great Britain survived the depression and the war, but at such a high cost that its citizens voted overwhelmingly in 1945 for a socialist government. Within a few years of the war's end it was apparent that Britons could no longer afford to maintain their worldwide Empire—on which, it had been said in 1914, the sun never set.

■ China

For China, the disasters of 1931-1945 were only part of the long, tragic epic of social and political revolution. Mao's communist army had fought the Japanese more effectively than Chiang's Nationalists; now the two sides were preparing for their showdown, with the Soviets helping Mao by facilitating a communist takeover of industrial Manchuria after Japan's defeat. Ahead lay four more years of civil war, followed by a half-century of violent social transformation.

■ U.S.S.R.

At the cost of millions of lives and totalitarian terror, the Soviet Union had achieved impressive industrial growth under the Five Year Plans of the 1930s. By 1945, it had borne the heaviest burden in lives and devastation in defeating Hitler. The war left Stalin in control in Eastern Europe, and his rule in the U.S.S.R. was total. His paranoia was also at high pitch. For Stalin sent to his *gulag* (concentration camp) system even liberated Soviet POWs and slave laborers whom the Nazis had deported, fearing that they might be so "contaminated" with foreign ideas as to be dangerous. Stalin may or may not have believed that postwar conditions would facilitate communism's expansion into Europe—evidence of his thinking is still fragmentary—but clearly his overriding obsession was with security. With such a despot ruling the Soviet Union, Roosevelt's wartime hopes for postwar Soviet-American cooperation were illusory. Within just a few years of V-E Day, the Cold War was underway.

For all the suffering and death that had been unleashed between 1933 and 1945, much of that which was of lasting good had also been achieved. Above all, the world had seen the face of evil in Nazism, and had crushed it. Before 1933, many of the elements that went into Nazism had been taken for granted in all advanced countries, including the United States. These included unbridled nationalism, a morbid fascination with the irrational, a naïve faith in such pseudo-sciences as eugenics and biological racism, an unwillingness to see how far dictatorship and the police state might go in terrorizing citizens, and above all racism and anti-Semitism. Hitlerite Germany merely took all these evils to their extreme. By 1945, almost everyone in the civilized world understood that "never again" was the only proper response. It would take time to eradicate all the roots—in the United States in 1945, for example, strong traces of anti-Semitism remained, and the struggle to overcome racism had only begun. Forever after, however, the specter of Hitlerism would arise as a reminder of where each of these manifestations of inhumanity was likely to lead.

The terrible ending of World War II, with the atomic bombing of Hiroshima and Nagasaki, also contained its own warning. World War II had been fought, on both sides, with increasing savagery and a toleration for indiscriminate slaughter. The German "blitzing" of Rotterdam, Coventry, and London and the Allies' incendiary attacks on such cities as Hamburg, Dresden, and Tokyo had all helped inure consciences to the use of nuclear weapons as a "normal" means of waging war. After August 1945, no one could think that way again. Nuclear weapons had the potential to destroy all life on the planet. And although the Cold War would be waged with both sides armed with this ultimate weapon, the price of deploying them was understood. Nuclear weapons—though frequently brandished—were never used in the U.S.-Soviet confrontation. Whether they will remain unused in the post-Cold War world of global terrorism is another question. ■

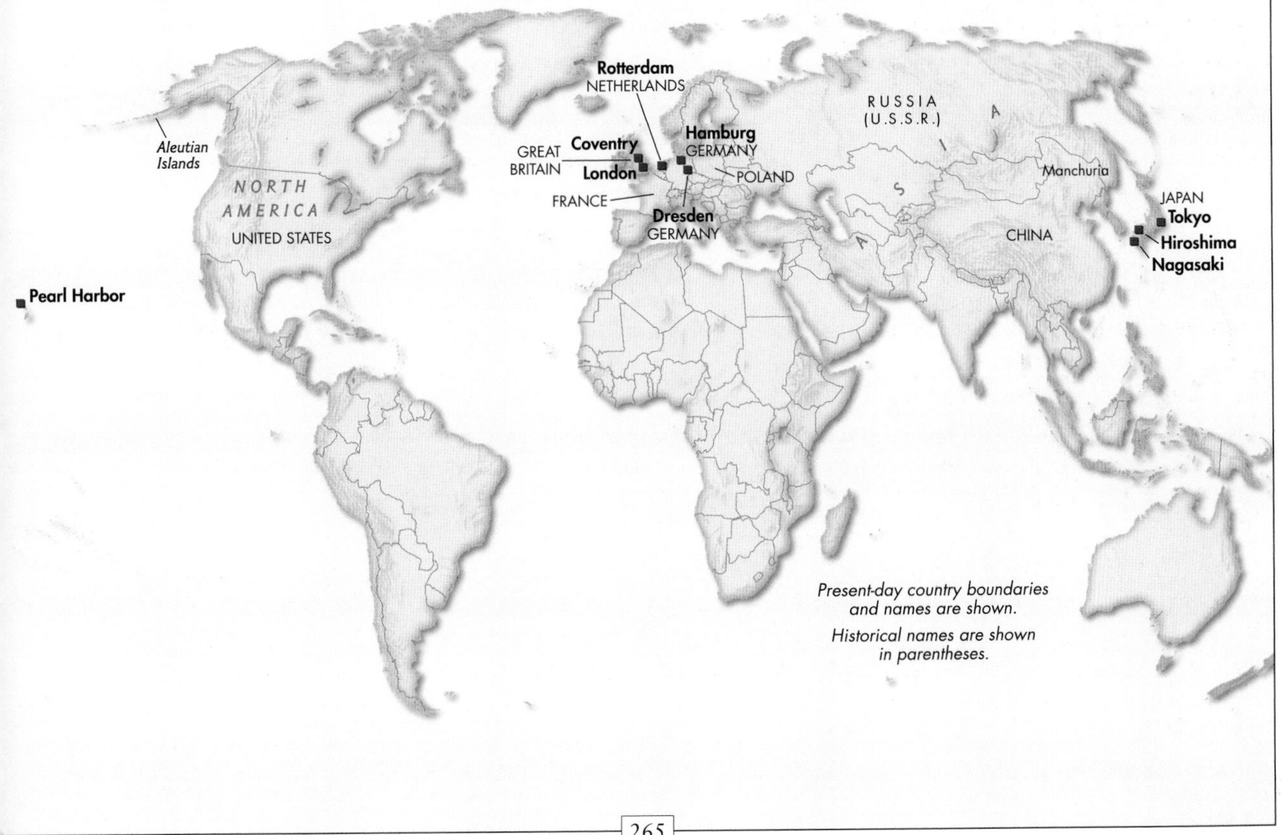

COLD WAR AMERICA 1945–1989

FOR TWENTY YEARS AFTER V-J DAY, THE UNITED STATES LED THE WORLD BY VIRTUALLY every measure. If ever there was an economy equally adept at producing guns and butter, it was postwar America.

Victory in World War II put the United States on high moral ground—shadowed by the use of the atom bomb. Overwhelmingly, though, Americans shared an uncritical faith that their country stood for all that was good in the world. Cold War debates differed over *how,* not *whether*, to oppose the Communist threat.

Still, Americans had to ask many questions about themselves: Was America actually losing moral purpose amid its affluence? What was the right response to the rising African-American demand for civil rights and social justice? And what of the unease that, by the late 1950s, was spreading among America's youngest generation, the baby boomers?

The Vietnam War not only deepened these questions about America's role in the world but also robbed many of their faith in government. The Watergate scandal added to the cynicism, and the economic crises of the seventies destroyed old illusions of limitless growth. The revival of American optimism in the eighties—fed by prosperity based on a spreading technological revolution—was matched by a polarization between deeply held values rooted in the cultural clashes of the sixties. ■

In May 1952 a class takes refuge in a Newark school during New Jersey's first statewide air-raid test. Such drills were common in the 1950s.

■ 1945	■ 1947	■ 1950	■ 1954	■ 1962
World War II ends with the fall of Hitler and the use of the atomic bomb on Japan; Potsdam Conference divides Germany into occupation zones.	Truman Doctrine and Marshall Plan mark beginning of U.S. Cold War strategy.	Korean War begins; Joseph McCarthy launches anticommunist hysteria.	Supreme Court declares school segregation unconstitutional.	Cuban Missile Crisis takes the world to the brink of nuclear war.

■ **1968**
Martin Luther King, Jr., and Robert F. Kennedy are assassinated; Richard Nixon elected President.

■ **1973**
First energy crisis begins with OPEC price increases and Arab oil embargo.

■ **1974**
Nixon resigns under threat of impeachment as a result of the Watergate affair.

■ **1981**
Ronald Reagan inaugurated as President, beginning a conservative era; Iran hostage crisis ends.

■ **1989**
Berlin Wall is torn down and communism begins to collapse in Eastern Europe and the U.S.S.R.

The Atomic Age

1945–1960

WHILE THE UNITED STATES demobilized, in Eastern Europe pro-Soviet dictatorships were imposed, culminating in a communist coup in Prague in February 1948.

The Cold War Begins

In 1947 the economically strapped British government asked Washington to protect Greece and Turkey against Soviet pressure. On March 12, 1947, Truman announced that the U.S. would aid nations resisting communism. In June, General Marshall, now secretary of state, proposed American assistance to reconstruct Europe. In four years, $13 billion in Marshall Plan aid reached Western Europe.

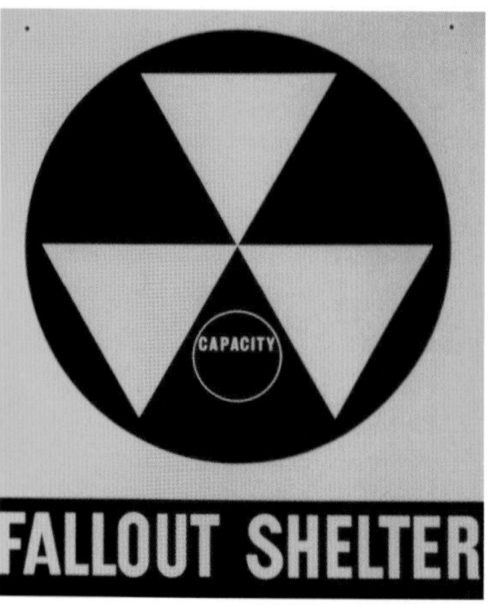

In 1948 Britain and the U.S. introduced currency reform in Germany; in response Stalin closed access to Western zones in Berlin, inside the Soviet sector. Truman mounted an airlift. In May 1949, Stalin lifted the blockade.

The Prague coup and the Berlin blockade focused Western leaders' attention on the "Iron Curtain"—Churchill's 1946 phrase—dividing Europe. Anglo-American policy aimed to create a non-communist democracy in West Germany. To reassure the French, Washington promised to commit forces. The result, in 1949, was the North Atlantic Treaty Organization (NATO), embracing the U.S., Canada, Great Britain, France, Italy, and smaller states. NATO, said a British diplomat, would "keep the Americans in, the Russians out, and the Germans down."

Truman's Faltering Fair Deal

American interest in reform ebbed. In 1946 the GOP took over Congress. People wanted to spend wartime savings—and they blamed Truman for inflation. "To err is Truman," they said. Efforts to rescind wartime concessions caused strikes. Congress overrode Truman's veto of the Taft-Hartley Bill, curbing union bosses' abuses. He also failed to add health insurance to Social Security.

Signs such as this proliferated during the Cold War. Americans wondered what to do if, during a nuclear attack, more people tried to crowd into a shelter than space allowed.

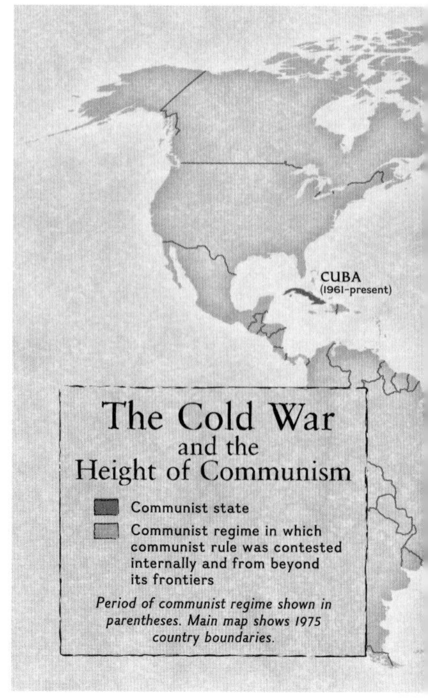

But there were policy successes, especially the GI Bill of Rights, which came into effect under Truman. It enabled veterans to buy homes at low interest over 30 years. Widespread home ownership stimulated economic growth. New subdivisions were home to children soon to become known as the baby boom generation.

The GI Bill democratized education, allowing 7.8 million veterans to finish school. A college degree became the ticket to upward mobility, and American universities, by attracting some of Europe's best brains, became world-class.

This Cold War-era map shows not only the U.S.S.R., China, and other communist-ruled countries but also countries in Africa and Asia that had pro-Soviet governments in the 1970s, including Angola, Afghanistan, and others.

In 1948, Democrats nominated Truman with little hope. He had offended southern Democrats by integrating the Armed Forces and opposing workplace discrimination; Strom Thurmond ran for President as a Dixiecrat. On the left was Henry Wallace, FDR's Vice President dumped from the ticket in 1944. He organized a new Progressive Party with tacit communist support.

The Republicans' Thomas A. Dewey—whom everyone expected to win—looked pompous and sounded platitudinous. Crowds shouted "Give 'em hell, Harry!" as Truman made his Fair Deal pitch. Truman won in a classic upset. Dewey had inspired no one, while rural and working-class Americans returned to the Roosevelt Coalition. Wallace seemed like Stalin's stooge, and too few Southerners defected to Thurmond.

The Second Great Red Scare

In 1947 the war and navy departments were merged in the Department of Defense, the Joint Chiefs of Staff and National Security Council were created to advise the President, and the wartime O.S.S. gave way to the more professional Central Intelligence Agency. Truman's two secretaries of state, George Marshall and Dean Acheson, overhauled the State Department. Truman ordered loyalty oaths and background checks for all federal employees. Abuses occurred, and Truman bore some responsibility for the hysteria.

Alger Hiss, high in the State Department, reported to Stalin's

NOTABLE DATES

■ 1945
Harry Truman becomes President upon Roosevelt's death; World War II ends with atom-bombing of Japan; imposition of communism in Eastern Europe begins.

■ 1947
Truman Doctrine and Marshall Plan announced; Defense Department and CIA created.

■ 1948
Communist coup in Prague; Berlin blockade begins; Truman elected President.

■ 1949
Berlin blocade ends; NATO formed; U.S.S.R. tests first nucelar weapon; communists win Chinese civil war.

■ 1950
Joseph McCarthy begins his anticommunist campaign; Korean War begins.

■ 1952
U.S. tests first hydrogen bomb; Dwight D. Eisenhower elected President.

■ 1953
Stalin dies; Rosenbergs executed for espionage; Korean War armistice signed.

■ 1954
French defeated in Indochina at Dienbienphu; Geneva Conference partitions Vietnam; Senate censures McCarthy.

■ 1956
Suez Crisis; Hungarian Revolution; Eisenhower reelected President.

■ 1957
U.S.S.R. launches Sputnik.

■ 1960
U-2 incident; John F. Kennedy elected President.

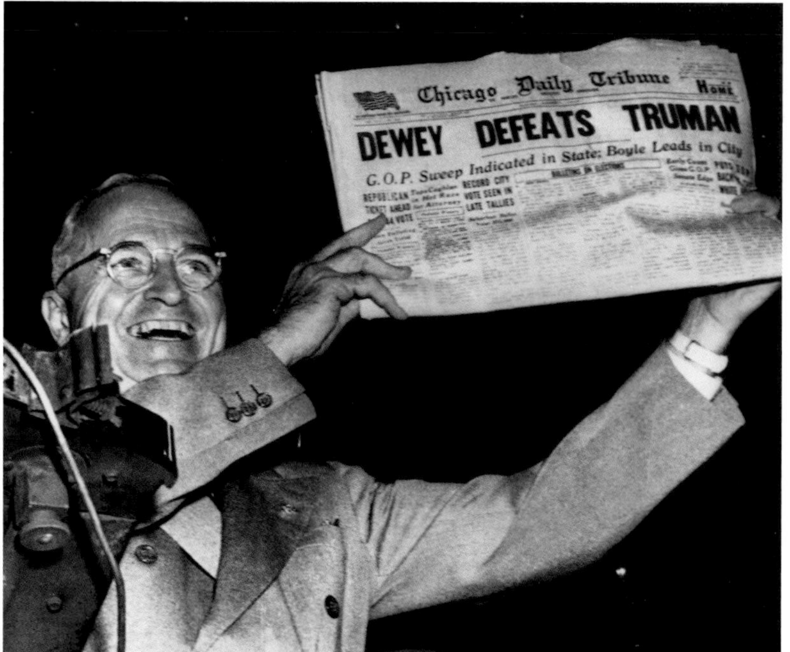

A triumphant Truman holds up a newspaper that, on the basis of early returns and pre-election polls, proclaimed him the loser. At the time, the *Chicago Tribune* was one of the country's most partisan Republican newspapers.

secret police. So did Klaus Fuchs, a German physicist in the Manhattan Project. Fuchs fled to East Germany, but his accomplices were caught. In 1953 two of them, Julius and Ethel Rosenberg, were electrocuted. Hiss was convicted of perjury, though the statute of limitations prevented his being tried for espionage. Not until the Cold War was over did the U.S. admit that it had proof of Hiss's and others' guilt—which could not be revealed lest Moscow know its sources of information.

News of a Soviet atomic bomb test in September 1949 frightened Americans. So did the establishment, on October 1, 1949, of the People's Republic of China. One-third of the human race now lived under communism. In June 1950, war erupted in Korea, while the demagogic Senator Joe McCarthy from Wisconsin orchestrated a new anticommunist hysteria.

I Like Ike

In 1952 Democrats nominated for President the governor of Illinois, Adlai Stevenson. Ohio's Robert Taft was the idol of anti-New Deal Republicans, but moderate Republicans persuaded General Eisenhower to run. Ike won the nomination, choosing as his running mate a young, communist-baiting senator, Richard M. Nixon.

The "I Like Ike" slogan demonstrated Americans' trust for the warm yet commanding Dwight Eisenhower. Nixon overcame accusations of corruption with a maudlin TV speech that included allusions to his daughters' "little dog Checkers," demonstrating the new power of television in politics. Ike's promise "I will go to Korea" clinched his landslide victory.

Eisenhower settled the Korean War with a truce. He did not repeal the New Deal, and he launched the greatest public works project in American history, the interstate highway system, which by 1991 pumped $128 billion gasoline-tax dollars into the economy. Cars and trucks, not mass transit, would be America's future. Environmental costs hardly mattered.

The fifties were good for most Americans. Defense spending created many high-paying jobs. Corporations raised benefits and wages, passing along the cost to consumers. By the mid-fifties, almost every family had a TV. Yet economic growth was not consistent; millions of elderly, minority, and Appalachian Americans lived in squalor.

The Cold War lurked beneath the surface. Schools held air-raid drills, and young men faced the draft. The Soviets' 1949 atom bomb jolted the Truman Administration into building a hydrogen bomb, first tested in 1952. Eisenhower thought the weaponry "more bang for the buck." Soon Soviets exploded an H-bomb, too, and proved adept at building intercontinental missiles. By the late 1950s, each side could destroy the other. This was the M.A.D. (Mutually Assured Destruction) doctrine—but it worked. In 1956 Hungary revolted against communism, and Eisenhower allowed Soviets to crush the rebels. It was not worth World War III.

Stalin died in 1953. His successors began preaching peaceful coexistence yet rejected inspections to verify disarmament. Eisenhower built alliances across Asia and Latin America, and in 1955 encouraged South Vietnam to fight a communist insurgency. The U.S. supported the Islamic Saudi Arabian monarchy, which supplied the U.S with cheap oil, and also backed Israel. When Egypt seized the Suez Canal and Britain, France, and Israel invaded in November 1956, Eisenhower forced a withdrawal. The same week, he was reelected in a landslide. Voters trusted Ike.

America received a rude shock in October 1957, when the U.S.S.R. orbited the world's first artificial satellite, Sputnik. Americans were alarmed at Soviet scientific expertise, especially after the first U.S. satellite launches fizzled. The U.S.S.R seemed to have purpose that the U.S. had lost. Democrats decried a missile gap. No such gap existed. But Eisenhower could not say this without revealing secret surveillance of the U.S.S.R. by U-2 spy planes. Only in the spring of 1960 did these flights become known, when a Soviet missile shot one down deep inside Russia, complete with the parachuting pilot. Ike first denied and then owned up to the flights. Americans' trust in his competence—though not their affection for him—plummeted. ■

The Rosenbergs

Electrical engineer Julius Rosenberg served during World War II in the U.S. Army Signal Corps. As a communist, he used his military position to pass information to a Soviet espionage courier, Harry Gold. Rosenberg's brother-in-law, David Greenglass, a sergeant in the U.S. military, had been assigned to work as a machinist in Los Alamos, where he was in touch with Klaus Fuchs, the communist physicist near the heart of the Manhattan Project. Greenglass reported from Fuchs to Julius Rosenberg, and thence to Gold. Thus Stalin eavesdropped on the making of the atom bomb.

After their arraignment on espionage charges, Ethel and Julius Rosenberg leave New York City's Federal Court on August 23, 1950.

In May 1950 the plot unraveled. Interrogated in Britain, Fuchs fled to East Germany. Gold was caught; then, in June 1950, came Greenglass and the Rosenbergs. Greenglass testified against his sister and brother-in-law, drawing a sentence of 15 years. (Gold got 30 years.) The Rosenbergs' trial began in March 1951 before federal judge Irving Kaufmann. Less than two years earlier the Soviets had tested their atom bomb. Kaufmann excoriated the couple for putting it into Stalin's hands. The nation applauded when they were convicted and Kaufmann sentenced them to death—the first civilians in the U.S. condemned to death for espionage.

Abroad, communists denounced the trial, and the American Communist Party tried to generate sympathy for the couple and their two young children. The couples' appeals were rejected, and in June 1953 they were electrocuted.

Later doubts about Julius's guilt faded after Soviet archives opened. But Ethel was probably only peripherally involved in espionage. Federal prosecutors apparently knew this, but threatened to electrocute her to pressure Julius into telling more about Soviet spying in the U.S. He refused, taking his wife to the electric chair with him. Even J. Edgar Hoover was reportedly shaken to learn it. ■

Korea and McCarthyism

1949–1957

On June 24, 1950, the Cold War turned hot. Egged on by Stalin, communist North Korea invaded the southern Republic of Korea. Within weeks, North Korea's large and well-supplied army controlled most of the peninsula.

Police Action

Truman urged the United Nations to resist North Korean aggression—and because the Soviets were boycotting the U.N. in a dispute over seating "Red China," Truman got what he wanted. Under a U.N. mandate, the U.S. and other forces were dispatched to Korea in a "police action" to repel the invasion. In September, MacArthur outflanked North Korea in a risky landing at Inchon, near Seoul. He quickly reconquered most of the peninsula. North Korean forces fled to the Yalu River, the border with China.

The new Chinese communist government warned that it would not tolerate U.S. forces reaching the Yalu River. MacArthur advised Truman to ignore Beijing's threats and carelessly divided his forces. Into that gap, in November 1950, poured an army of Chinese "volunteers." Now U.S. forces had to retreat, screened by Marines fighting a heroic rear-guard action. Seoul fell to the communists again before a front was stabilized across central Korea.

MacArthur, in World War II-era unconditional surrender mode, publicly maintained that "there is no substitute for victory." He also communicated strategic thoughts to bitter Republican critics of the President. In so doing, MacArthur ignored American traditions of civilian supremacy over the military. Truman had no alternative but to slap him down. "The son of a bitch isn't going to resign on me," snapped the President. "I want him fired." On April 10, 1951, MacArthur was relieved of his command. Soon, Army Chief of Staff Gen. Omar Bradley testified to the Senate that MacArthur's plan to broaden the Korean War would have been "the wrong war, at the wrong place at the wrong time and with the wrong enemy."

McCarthyism

The Soviet bomb and the "loss" of China help explain the sudden rise of Wisconsin Senator Joseph McCarthy. In February 1950 he made headlines by telling a Republican audience that he had a list of communists working in the State Department. What names (if any) were on this list, how he got them, and how many names there were, never was clear. McCarthy had discovered his tactic: Make a spectacular charge, don't bother proving it, and move on to a new one before too many questions get asked. Republican leaders embraced McCarthy as a club to beat Truman and the hated legacy of the New Deal.

Between 1951 and 1954, McCarthy chaired a Senate committee "investigating" communist infiltration of the government and American society. State Department and academic experts on China lost their jobs amid accusations they were "pro-communists" responsible for losing China. No matter that McCarthy couldn't tell the difference between Karl Marx and Groucho Marx, as one pundit put it—for millions, he was the nation's defender against an atheistic menace.

Hundreds of little McCarthys flourished across the country in state legislatures and local boards, firing anyone allegedly tainted with communist sympathies. Careers were ruined, families torn apart, and suicides precipitated by the whisper "communist."

Hollywood, too, was cleansed of "communist influence." Naming names—publicly identifying pro-communists—and blacklisting

Marilyn Monroe, sex symbol for America in the fifties, wiggles her way past GIs in Korea in February 1954. A tragic figure, confused by conflicts between her public and private personas, Monroe took her own life in 1962.

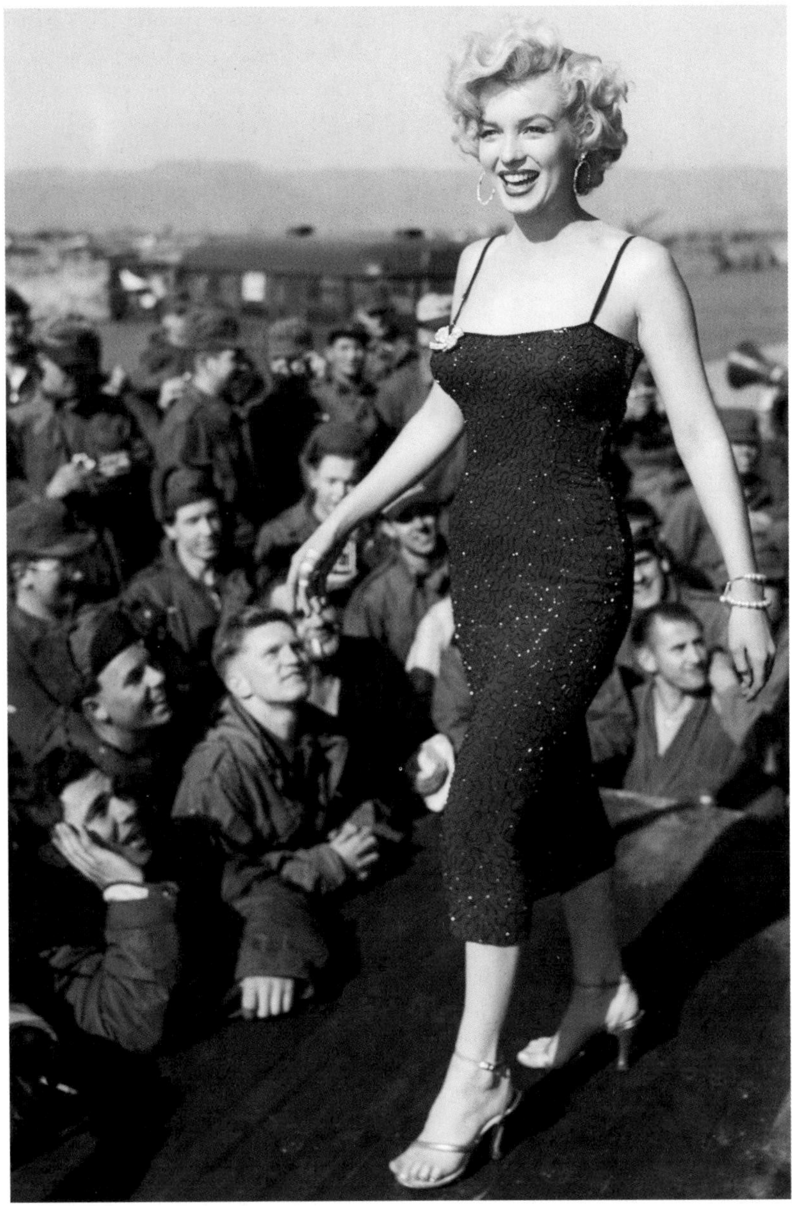

NOTABLE DATES

■ **1949**
U.S.S.R. tests a nuclear weapon; communists win the Chinese Civil War.

■ **1950**
Joseph McCarthy begins making allegations of communist influence in U.S. government; North Koreans attack South Korea; U.N. authorizes U.S. and other Western countries to undertake "police action" to repel aggression in Korea; Rosenbergs arrested; China intervenes in Korea.

■ **1951**
Truman relieves MacArthur of command in Korea; Rosenbergs tried and convicted of espionage; McCarthy begins conducting Senate investigations of communism in the U.S.

■ **1952**
Dwight D. Eisenhower elected President.

■ **1953**
Korean War ends with armistice; Rosenbergs electrocuted.

■ **1954**
During Army-McCarthy hearings, McCarthy's televised tactics begin to discredit him; Senate censures McCarthy.

■ **1957**
McCarthy dies.

those to be denied jobs preoccupied the entertainment industry. Actor Ronald Reagan became president of the Screen Actors' Guild and advocated the naming names tactic. The 1950 film *High Noon*, starring Gary Cooper (a namer of names), glorified the lonely hero who stands up for a cowering community unwilling to resist evil.

Television demonstrated its power in 1954, when McCarthy declared the U.S. Army riddled with communists. The ensuing hearings revealed McCarthy's boorish style, and CBS's Edward R. Murrow exposed McCarthy's shabby career. McCarthy was censured by the Senate in 1954 and died of alcoholism in 1957. ■

Fifties Society, Faith, and Science

1946–1964

BY 1952, THE CULTURE WARS of the twenties had been suspended for a quarter-century, first by hard times and then by postwar affluence. Americans' faith in their nation's values made unconventional opinions unpopular, though minorities had real reason to be satisfied.

The fifties were a decade of faith in God, country, and science. Congress put "In God We Trust" on coins and added "under God" to the Pledge of Allegiance. American families sought values for bringing up children by joining churches. Southern Baptist Billy Graham's televised crusades moved millions to make a "decision for Christ," and weekly telecasts by Bishop Fulton J. Sheen presented Catholicism and anticommunism in a reassuring way. Faith healer Oral Roberts used television to spread Pentecostal fundamentalism. The books of Norman Vincent Peale combined a psychologically sophisticated "power of positive thinking" with mainstream Protestantism to influence millions of middle-class Americans. Protestant philosophers Reinhold and H. Richard Niebuhr discussed making moral decisions in an amoral world.

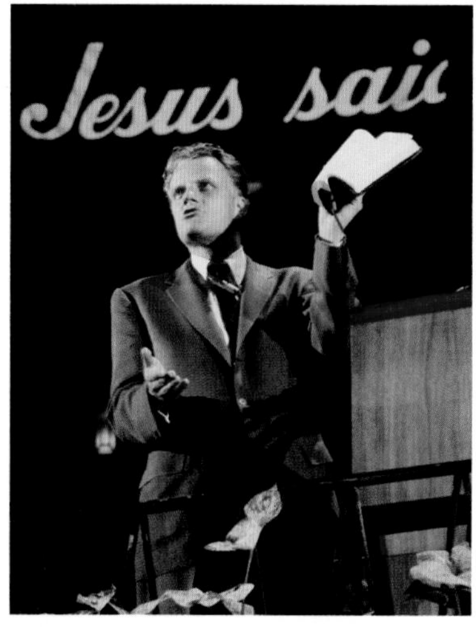

Billy Graham preaches at Madison Square Garden in New York City in 1957. His "Crusades for Christ" were very successful. Graham acquired public influence as a preacher of simple, heartfelt faith.

Uneasily juxtaposed with American religiosity was the faith of the middle class in Freudianism and science. Freud was taught to undergraduates as the epitome of sophisticated psychology, and adults obsessed about "complexes" and repressions. Zoologist Alfred Kinsey informed the American public, in widely read books with a barrage of statistics, that men and women alike enjoyed a much wider range of sexual experience than had been assumed. Sociological and psychological arguments figured heavily in the Supreme Court's *Brown* decision, striking down segregation. The prestige of cutting-edge physics soared in the atomic age. And for millions of parents, the last word on childrearing came from Dr. Benjamin Spock, whose books taught that children should not be brought up in an authoritarian, repressive atmosphere.

In the twenties, the split was between rural and small-town America and big-city America. But depression, war, and affluence had brought millions of rural and small-town Americans to the cities. Their traditional values were reinforced by the political and religious conservatism of cold-war America.

Films were subject to voluntary censorship. Too much sex, violence, or disrespect toward established institutions were taboo. Despite these restrictions, American filmmakers produced great films, but foreign-made films—ranging from profound dramas by Sweden's Ingmar Bergman to farces starring French sexpot Brigitte Bardot—challenged prudery. So did *Playboy* magazine, first published in 1953, which slickly implied that a beautiful "playmate" was simply one more possession to acquire.

For American women, the fifties were the decade of domesticity. Women had been urged to leave the wartime workplace for returning veterans. Those pursuing careers were underpaid and underrepresented in positions of authority. Staying home, raising a brood of well-adjusted children, and being a loving but subordinate partner to a busy husband were the ideals. But signs of middle-class women's disquiet were already being researched by author Betty Friedan. She published those views in her 1963 manifesto of a reviving feminism, *The Feminine Mystique*. Disillusionment, stress, and sometimes alcoholism showed that not all was well in the fifties household.

Advances in technology and science stand among notable events of the fifties. The rise of the computer and the transistor created the information sciences. Discovery in 1953 by Briton Francis Crick and American James Watson of the structure of the DNA molecule—and its method of self-replication—revolutionized biology and biochemistry. The dread disease polio was conquered in 1955 with a vaccine developed by Dr. Jonas Salk. The great American scientist Richard Feynman revolutionized most aspects of physics, including clarifying quantum electrodynamics and explaining much of the weak nuclear force—the key to understanding radioactive decay and particle physics. In 1964, American researchers at Bell Labs discovered cosmic background radiation—unambiguous evidence of the Big Bang and an expanding universe.

As the Eisenhower years drew to a close, there was talk of lost purpose and a sense of shame about the denial of equal rights to African Americans. Communism was still widely perceived as a menace, but so (increasingly) was the arms race. Some older Americans saw the wells of idealism and discontent among young people that had not been sufficiently tapped in a conformist decade. In his telecast farewell address of January 1961, Eisenhower startled the public with a solemn warning against allowing "the military-industrial complex" to gain too much influence over national decision making. ■

Computers of the 1950s were massive and frightening to some because of their capacity to store data on individuals and displace human workers. This 1955 IBM computer had a capacity and speed far below today's laptops.

NOTABLE DATES

■ 1946
Dr. Benjamin Spock publishes first edition of *Common Sense Book of Baby and Child Care.*

■ 1947
Invention of the transistor.

■ 1948
Alfred Kinsey publishes *Sexual Behavior of the Human Male.*

■ 1950
Billy Graham emerges as foremost spokesman for fundamentalism.

■ 1952
UNIVAC computer used on TV on election night to project outcome of 1952 presidential election, introducing Americans to the power of computers.

■ 1953
Discovery of structure of the DNA molecule by Francis Crick and James D. Watson, revolutionizing biology and medicine; *Playboy* magazine published.

■ 1954
"Under God" added to the Pledge of Allegiance.

■ 1956
Congress makes "In God We Trust" the official U.S. motto and orders it placed on all U.S. coinage.

■ 1959
Film *On the Beach* raises questions about the nuclear arms race and helps initiate peace movement.

■ 1961
Eisenhower warns against military-industrial complex.

■ 1963
Betty Friedan publishes *The Feminine Mystique,* initiating feminist movement.

Kennedy and the Space Race

1960–1972

GLAMOROUS JOHN F. KENNEDY won the Presidency in 1960 by a razor-thin margin over Richard Nixon. Kennedy's crafted image was enhanced by his sterling performances in the first televised presidential debates and by Democrats' arguments that President Eisenhower had allowed the nation to drift. At the time, the public knew nothing of Kennedy's reckless womanizing or his life-threatening ailments.

The New Frontier

So JFK called his program, and in a soaring Inaugural Address he called for national rededication. "The torch has passed to a new generation . . . ." America would, he promised, "pay any price, bear any burden . . . to assure the survival and the success of liberty."

Determined to confront communism and to build America's conventional warfare capabilities, Kennedy authorized a CIA plan to overthrow the pro-communist

John Kennedy and his wife, Jackie, were charismatic figures to millions. Minutes after this photo was taken, Kennedy was shot by Lee Harvey Oswald as this motorcade moved through downtown Dallas in November 1963.

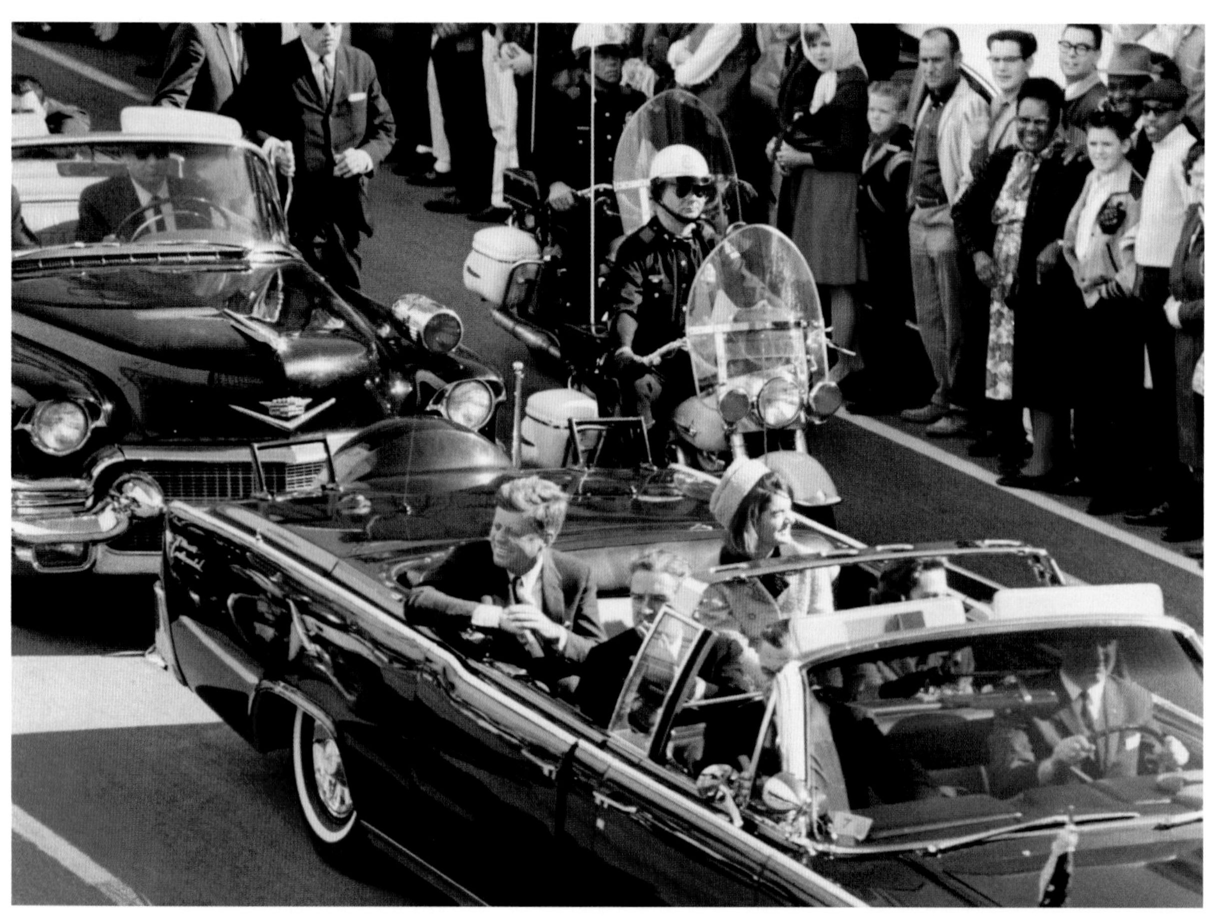

revolutionary regime of Fidel Castro in Cuba. In April 1961, CIA-supported Cuban exiles landed at the Bay of Pigs, but Castro's military wiped out their beachhead. Kennedy took personal responsibility—though CIA plots to kill Castro continued.

Kennedy's foreign policy focused heavily on West Berlin. Soviet leader Nikita Khrushchev aimed to stabilize communist East Germany by permitting authorities to stop the flight of Germans into West Berlin. In the summer of 1961, Kennedy mobilized the Army Reserves, increased draft calls, and suggested that Americans build bomb shelters. The crisis ebbed when East Germany erected a concrete wall around West Berlin.

In October 1962, an even worse crisis erupted. American U-2s discovered that the U.S.S.R. was installing in Cuba nuclear-tipped missiles capable of devastating the U.S. Kennedy's military advisers wanted to destroy the bases immediately, but instead he announced a "quarantine" of Cuba. For days, a Soviet convoy steamed toward Cuba, carrying potentially lethal cargoes, as American troops massed in Florida. Finally came Khrushchev's rambling message, seeming to admit that he would withdraw the missiles—and then a second message imposing stiffer conditions. Kennedy accepted the first message and ignored the second. "We're eyeball to eyeball and the other fellow just blinked," said Secretary of State Dean Rusk. After Soviet missiles were withdrawn, U.S. missiles aimed at the U.S.S.R. were pulled from Turkey, a NATO ally.

On November 22, 1963, in a motorcade through Dallas, Kennedy was shot by Lee Harvey Oswald. Questions of whether Oswald was the lone assassin or part of a wider conspiracy have never been fully answered, for Oswald was killed in the Dallas police headquarters two days later by Jack Ruby, a bystander with ties to organized crime. The official explanation of the assassination, by a commission headed by Chief Justice Warren, was rushed to the public before the 1964 election. Most historians regard the report as a generally accurate account of how a lonely ne'er-do-well managed to kill the most powerful man alive in mid-century America.

The Space Race

One of Kennedy's first acts had been to commit to landing on the moon by 1970. The Apollo Program was announced in May 1961, operating within the National Aeronautic and Space Administration (NASA). This was one of the largest scientific undertakings since the Manhattan Project, with enormous technical challenges. A spacecraft fire cost three astronauts their lives. But several Earth-orbit tests succeeded before, on December 21, 1968—barely more than five years after Kennedy's death—Apollo 8 carried the first humans into orbit around the moon and back. After more test flights, Apollo 11 accomplished its epoch-making goal: On July 20, 1969, Neil Armstrong became the first human being to set foot on a non-terrestrial surface. "One giant step for mankind," he radioed back to Earth. ■

NOTABLE DATES

■ 1960
John F. Kennedy elected President.

■ 1961
Kennedy delivers "Ask not" Inaugural Address; failure of Bay of Pigs invasion of Cuba; crisis over Berlin threatens war; Berlin Wall erected; Apollo moon-landing program begins.

■ 1962
Cuban Missile Crisis brings world to brink of nuclear war.

■ 1963
Kennedy assassinated; Lyndon B. Johnson becomes President.

■ 1964
Warren Commission Report issued, declaring Lee Harvey Oswald Kennedy's sole assassin; Civil Rights Act and tax cut enacted; Johnson elected President.

■ 1968
Apollo 8: first human flight to moon and back.

■ 1969
Apollo 11: first human landing on the moon.

■ 1972
Last Apollo mission to the moon.

Civil Rights Revolution

1954–1963

IN 1954, IN ONE OF THE LANDmark events of the Eisenhower years, the Supreme Court handed down an epoch-making, unanimous decision in *Brown* v. *Board of Education*. School segregation, it ruled, denied the equal protection of the law and was unconstitutional. The National Association for the Advancement of Colored People (NAACP), which had charted this course under the leadership of attorney Thurgood Marshall, had at last won a victory over the fiction of "separate but equal" enshrined by the 1896 *Plessy* v. *Ferguson* case.

Eisenhower had recently appointed the Court's chief justice, former California governor Earl Warren, who ensured the decision's unanimity. The President was not happy with *Brown*; he thought that segregation could only be eased gradually, over generations. But he upheld the decision as the law of the land. Many southern whites, led by southern Democrats in Congress, vowed massive resistance.

The Leadership of Martin Luther King, Jr.

In 1955, a new front in the African-American struggle for equality opened. Acting within a carefully planned strategy, an NAACP activist in Montgomery, Alabama, named Rosa Parks refused to give up her city bus seat to a white passenger, as required by a local ordinance. To force the city to rescind this and other Jim Crow laws, the city's black population organized a boycott of municipal buses, threatening to bankrupt a bus system heavily dependent on black fares. African Americans walked to and from work, or rode in carpools. And out of the boycott a profoundly eloquent and thoughtful leader emerged: the Rev. Dr. Martin Luther King, Jr.

A young preacher in a local black Baptist church, Dr. King was the son of a famous Atlanta minister and had just earned a doctorate at Boston University's School of Theology. There he had studied the non-violent, civil-disobedience messages of the Russian novelist Leo Tolstoy and of India's Mohandas Gandhi. These he joined with the spirit of the Christian gospels in a powerful, redemptive message to all Americans: To throw off racism, to embrace the cause of justice, and to realize the American dream of equal opportunity. The high principles and Christian foundations of his appeal became known throughout the nation during the yearlong boycott: "If we are arrested every day, don't ever let anyone pull you so low as to hate

Rosa Parks initiated the Montgomery, Alabama, bus boycott on December 1, 1955, when she refused to sit at the back of the bus. Here, she rides at the front after the Court ruled segregation of city buses unconstitutional.

Their clothes neatly starched and their books ready, on September 5, 1957, nine black students ran a gauntlet of abuse as they attempted to integrate Central High School in Little Rock, Arkansas, protected by National Guard troops.

them. We must use the weapon of love," he preached. By the time the boycott had finally succeeded—brought about by Montgomery white merchants' economic losses and reinforced by a Supreme Court ruling in November 1958 that segregation on public buses was illegal—King's powerful influence among African Americans was already firm. The next year he became president of the Southern Christian Leadership Conference, a coalition of southern black preachers dedicated to nonviolence; over the next few years he received great acclaim as a moral and spiritual leader, not only in the United States but also as southern defenders of segregated schools discredited themselves in the eyes of the world. In those northern and border states where segregation had been practiced, there was generally quiet compliance with the Supreme Court's order that desegregation proceed "with all deliberate speed." Not so in most of the old Confederacy. One county in Virginia shut down its public school system for two years rather than comply. In October 1957, ordered by a federal court to desegregate Little Rock Central High, local officials refused and turned for support to Arkansas governor Orval Faubus. He mobilized Arkansas guardsmen to "maintain order" and prevent a handful of young African Americans from starting classes—and his defiance of the court was backed by a howling white mob. Reluctantly, but

NOTABLE DATES

■ **1954**
Supreme Court declares school segregation unconstitutional in *Brown* v. *Board of Education.*

■ **1955**
Montgomery bus boycott makes Dr. Martin Luther King, Jr., leading black civil-rights leader.

■ **1957**
Eisenhower intervenes to enforce desegregation of Little Rock high school.

■ **1958**
Supreme Court rules segregation on public buses unconstitutional.

■ **1960**
Sit-in demonstrations begin in Greensboro, North Carolina.

■ **1961**
Freedom Rides begin, aiming to desegregate southern public transportation.

■ **1962**
Birmingham church bombing kills three black girls; Kennedy enforces desegregation of University of Mississippi.

■ **1963**
King delivers "I Have a Dream" speech at the March on Washington.

fully aware that federal authority was on the line, President Eisenhower turned the troops into U.S. National Guardsmen and ordered them to hold back the crowds while escorting the black students into the school. The incident received worldwide publicity—not only by contrasting the dignity and composure of the black children with the ugliness of the mob barring them from school but also by highlighting the contradiction between U.S. claims to represent freedom in the face of communist totalitarianism and the brutal reality of American racism. If no other considerations motivated uncommitted Americans to see the justice of the civil rights struggle, this Cold War reasoning often carried the day.

King's message of nonviolent protest resonated deep within the black community. At historically black colleges across the South, students studied his writings and those of Gandhi, Tolstoy, and Thoreau, preparing to offer themselves as nonviolent protesters for civil rights. In the winter of 1960, beginning at Greensboro, North Carolina, and later spreading to many other southern cities, college and high-school black students organized sit-ins to call for desegregating lunch counters and other eating facilities. Defying Jim Crow rules, they simply occupied seats and, when they were refused service, held their ground despite every insulting or painful effort of jeering whites to drive them away. It took great courage and inner resolve to sit-in, and many participants would go on to still more dangerous protests during the 1960s. Although as yet no federal courts or laws protected them or responded to their demands, those who participated in the sit-ins received the admiration of white liberals everywhere.

Black Radicalization, 1963-1969

Twice in the sixties, *Newsweek* reported on surveys among the African-American middle class. The first was released on July 29, 1963, just before King's "I Have a Dream" speech. The second dates from 1969, after Congress enacted Civil Rights laws in 1964 and 1965 and Lyndon Johnson's Great Society attacked poverty. It reflected African-American frustration with the slow pace of change.

Percentages	1963	1969
Think whites want to keep blacks down:	19	47
Don't think whites have gotten better:	25	47
Don't think whites will get better:	9	32
Feel whites will budge only when forced by blacks:	16	44
Would like a separate black nation:	0	18
Don't think U.S. is worth fighting for:	7	20
Feel NAACP is doing good job:	79	19
Feel Urban League is doing good job:	37	19
Think violence will be necessary:	9	33
Believe riots have helped:	*	50
Would like a separate black nation	0	18

* Not asked

A Violent Backlash

The Civil Rights Revolution heated up considerably on Kennedy's White House watch, not always to the President's liking. He regarded African-American demands for broader rights as a distraction from his game of global chess with Khrushchev and as an unpleasant reminder to the rest of the world of America's grievous shortcomings. Pressured by FBI director J. Edgar Hoover (a racist who hated the civil- rights movement and also had a thick dossier on Kennedy's sex life, which went back decades), the President agreed to allow the FBI secretly to wiretap Martin Luther King, Jr., for (non-existent) evidence that he was involved with communists.

But the momentum of the African-American struggle for rights and dignity forced the President's hand, and that of his brother Robert, the attorney general. In 1961-62, the sit-in movement morphed into the Freedom Rides, as black and white volunteers took life-threatening risks to ride buses into the Deep South challenging segregation in interstate transportation. They were greeted with mobs, the Ku Klux Klan, and police-sanctioned violence, and some sustained permanent injuries.

The Kennedy brothers had to intervene with federal injunctions to stop the Jim Crow practices that the riders dramatized. In 1962, a black Air Force veteran attempted to enroll at the University of Mississippi, setting off a violent white reaction (egged on by inflammatory radio broadcasts by the state's governor); Kennedy had to send in federal troops to quiet the campus and permit the lone black man to attend classes. The 1962 bombing, by local white racists, of a Birmingham, Alabama, church used as a headquarters by civil-rights activists, resulted in the deaths of three young black girls and attacks on civil-rights demonstrators.

The attacks were carried out with police dogs on the authority of the city's police commissioner, "Bull" Connor, and again Kennedy was forced to intervene. This time he finally promised to support a civil-rights bill that faced an uphill congressional battle against strong conservative opposition.

Kennedy's promise was largely forced by the soaring eloquence of Dr. Martin Luther King, Jr. Arrested during the Birmingham, Alabama, demonstrations, he smuggled out his dramatic "Letter from the Birmingham Jail" calling upon white liberals and Christians to witness the truth of the nonviolent black struggle for justice. The ultimate pressure brought to bear on President Kennedy was the March on Washington in July 1963, organized by a coalition of labor unions and civil-rights organizations. Dr. King delivered before this throng, and a nationwide television audience, his soul-stirring "I Have a Dream" speech. At the end, in stirring tones, Dr. King asked: "When will be able to join hands and sing in the words of the old Negro spiritual, 'Free at last! Free at last! Thank God Almighty, we are free at last!'" Despite such an appeal, resistance to the civil-rights movement remained strong. ■

Jackie Robinson Desegregates Baseball

Major league baseball was segregated before World War II. Some of the greatest baseball players competed in the Negro League, and discerning white fans sometimes came to watch, and occasionally black-white exhibition games were held.

All that changed in 1947, when Jackie Robinson put on a Brooklyn Dodgers uniform. Robinson (born in 1919) had been signed in 1945 by the Dodgers' president, Branch Richey, and played for two years in the Brooklyn farm system before Richey decided that he was ready for the big leagues. Richey did not want Robinson to fail under pressure. He had chosen Robinson not only for his phenomenal talent but also for his emotional steadiness, and he prepared Robinson for the racist taunts that he would encounter. Robinson, a star football and baseball player at UCLA before the war, had received officer training and been commissioned. If any athlete was ready for this assignment, it was Robinson.

Jackie Robinson, shown here in 1953, was one of the great baseball players of all time as well as a hero for his role in desegregating the sport.

Robinson did face great hostility, but he silenced all his detractors with his skill, his cool, and his dignity. He led the National League in stolen bases and was named Rookie of the Year. His .342 batting average made him the league's top hitter in 1949 and its Most Valuable Player. Retiring in 1957, he had compiled a lifetime batting average of .311, and was soon voted into the Hall of Fame. Thereafter, until his death in 1972, he was a highly successful businessman.

Robinson opened the door for black athletes in all major-league sports. Reticent about stirring more public controversy, he held back from giving all-out public support to the civil-rights movement. But his place as an American hero for all races was already secure. ■

The Vietnam War Begins

1963–1968

THE TRAGEDY OF JOHN F. Kennedy's assassination swiftly blended with the triumph of his New Frontier. "Let us continue," intoned his successor, former Vice President Lyndon B. Johnson in his first speech to Congress after Kennedy's somber funeral. Honoring the fallen hero, Congress enacted his tax cut in 1964, delivering the first planned Keynesian stimulus to the economy. That same year, a Civil Rights Act, guaranteeing increased protections for African Americans and women, promised that "affirmative action" would break patterns of discrimination in everyday life.

Johnson was unlike John F. Kennedy in everything but womanizing and ruthless political instincts. As Senate majority leader in the 1950s, Johnson had wielded immense power while Kennedy played almost no role in crafting legislation. LBJ was a crude wheeler-dealer; JFK had been polished and highly articulate. As one of Kennedy's rivals for the 1960 nomination, Johnson had been picked for the Vice Presidency largely to hold southern and Texas electoral votes for the northern liberal presidential candidate. Johnson knew poverty firsthand, from his Texas childhood; Kennedy, the son of enormous wealth and privilege, knew it only from reading books and staff memos. Johnson yearned to improve the lives and win the love of the disadvantaged, whom Kennedy saw abstractly. Johnson wanted to make his mark as a second FDR, a great domestic reformer; Kennedy saw himself as an American Churchill, triumphant in global politics. Johnson thought Kennedy insufficiently liberal. Kennedy's life ended in a blaze of martyred glory; Johnson left public life discredited.

Johnson routed Barry Goldwater for the Presidency in 1964. Goldwater looked both backward and forward. He favored dismantling much of the New Deal—by making Social Security voluntary, for example—but his conservatism was that of southwestern libertarianism. He admired freewheeling capitalism and—though not a racist himself—courted southern segregationists in the name of states rights. Abroad, he favored an aggressively anti-communist policy to roll back the Iron Curtain in Europe and resist "Red China" in Asia. Only half-jokingly, Goldwater confessed to an urge to "lob one [a nuclear bomb] into the men's room at the Kremlin." "Extremism in the defense of liberty is no vice," Goldwater told the Republican convention. Most Americans judged *him* the extremist. Johnson won as the peace candidate, and a Democratic Congress enacted the liberal agenda. Conservatism

There were few set battles in the Vietnam War, but when they occurred they were bloody. Here, in 1966, a wounded Marine tries to help another in a struggle near the demilitarized zone separating North and South Vietnam.

NOTABLE DATES

■ **1963**
Assassination of South Vietnamese president in U.S.-backed coup; Kennedy assassinated; Johnson becomes President.

■ **1964**
Tonkin Gulf incident and Tonkin Gulf Resolution; Johnson begins planning U.S. military intervention in South Vietnam; Johnson elected President.

■ **1965**
U.S. bombing of North Vietnam and military intervention in South Vietnam begin; antiwar protest movement begins among students and peace activists.

■ **1968**
Tet Offensive and My Lai Massacre in South Vietnam; Eugene McCarthy runs strongly against Johnson in New Hampshire primary and Johnson withdraws from presidential race.

seemed dead. Yet Goldwater was Ronald Reagan's precursor.

Johnson's Vietnam Failure

Johnson's Presidency was fatally damaged by the Vietnam War. LBJ remembered the early fifties Republican charges of "losing" China and uncritically accepted Eisenhower's well-known dictum that the countries of Southeast Asia were lined up like dominoes on end—knock one over and all would fall to Red China. This, it seemed, might be starting in 1963. Such a defeat, he feared, would destroy American credibility around the world. But neither did he want to allow war in Vietnam—"that raggedy-ass little fourth-rate country"—to distract him from domestic reforms.

In July 1964, Johnson resolved to stop South Vietnam's slide. Using a shadowy naval incident in the Gulf of Tonkin (an American destroyer *may* have been fired on by North Vietnamese gunboats), Johnson extracted from Congress a resolution empowering him to protect American lives in Vietnam. It was, Johnson said, "Like Grandma's nightshirt—it covered everything." Only two senators voted against this virtual declaration of war. Johnson then did what Ike and JFK had done: He sent military advisors and prodded the South Vietnamese generals to make their regime more popular.

But while Johnson's election campaign portrayed him as a man of peace and Goldwater as an extremist whose finger could not be trusted on the nuclear trigger, he and the Pentagon secretly planned a massive bombing campaign against North Vietnam. In February 1965, Operation Rolling Thunder was unleashed against northern targets, while combat contingents landed in the south. The plan was to stabilize the south and force North Vietnamese leader Ho Chi Minh to negotiate. Rolling Thunder was the stick; the carrot was Johnson's offer to build a TVA-style Mekong River project. "Uncle Ho" would have no part of it.

That set the pattern. General after general took power in Saigon, winning neither hearts nor minds. More and more American ground troops tried to flush out elusive communist Vietcong guerrillas. Every night in the White House "situation room," Johnson picked bombing targets. Secretary of State Rusk kept warning that abandoning South Vietnam would be "another Munich," and Secretary of Defense Robert McNamara kept seeing light at the end of the long, dark tunnel.

At first, most Americans supported the war. Impatience was directed at the Pentagon and White House for not getting the job done quickly enough. Draft calls rose, though college students were exempt until 1969. By 1968, American troop strength in Vietnam reached 536,000. Except for the Marines (all volunteers), American "grunts" in Vietnam were mostly draftees on a one-year tour and with only one thought—to survive

Marines try to keep their weapons dry as they slog through a marsh in 1965. Much of the ground action in the Vietnam War consisted of American patrols to flush out the enemy.

clashes with a shadowy enemy and get home alive. As morale and discipline began to crack, drug use and insubordination increased. Pilots shot down over North Vietnam were often tortured to elicit anti-war statements, though very few ever broke.

Antiwar protests started on campuses—first "teach-ins," then marches, then resistance. Television brought the war into every living room, as well as images of students chanting "Hell no, we won't go!" In 1965, Quaker Norman Morrison immolated himself in view of McNamara's Pentagon window; Martin Luther King denounced the war; students protested on the Washington Mall; and young men burned draft cards. A growing contingent of Democratic senators held skeptical hearings, at which LBJ's spokesmen insisted that everything was going according to plan. LBJ's credibility sank. "How can you tell when he's lying?" went a joke. "Whenever his lips are moving."

In South Vietnam, little changed. U.S. forces always prevailed if directly attacked by Vietcong guerrillas or regular North Vietnamese soldiers. But American forays seldom permanently regained territory. American napalm was just as apt to kill and maim civilians (if they *were* civilians and not Vietcong—no one could tell). Inevitably, atrocities occurred; the worst reported was the My Lai Massacre in March 1968, in which a poorly led platoon killed 347 women, children, and old men, who may or may not have been loyal to the Vietcong. Even permissible violence got out of hand.

Costs of the Vietnam War

Americans killed or missing in action: More than 47,000

Americans dead from other war-related causes; More than 11,000

Americans wounded: More than 303,000

South Vietnamese troops killed: 185,000-227,000 (estimated)

North Vietnamese, Vietcong combatants killed: More than 900,000

Vietnamese civilians killed: More than 1 million (estimated)

American war effort: More than $200 billion

Other costs: devastation of neighboring Laos and Cambodia; genocide by the victorious Cambodian Khmer Rouge; defoliation of large areas of Vietnam by the defoliant Agent Orange; and more than a generation of disillusionment, cynicism, and bitterness in U.S. society and politics.

"In order to save the village, it was necessary to destroy it," one officer told a reporter.

In January 1968 the Vietnamese prepared to hold their lunar New Year holiday, Tet. In the midst of festivities in South Vietnam's cities (which had largely been spared wartime violence), infiltrated Vietcong and North Vietnamese soldiers opened fire. The United States embassy in Saigon came under attack; the ancient capital Hue fell, and the insurgents dug in behind its heavily walled citadel. But South Vietnamese city dwellers rejected the communist appeal to rise, and after several weeks the Americans regained control. For North Vietnam, Tet was a military debacle.

Yet politically, Tet was a brilliant victory. On television, the American public saw the fighting in all its gory detail and heard the avuncular anchorman Walter Cronkite of CBS ask, "What the hell is going on? I thought we were winning the war." General William Westmoreland, the ground commander, asked for one more infusion of United States troops. Johnson refused. In the New Hampshire Democratic primary, the President almost lost to an antiwar senator, Eugene McCarthy of Minnesota. He had the passionate support of thousands of idealistic college-student volunteers, shaved and "clean for Gene." The New Hampshire protest voters for McCarthy, however, included almost as many hawks, demanding a quick victory, as antiwar doves who wanted an immediate exit from the quagmire.

President Johnson by now was unable to travel anywhere in the country—except to military bases—without demonstrators chanting, "Hey, hey, LBJ, how many kids did you kill today?" After his near-loss to Eugene McCarthy in New Hampshire, Johnson acknowledged that the war had destroyed his Presidency. He summoned to the White House a panel of "wise men"—veterans of the Truman Administration like former secretary of state Acheson, all of them staunch anticommunists—who bluntly advised him to cut his Vietnam losses. On March 31, announcing that he would begin peace negotiations with North Vietnam, President Johnson also delivered the bombshell that he would not be a candidate in the upcoming election of 1968. ■

Great Society and Great Unrest

1962–1976

LIBERALISM REACHED ITS HIGH-water mark with LBJ's election and the Democratic Congress's enactment of sweeping reforms. During the sixties, meanwhile, Earl Warren's Supreme Court issued landmark decisions increasing civil liberties protections for criminal defendants, separating church and state, and otherwise offending many ordinary Americans' values. African-American unrest sparked a white backlash, and America found itself in an unpopular war. The peace and freedom protests of unconventional-looking young people repelled countless adults.

The Great Society and Civil Rights

In his Inaugural Address, Johnson boasted of ushering in the Great Society. The cornerstone of the Great Society was health insurance for the elderly, which neither FDR nor Truman had been able to enact. Johnson finally pushed through Congress the bill establishing Medicare and, for the destitute, Medicaid. By paying most bills associated with old-age illness, Medicare helped raise the elderly from the nation's least to its most affluent segment. Medicaid imposed heavy burdens on the

This float was part of the bicentennial parade in Washington, D.C., on July 4, 1976. The symbolism was typical of the era. Despite the upbeat message, the 1970s were a period of social and economic strain and cultural anguish.

states to provide medical care to the poor and to indigent nursing-home residents. Neither program controlled medical costs.

The Great Society helped raise millions above the poverty line, but not all of its programs worked well. Urban renewal often moved people from squalid slums to public housing projects that became squalid. The disadvantaged were offered community organizers to lobby city-hall bureaucracies, outraging mayors. Job training often taught obsolete skills while inner-city public schools deteriorated. Welfare spending increased, yet it still gave single mothers a pittance while males evaded responsibility. Meanwhile northern black ghettos exploded in riots every long, hot summer beginning in 1964, and middle-class northern whites recoiled as northern black youths shouted "burn, baby, burn!"

The peaceful African-American struggle for civil rights in the South still went on. In 1965, Johnson urged Congress to pass a strong voting-rights act, quoting the civil-rights anthem, "We Shall Overcome." The change was enormous as southern blacks began voting. Southern white politicians learned to court black voters. But southern whites also moved into the conservative Republican Party.

The year 1968 brought together all these swirling currents. First came Tet, McCarthy's run against Johnson, and LBJ's abdication. Five days later, on April 4, 1968, while visiting Memphis to support striking black garbage workers, Martin Luther King, Jr., was killed by a white sniper. Into the political fray jumped New York Senator Robert F. Kennedy, JFK's younger brother and attorney general. RFK embraced the antiwar movement. His primary victories climaxed on June 2 in California. Immediately after Kennedy's victory speech, Palestinian Sirhan Sirhan shot him dead. The party's establishment—labor leaders, big-city bosses, and elected officials—stood by Vice President Hubert Humphrey, a staunch liberal who had defended the Vietnam War. In August the Democrats nominated him at their Chicago convention, while outside antiwar protesters were clubbed by Mayor Richard Daley's police.

No such unpleasantness marred the Republican convention, which nominated Richard Nixon. And as a third-party candidate, Alabama governor George Wallace, put

Quality of Life Report, 1964

Compared to 1900, African-American life had improved enormously: Life spans almost doubled and lynchings ended. Congress passed civil-rights legislation; racism was discredited. But statistics still showed wide black-white disparities.

Life Expectancy (in years):

Non-white	White
61.1 (male)	67.7 (male)
67.2 (female)	74.6 (female)

Fetal Death Rate (in 1,000 live births):

Non-white	White
28.1	14.1

Median Years Schooling Completed:

Blacks	Whites
8.7	11.9

Mean Income of Heads of Families:

Blacks	Whites
$4,186	$6,771

NOTABLE DATES

■ 1963
Kennedy assassinated; Johnson becomes President.

■ 1964
Johnson elected President.

■ 1965
Immigration reform, Medicare/Medicaid, and other Great Society reform legislation enacted.

■ 1968
King and Robert Kennedy assassinations; riots at Chicago's Democratic convention; Richard Nixon elected President.

■ 1970
Kent State University shootings kill four students in antiwar demonstration.

■ 1972
Equal Rights Amendment proposed and sent to states; death of J. Edgar Hoover; Watergate break-in; Nixon visits China and Soviet Union, initiating détente policy; Nixon reelected President.

■ 1973
Watergate revelations begin; Nixon tries to fire special prosecutor in Saturday Night Massacre; draft abolished.

■ 1974
Nixon releases Oval Office tapes, revealing "smoking gun"; Nixon resigns as Congress prepares impeachment and trial; Gerald Ford becomes President.

The New Left

"We are people of this generation, bred in at least modest comfort, housed now in universities, looking uncomfortably to the world we inherit." So began the "Port Huron Statement," a sometimes eloquently insightful but mostly turgid manifesto of Students for a Democratic Society. About 60 attendees at a rundown lakeside camp near Detroit, there to organize SDS in June 1962, endorsed it. This was the most important—really, the only—coherent statement of New Left ideas.

Some in the New Left had family roots in Marxism. But not all: Tom Hayden, the University of Michigan student who drafted the "Port Huron Statement," grew up attending the parish church of the long-silenced Father Charles Coughlin. They had in common hostility to communist ideology, fear of nuclear war, revulsion at facing lives of meaningless work, and idealistic faith in "participatory democracy"—the control of peoples' lives by people themselves, not by nameless bureaucrats. They disliked capitalism, hated apathy, and yearned for commitment.

SDS never was a mass movement, its aims too amorphous and esoteric. It disappeared into the general current of activism. A handful of ideologues called the Weathermen tried to revive SDS as a revolutionary organization, but failed. Older thinkers of the time, like German-born philosopher Herbert Marcuse, were admired by New Left students for their attempts to combine Marxist and Freudian theories. That was the limit of the New Left as an intellectual movement. Its idealism and lack of staying power were symptomatic of sixties student life. ■

The Chicago Seven, tried for conspiracy to incite riots during the 1968 Chicago Democratic Convention, became New Left heroes. Tom Hayden appears on the right.

himself forward as the champion of white working-class Americans shocked by protesters, rioters, and "pointy-head intellectuals."

Humphrey came on strong at the close of the campaign, after he broke with Johnson over Vietnam, but Nixon won with silent majority votes. Law and order were Nixon's watchwords in mobilizing the white middle class against the excesses of liberalism. Indeed, liberalism became a dirty word.

Yet after Nixon's Inauguration the violence continued. Nixon's much-touted secret plan to end the war was "Vietnamization"—preparing South Vietnam's army to take on most of the fighting. More antiwar protests erupted when Nixon invaded Vietnam's neighbor Cambodia in 1970 to wipe out communist bases. On May 4, at Kent State University in Ohio, National Guardsmen called out to control a demonstration let loose a fusillade that killed four students. Polls showed that Americans sympathized with the guardsmen, not with the protesters.

The Imperial Presidency

A Red-baiter in the early 1950s, by 1960 Nixon's politics were centrist. As President, he created the Environmental Protection Agency, responding to public alarm about the environment. The Nixon Administration codified affirmative action policies by imposing hiring guidelines on government agencies, colleges, and businesses with federal contracts. Nixon supported the Equal Rights Amendment in 1972. He endorsed most federal actions to enforce civil-rights legislation,

FBI agent Mark Felt posed for this picture in Salt Lake City in 1958. In 1973, he was Deep Throat, informant to the *Washington Post* who supplied information about the unfolding Watergate scandal. He disclosed his identity in 2005.

except for federal courts' attempts to bus schoolchildren to achieve racial balance. His only serious attempt to limit the government's reach was to institute revenue sharing, redistributing federal monies to states. He achieved foreign-policy breakthroughs in 1972 as he visited both Beijing and Moscow, laying the basis for U.S. recognition of "Red China" and for détente with the Soviet Union.

In 1971, Defense Department analyst Daniel Ellsberg released to the *New York Times* a secret Pentagon study of how the government had blundered into the war. Infuriated, Nixon created a secret White House unit, "the Plumbers," to plug "leaks." They sought information by burglarizing Ellsberg's psychiatrist's files and in 1972 bugged Democratic headquarters in Washington's Watergate building. When the burglars were caught, Nixon denied any knowledge of the break-in.

In 1972 Nixon won in a landslide against the Democrats' ultraliberal antiwar candidate, Senator George McGovern. Then the Watergate affair began to unravel. In early 1973 the federal judge trying the case rejected the burglars' claim that they had acted alone. Congress opened inquiries. Some White House officials began to talk, revealing the secret taping system in Nixon's Oval Office. Nixon refused to surrender the tapes, but Congress forced him to accept a special prosecutor, former Solicitor General Archibald Cox. When in October 1973 Nixon fired Cox, Congress installed another prosecutor, Leon Jaworski, just as relentless in demanding the tapes; Nixon issued expurgated versions. But the Supreme Court unanimously ruled that he must surrender the original tapes. When he did, there was the "smoking gun": evidence that Nixon had conspired to cover up Watergate. On July 27-30, 1974, the House Judiciary Committee adopted articles of impeachment, charging Nixon with abuse of power. Nixon resigned on August 9, 1974. Vice President Gerald Ford took office and a month later pardoned Nixon.

Watergate did prove that the system worked. A President guilty of criminal wrongdoing was constitutionally removed from office. But Watergate also proved that much had gone wrong in public life. Nixon had evaded taxes, and his first Vice President, Spiro Agnew, resigned after bribe taking was revealed. Watergate reinforced public perceptions, already created in Vietnam years, that the government could not be trusted. Exposés of FBI and CIA abuses poured forth after the death of J. Edgar Hoover in 1972. The American intelligence community had to be rebuilt on a law-abiding basis, amid questions by liberals about the legitimacy of the Cold War. Critics called Nixon's tenure "the Imperial Presidency." It was time to establish limits. ■

Personal Freedom

1956–1981

BABY BOOMERS FIRST REVEALED their longing for a distinctive style in the early fifties, when rock 'n' roll appeared. In 1956, Elvis Presley created a national sensation. His music earned him millions—and appalled most adults. Until the boomers themselves became parents, there would be a strong generational conflict in young people's quest for personal "space" and "freedom." Rock unified the boomer generation. So did *Mad* magazine, leering at the adult world, and J.D. Salinger's novel, *Catcher in the Rye*, whose anti-hero rebels against such "phonies" as his distant parents.

Counterculture

Sixties lifestyles mainly arose after 1963 and lasted into the 1970s. The Beatles took America by storm in 1964. Their music became edgier —and better—as the decade wore on and political tensions rose. Meanwhile came the hard rock of the Rolling Stones, the Grateful Dead, and others. Very different, but also popular, was the politically articulate folk singing of Joan Baez and Judy Collins; Bob Dylan's "Blowin' in the Wind" became the antiwar anthem. Film censorship also collapsed in the late sixties. Graphic violence, nudity, and sex ceased to shock.

Around 1960, oral contraceptives arrived in American bedrooms. Offering protection from pregnancy, the Pill allowed couples to separate sexuality from procreation. Sixties music, dancing, dress, films, and lifestyles were suffused with sexuality. Abortion remained taboo, but the pressure was on to legalize it. Nothing stopped the sexual revolution born in the sixties—until AIDS was diagnosed among American gay men in 1981.

There was talk in the late sixties of a youth counterculture—a principled rejection of older generations' "uptight" values. There *was* a heavy tinge of idealism to the peace-and-freedom movements. But there was also much self-indulgence, especially among hippies and dropouts who congregated at the fringes of campuses and in neighborhoods like San Francisco's Haight-Ashbury, experimenting with communal living and drugs.

From the sixties ferment grew a new feminism, powerfully influenced by the experiences of young women who joined "the movement," only to find themselves coffee makers and sex partners. By about 1968, many bluntly asserted their independence.

The counterculture appalled many older Americans. Suburban whites started rediscovering the old-fashioned values that would make them the Silent Majority. Going to church, building your career, loving your family, dressing neatly, and being patriotic all became political statements.

The federal courts provoked a backlash, too. After 1960, the Warren Court issued a stream of decisions curbing government's ability to abridge civil liberties, banning public school prayer and Bible reading, and striking down restrictions on pornography. When in *Roe* v. *Wade* (1973) the Court established a woman's right to an abortion, the most explosive cultural issue of the last quarter of the 20th century ignited. *Roe* offended the Catholic Church, orthodox Jews, and conservative Protestant evangelicals, for whom abortion was murder; it was hailed by feminists and liberals as a vindication of a woman's right to control her own body. Pro-Choice abortion-rights defenders came to dominate the national Democratic Party, and the anti-abortion Right to Life position became stronger among Republicans, narrowing space for pragmatic compromise. In the middle, the majority of Americans uneasily accepted *Roe*.

The "Me" Generation

In the early 1970s, protest movements grew quieter and more personal. Former activists sought their fulfillment through Eastern

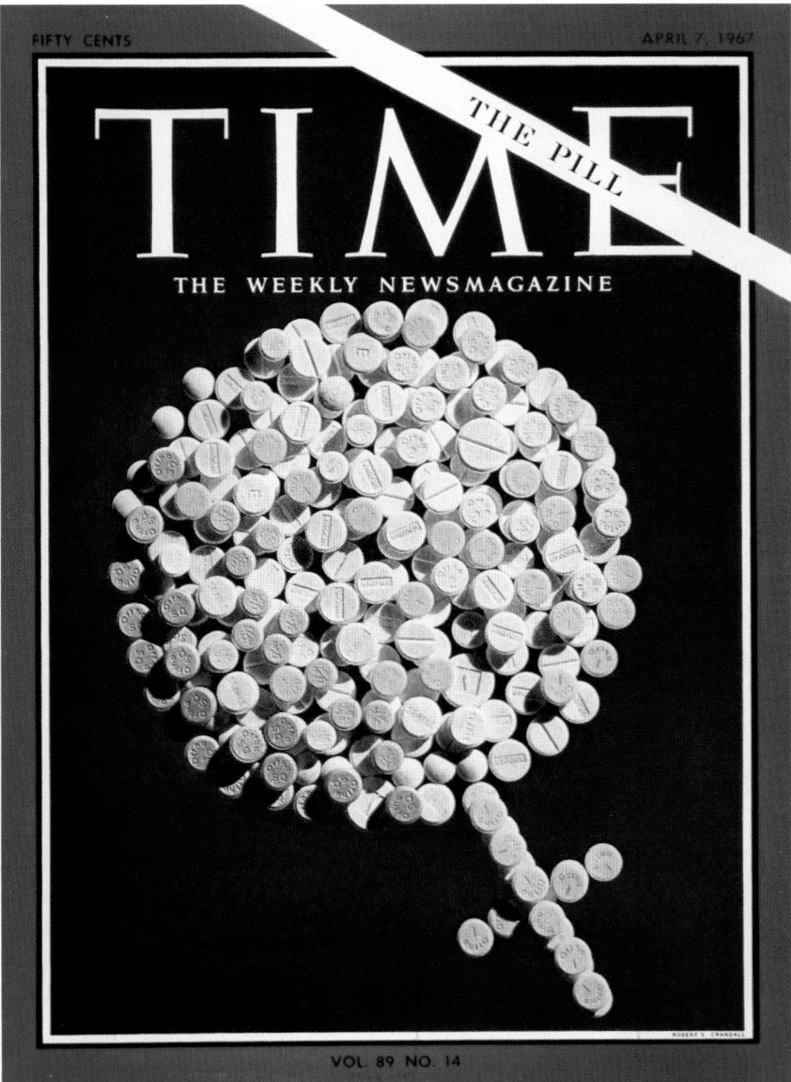

In April 1967, at the height of the sexual revolution of the 1960s, *Time* magazine celebrating both the pill and its liberation of women.

spirituality, New Age cults, recreational drugs, sex, and career building. "The 'Me' Generation," satirist Tom Wolfe labeled them. Yuppies (young upwardly mobile professionals) replaced protesters of the 1960s. The stereotypical yuppie was preoccupied with how "I" fit into everything and obsessed about fulfillment and fitness.

Evangelical Protestantism emerged in the late 1970s, matching the growing size and wealth of evangelical and charismatic churches in American communities and of "televangelists" reaching millions on TV. Evangelicals opposed abortion, wanted to bring back school prayer, attacked the teaching of evolution, and condemned pornography, homosexuality, and other manifestations of sexual freedom. ■

NOTABLE DATES

■ **1956**
Elvis Presley appears on national TV.

■ **1960**
Oral contraceptives initiate sexual revolution; Supreme Court begins issuing liberal decisions in sensitive values cases.

■ **1964**
Beatles begin performing in U.S.

■ **1967**
Film *Bonnie and Clyde* sympathetically portrays outlaws; Beatles extol LSD.

■ **1968**
Women's liberation movement gains attention.

■ **1969**
Film *Easy Rider* sympathetically portrays the drug culture.

■ **1973**
Supreme Court, in *Roe* v. *Wade*, legalizes abortion.

■ **1981**
AIDS publicly identified, slowing the sexual revolution.

A Post-Imperial Presidency

1972–1984

SUPREME COURT DECISIONS about sexuality, religion, and crime control politicized the federal judiciary like nothing since *Dred Scott*. After *Roe*, Senate hearings on Supreme Court nominations increasingly turned into donnybrooks over abortion rights.

Discovering Limits

Nixon's January 1973 peace agreement with North Vietnam provided for mutual withdrawal from South Vietnam. Neither Congress nor the American public had any stomach for continuing the war. In 1974 it passed (over Ford's veto) the War Powers Act, forcing Presidents to obtain congressional approval before committing American forces abroad. In March 1975, North Vietnamese forces struck a powerful blow in South Vietnam, which, with no American help, quickly collapsed. American TV watchers' last view of the war, on April 30, 1975, was of South Vietnamese trying desperately to board helicopters on the roof of the U.S. embassy in Saigon as personnel evacuated. In Cambodia, the communist insurgency provoked by Nixon's 1970 invasion launched one of history's worst genocides against the country's urban population.

Nixon's two successors were good men, but neither inspired confidence. Ford could not live down his pardon of Nixon, and though he struggled with economic woes, he failed. In 1976 Ford lost to Democrat Jimmy Carter, a one-term Georgia governor. Carter exuded born-again piety, which voters welcomed as the antithesis of Nixon's hypocrisy, but events overwhelmed him also.

The 1964 tax cut and Great Society spending had stimulated growth, but taxes were not raised in the late sixties as growth became a boom and war spending touched off inflation. Nixon imposed price controls before the 1972 election; when they were removed, inflation surged again. Watergate unraveled to the drumbeat of bad news, especially the 1973 energy crisis. Federal transfer payments—principally Social Security, Medicare, and welfare—worsened inflation by pumping too many dollars into the economy. Facing higher living costs, workers demanded wage increases not matched by productivity gains; new technologies were not yet sufficiently developed to cut costs and raise output.

When Ronald Reagan took the oath of office on January 20, 1981, a new era began. Ideas governing the U.S. since FDR's New Deal were on the defensive. Reagan called government "the problem," not "the solution."

The Misery Index

In the 1970s economist Robert Barro devised the misery index—inflation rate plus unemployment rate. Here is the misery rate from 1968 (beginning of Vietnam-era inflation), through oil shocks, high unemployment, stagflation, and into the Reagan years.

1968	7.30	**1977**	13.55
1969	8.95	**1978**	13.69
1970	10.82	**1979**	17.07
1971	10.25	**1980**	20.76
1972	8.87	**1981**	17.97
1973	11.02	**1982**	15.87
1974	16.67	**1983**	12.82
1975	17.68	**1984**	11.81
1976	13.45		

(In May 2005 the misery index was 7.90.)

Morning in America

The years 1979-80 were disheartening. The February 1979 overthrow of Iran's shah by anti-American Islamists led to a takeover of the U.S. embassy in Tehran and seizure of personnel as hostages. Carter failed to rescue them, as the Soviet Union invaded next-door Afghanistan with seeming success. Economically, these years were equally painful as the Federal Reserve sought to "wring inflation out of the economy," at the price of recession and soaring interest rates. Carter's chances for reelection looked dim.

Republicans nominated a former movie star and California governor, Ronald Reagan. Though he had compromised with California's Democratic legislature and signed an abortion law, Reagan was Goldwater's heir as the champion of free-market capitalism and militant anticommunism. He wanted government "off the backs" of Americans, and by convincing a majority of voters that he was trustworthy and likeable, he easily won.

Reagan asked Congress for large tax cuts, which he said would increase spending. He also urged slashes in spending on social welfare, environmental, and regulatory programs. This was his unorthodox supply-side remedy to stagflation. Reagan got his tax cuts, which benefited high-income Americans, but only modest spending cuts. These hurt the poor, but Congress refused to impose hardships on the middle class. Reagan also dramatically increased military spending, generating huge deficits, while the Fed kept interest rates high.

Reagan's recession was bitter medicine to stop inflation. But the economy began turning around in August 1982, heralded by falling interest rates and a stock-market surge. Tax cuts stimulated spending, and Reagan's defense buildup had a multiplier effect. By 1984, inflation had dropped, economic growth and employment were gaining, and computers were enhancing productivity—and Reagan proposed a space-based missile defense system. Opponents labeled it Star Wars. Did Reagan know that it would never work but cleverly began the project simply to bankrupt the U.S.S.R.? Or did he genuinely think that anti-missile defenses could save America from attack? We may never know. Star Wars did go forward—and Reagan also insisted on basing cruise missiles in Western Europe. ■

NOTABLE DATES

■ 1972
Nixon Administration imposes price controls; Watergate break-in; Nixon reelected President.

■ 1973
Paris peace agreements with North Vietnam end U.S. intervention in Vietnam War; Watergate scandal begins; U.S. supports overthrow of elected Chilean government by Pinochet; Energy Crisis begins with Yom Kippur War and Arab oil embargo.

■ 1974
Nixon resigns Presidency; Congress enacts War Powers Act over Ford's veto.

■ 1975
South Vietnam collapses; Vietnam united under communist rule.

■ 1976
Jimmy Carter elected President; death of Mao Tse-Tung initiates economic liberalism in China.

■ 1979
Anti-American Islamists lead revolution in Iran; U.S. embassy in Tehran occupied and hostages taken; U.S.S.R. invades Afghanistan.

■ 1980
Tehran hostage-rescue operation fails; U.S. stagflation worsens; Ronald Reagan elected President.

■ 1981
Heavy tax cuts enacted; military spending substantially increases.

■ 1982
Inflation and interest rates abate; U.S. economic turnaround begins.

■ 1984
Reagan reelected.

Looking Out for the Environment

1962–1992

ALTHOUGH THE PRESERVATIONIST Sierra Club was founded in 1892 and progressives cared about conservation, contemporary American environmentalism dates from the 1962 book *Silent Spring* by the popular science writer Rachel Carson. In spelling out the disastrous ecological effects of the common insecticide and disinfectant DDT, Carson opened Americans' eyes to the ecological cost of progress. Because of competition with other issues, it took until the end of the 1960s for environmentalist concerns to be taken seriously by the younger generation. But in 1970 the first Earth Day was celebrated in the U.S.: Young idealists were broadening their consciousness to include concern for the fate of Earth.

The major environmental issues that worried Americans included air and water pollution, the effects of human-produced chemicals on the environment and humans, and destruction of natural habitats and ecological balances. To meet these challenges, in 1972 Congress and President Nixon established the Environmental Protection Agency, to investigate environmental hazards, make environmental-impact reports, and—perhaps most importantly—to ban dangerous substances and clean up contamination. Polluting indutries contributed to a superfund to pay for the worst damages. Although later the EPA and its myriad regulations would become a target of antiregulatory ire, its creation was relatively uncontroversial.

Finite Resources

Environmentalist concerns broadened after publication in 1972 of *Limits to Growth*, a manifesto

In June 1989, an oil spill from an Exxon tanker caused enormous damage to wildlife and habitat in Alaska. Here, workers attempt to clean oil-drenched rocks. Exxon was ordered by a court to pay for the cleanup.

warning that within a century many essential non-renewable resources would be fatally depleted. Petroleum headed everyone's list of non-renewable resources being depleted by the modern way of life, epitomized by automobiles. And in 1973 there was a sudden, steep leap in oil prices. First, the Organization of Petroleum Exporting Countries (OPEC) deployed its power against the oil-consuming West; then, in October, Arab producers embargoed oil shipments during the Yom Kippur War with Israel, causing American filling stations to literally run out of gas. Skyrocketing oil prices contributed to the stagflation that afflicted the economy—and in 1979 another cutoff of petroleum by the Iranian Revolution led to a second energy crisis.

The search now was on to develop economically feasible alternatives to fossil fuels. Hydroelectric, geothermal, solar energy—even massed windmills—were tried, as was ethanol, produced from corn. Clearly, nuclear power was another alternative that had to be considered. The Carter Administration struggled with the energy crisis, creating the Department of Energy to encourage fuel conservation and research on alternatives, and the President appeared on TV wearing a sweater urging Americans to save energy by bundling up and turning down thermostats. But in 1979 a near-meltdown at the Three Mile Island nuclear plant in Pennsylvania frightened the public about nuclear energy. No new nuclear plants were authorized after that time. Alternative energy sources remained elusive, though breakthroughs came with building fuel-efficient engines and reducing air pollution. Transitioning from smokestack to a high-tech industrial base achieved gains.

Meanwhile a series of disturbing environmental catastrophes occurred, including an industrial disaster at a chemical plant operated by Union Carbide in Bhopal, India, in 1984, and a disastrous oil spill off the pristine shores of Alaska in 1989. Public awareness was again heightened.

Environmentalism also became controversial. Business interests found the costs of EPA mandates and other environmental regulations both expensive and burdensome. Workers whose livelihood depended on polluting factories or depleting industries—including loggers in the Northwest whose timber cutting was destroying the habitat of a threatened spotted owl species—denounced attempts to eliminate their jobs. The Reagan Administration tried to eliminate environmental regulations in the interest of stimulating growth. In 1992, at a meeting with leaders of 107 countries in Rio de Janeiro, George H.W. Bush found himself isolated by insisting that meeting environmental goals must not hurt American prosperity. As the U. S. entered the last decade of the 20th century—and as a consensus developed among scientists that atmospheric pollution was causing potentially catastrophic global warming—the limits to which the American people and their government would go in curbing environmentally damaging economic growth were clearly limited. ■

NOTABLE DATES

■ **1962**
Rachel Carson publishes *Silent Spring*, initiating public awareness of environmental issues.

■ **1970**
First Earth Day celebrated.

■ **1972**
Environmental Protection Agency established; Club of Rome publishes *Limits to Growth*.

■ **1973**
OPEC begins raising global oil prices; Yom Kippur War marks onset of Arab oil embargo; energy crisis begins.

■ **1978**
Revelations about Love Canal pollution in Buffalo, New York.

■ **1979**
Iranian Revolution initiates another oil embargo; near-meltdown of Three Mile Island nuclear plant raises questions about nuclear power-plant safety.

■ **1984**
Accident at Bhopal (India) chemical plant.

■ **1989**
Exxon *Valdez* oil spill in Alaska.

■ **1992**
President Bush defends preference for economic growth over environmental protection at meeting in Rio de Janeiro.

WORLD SURVEY

1945–1989

The Cold War divided the world three ways. There was the Free World, led by the United States. There was the world of communist totalitarianism, dominated by the Soviet Union but challenged from within by Mao's China. And by the early 1960s there was a neutral Third World of former colonial lands.

West and East

Prodded by the Marshall Plan, West European governments in 1948 began creating institutions for economic, and later political, integration. By the 1980s these culminated in the European Community. In 1992 the Maastricht Treaty would set the goal of uniting Europe politically.

Japan became a great success story. After World War II, it renounced militarism and embraced pacifism and democracy, turning its energies to export-oriented industrial reconstruction.

The Soviet Union forced the economic and political integration of its East European satellites, all of them rigid dictatorships with state-dominated economies.

Stalin died in 1953, ultimately succeeded by Nikita Khrushchev—perhaps the last Soviet ruler who truly believed that Communism would work. He set the goal of "overtaking" the capitalist world within a generation. But when he accused the hitherto-revered Stalin of committing innumerable "crimes," Khrushchev stimulated far-reaching ferment, including the 1956 Hungarian revolt. Soviet prestige was enhanced by the successful Sputnik launch in 1957, and for a while the U.S.S.R. seemed to fulfill Khrushchev's boasts of economic progress. But Soviet growth was a mirage. Khrushchev's attempts to improve Soviet agriculture caused ecological disasters, and Soviet industry proved resistant to innovation. In 1964, Khrushchev's Kremlin colleagues deposed him for "harebrained scheming." The long decline of the U.S.S.R. had begun, and would continue steadily in the 1970s and 1980s despite a vast Soviet military buildup.

China diverged from the Soviet model after 1958, when Chinese leader Mao Tse-tung tried a "Great Leap Forward" to accelerate economic growth. It was an unmitigated disaster. Things got still worse when Mao unleashed the "Cultural Revolution" in the early 1960s. Until 1971, the United States failed to exploit the Sino-Soviet rift. But after Mao's death, the country's new leader, Deng Xiaoping, in 1979, put China on the "capitalist road" to economic modernization and rapid growth.

The Third World

Neutrality in the Cold War seemed to the Eisenhower administration "immoral." But it was the path chosen by almost all the countries that were set free from European colonial control after World War II. India, where British rule ended in 1947 (after Muslim areas broke away to form Pakistan), was the most important of these newly independent countries, and remained democratic. Its leaders regularly lectured the U.S. about its racism and its Cold War ideology. Most other ex-colonial lands became dictatorships, their leaders learning to play off Western powers against the Soviets. But the colonial powers had done little to prepare these lands for independence. When the AIDS epidemic appeared in Africa, in the late 1970s, its effects were devastating.

The Middle East

The State of Israel was founded in 1948, and from the outset was under siege by its Arab neighbors. Though some Arab countries grew wealthy from oil, none became democracies, and none matched Israel's military prowess. Israel withstood Arab attacks in the 1967 Six Day War, which ended in Israel's occupation of the West Bank, and in the 1973 Yom Kippur War. An Islamic revival competed with pan-Arab nationalism for the loyalty of the Arab people, while the region's problems—corruption and authoritarianism—only worsened.

Economic development proceeded rapidly in oil-rich Iran, where the modernizing but tyrannical Shah Reza Pahlavi had seized power in 1953. Beneath the surface, however, the fast pace of social and economic change that the shah fostered outraged Iran's conservative Muslim population. The tinder exploded in the 1979 Iranian Revolution, led by the fanatically anti-Western Ayatollah Ruhollah Khomeini.

■ Latin America

Washington largely took the rest of the Western Hemisphere for granted, though in 1954 a reform-minded Guatemalan president who threatened United Fruit's interests and tried to buy arms from the Soviets was overthrown by a CIA coup. Anti-*Yanqui* feeling escalated. The greatest shock to Americans was the revolution in Cuba that began in 1959, when a Marxist-Leninist, Fidel Castro, led a guerrilla movement that ousted the country's U.S.-backed dictator. Castro took his country into the Soviet bloc, almost causing a nuclear war in 1962.

It was not U.S. aid but a gradual opening to the world economy that fitfully promoted Latin American development in the seventies and eighties—punctuated by economic crises and several nasty reversions to dictatorship and severe internal repression. The most notorious Latin tyranny in these years was the Chilean dictatorship of General Augusto Pinochet, born in a U.S.-backed 1973 coup against a democratically elected leftist president. As late as the 1980s, Washington was still promoting right-wing terror against left-wing movements in Nicaragua and El Salvador. ■

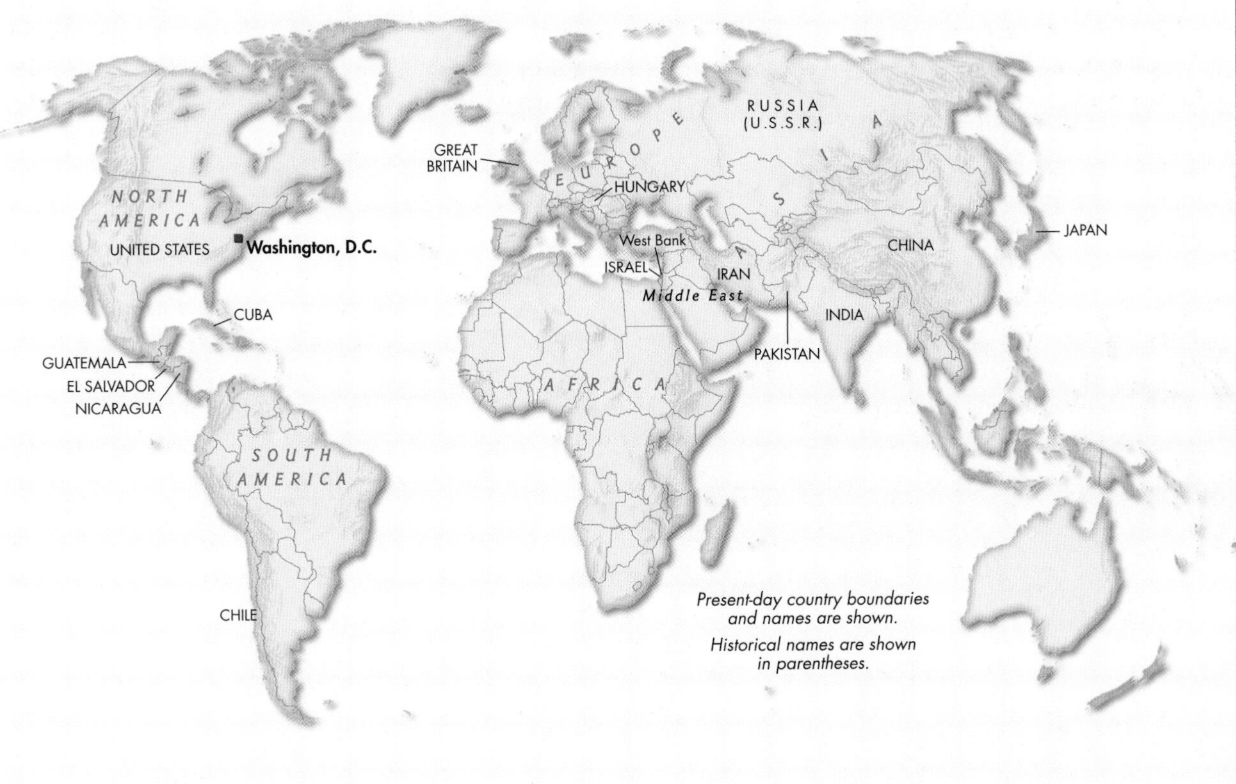

Global Hegemony 1985–Present

THE YEAR 1989, IN WHICH THE BERLIN WALL CAME DOWN AND COMMUNISM COLLAPSED, ranks as a milestone as significant as 1789, the year of the French Revolution and the birth of constitutional government in the U.S. It brought to an end the "true" 20th century, which opened in 1914 with World War I and imposed the baleful legacies of totalitarian fascism and communism, the poisoned fruits of Auschwitz, Hiroshima, and Stalin's Gulag—but had also been the era of Gandhi, King, Einstein, and the double helix.

American political theorist Francis Fukuyama asserted that 1989 marked "the end of history." Fukuyama was speaking of rival ideas, totalitarianism and freedom, struggling for realization. The way was open for freedom to march forward and for history, the struggle of opposites, to end. But history was not over. The Cold War division of the globe into communist and Western camps had ensured a rough stability and kept Third World clients on a leash. The Cold War's end removed these stabilizers and raised ominous new challenges—including bids by unstable Iran and North Korea to acquire nuclear weapons.

Globalization carried the promise of prosperity and the risk of global climatic change. It also highlighted a dangerous confrontation between worldwide modernism and Islamic fundamentalism bent on holy war against the ungodly—of which America was the epitome. ■

Defying terrorism, New York City firefighters raise the flag over the ruins of the collapsed World Trade Center on September 11, 2001.

■ 1985
Soviet leader Mikhail Gorbachev begins reforms in U.S.S.R. and signals willingness to ease Cold War tensions.

■ 1989
Fall of communist regimes in East European Soviet satellite states; Berlin Wall falls; Chinese democratic movement stifled in Beijing.

■ 1991
In Gulf War, U.S.-organized global coalition drives Iraqi forces from Kuwait; Saddam Hussein holds power in Iraq; U.S.S.R. dissolves.

■ 1992
Yugoslavia breaks up amid ethnic conflict; Bill Clinton elected President.

■ 1999
Senate fails to convict President Clinton, impeached for perjury; in brief war, U.S. and NATO forces drive Serb forces from Albanian-inhabited Kosovo.

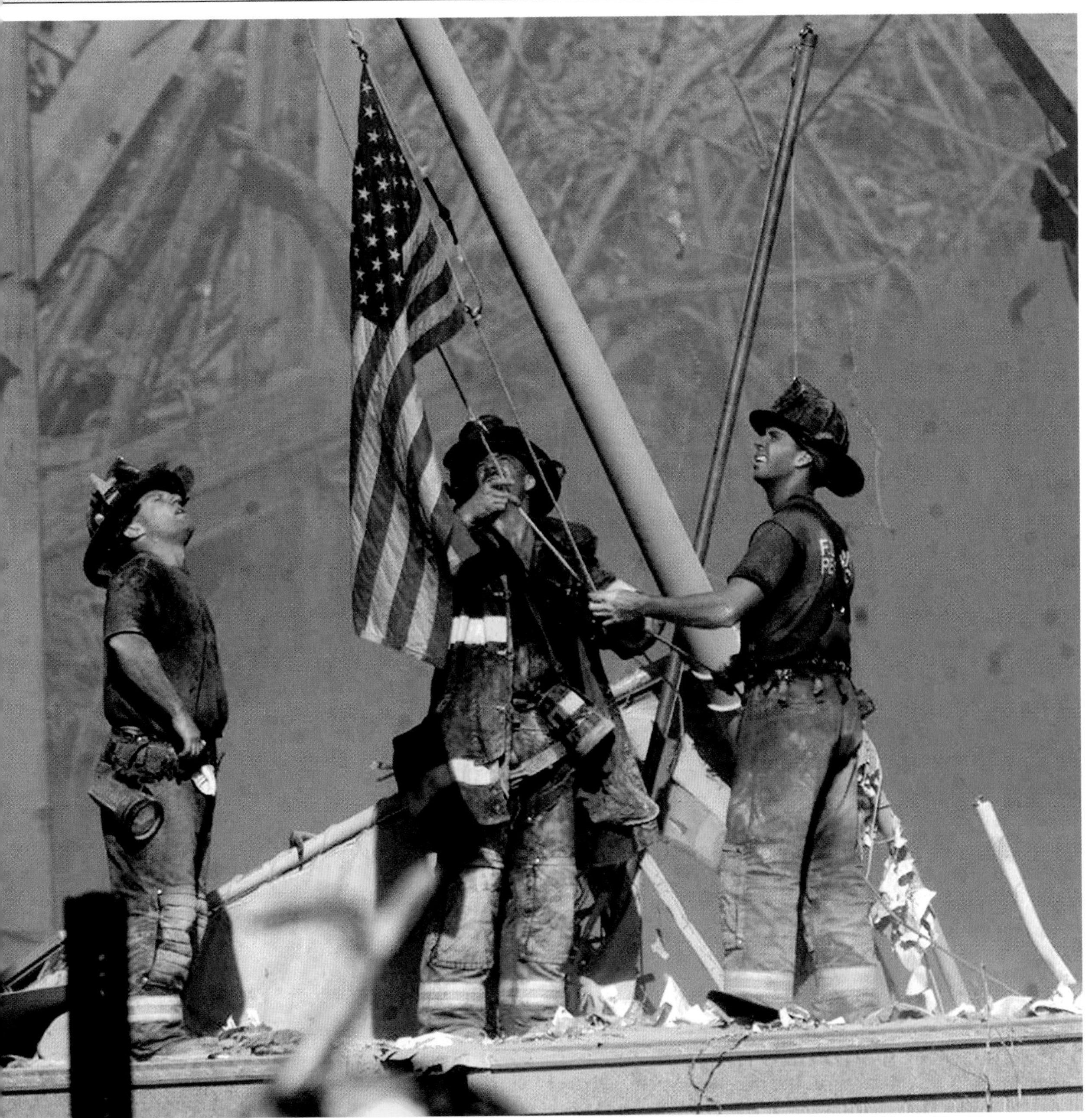

■ 2000	■ 2001	■ 2003	■ 2004	■ 2005
Vladimir Putin elected President of Russia; in disputed election outcome, Supreme Court awards Presidency to George W. Bush.	September 11 terrorist attacks destroy New York's World Trade Center, damage Pentagon; U.S. destroys Taliban in Afghanistan but fails to capture Osama bin Laden.	U.S. invasion topples Saddam Hussein but fails to find WMDs; U.S. forces face growing insurgency; human genome mapped.	George W. Bush reelected President; violent insurgency grows in Iraq.	Iraq elects provisional national assembly and drafts a new constitution amid continuing insurgency.

The Cold War Ends

1981–1991

DURING HIS FIRST TERM, Reagan heated up America's Cold War confrontation with the Soviet Union. He encouraged East Bloc dissidents by citing the Helsinki Accords, a multilateral agreement that President Ford had signed in 1975, which bound communist governments to respect human rights. Reagan also assisted forces abroad fighting communism. The covert aid that the Reagan Administration gave to the anti-Soviet Islamic resistance in Afghanistan eventually produced a Soviet defeat in the late 1980s, but it also trained Muslim militants who would turn against the United States. In Latin America, Reagan opposed a leftist revolutionary movement in El Salvador and a leftist government in Nicaragua by supporting in both countries anticommunist paramilitaries, called Contras in Nicaragua. When Congress cut off funding to the often-murderous Contras, the White House contrived a secret deal by which arms were sold to Iran and the profits passed on to the Contras. The scheme came to light in Reagan's second term. (He denied knowledge of it, calling into question either his truthfulness or his competence.) Reagan enjoyed one unambiguous success in Latin America, in 1983, when the Marines invaded the tiny Caribbean island of Granada to oust a pro-Castro president. These were the last volleys of the East-West Cold War.

The Iranian Revolution, with its passionate anti-U.S. rhetoric and support for Middle Eastern terrorists, had obsessed Americans throughout the 1980s. Just as Reagan was taking his first presidential oath, in January 1981, the Iranians had released the embassy hostages. In 1982 Reagan sent Marines to Lebanon to help stop internal violence. But an Iranian suicide bombing that killed 241 Marines caused him to pull out of Lebanon in 1984. Thereafter Reagan tried to persuade the Iranian Islamic Republic to be more accommodating. But except for entering into the shady Iran-Contra deal, the Iranian mullahs refused to cooperate with the United States.

A Cold War Truce

A major turning point in Soviet-American relations occurred with the advent of a new Kremlin leader in 1985. Mikhail Gorbachev knew the deficiencies of totalitarianism. He intended to win internal support by modernizing the Soviet economy through glasnost (openness) and perestroika (restructuring)—Russian words that quickly entered the global vocabulary. British Prime Minister Margaret Thatcher visited "Gorby" in Moscow and signaled to Washington that "we can do business together."

Reagan kept up the pressure. Visiting West Berlin, he demanded: "Mr. Gorbachev, tear down this Wall!" But he also suggested that the U.S. and the Soviet Union complete long-stalled efforts to end the arms race. Gorbachev was facing demands for more rapid democratization—demands he had hoped not to face, for his intention was to update Marxist-Leninism, not to replace it. But the meltdown of the Chernobyl nuclear power plant in the Soviet Ukraine in 1986 shook the Soviet people's confidence in the regime, in communism, and in him. Reagan visited Moscow, strolled about Red Square with Gorbachev, and promised a friendly relationship. Cold Warrior Reagan became the apostle of East-West concord.

It is too early to evaluate Reagan. He was no "amiable dunce," as detractors sneered, nor was he an intellectual. He relied on instinct, like his Depression-era idol Franklin Roosevelt. (Reagan had once been a "liberal" New Deal Democrat.) His stature, even among academic historians unsympathetic to conservatism, has grown. How much credit he deserves for defeating communism, ending the Cold War, and turning

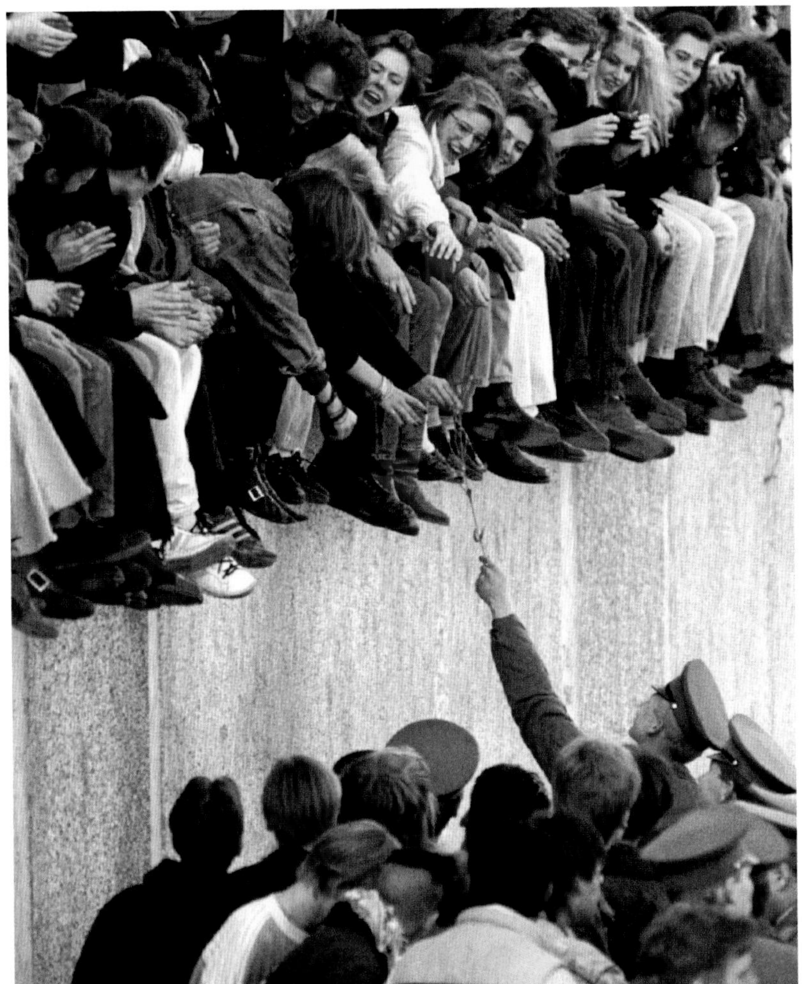

On November 10, 1989, East Germans opened the Berlin Wall. Here, celebrating West Berliners atop the Wall take a flower handed back to them from an East German policeman.

around the American economy still must be answered. There is more consensus among historians that Reagan's political skills and well-crafted persona raised American spirits after the cynical, doleful 1970s, and that he provided every possible opportunity to let the emerging technologies of the 1980s work their transforming magic both on the American and the global economies.

In 1988, United States relations with the Soviet Union steadily warmed as the end of Reagan's presidential term approached. His Vice President, George H.W. Bush, ran against a colorless technocrat, Massachusetts Democratic governor Michael Dukakis. The campaign had little substance. The Republicans "defined" Dukakis as an ineffectual liberal, and Bush got campaign mileage out of reminding voters of the shocking crimes committed by a black rapist furloughed from prison under a Dukakis program. Furthermore,

NOTABLE DATES

■ 1978
Camp David Accords promise Israeli-Egyptian peace.

■ 1984
Reagan reelected President.

■ 1985
Mikhail Gorbachev becomes leader of U.S.S.R., initiates reform policies.

■ 1986
Chernobyl nuclear power plant meltdown in U.S.S.R. shakes confidence in communist system.

■ 1987
Palestian intifada revolt against Israeli rule begins.

■ 1988
George H.W. Bush elected President.

■ 1989
Democracy peacefully restored in Poland, Czechoslovakia, Hungary, and Bulgaria; fall of Berlin Wall; communism forcibly overthrown in Romania; Tiananmen Square demonstrations for liberty in Beijing crushed by Chinese communist authorities.

■ 1990
Iraqi dictator Saddam Hussein occupies Kuwait, opposed by U.S.-organized global coalition.

■ 1991
Gulf War: liberation of Kuwait by U.S.-led coalition; Saddam Hussein survives in power; disintegration of Yugoslavia begins; Moscow coup briefly ousts Gorbachev but soon collapses; U.S.S.R. disintegrates as Soviet republics declare independence.

The Gulf War

By late 1990, 700,000 troops from Bush's global alliance—540,000 of them American—massed in the Saudi Arabian desert opposite Kuwait, and the United Nations imposed economic sanctions on Iraq.

Many Americans opposed moving beyond sanctions and initiating hostilities. Memories of the Vietnam War had not died. Saddam's formidable army possessed chemical and biological weapons. There was talk on the Left that President Bush's real aim was United States seizure of Middle Eastern oil, and indeed Bush did not intend to allow Saddam to control any more of the world's oil supply. After Kuwait, might Saudi Arabia and the oil-rich Persian Gulf states follow?

Retreating from Kuwait, Iraqi forces set hundreds of oil wells ablaze. These firefighters are attempting to extinguish the fires.

Most congressional Democrats claimed that sanctions alone would squeeze Saddam out of Kuwait. But by a close vote Congress authorized Bush to liberate Kuwait by force.

On January 16, 1991, war erupted. American bombers and cruise missiles pounded Iraqi military targets with startling, high-tech precision (unfortunately also accidentally hitting a few civilian sites). All this was shown in vivid detail on global television. After a month of aerial bombardment, coalition armies on February 24, 1991, launched Operation Desert Storm, pouring into Kuwait and into southern Iraq. Within a hundred hours the Iraqi Army was crushed; more American troops died of accidents than of enemy fire. Thinking that Saddam Hussein's regime was about to fall, Bush refused to march on Baghdad for which he had no allied suppport.

American propaganda had incited uprisings by long-oppressed Sunni Kurds and by Shiite Arabs. Both took this opportunity to rebel against Saddam's brutal rule, but President Bush did not back up their rebellion. Other regional powers dreaded the ethnic conflict that would follow Iraq's disintegration. Saddam signed an armistice promising to destroy his weapons of mass destruction—but now he clearly had breathing space for his elite Republican Guard to crush the Shiites and to drive Kurds into a northern strip of Iraq protected by American air power. Saddam Hussein had survived to fight another day. ■

the economy had briskly recovered from the stock market crash of October 1987, skillfully handled by Federal Reserve chairman Alan Greenspan to avert a 1929-like debacle. By Election Day 1988 things were starting to boom again—always a good omen for the incumbent party.

Winning handily, President Bush promised a "kinder, gentler" approach. This tone befitted Bush's patrician background. He was a Connecticut Yankee, son of a Republican senator; in the fifties he moved to Texas to make money in oil. His politics, for a Texas Republican, were moderate, but he drifted to the right. For example, once an advocate of abortion choice, he evolved toward a pro-life position. For the most part, he managed diplomacy adeptly. At home, Bush opposed tax increases. "Read my lips: No new taxes," he promised dramatically. He would later rue that vow.

The Fall of European Communism

Meanwhile the disintegration of communism in the Soviet Union and Eastern Europe was gaining momentum. Mikhail Gorbachev promised not to interfere as East Europeans took their countries' destinies back into their hands. In early 1989, free elections in Poland brought a landslide for noncommunist democrats. Hungary quietly restored democracy. Then East Germany's rulers had to open the Berlin Wall in November 1989 as East Germans demanded unification with West Germany. In Czechoslovakia, dissidents led a peaceful Velvet Revolution. Communism fell quietly in Bulgaria and Albania as well. Only in Romania was there violence: After dictator Nicolae Ceauşescu ordered security forces to crack down, he was deposed and shot. In Yugoslavia, which had never been a Soviet satellite, communism died a little later, in 1991-92, amid bloody civil wars. The communist dictatorship in the U.S.S.R. itself began to fall. The Baltic republics (annexed in 1940) demanded independence, and one—Lithuania—seceded. Then, in August 1991, a coup by Kremlin hardliners temporarily toppled Gorbachev. But when Boris Yeltsin, the president of the Russian Federation (the gigantic republic at the core of the U.S.S.R.) virtually declared Russian independence, the coup collapsed. The U.S.S.R. was dissolved as the year 1991 ended.

Bush watched these momentous events quietly, wisely refraining from gloating or interfering. He offered the new democratic leaders support in building free institutions. He also watched as reformist impulses spread in China, culminating tumultuously in May and early June 1989 in a student demonstration in Beijing's vast Tiananmen Square that featured a statue called "the goddess of liberty," strikingly similar to America's Statue of Liberty. But the cause of Chinese democracy failed. On June 4, troops killed at least a thousand protestors. The building of a vibrant market economy continued, and Western businessmen, eager for a foothold, helped ensure China's continued respectability. President Bush muted his protests, too.

A Still Dangerous World

In the volatile Middle East, the loss of the checks and balances of superpower rivalry allowed regional tensions to escalate into full-scale war. Saddam Hussein, the dictator of Iraq, had been a Soviet client but during the 1980s had also been wooed by the Americans as a counterweight to Iran. In 1990 Saddam ended the decade-long war that he had been fighting with Iran—and he seems to have assumed that the United States would allow him to annex oil-rich Kuwait. Not for the last time, Saddam misjudged. When on August 2, 1990, the Iraqi Army occupied Kuwait, Bush vowed that this aggression "would not stand." And it did not. With great skill, Bush put together a global coalition that included France, often critical of American foreign policy, and several Arab countries, alarmed by Iraqi expansionism. The dying Soviet Union backed America's stand, and on this occasion the United Nations worked as was originally intended.

In a brief war in early 1991, the American-led coalition expelled Iraqi forces from Kuwait. Bush refused to attempt to overthrow Saddam, for which he had no international mandate. He also realized that occupying Iraq, with its complex ethnic and religious conflicts, would destabilize the entire Middle East and impose too heavy a political and economic burden on the United States.

In the spring of 1991 Bush stood at the height of his popularity and global respect. But this high point would not be enough to secure his Presidency. ■

Politics of Culture War

1991–2001

Defense-spending cuts led to a recession in 1991. Preoccupied with international affairs, President Bush seemed insensitive to victims of the recession. Enormous budget deficits precluded the peace dividend (increased social spending) for which Democrats pined. When Bush agreed with Democrats to raise taxes—violating his "read my lips" vow—conservatives howled and his poll numbers plummeted.

Yet for the first time in 60 years the United States seemed unthreatened abroad. The Democrats' 1992 candidate for President, Governor Bill Clinton of Arkansas was an exceptional campaigner, attuned to domestic needs. A man of humble origins and high intelligence, Clinton also had liabilities. Arkansas enemies called him Slick Willie. He had managed to avoid the Vietnam-era draft through political connections, and there were rumors of youthful marijuana use. He also had a reputation for womanizing; an ex-girlfriend's revelations almost derailed his candidacy. Clinton survived when his wife, Hillary Rodham Clinton, came to his defense.

A Centrist President

Clinton bonded with ordinary Americans, declaring that he could "feel your pain." The Republican convention offended middle-of-the-road voters with rhetoric about a culture war. Then eccentric Texas billionaire Ross Perot financed an independent run for the White House. Perot's talk of simple solutions to complex issues and his attacks on the North American Free Trade Agreement (NAFTA) attracted Reagan Democrats. Clinton got only 43 percent of the popular vote, but with Perot siphoning off 19 percent (more than any earlier third-party candidate), he trounced George Bush.

Clinton was a pragmatic centrist. He favored a balanced budget and broadened health insurance, and mostly with Republican votes he got NAFTA ratified. But he made serious initial mistakes. One was to arrange a "don't ask, don't tell" compromise allowing homosexuals to serve in the military if they kept their orientation quiet, infuriating cultural conservatives. Another misstep was to name his wife to head a commission to recommend a national health-care plan; deliberations produced a complicated, expensive scheme. Insurance companies, doctors, and Republicans attacked it. When Congress rejected it, 35 million Americans remained without health insurance.

Clinton proposed to combat the 1991 recession with heavy new

Bill Clinton, looking beleaguered, confronts a press conference in 1997, soon after revelations surfaced of his affair with Monica Lewinsky. He denied improprieties. Later, he admitted that he had lied to his wife, his staff, and the nation.

On March 18, 1999, the Dow Jones industrial average passed the 10,000 mark for the first time. These traders cheer the news. Later the Dow would climb to still dizzier heights—before sagging badly in 2000-2001.

spending. But Republicans blocked the plan. By 1993, an exuberant expansion was under way, led by the high-tech sector and export-oriented industries.

Capitalizing on voters' disenchantment, Republicans swept the1994 midterm elections. They won the Senate and, for the first time since 1953, took the House too. The Republicans' manifesto, the Contract with America, called for ending welfare abuses, reforming education, promoting free trade, imposing term limits on incumbents, lowering taxes, reducing the deficit, and curbing liberal excesses.

Clinton's superb political skills now came into full flower. "The era of big government is over," he proclaimed in his 1995 State of the Union address. Preempting the Contract with America, and over liberal opposition, he agreed with Congress "to end welfare as we know it." Long-run subsidies to single mothers of young children gave way to a three-year lifetime limit on welfare payments in all but special cases, and states were mandated to create "workfare" training and job placement for welfare clients. That caused real pain, though the booming economy made it easier to find low-paying jobs. The middle class credited Clinton, not the GOP.

As the 1996 election approached, Clinton basked in the economic expansion. A tussle between the President and the House of Representatives, which threatened to stop the issuance of federal checks, enabled Clinton to brand the Republicans as extremists, threatening middle-class benefits. For President, the GOP nominated a veteran senator, Kansan Bob Dole, with no program except tax cuts. Perot ran again, getting only half his 1992 vote tally—still, enough to kill Dole's chances. Clinton was reelected with just under a

NOTABLE DATES

■ **1991**
Defense spending cuts initiate recession.

■ **1992**
Bush, at Rio de Janeiro Earth Summit, criticized for failing to back environmental initiatives; Bill Clinton elected President.

■ **1993**
U.S. recession ending; Senate ratifies NAFTA trade pact; Clinton health-care initiative fails; Hubble Space Telescope repaired, begins functioning correctly.

■ **1994**
Republicans sweep midterm elections.

■ **1995**
Oklahoma City terrorist bomb attack destroys federal office building; O.J. Simpson acquitted on murder charges after sensational trial.

■ **1996**
Congress reforms immigration laws in unusccessful attempt to end illegal immigration; Clinton reelected President.

■ **1997**
Kyoto Treaty on global emissions signed but not ratified; Clinton sex scandal erupts.

■ **1998**
Clinton impeached on perjury charges but Senate later refuses to convict.

■ **2000**
Gore-Bush presidential election deadlock over disputed Florida results; Supreme Court awards victory to George W. Bush.

■ **2001**
No Child Left Behind education reform law enacted; September 11 terrorist attacks.

popular-vote majority. The Republicans held Congress.

As so often happens with reelected Presidents, Clinton's second term was troubled. Corruption charges involving the Clintons and Arkansas moneymen, called the Whitewater affair, generated much noise, a few convictions, and no clear determination of presidential malfeasance (or innocence). But Whitewater was overshadowed by a presidential sex scandal. An Arkansas woman sued Clinton for sexual harassment while he was governor, and ultimately he paid her $850,000 to settle out of court. Seeking evidence of presidential philandering, her lawyers meanwhile discovered Monica Lewinsky, a White House intern who had caught Clinton's roving eye. The two had a torrid affair in 1995-96. Clinton initially denied any dalliance with "that woman," testifying to that effect before a grand jury, and Mrs. Clinton blamed everything on a "gigantic right-wing conspiracy." Caught when Lewinsky produced a dress stained with the President's semen, Clinton dolefully admitted the truth. The dour, puritanical special prosecutor appointed by the Republican Congress, Kenneth Starr, laid out the lurid details. House Republicans impeached Clinton for perjury.

The scandal sickened the country. It was the first time a sitting President had been plausibly accused of sexual misconduct—and presidential perjury was serious. Yet to seek a President's removal from office on such grounds also seemed highly questionable—or so a majority of Americans told pollsters. In the summer of 1999 the Senate held the second presidential impeachment trial in history. Less than the required two-thirds of the senators thought the charges warranted removing the President. Clinton was acquitted.

Public Opinion Polls on Values Issues

Percentage by Year

Should gun-control laws be

	1993	2004
More strict?	70	54
Kept as now?	24	34
Less strict?	4	11

Would you say that Darwin's theory of evolution is

	2004
Supported by evidence?	35
Not supported by evidence?	35
Don't know enough to say	29

Would you describe yourself as "born again" or evangelical?

	2005
Yes	42
No	53

Do you think that abortion should be (yearly averages)

	1975	2005
Legal under all circumstances?	21	23
Legal under certain circumstances?	54	53
Illegal under all circumstances?	22	22
No opinion	3	2

Should homosexual relations between consenting adults

	1977	2005
Be legal?	43	52
Not be legal?	43	42
No opinion	14	5

In which do you have "a great deal" or "quite a lot" of confidence?

	1993	2005
The military	68	74
The police	52	63
The church	53	53
Banks	37	49
The Presidency	45	44
Medical system	34	42
Supreme Court	44	41
Public schools	39	37
TV news	46	28
Newspapers	31	28
U.S. Congress	18	22

The Formidable Mrs. Clinton

Born in 1947, Hillary Rodham was the classic overachieving middle-class daughter. She earned every Girl Scout merit badge, graduated at the top of her high school and college classes (Wellesley, 1969), earned a Yale law degree, joined the House staff for Nixon's impeachment, and advocated children's legal rights—all before moving to the University of Arkansas to teach and, in 1975, marrying her Yale classmate, Bill Clinton.

When her husband was elected governor in 1978, she had not adopted his surname—a shocking thing to many Arkansas voters, which contributed to his defeat in 1980. (In 1982, when he ran again, she was Hillary Rodham Clinton.) Meanwhile she had become both a partner in Little Rock's premier law firm and the mother of the couple's only child, Chelsea.

During the 1992 presidential campaign, in an interview on prime-time TV, Hillary said, "I suppose I could have stayed home and baked cookies . . . but what I decided to do is fulfill my profession." Never were words so polarizing ever uttered by a presidential candidate's spouse. Conservatives leaped on this remark to pillory her as a liberal feminist, contemptuous of at-home women. That would forever be her image on the Right; to liberals and career women, such hostility made her a hero.

She faced her first political crisis when, in Bill's 1992 run for President, an ex-girlfriend surfaced. On TV, Hillary stood by him, saving his candidacy. She had to do it again when the Monica Lewinsky scandal broke, to her deep inward grief. Somehow, though, the marriage survived.

Eleanor Roosevelt was her role model, and as with FDR's First Lady, her activism made her a symbol, equally admired and hated. In 2000, she would become the first presidential spouse to win political office, as senator from New York, and after the Democrats failed to regain the White House in 2004, she instantly headed everyone's list of potential 2008 contenders.

Values Politics

In the late 20th century, the intensity of the Lewinsky scandal reflected the importance that so many Americans placed on religiously tinged values. Since the 1960s, politics had stirred passions about many issues that earlier generations had regarded as outside the purview of government. Why?

There was, above all, the legacy of the civil-rights struggle. African Americans believed that killing Jim Crow had been a fragile victory and affirmative action was still needed; many whites opposed "reverse discrimination" and thought black leaders harped too much on white guilt. With civil rights never ceasing to be an area of contention in national politics, there was ample ground for hypocrisy and double-talk on all sides.

O.J. Simpson

ORENTHAL JAMES SIMPSON HAD BEEN ONE OF THE GREATEST running backs in football history. Retiring in 1979, he remained a celebrity with his commercials, sports commentary, and film and TV roles. Simpson and his white wife, Nicole Brown, divorced in 1992 after many complaints of spousal abuse. On June 12, 1994, her body and that of a male acquaintance were discovered in Los Angeles, murdered with a knife. Simpson was charged with the murders on June 17.

His 133-day televised trial in 1995, in which Johnnie Cochran, one of America's most flamboyant defense lawyers, defended him, riveted the world. Despite gloves found at the crime scene soaked in blood matching his DNA, he was acquitted. Cochran raised doubts about the validity of DNA testing and also argued that Simpson had been framed with evidence planted by a "racist cop." Indeed, there were signs of sloppy police work, and the Los Angeles Police Department had a history of brutality against blacks. Sentiment ran high in Simpson's favor in black communities nationwide; whites thought him guilty. The largely black jury's verdict may have been affected by memories of race riots accompanying the trial of Los Angeles police videotaped beating a black suspect named Rodney King. At a subsequent civil trial before a mostly white jury, Simpson was found guilty of his wife's "wrongful death."

Would Simpson have been acquitted had he been a poor man without a famous lawyer? Were white and black ideas of justice so racially tainted that objectivity was not possible? Such were Americans' questions after the trial, and the years have not erased their memories. ■

O. J. Simpson, on the right, confers with his lawyer Johnnie Cochran during his Los Angeles murder trial. Simpson's trial and acquittal polarized the nation.

Second, so-called family values had been politicized: sexual behavior and sexual identity, abortion and reproductive rights, and end-of-life decisions. And closely linked to family values was a third sphere of bitter contention: the nation's troubled system of public education. Here, too, what had once been the domain of state and local governments and parents' private decisions now became matters of federal politics. Presidents, Congress, and the federal courts all had to make pronouncements and policy with regard to public versus private (including religious) schooling, school prayer and Bible reading, curricular content (such as teaching evolution), and multiculturalism—the effort to emphasize the diversity and dark sides of the American experience rather than presenting American history as a triumph of traditional values. Conservatives saw the public schools as the bastion of incompetent teachers and as dens of secularism, multiculturalism, disorder, and Darwinism; liberals defended public schooling as the great leveler of American society.

Fourth, environmentalism presented another host of contentious issues: Was Earth the realm of humans to exploit for economic opportunity or a fragile inheritance to be preserved?

A fifth area of contention was debate over private gun rights, rooted in the Second Amendment's guarantee of the right "to keep and bear arms." Did this empower citizens to collect arsenals of unregistered assault weapons and machine guns? Yes, said conservatives and libertarians, invoking images of the state impounding hunters' shotguns; no, replied liberals, pointing to a rash of public-school massacres and extremist militia movements.

And finally, there was political correctness, the alleged domination in academia by tenured faculty, educated in graduate schools since the 1960s and sharing left-wing interpretations of history, literature, and the social sciences. College speech codes, intended to discourage insensitivity about sexual identity, gender, and race, *did* have a chilling effect on the exchange of ideas, and very few conservatives taught in university liberal-arts departments. The right denounced political correctness; the left denied its existence or retorted that conservatism reflected deficient intelligence.

Sandra Day O'Connor, the first woman to serve on the Supereme Court, testifies in 1981 during pre-confirmation hearings. By her retirement in 2005, she had earned great respect as a centrist and pragmatist on a divided Court.

Fitting this cultural contention into end-of-the-centuryAmerican life is puzzling because the United States remains a peaceful society. Overwhelmingly, Americans reject extremes. Evangelicals, a loosely defined category of religious believers variously estimated at between 20 and 40 percent of the population, are not politically monolithic; they include people of all races and political views ranging from deeply conservative to progressive to apolitical. Lynching mobs, race riots, and McCarthyism are gone; the militia movement is fading fast. Bizarre violence by environmentalist extremists, right-wing attacks on abortion clinics, and homophobic beatings are aberrations that practically no Americans condone.

The impeachment of Bill Clinton was political theater, fought over symbols. The Clintons—the first baby boomers to win the White House—evoked passionate conservative hatred, for both of them flouted what traditionalists considered core values and symbolized sixties attitudes. These included Bill's sexual behavior, his youthful drug dabbling, and his draft dodging; they also included Hillary's career as an assertive professional woman. The Clintons also attracted deep admiration—from blacks, for whom Clinton was among the most sympathetic and understanding white men of power they had ever encountered; from journalists,who admired the couple's charisma; and from liberals and intellectuals, who saw both Clintons as hounded by the same traditionalists who had been Nixon's Silent Majority of 1968.

The Election of 2000

The millennial election of 2000 continued this political theater, and it showed how the American electorate was divided almost 50-50 between Democrats and Republicans, even though most voters were centrists. The nation was at peace, and the biggest issue was mounting budget *surpluses*—should they be spent, or used to cut taxes? Serious economic and foreign policy issues that had roiled Americans since 1929 appeared to have vanished. Clinton left a booming economy, a surging stock market, low unemployment, and a shrinking national debt.

Clinton's Vice President, Al Gore, a moderate liberal with strong environmentalist convictions, easily won the 2000 Democratic nomination. On the Republican side there was a bitter contest between President Bush's son, Governor George W. Bush of Texas, and a maverick Arizona senator, John McCain. A Vietnam veteran who survived torture as a POW, McCain won admiration across the spectrum for his independence, problem-solving bent, and tell-it-like-it-is manner. But McCain's criticism of conservative evangelicals enabled Bush to rally the Religious Right and win the nomination.

The election was one of the closest contests in American history. Gore won a 150,000-vote majority of the popular vote (out of 104 million cast), but the Electoral College outcome hinged on a few hundred votes in Florida. After weeks of agonizing recounts, the Supreme Court intervened to award the Presidency to George W. Bush.

Oklahoma City Bombing

THOUSANDS OF CITIZENS ROUTINELY VISITED THE ALFRED P. Murrah Building in Oklahoma City. At 9:02 a.m. on April 19, 1995, a Ryder truck was parked in front—loaded with 5,000 pounds of ammonium nitrate, a common agricultural fertilizer—where it exploded, taking 168 lives.

Most Americans' immediate reaction was to assume Arab terrorists were responsible. Instead, a Gulf War veteran, Timothy McVeigh, stopped an hour after the explosion for driving without a license plate, was charged with the crime, up to then the most deadly act of terrorism on U.S. soil.

The explanation emerged at McVeigh's trial, which ended in his conviction and 2001 execution. Accomplice Terry Nichols drew a life sentence; another accomplice received a 12-year sentence. All were participants in the militia movement, an assortment of gun-rights enthusiasts and white supremacists with grudges against the federal government. McVeigh's chief grievance was the Ruby Ridge shootout in Idaho in 1993—he bombed the Murrah Building to mark its second anniversary—in which federal agents attempting to arrest the possessor of a weapons cache instead killed him and his son. Discredited, organized militias faded away in the late 1990s, although their participants and their grievances have by no means vanished. ■

A fireman attempted to save this young child from the Oklahoma City bomb blast. The child later died.

Gay Marriage

On February 4, 2004, the Massachusetts Supreme Judicial Court ruled 4-3 that the commonwealth's legislature had six months to enact a law giving same-sex couples the right to marry. Instantly, gay marriage became a political issue—particularly because the leading candidate for the Democratic presidential nomination, John Kerry, was from Massachsetts. He declared that gay marriage was going too far. President Bush quickly promised to support a constitutional amendment against it, though he (like Kerry) supported civil unions. Antigay marriage sentiment was credited, however, with mobilizing conservative Christians to vote against Kerry, perhaps costing him the election.

This same-sex couple share a wedding cake at a mock ceremony in April 2004 in Seattle, sponsored by vendors of wedding supplies.

Meanwhile, during the spring of 2004, gay marriages went ahead in a number of locales. The mayor of San Francisco issued about four thousand marriage licenses to same-sex couples between February 12 and March 11, before being stopped by the state's supreme court. (All were subsequently declared invalid.) New Jersey, Maine, Connecticut, and the District of Columbia, as well as California, subsequently adopted civil-union laws. But thirteen states constitutionally limited marriage to a man and a woman. In Massachusetts, where the court order had obliged the legislature to legalize gay marriage, about six thousand same-sex couples married by May 2005, and a majority of residents polled said that they supported legalization.

The issue remains deeply divisive among Americans. In May 2005, 45 percent favored an antigay marriage amendment to the federal Constitution; 47 percent opposed. Of those who said they attended church weekly, 80 percent opposed. Most Protestant churches were deeply split, and the Catholic Church and evangelicals condemned it.

America took a more conservative stance than other Western countries: By 2005, gay marriage had been legalized in Canada, Spain, Belgium, and the Netherlands, and most other European Union member states either provided for civil unions or were considering such legislation. ■

The closeness of the election demonstrated how issues could be framed to mobilize equally strong turnouts. Both parties represented special interests: The Democrats' largest contributors were public-employee unions, teachers' unions, and trial lawyers; big business bankrolled the Republicans and conservative evangelicals supplied foot soldiers. Both sides used e-mail and websites to extract millions of dollars from ideological supporters. Gerrymandering ensured that few House seats changed hands, and efforts to reform political fundraising—an issue that McCain pursued—made little difference in elections. Entrenched in safe seats, most House members saw no reason to compete for the center. Despite the centrist attitudes of most voters, political polarities aggravated cultural warfare.

An Ideological President

Half the electorate felt enraged at Bush's "illegitimate" triumph, but despite his razor-thin victory he concentrated on conservative goals.

His opponents held him in contempt for his troubles with English syntax, his swaggering gait, and his wooing of the Religious Right. Graduating in the late sixties from Yale, Bush followed a self-admitted aimless path. Connections got him a relatively safe berth in the Air National Guard during the Vietnam War. He developed a drinking problem. But in his late thirties, he had a conversion, swore off alcohol, and entered politics. In 1994 he was elected governor of Texas and reelected by a wide margin in 1998. His Republicanism was harder-edged than his father's, anchoring "Dubya" on the conservative side of the great post-1963 cultural divide. He was as despised on the left as Clinton had been detested on the right.

There was a crucial difference between Bush and Clinton. Clinton was a centrist, praised or condemned by partisans on both sides of the culture wars. Bush, never a consensus builder, planted his standard on the right. "I don't do nuance," he boasted.

Bush and the Republican Congress enacted the long-term conservative objective of a massive tax cut, favoring high-income taxpayers and meant to shrink the scope of government. Only in the No Child Left Behind (NCLB) Act of his first year did Bush come close to governing from the center. There was a consensus that something should be done about raising American children's low achievement scores. NCLB required schools to improve test scores or lose funding. Archliberal Senator Edward Kennedy helped pass NCLB. As a result, public schools began teaching for the test, with uncertain consequences. Soon, complaints multiplied that President Bush was not funding educational reform enough to permit it to succeed. ■

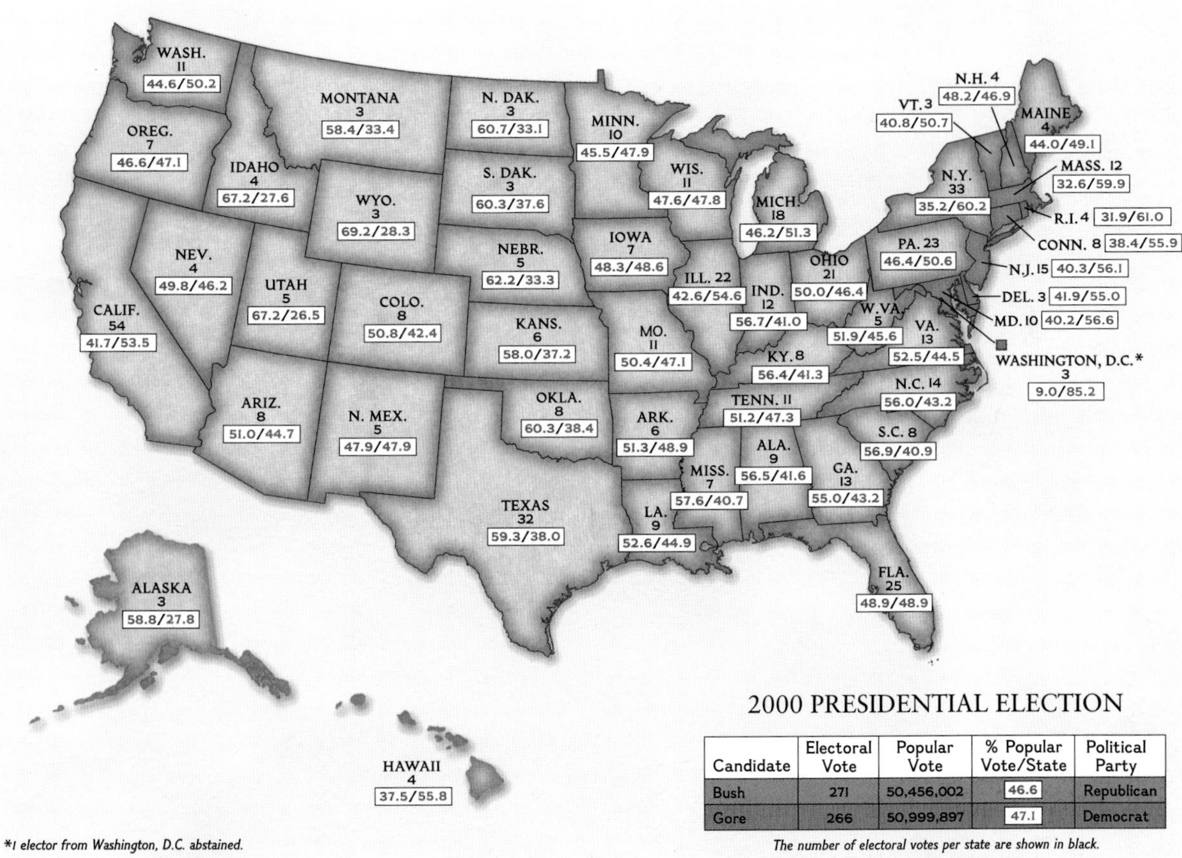

Candidate	Electoral Vote	Popular Vote	% Popular Vote/State	Political Party
Bush	271	50,456,002	46.6	Republican
Gore	266	50,999,897	47.1	Democrat

In the sharply polarizing presidential elections of 2000 and 2004, journalists and then the general public came to distinguish the social conservative "red" states that voted Republican from the more liberal "blue" states in the Democratic column.

Globalization

Since 1945

THE WORD "GLOBALIZATION" originated in the 1990s, denoting the spread across borders of modern industrial and agricultural production, trade, finance, technology, services, ideas, culture—along with workers, jobs, and environmental consequences.

For Americans, globalization typically meant manufacturing auto parts in Mexico or Brazil, with the final assembly of the car in Detroit, or building German and Japanese cars in Tennessee or South Carolina. It meant the merger of one of America's Big Three automakers with a giant German company to form Daimler-Chrysler in 1998. It meant the eclipse of American textile manufacturing and the importation of inexpensive clothing from huge Chinese factories. It also meant outsourcing data processing, programming, and even telemarketing jobs to India.

Globalization began during World War II, when the Roosevelt Administration insisted that postwar reconstruction include liberalized international trade, an international currency designed to avert depression, and the freest possible movement of American capital worldwide. The war's end saw creation of the International Monetary Fund (IMF), the World Bank, and the General Agreement on Trade and Tariffs (GATT)—in 1994 renamed the World Trade

This advertisement features the trademark white cord of Apple's iPod, one of the hottest consumer items of contemporary global trade.

Organization, or WTO. Facilitated by these institutions, in the 1950s corporations went multinational, investing around the world and locating operations wherever economic conditions best suited.

The Rise of the Computer

The modern electronic computer was another prerequisite for globalization, permitting immense increases in the speed, volume, and distance with which information is processed and projected.

Most Americans' first glimpse of computing came on election night 1952, when a TV network predicted Ike's landslide on "an electronic brain." World War II had required lightning calculations to develop weaponry and break codes. In Britain, Alan Turing's decoding center in 1943 constructed Colossus, a computer with 1,500 vacuum tubes. American weapons developers by 1946 completed ENIAC, a high-speed, 18,000-tube digital computer measuring 8 feet by 46 feet and controlled with wires plugging into outlets.

John von Neumann, a mathematical genius born in Hungary, suggested adding to ENIAC a data-storage capacity using binary numbers. The result was the first commercial computer, Mark 1; eight were sold. UNIVAC-1, built in 1951 for the Census Bureau and corporations, was TV's election-predicting "electronic brain."

In 1947 the transistor was invented, an innovation of enormous import. Transistors slowly replaced vacuum tubes—in the mid-1950s in radios and, about 1960, in computers. This marked computing's second generation. Meanwhile IBM used its mastery of punch cards (invented for adding machines) to develop the technology of data input. Laypeople knew of computers through IBM cards full of mysterious holes. Computing evoked much fear of control by invisible Big Government or Big Business, displacing human labor and killing the human spirit.

In the early 1960s, huge vacuum-tube machines yielded to compact, cheaper, and faster transistorized digital computers. They proliferated in large institutions and required much training to operate; many people feared them as dehumanizing. Computer science also aroused interest in artificial intelligence. The 1969 film *2001: A Space Odyssey*, whose anti-hero was a supercomputer named HAL, made that clear.

Third-generation computers, introduced around 1970, implanted circuits on tiny silicon chips; in the fourth-generation machines of the 1980s, miniaturization and integration increased. Key innovations included Intel Corporation's first microprocessor chip in 1974 and random-access memory (RAM) chips. To create operating systems, in the mid-1970s Harvard dropout Bill Gates launched Microsoft Corporation, which made him one of the world's richest men. In a garage, Steve Jobs and Steve Wozniak created the Apple, a cheap personal computer for consumers that substituted a mouse and menus for the IBM machine's complicated codes.

These technologies and, about 1980, the advent of the personal computer radically transformed

NOTABLE DATES

■ 1945
1945 International Monetary Fund, World Bank, and General Agreement on Trade and Tariffs create framework of an open postwar global economy.

■ 1946
1946 ENIAC computer completed.

■ 1947
Transistor invented.

■ 1953
Crick and Watson discover the double-helix structure of DNA.

■ 1970
"Third generation" computers feature silicon-chip circuitry.

■ 1974
Intel Corporation introduces first microprocessor and RAM chips.

■ 1993
Congress ratifies NAFTA free-trade agreement with Canada and Mexico.

■ 1996
Congress attempts but fails to reform U.S. immigration law.

■ 1997
Kyoto Treaty for environmental protection signed but not ratified.

■ 2003
Completion of project to map the human genome.

■ 2005
Congress ratifies CAFTA free-trade agreement with Guatemala, El Salvador, Honduras, Nicaragua, Costa Rica, and the Dominican Republic.

work and entrepreneurship. Their prices dropping steadily, the new computers vastly increased the speed with which research could be conducted and disseminated. Public fears of the computer as Big Brother's sinister tool gave way to myriad opportunities for employment, investment, and fun. Computers diffused rather than hoarded information. By the late 1980s e-mail, and by the early 1990s the Internet (which had been created by the Pentagon in the 1960s to connect bases, defense industries, and command-and-control centers), became available to businesses and the public, revolutionizing communications more radically than the telegraph and the telephone had done in the 19th century. By 1995, the first successful e-commerce venture emerged, amazon.com.

The Outreach of Globalization

Globalization demanded reducing or eliminating tariffs and other impediments to trade, as well as international standards of intellectual property rights to prevent pirating. It also required computer-driven information technology, enabling corporations to move data and funds across borders and facilitating "just in time" delivery systems to slash inventory costs.

By 2000, the penetration of multinational corporations was transforming parts of the Third World and ex-communist countries by substituting capitalist markets for central planning. Among the most dramatic instances were the absorption of former Soviet satellites into the European Union and the emergence of China as a global economic

Biomedicine

THE REVOLUTION IN BIOLOGY, BEGUN IN 1953 WITH THE discovery of DNA's molecular structure, was gathering momentum by the early 1960s. That momentum made the late 20th century the most astonishing in the history of the life sciences.

One path of this revolution led to the biochemistry of proteins and nucleic acids. After 1960, knowledge of protein structure immensely broadened the ability of physicians to diagnose and of pharmaceutical researchers to design drugs. Although curing cancer remained elusive, better understanding emerged of cancer's causes in failures of the human immune system, and hopes rose that many cancers could be controlled as chronic rather than fatal diseases. The revolution's second path led to investigation of the genetic code and of genes' chemical structure. By 1978, genetic engineering yielded the first successful human in vitro fertilization, while later studies in recombinant DNA broadened avenues for diagnosis and treatment and made possible identification of hereditary clues to life-threatening conditions. In 2003, half a century after Crick and Watson's discovery, sequencing the human genome capped one biological revolution and initiated another.

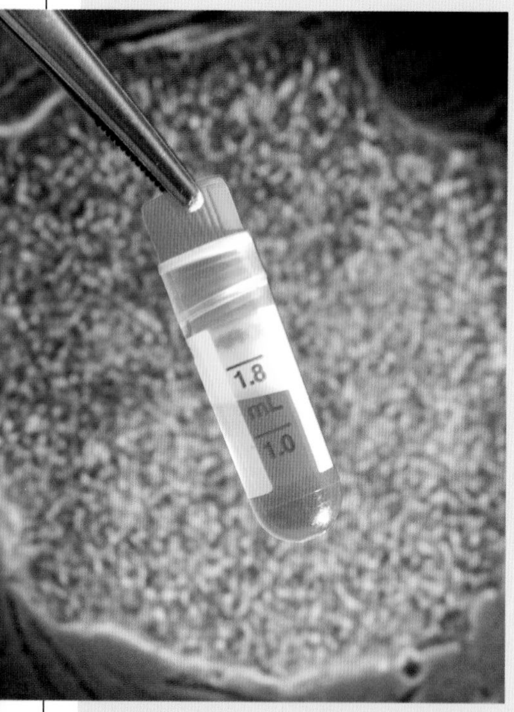

In 2004 the first stem-cell bank opened in London, heralded by this photo of an ampoule and an enlarged image of a human stem cell.

Such work was expensive, requiring federal, foundation, and drug-company funding—and stirred political controversy and religious objections. On right-to-life grounds, the Bush Administration limited research on stem cells from human embryos, not used for in vitro fertilization. Genetic testing raised ethical issues; so did fears of attempts to clone humans. Medical success in extending life forced decisions about rationing and terminating care. All this was stressful in a society in which almost half the population dismissed Darwinism as "just a theory." ■

player. Benefits and the costs were most visible to Americans in northern Mexico's booming maquiladora enterprises, manufacturing parts and goods for the U.S. market. Providing good jobs by Mexican standards, they often cut corners with environmental and safety standards.

Asia provided the most dramatic instances of globalization. In the 1950s and 1960s, Asian countries except Japan were desperately poor. But far from the rest of Asia falling to communism after the toppling of the South Vietnamese "domino" in 1975, the so-called Asian tigers surged. South Korea, Taiwan, Malaysia, Singapore, and Thailand reached sustained growth first. By the late 1980s came the Philippines and Indonesia. China itself took the capitalist road after Mao Tse-tung's death in 1976 and the accession of Communist Party leader Deng Xiaoping. Under Deng, China restored many elements of a market economy and welcomed foreign investment. All these countries followed a strategy similar to Japan's early in the century and after World War II: They used their low-cost but well-educated workforces to build export industries in consumer goods and high-tech components. As they began achieving economic modernization, most gradually shed dictatorships. By the 1990s, only Cambodia, totalitarian Myanmar, and communist North Korea and Laos remained stagnant. Even communist Vietnam introduced a market economy and sought American investment. India, too, largely abandoned central planning.

American graduate schools drew tens of thousands of Asian and other foreign students, particularly in engineering and science. Many remained in the U.S. to teach, do research, and launch high-tech companies. By century's end, America faced stiff competition from rival Asian firms. This was felt in stem-cell research, where concerns of the Bush Administration restricted researchers' access to stem cell lines.

Milestones in Globalization

1992 — European Union (EU) replaces European Community

1994-2003 — Trade among U.S., Canada, and Mexico increases from $302 billion to $652 billion.

1994 — NAFTA goes into effect.

2005 — EU has 25 members; EU and U.S. account for 20 percent of mutual bilateral trade.

— U. S. ratifies CAFTA trade pact

— Asian Pacific Economic Conference (formed 1989 with 12 members) has 21 members and accounts for 60 percent of global trade.

— Foreign investment in U.S. business and real estate: $1.4 trillion; U.S. investment abroad: $2.1 trillion.

Globalization's Challenge to America

One major issue in the 2004 presidential election was outsourcing jobs to countries like India, where skilled, English-speaking technicians could be hired at a fraction of U.S. pay.

Blue-collar Americans had felt the strains of globalization since the 1980s. It was becoming less efficient for the high-wage U.S. economy to maintain "smokestack" industries like steel and automobile manufacturing; these were cheaper to operate where wages were low, unions weak, and environmental regulations loose. Under Reagan, manufacturing jobs declined; most job growth was in high technology and services (from burger flippers to stockbrokers). Still, despite erosion of manufacturing jobs during the eighties, Reagan won a significant part of the white-male blue-collar vote, often over such cultural issues as patriotism, religious values, and dislike of affirmative action; pundits used "Reagan Democrat" to describe this pattern. George H.W. Bush kept enough Reagan Democrat votes to win in 1988, an election laden with cultural baggage.

But Bush's negotiation of the North American Free Trade Association (NAFTA), a free-trade pact with Canada and Mexico, aroused strong blue-collar opposition. Globalization became a divisive issue. Many workers and businesses stood to gain from NAFTA, whose advocates also ranged from corporate bosses to economics professors; and many consumers also realized that free trade often meant lower prices on imported goods. But visions of companies exporting manufacturing jobs to Mexico frightened American workers. Unions, most liberals, and environmentalists fought NAFTA. In 1992, anti-NAFTA fears gave traction to Ross Perot's independent candidacy, defeating George H.W. Bush. In winning, Bill Clinton took the position of promising environmental and wage protections but otherwise supporting trade liberalization, and in his first term gained Senate ratification of NAFTA.

NAFTA has neither worked miracles nor wreaked havoc. Twenty-two million jobs were created in the U.S. during the Clinton Administration, most generated by the high-tech-based New Economy that boomed until 2000. But NAFTA too was more a job creator than a job destroyer. Even with barriers down, jobs never automatically migrated to low-wage countries; workers' skills, efficiency, and literacy, as well as legal and political environments and infrastructure, all affected corporate decisions about relocating jobs. Yet these factors underscored the need for American workers to maintain a competitive advantage; further, the U.S. government did not always adequately compensate or retrain workers who lost jobs or suffered pay reductions because of globalization. And anemic American net job growth since 2001 (almost entirely in services) may yet challenge optimism about globalization.

In tandem with globalization, a wave of immigration inundated the U.S. By 2005, about 34 million immigrants lived in the U.S., perhaps one-third of them illegal. About one-third lacked health insurance—and about 30 percent were Mexican-born, few with a high school education or advanced skills.

In 1996 Congress amended immigration laws but did not achieve the desired stabilization. Problems remained of controlling U.S. borders and preventing both illegal immigration and the exploitation of illegals by employers. An argument for NAFTA was that raising wages and living standards in Mexico would reduce immigration to the U.S., but that goal had to be long-range. George W. Bush's attempt to create a guest-worker program—favored by business and agribusiness—drew fire from both liberals and cultural conservatives. As they gained citizenship, Hispanics—a label covering disparate ethnicities and races—increased their political clout and were courted by both parties. They surpassed blacks as the country's largest minority, produced half of the U.S. population growth in 2000-2005, and in 2005 numbered more than 41 million of the country's estimated 293 million.

In July 2003, 12 Cubans attempted to flee in a makeshift boat fashioned from a 1951 Chevrolet pickup. They got within 40 miles of the U.S. before the Coast Guard picked them up and returned them to Cuba.

Questioning Globalization

By 2000, passionate anti-globalization became a cause for young idealists and old leftists, occasioning protest when leaders of the IMF and the World Bank convened in public. Liberals abandoned their historical commitment to free trade—a core principle for Wilson, FDR, and Kennedy—and criticized globalization, citing corporate power, worker protection, and environmental issues.

The deepest concerns about globalization focused on the environment. Worries in the 1970s about resource depletion receded as technology facilitated the substitution of critical materials. Conservation and pollution control, especially when linked to economic incentives, showed impressive results. But in the 1990s, more serious problems were disclosed: threats to biodiversity, and global warming. These issues had embarrassed President George H.W. Bush at a 107-nation

The Hubble Space Telescope

In 1977, Congress authorized NASA to build an orbiting telescope, capable of making observations beyond the distortions created by Earth's atmosphere. The result was a schoolbus-size instrument that the crew of the shuttle *Discovery* placed in orbit in 1990. Immediately, it was noticed that the telescope's main mirror had been incorrectly ground, causing fuzzy images, and that its stabilizing gyroscopes were malfunctioning. These defects were corrected with instruments installed by the crew of the shuttle *Endeavor* in December 1993, and thereafter the telescope worked flawlessly. Appropriately, it was named in honor of Edwin Hubble, the great American astronomer whose work in the 1920s laid the foundations of present-day knowledge of the expanding universe and the Big Bang.

Among the spectacular images captured by the Hubble were these sharp photographs of the Whirlpool Galaxy (left) and the Eagle Nebula (right).

Capturing images with ten times the resolution of the largest ground-based astronomical cameras, the Hubble has recorded some 700,000 breathtakingly spectacular images. It has probed beyond 10 billion light-years from Earth, observing light emitted by the earliest stars, quasars, and galaxies, thus enabling cosmologists to reach consensus as to the universe's 13-billion-year-old age. It has confirmed the reality and behavior of black holes, photographed planets orbiting nearby stars, and produced data that may resolve questions regarding mysterious dark matter, believed to constitute the bulk of the known cosmic mass. Much tested knowledge about the origin, size, composition, and fate of the universe would still be untested hypothesizing without the Hubble.

Larger space telescopes are now being built, but it will be years before they are orbited. Meanwhile the Hubble's future is cloudy. It will probably cease functioning before the decade ends, yet since the disintegration of the *Columbia* in 2003, NASA has been unable to safely send a crew to do the work. Whether the job can feasibly be done by robotics—given current budgets—is uncertain. ■

Earth Summit in Rio de Janeiro in 1992; he alone among world leaders insisted that economic growth take priority over environmental concerns. For a while, doubts lingered over the validity of scientists' warnings that emissions of atmospheric contaminants—particularly those derived from burning fossil fuels—were driving up temperatures dangerously; doomsday scenarios foretold melting polar ice caps and disrupted ocean currents. The drive of developing countries, led by China and India, to reap the benefits of industrialization clearly clashed with a global imperative to rein in growth and avert global warming. In 1997, the Kyoto Treaty was negotiated, by which industrialized countries pledged to cut dangerous carbon emissions. Yet implementing it would have serious negative effects on American economic growth and living standards. The Senate rejected it, 95-0.

No critics of the Kyoto Treaty were more adamant than George W. Bush. The Toxic Texan, many called him. His refusal to take global warming seriously took on darker overtones in 2005 with revelations that policy was influenced by oil company representatives' editing of government scientific reports on the issue. ■

Perils of the New Millennium

SINCE 2001

GEORGE W. BUSH'S APPROVAL rating approached 90 percent as he rallied the nation for a War on Terror after the 9/11 attack (page 321). The Patriot Act broadened the government's authority to pursue terrorists, trading a bit of liberty for a bit more security. Democrats prodded Bush to unify existing agencies within a Department of Homeland Security.

Going to War

The Islamic terrorist group Al Qaeda, based in Afghanistan, claimed responsibility for the attack. Bush won U.N. and congressional authorization to invade Afghanistan should it refuse to surrender Al Qaeda's leaders, including Osama bin Laden. The high-tech assault on primitive Afghanistan began on October 7, 2001. Resistance crumbled, but tribal warriors failed to capture Osama bin Laden. By 2004 American-brokered negotiations produced a president and national assembly, but security was tenuous.

Immediately after 9/11, Vice President Dick Cheney and Defense Secretary Donald Rumsfeld began arguing that Iraq was complicit in Al Qaeda's attacks. Saddam Hussein's actions kindled suspicions that he was hiding weapons of mass destruction (WMDs). Bush branded Iraq, Iran, and North Korea an "axis of evil."

Intelligence data seemingly confirmed worst-case scenarios. The U.N. Security Council on November 8, 2002, ordered Iraq to admit arms inspectors. But they found no sign of the WMDs that Saddam had possessed in the mid-1990s. Still, CIA chief George Tenet assured Bush and skeptical Secretary of State Colin Powell that it was a "slam dunk" that Saddam had WMDs. In February 2003, Powell presented the Administration's case on Iraqi WMDs to the Security Council. When Russia, China, France, and Germany demanded further inspections, Bush assembled a "coalition of the willing"—principally Britain, Italy, Spain, Australia, and East European countries.

War in Iraq

A "shock and awe" display of American military power exploded on March 20, 2003, beginning a swift march on Baghdad. When Baghdadis tore down a gigantic statue of Saddam on April 10, most Americans felt vindicated. In May, Bush dramatically landed on the carrier *Abraham Lincoln* beneath a "Mission Accomplished" banner.

Saddam's WMDs were never found. As Saddam and his accomplices hid, law and order in Iraq collapsed. Sure that American troops would be greeted as liberators, the Pentagon had not sent enough troops to ensure security nor planned Iraq's occupation nor anticipated the breakdown of infrastructure. The long-dominant Sunni minority feared for its future as the Shiite majority asserted itself. Only Kurds welcomed the Americans. American troops and contractors struggled to get utilities back in service, restrain Shiite militias, and combat an insurgency of Saddamist die-hards, fearful Sunni civilians, and Al Qaeda-affiliated terrorists.

Bush's popularity ebbed as American deaths increased. A bloody struggle was required to reduce the defiant Sunni city of Fallujah in November 2004; car bombs and ambushes took a grim toll, and Americans were kidnapped and beheaded. Saddam's capture in December 2003 had no apparent effect on the insurgency.

Charges mounted that the Bush Administration had misinterpreted or manipulated evidence on the basis of which it invaded Iraq, and that the war was a distraction from the main objective—bin Laden and Al Qaeda. Photos surfacing in May 2004 of detainees being abused in Baghdad's Abu Ghraib prison and exposés of mistreatment of "enemy combatants" in the U.S. prison at Guantánamo Naval Base suggested that the administration overstepped international law in its quest for

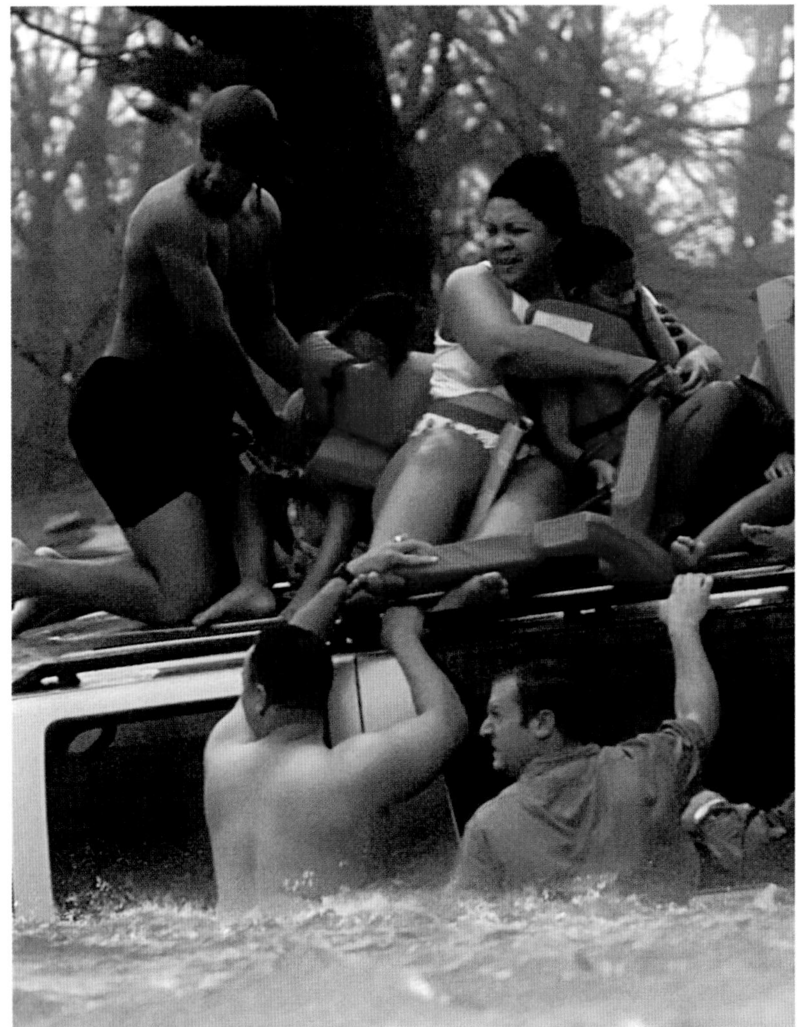

Emergency crews rescue a family, trapped on U.S. Interstate 90 near Bay St. Louis, Mississippi, on August 29, 2005. The family was trapped on the roof of their car in the flooding caused by Hurricane Katrina, one of the worst natural disasters ever experienced in the U.S.

intelligence. In the fall of 2004 the blue-ribbon 9/11 Commission issued a scathing report citing numerous instances of intelligence failures before Al Qaeda's attack.

Bush stressed America's war aim as encouragement of democracy in the Middle East. This goal seemed elusive. In January 2005, mostly Shiite and Kurdish voters chose a national assembly. A coalition government tried but failed to conciliate the Sunni minority. In August 2005, a draft constitution promised autonomy to Kurds and Shiites, but Sunni objections and continuing terrorist attacks raised the specter of civil war.

Bush Reelected

In the 2002 elections, fears of terrorism had swelled Republican majorities. Democrats with reservations about the Patriot Act were defeated for lacking patriotism.

NOTABLE DATES

■ 2001
George W. Bush inaugurated as President; 9/11 attack; U.S. invades Afghanistan and overthrows Taliban regime, but fails to find Osama bin Laden.

■ 2002
Bush defines Iraq, Iran, and North Korea as the "axis of evil"; U.N. Security Council orders Iraq to admit arms inspectors; Republicans gain in midterm elections; Enron scandal shocks the corporate world and leads to thousands of employees losing their life savings.

■ 2003
U.S. invades Iraq and overthrows Saddam Hussein; Bush proclaims "mission accomplished," but U.S. fails to find WMDs; insurgency begins; Saddam Hussein captured.

■ 2004
Death of Yasser Arafat raises hopes for end of Israeli-Palestinian stalemate; Mahmoud Abbas elected to head Palestinian Authority government; revelations of Abu Ghraib prison abuses; terrorists attack in Madrid; 9/11 Commission finds serious security lapses before terrorist attacks; Bush narrowly reelected.

■ 2005
Iraqis vote for provisional national assembly; terrorist attacks in London; polls show declining public support for war in Iraq; Israel withdraws from Gaza Strip; amid continuing insurgency and terrorist attacks, Iraqi constitution drafted; Katrina, one of the worst hurricanes ever to hit the U.S., devastates the Gulf Coast, leaving 80 percent of New Orleans underwater.

This riot took place in April 2000 in Washington, D.C., when World Bank and International Monetary Fund leaders convened. Protesters saw the Bank and IMF as spearheading capitalist domination, exploiting Third World workers, and plundering Earth's environment.

Bush faced the 2004 electorate amid the steady drip of bad news from Iraq and with a sluggish economy. The bubble of inflated tech-stock prices had burst in 2000-2001, and accounting scandals in corporations like WorldCom and Enron shook confidence in the New Economy. More jobs were lost than created in Bush's first term, for the first time since Hoover's day, and federal budget deficits once again yawned far and deep—consequences of Bush's tax cuts, the War on Terror, and an extremely expensive drug benefit Bush and Congress added to Medicare.

Yet the 2004 elections turned on culture-war issues—and on George W. Bush himself. In journalistic shorthand, the U.S. consisted of GOP red states and Democratic blue states. New England, the Middle Atlantic, parts of the Midwest, and the West Coast were blue; the South, the Sun Belt (except for California), the Rockies, and the Great Plains were red. Only a few states, mostly midwestern, were up for grabs. Cultural issues were dominated by the question of civil marriage rights for gays. Social Security and Medicare got little attention.

John F. Kerry won the Democratic nomination. A Catholic liberal with an aloof manner, he was the antithesis of George W. Bush in everything except wealth and a Yale degree. In the 1960s Kerry was decorated in Vietnam, then led Vietnam Veterans Against the War, and eventually became a senator from Massachusetts.

Political mud flew freely. Kerry charged that the wars on Al Qaeda and Saddam had been waged incompetently, while Bush touted his steadfastness and implied that Democrats were soft on terrorism. Vietnam-era vitriol was recycled: Right-wing veterans attacked Kerry's decorations as fraudulently gained and liberals implied that Bush had evaded combat through preferential treatment in the National Guard. Both evangelical and Catholic conservatives voted Republican to block gay marriage. Bush won: 51 percent to 48 percent in popular votes, but his victory was razor-thin in the Electoral College. By a few thousand votes, Ohio went for Bush, and decided the contest.

Issues largely ignored during the campaign surfaced in Bush's second term. It was estimated that by 2042 the Social Security system would need massive infusions of revenues to stay afloat. Bush proposed to meet the challenge by cutting future benefits, offset by allowing younger workers to shift part of their contributions to individual retirement accounts with faster growth through investment in equities. Transition costs would be at least a trillion borrowed dollars. But Bush offered no proposal to meet the immediate need of fixing Medicare and Medicaid. These entitlements threatened to engulf the budget as the population aged and medical costs outstripped GDP growth.

Unpalatable choices loomed—a combination of sustaining growth, encouraging immigration, raising taxes, and rationing health care. But for politicians, "exciting the base" with cultural issues was more important than winning votes in the middle or solving national problems. Faith, home, family, reproduction, education, race, and gender became battlegrounds. And yet—Americans asked in 2005, as right-wing evangelicals and Republican politicians made a federal case out of a Florida family's struggle with a tragic end-of-life decision—had the politicization of private life finally gone too far?

9/11

JUST BEFORE 9 A.M. IN NEW YORK CITY ON September 11, 2001, two commercial jetliners, flying out of Boston, smashed into the World Trade Center, the symbol of globalizing capitalism. Within minutes, another jet crashed into the Pentagon; an hour later, a fourth went down in Pennsylvania—intended, it appeared, to hit either the White House or the Capitol. Almost 3,000 perished in the fiery collapse of the Twin Towers, and 125 at the Pentagon; besides the hijackers, 286 died aboard the doomed airliners. The heroism of New York City firefighters and police in rescuing victims, only to perish in the calamity, along with the heroism of the passengers on the hijacked plane over Pennsylvania who overpowered their captors and crashed the jet, became legendary. The loss of life on 9/11 exceeded the death toll at Pearl Harbor in World War II and, like that earlier "day of infamy," was seared into the American memory.

The hijackers were 19 Arab men, members of the fanatical Islamist group Al Qaeda, based in Afghanistan and supporting the fundamentalist Taliban regime. Its founder, Osama bin Laden, a wealthy Saudi, boasted on videotape of having planned the attacks. Al Qaeda aimed to convert the world to its ultra-strict brand of Islam. It was linked to earlier terrorist assaults on the U.S.: a 1993 attempt to bring down the Twin Towers by car-bombing an underground garage, the 1998 destruction of embassies in Kenya and Tanzania, and the 2000 attack on the U.S.S. *Cole* in Aden.

The Clinton Administration had retaliated against Al Qaeda for the embassy bombings with cruise missile attacks on its Afghan bases. Both under Clinton and during George W. Bush's first months as President, antiterrorism experts in Washington knew that some kind of assault might come, but intelligence "dots" never got connected.

Now, belatedly, they were. ■

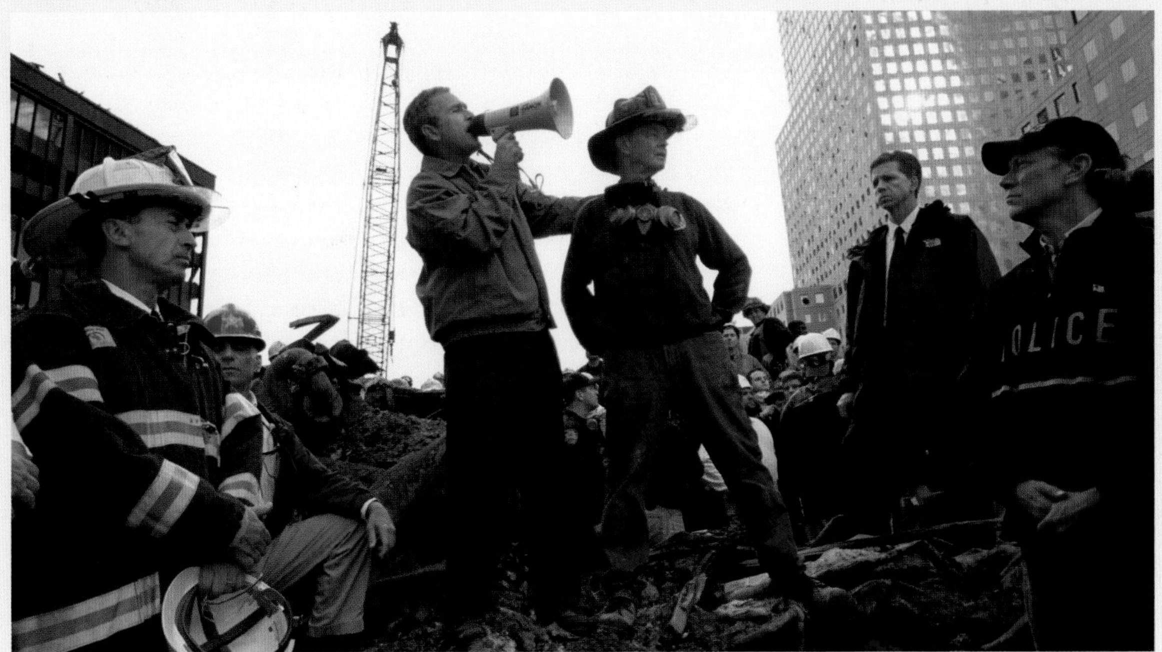

"I can hear you," George W. Bush shouted through a bullhorn to rescue workers on the ruins of the World Trade Center on September 14, 2001. "The rest of the world hears you. And the people who knocked these buildings down will hear all of us soon."

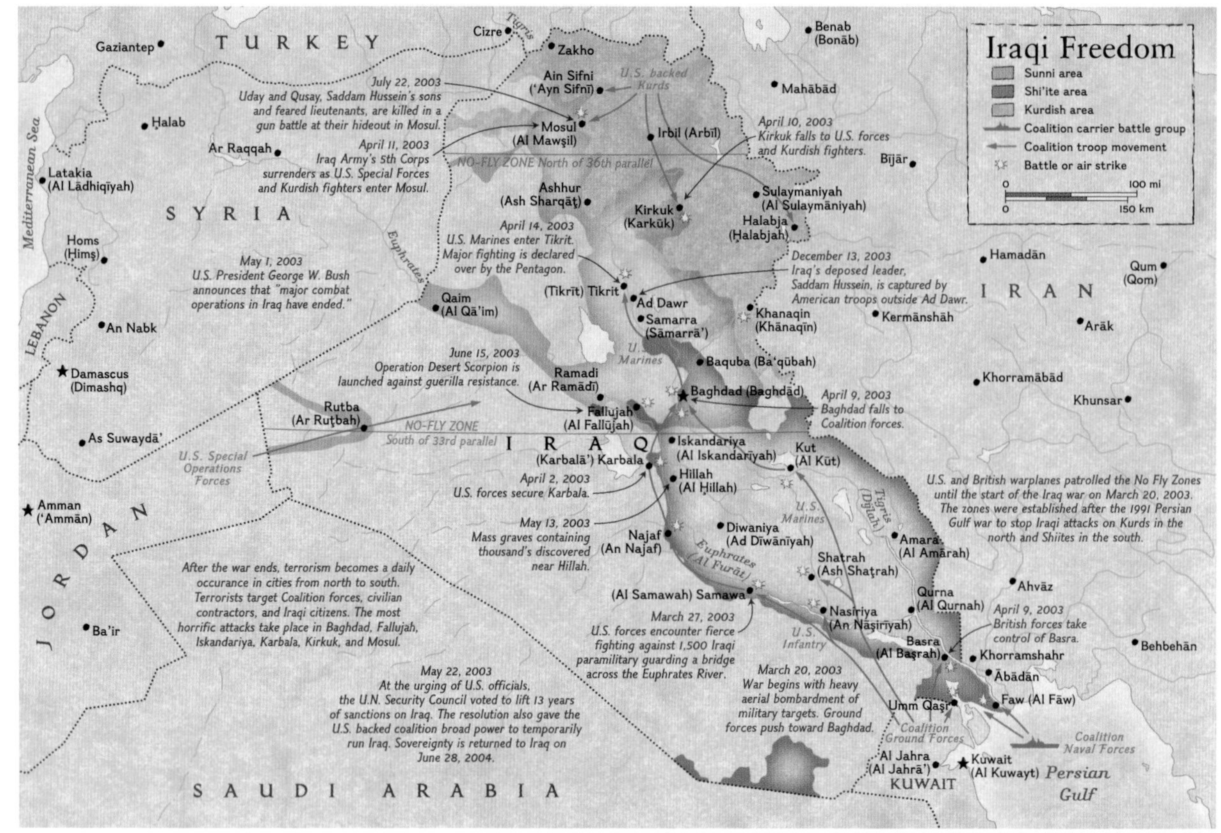

Operation Iraqi Freedom succeeded almost as quickly as its planners expected. Unexpected, however, were the sabotage of the country's infrastructure, collapse of Iraqi society, and emergence of a fierce Sunni insurgency—not to mention the absence of Saddam's WMDs.

The Islamist Challenge

Although Americans were told after 9/11 that most Muslims were peaceable and that Islam encompasses many varieties, it was frightening to discover that some strains of the Islamic faith regard the West as evil. At the dawn of the 21st century, Westerners found it incredible to face religious zealots seemingly straight from the Middle Ages.

Medieval Islam had been in decline since the 13th century. By 1800, Islamic reformers were pointing Muslims in two contradictory directions—toward emulating the West or recovering the purity of early Islam. One manifestation of the latter was the Wahhabi movement, allied since the 18th century with the House of Saud in central Arabia. After the collapse of the Ottoman Empire, chieftain Ibn Saud unified Arabia and gave Wahhabist clerics power to enforce their brand of Sunni Islam. They denounced all other strains of Islam as impure—particularly Shiism, dominant in Iraq and Iran.

Especially from 1920 to 1970, neo-Islamic appeals such as Wahhabism had to compete with other Western ideologies: secularism, nationalism, democracy, socialism, capitalism, Marxism, and fascism. But by the 1970s, the brutal and corrupt "modernizing" regimes dominating the Middle East were discredited—especially because they could not defeat Israel.

In June 1967, Americans and Europeans had cheered when Israel forestalled an invasion by preemptively attacking Egypt, Syria, and Jordan. Israeli armies occupied East Jerusalem, the West Bank, Gaza, and the Sinai Peninsula. Soon, though, Yasser Arafat founded the Palestinian Liberation Organization (PLO), which at the 1972 Munich Olympics killed 11 Israeli athletes; later there would be many other attacks. Egypt and Syria attacked again in 1973, on Yom Kippur.

Reinforced by America, Israel again prevailed.

But in the Yom Kippur War the Arabs also embargoed oil shipments to the West, and Israel's repressive occupation of Palestinian lands made it seem more an oppressor than a victim. Israeli intransigence, especially to Europeans, became a stumbling block. In 1978, Jimmy Carter brought together Egyptian president Anwar Sadat and hard-line Israeli Prime Minister Menachem Begin. In return for Egyptian recognition, Israel gave up Sinai. But neither Palestinian guerrilla attacks nor harsh Israeli responses abated.

Israel never trusted Arafat, and Arafat was not strong enough to make peace with Israel. In 1987 the Palestinians proclaimed the intifada (meaning "shaking") uprising. Peace process talks took place, often under American auspices; Israel offered land for peace. But the PLO demanded all the occupied land, including East Jerusalem, and the right of return for post-1948 refugees (which would have swamped Israel with Arabs). In 2000, Clinton and a center-left Israeli cabinet thought that a bargain had been struck, giving the PLO almost all it asked. Arafat rejected the deal, unable to withstand his hardliners. The intifada resumed, and hawkish Ariel Sharon came to power in Israel.

Many hoped that Arafat's death in 2004 would break the impasse. His democratically elected successor, Mahmoud Abbas, strove to control terrorism. Sharon defied Israeli settlers by withdrawing from Gaza, though he promised no concessions on the West Bank. But everything was complicated by the rise of militant Islamism across the Muslim world.

"Islam is the Answer" was the passionate response of many young Muslims to the humiliation they felt confronting Israel and the West. Salafism—"following the pious ancestors"—was a tradition of fundamentalist faith in Islam, and to young Islamists strict enforcement

Osama bin Laden got insurgency training in the U.S.-backed jihad against Soviet occupation of Afghanistan. He turned against the U.S., he said, because they supported Israel and stationed troops on Saudi Arabia's holy Islamic soil.

of the traditional law code was a cornerstone demand. Youths steeped in salafism emerged from *madrasas* (Koranic schools) and preached across the Muslim world. But only in Shiite Iran did Islamic revolutionaries take power, in 1979; elsewhere, Islamists met repression.

The Islamist movement spread to Muslim communities in Europe and America. Lavish Saudi subsidies brought many American mosques, schools, and charities under Wahhabist influence. Islamism rejected pluralism, secularism, individualism, women's rights, the separation of personal religion from the public sphere, and skeptical attitudes toward literally interpreted revelation.

Al Qaeda took Islamism still further, demanding jihad against everything Western. Unlike most Muslims, Al Qaeda saw jihad as literal warfare and suicide as martyrdom. (The Koran forbids suicide and taking innocent life.) Osama bin Laden was a product of a Wahhabite strain that condemned the House of Saud both for its corruption and for its alliance with the United States.

The attacks on 9/11, the war in Iraq, Kashmiri violence against Hindu India, and other lethal outbreaks of al Qaeda-inspired terrorism—most spectacularly in Bali, Madrid, and London—frightened the entire world. Al Qaeda-affiliated terrorists from all over the Arab world took a leading role in the Sunni Muslim insurgency in Iraq. Could Islamic minorities in Europe and America live, long-term, within pluralist, secular Western communities and traditions? Could Muslim societies, from the Middle East to Indonesia, as well as other Muslim subcultures in Western countries, adapt to Western pluralism—for example, by according women greater rights and by embracing the pragmatism of democratic politics? Some Islamists were quite open to accommodation and pluralism; many were not. ■

WORLD SURVEY

1985 – PRESENT

How should the pluralist, secular world respond to the Islamic world's anti-Western stance?

Europe and the Former Soviet Union

With the Cold War's end, NATO and the European Union (EU) absorbed much of the former Soviet Bloc. In 1992, EU members committed to write a constitution. But in 2005 French and Dutch voters rejected the constitution, while Great Britain grew more Euroskeptical. Concerns that too much liberty and identity were being lost to political elites and to "Eurocrats" in Brussels stalled a "United States of Europe."

Europe's economy suffered high unemployment and almost no job growth. Such stagnation—an American judgment—seemed to most Europeans the price, along with high taxes, for a better social safety net and a less hectic lifestyle. Could it be sustained, or would globalization force Europe's Americanization? Europe was less religious than America and less divided by culture wars, deepening mutual disdain. Yet West Europeans faced cultural dilemmas too, consequences of globalization. How to integrate economically laggard former communist countries? And how to assimilate non-European immigrants, often alienated Muslims? The U.S. found it far easier to assimilate newcomers into its already multicultural society than did Europeans, with their thousand- year-old ties of language, community, blood, and soil.

Russia, floundering in corruption and cynicism, failed to establish a market economy and political liberty after 1991. When the Chechen Muslim minority tried to break away, civil war and terrorism ensued. In 2000, ex-KGB officer Vladimir Putin was overwhelmingly elected President. Putin could not crush the Chechens, but he eroded Russia's remaining free institutions. As he did, his popularity rose.

A Violent World

Yugoslavia's breakup after 1992 was punctuated by bloody civil wars and Serb massacres of Muslim Bosnians and Albanians. Belatedly, Europe and the U.N. intervened, but it was the U.S. that in 1996 finally brokered the Dayton Accords, stabilizing multiethnic Bosnia. In 1999, new massacres loomed in the Albanian-populated province of Kosovo. Reluctantly, the Clinton administration led a NATO intervention that forced the Serbs to withdraw.

Africa, devastated by AIDS, got little attention once it ceased to be a Cold War battlefield. America withdrew from Somalia in 1993 when its peacekeepers came under fire. Genocide in Rwanda in 1994 killed an estimated 800,000 as ethnic-majority Hutus butchered minority Tutsis, with virtually no outside effort to stop it. One of the more hopeful signs was South Africa's peaceful transition from apartheid to multiracial democracy after Nelson Mandela's election as president in 1994.

Part of the Middle East's threat to global stability lay in the Israeli-Palestinian conflict. In 1978, Carter achieved his most important success by mediating the Camp David Accords, a peace deal between Egypt and Israel. But Israel never trusted PLO leader Yasser Arafat, nor was he strong enough to make peace. In 1987 the Palestinians launched an uprising, the intifada, ranging from suicide bombing to rock throwing. Israel offered to exchange some occupied land to end the terrorism. But the PLO demanded all Israeli-occupied land, including East

Jerusalem, and the right of return for all refugees. In 2000, Clinton almost struck a bargain giving the PLO almost everything except the right of return. Arafat rejected the deal, and Ariel Sharon came to power in Israel. After Arafat's death in 2004, his successor, Mahmoud Abbas, was democratically elected. Whether this heralded a more peaceful future depended on Abbas reining in terrorism and Israel choosing between Sharon's plan to confine independent Palestine to small enclaves and the more generous settlement envisioned in 2000.

Israel's existence and its control of Jerusalem—holy to Muslims—partly explain the upsurge of militant Islam. But this would have occurred even without Israel's presence, growing out of the Muslim movement called Salafism—"following the pious ancestors." This ultra-fundamentalist trend had in the 18th century produced the Wahhabist sect, which dominates modern Saudi Arabia and nurtured Al Qaeda.

By the 1970s, Western-derived ideologies—nationalism (like Saddam's) and Marxism—failed in the Middle East. "Islam is the Answer" was the passionate response of some young Muslims, steeped in Salafism. Such "Islamism" was preached in mosques and schools throughout the Muslim world and in Muslim communities in Europe and America. Only in Shiite Iran did Islamist revolutionaries take power, in 1979. Nowhere was Islamism a majority opinion among Muslims.

Al Qaeda interpreted Islam as demanding jihad against the West. Jihad, which most Muslims consider a duty, means "struggle," but Al Qaeda saw it as literal warfare and lauded suicide—condemned by the Koran—as martyrdom.

Nine-eleven frightened the entire world. Would Al Qaeda's extremism become the vehicle for a jihad against non-Muslims? Or could Muslim societies adapt to Western pluralism? These were questions that Americans of all faiths and traditions had to contemplate as the 21st century began. But the answers were not entirely for Americans to give. ■

AT A GLANCE

1 Native Americans Today

2 Notable Accomplishments

3 Leaders and People of Note

4 Sports

5 Scientists and Inventors

6 Artists

7 Explorers

8 Periods and Movements

9 Religious Groups

San Francisco after the devastating earthquake of 1906. Troops walk east along Market Street. In the distance, the tall Call building burns.

Native Americans Today

ALABAMA

Poarch Band of Creek Indians

ALASKA

Village of Afognak
Agdaagux Tribe of King Cove
Native Village of Akhiok
Akiachak Native Community
Akiak Native Community
Native Village of Akutan
Village of Alakanuk
Alatna Village
Native Village of Aleknagik
Algaaciq Native Village (St. Mary's)
Allakaket Village
Native Village of Ambler
Village of Anaktuvuk Pass
Yupiit of Andreafski

Sequoyah, a Cherokee, began to develop a syllabary for his language in 1909.

Angoon Community Association
Village of Aniak
Anvik Village
Arctic Village (See Native Village of Venetie Tribal Government)
Asa'carsarmiut Tribe
Native Village of Atka
Village of Atmautluak
Atqasuk Village (Atkasook)
Native Village of Barrow Inupiat Traditional Government
Beaver Village
Native Village of Belkofski
Village of Bill Moore's Slough
Birch Creek Tribe
Native Village of Brevig Mission
Native Village of Buckland
Native Village of Cantwell
Native Village of Chanega (aka Chenega)
Chalkyitsik Village
Cheesh-Na Tribe
Village of Chefornak
Chevak Native Village
Chickaloon Native Village
Native Village of Chignik
Native Village of Chignik Lagoon
Chignik Lake Village
Chilkat Indian Village (Klukwan)
Chilkoot Indian Association (Haines)
Chinik Eskimo Community(Golovin)
Native Village of Chitina
Native Village of Chuathbaluk (Russian Mission, Kuskokwim)
Chuloonawick Native Village
Circle Native Community
Village of Clarks Point
Native Village of Council
Craig Community Association
Village of Crooked Creek
Curyung Tribal Council
Native Village of Diomede (aka Inalik)
Village of Dot Lake
Douglas Indian Association
Native Village of Eagle
Native Village of Eek
Egegik Village
Eklutna Native Village

Native Village of Ekuk
Ekwok Village
Native Village of Elim
Emmonak Village
Evansville Village (aka Bettles Field)
Native Village of Eyak (Cordova)
Native Village of False Pass
Native Village of Fort Yukon
Native Village of Gakona
Galena Village (aka Louden Village)
Native Village of Gambell
Native Village of Georgetown
Native Village of Goodnews Bay
Organized Village of Grayling
(aka Holikachuk)
Gulkana Village
Native Village of Hamilton
Healy Lake Village
Holy Cross Village
Hoonah Indian Association
Native Village of Hooper Bay
Hughes Village
Huslia Village
Hydaburg Cooperative Association
Igiugig Village
Village of Iliamna
Inupiat Community of Arctic Slope
Iqurmuit Traditional Council
Ivanoff Bay Village
Kaguyak Village
Organized Village of Kake
Kaktovik Village (aka Barter Island)
Village of Kalskag
Village of Kaltag
Native Village of Kanatak
Native Village of Karluk
Organized Village of Kasaan
Kasigluk Traditional Elders Council
Kenaitze Indian Tribe
Ketchikan Indian Corporation
Native Village of Kiana
King Island Native Community
King Salmon Tribe
Native Village of Kipnuk
Native Village of Kivalina
Klawock Cooperative Association
Native Village of Kluti Kaah (aka
Copper Center)
Knik Tribe
Native Village of Kobuk
Kokhanok Village

Native Village of Kongiganak
Village of Kotlik
Native Village of Kotzebue
Native Village of Koyuk
Koyukuk Native Village
Organized Village of Kwethluk
Native Village of Kwigillingok
Native Village of Kwinhagak
(aka Quinhagak)
Native Village of Larsen Bay
Levelock Village
Lesnoi Village (aka Woody Island)
Lime Village
Village of Lower Kalskag
Manley Hot Springs Village
Manokotak Village
Native Village of Marshall
(aka Fortuna Ledge)
Native Village of Mary's Igloo
McGrath Native Village
Native Village of Mekoryuk
Mentasta Traditional Council
Metlakatla Indian Community,
Annette Island Reserve
Native Village of Minto
Naknek Native Village
Native Village of Nanwalek
(aka English Bay)
Native Village of Napaimute
Village of Napakiak
Native Village of Napaskiak
Native Village of Nelson Lagoon
Nenana Native Association
New Koliganek Village Council
New Stuyahok Village
Newhalen Village
Newtok Village
Native Village of Nightmute
Nikolai Village
Native Village of Nikolski
Ninilchik Village
Native Village of Noatak
Nome Eskimo Community
Nondalton Village
Noorvik Native Community
Northway Village
Native Village of Nuiqsut
(aka Nooiksut)
Nulato Village
Nunakauyarmiut Tribe
Native Village of Nunapitchuk

Village of Ohogamiut
Village of Old Harbor
Orutsararmuit Native Village
(aka Bethel)
Oscarville Traditional Village
Native Village of Ouzinkie
Native Village of Paimiut
Pauloff Harbor Village
Pedro Bay Village
Native Village of Perryville
Petersburg Indian Association
Native Village of Pilot Point
Pilot Station Traditional Village
Native Village of Pitka's Point
Platinum Traditional Village
Native Village of Point Hope
Native Village of Point Lay
Native Village of Port Graham
Native Village of Port Heiden
Native Village of Port Lions
Portage Creek Village
(aka Ohgsenakale)
Pribilof Islands Aleut Communities
of St. Paul & St. George Islands
Qagan Tayagungin Tribe of Sand
Point Village
Qawalangin Tribe of Unalaska
Rampart Village
Village of Red Devil
Native Village of Ruby
Native Village of Saint Michael
Village of Salamatoff
Native Village of Savoonga
Organized Village of Saxman
Native Village of Scammon Bay
Native Village of Selawik
Seldovia Village Tribe
Shageluk Nativeive Village
Native Village of Shaktoolik
Native Village of Sheldon's Point
Native Village of Shishmaref
Native Village of Shungnak
Sitka Tribe of Alaska
Skagway Village
Village of Sleetmute
Village of Solomon
South Naknek Village
Stebbins Community Association
Native Village of Stevens
Native Village
of Stony River Point

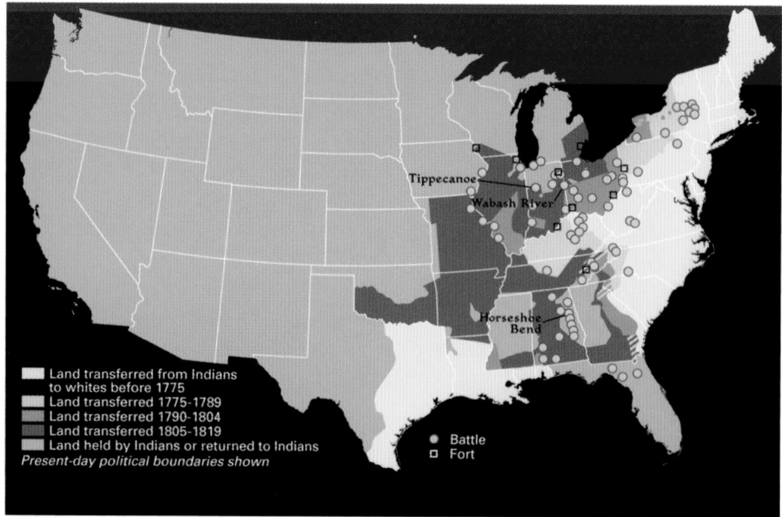

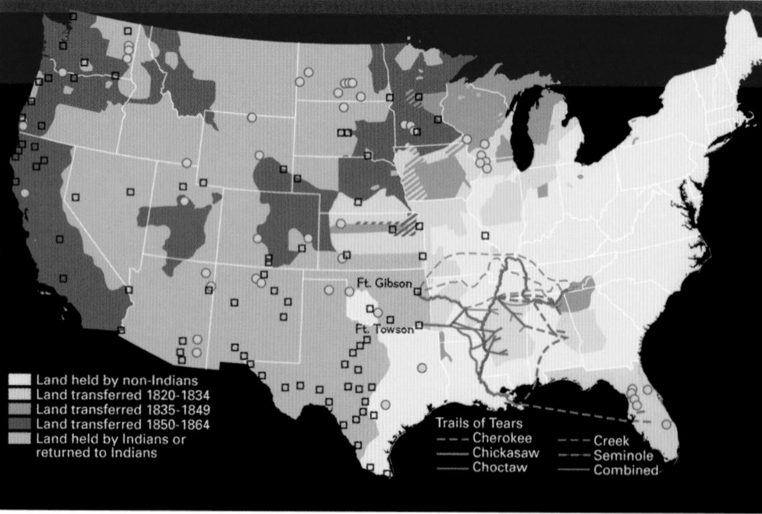

1775-1819 (top) A Nation Expands

Recognizing that Indians could swing the balance of power in the Revolution, George Washington authorized the first U.S.-Indian treaty, with the Delaware tribe in 1778. Hundreds of treaties followed, but settlers continued to move onto Indian lands. "First one, and then another, come," Seneca Chief Cornplanter complained to Washington. Liquor and European diseases ravaged many tribes. Some Indians fought back. In 1791 an alliance of midwestern tribes killed about 600 American troops at the Wabash River. But from 1811 to 1814, U.S. armies defeated Indian forces at Tippecanoe and Horseshoe Bend and thwarted Britain and its Indian allies in the War of 1812, solidifying U.S. control east of the Mississippi.

1820-1864 (bottom) Forced Exodus

In an 1830 address to Congress, President Jackson, a former Indian fighter, declared, "What good man would prefer a country covered with forests and ranged by a few thousand savages to our extensive Republic?" Earlier that year he had pressed Congress to pass the Indian Removal Act, which led to the forced relocation of many tribes to a designated Indian territory (present-day Oklahoma). Some resisted, including the Sauk and the Seminole, but virtually all were subdued. Most Cherokee reluctantly agreed to move, but their 1838 winter relocation and march—along one of the Trails of Tears—killed one-fourth of the group. Death also reigned out West. In the 1850s bands of California miners and vigilantes murdered Indians with impunity.

Sun'aq Tribe of Kodiak
Takotna Village
Native Village of Tanacross
Native Village of Tanana
Native Village of Tatitlek
Native Village of Tazlina
Telida Village
Native Village of Teller
Native Village of Tetlin
Central Council of the Tlingit & Haida Indian Tribes
Traditional Village of Togiak
Tuluksak Native Community
Native Village of Tuntutuliak
Native Village of Tununak
Twin Hills Village
Native Village of Tyonek
Ugashik Village
Umkumiute Native Village
Native Village of Unalakleet
Native Village of Unga
Native Village of Venetie Tribal Government (Arctic Village and Village of Venetie)
Village of Wainwright
Native Village of Wales
Native Village of White Mountain
Wrangell Cooperative Association
Yakutat Tlingit Tribe

ARIZONA

Ak Chin Indian Community of the Maricopa (Ak Chin) Indian Reservation
Cocopah Tribe
Fort McDowell Yavapai Nation
Gila River Indian Community of the Gila River Indian Reservation
Havasupai Tribe of the Havasupai Reservation
Hopi Tribe
Hualapai Indian Tribe of the Hualapai Indian Reservation
Kaibab Band of Paiute Indians of the Kaibab Indian Reservation
Pascua Yaqui Tribe
Salt River Pima-Maricopa Indian Community of the Salt River Reservation
San Carlos Apache Tribe of the San Carlos Reservation

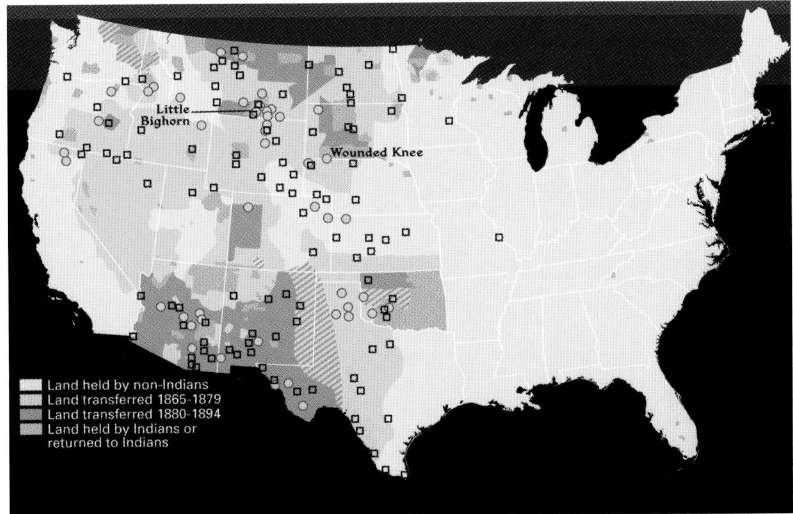

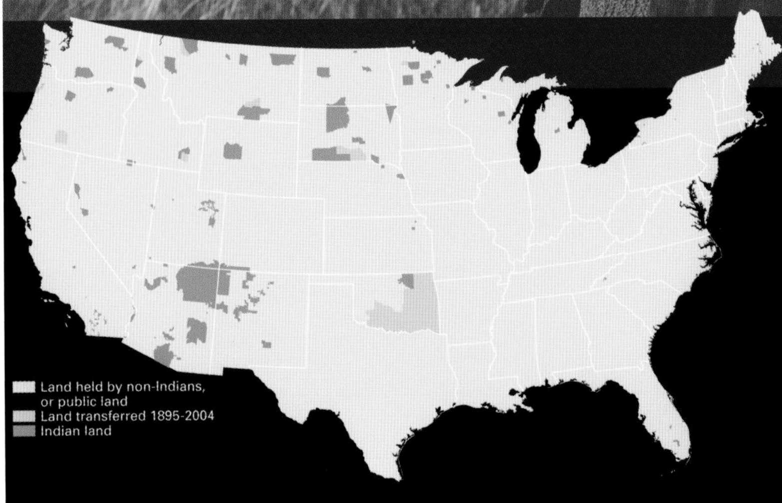

1865-1894 (top) Land Rush

The Civil War's end and the railroad's expansion brought land-hungry settlers to the West. The U.S. voided its treaties with tribes in Indian Territory, forcing them to give up lands promised "for as long as the grass grows." The U.S. Army spent the next two decades building forts and subduing tribes in the Great Plains and Southwest. Apache leader Geronimo surrendered in 1886, technically ending the Indian Wars (though the massacre of Indians at Wounded Knee followed in 1890). In 1887 Congress passed the Dawes General Allotment Act, allowing the government to partition a tribe's reservation land into parcels and give each adult a plot of 80 or 160 acres. The U.S. then opened what was left to settlers, sparking land rushes.

1895-2005 (bottom) New Battlefields

In the half century following the Dawes Act, Indians lost more than 90 million acres—much of it to swindlers. Then the struggle for land and rights shifted from battlefield to Congress and the courts. In 1934 the Indian Reorganization Act ended forced land allotments and bolstered the power of tribal governments. From 1946 until its expiration in 1978 the Indian Claims Commission reviewed hundreds of land claims and awarded millions of dollars in compensation. The United States began to acknowledge tribal sovereignty with the Indian Self-Determination Act of 1975, a major turning point.

San Juan Southern Paiute Tribe
Tohono O'odham Nation
Tonto Apache Tribe
White Mountain Apache Tribe of the Fort Apache Reservation
Yavapai-Apache Nation of the Camp Verde Indian Reservation
Yavapai-Prescott Tribe of the Yavapai Reservation

CALIFORNIA

Agua Caliente Band of Cahuilla Indians of the Agua Caliente Indian Reservation
Alturas Indian Rancheria
Augustine Band of Cahuilla Mission Indians of the Augustine Reservation
Bear River Band of the Rohnerville Rancheria
Berry Creek Rancheria of Maidu Indians
Big Lagoon Rancheria
Big Pine Band of Owens Valley Paiute Shoshone Indians of the Big Pine Reservation
Big Sandy Rancheria of Mono Indians
Big Valley Band of Pomo Indians of the Big Valley Rancheria
Blue Lake Rancheria
Bridgeport Paiute Indian Colony
Buena Vista Rancheria of Me-Wuk Indians
Cabazon Band of Mission Indians
Cachil DeHe Band of Wintun Indians of the Colusa Indian Community of the Colusa Rancheria
Cahuilla Band of Mission Indians of the Cahuilla Reservation
Cahto Indian Tribe of the Laytonville Rancheria
California Valley Miwok Tribe
Campo Band of Diegueno Mission Indians of the Campo Indian Reservation
Capitan Grande Band of Diegueno Mission Indians: Barona Group of Capitan Grande Band of Mission Indians of the Barona

Reservation, Viejas (Baron Long) Group of Capitan Grande Band of Mission Indians of the Viejas Reservation
Cedarville Rancheria
Chemehuevi Indian Tribe of the Chemehuevi Reservation,
Cher-Ae Heights Indian Community of the Trinidad Rancheria
Chicken Ranch Rancheria of Me-Wuk Indians
Cloverdale Rancheria of Pomo Indians
Cold Springs Rancheria of Mono Indians
Cortina Indian Rancheria of Wintun Indians
Coyote Valley Band of Pomo Indians
Death Valley Timbi-Sha Shoshone Band
Dry Creek Rancheria of Pomo Indians
Elem Indian Colony of Pomo Indians of the Sulphur Bank Rancheria
Elk Valley Rancheria
Enterprise Rancheria of Maidu Indians
Ewiiaapaayp Band of Kumeyaay Indians
Federated Indians of Graton Rancheria
Fort Bidwell Indian Community of the Fort Bidwell Reservation
Fort Independence Indian Community of Paiute Indians of the Fort Independence Reservation
Greenville Rancheria of Maidu Indians
Grindstone Indian Rancheria of Wintun-Wailaki Indians
Guidiville Rancheria
Habematolei Pomo of Upper Lake
Hoopa Valley Tribe
Hopland Band of Pomo Indians of the Hopland Rancheria
Inaja Band of Diegueno Mission Indians of the Inaja and Cosmit Reservation
Ione Band of Miwok Indians

Wilma Mankiller was the first woman elected to serve as leader of the Cherokee Nation.

Jackson Rancheria of Me-Wuk Indians
Jamul Indian Village
Karuk Tribe
Kashia Band of Pomo Indians of the Stewarts Point Rancheria
La Jolla Band of Luiseno Mission Indians of the La Jolla Reservation
La Posta Band of Diegueno Mission Indians of La Posta Reservation
Lower Lake Rancheria
Los Coyotes Band of Cahuilla and Cupeno Indians of the Los Coyotes Reservation
Lytton Rancheria
Manchester Band of Pomo Indians of the Manchester-Point Arena Rancheria
Manzanita Band of Diegueno Mission Indians of the Manzanita Reservation
Mechoopda Indian Tribe of Chico Rancheria
Mesa Grande Band of Diegueno Mission Indians of the Mesa Grande Reservation
Middletown Rancheria of Pomo Indians
Mooretown Rancheria of Maidu Indians
Morongo Band of Cahuilla Mission Indians of Morongo Reservation
Northfork Rancheria of Mono Indians
Paiute-Shoshone Indians of the Bishop Community of the Bishop Colony
Paiute-Shoshone Indians of the Lone Pine Community of the Lone Pine Reservation
Pala Band of Luiseno Mission Indians of the Pala Reservation
Paskenta Band of Nomlaki Indians
Pauma Band of Luiseno Mission Indians of Pauma & Yuima Reservation

Pechanga Band of Luiseno Mission Indians of the Pechanga Reservation
Picayune Rancheria of Chukchansi Indians
Pinoleville Rancheria of Pomo Indians
Pit River Tribes: Big Bend, Likely, Lookout, Montgomery Creek Rancheria, Roaring Creek Rancheria, XL Ranch
Potter Valley Tribe
Quartz Valley Indian Community of the Quartz Valley Reservation
Ramona Band or Village of Cahuilla Mission Indians
Redding Rancheria
Redwood Valley Rancheria of Pomo Indians
Resighini Rancheria
Rincon Band of Luiseno Mission Indians of the Rincon Reservation
Robinson Rancheria of Pomo Indians
Round Valley Indian Tribes of the Round Valley Reservation
Rumsey Indian Rancheria of Wintun Indians
San Manual Band of Serrano Mission Indians of the San Manual Reservation
San Pasqual Band of Diegueno Mission Indians
Santa Rosa Indian Community of the Santa Rosa Rancheria
Santa Rosa Band of Cahuilla Mission Indians of Santa Rosa Reservation
Santa Ynez Band of Chumash Indians of Santa Ynez Reservation
Santa Ysabel Band of Diegueno Mission Indians of the Santa Ysabel Reservation
Scotts Valley Band of Pomo Indians
Sherwood Valley Rancheria of Pomo Indians
Shingle Springs Band of Miwok Indians, Shingle Springs Rancheria (Verona Tract)
Smith River Rancheria
Soboba Band of Luiseno Indians
Susanville Indian Rancheria
Sycuan Band of the Kemeyaay Nation
Table Mountain Rancheria
Torres Martinez Desert Cahuilla Indians
Tule River Indian Tribe of the Tule River Reservation
Tuolumne Band of Me-Wuk Indians of the Tuolumne Rancheria
Twenty-Nine Palms Band of Mission Indians
United Auburn Indian Community of the Auburn Rancheria
Upper Lake Band of Pomo Indians of Upper Lake Rancheria
Utu Utu Gwaitu Paiute Tribe of the Benton Paiute Reservation
Yurok Tribe of Yurok Reservation

COLORADO

Southern Ute Indian Tribe of the Southern Ute Reservation

CONNECTICUT

Mashantucket Pequot Tribe
Mohegan Indian Tribe
Miccosukee Tribe of Indians
Seminole Tribe of Florida: Dania, Big Cypress, Brighton, Hollywood, and Tampa Reservations

IDAHO

Coeur D'Alene Tribe of the Coeur D'Alene Reservation
Kootenai Tribe
Nez Perce Tribe
Shoshone-Bannock Tribes of the Fort Hall Reservation

IOWA

Sac & Fox Tribe of the Mississippi

KANSAS

Kickapoo Tribe of Indians of the Kickapoo Reservation
Prairie Band of Potawatomi Nation

LOUISIANA

Chitimacha Tribe
Jena Band of Choctaw Indians
Coushatta Tribe
Tunica-Biloxi Indian Tribe

MAINE

Aroostook Band of Micmac Indians
Houlton Band of Maliseet Indians
Passamaquoddy Tribe
Penobscot Tribe

MASSACHUSETTS

Wampanoag Tribe of Gay Head (Aquinnah)

MICHIGAN

Bay Mills Indian Community
Grand Traverse Band of Ottawa and Chippewa Indians
Hannahville Indian Community
Huron Potawatomi, Inc
Keweenaw Bay Indian Community
Little River Band of Ottawa Indians
Little Traverse Bay Bands of Odawa Indians
Lac Vieux Desert Band of Lake Superior Chippewa Indians
Match-e-be-nash-she-wish Band of Pottawatomi Indians
Saginaw Chippewa Indian Tribe
Sault Ste. Marie Tribe of Chippewa Indians

MINNESOTA

Minnesota Chippewa Tribe, Minnesota: Bois Forte Band (Nett Lake), Fond du Lac Band, Grand Portage Band, Leech Lake Band, Mille Lacs Band, White Earth Band
Lower Sioux Indian Community
Prairie Island Indian Community
Red Lake Band of Chippewa Indians
Shakopee Mdewakanton Sioux Community
Upper Sioux Community

MISSISSIPPI

Mississippi Band of Choctaw Indians

MONTANA

Assiniboine and Sioux Tribes of the

Fort Peck Indian Reservation
Blackfeet Tribe of the Blackfeet Indian Reservation
Chippewa-Cree Indians of the Rocky Boy's Reservation
Confederated Salish & Kootenai Tribes of the Flathead Reservation
Crow Tribe
Fort Belknap Indian Community of the Fort Belknap Reservation
Northern Cheyenne Tribe of the Northern Cheyenne Indian Reservation

NEBRASKA
Iowa Tribe of Kansas and Nebraska
Omaha Tribe of Nebraska
Ponca Tribe of Nebraska
Santee Sioux Nation, Nebraska
Winnebago Tribe of Nebraska

NEVADA
Duckwater Shoshone Tribe of the Duckwater Reservation
Ely Shoshone Tribe
Las Vegas Tribe of Paiute Indians of the Las Vegas Indian Colony
Lovelock Paiute Tribe of the Lovelock Indian Colony
Moapa Band of Paiute Indians of the Moapa River Indian Reservation
Paiute-Shoshone Tribe of the Fallon Reservation and Colony
Pyramid Lake Paiute Tribe of the Pyramid Lake Reservation
Reno-Sparks Indian Colony
Shoshone-Paiute Tribes of the Duck Valley Reservation
Summit Lake Paiute Tribe
Te-Moak Tribes of Western Shoshone Indians: Battle Mountain Band, Elko Band, South Fork Band, Wells Band
Walker River Paiute Tribe of the Walker River Reservation
Winnemucca Indian Colony
Yerington Paiute Tribe of Yerington Colony & Campbell Ranch
Yomba Shoshone Tribe of the Yomba Reservation

NEW MEXICO
Jicarilla Apache Nation
Mescalero Apache Tribe of the Mescalero Reservation
Pueblo of Acoma
Pueblo of Cochiti
Pueblo of Jemez
Pueblo of Isleta
Pueblo of Laguna
Pueblo of Nambe
Pueblo of Picuris
Pueblo of Pojoaque
Pueblo of San Felipe
Pueblo of San Juan
Pueblo of San Ildefonso
Pueblo of Sandia
Pueblo of Santa Ana
Pueblo of Santa Clara
Pueblo of Santo Domingo
Pueblo of Taos
Pueblo of Tesuque
Pueblo of Zia
Zuni Tribe of the Zuni Reservation

NEW YORK
Cayuga Nation
Oneida Nation Onondaga Nation
St. Regis Band of Mohawk Indians
Seneca Nation
Tonawanda Band of Seneca Indians
Tuscarora Nation

NORTH CAROLINA
Eastern Band of Cherokee Indians

NORTH DAKOTA
Three Affiliated Tribes of the Fort Berthold Reservation
Turtle Mountain Band of Chippewa Indians

SOUTH DAKOTA
Spirit Lake Tribe
Yankton Sioux Tribe of South Dakota

OKLAHOMA
Absentee-Shawnee Tribe of Indians
Alabama-Quassarte Tribal Town
Apache Tribe
Caddo Nation
Cherokee Nation
Cheyenne-Arapaho Tribes
Chickasaw Nation
Comanche Nation
Delaware Nation
Eastern Shawnee Tribe
Fort Sill Apache Tribe
Iowa Tribe
Kaw Nation
Kialegee Tribal Town
Kickapoo Tribe
Kiowa Indian Tribe
Miami Tribe
Modoc Tribe
Muscogee (Creek) Nation
Osage Tribe
Ottawa Tribe
Otoe-Missouria Tribe of Indians
Pawnee Nation
Peoria Tribe of Indians
Ponca Tribe of Indians
Quapaw Tribe of Indians,
Sac & Fox Nation
Seminole Nation
Seneca-Cayuga Tribe
Shawnee Tribe
Thlopthlocco Tribal Town,
Tonkawa Tribe of Indians
United Keetoowah Band of Cherokee Indians
Wichita and Affiliated Tribes: Wichita, Keechi, Waco, Tawakonie
Wiyot Tribe, California Wyandotte Nation

OREGON
Burns Paiute Tribe of the Burns Paiute Indian Colony
Confederated Tribes of Coos, Lower Umpqua, Siuslaw Indians
Confederated Tribes of the Siletz Reservation
Confederated Tribes of the Umatilla Reservation
Confederated Tribes of the Grand Ronde Community
Confederated Tribes of the Warm Springs Reservation
Cow Creek Band of Umpqua Indians

Coquille Tribe
Klamath Indian Tribes

SOUTH CAROLINA

Catawba Indian Nation

SOUTH DAKOTA

Crow Creek Sioux Tribe of the Crow Creek Reservation
Flandreau Santee Sioux Tribe
Oglala Sioux Tribe of the Pine Ridge Reservation
Rosebud Sioux Tribe of the Rosebud Indian Reservation
Cheyenne River Sioux Tribe of the Cheyenne River Reservation
Lower Brule Sioux Tribe of the Lower Brule Reservation
Sisseton-Wahpeton Oyate of the Lake Traverse Reservation

RHODE ISLAND

Narragansett Indian Tribe

TEXAS

Alabama-Coushatta Tribes
Kickapoo Traditional Tribe
Ysleta Del Sur Pueblo

UTAH

Northwestern Band of Shoshoni Nation (Washakie)
Paiute Indian Tribe: Cedar City Band, Kanosh Band, Koosharem Band, Indian Peaks Band, Shivwits Band
Skull Valley Band of Goshute Indians
Ute Indian Tribe of the Uintah & Ouray Reservation

WASHINGTON

Muckleshoot Indian Tribe of the Muckleshoot Reservation
Confederated Tribes of the Chehalis Reservation
Confederated Tribes of the Colville Reservation
Confederated Tribes and Bands of the Yakama Nation
Cowlitz Indian Tribe
Hoh Indian Tribe, Hoh Reservation
Jamestown S'Klallam
Kalispel Indian Community of the Kalispel Reservation
Lower Elwha Tribal Community of the Lower Elwha Reservation
Lummi Tribe of Lummi Reservation
Makah Indian Tribe of the Makah Indian Reservation
Nisqually Indian Tribe of the Nisqually Reservation
Nooksack Indian Tribe
Port Gamble Indian Community of the Port Gamble Reservation
Puyallup Tribe of Puyallup Reservation
Quileute Tribe of Quileute Reservation
Quinault Tribe of the Quinault Reservation
Samish Indian Tribe
Sauk-Suiattle Indian Tribe
Shoalwater Bay Tribe of the Shoalwater Bay Indian Reservation
Skokomish Indian Tribe of the Skokomish Reservation
Snoqualmie Tribe
Spokane Tribe of Spokane Reservation
Squaxin Island Tribe of the Squaxin Island Reservation
Stillaguamish Tribe
Suquamish Indian Tribe of the Port Madison Reservation
Swinomish Indians of the Swinomish Reservation
Tulalip Tribes of Tulalip Reservation
Upper Skagit Indian Tribe

WISCONSIN

Bad River Band of the Lake Superior Tribe of Chippewa Indians of the Bad River Reservation
Forest County Potawatomi Community
Ho-Chunk Nation
Lac Courte Oreilles Band of Lake Superior Chippewa Indians
Lac du Flambeau Band of Lake Superior Chippewa Indians of Lac du Flambeau Reservation
Menominee Indian Tribe
Oneida Tribe of Indians
Red Cliff Band of Lake Superior Chippewa Indians
St. Croix Chippewa Indians
Sokaogon Chippewa Community
Stockbridge Munsee Community

WYOMING

Arapahoe Tribe of the Wind River Reservation
Shoshone Tribe of the Wind River Reservation

INTERSTATE

Colorado River Indian Tribes of the Colorado River Indian Reservation, Arizona and California
Confederated Tribes of the Goshute Reservation, Nevada and Utah Navajo Nation, Arizona, New Mexico, and Utah
Fort McDermitt Paiute and Shoshone Tribes of the Fort McDermitt Indian Reservation, Nevada and Oregon
Fort Mojave Indian Tribe of Arizona, California, and Nevada
Pokagon Band of Potawatomi Indians, Michigan and Indiana
Quechan Tribe of the Fort Yuma Indian Reservation, California and Arizona
Sac & Fox Nation of Missouri in Kansas and Nebraska
Standing Rock Sioux Tribe of North and South Dakota
Ute Mountain Tribe of the Ute Mountain Reservation, Colorado, New Mexico, and Utah
Washoe Tribe of Nevada and California: Carson Colony, Dresslerville Colony, Woodfords Community, Stewart Community, Washoe Ranches ■

Notable Accomplishments

1752 Benjamin Franklin flies a kite in a thunderstorm and proves lightning is electricity; he then invents a lightning rod.

1777 United States flag is authorized: "Thirteen stripes alternative red and white; that the Union be thirteen stars, white in a blue field, representing a new constellation."

1787 The Constitutional Convention, held in Philadelphia, creates the U.S. Constitution.

1804-06 The Lewis and Clark expedition successfully crosses the American continent and returns to Missouri.

1825 Erie Canal completed.

1828 Noah Webster publishes *American Dictionary of the English Language.*

1844 First message sent over a telegraph line by inventor Samuel F.B. Morse.

Daniel Boone comes through the Cumberland Gap with his band of pioneers.

1851 *The Flying Cloud*, a clipper ship, sails from New York to San Francisco in 89 days, 8 hours.

1852 Harriet Beecher Stowe publishes *Uncle Tom's Cabin*, which sells 300,000 copies the first year.

1858 First transatlantic cable completed by Cyrus W. Field.

1861 First transcontinental telegraph line is put in service.

1869 Transcontinental railroad is completed.

1872 World's first national park is established—Wyoming's Yellowstone.

1876 First telephone conversation between inventor Alexander Graham Bell and assistant Thomas Watson.

1878 Thomas Edison founds the Edison Electric Light Company.

1881 Booker T. Washington founds the Tuskegee Institute for blacks.

1883 The Brooklyn Bridge is completed.

1890 Jacob Riis publishes *How the Other Half Lives*, spurring reforms.

1892 Ellis Island opens. The first of 12 million immigrants passes through its "golden door."

1899 Scott Joplin writes "Maple Leaf Rag." Ragtime's vibrant piano compositions introduce African American rhythms into popular music.

1900 L. Frank Baum writes *The Wonderful Wizard of Oz*, an allegory of Populist politics.

1903 First cross-country automobile

trip completed from San Francisco to New York, May 23-Aug. 1. First successful heavier-than-air airplane flight, by Orville Wright Dec. 17.

1903 President Roosevelt designates Pelican Island, Florida, as the first national wildlife refuge.

1904 New York City's first subway line opens.

1908 Henry Ford introduces the Model T automobile, costing $850.

1909 W. E. B. Du Bois helps found the National Association for the Advancement of Colored People.

1914 Panama Canal is opened..

1921 Comedian Charlie Chaplin stars in *The Kid* as his own mustachioed creation, the Tramp.

1924 George Gershwin writes "Rhapsody in Blue."

1927 Charles Lindbergh completes the first solo nonstop transatlantic flight.

1931 The Empire State Building opens.

1936 Margaret Mitchell publishes *Gone With the Wind.*

1940 Richard Wright publishes *Native Son.*

1945 First atomic bomb produced and tested; dropped on two Japanese cities.

1946 ENIAC, the first computer, comes on line.

1947 Radiocarbon dating developed.

1953 A revolution in biology follows the discovery of the double-helix structure of the DNA molecule by American James D. Watson and Englishman Francis Crick.

1954 Jonas Salk's polio vaccine is tested on more than 400,000 children nationwide.

1954 First nuclear-powered submarine, *Nautilus*, launched in Connecticut.

1956 First transatlantic telephone cable becomes operational.

1956 Don Larsen of the New York Yankees pitches the first "perfect" game in a World Series.

1957 Jack Kerouac publishes *On the Road.* It quickly establishes itself as the bible of the beatniks, a small group of bohemians and self-styled fugitives from the great American middle class.

1958 First U.S. satellite, Explorer I, goes into orbit.

1959 St. Lawrence Seaway opens.

1960 The Pill, the first oral contraceptive available in the U.S., is approved by the Food and Drug Administration.

1960 First operational laser pulse used.

1962 Rachel Carson publishes *Silent Spring.*

1962 John Glenn is the first American to orbit Earth.

1963 The U.S., Soviet Union, and Britain sign a limited nuclear test-ban treaty.

1969 The U.S. puts the first men, Neil A. Armstrong and Edwin E. Aldrin, Jr., on the moon.

1971 The silicon microprocessor is developed.

1972 *Washington Post* reporters Carl Bernstein and Bob Woodward begin their coverage of "a third-rate burglary attempt" at the Watergate office complex. Less than 16 months later, President Richard M. Nixon resigns.

1976 Vikings I and II land on Mars.

1977 Treaties are signed for the gradual return of the Canal Zone and canal to Panama.

1978 President Jimmy Carter mediates Camp David accords between Israel and Egypt.

1981 Space Shuttle *Columbia*, first reusable spacecraft, is launched.

1981 Personal computers introduced.

1981 Sandra Day O'Connor becomes the first female Justice of the Supreme Court.

1987 More than 200,000 gays, lesbians, and sympathizers march on Washington, D.C., to demand civil rights and stronger action against AIDS, an affliction first reported in the U.S. in 1981.

2001 Human DNA is successfully decoded.

2004 Nuclear-powered spacecraft Cassini enters into orbit around Saturn, in a joint project of NASA, the European Space Agency, and the Italian Space Agency.

2005 Space Shuttle *Discovery* makes a successful round-trip visit to the International Space Station. ■

Leaders and People of Note

Adams, Abigail (Abigail Smith) (1744-1818) Avid letter writer and trusted adviser to her husband, John. Her correspondence, particularly with her husband, provides insight into 18th-century life in the new nation. She supported the decision to break from Great Britain, was a strong and influential advocate for women's rights, and a vigorous opponent of slavery.

Adams, Charles Francis (1807-1886) Son of John Quincy Adams; abolitionist congressman, leader of Free-Soil Party; served as U.S. minister to Great Britain during Civil War, successfully keeping Britain from recognizing and possibly allying with the Confederacy.

Reformer Jane Addams, seen here about 1914, was a founder of the National Progressive Party.

Adams, John (1735-1826) Political philosopher, George Washington's Vice President (1789-1797), second President (1797-1801).

Adams, John Quincy (1767-1848) Son of John and Abigail, skillful diplomat instrumental in acquiring Florida and in writing the Monroe Doctrine; prominent abolitionist while serving in House of Representatives; sixth president (1825-1829).

Addams, Jane (1860-1935) Social reformer, founded Chicago's Hull House, where people came for assistance with everything from education to health care. She also helped form the National Progressive Party in 1912, the Women's Peace Party in 1915, and the American Civil Liberties Union (ACLU) in 1920.

Arnold, Benedict (1741-1801) Hero, traitor. Fought valiantly on patriot side until 1779, when, passed over for promotion and having married a Loyalist sympathizer, he sold his services to the British. Subsequently alienated the Loyalists and the British when he abandoned his English contact, Maj. John Andre, to be hanged as a spy by the Americans. He retired in England in 1781, where he spent the rest of his sickly life ostracized by all sides.

Barton, Clara (1821-1912) Nursed soldiers during America's Civil War. After the war, she organized searches for missing soldiers. During the Franco-Prussian War (1869-1873), she opened hospitals in Europe. In 1881 she founded the American Red Cross—an organization that provides neutral wartime relief and peacetime disaster relief—serving as its president from 1881 to 1904. She helped gain it worldwide respect and recognition.

Burr, Aaron (1756-1836) Third vice president (1801-1805). Challenged Alexander Hamilton to a duel after Hamilton's opposition cost Burr important political positions. Fled to Mexico after killing Hamilton, where he made tentative plans to form an independent government and possibly to foment a secessionist movement in the western U.S. Tried for treason in 1807; acquitted.

Carter, Jimmy (1924-) While President of the United States, signed the Panama Canal Treaty in 1977. Founded the Carter Center of Emory University in 1982 after losing a bid for a second term. The center works on human rights and democracy issues. Awarded the Presidential Medal of Freedom—the nation's highest civilian honor—with wife Rosalynn in 1999. Won the Nobel Peace Prize in 2002.

Chavez, Cesar (1927-1993) Labor leader and union organizer of Mexican-American descent. A farm laborer himself, and the son of farm laborers, Chavez knew first-hand the problems faced by migrant workers. He created the National Farm Workers Association (NFWA) in 1962; organized nation-wide boycotts of agribusinesses that refused to negotiate, resulting in much-needed reforms.

Clay, Henry (1777-1852) Influential U.S. Senator and Speaker of the House; earned nickname "Great Pacificator" for his role in the Missouri Compromise; later brokered the Compromise of 1850, which helped avoid a civil war.

Crazy Horse (Ta-sunko-witko) (c.1842-1877) Oglala Sioux leader of Red Cloud's War (1866-68) and Sioux agitation (1876-77); helped defeat Custer at Little Bighorn (1876); was killed in prison.

Debs, Eugene V. (1855-1926) Socialist and union organizer who led a strike against the Great Northern Railway; Socialist candidate for President five times; helped found Industrial Workers of the World.

Decatur, Stephen (1779-1820) Naval officer famous for commanding a successful expedition into the harbor of Tripoli to burn the U.S. frigate *Philadelphia* which had fallen into Tripolitan hands; subsequently fought with great distinction in the War of 1812, and later against the Barbary Pirates in the Mediterranean.

Dix, Dorothea (1802-1887) Helped create distinct institutions for the poor and mentally ill, replacing those that treated poverty and mental illness as a crime. Her dedication led her to work in 21 states and Canada.

Douglass, Frederick (original name Frederick Augustus Washington Bailey) (1817-1895) Brilliant orator and writer; leader in Abolition movement; consultant to President Lincoln; first black citizen to hold high rank in U.S. government. Born a slave, escaped to New York in the late 1830s, changing his name to elude slave hunters. Found his voice as a natural orator at an antislavery convention in 1841; decried violent abolitionist raid on Harpers Ferry in 1859; published his autobiography in 1882; appointed U.S. minister and consul general to Haiti (1889-91). Staunch supporter of women's rights movement.

Franklin, Benjamin (1706-1790) Statesman, scientist, writer, and philosopher. Created foundation of public libraries, invented an improved heating stove, experimented with electricity (most famously with kites in 1752). Signed Declaration of Independence, helped negotiate the Treaty of Paris, which ended the Revolutionary War.

Geronimo (Goyathlay, "One Who Yawns) (1829-1909) Leader of Chiricahua Apache. Resisted forced removal of Apaches to reservation in Arizona, leading raiding parties that wreaked havoc throughout the region. Surrendered and taken prisoner in 1886. Attempted unsuccessfully to "take the white man's role" by farming and joining the Dutch Reformed Church.

Grant, Ulysses S. (1822-1885) Commanded Union forces from 1864 until end of Civil War; U.S. President 1869-1877. The courtesy with which he accepted Robert E. Lee's surrender at Appomattox and his leniency toward the rebel army are considered to have been instrumental in the relatively peaceful way in which the country reunited. Grant's memoirs are considered among the finest of military autobiographies.

Grimke, Sarah Moore (1792-1873) **and Angelina Emily** 1805-1879) Daughters of a Southern slaveowner; made advances in abolition; raised women's rights issues.

Hamilton, Alexander (c.1755/57-1804) The nation's first secretary of state, appointed by George Washington. Hamilton, a committed nationalist, believed that power should reside in a central government, not in separate state governments. A delegate to the Constitutional Convention in Philadelphia in 1787, he helped to write the United States Constitution, later joining with James Madison and John Jay to write *The Federalist*, a series of newspaper essays that explained and promoted the Constitution to the general public. Hamilton was killed in a duel with political adversary Aaron Burr.

Hoover, J. Edgar (1895-1972) Controversial director of the FBI from 1924 until his death in 1972. Responsible for increasing the agency's size and responsibilities, focusing its attention on radicals, or people Hoover considered to be radicals, of every kind—from the KKK to Martin Luther King. Stayed in office through 8 presidents and 18 attorneys general, apparently by threatening to leak damaging information about them.

Jefferson, Thomas (1743-1826) The third President of the United States (1801-1809), and one of early America's greatest political minds. He wrote the Declaration of Independence. He also had interests in philosophy, education, nature, science, architecture, farming, music, and writing.

Jones, John Paul (1747-1792) Original name John Paul. First American naval hero. In 1779, commanding the French ship *Bonhomme Richard*, Jones and a fleet of four smaller ships successfully engaged British ships *Serapis* and *Countess of Scarborough* in a grueling battle off the British coast. At the battle's outset, when called upon to surrender, Jones famously responded "I have not yet begun to fight."

Kennedy, John Fitzgerald (1917-1963) Served as the 35th U.S. President (1961-63). Challenged Americans to "Ask not what your country can do for you—ask what you can do for your country." Handled the Cuban Missile Crisis; assassinated before he completed his third year as President.

King, Martin Luther, Jr. (1929-1968) Advocated nonviolence and racial brotherhood in the struggle for racial equality. He led the boycott of segregated public transportation in Montgomery, Alabama. Major organizer of March on Washington, where he delivered his "I Have a Dream" speech. Won the Nobel Peace Prize in 1964; was assassinated in Memphis, Tennessee.

Lee, Robert E. (1807-1870) Commanded the Army of Northern Virginia during the Civil War; one of the nation's ablest military leaders; surrendered to Ulysses Grant in 1865. His conduct helped prevent guerilla war after the surrender.

Lincoln, Abraham (1809-1865) Born in Kentucky, where he received little formal education. Moved to Illinois and was elected to the legislature, which kicked off a political career. Elected 16th President of the United States in 1860; guided country through the Civil War. He issued the Emancipation Proclamation in 1863 and delivered the Gettysburg Address that same year. He was shot in Ford's Theater in 1865.

MacArthur, Douglas (1880-1964) Commanded the Southwest Pacific Theater in World War II; skillfully administered postwar Japan during the Allied occupation afterwards; led United Nations forces during the first nine months of the Korean War. Widely criticized for sending in regular troops to Washington, D.C. to disperse the veterans of the Bonus Army in 1932. Served as military adviser to the Phillippines from1935 to 1942.

Malcolm X (1925-1965) Original name Malcolm Little; Muslim name el-Hajj Malik El-Shabazz. Leader of black militants, encouraged racial pride, black nationalism. In the beginning rejected integration of the races, urging instead black separatism and elitism, through violent means if necessary. Later had a change of heart—perhaps a melding of the races would be possible. Assassinated in Harlem, three Black Muslims were convicted of the murder.

Mankiller, Wilma (1945-) Her family was involved in the 1969 Indian occupation of Alcatraz. She was later elected first female principal chief of the Cherokee Nation (1985-1995).

Mather, Cotton (1663-1728) American Congregational minister and author, son and grandson of Puritan ministers. A man of contradictions, he was fascinated by science and was selected for membership in the Royal Society in London; at the same time, he believed in witchcraft. However, his was a cautionary voice during Salem's witch trials.

Paine, Thomas (1737-1809) British-American political philospher and writer whose pamphlet "Common Sense" urged the colonies to break with England; the "American Crisis" papers encouraged the Continental Army to continue fighting the British.

Perry, Oliver Hazard (1785-1819) Naval officer who commanded squadron which successfully took on the British fleet in Lake Erie during the War of 1812, ending British control of the Great Lakes. His official report regarding the British surrender read "We have met the enemy and they are ours."

Powell, John Wesley (1834-1902) Geologist and explorer of the Green and Colorado Rivers; wrote extensively on western Indian languages and customs. Ran the Colorado River and reported on the hydrology of the West.

Roosevelt, Anna Eleanor (1884-1962) Humanitarian First Lady and wife of Franklin D. Roosevelt who fought for the Universal Declaration of Human

Explorer John Wesley Powell , at left, poses with three members of his team, about 1870.

Rights, adopted by the United Nations in 1948.

Roosevelt, Franklin Delano (1882-1945) Served as the 32nd U.S. President for four terms (1933-1945), longer than any other President. (After he died, the 22nd Amendment to the U.S. Constitution was passed, allowing only two consecutive terms of office.) His domestic program, the New Deal, promised relief, recovery, and reform during the Great Depression of the 1930s. He declared war on Japan after it attacked Pearl Harbor on December 7, 1941; thus the United States entered World War II.

Roosevelt, Theodore (1858-1919) Served as the 26th U.S President (1901-09). Acquired the Panama Canal Zone and began construction of Panama Canal; won the Nobel Peace Prize (1906) for helping end Russo-Japanese War; helped break up Standard Oil Company and other trusts; well known for his conservation of land and natural resources.

Seton, Saint Elizabeth Ann (maiden name Elizabeth Ann Bayley) (1774-1821) First native-born American to be canonized by the Roman Catholic Church (in 1975). One of the founders of New York's first charitable institution, the Society for the Relief of Poor Widows with Small Children. Later converted to Roman Catholicism and founded the Sisters of Charity, the first religious society in America.

Sitting Bull (Tatanka Iyotake) (c.1831-1890) Sioux chief who defeated Gen. George Custer in the Battle of Little Bighorn (1876); gained worldwide recognition in Buffalo Bill's "Wild West" Show; a leader in the Ghost Dance movement, he was shot and killed by Indian guards attempting to arrest him.

Tecumseh (1768-1813) Shawnee Indian chief. A skilled orator and military strategist, he formed intertribal alliances to fight white rule in the Ohio River valley. Fought with British forces during the War of 1812, participating in the capture of Detroit and the invasion of Ohio.

Truth, Sojourner (Legal name Isabella Van Wagener) (c.1797-1883) Evangelist and reformer. Born to slaves, was herself a slave owned by Dutch masters in New York until she was set free by Isaac Van Wagener. She believed her God-given purpose in life was to travel about the country, singing and preaching about the brotherhood of man. A tireless campaigner for abolition and women's rights, she helped integrate the streetcars of Washington, D.C., and was received at the White House by President Lincoln in 1864.

Tubman, Harriet (ca 1820-1913) Escaped slavery and became a prominent force in the Underground Railroad. Served as nurse, laundress, and spy for the Union Army during the Civil War.

Webster, Daniel (1782-1852) United States Senator from Massachusetts and Secretary of State; a candid, gifted orator who, with Clay, helped steer the country away from civil war. Voted against war with Great Britain in 1812; politically conservative, he believed—contrary to Andrew Jackson's agrarian policies—that helping business interests was the surest way to help the general public. Daniel Webster's outspoken, opinionated personality won him staunch detractors as well as dedicated admirers. John Quincy Adams's memoirs make reference to "the gigantic intellect, the envious temper, the ravenous ambition, and the rotten heart of Daniel Webster." ■

Sports

Aaron, Henry Louis (Hank) (1934-) Baseball great who hit 755 home runs during his career, a record that remains unbroken in U.S. professional baseball.

Ali, Muhammad (Cassius Marcellus Clay) (1942-) Called The Greatest; he won a boxing gold medal at the 1960 Olympic Games; he defeated Sonny Liston to become heavyweight boxing champion of the world in 1964. He successfully defended the title nine times, until 1967, when he was stripped of the title and sentenced to five years in prison for refusing to submit to the draft, claiming a religious exemption as a minister in the Nation of Islam. In 1971, he was cleared of the charges; in 1974, at age 32, he won back the title.

Armstrong, Lance (1971-) Winner of the grueling Tour de France bicycle race an unprecedented seven times (1999 through 2005).

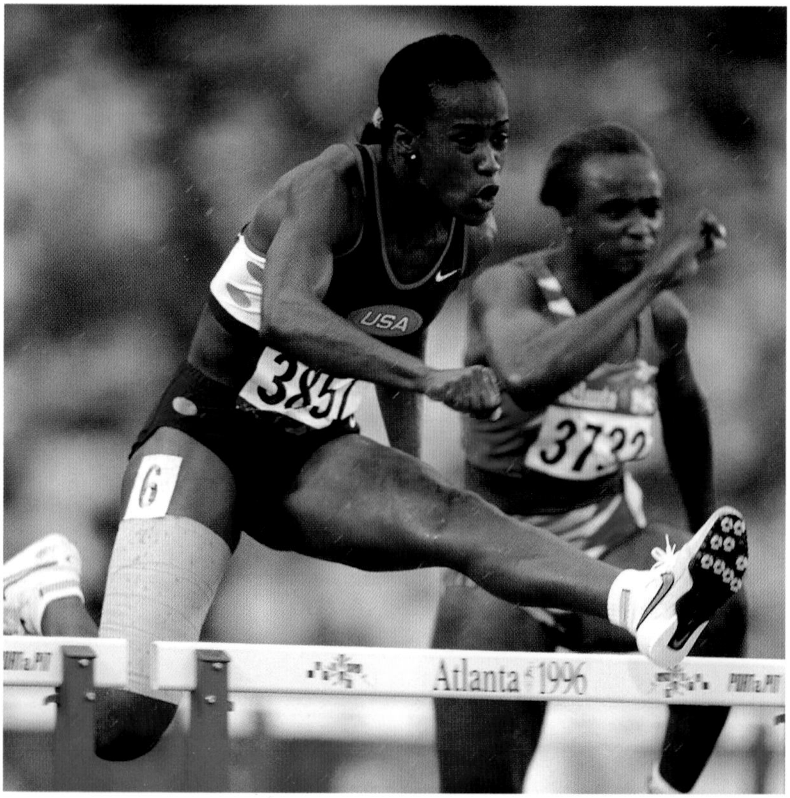

Berra, Lawrence Peter(Yogi) (1925-) Baseball player, manager, coach. Played with the New York Yankees from 1946 until he retired in 1963. He was named the American League's most valuable player in 1951, 1954, and 1955. Berra caught in more World Series games (75) than any other catcher, and hit at least 20 home runs a season through 1958. He managed the Yankees until he was fired in 1964, managed and coached the New York Mets (1965-1975), then returned to coach the Yankees from 1976 to 1983. He became Yankee manager again from 1983 to 1985. He's known for such phrases as "it ain't over til it's over" and "it's deja vu all over again."

Brown, James Nathaniel (Jim) (1936-) Football legend; he played fullback for the Cleveland Browns (1957-1965), his career rushing record of 12,312 yards remained unbroken until 1984.

Grange, Harold (Red) (1903-1991) Star running back at the University of Illinois (1922-1925), where he earned the nickname Galloping Ghost, and with the Chicago Bears (1925-1934). His exploits helped promote public interest in professional football.

Jones, Robert Tyre (Bobby) (1902-1971) Golfer; a practicing lawyer, he never turned professional. He was the first to achieve golfing's Grand Slam, winning the four major tournaments of his time in a single year. From 1923 through 1930, Jones won 13 championships in the four annual tournaments that make up the Grand Slam—a record held until Jack Nicklaus surpassed it in 1973. In 1958, Jones was awarded the freedom of the burgh of St. Andrews, Fife, Scotland

Jackie Joyner-Kersee holds the world's record in the heptathlon.

(site of the world's premier golf club), the first American since Benjamin Franklin (in 1759) to receive such an honor.

Jordan, Michael (1963-) Nicknamed Air Jordan, and considered by most to be the greatest all-around basketball player in history; led his team, the Chicago Bulls, to six championships (1991-1993, 1996-1998); led the U.S. Olympic team to two gold medals (1984 and 1992).

Joyner-Kersee, Jaqueline (Jackie) (1962-) One of the greatest female athletes ever to compete, she holds the world's record in the seven-event heptathlon.

King, Billie Jean (1943-) Tennis champion and crusader for women's equality in sport. She won at Wimbledon (6 singles titles, 5 mixed doubles, 10 doubles titles), at the U.S. Open (4 singles, 4 mixed doubles, 4 doubles), took one Australian Open singles title, and one singles and one doubles title at the French Open. She also beat Bobby Riggs in a 1973 "Battle of the Sexes" match.

Louganis, Gregory Efthimios (Greg) (1960-) Diver; perhaps the best in history. Retired in 1984 after having won 47 national and 13 world championships. Competing in the 1976, 1984, and 1988 Olympics (the U.S. boycotted the 1980 Olympics), he won five medals: a silver in 1976 at age 16; thereafter, it was all gold.

Man o' War (Big Red) (1917-1947) Thoroughbred racehorse, voted the greatest horse of the first half of the 20th century in a 1950 Associated Press poll. Raced only two seasons (1919-1920), he won 20 of 21 races (beaten by a horse named Upset); establishing five track records at various distances; won the Preakness Stakes and the Belmont Stakes in 1920 (did not race in the Kentucky Derby). Retired to stud in late 1920. He sired 64 stakes horses, including War Admiral (winner of the 1937 Triple Crown).

Murphy, Isaac (1856-1896) Jockey who won 628 races out of 1,412 entered during his career (1873-1896); first jockey to ride three Kentucky Derby winners (1884, 1890, 1891), won a total of $250,000.

Nicklaus, William (Jack) (1940-) Golfer who won the Masters Tournament six times, the U.S. Open four times, the PGA Championship five times, the British Open three times, and the Australian Open six times. He played on winning U.S. World Cup teams six times, and won a record three individual World Cup tournaments. He was named PGA Player of the year five times.

Owens, Jesse (1913-1980) Track and field; won four gold medals in the 1936 Olympics in Berlin.

Robinson, Jack Roosevelt (Jackie) (1919-1972) Legendary player who broke the color barrier in the game of baseball, playing first with the Kansas City Monarchs of the Negro National League (1945-1947), then with the Brooklyn Dodgers of the (until then) all-white National League (1947-1956). He was voted the league's most valuable player in 1949.

Ruth, George Herman (Babe) (1895-1948) Nicknamed the Bambino or the Sultan of Swat; hit a record 60 home runs in 1927 (a 156-game season); a career total of 714, a record that lasted until 1974.

Shoemaker, William Lee (Willlie) (1931-) Jockey; In a career that spanned 41 years (1949-1990), he won a world-record 8,833 races, $120,000,000 in purses.

Spitz, Mark (1950-) Olympic swimmer, won seven gold medals at the 1972 summer games, setting world records in all seven events.

Sullivan, John L. (1858-1918) Pugilist, also known as the Great John L. and the Boston Strong Boy; won heavyweight championship (1882) fighting with bare knuckles, on turf.

Thorpe, Jim (1886-1953) Of mostly Sauk and Fox Indian descent, he won decathlon and pentathlon in 1912 Olympic Games (though later disqualified for having briefly played minor-league baseball, his Olympic medals were restored to him in 1982); played professional baseball (1913-1919) and football (1919-1926); first president of the National Football League (1920-1921); Pennsylvania town of Jim Thorpe is named after him.

Tilden, Bill (1893-1953) Tennis great called "Big Bill," he was the first American to win Wimbledon; ranked number one in the world from 1920 to 1925; won seven U.S. Nationals; captained seven winning Davis Cup teams for the U.S.

Zaharias, Mildred Ella Didrikson (Babe) (1914-1956) Played on the women's All-America Basketball team (1930-1932); at the 1930 to 1932 women's national track and field championships, she won eight events and tied for a ninth; at the 1932 Olympic Games she won gold medals in hurdles and in javelin throw. She later took up golf, winning the National Women's Amateur title in 1946 and 17 consecutive amateur tournaments in 1947; she then turned professional and won three U.S. Women's Open titles. ■

Scientists and Inventors

Baekeland, Leo Hendric (1863-1944) Chemist and inventor. Discovered Bakelite, the first synthetic plastic.

Bardeen, John (1908-1991) Physicist, with Walter Brattain and William Shockley developed the point-contact transistor in 1947 for which they received the Nobel prize for physics in 1956. Won the same award in 1972, with Leon N. Cooper and John R. Schreiffer for formulating the theory of superconductivity in 1957.

Bell, Alexander Graham (1847-1922) Invented the telephone, the induction balance for finding metal objects in the body, and a precursor of the iron lung, among other things. He experimented with flight, with hydrofoils, and with selective breeding in sheep. He taught the visible speech system that his father created. Founded the journal *Science* (1883), and was second president of the National Geographic Society (1898-1903).

Berg, Paul (1926-) Working at Stanford, combined the DNA of two different types of virus, creating the first recombinant DNA molecule. He was awarded (with Walter Gilbert and Frederick Sanger) the 1980 Nobel Prize for Chemistry.

Bigelow, Erastus Brigham (1814-1879 Invented power looms for manufacturing fabrics and weaving carpets (1845-51); helped found Massachusetts Institute of Technology in 1861.

Blanchard, Thomas (1788-1864) Devised an automatic tack-making machine and a lathe for turning gunstocks.

Boyer, Herbert W. (1936-) Working with fellow biochemist Stanley N. Cohen, pioneered genetic engineering—the splicing together of DNA from different organisms to create new genes that alter nature.

Burden, Henry (1791-1871) Invented a horseshoe-making machine used during the Civil War.

Burroughs, William Seward (1855-1898) Invented the mechanical calculating machine (1885) and patented a recording adding machine(1892).

Carver, George Washington (c.1864-1943) Son of slaves who promoted crop diversification and peanuts, soybeans, and other soil enhancers; developed more than 300 by-products of peanuts, and 118 from sweet potatoes.

Colt, Samuel (1814-1862) Invented the revolver, patented in 1836. Built a firm (1842) to manufacture the revolver for its use by U.S. troops during the Mexican War.

Corliss, George Henry (1817-1888) Developed and manufactured the steam engine that furnished the power for the displays at Philadelphia's U.S. Centennial Exhibition of 1876. The Corliss steam engine produced power enough to drive 13 acres of machinery inside Machinery Hall "without a moment's derangement," according to an observer.

de Forest, Lee (1873-1961) Broadcasting industry pioneer, he invented the vacuum tube, which he patented as a "Device for Amplifying Feeble Electrical Currents."

Duryea, Charles (1861-1938) and **Frank** (1869-1967) Brothers and bicycle mechanics in Springfield, Massachusetts; built America's first successful car, which they exhibited in 1895.

Eastman, George (1854-1932) Developed the Kodak box camera in 1888 after perfecting the process for making photographic dry plates and flexible film.

Edison, Thomas Alva (1847-1931) Patented more than 1,000 inventions, including an electric vote recorder, a printing telegraph, a microphone, a phonograph, an incandescent electric lightbulb, an alkaline storage battery, and a high-speed camera and kinetograph.

Edgerton, Harold E. (1903-1990) An electrical engineer and photographer, he invented the electronic flash, or strobe. During World War II, he devised stroboscopic units for photographing the enemy at night. He later developed methods and equipment for underwater photography at unprecedented depths.

Einstein, Albert (1879-1955) Deduced the theory of relativity, Brownian motion, and the photoelectric effect. Made key contributions to the quantum theory. After being forced to leave Germany before World War II, he immigrated to the United States and

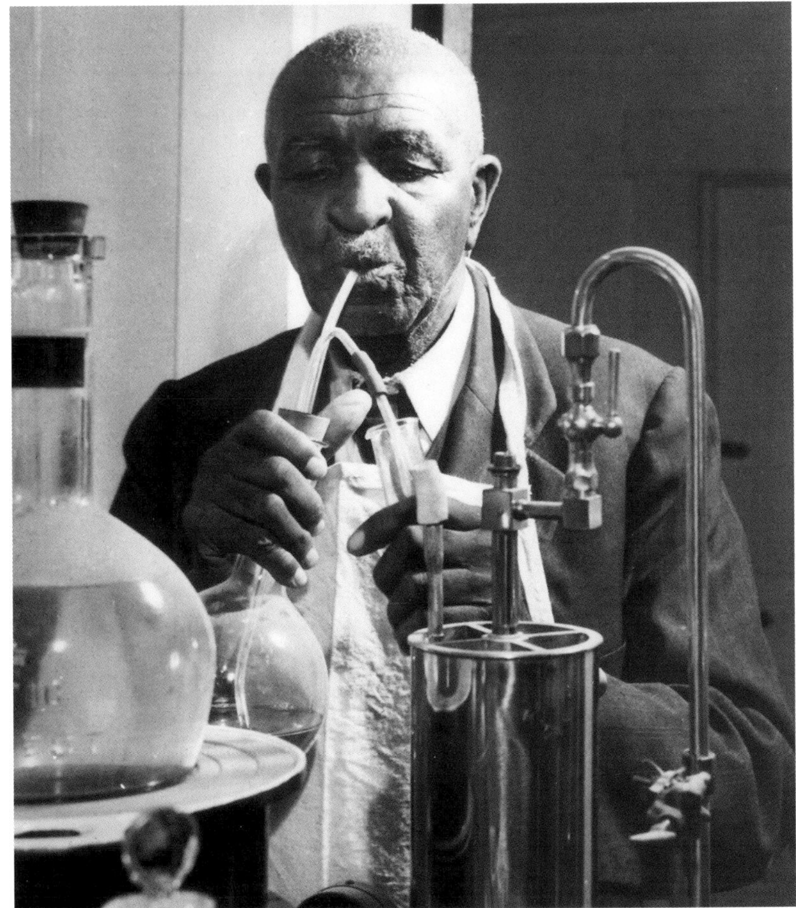

George Washington Carver conducts an expiriment at Tuskegee Institute, about 1925.

served at the Institute for Advanced Study at Princeton, New Jersey. He was awarded the Nobel Prize in physics in 1921.

Ericsson, John (1803-1889) Swedish born engineer, devised screw propeller, designed and built ironclad *Monitor* for Union Army in 1862.

Evans, Oliver (1755-1819) Inventor of the high-pressure steam engine. Devised machines and methods to improve the manufacture of flour in particular and of milling in general. George Washington used his machinery at Mt. Vernon. Also built steam-powered dredge for the Philadelphia waterfront in 1805.

Farnsworth, Philo Taylor (1906-1971) Engineer. Demonstrated the world's first all-electronic television system in 1928. After unsuccessfully attempting to produce his system commercially, licensed his innovations to RCA.

Fitch, John (1743-1798) steamboat pioneer. Built first operating steamboat.

Franklin, Benjamin (1706-1790) Statesman, scientist, and philosopher. Created foundation of public libraries, invented an improved heating stove, and experimented with electricity (most famously with kites in 1752). Signed the Declaration of Independence, and helped negotiate the Treaty of Paris, ending the Revolutionary War.

Fulton, Robert (1765-1815) Built first affordable steamboat, opening up river transportation routes to commercial steamboats. Designed first submarine and war steamboat. Patented machines that sawed marble, spun flax, and twisted hemp into rope. Suggested improvements to canal construction.

Goddard, Robert H. (1882-1945) Built the first liquid-fuel rocket and the first rocket-firing bazooka.

Goethals, George Washington (1858-1928) Army officer and chief engineer for Panama Canal who saw canal construction through to completion.

Goodyear, Charles (1800-1860) Developed vulcanization process for treating rubber in 1839.

Henry, Joseph (1797-1878) Induced electricity through electromagnetism. Planner and first secretary of the Smithsonian Institution.

Hine, Lewis Wickes (1874-1940) Pioneer of documentary photography, he documented the construction of the Empire State Building in the 1920s, New York City tenements, and the immigrant processing center on Ellis Island in New York Harbor.

Hollerith, Herman (1860-1929) Invented the Hollerith Electric Tabulating Machine, which revolutionized data processing. It also prompted the catchphrase "do not fold, spindle or mutilate." His company was later renamed International Business Machines Corporation (IBM).

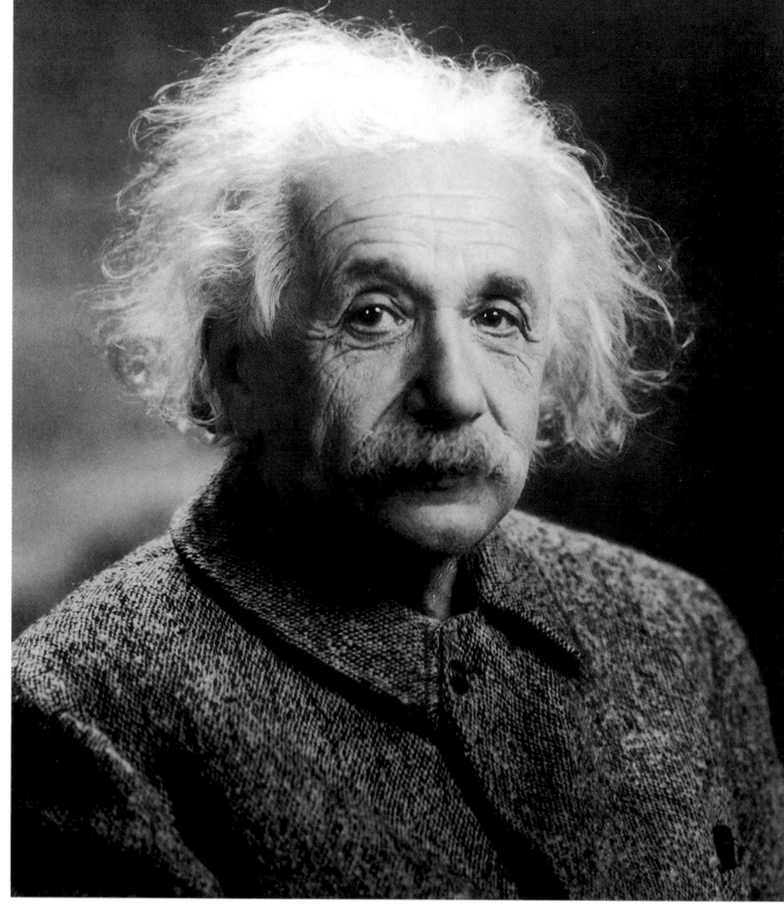

Albert Einstein, developer of the theory of relativity, about 1939.

Howe, Elias (1819-1867) Designed sewing machine, patented in 1846. Nephew of William Howe.

Howe, William (1803-1852) Uncle of Elias Howe; invented improved Howe truss bridge, patent awarded in 1840.

Hubble, Edwin Powell (1889-1953) Astronomer who proved that most nebulae are galaxies rushing away from one another in space beyond our Milky Way. His discoveries showed the universe is expanding—not staying the same size. He deduced the Hubble constant for measuring expansion of visible universe.

Hunt, Walter (1796-1859) Invented the safety pin, patented in 1849. Later sold all rights to his invention for $400.

Hyatt, John Wesley (1837-1920) Developed composition billiard balls, water filter and purifier, a new type of sewing machine, and a process for solidifying hardwood.

Jefferson, Thomas (1743-1826) The third President of the United States (1801-1809) and one of early America's greatest political minds. He wrote the Declaration of Independence. He also had interests in philosophy, education, nature, science, architecture, farming, music, and writing.

Kettering, Charles Franklin (1876-1958) Created first electric cash register, automotive electric self-starter engine, and numerous automobile improvements.

Kuiper, Gerard Peter (1905-1973) Dutch-American astronomer, discovered Uranus's moon Miranda in 1948 and Neptune's moon Nereid in 1949. In 1951, predicted belt of rocky, orbiting bodies would be found just outside Neptune's orbit. The Kuiper belt was discovered in 1990.

Land, Edwin Herbert (1909-1991) Physicist and inventor, devised first light polarizing apparatus (1932), invented Polaroid Land Camera, which developed and printed photographs in 60 seconds; had patents for more than 530 inventions.

Leavitt, Henrietta Swan (1868-1921) Discovered that the periods of Cepheid variable stars are directly related to their intrinsic brightness: this period-to-luminosity relationship provides astronomers with a star's absolute magnitude. Also discovered 4 novas and some 2,400 variable stars.

Lawrence, Ernest Orlando (1901-1958) Physicist who produced radioactive isotopes and used radioactivity in medicine. Introduced use of neutron beams in cancer treatment. Invented the cyclotron.

Morse, Samuel Finley Breese (1791-1872) Artist and inventor. Created Morse code, received patent for it in 1837.

McCormick, Cyrus Hall (1809-1884) Innovative industrialist. Invented the reaper in 1831. Later, as a businessman, he pioneered modern marketing techniques, advertising heavily, sending out agents, and selling on the installment plan.

Muir, John (1838-1914) Naturalist who wandered widely in the West; helped establish Yosemite National Park and influenced President Theodore Roosevelt's conservation initiatives.

Neumann, John von ((1903-1957) Mathematical and computer genius, born in Budapest, Hungary. He contributed to the theories of numbers and games and the science of cybernetics (a word he coined), but his greatest contributions were in the field of computer development. He was on the original roster of the Institute for Advanced Study in Princeton (1933-1957), and later worked at Los Alamos, developing both the atomic bomb and the hydrogen bomb.

Oppenheimer, Julius Robert (1904-1967) Physicist who directed the Manhattan Project (1942-45), which developed the atom bomb.

Parmly, Levi Spear (1790-1859) Dentist who invented modern dental floss (1815). He used silk thread.

Penzias, Arno (1933-) Working at Bell Labs in 1965 with fellow astrophysicist Robert Wilson discovered remnants of cosmic microwave background radiation, effectively validating the Big Bang theory. They shared the 1978 Nobel prize for physics.

Pincus, Gregory (1903-1967) Endocrinologist who directed the development of oral contraceptives, popularly known as the pill, which was approved by the FDA in 1960

Reed, Walter (1851-1902) Army surgeon and bacteriologist, proved in 1900 that yellow fever is transmitted by mosquitoes.

Rillieux, Norbert (1806-1894) Invented the multiple-effect evaporator, patented in 1843, which transformed cane-juice processing, and is still in use today.

Salk, Jonas (1914-1995) Physician who discovered the first successful vaccine for poliomyelitis in 1954.

Sequoyah (c.1765-1843) Cherokee who created a syllabary, a set of written characters each representing a syllable in the Cherokee language, and thus taught thousands of Indians to read and write.

Shockley, William Bradford (1910-1989) Physicist who developed, with John Bardeen and Walter H. Brattain, the transistor for which they received the 1956 Nobel prize for physics.

Spangler, James Murray (1848-1915) Patented (in 1908) the first widely marketed vacuum cleaner. He and his cousin William B. Hoover founded the Hoover Company.

Stevens, John (1749-1838) Initiated federal legislation establishing patent laws in the U.S. (1790); built the first seagoing steamship, the *Phoenix* (1808); also built the first experimental steam locomotive in the United States (1825).

Tesla, Nikola (1856-1943) Croatian-born American electrician and inventor who created artificial lighting and demonstrated the wireless communication system. Installed electric power machinery at Niagara Falls. Discovered the principle of rotating magnetic field.

Tombaugh, Clyde William (1906-1997) Astronomer who discovered the planet Pluto in 1930.

Townes, Charles H. (1915-) Developed the maser (Microwave Amplification by Stimulated Emission of Radiation) in 1954, instrumental in developing the laser in 1960. Won the Nobel Prize for physics in 1964, with Russian scientists N.G. Basov and A.M. Prokhorov, for their contributions to quantum electronics.

Waksman, Selman Abraham (1888-1973) Ukraine-born biochemist who discovered in 1943 the antibiotic streptomycin, which successfully treats tuberculosis.

Watson, James Dewey (1928-) American biologist, working with British biophysicist Francis Crick, discovered the double-helix molecular structure of DNA, for which they were awarded the Nobel Prize in physiology or medicine.

Whitney, Eli (1765-1825) Inventor of the cotton gin, in 1793.

Wright, Wilbur (1867-1912) **and Orville** (1871-1948) In 1903 the Wright brothers became the first to successfully fly a motor-powered airplane in Kitty Hawk, North Carolina.

Zworykin, Vladimir Kosma (1889-1982) Russian-born engineer, invented many electronic devices, including the iconoscope in 1923, and kinescope in 1929, which together made up the first electronic television system. ■

Artists

Alcott, Louisa May (1832-1888) Wrote immensely popular children's stories, including the autobiographical *Little Women* (1868-69) and *Little Men* (1871). Active in women's suffrage and also in temperance reform movements.

Angelou, Maya (1928-) Poet and writer whose work emphasizes the strength of black women; best known for *I Know Why the Caged Bird Sings*.

Armstrong, Louis (1900-1971) Jazz trumpeter and singer whose virtuosity and distinctive syle continues to influence musicians; international celebrity as soloist, band leader, and film actor.

Bernstein, Leonard (1918-1990) Conductor, composer, pianist, and educator. Conducted New York City Symphony (1945-1948) and the New York Philharmonic (1958-1969), served on the faculties at Berkshire Music Center (1948-1955), Brandeis University (1951-1956), wrote symphonies, ballets, musicals (including *West Side Story*). Gave concerts to introduce children from all economic backgrounds to classical music.

Bulfinch, Charles (1763-1844) America's first professional architect. His work includes the central part of the Boston State House (1795-98) and the west portico of the national Capitol (1818-30).

Cassatt, Mary (1844-1926) Painter who captured the play of light on objects (for example, the fabric in "The Cup of Tea" appeared iridescent) and the informal gesture or moment.

Cather, Willa (1873-1947) Novelist who wrote many novels dealing with the passing frontier and the heroic strength and bravery of the immigrants that settled America's plains and prairies. Among her best-known work, *O Pioneers!* (1913), takes place on the Nebraska prairies; *My Antonia* (1918) follows a Bohemian immigrant girl's struggles on the frontier; and *Death Comes for the Archbishop* (1927) is Cather's tribute to the Roman Catholic Church as spiritual pioneer in New Mexico.

Church, Frederic Edwin (1826-1900) Painter, best known for landscapes that include striking effects of light.

Copley, John Singleton (1738-1815) Boston-born painter, moved to London in 1774. Considered by many of his contemporaries the outstanding American portraitist of his day; sitters included John Adams, John Hancock, Lord Cornwallis. Later turned to historical painting, producing "Death of Lord Chatham," and "Siege of Gibraltar," among others.

Dana, Richard Henry (1815-1882) Wrote *Two Years Before the Mast* (1840), an immensely popular and influential account of time he spent working as a common sailor.

Dickinson, Emily (1830-1886) Reclusive poet of Amherst, Massachusetts, she led an outwardly quiet, sheltered, and solitary life, never marrying and keeping her writing secret even from her family. Her poetry reveals a woman of insight, paradox, and gentle wit. Only six of her poems were published during her lifetime—and even those were published without her consent.

Eakins, Thomas (1844-1916) Painter, sculptor who promoted studies in anatomy and dissection and stressed the importance of nude models.

Faulkner, William (1897-1962) Novelist and Nobel laureate who in *The Sound and the Fury, As I Lay Dying, Light in August*, and other novels and short stories explored universal truths of human nature through long, complex sentences and small-town southern characters.

Fitzgerald, F. Scott (1896-1940) Writer whose portaits of the glittering Jazz Age portrayed the optimism and indulgence produced by American capitalism; best known for his novel *The Great Gatsby*.

Franklin, Benjamin (1706-1790) Statesman, scientist, writer, and philosopher who created America's first subscription libraries, invented an improved heating stove, and experimented with electricity (most famously with kites in 1752). Signed the Declaration of Independence and helped to negotiate the Treaty of Paris, which ended the American Revolution.

Frost, Robert Lee (1874-1963) Poet whose language and verse made his poetry deceptively accessible.

Guthrie, Woodrow Wilson (Woody) (1912-1967) Folksinger, composer. Traveled about the United States, frequently in support of labor unions and populist causes. Composed more than a thousand songs. Among his best known: "So Long (It's Been Good to Know Yuh)," "This Land Is Your Land."

Hawthorne, Nathaniel (1804-1864) The author of *The House of Seven Gables* (1851) and *The Scarlet Letter* (1850) was born in Salem, Massachusetts to a prominent Puritan family; both the theme of Puritanism and the theme of family loom large in the author's work.

Hemingway, Ernest (1899-1961) In his youth, Hemingway made frequent forays into the wilds of northern Michigan on hunting and fishing trips, passions later reflected in his writings and in his primitivistic attitude. His writing is known for its understatement and spare style. His heroes are often simple people with honest emotions, contrasted with the artificiality of civilized society. His works include *The Sun Also Rises* (1926), *A Farewell to Arms* (1929), and *For Whom the Bell Tolls* (1940). His allegorical short novel, *The Old Man and the Sea*, won a Nobel Prize in 1954.

This self-portrait of painter Mary Cassatt captures the artist at the age of 36 in 1880.

Homer, Winslow (1836-1910) Painter and illustrator, he contributed drawings to *Harper's Weekly*, many of them depicting scenes from the Civil War. He was especially noted for his watercolors, which are imbued with striking effects of light, color, and atmosphere. Many of his seascapes portray New England's rugged coastline, especially near Prouts Neck, Maine, where he lived. His most famous paintings include "Breezing Up," "Snap the Whip," and "The Gulf Stream."

Hopper, Edward (1882-1967) Painter known for stark, realistic scenes emphasized with a masterful use of light and shadow, often portraying the loneliness and isolation of urban life. His works include "Nighthawks" and "Early Sunday Morning" as well as scenes of rural New England.

James, Henry Jr. (1843-1916) Born in New York City to a well-to-do family of intellectuals (his brother William, 1842-1910, was the famous philosopher), much of James' work portrays upper-class life in 19th-century America; his deftly drawn characters strive to find meaning and value within the confines and constructs of society. Some of his best-known works, including *The Portrait of a Lady* (1881), are set in Europe, comparing and contrasting Americans and Europeans. Other titles (he was a prolific writer) include: *The American* (1877), *The Europeans* (1878), *The Bostonians*

(1886), *The Ambassadors* (1903), his last completed novel, *The Golden Bowl* (1904), and the short story "The Turn of the Screw."

Lewis, Sinclair (1885-1951) Novelist (*Babbitt, Arrowsmith*) who chronicled the moral decay of professionals in the Midwest; first American awarded Nobel Prize in literature (1930).

Mailer, Norman (1923-) Perhaps best known for his first novel, *The Naked and the Dead*, in which he drew upon his experiences serving with the U.S. Army in the Pacific.

Melville, Herman (1819-1891) Had great success with his early novels, including *Typee* (1846) and *White-Jacket* (1850), inspired by his own adventures as a young man at sea and on the Marquesas Islands. His greatest work, *Moby Dick* (1851—"Call me Ishmael" is considered one of literature's great first lines) was not a success, however; and he died in penurious obscurity

Mies van der Rohe, Ludwig (1886-1969) German-American modernist architect; used steel and glass in skyscraper designs. Kept walls to a minimum and often used rare wood or marble to construct them.

O'Keeffe, Georgia (1887-1986) Painter known for abstract florals ("Black Iris") that appear surprising or suggestive of human anatomy.

Olmsted, Frederick Law (1822-1903) Influential landscape architect, designed Central Park in New York City as well as the United States Capitol grounds.

O'Neill, Eugene (1888-1953) Playwright, Nobel laureate. In such works as *Long Day's Journey into Night*, *The Emperor Jones*, and *The Iceman Cometh* he used archetypal themes from religion and mythology to explore the psychology of stressed individuals and families.

Samuel L. Clemens, aka Mark Twain, relaxes aboard ship, about 1901.

Paine, Thomas (1737-1809) British-American philospher and writer whose pamphlet "Common Sense" urged the colonies to break with England; "American Crisis" papers encouraged Continental Army to continue fighting the British.

Peale, Charles Wilson (1741-1827). Portrait painter and patriarch of a family of artists: sons Raphaelle (1774-1825), Rembrandt (1778-1860), and Titian Ramsay (1799-1885), and daughter Sarah Miriam (1800-1885); his brother James (1749-1831) was also a painter, a noted miniaturist.

Poe, Edgar Allan (1809-1849) Baltimore, Maryland, poet and short-story writer, credited with setting the standard for the modern detective story. His poetry includes "The Raven," "Ulalume," and "Annabel Lee," all written in the 1840s. His best-known short stories include "The Pit and the Pendulum" and "The Tell-Tale Heart," both dark tales of horror which, like most of his other works, he published in the 1840s.

Pollack, (Paul) Jackson (1912-1956) Abstract painter who produced interlaced lines by pouring or dripping paint onto canvas ("One"); influenced by Jungian symbolism and surrealism.

Salinger, Jerome David (1919-) The reclusive author's work includes the quintessential novel of teenage angst and disillusionment, *The Catcher in the Rye* (1951).

Sargent, John Singer (1856-1925) Painter, perhaps best known for his portrait entitled "Madame X," which caused a scandal at the Paris Salon of 1884.

Stein, Gertrude (1874-1946) Author who wrote in a distinct style that used little punctuation and often repeated basic words as in "Rose is a rose is a rose is a rose." Her salon in Paris, where she lived from 1902 until her death, attracted many painters and writers. Matisse and Picasso were regulars, as was American writer Ernest Hemingway.

Steinbeck, John (1902-1968) Novelist who chronicled the lives of migrant agricultural laborers in *Of Mice and Men* (1937) and *The Grapes of Wrath* (1939).

Stuart, Gilbert Charles (1755-1828) Portrait painter, best known for his portrayals of George Washington, including five full-length portraits.

Thoreau, Henry David (1817-1862) Essayist, philosopher, abolitionist, poet, and naturalist. He abhorred the strict Calvinist religion of his native New England, believing instead in the natural goodness of man and nature. He was, as was his friend Ralph Waldo Emerson, a transcendentalist, but at the same time he enjoyed the science of nature. While his fellow transcendentalists sought to live communally at a retreat called Brook Farm, Thoreau built a hut for himself in the woods near Concord, Massachusetts, on Walden Pond. It was there that he felt he could live a life of simplicity, independence and wisdom, and it was there that he wrote his most famous book, *Walden* (1854).

Twain, Mark (Samuel Langhorne Clemens) (1835-1910) Novelist and humorist who captured American diction and coined the term "Gilded Age" to describe the excesses of his time; his *Adventures of Huckleberry Finn* explores the moral dilemma of slavery.

Updike, John (1932-) Pennsylvania-born novelist and poet. An early work, *Rabbit, Run* (1960), follows a young man who, yearning for the glory and applause of his days as a high-school athlete, leaves his wife and child. A sequel, *Rabbit is Rich*, won a Pulitzer Prize in 1981. Though best known for these and other novels, Updike has also produced several poetry collections.

Venturi, Robert (1925-) Architect whose criticism of modern architecture led to postmodernism; valued decoration and symbolism over functionality in design.

Warhol, Andy (1928-1987) Painter and filmmaker who led and shaped the American pop art movement. Works include silk screens of actress Marilyn Monroe and of a Campbell's soup can.

Whistler, James Abbott McNeil (1834-1903) Artist known especially for his use of shades of gray rather than contrasting colors. His most famous painting is one he did of his mother.

Whitman, Walt (1819-1892) Poet who believed in the pursuit of emotional freedom through love, social freedom through democracy, and freedom of the soul through religion. His writing is simple, devoid of the usual use of rhyme or meter, a style later known as free verse. *Leaves of Grass,* a collection of poems, was first published in 1855.

Williams, Hank (1923-1953) Country singer, songwriter. Wrote more than 100 songs during his short life, including "Your Cheatin' Heart," "Jambalaya," "Cold, Cold Heart," and "Hey, Good Lookin."

Williams, Tennessee (1911-1983) Playwright known for his works of "poetic realism" and experiments with settings and symbolism. *The Glass Menagerie, A Streetcar Named Desire,* and *Cat on a Hot Tin Roof* feature suppressed emotions that flare into violence.

Wolfe, Thomas Clayton (1900-1938) Novelist whose works include *Look Homeward, Angel* (1929); *Of Time and the River* (1935); and *You Can't Go Home Again* (published posthumously, 1940).

Wright, Frank Lloyd (1867-1959) Architect known for his organic design; believed that buildings and nature should relate to each other. His cantilevers and floor plans broke with traditional square shapes; best known for Fallingwater.

Wyeth, Newell Convers (1882-1945) Illustrator and painter, illustrated works of Robert Louis Stevenson. Father of painter Andrew Wyeth ("Christina's World"), grandfather of painter Jamie Wyeth (portrait of JFK), both of Chadd's Ford, Pennsylvania; brother-in-law of illustrator Howard Pyle (*The Merry Adventures of Robin Hood*, 1883, and others).

Explorers

Anderson, Maxie (1934-1983) Made first transatlantic crossing by balloon, *Double Eagle II*, with Ben Abruzzo and Larry Newman (1978); made his first nonstop balloon transit of North America, with his son Kristian, on the balloon *Kitty Hawk* (1980).

Ballard, Robert D. (1942-) Explored the mid-Atlantic Ridge and discovered the Pacific Ocean's hydrothermal vents; discovered the wreck of the *Titanic* in September 1985.

Beebe, C. William (1877-1962) Dived to record 3,028 feet in bathysphere (1934).

Bingham, Hiram (1875-1956) Explored a route across Venezuela and Colombia; explored trade route from Buenos Aires to Lima; discovered Machu Picchu (1911-15).

Boone, Daniel (c.1734-1820) Pioneer whose expeditions through the Cumberland Gap opened up the Kentucky country to settlers moving west.

Amelia Earhart was the first woman to fly solo across the Atlantic Ocean.

Borman, Frank (1928-) Commander of Apollo 8, which first orbited the moon; accompanied by James A. Lovell, Jr., and Willliam A. Anders (1968).

Byrd, Richard E. (1888-1957) First to fly over North Pole (1926); first to fly over South Pole (1929); established American base in Antarctica (1929).

Collins, Michael (1930-) Astronaut; piloted the command module *Columbia* during Apollo 11, the mission that put Neil Armstrong and Buzz Aldrin on the moon. Collins later called his orbit around the moon—48 minutes of it beyond all contact with the Earth—"the ultimate solo flight."

Davis, Wade (1953-) Anthropologist, ethnobotanist. A citizen of Canada, Ireland, and the United States. He spent more than three years in the Amazon and Andes as a plant explorer, living among 15 indigenous groups in eight Latin American nations while making some 6,000 botanical collections.

Earhart, Amelia Mary (1897-1937) First woman to fly across the Atlantic Ocean, Newfoundland to Wales (1928); first woman to fly solo across the Atlantic (1932); first Hawaii-to-mainland solo flight (1935); first to fly Mexico City to New York (1935); lost with navigator Fred Noonan on attempted round-the-world flight (1937).

Earle, Sylvia (1935-) Marine biologist; undersea explorer. In 1979, off the Hawaiian island of Oahu, Earle stepped off a research sub and strolled upon the ocean floor for more than two hours at a depth of 1,250 feet, the only person ever to walk at that depth untethered to the surface. Connected to the sub by an 18-foot communications cable, she was encased in a wearable undersea environment known as a Jim suit.

Fay, Michael (1956-) Conducted a year-long walk across central Africa seeking correlations between large animal populations and human influences (1999).

Fremont, John C. (1813-1890) Mapped the Oregon Trail (1842); crossed the Rocky Mountains to California (1843-45).

Glenn, John H., Jr. (1921-) First American to orbit Earth, in Mercury capsule Friendship 7 (1962).

Greely, Adolphus Washington (1844-1935) Army officer, commanded the 1881 U.S. expedition to establish Arctic meteorological station; attained the most northerly point reached up to that time; explored Ellesmere Island and northern Greenland (1883-1884).

Henson, Matthew A. (1886-1955) Originally hired as a valet by Robert Peary in 1887, Henson became the explorer's traveling companion and indispensable assistant for the next 20 years. He accompanied Peary to Central America (1887); to Greenland (1895 and 1900); and finally to the Arctic, including the 1909 expedition to the North Pole. Unlike Peary, Henson learned to speak Inuit and became an expert dog handler and driver.

Kane, Elisha Kent (1820-1857) Led expedition into Arctic in search of Sir John Franklin (1853-1855); reached previously undiscovered territory.

Lewis, Meriwether (1774-1809) With William Clark led first crossing of the continent to the Pacific via the Missouri and Columbia Rivers (1804-1806).

Lindbergh, Charles (1902-1974) Aviator and national hero who made the first solo nonstop flight across the Atlantic (1927) in *The Spirit of St. Louis*, also the title of his Pulitzer-prize winning 1953 autobiography.

Maury, Matthew Fontaine (1806-1873) Directed history's first major deep-sea survey, in Atlantic (1849).

Peary, Robert E. (1856-1920) Made four attempts to reach the North Pole; might have succeeded on fourth try in 1909.

Pike, Zebulon Montgomery (1779-1813) Mapped territory westward from St. Louis to Colorado (1806).

Plaisted, Ralph (1927-) Completed first confirmed arrival at the North Pole (1968).

Powell, John Wesley (1834-1902) Explorer who investigated the Grand Canyon by boat, traveling some 1,000 miles in 98 days.

Reinhard, Johan (1943-) Anthropologist and archaeologist who discovered Inca "Ice Maiden"; explored the summits of three Andean volcanoes for Inca burials and artifacts; excavated highest known archaeological site, atop 22,000-foot-high Mount Llullaillaco (1995-1999).

Rock, Joseph F. (1884-1962) Explored central China and unmapped borderlands of China's southwest (1922-1949).

Russell, Israel Cook (1852-1906) Geologist who carried out both geologic and geographic studies in Alaska's Mount St. Elias region; recalculated the height of Mount St. Elias and made an attempt to climb it; also discovered Mount Logan (1890).

Shepard, Alan B. Jr. (1923-) First American to travel in space (1961) aboard Freedom 7.

Smith, Jedediah Strong (1700-1831) Explorer who was the first to cross the Great Basin into California (1826).

Smith, John (1580-1631) Explored and produced the first map of the Chesapeake Bay (c. 1608).

Stanley, Henry Morton (1841-1904) Welsh-born, settled in U.S.; commissioned by New York Herald to find David Livingstone in Africa (1871); circumnavigated Lake Victoria; discovered Lake Edward; descended Congo (Zaire) River (1874-77).

Steger, Will (1943-) Attempted a solo trek from the North Pole to Canada (1997).

Stirling, Matthew Williams (1896-1975) Archaeologist who discovered the remains of the Olmec culture along the Gulf coast of Mexico (1938-1946).

Washburn, Bradford (1910-) Explored and mapped unknown portions of northern Canada; member of team who was first group to cross the St. Elias Range from Canada to Alaska (1935).

Whittaker, James W. (1929-) First American to reach the summit of Mount Everest, with Sherpa Nawang Gombu (1963); four other Americans also made it to the top on the same expedition: Thomas F. Hornbein, William F. Unsoeld, Luther G. Jerstad, and Barry C. Bishop.

Wilkes, Charles (1798-1877) Charted Melanesian regions of the Pacific Ocean and also confirmed the existence of Antarctica (1838-1842).

Periods and Movements

Abolitionism (early 1800s-1900) This worldwide movement to abolish slavery came out of the Enlightenment. In America, Quakers objected to slavery in the 17th century; during the Revolutionary era Thomas Jefferson (himself a slaveowner) and others condemned slavery. Abolitionism spread as a moral crusade in the 1800s, almost exclusively in the North—among its proponents were publisher William Lloyd Garrison, poet James Russell Lowell, and ex-slave Frederick Douglass. After the Civil War, the 13th Amendment to the Constitution abolished slavery in 1865.

Civil Rights Movement (mid 1950s –mid 1960s) This social reform movement fought against discrimination—including segregation—of black Americans. Supporters of civil-rights reform united in 1955 after Rosa Parks refused to give up her seat to a white man on a Montgomery, Alabama, bus. Many legal rights were gained after the 1964 Civil Rights Act struck down discrimination based upon race, creed, national origin, or sex. Dr. Martin Luther King, Jr., was one of movement's notable leaders.

Cold War (1940s-1990s) A period of intense rivlary between the U.S. and the U.S.S.R. and their respective allies. Existing tensions grew after World War II, when Soviet leader Joseph Stalin sought to expand communism and the U.S. sought to "contain" it. A nuclear arms race developed, and key moments ranged from the building of the Berlin Wall and the Cuban Missile Crisis, to the Vietnam War and the breakup of the Soviet Union.

Computer Age (late 1900s) The first electronic computers were built in the 1940s to solve complex mathematical equations. They were as large as a room in a house. In the late 1940s, the transistor was developed, setting the groundwork for making the computer smaller, lighter, faster, and less expensive. Soon computers were linked to transfer information among people; these networks were linked in the 1980s to create the Internet. Today computers are used in almost all businesses, large and small, and are rapidly becoming essential school and household tools.

Conservation/Environmental Movement (20th century) With an expanding nation's continuing need for forest products and other natural resources, a national environmental movement sprang to life. Dedicated to conservation, John Muir founded the Sierra Club in 1892 and influenced President Theodore Roosevelt's decision to create the U.S. Forest Service and set aside nearly 150 million acres of forest. Founded in 1905, the Audubon Society is dedicated to protection of land, water, and wildlife. The Environmental Protection Agency is the government's arm for guarding the nation against pollution.

Feminist Movement (mid 1800s – late 1900s) The stuggle for equal rights for women grew from rumblings of discontent to a groundswell political movement in the late 1800s and early 1900s. At first, the movement concentrated on gaining suffrage; in 1920 the 19th Amendment to the Constitution gave women the right to vote. Feminism died out until mid-century, when women began entering the work force in large numbers. With many professions still closed to women, organizations such as the National Organization for Women worked for non-discrmination in education and the workplace. The women's liberation movement likewise sought equality in the home and in society.

Gilded Age (late 1800s – early 1900s) Expanding industrialization created a new breed of ultra-rich American capitalists called captains of industry, or robber barons. Grabbing monopolies in everything from oil and steel to sugar and rubber, they worked the strings, while underpaid laborers toiled away in mines and sweatshops. Writer Mark Twain called it the Gilded Age—glittering on the surface, but concealing base metal underneath.

Gold Rush (mid 1800s) The California gold rush of 1849—the largest gold rush in America—actually began in 1848 with the discovery of gold at Sutter's Mill. By 1850 so many thousands of fortune-seekers had poured into California that it gained statehood. Later gold rushes in other parts of the West and in Alaska also brought floods of settlers into previously wild territories.

Great Depression (1929-1941) The United States stock market crash in October 1929 triggered a worldwide economic crisis that left many

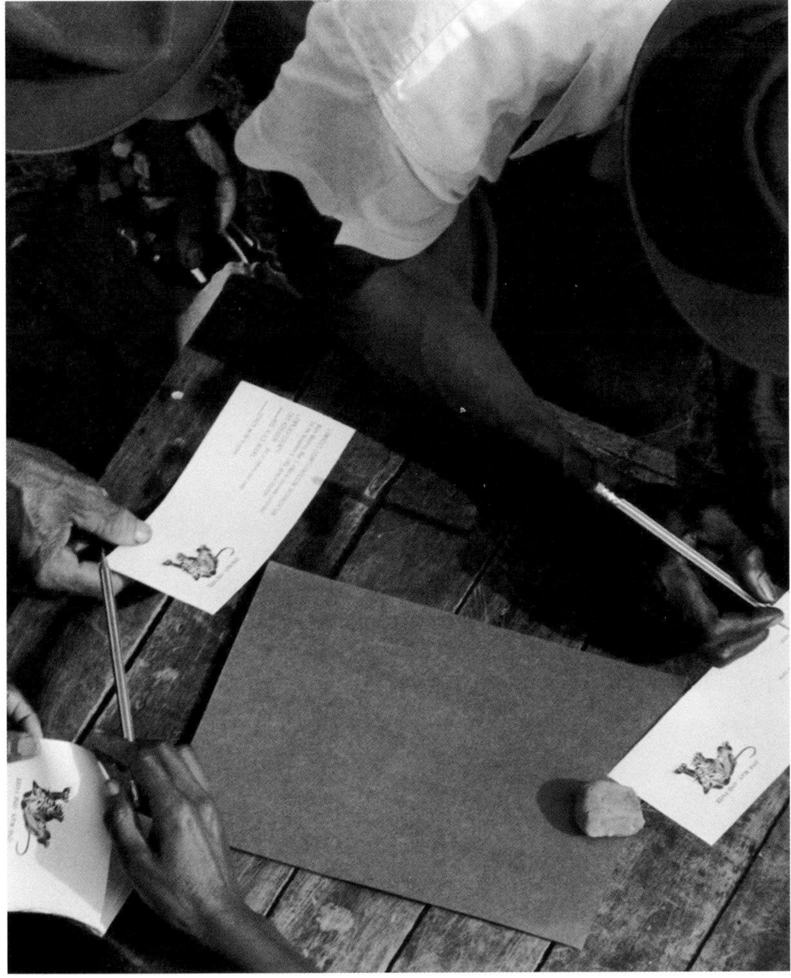

Voting in Alabama

people unemployed and dependent on governments or charities for food and other necessities. The United States had invested heavily in other countries, but now those investments were recalled, sending Europe into the same downward spiral. President Franklin D. Roosevelt initiated the New Deal, a program of government reforms to help ease the effects of the Great Depression and the Dust Bowl, the drought-and-dust-storm-plagued Great Plains. The period ended with the increased level of production brought about by America's entry into World War II.

Industrial Revolution (late 1700s–early 1800s) A time of great change for humanity, the industrial revolution began in Britain and spread throughout Europe and then to North America. Power-driven machinery and factory organization created an abundance of merchandise quickly. Many people migrated to the cities to work in factories. Overcrowded and unsanitary living conditions developed as a result. Yet quality of life improved dramatically for others. Business leaders, called capitalists, found their niche, as did bankers and investors. Material benefits still exist today from this period of change, as do the problems—such as air, water, and land pollution.

Reconstruction (1865-1877) Following the Civil War, the North and South sought to mend relations. Issues such as how to repair war-damaged southern states and protect the rights of the four million freed slaves were addressed as well as what criteria should be used to admit seceded states (Alabama, Arkansas, Florida, Georgia, Louisiana, Mississippi, North Carolina, South Carolina, Tennessee, Texas, and Virginia) back into the Union. In the end, Reconstruction failed to bring racial harmony to the country. Instead, feelings of sectional bitterness intensified in many areas.

Roaring Twenties (1920s) With President Calvin Coolidge's observation that "The business of America is business" for a motto, the 1920s were a period of extravagant living after the troubles of a world war. Big band jazz, the Charleston, illegal drinking, and unbridled speculation in real estate and the stock market were pastimes of an era fueled by the automobile, radio, and other industries. The high life came to an abrupt end with the stock market crash of 1929.

Space Race (1960s) In October1957 the Soviets launched the first artificial satellite into space, beginning a race between the United States and the U.S.S.R. to place the first man in space. The Soviets won: Cosmonaut Yuri Gagarin orbited above Earth in 1961. A month later, President Kennedy announced plans to put a man on the moon before the end of the decade. The United States won that race in 1969. With the Cold War coming to an end, Russians and Americans have cooperated in ventures, sharing space stations and conducting experiments that cannot be duplicated on Earth.

Religious Groups

Amish The Amish, members of a strict, 17th-century fundamentalist derivative of the European Mennonite Church, began to migrate to North America in the early 1700s. Divisions arose within the community after 1850 between "old order" Amish who believed in keeping strictly to traditional dress and behavior, and "new order" Amish who wanted to adopt more modern, or progressive methods. Those that backed the new order generally left to form new churches or joined the Mennonite Church. Most of the remaining traditionalists are members of the Old Order Amish Mennonite Church. They are known for their plain, drab clothes, fastened with hooks and eyes rather than buttons, and their shunning of telephones, electric lights and modern methods of farming. The men wear beards (no moustaches) and broad-brimmed black hats, the women wear bonnets, long dresses with capes, black shoes and stockings, no jewelry. They have no automobiles, using instead horses and buggies. Services are conducted in a mix of German and English called Pennsylvania Dutch. The largest Amish settlements are in Pennsylvania, Ohio, Indiana, Iowa, Illinois, and Kansas. No Amish remain in Europe.

Baptist The Baptist movement began in England in the early 17th century as a protest to infant baptism. In the United States, the southern and northern Baptists parted ways in 1845 over the issue of whether slaveowners could be missionaries. Of more than 30 million Baptists in the United States, the Southern Baptist Convention is the largest group with 16.2 million adherents. Southern Baptists tend to be socially conservative and

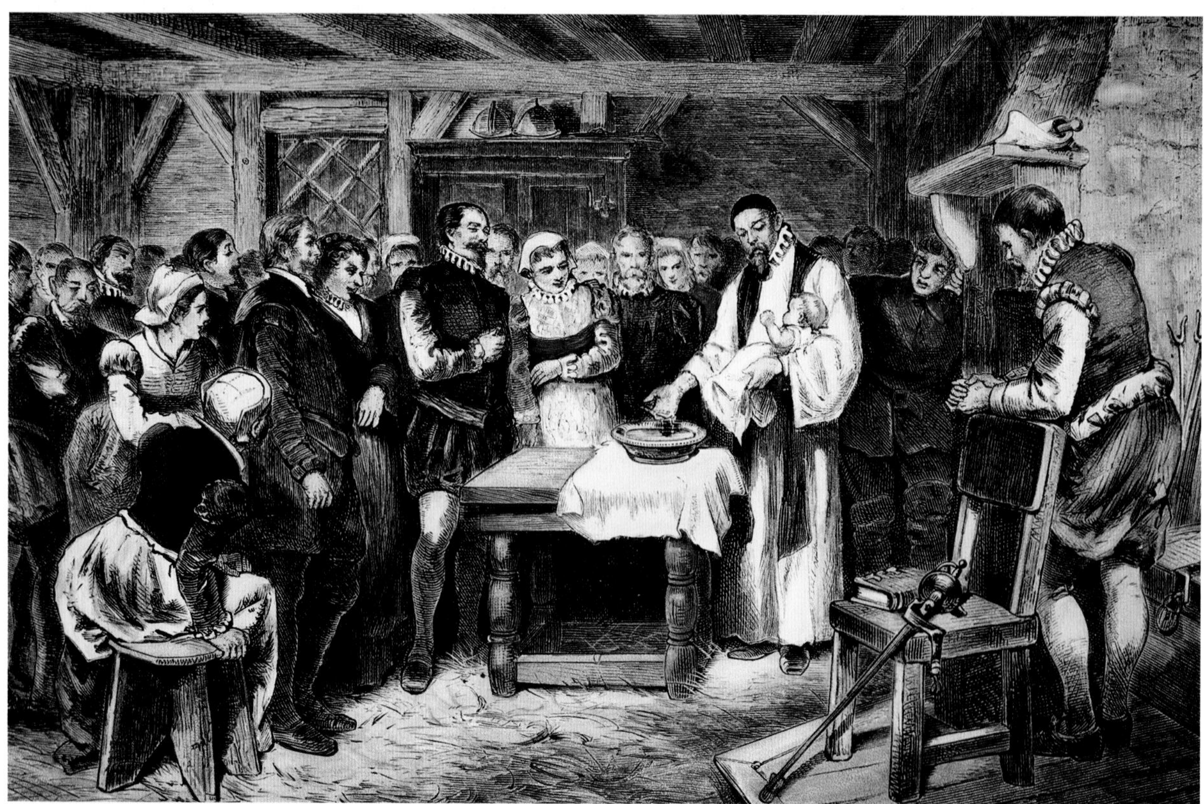

The baptism of Virginia Dare, first baby born to English parents in the New World.

evangelical—that is, they believe in salvation through faith in Christ. Many are also fundamentalists, taking the Bible as the literal word of God. Missionary outreach plays an important part in the life of the church. Baptists practice total immersion baptism. Strong believers in the separation of church and state, Baptists embrace the idea of congregational autonomy, though Southern Baptists have the largest central authority of all Baptist groups.

Claiming 7.5 million members, the National Baptist Convention, U.S.A., Inc., and the National Baptist Convention of America are mainly black congregations; they originated in 1880 and split into separate bodies in 1915. The latter emphasizes missionary work. The newer Progressive National Baptist Convention is also primarily black and includes about 2.5 million members.

Buddhist Buddhism began with Siddhartha Gautama, born in present-day Nepal about 563 B.C. After meditating and attaining Enlightenment, Gautama began teaching the Four Noble Truths—life is filled with anguish; this leads to seeking permanence in a transient world; nirvana terminates this seeking; nirvana is attainable through the Eightfold Path: right understanding, right aspiration, right speech, right action, right mode of livelihood, right endeavor, right mindedness, and right concentration. Some 2.9 million people practice Buddhism in the United States. Zen, a form of Buddhism from Japan, became popular with 1960s American counterculturists because of its emphasis on seeking strength from within rather than from society.

Eastern Orthodox After disputes about liturgy and papal authority, the Eastern and Western branches of Christianity split in 1054. Not until 1965, after a meeting of Ecumencial Patriarch Athenagoras I and Pope Paul VI did the two branches lift their excommunication of each other. Unlike the Roman Catholic Church, the many Eastern Orthodox churches have no central authority, though the ecumenical patriarch of the Church of Constantinople is held in special esteem. Eastern Orthodox priests may marry before ordination; bishops must be unmarried. Church members believe in the original Nicene-Constantinopolitan Creed, which says that the Holy Spirit proceeds from the Father, not, as Catholics believe, from the Father and from the Son. This and the infallability of the Pope are the main doctrinal differences between the two religions. Icons play a key part in worship. About 4.1 million Americans belong to Eastern Orthodox churches, including the Greek, Armenian, Antiochian, Coptic, and Russian Orthodox churches.

Episcopal The Episcopal Church grew from the Church of England, or Anglican Church, which separated from Rome in 1534. It began in the United States in 1789, in Philadelphia. The most Catholic of the Protestant denominations, the Episcopal Church emphasizes liturgy, formal ritual, and weekly Eucharist, which is viewed as symbolic rather than a literal transubstantiation of the Lord's Supper. The Bible and Book of Common Prayer are the main texts. Current concerns over gay ministers have caused rifts, though the church remains socially broad and ecumenical in outlook, accepting of many forms of Christianity. Some 2.3 million Episcopalians reside in the U.S.

Jehovah's Witnesses The church began in the 19th century in the United States. They believe in the Second Coming of Christ after Armageddon (the end of the "times of the gentiles") and the subsequent emergence of God's Kingdom—which will be inhabited only by those who witness Jehovah, the true God. The Witnesses regard secular governments and world powers as unwitting allies of Satan. The life mission of every Jehovah's Witness is to convert others through doorstep preaching or religious tracts.

Jewish Ranking sixth among all U.S. religious groups, Jews number some 6.2 million. Emerging from Mesopotamia around the 13th century B.C., Judaism sprang from Hebrew monotheism and the laws of Moses, an Israelite. From about the fifth to the second century B.C., the Hebrew Bible was recorded; it includes the Torah (the first five books of the Old Testament). Among the three major branches of Judaism in America, Orthodox Jews are the most conservative: They wear head coverings, observe strict kosher dietary laws, study Hebrew, and look for the coming of a messiah. Conservative Judaism has a somewhat more liberal outlook, seeking to adapt old teachings to modern times. Reform Judaism is the most relaxed, holding the belief in a future messianic era rather than a messiah.

Lutheran Based on the tenets of Martin Luther, the Lutheran church is the largest Protestant denomination in the world, with about 60 million members. Some 8.1 million Lutherans live in the United States; of these, 5.5 million belong to the Evangelical Lutheran Church in America. Lutherans began coming to America in the mid-1600s and continued immigrating from Germany and Scandinavia; most settled in the Midwest.

Lutherans put emphasis on the forgiveness of sin through God's grace, which then allows the forgiven to show kindness to others. Hymns and congregational participation are important in worship. The ultimate church authority is the Bible.

Mennonite A Protestant church rising from the Anabaptist reform movement of the 16th-century Protestant Reformation. Mennonites believe in adult baptism, a complete separation between the church and the state, and that the church receives its guidance from Christ himself, not through clergy—though they recognize their leaders as divinely summoned prophets and apostles. They live in communities, isolated somewhat from the general populace, subsisting on farming. They are pacifists. While there are Mennonite communities in many countries, Canada and the United States have the heaviest concentration of believers.

Methodist Some 8.3 million members make the United Methodists the leading group of 12.4 million Methodists. Reverend John Wesley started the Methodist movement as an evangelical branch of the Church of England in 1738. Devotees were methodical in their Bible studies, praying, and good works. The first denomination in the United States was established in Baltimore in 1784. Circuit riding preachers then helped the rapid spread of Methodism. The black African Methodist Episcopal church was founded in 1787; today's membership totals 2.5 million. The United Methodist Church came into being in 1968, joining the Methodist Church with the Evangelical United Brethren Church. Among rituals are infant or adult baptism and the Lord's Supper.

Mormon Calling themselves Mormons, the 5.4 million members of the Church of Jesus Christ of Latter-day Saints take their name from the Book of Mormon, which members believe was translated from golden plates given by an angel to church founder Joseph Smith in 1827. As Smith's church swelled it moved west to avoid conflict with locals, finally settling in Utah under leader Brigham Young in the 1840s. Mormons believe theirs is the one true church; the Bible and *Book of Mormon* are their main scriptures. In the Mormon faith, marriage is for eternity, and family life continues corporeally after death. Geneology is important because Mormons believe they can baptize dead relatives who were non-Mormons and thus be reunited in the afterlife. Faith and good deeds are responsible for reward or punishment after death. The Mormon ethic of temperance, thrift, industry, and tithing, coupled with their patriotism and family emphasis have made the Mormon church one of the most successful of indigenous American religions.

Muslim Muslims are the followers of Islam who believe in surrendering, or committing to "the God" known as Allah. Islam founder Muhammad was born about A.D. 570 in Mecca. The Koran, a record of Muhammad's work, is Islam's sacred text. There are five pillars or duties: declaration of faith, daily prayer at five appointed times, alms to the needy, fasting during Ramadan (the ninth month of the lunar year), and, if possible, a pilgrimage to the Sacred Mosque at Mecca. At the end of time, Muslims believe, is a judgment day when God assigns humankind to heaven or hell. There are currently about 5.4 million Muslims in the United States, with headquarters in Plainfield, Indiana.

Pentecostal The Pentecostal movement began as a religious revival in Kansas in 1901. Pentacostals believe in baptism in the Holy Spirit—specifically, in the ability to speak in tongues. Faith healing and prophecy are other abilities possessed by some believers. Pentecostals look for signs of the second coming of Christ, marking the end of the world, as prophesied in the Bible. Worship services emphasize emotions and physical involvement, or holiness experiences. Of 11.5 million Pentacostals in some 30 denominations, 5.5 million belong to the Church of God in Christ, which was organized in Jackson, Mississippi, in 1894. The Assemblies of God holds 2.7 million members. Originating in Hot Springs, Arkansas, in 1914, it stresses the infallibility of the Bible and eternal damnation for non-believers.

Presbyterian The Presbyterian church grew out of the Reformed church movement in Europe in the 16th century, led by John Calvin and others. The name stems from "presbyter," a New Testament term for "elder," and refers to a system of church government. Church councils, "presbyteries," are formed of ministers and lay elders. Worship services are usually simple and include preaching, hymn singing, and the sacraments of baptism and the Lord's Supper. Of the 4 million Presbyterians in the United States, the vast majority belong to the Prebyterian Church (U.S.A.), a 1983 unification of the northern and the southern branches.

Quaker The Society of Friends is a Christian group founded in the mid 1700s in England and the American colonies. Quakers believe in direct communication with God without the intervention of creeds, clergy, or church. Early Quakers held gatherings without liturgy or appointed preacher, believing that God might speak through any of the expectant worshippers. Today, many Friend's services include hymns, prayers, and sermons, but they still do not participate in outward observances of the sacraments,

Muslims pray at the Islamic Center of America.

believing instead in spiritual baptism and communion.

Roman Catholic With 66.4 million members, the Roman Catholic Church ranks as the most populous religious group in the United States. As such it is the major denomination of Christianity in the nation, as it is worldwide. St. Paul and others spread the teachings of Jesus Christ, helping to make Christianity the official religion of the Roman Empire nearly 300 years after the death of Jesus Christ. In 1054 the Great Schism split the empire and religion into Roman Catholic (centered in Rome) and Eastern Orthodox (centered in present-day Istanbul). Protestants split from the Catholic Church during the Reformation in the 1500s. The Pope has supreme authority over the church, which is organized under celibate bishops and priests. Most recent United States Presidents have visited with the Pope. A highly ritualized religion, Roman Catholicism observes the rites of Mass, baptism, Eucharist, reconciliaton, confirmation, marriage, ordination, and unction (anointing the sick). Roman Catholics believe in salvation through merit and grace; Mary, mother of Jesus, holds high status in Roman Catholic ideology.

Shaker The United Society of Believers in Christ's Second Appearing began in Manchester, England, with a textile worker and Quaker named Ann Lee, who, her followers believed, was the female embodiment of the Second Coming of Christ. They believed in good works, plain living, productive labor, and celibacy.

Lee and eight disciples brought their faith to the New World in 1776. The small group found a responsive chord among their fellow settlers in New York, and they attracted several thousand converts. By 1826, 18 Shaker communities had been set up in 8 states. They reflected a distintive style of communal living dedicated to the pursuit of perfection, and led by elders of the church.

The Shaker community's numbers declined to the point of extinction in the 20th century. They are perhaps best remembered for their simple, utilitarian furniture as well as their distinctive architecture.

Unitarian The name refers to Unitarians' belief in God as a single personality, as opposed to Trinitarians who believe in God the father, the son, and the holy ghost—the Trinity. At its inception in 18th-century England, Unitarianism was an amalgam of deism and Congregationalism. Many early thinkers in the U.S. were Unitarians; having escaped the religious dogmas of Europe, many were suspicious of organized religions. Religious humanists, Unitarians stress reason and individual freedom of belief, believing that God works through the laws of nature.

The American Unitarian Association, an association of individuals, was organized in 1825. Controversy arose within the association in 1865 at the National Conference of Unitarian Churches over the Christian bias of its new constitution. A separatist Free Religious Association formed, with the core belief that Unitarianism should include people whose beliefs were nontheist and non-Christian. The two associations merged in 1925, keeping the name American Unitarian Association. Another merger, with the Universalist Church of America in 1961, resulted in the Unitarian Universalist Association (UUA), which has a current membership of more than a thousand congregations.

Voodoo Voodoo is practiced in areas of the southern U.S., particlarly Louisiana. Rituals combine elements of Catholicism (candles, crosses, prayers, baptism) with elements of West African tribal religions (dances, drums, and worship of ancestors).

IROQUOIS FEDERATION CONSTITUTION

Five Finger Lakes and Mohawk Valley Indian nations—the Mohawk, Oneida, Onondaga, Cayuga, and Seneca—confederated under the name Iroquois about 1570. A new structure of governance was set up, one that may indirectly have influenced the structure of the United States government.

THIS IS WISDOM AND JUSTICE ON THE PART OF THE GREAT SPIRIT to create and raise chiefs, give and establish unchangeable laws, rules and customs between the Five Nation Indians, the Mohawks, Oneidas, Onondagas, Cayugas, and Senecas and the other nations of Indians here in North America. The object of these laws is to establish peace between the numerous nations of Indians, hostility will be done away with, for the preservation and protection of life, property and liberty.

And the number of chiefs in this confederation of the five Nation Indians are fifty in number, no more and no less. They are the ones to arrange, to legislate and to look after the affairs of their people.

And the Mohawks, an Indian Nation, forms a party of the body of this Five Nation Indians confederation, and their representatives in this confederation is nine chiefs.

And the Oneidas, an Indian Nation, forms a party of the body of this Five Nation Indians confederation, and their representatives in this confederation is nine chiefs.

And the Onondagas, an Indian Nation, forms a party of the body of this Five Nation Indians confederation, and their representatives in this confederation is fourteen chiefs.

And the Cayugas, an Indian Nation, forms a party of the body of this Five Nation Indians confederation, and their representatives in this confederation is ten chiefs.

And the Senecas, an Indian Nation, forms a party of the body of this Five Nation Indians confederation, and their representatives in this confederation is eight chiefs.

And when the Five Nation Indians confederation chiefs assemble to hold a council, the council shall be duly opened and closed by the Onondaga chiefs, the Firekeepers. They will offer thanks to the Great Spirit that dwells in heaven above: the source and ruler of our lives, our daily wants and daily health, and they will then declare the council open for the transaction of business, and give decisions of all that is done in the council.

And there are three totems or castes of the Mohawk nation, the Tortoise, the Wolf, and the Bear; each has three head chiefs, nine in all. The chiefs of the Tortoise and Wolf castes are the council by themselves, and the chiefs of the Bear caste are to listen and watch the progress of the council or discussion of the two castes; and if they see any error they are to correct them, and explain, where they are wrong; and when they decide with the sanction of the Bear castes then their speaker will refer the matter to the other side of the council fire, to the second combination chiefs, the Oneidas and Cayugas.

And the council of the five Nations shall not be opened until all of the three castes of the Mohawk chiefs are present; and if they are not all present it shall be legal for them to transact the business of the council if all the three totems have one or more representatives present, and if not it shall not be legal except in small matters; for all the three castes of the Mohawk chiefs must be present to be called a full council.

THE DECLARATION OF INDEPENDENCE

The Unanimous Declaration of the Thirteen United States of America, July 4, 1776:

WHEN IN THE COURSE OF HUMAN EVENTS, IT BECOMES NECESSARY for one People to dissolve the Political Bands which have connected them with another, and to assume among the Powers of the Earth, the separate and equal Station to which the Laws of Nature and of Nature's God entitle them, a decent respect to the opinions of mankind requires that they should declare the causes which impel them to the separation.

We hold these Truths to be self-evident, that all Men are created equal, that they are endowed by their Creator with certain unalienable Rights, that among these are Life, Liberty and the pursuit of Happiness—That to secure these Rights, Governments are instituted among Men, deriving their just powers from the Consent of the Governed, That whenever any Form of Government becomes destructive of these Ends, it is the Right of the People to alter or to abolish it, and to institute new Government, laying its Foundation on such Principles and organizing its powers in such form, as to them shall seem most likely to effect their Safety and Happiness. Prudence, indeed, will dictate that Governments long established should not be changed for light and transient Causes; and accordingly all Experience hath shewn, that Mankind are more disposed to suffer, while Evils are sufferable, than to right themselves by abolishing the Forms to which they are accustomed. But when a long Train of Abuses and Usurpations, pursuing invariably the same Object evinces a Design to reduce them under absolute Despotism, it is their Right, it is their Duty, to throw off such Government, and to provide new Guards for their future Security. Such has been the patient Sufferance of these Colonies; and such is now the Necessity which constrains them to alter their former Systems of Government. The History of the present King of Great Britain is a History of repeated Injuries and Usurpations, all having in direct Object the Establishment of an absolute Tyranny over these States. To prove this, let Facts be submitted to a candid World.

He has refused his Assent to Laws, the most wholesome and necessary for the public good.

He has forbidden his Governors to pass Laws of immediate and pressing Importance, unless suspended in their Operation till his Assent should be obtained; and when so suspended, he has utterly neglected to attend to them.

He has refused to pass other Laws for the Accommodation of large Districts of People, unless those People would relinquish the right of Representation in the Legislature, a Right inestimable to them and formidable to Tyrants only.

He has called together legislative Bodies at Places unusual, uncomfortable, and distant from the Depository of their public Records, for the sole Purpose of fatiguing them into Compliance with his Measures.

He has dissolved Representative Houses repeatedly, for opposing with manly Firmness his invasions on the Rights of the People.

He has refused for a long Time, after such Dissolutions, to cause others to be elected; whereby the Legislative Powers, incapable of Annihilation, have returned to the People at large for their Exercise; the State remaining in the mean time exposed to all the Dangers of Invasion from without, and Convulsions within.

He has endeavoured to prevent the Population of these States; for that Purpose obstructing the Laws for Naturalization of Foreigners; refusing to pass others to encourage their Migrations hither, and raising the Conditions of new Appropriations of Lands.

He has obstructed the Administration of Justice, by refusing his Assent to Laws for establishing Judiciary Powers.

He has made Judges dependent on his Will alone, for the Tenure of their Offices, and Amount and payment of Salaries.

He has erected a Multitude of New Offices, and sent hither Swarms of Officers to harrass our people, and eat out their Substance.

He has kept among us, in Times of Peace, Standing Armies without the Consent of our Legislatures.

He has affected to render the Military independent of and superior to the Civil power.

He has combined with others to subject us to a Jurisdiction foreign to our Constitution, and unacknowledged by our laws; giving his Assent to their Acts of pretended Legislation: For quartering large Bodies of Armed Troops among us:

For protecting them, by a mock Trial, from Punishment for any Murders which they should commit on the Inhabitants of these States:

For cutting off our Trade with all parts of the World:

For imposing Taxes on us without our Consent:

For depriving us in many cases, of the benefits of Trial by Jury:

For transporting us beyond Seas to be tried for pretended Offences:

For abolishing the free System of English Laws in a neighbouring Province, establishing therein an Arbitrary government, and enlarging its Boundaries so as to render it at once an example and fit Instrument for introducing the same absolute Rule into these Colonies:

For taking away our Charters, abolishing our most valuable Laws, and altering fundamentally the Forms of our Governments:

For suspending our own Legislatures, and declaring themselves invested with Power to legislate for us in all Cases whatsoever.

He has abdicated Government here, by declaring us out of his Protection and waging War against us.

He has plundered our Seas, ravaged our Coasts, burnt our towns, and destroyed the Lives of our People.

He is at this time transporting large Armies of foreign Mercenaries to compleat the works of Death, Desolation and Tyranny, already begun with circumstances of Cruelty & Perfidy scarcely paralleled in the most barbarous Ages, and totally unworthy the Head of a civilized Nation.

He has constrained our fellow Citizens taken Captive on the high Seas to bear Arms against their Country, to become the Executioners of their Friends and Brethren, or to fall themselves by their Hands.

He has excited domestic Insurrections amongst us, and has endeavoured to bring on the Inhabitants of our Frontiers, the merciless Indian Savages, whose known Rule of Warfare, is an undistinguished Destruction of all Ages, Sexes and Conditions.

In every stage of these Oppressions We have Petitioned for Redress in the most humble Terms: Our repeated Petitions have been answered only by repeated Injury. A Prince whose Character is thus marked by every act which may define a Tyrant, is unfit to be the Ruler of a free People.

Nor have we been wanting in Attentions to our British Brethren. We have warned them from Time to Time of Attempts by their Legislature to extend an unwarrantable jurisdiction over us. We have reminded them of the circumstances of our Emigration and Settlement here. We have appealed to their native Justice and Magnanimity, and we have conjured them by the Ties of our common Kindred to disavow these Usurpations, which, would inevitably interrupt our connections and correspondence. They too have been deaf to the voice of Justice and of Consanguinity. We must, therefore, acquiesce in the Necessity, which denounces our Separation, and hold them, as we hold the rest of Mankind, Enemies in War, in Peace, Friends.

We, therefore, the Representatives of the UNITED STATES of AMERICA, in General Congress, Assembled, appealing to the Supreme Judge of the world for the Rectitude of our Intentions, do, in the Name, and by Authority of the good People of these Colonies, solemnly Publish and Declare, That these United Colonies are, and of Right ought to be, Free and Independent States; that they are Absolved from all Allegiance to the British Crown, and that all political Connection between them and the State of Great Britain, is and ought to be totally dissolved; and that as Free and Independent States, they have full Power to levy War, conclude Peace, contract Alliances, establish Commerce, and to do all other Acts and Things which Independent States may of right do. And for the support of this Declaration, with a firm Reliance on the Protection of Divine Providence, we mutually pledge to each other our Lives, our Fortunes and our sacred Honor.

GEORGIA:
Button Gwinnett
Lyman Hall
George Walton

NORTH CAROLINA:
William Hooper
Joseph Hewes
John Penn

SOUTH CAROLINA:
Edward Rutledge
Thomas Heyward, Jr.
Thomas Lynch, Jr.
Arthur Middleton

MASSACHUSETTS:
John Hancock

MARYLAND:
Samuel Chase
William Paca
Thomas Stone
Charles Carroll
of Carrollton

VIRGINIA:
George Wythe
Richard Henry Lee
Thomas Jefferson
Benjamin Harrison
Thomas Nelson, Jr.
Francis Lightfoot Lee
Carter Braxton

PENNSYLVANIA:
Robert Morris
Benjamin Rush
Benjamin Franklin
John Morton
George Clymer
James Smith
George Taylor
James Wilson
George Ross

DELAWARE:
Caesar Rodney
George Read
Thomas McKean

NEW YORK:
William Floyd
Philip Livingston
Francis Lewis
Lewis Morris

NEW JERSEY:
Richard Stockton
John Witherspoon
Francis Hopkinson
John Hart
Abraham Clark

NEW HAMPSHIRE:
Josiah Bartlett
William Whipple

MASSACHUSETTS:
Samuel Adams
John Adams
Robert Treat Paine
Elbridge Gerry

RHODE ISLAND:
Stephen Hopkins
William Ellery

Connecticut:
Roger Sherman
Samuel Huntington
William Williams
Oliver Wolcott

New Hampshire:
Matthew Thornton

THE CONSTITUTION OF THE UNITED STATES

WE THE PEOPLE OF THE UNITED STATES, IN ORDER TO FORM A more perfect Union, establish Justice, insure domestic Tranquility, provide for the common defense, promote the general Welfare, and secure the Blessings of Liberty to ourselves and our Posterity, do ordain and establish this Constitution for the United States of America.

Article I

Section 1
All legislative Powers herein granted shall be vested in a Congress of the United States, which shall consist of a Senate and House of Representatives.

Section 2
The House of Representatives shall be composed of Members chosen every second Year by the People of the several States, and the Electors in each State shall have the Qualifications requisite for Electors of the most numerous Branch of the State Legislature.

No Person shall be a Representative who shall not have attained to the Age of twenty-five Years, and been seven Years a Citizen of the United States, and who shall not, when elected, be an Inhabitant of that State in which he shall be chosen.

Representatives and direct Taxes shall be apportioned among the several States which may be included within this Union, according to their respective Numbers, which shall be determined by adding to the whole Number of free Persons, including those bound to Service for a Term of Years, and excluding Indians not taxed, three fifths of all other

Persons. The actual Enumeration shall be made within three Years after the first Meeting of the Congress of the United States, and within every subsequent Term of ten Years, in such Manner as they shall by Law direct. The Number of Representatives shall not exceed one for every thirty Thousand, but each State shall have at Least one Representative; and until such enumeration shall be made, the State of New Hampshire shall be entitled to chuse three, Massachusetts eight, Rhode-Island and Providence Plantations one, Connecticut five, New-York six, New Jersey four, Pennsylvania eight, Delaware one, Maryland six, Virginia ten, North Carolina five, South Carolina five, and Georgia three.

When vacancies happen in the Representation from any State, the Executive Authority thereof shall issue Writs of Election to fill such Vacancies.

The House of Representatives shall chuse their Speaker and other Officers; and shall have the sole Power of Impeachment.

Section 3

The Senate of the United States shall be composed of two Senators from each State, chosen by the Legislature thereof for six Years; and each Senator shall have one Vote.

Immediately after they shall be assembled in Consequence of the first Election, they shall be divided as equally as may be into three Classes. The Seats of the Senators of the first Class shall be vacated at the Expiration of the second Year, of the second Class at the Expiration of the fourth Year, and of the third Class at the Expiration of the sixth Year, so that one third may be chosen every second Year; and if Vacancies happen by Resignation, or otherwise, during the Recess of the Legislature of any State, the Executive thereof may make temporary Appointments until the next Meeting of the Legislature, which shall then fill such Vacancies.

No Person shall be a Senator who shall not have attained to the Age of thirty Years, and been nine Years a Citizen of the United States, and who shall not, when elected, be an Inhabitant of that State for which he shall be chosen.

The Vice President of the United States shall be President of the Senate, but shall have no Vote, unless they be equally divided.

The Senate shall chuse their other Officers, and also a President pro tempore, in the Absence of the Vice President, or when he shall exercise the Office of President of the United States.

The Senate shall have the sole Power to try all Impeachments. When sitting for that Purpose, they shall be on Oath or Affirmation. When the President of the United States is tried, the Chief Justice shall preside: And no Person shall be convicted without Concurrence of two thirds of the Members present.

Judgment in Cases of Impeachment shall not extend further than to removal from Office, and disqualification to hold and enjoy any Office of honor, Trust or Profit under the United States: but the Party convicted shall nevertheless be liable and subject to Indictment, Trial, Judgment and Punishment, according to Law.

Section 4

The Times, Places and Manner of holding Elections for Senators and Representatives, shall be prescribed in each State by the Legislature thereof; but the Congress may at any time by Law make or alter such Regulations, except as to the Places of chusing Senators.

The Congress shall assemble at least once in every Year, and such Meeting shall be on the first Monday in December, unless they shall by Law appoint a different Day.

Section 5

Each House shall be the Judge of the Elections, Returns and Qualifications of its own Members, and a Majority of each shall constitute a Quorum to do Business; but a smaller Number may adjourn from day to day, and may be authorized to compel the Attendance of absent Members, in such Manner, and under such Penalties as each House may provide.

Each House may determine the Rules of its Proceedings, punish its Members for disorderly Behaviour, and, with the Concurrence of two thirds, expel a Member.

Each House shall keep a Journal of its Proceedings, and from time to time publish the same, excepting such Parts as may in their Judgment require Secrecy; and the Yeas and Nays of the Members of either House on any question shall, at the Desire of one fifth of those Present, be entered on the Journal.

Neither House, during the Session of Congress, shall, without the Consent of the other, adjourn for more than three days, nor to any other Place than that in which the two Houses shall be sitting.

Section 6

The Senators and Representatives shall receive a Compensation for their Services, to be ascertained by Law, and paid out of the Treasury of the United States. They shall in all Cases, except Treason, Felony and Breach of the Peace, be privileged from Arrest during their Attendance at the Session of their respective Houses, and in going to and returning from the same; and for any Speech or Debate in either House, they shall not be questioned in any other Place.

No Senator or Representative shall, during the Time for which he was elected, be appointed to any civil Office under the Authority of the United States, which shall have been created, or the Emoluments whereof shall have been encreased during such time; and no Person holding any Office under the United States, shall be a Member of either House during his Continuance in Office.

Section 7

All Bills for raising Revenue shall originate in the House of Representatives; but the Senate may propose or concur with Amendments as on other Bills.

Every Bill which shall have passed the House of Representatives and the Senate, shall, before it become a Law, be presented to the President of the United States: If he approve he shall sign it, but if not he shall return it, with his Objections to that House in which it shall have originated, who shall enter the Objections at large on their Journal, and proceed to reconsider it.If after such Reconsideration two thirds of that House shall agree to pass the Bill, it shall be sent, together with the Objections, to the other House, by which it shall likewise be reconsidered, and if approved by two thirds of that House, it shall become a Law. But in all such Cases the Votes of both Houses shall be determined by Yeas and Nays, and the Names of the Persons voting for and against the Bill shall be entered on the Journal of each House respectively. If any Bill shall not be returned by the President within ten Days (Sundays excepted) after it shall have been presented to him, the Same shall be a Law, in like Manner as if he had signed it, unless the Congress by their Adjournment prevent its Return, in which Case it shall not be a Law.

Every Order, Resolution, or Vote to which the Concurrence of the Senate and House of Representatives may be necessary (except on a question of Adjournment) shall be presented to the President of the United States; and before the Same shall take Effect, shall be approved by him, or being disapproved by him, shall be repassed by two thirds of the Senate and House of Representatives, according to the Rules and Limitations prescribed in the Case of a Bill.

Section 8

The Congress shall have Power To lay and collect Taxes, Duties, Imposts and Excises, to pay the Debts and provide for the common Defence and general Welfare of the United States; but all Duties, Imposts and Excises shall be uniform throughout the United States;

To borrow Money on the credit of the United States;

To regulate Commerce with foreign Nations, and among the several States, and with the Indian Tribes;

To establish an uniform Rule of Naturalization, and uniform Laws on the subject of Bankruptcies throughout the United States;

To coin Money, regulate the Value thereof, and of foreign Coin, and fix the Standard of Weights and Measures;

To provide for the Punishment of counterfeiting the Securities and current Coin of the United States;

To establish Post Offices and post Roads;

To promote the Progress of Science and useful Arts, by securing for limited Times to Authors and Inventors the exclusive Right to their respective Writings and Discoveries;

To constitute Tribunals inferior to the supreme Court;

To define and punish Piracies and Felonies committed on the high Seas, and Offences against the Law of Nations;

To declare War, grant Letters of Marque and Reprisal, and make Rules concerning Captures on Land and Water;

To raise and support Armies, but no Appropriation of Money to that Use shall be for a longer Term than two Years;

To provide and maintain a Navy;

To make Rules for the Government and Regulation of the land and naval Forces;

To provide for calling forth the Militia to execute the Laws of the Union, suppress Insurrections and repel Invasions;

To provide for organizing, arming, and disciplining, the Militia, and for governing such Part of them as may be employed in the Service of the United States, reserving to the States respectively, the Appointment of the Officers, and the Authority of training the Militia according to the discipline prescribed by Congress;

To exercise exclusive Legislation in all Cases whatsoever, over such District (not exceeding ten Miles square) as may, by Cession of particular States, and the Acceptance of Congress, become the Seat of the Government of the United States, and to exercise like Authority over all Places purchased by the Consent of the Legislature of the State in which the Same shall be, for the Erection of Forts, Magazines, Arsenals, dock-Yards, and other needful Buildings;--And

To make all Laws which shall be necessary and proper for carrying into Execution the foregoing Powers, and all other Powers vested by this Constitution in the Government of the United States, or in any Department or Officer thereof.

Section 9

The Migration or Importation of such Persons as any of the States now existing shall think proper to admit, shall not be prohibited by the Congress prior to the Year one thousand eight hundred and eight, but a Tax or duty may be imposed on such Importation, not exceeding ten dollars for each Person.

The Privilege of the Writ of Habeas Corpus shall not be suspended, unless when in Cases of Rebellion or Invasion the public Safety may require it.

No Bill of Attainder or ex post facto Law shall be passed.

No Capitation, or other direct, Tax shall be laid, unless in Proportion to the Census or enumeration herein before directed to be taken.

No Tax or Duty shall be laid on Articles exported from any State.

No Preference shall be given by any Regulation of Commerce or Revenue to the Ports of one State over those of another; nor shall Vessels bound to, or from, one State, be obliged to enter, clear, or pay Duties in another.

No Money shall be drawn from the Treasury, but in Consequence of Appropriations made by Law; and a regular Statement and Account of the Receipts and Expenditures of all public Money shall be published from time to time.

No Title of Nobility shall be granted by the United States: And no Person holding any Office of Profit or Trust under them, shall, without the Consent of the Congress, accept of any present, Emolument, Office, or Title, of any kind whatever, from any King, Prince, or foreign State.

Section 10

No State shall enter into any Treaty, Alliance, or Confederation; grant Letters of Marque and Reprisal; coin Money; emit Bills of Credit; make any Thing but gold and silver Coin a Tender in Payment of Debts; pass any Bill of Attainder, ex post facto Law, or Law impairing the Obligation of Contracts, or grant any Title of Nobility.

No State shall, without the Consent of the Congress, lay any Imposts or Duties on Imports or Exports, except what may be absolutely necessary for executing it's inspection Laws: and the net Produce of all Duties and Imposts, laid by any State on Imports or Exports, shall be for the Use of the Treasury of the United States; and all such Laws shall be subject to the Revision and Controul of the Congress.

No State shall, without the Consent of Congress, lay any Duty of Tonnage, keep Troops, or Ships of War in time of Peace, enter into any Agreement or Compact with another State, or with a foreign Power, or engage in War, unless actually invaded, or in such imminent Danger as will not admit of delay.

Article II

Section 1

The executive Power shall be vested in a President of the United States of America. He shall hold his Office during the Term of four Years, and, together with the Vice President, chosen for the same Term, be elected, as follows:

Each State shall appoint, in such Manner as the Legislature thereof may direct, a Number of Electors, equal to the whole Number of Senators and Representatives to which the State may be entitled in the Congress: but no Senator or Representative, or Person holding an Office of Trust or Profit under the United States, shall be appointed an Elector.

The Electors shall meet in their respective States, and vote by Ballot for two Persons, of whom one at least shall not be an Inhabitant of the same State with themselves. And they shall make a List of all the Persons voted for, and of the Number of Votes for each; which List they shall sign and certify, and transmit sealed to the Seat of the Government of the United States, directed to the President of the Senate. The President of the Senate shall, in the Presence of the Senate and House of Representatives, open all the Certificates, and the Votes shall then be counted. The Person having the greatest Number of Votes shall be the President, if such Number be a Majority of the whole Number of Electors appointed; and if there be more than one who have such Majority, and have an equal Number of Votes, then the House of Representatives shall immediately chuse by Ballot one of them for President; and if no Person have a Majority, then from the five highest on the List the said House shall in like Manner chuse the President. But in chusing the President, the Votes shall be taken by States, the Representation from each State having one Vote; A quorum for this purpose shall consist of a Member or Members from two thirds of the States, and a Majority of all the States shall be necessary to a Choice. In every Case, after the Choice of the President, the Person having the greatest Number of Votes of the Electors shall be the Vice President. But if there should remain two or more who have equal Votes, the Senate shall chuse from them by Ballot the Vice President.

The Congress may determine the Time of chusing the Electors, and the Day on which they shall give their Votes; which Day shall be the same throughout the United States.

No Person except a natural born Citizen, or a Citizen of the United States, at the time of the Adoption of this Constitution, shall be eligible to the Office of President; neither shall any Person be eligible to that Office who shall not have attained to the Age of thirty five Years, and been fourteen Years a Resident within the United States.

In Case of the Removal of the President from Office, or of his Death, Resignation, or Inability to discharge the Powers and Duties of the said Office, the Same shall devolve on the Vice President, and the Congress may by Law provide for the Case of Removal, Death, Resignation or Inability, both of the President and Vice President, declaring what Officer shall then act as President, and such Officer shall act accordingly, until the Disability be removed, or a President shall be elected.

The President shall, at stated Times, receive for his Services, a Compensation, which shall neither be increased nor diminished during the Period for which he shall have been elected, and he shall not receive within that Period any other Emolument from the United States, or any of them.

Before he enter on the Execution of his Office, he shall take the following Oath or Affirmation:—"I do solemnly swear (or affirm) that I will faithfully execute the Office of President of the United States, and will to the best of my Ability, preserve, protect and defend the Constitution of the United States."

Section 2

The President shall be Commander in Chief of the Army and Navy of the United States, and of the Militia of the several States, when called into the actual Service of the United States; he may require the Opinion, in writing, of the principal Officer in each of the executive Departments, upon any Subject relating to the Duties of their respective Offices, and he shall have Power to grant Reprieves and Pardons for Offences against the United States, except in Cases of Impeachment.

He shall have Power, by and with the Advice and Consent of the Senate, to make Treaties, provided two thirds of the Senators present concur; and he shall nominate, and by and with the Advice and Consent of the Senate, shall appoint Ambassadors, other public Ministers and Consuls, Judges of the supreme Court, and all other Officers of the United States, whose Appointments are not herein otherwise provided for, and which shall be established by Law: but the Congress may by Law vest the Appointment of such inferior Officers, as they think proper, in the President alone, in the Courts of Law, or in the Heads of Departments.

The President shall have Power to fill up all Vacancies that may happen during Recess of the Senate, by granting Commissions which shall expire at End of the next Session.

Section 3

He shall from time to time give to the Congress Information of the State of the Union, and recommend to their Consideration such Measures as he shall judge necessary and expedient; he may, on extraordinary Occasions, convene both Houses, or either of them, and in Case of Disagreement between them, with Respect to the Time of Adjournment, he may adjourn them to such Time as he shall think proper; he shall receive Ambassadors and other public Ministers; he shall take Care that the Laws be faithfully executed, and shall Commission all the Officers of the United States.

Section 4

The President, Vice President and all civil Officers of the United States, shall be removed from Office on Impeachment for, and Conviction of, Treason, Bribery, or other high Crimes and Misdemeanors.

Article III

Section 1

The judicial Power of the United States shall be vested in one supreme Court, and in such inferior Courts as the Congress may from time to time ordain and establish. The Judges, both of the supreme and inferior Courts, shall hold their Offices during good Behaviour, and shall, at stated Times, receive for their Services a Compensation, which shall not be diminished during their Continuance in Office.

Section 2

The judicial Power shall extend to all Cases, in Law and Equity, arising under this Constitution, the Laws of the United States, and Treaties made, or which shall be made, under their Authority;—to all Cases affecting Ambassadors, other public Ministers and Consuls;—to all Cases of admiralty and maritime Jurisdiction;—to Controversies to which the United States shall be a Party;—to Controversies between two or more States;—between a State and Citizens of another State;--between Citizens of different States;—between Citizens of the same State claiming Lands under Grants of different States, and between a State, or the Citizens thereof, and foreign States, Citizens or Subjects.

In all Cases affecting Ambassadors, other public Ministers and Consuls, and those in which a State shall be Party, the supreme Court shall have original Jurisdiction. In all the other Cases before mentioned, the supreme Court shall have appellate Jurisdiction, both as to Law and Fact, with such Exceptions, and under such Regulations as the Congress shall make.

The Trial of all Crimes, except in Cases of Impeachment, shall be by Jury; and such Trial shall be held in the State where the said Crimes shall have been committed; but when not committed within any State, the Trial shall be at such Place or Places as the Congress may by Law have directed.

Section 3

Treason against the United States, shall consist only in levying War against them, or in adhering to their Enemies, giving them Aid and Comfort. No Person shall be convicted of Treason unless on the Testimony of two Witnesses to the same overt Act, or on Confession in open Court.

The Congress shall have Power to declare the Punishment of Treason, but no Attainder of Treason shall work Corruption of Blood, or Forfeiture except during the Life of the Person attainted.

Article IV

Section 1

Full Faith and Credit shall be given in each State to the public Acts, Records, and judicial Proceedings of every other State. And the Congress may by general Laws prescribe the Manner in which such Acts, Records and Proceedings shall be proved, and the Effect thereof.

Section 2

The Citizens of each State shall be entitled to all Privileges and Immunities of Citizens in the several States.

A Person charged in any State with Treason, Felony, or other Crime, who shall flee from Justice, and be found in another State, shall on Demand of the executive Authority of the State from which he fled, be delivered up, to be removed to the State having Jurisdiction of the Crime.

No Person held to Service or Labour in one State, under the Laws thereof, escaping into another, shall, in Consequence of any Law or Regulation therein, be discharged from such Service or Labour, but shall be delivered up on Claim of the Party to whom such Service or Labour may be due.

Section 3

New States may be admitted by the Congress into this Union; but no new State shall be formed or erected within the Jurisdiction of any other State; nor any State be formed by the Junction of two or more States, or Parts of States, without the Consent of the Legislatures of the States concerned as well as of the Congress.

The Congress shall have Power to dispose of and make all needful Rules and Regulations respecting the Territory or other Property belonging to the United States; and nothing in this Constitution shall be so construed as to Prejudice any Claims of the United States, or of any particular State.

Section 4
The United States shall guarantee to every State in this Union a Republican Form of Government, and shall protect each of them against Invasion; and on Application of the Legislature, or of the Executive (when the Legislature cannot be convened), against domestic Violence.

Article V

The Congress, whenever two thirds of both Houses shall deem it necessary, shall propose Amendments to this Constitution, or, on the Application of the Legislatures of two thirds of the several States, shall call a Convention for proposing Amendments, which, in either Case, shall be valid to all Intents and Purposes, as Part of this Constitution, when ratified by the Legislatures of three fourths of the several States, or by Conventions in three fourths thereof, as the one or the other Mode of Ratification may be proposed by the Congress; Provided that no Amendment which may be made prior to the Year One thousand eight hundred and eight shall in any Manner affect the first and fourth Clauses in the Ninth Section of the first Article; and that no State, without its Consent, shall be deprived of its equal Suffrage in the Senate.

Article VI

All Debts contracted and Engagements entered into, before the Adoption of this Constitution, shall be as valid against the United States under this Constitution, as under the Confederation.

This Constitution, and the Laws of the United States which shall be made in Pursuance thereof; and all Treaties made, or which shall be made, under the Authority of the United States, shall be the supreme Law of the Land; and the Judges in every State shall be bound thereby, any Thing in the Constitution or Laws of any State to the Contrary notwithstanding.

The Senators and Representatives before mentioned, and the Members of the several State Legislatures, and all executive and judicial Officers, both of the United States and of the several States, shall be bound by Oath or Affirmation, to support this Constitution; but no religious Test shall ever be required as a Qualification to any Office or public Trust under the United States.

Article VII

The Ratification of the Conventions of nine States, shall be sufficient for the Establishment of this Constitution between the States so ratifying the Same.

Done in Convention by the Unanimous consent of the States present the Seventeenth Day September in the Year of our Lord one thousand seven hundred and Eighty seven and of the Independence of the United States of America the Twelfth In witness whereof We have hereunto subscribed our Names, George Washington, President and deputy from Virginia

Delaware
George Read
Gunning Bedford Jun
John Dickinson
Richard Bassett
Jacob Broom

Maryland
James McHenry
Daniel of St Thomas Jenifer
Daniel Carroll

Virginia
John Blair
James Madison Jr.

North Carolina
William Blount
Richard Dobbs Spaight
Hugh Williamson

South Carolina
John Rutledge
Charles Cotesworth Pinckney
Charles Pinckney
Pierce Butler

Georgia
William Few
Abraham Baldwin

New Hampshire
John Langdon
Nicholas Gilman

Massachusetts
Nathaniel Gorham
Rufus King

Connecticut
William Samuel Johnson
Roger Sherman

New York
Alexander Hamilton

New Jersey
William Livingston
David Brearley
William Paterson
Jonathan Dayton

Pennsylvania
Benjamin Franklin
Thomas Mifflin
Robert Morris
George Clymer
Thomas FitzSimons
Jared Ingersoll
James Wilson
Gouverneur Morris
ATTEST
William Jackson,
Secretary

THE TEN ORIGINAL AMENDMENTS: THE BILL OF RIGHTS

Passed by Congress September 25, 1789. Ratified December 15, 1791.

AMENDMENT I: Congress shall make no law respecting an establishment of religion, or prohibiting the free exercise thereof; or abridging the freedom of speech, or of the press; or the rightof the people peaceably to assemble, and to petition the government for a redress of grievances.

AMENDMENT II: A well regulated Militia, being necessary to the security of a free State, the right of the people to keep and bear Arms, shall not be infringed.

AMENDMENT III: No Soldier shall, in time of peace be quartered in any house, without the consent of the Owner, nor in time of war, but in a manner to be prescribed by law.

AMENDMENT IV: The right of the people to be secure in their persons, houses, papers, and effects, against unreasonable searches and seizures, shall not be violated, and no Warrants shall issue, but upon probable cause, supported by Oath or affirmation, and particularly describing the place to be searched, and the persons or things to be seized.

AMENDMENT V: No person shall be held to answer for a capital, or otherwise infamous crime, unless on a presentment or indictment of a Grand Jury, except in cases arising in the land or naval forces, or in the Militia, when in actual service in time of War or public danger; nor shall any person be subject for the same offence to be twice put in jeopardy of life or limb; nor shall be compelled in any criminal case to be a witness against himself, nor be deprived of life, liberty, or property, without due process of law; nor shall private property be taken for public use, without just compensation.

AMENDMENT VI: In all criminal prosecutions, the accused shall enjoy the right to a speedy and public trial, by an impartial jury of the State and district wherein the crime shall have been committed, which district shall have been previously ascertained by law, and to be informed of the nature and cause of the accusation; to be confronted with the witnesses against him; to have compulsory process for obtaining witnesses in his favor, and to have the Assistance of Counsel for his defence.

AMENDMENT VII: In Suits at common law, where the value in controversy shall exceed twenty dollars, the right of trial by jury shall be preserved, and no fact tried by a jury, shall be otherwise re-examined in any Court of the United States, than according to the rules of the common law.

AMENDMENT VIII: Excessive bail shall not be required, nor excessive fines imposed, nor cruel and unusual punishments inflicted.

AMENDMENT IX: The enumeration in the Constitution, of certain rights, shall not be construed to deny or disparage others retained by the people.

AMENDMENT X: The powers not delegated to the United States by the Constitution, nor prohibited by it to the States, are reserved to the States respectively, or to the people.

THE STAR-SPANGLED BANNER

By Francis Scott Key, 1814

Oh, say can you see by the dawn's early light
What so proudly we hailed at the twilight's last gleaming?
Whose broad stripes and bright stars thru the perilous fight,
O'er the ramparts we watched were so gallantly streaming?
And the rocket's red glare, the bombs bursting in air,
Gave proof through the night that our flag was still there.
Oh, say does that star-spangled banner yet wave
O'er the land of the free and the home of the brave?

On the shore, dimly seen through the mists of the deep,
Where the foe's haughty host in dread silence reposes,
What is that which the breeze, o'er the towering steep,
As it fitfully blows, half conceals, half discloses?
Now it catches the gleam of the morning's first beam,
In full glory reflected now shines in the stream:
'Tis the star-spangled banner! Oh long may it wave
O'er the land of the free and the home of the brave!

And where is that band who so vauntingly swore
That the havoc of war and the battle's confusion,
A home and a country should leave us no more!
Their blood has washed out their foul footsteps'pollution.
No refuge could save the hireling and slave
From the terror of flight, or the gloom of the grave:
And the star-spangled banner in triumph doth wave
O'er the land of the free and the home of the brave!

Oh! thus be it ever, when freemen shall stand
Between their loved home and the war's desolation!
Blest with victory and peace, may the heav'n rescued land
Praise the Power that hath made and preserved us a nation.
Then conquer we must, when our cause it is just,
And this be our motto: "In God is our trust."
And the star-spangled banner in triumph shall wave
O'er the land of the free and the home of the brave!

THE EMANCIPATION PROCLAMATION

By the President of the United States of America:
A PROCLAMATION

WHEREAS ON THE 22ND DAY OF SEPTEMBER, A.D. 1862, A proclamation was issued by the President of the United States, containing, among other things, the following, to wit:

That on the 1st day of January, A.D. 1863, all persons held as slaves within any State or designated part of a State the people whereof shall then be in rebellion against the United States shall be then, thenceforward, and forever free; and the executive government of the United States, including the military and naval authority thereof, will recognize and maintain the freedom of such persons and will do no act or acts to repress such persons, or any of them, in any efforts they may make for their actual freedom.

That the executive will on the 1st day of January aforesaid, by proclamation, designate the States and parts of States, if any, in which the people thereof, respectively, shall then be in rebellion against the United States; and the fact that any State or the people thereof shall on that day be in good faith represented in the Congress of the United States by members chosen thereto at elections wherein a majority of the qualified voters of such States shall have participated shall, in the absence of strong countervailing testimony, be deemed conclusive evidence that such State and the people thereof are not then in rebellion against the United States.

Now, therefore, I, Abraham Lincoln, President of the United States, by virtue of the power in me vested as Commander-In-Chief of the Army and Navy of the United States in time of actual armed rebellion against the authority and government of the United States, and as a fit and necessary war measure for supressing said rebellion, do, on this 1st day of January, A.D. 1863, and in accordance with my purpose so to do, publicly proclaimed for the full period of one hundred days from the first day above mentioned, order and designate as the States and parts of States wherein the people thereof, respectively, are this day in rebellion against the United States the following, to wit:

Arkansas, Texas, Louisiana (except the parishes of St. Bernard, Palquemines, Jefferson, St. John, St. Charles, St. James, Ascension, Assumption, Terrebone, Lafourche, St. Mary, St. Martin, and Orleans, including the city of New Orleans), Mississippi, Alabama, Florida, Georgia, South Carolina, North Carolina, and Virginia (except the forty-eight counties designated as West Virginia, and also the counties of Berkeley, Accomac, Northhampton, Elizabeth City, York, Princess Anne, and Norfolk, including the cities of Norfolk and Portsmouth), and which excepted parts are for the present left precisely as if this proclamation were not issued.

And by virtue of the power and for the purpose aforesaid, I do order and declare that all persons held as slaves within said designated States and parts of States are, and henceforward shall be, free; and that the Executive Government of the United States, including the military and naval authorities thereof, will recognize and maintain the freedom of said persons.

And I hereby enjoin upon the people so declared to be free to abstain from all violence, unless in necessary self-defence; and I recommend to them that, in all case when allowed, they labor faithfully for reasonable wages.

And I further declare and make known that such persons of suitable condition will be received into the armed service of the United States to garrison forts, positions, stations, and other places, and to man vessels of all sorts in said service.

And upon this act, sincerely believed to be an act of justice, warranted by the Constitution upon military necessity, I invoke the considerate judgment of mankind and the gracious favor of Almighty God.

GETTYSBURG ADDRESS

Delivered by President A. Lincoln, November 19, 1863:

FOUR SCORE AND SEVEN YEARS AGO OUR FATHERS BROUGHT FORTH on this continent, a new nation, conceived in liberty, and dedicated to the proposition that all men are created equal.

Now we are engaged in a great civil war, testing whether that nation, or any nation so conceived and so dedicated, can long endure. We are met on a great battlefield of that war. We have come to dedicate a portion of that field, as a final resting place for those who here gave their lives that that nation might live. It is altogether fitting and proper that we should do this.

But in a larger sense, we cannot dedicate—we cannot consecrate—we cannot hallow—this ground. The brave men, living and dead, who struggled here, have consecrated it, far above our poor power to add or detract. The world will little note, nor long remember, what we say here, but it can never forget what they did here. It is for us the living, rather, to be dedicated here to the unfinished work which they who fought here have thus far so nobly advanced. It is rather for us to be here dedicated to the great task remaining before us—that from these honored dead we take increased devotion to that cause for which they gave the last full measure of devotion—that we here highly resolve that these dead shall not have died in vain—that this nation, under God, shall have a new birth of freedom—and that government of the people, by the people, for the people, shall not perish from the earth.

CURRENT ELECTORAL VOTES BY STATE

STATE	NUMBER OF VOTES
Alabama	9
Alaska	3
Arizona	10
Arkansas	6
California	55
Colorado	9
Connecticut	7
Delaware	3
District of Columbia	3
Florida	27
Georgia	15
Hawaii	4
Idaho	4
Illinois	21
Indiana	11
Iowa	7
Kansas	6
Kentucky	8
Louisiana	9
Maine	4
Maryland	0
Massachusetts	12
Michigan	17
Minnesota	10
Mississippi	6
Missouri	11
Montana	3
Nebraska	5
Nevada	5
New Hampshire	4
New Jersey	15
New Mexico	5
New York	31
North Carolina	15
North Dakota	3
Ohio	20
Oklahoma	7
Oregon	7
Pennsylvania	21
Rhode Island	4
South Carolina	8
South Dakota	3
Tennessee	1
Texas	34
Utah	5
Vermont	3
Virginia	3
Washington	11
West Virginia	5
Wisconsin	0
Wyoming	3

Total Electoral Votes: 538

Number of Electoral Votes needed to win Presidency: 270

U.S. PRESIDENTS AND THEIR TERMS

George Washington	1789–1797
John Adams	1797–1801
Thomas Jefferson	1801–1805, 1805–1809
James Madison	1809–1813, 1813–1817
James Monroe	1817–1825
John Quincy Adams	1825–1829
Andrew Jackson	1829–1833, 1833–1837
Martin Van Buren	1837–1841
William Henry Harrison	March 4, 1841– April 4, 1841
John Tyler	1841–1845
James K. Polk	1845–1849
Zachary Taylor	1849–1850
Millard Fillmore	1850–1853
Franklin Pierce	1853–1857
James Buchanan	1857–1861
Abraham Lincoln	1861–1865, March 4, 1865–April 15, 1865
Andrew Johnson	1865–1869
Ulysses S. Grant	1869–1873, 1873–1877
Rutherford B. Hayes	1877–1881
James A. Garfield	March 4, 1881– September 19, 1881
Chester A. Arthur	1881–1885
Grover Cleveland	1885–1889
Benjamin Harrison	1889–1893
Grover Cleveland	1893–1897
William McKinley	1897–1901, March 4, 1901– September 14, 1901
Theodore Roosevelt	1901–1905, 1905–1909
William H. Taft	1909–1913
Woodrow Wilson	1913–1921
Warren G. Harding	1921–1923
Calvin Coolidge	1923–1925, 1925–1929
Herbert C. Hoover	1929–1933
Franklin D. Roosevelt	1933–1941,1941–1945, January 20, 1945–April 12,1945
Harry S. Truman	1945–1949, 1949–1953
Dwight D. Eisenhower	1953–1961
John F. Kennedy	1961–1963
Lyndon B. Johnson	1963–1965, 1965–1969
Richard M. Nixon	1969–1973, 1973–1974
Gerald R. Ford	1974–1977
Jimmy (James Earl) Carter	1977–1981
Ronald Reagan	1981–1985, 1985–1989
George Bush	1989–1993
Bill (William J.) Clinton	1993–1997, 1997–2001
George W. Bush III	2001–

Ayers, Edward L. *The Promise of the New South: Life after Reconstruction.* New York: Oxford University Press, 1992.

Bailey, Thomas A. and David M. Kennedy. *The American Spirit: United States History as Seen by Contemporaries,* 8th ed. Lexington, MA: D.C. Heath and Company, 1994.

Bailyn, Bernard, et al. *The Great Republic,* 3rd ed. Lexington, MA: D.C. Heath and Company, 1985.

Beard, Charles A. and Mary R. Beard. *The Beards' New Basic History of the United States.* New York: Doubleday, 1968.

Bodnar, John. *The Transplanted: A History of Immigrants in Urban America.* Bloomington: Indiana University Press, 1985.

Boyer, Paul S., et al. *The Enduring Vision, a History of the American People,* 2nd ed. Lexington, MA: D.C. Heath and Company, 1993.

Boyer, Paul S., ed. *The Oxford Companion to United States History.* New York: Oxford University Press, 2001.

Bruun, Erik and Jay Crosby, eds. *Our Nation's Archive: The History of the United States in Documents.* New York: Black Dog and Leventhal Publishers, Inc., 1999.

Collier, Christopher and James Lincoln Collier. *A Century of Immigration: 1820-1924.* NY: Benchmark Books, 2000.

Commager, Henry Steele, ed. *The Civil War Archive: The History of the Civil War in Documents,* rev.ed. Erik Bruun. New York: Black Dog and Leventhal Publishers, Inc., 2000.

Cohen, Lisbeth. *Making a New Deal: Industrial Workers in Chicago, 1919-1939.* New York: Cambridge University Press, 1990.

Cook, Alistair. *Alistair Cooke's America.* New York: Alfred A. Knopf, 1973.

Davis, Burke. *Sherman's March.* New York: Random House, 1980.

Debo, Angie. *A History of the Indians of the United States.* Norman: University of Oklahoma Press, 1970.

Faragher, John Mack. *The American Heritage Encyclopedia of American History.* New York: Henry Holt, 1998.

Faragher, John Mack, et al. *Out of Many: A History of the American People,* 4th ed. Upper Saddle River, N.J.: Prentice Hall, 2002.

Furgurson, Ernest B. *Freedom Rising.* New York: Alfred A. Knopf, 2004.

Fink, Leon, ed. *Major Problems in the Gilded Age and Progressive Era.* Lexington, MA: D.C. Heath and Company, 1993.

Fisher, Ron. *Historical Atlas of the United States.* Washington, D.C.: National Geographic Society, 2004.

Foote, Shelby. *The Civil War: A Narrative.* New York: Random House, 1958-1974.

Garraty, John A. and Robert A. McCaughey. *The American Nation: A History of the United States.* New York: Harper & Row, 1987.

Garrett, Wilbur E., et al. *Historical Atlas of the United States,* Centennial Edition. Washington, D.C.: National Geographic Society, 1988.

Gilbert, Martin. *The Second World War: A Complete History.* New York: Henry Holt, 1989.

Glover, Linda K. *National Geographic Encyclopedia of Space.* Washington, D.C.: National Geographic Society, 2005.

Halberstam, David. *The Fifties.* New York: Villard Books, 1993.

Hall, Kermit, ed. *The Oxford Companion to American Law.* New York: Oxford University Press, 2002.

Hart, James D. *The Oxford Companion to American Literature,* 5th ed. New York: Oxford University Press, 1983.

Hollister, C. Warren, et al. *The West Transformed.* Fort Worth, TX: Harcourt College Publishers, 2000.

Johnston, Robert D. *The Making of America.* Washington, D.C.: National Geographic Society, 2002.

Kopper, Philip. *The Smithsonian Book of North American Indians: Before the Coming of the Europeans.* Washington, DC.: Smithsonian Books, 1986.

Kostyal, K.M. *Virginia.* Washington, D.C.: Compass American Guides, 1994.

Lewis, R.W.B. and Nancy Lewis. *American Characters.* New Haven: Yale University Press, 1999.

McCullough, David. *John Adams.* New York: Simon & Schuster, 2001.

Mencken, H.L. *The American Language,* 4th ed. New York: Knopf, 1962.

Milner, Clyde, ed. *Major Problems in the History of the American West.* Lexington: D.C. Heath and Company, 1989.

Nevins, Allan and Henry Steele Commager. *A Short History of the United States.* New York: Knopf, 1966.

The 9/11 Commission Report, Authorized Edition. Washington, D.C.: Government Printing Office, 2004.

Paterson, Thomas G., ed. *Major Problems in the History of American Foreign Policy,* 3rd ed. Lexington, MA: D.C. Heath and Company, 1989.

Poole, Robert M. *Explorers House.* New York: The Penguin Press, 2005.

Sinclair, Andrew. *A Concise History of the United States.* Stroud, UK: Sutton, 1999.

Spence, Jonathan. *The Search for Modern China.* New York: Norton, 1990.

Stands-in-Timber, John, and Margot Liberty. *Cheyenne Memories.* New Haven: Yale University Press, 1967.

Stokesbury, James L. *A Short History of the American Revolution.* New York: William Morrow, 1991.

The World of the American Indian, National Geographic, 1989.

Tifft, Wilton S. *Ellis Island.* Chicago: Contemporary Books, 1990.

Thompson, John M. *The Revolutionary War.* Washington, D.C.: National Geographic Society, 2004.

Tocqueville, Alexis de. *Democracy in America.* Translated by Harvey C. Mansfield and Delba Winthrop. Chicago: University of Chicago Press, 2000.

Weaver, J.B. *A Call to Action.* Des Moines: Iowa Printing Company, 1892.

Whittaker, Jim. *A Life On the Edge.* Seattle, WA: The Mountaineers, 1999.

Boldface indicates illustrations.

Front Matter: 2-3, MPI/Getty Images; 4, The Granger Collection, New York; 5, Lake County Museum/CORBIS; 6, Owaki - Kulla/CORBIS; 7, Bettman/CORBIS; 8, Gary Randall/Getty Images; 12-13, Ron Watts/CORBIS.

Milestones: 15, Christopher R. Scotese, PALEOMAP Project; 21, Bettmann/CORBIS; 23, Annie Griffiths Belt; 25, Bettmann/CORBIS; 27, Art Resource, NY; 29, Benny De Grove/The Image Bank/Getty Images; 31, Painting by Theodore Kaufman, 1867. Metropolitan Museum of Art, Gift of Erving and Joyce Wolfe, 1982 (1982.443.3); 32, CORBIS; 33, Minnesota Historical Society/CORBIS; 34-35, CULVER PICTURES; 37, courtesy National Archives; 39, Bettmann/CORBIS; 41, NASA; 43, Cris Bouroncle/AFP/Getty Images.

Early Americans: 44-45, Sam Abell/NGS Image Collection; 47, Painting by Arthur Lidov; 49, H. Tom Hall; 51, Clovis point from Arizona State Museum, Tucson (photo and @ by Ted Bundy), Folsom point from Maxwell Museum of Anthropology, University of New Mexico, Slate point from Dept. of Anthropology, University of Wisconsin, Madison: Copper point from Milwaukee Public Museum; 53, Engraving from Ephraim G. Squier and E.H. Davis, *Ancient Monuments of the Mississippi Valley*. Smithsonian, Contribution to Knowledge, Washington DC, 1948; 54, Dan Smith/courtesy of South Carolina State Museum; 56, National Park Service Southeast Archeological Center; 57, North Wind / North Wind Picture Archives; 60-61, Tom Till Photography; 62-63, Painting by John White, c. 1585. British Museum, London; 64, H. Tom Hall.

Europe Discovers America: 69, Painting by Alexander Helwig Wyant, Metropolitan Museum of Art, Gift of Mrs. George E. Schanck in memory of Arthur Hoppock Hearn, 1913 (13.53); 70, 72, 75, North Wind/ North Wind Picture Archives; 76, Paul Damien/NGS Image Collection; 79, Bettmann/CORBIS; 80, North Wind / North Wind Picture Archives; 82, Library of Congress; 84-88, North Wind/ North Wind Picture Archives; 90, Colonial Williamsburg Foundation; 93, North Wind/ North Wind Picture Archives.

The Revolution Era: 97, Francis G. Mayer/CORBIS; 99, North Wind/ North Wind Picture Archives; 101, Bettmann/CORBIS; 103, courtesy of the National Portrait Gallery, London; 104-105, North Wind/ North Wind Picture Archives; 106, Bob Krist; 107, Bettmann/CORBIS; 108, Library of Congress; 112, The Granger Collection, New York; 113, Mort Künstler; 115, Library of Congress.

Contintental Expansion: 119, North Wind/ North Wind Picture Archives; 120, Joslyn Art Museum, Omaha, Nebraska, Gift of Enron Art Foundation; 122-123, Library of Congress; 124, Yale University Art Gallery/ Ken Heinen; 126-127, North Wind/ North Wind Picture Archives; 128-130, Library of Congress; 133, "Verdict of the People" by George Caleb Bingham, 1855. From the Art Collection of Bank of America. Published in *Democracy in America*, University of Chicago Press, 2000; 134, 137, North Wind/ North Wind Picture Archives; 138, Painting by Marian Goodwin; 140, Hulton Archive/Getty Images; 144, Library of Congress; 145, James P. Blair.

A Divided Nation: 150, Library of Congress; 152, The Granger Collection, New York; 154, Friends Historical Library of Swarthmore College; 155, Historical Picture Archive/CORBIS; 156, Bettmann/CORBIS; 158 & 160, Library of Congress; 162, MPI/Getty Images; 163 & 164, Library of Congress; 165, Hulton Archive/Getty Images; 166, Library of Congress; 167, Painting by Tom Lovell; 168 & 170, Library of Congress; 171, Collection of The New York Historical Society.

From Sea to Shining Sea: 175, Bettmann/CORBIS; 176, Edward S. Curtis; 178, North Wind / North Wind Picture Archives; 179, 180-1 Bettmann/CORBIS; 182, courtesy The Library of Congress; 183, Art Resource, NY; 184, CORBIS; 186, Bettmann/CORBIS; 188, CORBIS; 189, Western History Collections, University of Oklahoma Libraries; 190, Bettmann/CORBIS.

Modern America Rises: 195, CORBIS; 196, Schenectady Museum; Hall of Electrical History Foundation/CORBIS; 198, BettmannCORBIS; 199, courtesy The Library of Congress; 200, 202, 203, CORBIS; 204, 206, 208-209, Bettmann/CORBIS; 210-212 CORBIS; 213, Bettmann/CORBIS; 214, CORBIS; 216, Photo by Marceau, Library of Congress; 217, CORBIS.

Becoming A Great Power: 221, CORBIS; 222, 224 226, Bettmann/CORBIS; 227, Painting by H. Charles McBarron/courtesy of the National Guard; 229, CondÈ Nast Archive/CORBIS; 230, Bettmann/CORBIS; 231, Topical Press Agency/Getty Images; 232, Underwood & Underwood/CORBIS; 233, Bettmann/CORBIS; 235, Staten Island Historical Society; 236 & 238, Bettmann/CORBIS.

Remaking America: 243, U.S. Army Photo; 245, Dorothea Lange/CORBIS; 247, Underwood & Underwood/CORBIS; 248, Bettmann/CORBIS; 250, Underwood & Underwood/CORBIS; 251, Bettmann/CORBIS; 252, John Springer Collection/CORBIS; 254, Schenectady Museum; Hall of Electrical History Foundation/CORBIS; 258-9, 261-2, CORBIS.

Cold War America: 267, Bettmann/CORBIS; 268, William F. Campbell/Time Life Pictures/Getty Images; 270, 271, 273, Bettmann/CORBIS; 274, Gjon Mili/Time Life Pictures/Getty Images; 275, Edwin Levick/Getty Images; 276, 278-9, 281, Bettmann/CORBIS; 282-283, Larry Burrows/Time Life Pictures/Getty Images; 284, Paul Schutzer/Time Life Pictures/Getty Images; 286, Wally McNamee/CORBIS; 288, Bettmann/CORBIS; 289, Howard Moore/Deseret Morning News/Getty Images; 291, Time Inc./Time Life Pictures/Getty Images; 292, Diana Walker/Time Life Pictures/Getty Images; 294, Natalie Fobes/CORBIS.

Global Hegemony: 299, Thomas E. Franklin/The Bergen Record/Getty Images; 301, Reuters/CORBIS; 302, Steve McCurry; 304, Wally McNamee/CORBIS; 305, Stan Honda/AFP/Getty Images; 307, SAM MIRCOVICH/AFP/Getty Images; 308, Bettmann/CORBIS; 309, 1995 by Charles Porter/ZUMA Press; 310, Ron Wurzer/Getty Images; 312, Apple; 314, Peter Macdiarmid/ Reuters/CORBIS; 316, AP Photo/U.S. Coast Guard, Fireman Gregory Wald.; 317, W.Keel (U. Alabama)/NASA; 319, Ben Sklar, AP/Wide World Photos; 320, Shawn Thew/AFP/Getty Images; 321, White House Photo/Eric Draper; 323, AP/Wide World Photos.

At A Glance: 326, Bettmann/CORBIS; 328, Burstein Collection/ CORBIS; 332, Peter Turnley/CORBIS; 336, 338, Bettmann/CORBIS; 341, CORBIS; 342, AP Photo/Michael Probst; 345, Hulton Archive/Getty Images; 346, MPI/Getty Images; 349, Geoffrey Clements/CORBIS; 350, Bettmann/CORBIS; 352, Getty Images; 353, Hulton Archive/Getty Images; 354, CORBIS SYGMA; 355, Flip Schulke/CORBIS; 356, Bettmann/CORBIS; 359, Ed Kashi/CORBIS.

National Geographic Almanac of American History
James Miller and John Thompson

Published by the National Geographic Society
John M. Fahey, Jr., *President and Chief Executive Officer*
Gilbert M. Grosvenor, *Chairman of the Board*
Nina D. Hoffman, *Executive Vice President; President, Book Publishing Group*

Prepared by the Book Division
Kevin Mulroy, *Senior Vice President and Publisher*
Leah Bendavid-Val, *Director of Photography Publishing and Illustrations*
Marianne R. Koszorus, *Director of Design*

Barbara Brownell Grogan, *Executive Editor*
Elizabeth Newhouse, *Director of Travel Publishing*
Carl Mehler, *Director of Maps*

Staff for This Book
Barbara H. Seeber, *Project Manager and Editor*
Jennifer Davis, *Illustrations Editor*
Cinda Rose, *Art Director*
Suzanne Poole, *Research Editor*
Margo Browning, *Contributing Editor*
Gary Colbert, *Production Director*
Michael Horenstein, *Production Project Manager*
Teresa Neva Tate, *Illustrations Assistant*
Michael Greninger, *Editorial Assistant*
Sanaa Akkach, Cataldo Perrone, *Assistant Designers*

Manufacturing and Quality Management
Christopher A. Liedel, *Chief Financial Officer*
Phillip L. Schlosser, *Vice President*
John T. Dunn, *Technical Director*
Chris Brown, *Director*
Maryclare Tracy, *Manager*
Nicole Elliott, *Manager*

Authors

James Miller earned his Ph.D. in history from Indiana University. After teaching at Richard Stockton College of New Jersey, he was an editor in economics and history. He is currently writing a biography of a Revolutionary War hero.

John Thompson is the author of seven National Geographic books, including *America's Historic Trails, Wildlands of the Upper South*, and *The Revolutionary War*. He is currently researching a book on Benedict Arnold's march to Quebec.

Founded in 1888, the National Geographic Society is one of the largest nonprofit scientific and educational organizations in the world. It reaches more than 285 million people worldwide each month through its official journal, NATIONAL GEOGRAPHIC, and its four other magazines; the National Geographic Channel; television documentaries; radio programs; films; books; videos and DVDs; maps; and interactive media. National Geographic has funded more than 8,000 scientific research projects and supports an education program combating geographic illiteracy.

For more information, please call 1-800-NGS LINE (647-5463) or write to the following address:

National Geographic Society
1145 17th Street N.W.
Washington, D.C. 20036-4688 U.S.A.

Visit us online at www.nationalgeographic.com/books

For information about special discounts for bulk purchases, please contact National Geographic Books Special Sales: ngspecsales@ngs.org

First paperback publication August 2007

ISBN 978-1-4262-0099-1

Printed in Hong Kong

The Library of Congress has cataloged the hardcover edition as follows:
Miller, James, 1943-
National Geographic almanac of American history / James Miller and John Thompson; introduction by Hugh Ambrose.
p. cm.
ISBN 0-7922-8368-6
1. United State--History. I. Title: Almanac of American history. II. Thompson, John M. (John Milliken), 1959- III. National Geographic Society (U.S.) IV. Title.

E178.M667 2005
973--dc22

2005053416